C000140830

1 MONTH OF
FREE
READING

at
www.ForgottenBooks.com

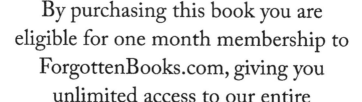

By purchasing this book you are eligible for one month membership to ForgottenBooks.com, giving you unlimited access to our entire collection of over 1,000,000 titles via our web site and mobile apps.

To claim your free month visit:

www.forgottenbooks.com/free185822

* Offer is valid for 45 days from date of purchase. Terms and conditions apply.

ISBN 978-0-428-98732-9
PIBN 10185822

This book is a reproduction of an important historical work. Forgotten Books uses
state-of-the-art technology to digitally reconstruct the work, preserving the original format
whilst repairing imperfections present in the aged copy. In rare cases, an imperfection in
the original, such as a blemish or missing page, may be replicated in our edition. We do,
however, repair the vast majority of imperfections successfully; any imperfections that
remain are intentionally left to preserve the state of such historical works.

Forgotten Books is a registered trademark of FB &c Ltd.
Copyright © 2018 FB &c Ltd.
FB &c Ltd, Dalton House, 60 Windsor Avenue, London, SW19 2RR.
Company number 08720141. Registered in England and Wales.

For support please visit www.forgottenbooks.com

The Critic

An Illustrated Monthly Review of Literature, Art
and Life

VOL. XLVIII.   JANUARY–JUNE, 1906

PUBLISHED FOR
THE CRITIC COMPANY
BY G. P. PUTNAM'S SONS
NEW ROCHELLE   NEW YORK

(RECAP)

v.48

UNIVERSITY
LIBRARY
PRINCETON, N.J.

EDITH WHARTON

Sketched from life for THE CRITIC by Kate Rogers Nowell
Copyright, 1906, by THE CRITIC Co.

Vol. XLVIII JANUARY, 1906 No. 1

1881-1906

*Twenty-five years ago—January, 1881—*THE CRITIC *was born. It was not much to look at at first, but it was received most kindly, for the public realized that it was like the famous singed cat—better than it looked. The typography was poor, the size insignificant, the illustrations wretchedly printed; but it had a fine list of contributors—an essay by E. C. Stedman, and essays and poems by Emma Lazarus, Charles de Kay, Sidney Howard Gay. Not only these, but it promised essays and poems by Walt Whitman, folk-lore stories by " Uncle Remus," and many other attractive things. And they all came—and* THE CRITIC *grew and flourished, so that it is to-day what it aimed to be at the start—the leading literary magazine in America. This verdict it owes to its readers—they never hesitate to say this of it—and the Editor is proud of their compliments and of their confidence.*

The Lounger

THE CRITIC has been most fortunate in getting an exclusive portrait of Mrs. Wharton. Many publications have appealed to the author of "The House of Mirth" to grant their artists permission to make a sketch of her, all of which propositions she has politely but firmly declined except that of THE CRITIC. Mrs. Kate Rogers Nowell went up to Lenox and spent several days there making sketches of Mrs. Wharton in her own home. The portrait is most successful and no one is better pleased with it than Mrs. Wharton herself.

Mrs. Wharton has not come to town yet, and will not till late in the month. In the meantime Messrs. Scribners' presses have been kept running steadily since the 15th of September on her now famous story. At the present time "The House of Mirth" is well on towards its two hundredth thousand. Here is an instance of a book which both as fiction and as literature is well worth all the honors that have been heaped upon it. The average reader and the discerning critic alike have been carried away by Mrs. Wharton's powerful portrayals of character.

In the Editor's Clearing House will be found a contribution with "The House of Mirth" for its subject. It is a burst of wild enthusiasm over the book, but it voices the opinion of hosts of its readers in America and England. The writer of it can see nothing to criticise in the story,—she loves every word of it,—and she is to be envied her emotions.

COPYRIGHT 1906, BY THE CRITIC COMPANY.
ENTERED AT NEW ROCHELLE, N. Y., POST OFFICE AS SECOND CLASS MATTER.

HON. JOSEPH H. CHOATE

From the painting by Herman G. Herkomer. Mr. Choate's address on Franklin will be found on page 51.

There is some talk of the dramatization of "The House of Mirth." If the dramatization is made it will doubtless be done by Mrs. Wharton herself, or certainly under her supervision, but I cannot see a play in the story. It is better as it was written. A play must have both light and shade. The story of Lily Bart is all shade.

Captain Harry Graham, whose portrait from a recent photograph is here

Ballads," there is no telling when their clever author may strike as humorous and as popular a note as the elder verse writer. Captain Graham, it will be remembered, is engaged to be married to that charming young actress Miss Ethel Barrymore.

John Bartlett is dead. To many people this name means nothing. but when you add that it is that of the compiler of "Familiar Quotations"

CAPTAIN HARRY GRAHAM
Author of "Misrepresentative Men"

reproduced, has succeeded to the mantle, or at least a portion of the mantle, of W. S. Gilbert. While his humorous verses, "Misrepresentative Men," have not attained the popularity of the "Bab

thousands and hundreds of thousands will recall it with delight. "Familiar Quotations" was first issued in 1855— a small volume of two hundred pages. Since then it has gone through nine

NOV 26 1906   209098

editions and has reached the dignified proportions of 1200 pages. No better book of its kind was ever made, and it has been indispensable to writers and readers alike. Mr. Bartlett was eighty-five years old at the time of his death. He was connected with the publishing firm of Little, Brown, & Company, of Boston, and lived in Cambridge, where he died. For the last few years he has not been very actively engaged in business. If his death is regretted by every reader of "Familiar Quotations" he will need no other monument.

From *The Sphere*

THE LATE LADY FLORENCE DIXIE

Lady Florence Dixie, whose death occurred at her home in England during the early part of December, was well known in this country. She was the youngest daughter of the seventh Marquis of Queensberry, and was born in 1857. She was a poet, novelist, sportswoman, explorer, and woman suffragist. Although a devoted sportswoman, she was as violently opposed to shooting for amusement as is President Roosevelt; and in a book called "Rambles in Hell" she mercilessly scored those who killed for sport. A short time before her death, Lady Florence had made arrangements for the publication of a new book called "Izra," which will be published before long in New York and London.

❧

Mrs. Craigie in her recent lecture before the students of Barnard College took Dante and Botticelli for her subject. She argued against the strenuous life of the day because those who live it do not take time to cultivate an appreciation for literature and the arts. To prove that one might be strenuous and at the same time cultivated she pointed to the subjects of her address —one a poet, the other a painter, both of whom were men of affairs, interested in the commercial and political doings of their day. In this twentieth century we scoff at philosophers, but Mrs. Craigie thinks perhaps we would not do so if we realized that Plato had made a success in the oil trade. He was not, so far as she knows, a member of a trust,—certainly not of *the* trust, —but notwithstanding that he did a flourishing business he found time to philosophize.

❧

Mrs. Craigie not only denounced the strenuous life but she scoffed at the idea of the simple life being a strong factor in the development of culture. To lead the simple life, she said, "one must be very healthy and wealthy, for the poor could not afford it and it would kill the delicate." Mrs. Craigie was introduced to her audience by the Hon. Joseph H. Choate, who said that it was from reading her play "The Ambassador" that he learned many of the duties of his office.

❧

Mrs. John W. Elliot has made an unusually attractive calendar which is published by the Massachusetts Audubon Society, 234 Berkeley Street, Boston. It was printed in Japan, Mr. Matzaki of Boston attending to the printing, which gives it an added artistic interest. All moneys received from the sale of this calendar will be devoted to carrying on the good work of the Audubon Society. Instead of the usual garish pictures that go with the average calendar, the prints accompanying this one are exquisite reproductions of Japanese color work, the subjects naturally being birds.

moiselle Blanche," a curious realistic study of the career of a circus-acrobat; and of "A Daughter of Thespis," pronounced by Mr. W. D. Howells the best novel of stage-life ever written. Mr. Barry was for several years dramatic critic of *Harper's Weekly* and of

Photo by Parkinson, Boston

MR. JOHN D. BARRY
Author of "Our Best Society"

The secret of the authorship of "Our Best Society," the novel of life among New York millionaires, which was the principal CRITIC serial of 1905, is out. The book is by Mr. John D. Barry, known as the author of "The Congressman's Wife," a novel dealing with graft in national politics which, several years ago, won the first prize in the *Smart Set* competition for novels; of "Made-

Collier's and he is now devoting himself wholly to the writing of fiction. His name is to appear on the third edition of "Our Best Society," which is now in press.

Mr. George Bernard Shaw's attacks upon the dead actor, Sir Henry Irving, have not added to his popularity in

DR. MAX NORDAU

England. Mr. Shaw might have waited till Irving was fairly cold in his grave before he let fly the poisoned arrows of his curious mind. In his much-dis-

acting as private secretary to Irving, may have helped the busy and absorbed actor in putting his material into shape; but that he was responsible for its ideas

MR. NORMAN DUNCAN AND MR. WILFRED CAMPBELL

cussed letter to *Die Neue Freie Presse* of Vienna, Mr. Shaw says among other things:

> His learning and knowledge in matters of art and literature were imaginary. He took care to have a following of authors, with Lord Tennyson, the Poet Laureate, at their head, and the journalists who helped him to write his lectures and speeches, behind, but he had no literary taste, and not the very slightest relations with the intellectual life of his time.

Even if this were true it would be very poor taste on the part of Mr. Shaw to make the statement when he did; but being untrue it is in something worse than bad taste. I know from my own conversations with Irving that he was a lover of literature, and of good literature; and that he read more than one would think that a man who led his busy life could read. As to his speeches and lectures being written by others, I doubt it; though the late L. F. Austin told me one day while he was sitting in this office that he wrote the lecture on "Acting" that Irving delivered at Saunders Theatre, Cambridge, before the undergraduates of Harvard University. Mr. Austin, who was then

or their expression I did not believe at the time nor do I believe it now.

Dr. Max Nordau has written a book of fairy tales which have been translated into English by Miss Mary J. Safford, and published at Christmas for the delectation of children of all ages. It has twenty-five illustrations by Miss Florence Safford, a niece of the translator. Both the older and the younger Miss Safford had every opportunity of discussing their work with Nordau in Paris, while a collaborator not to be forgotten was the author's little daughter Maxa. Each tale as it was finished was read aloud to her for final approval, and what Maxa liked stayed in, and what Maxa did n't like had to come out. Fairy tales by the caustic author of "Degeneration" seem rather incongruous. As yet (I think) the only thing of the kind to appear in English has been the pretty fantasy about the little girl and the big ship in a recent number of the *Cosmopolitan*.

Good wine needs no bush, but no doubt it sells more readily when well advertised. In the publishers' announcement of Mr. Wilfred Campbell's "Collected Poems," just issued we find the author's work praised not only by the publishers themselves, but in quotations from Mr. Stedman, Mr. Howells, and "a distinguished English critic" (name not given), as well as by a number of periodicals, including *the Nation*. But what has attracted the attention of the public to the book is the fact that Mr. Carnegie — whose reputation cannot be said to rest upon his work in literary criticism — has found it good, and has bought an edition of five hundred copies for his globe - encircling chain of libraries. This will mean much to the author and his publishers; but it is important to remember that, while it is not a guarantee of merit, it is equally remote from proving any lack of quality in the poems themselves. If Mr. Robinson's poetry is not as fine as one might fancy from President Roosevelt's commendation of it, it is certainly none the worse for his having praised it. Mr. Campbell's companion in the photograph printed herewith, though an American by residence, was born in Canada, and, like the poet, was educated at the University of Toronto.

∂≈

The most interesting event in the periodical world is that of the absorption of the *Country Calendar* by *Country Life in America*. The first number of the *Country Calendar* was printed in May last, since which time it had reached a paid-up subscription of thirty thousand copies—an unusually good showing for a new magazine, but, of course, nowhere near a paying circulation for a periodical so expensive to produce. The reason given for the absorption is that it seemed better to have one big comprehensive magazine, one that would give the public all it wanted of country life, rather than to divide the field between two. But I have a shrewd suspicion that the real reason was that Mr. Charles D. Lanier, the president of the Review of Reviews Company, who was the prime mover in the foundation and carrying out of the *Country Calendar* idea, had more work

to do than he could accomplish to his own satisfaction, and that he was glad to make a graceful exit from the new periodical to devote his entire time to the old.

∂≈

Mr. Marion Crawford's latest novel, "Fair Margaret," is called "The Soprano" in England. The probable explanation for this change of title is that there has been a book published in England by the name of "Fair Margaret." It is not an uncommon thing for the names of American books to be changed in London, or *vice versa*. On the whole I think "The Soprano" a better title than "Fair Margaret," it is less sentimental.

∂≈

Mr. Owen Johnson's novel, "In the Name of Liberty," is published in England under the name of "Nicole." Here is another instance of a change of name. Perhaps the English censor thinks that "In the Name of Liberty" sounds too much like a trumpet call to the populace!

∂≈

Mrs. Baillie-Saunders's much-advertised prize novel, "Saints in Society," is about to be published in this country. The prize that Mrs. Baillie-Saunders won for her novel was not such a big one—$500. Three and four times that much has been paid as prize money for a comparatively short story on this side of the water. It is a question whether anything is gained beyond advertising by prize stories. I cannot think of any prize novel that has taken its place among the masterpieces of fiction.

∂≈

It is most fortunate and appropriate that Mrs. Josephine Shaw Lowell's features have been preserved in the beautiful bas-relief portrait by Mr. Augustus Saint-Gaudens, whose equestrian portrait of Mrs. Lowell's brother, Colonel Shaw, is the principal feature of one of America's greatest and most thrilling monuments. On another page is printed a poem to the memory of

Courtesy of Miss Lowell

MRS. JOSEPHINE SHAW LOWELL
From a bas-relief by Mr. Augustus Saint-Gaudens

Photo by Kuno Mueller, Baden-Baden
MR. AND MRS. C. N. WILLIAMSON

Mrs. Lowell, who, like her brother, died in the service of her country; for

Peace hath her victories
No less renown'd than war.

My hearty congratulations to President Nicholas Murray Butler, of Columbia University, for being the first president to abolish football from his university. President Butler has the courage of his convictions, and I hope that other college presidents will be equally courageous. The game of football as played in America is more brutal than prize-fighting. Prize-fighting is at least done in the open, and the umpire can easily see that the rules of the game are followed. Not so in football. A man may kill his antagonist or maim him for life and never be punished, for he cannot be discovered. The only thing to do is what President Butler has done, and the sooner other college presidents find this out the better.

Mr. and Mrs. C. N. Williamson, whose latest book, "My Friend the Chauffeur," seems to be quite as great a success as their first automobile novel, "The Lightning Conductor," will probably in the near future put a new twist to their motor tales. All their stories have been based to a certain degree on their own experiences. A very large part of "My Friend the Chauffeur" is strictly in accordance with the facts. They were entertained at Venice at just such a water picnic as they describe. They were taken out into the lagoons by friends, whose gondoliers served them the most exquisite hot dinner in many courses (and how it was managed was a delightful mystery) while the boats floated on the still, opal water at sunset, rose-colored fairy lamps lighting the improvised dinner tables. Even the incident of dropping the gold bag in the Grand Canal was actually true. Mrs. Williamson's bag fell overboard, and in it was a lucky amulet and purse. A very handsome and delightful young Venetian artist did exactly as did Terry in the book: rushed into the old palazzo; appearing again in the moonlight in a sketchy but becoming bathing costume, and diving several times, he at last recovered the missing treasure. To reward him, Mr. and Mrs. Williamson introduced him to a charming young American woman, whom they thought might be interested in his pictures. The two fell in love at first sight, were married in a few weeks, and Mrs. Williamson gave the bride for a wedding present, set in a bracelet, the lucky amulet her husband had fished out of the canal.

A new departure of the Williamsons will come as the result of their last summer's vacation, which was spent in Holland travelling in a motor-boat through the canals, and a motor-boat romance can be expected in consequence. It is understood, however, that the next Williamson book to see the light will be a motor-car story, the scene of which is laid in the United States.

⁂

Apropos of the Williamsons, their first book, "The Lightning Conductor,"

which has gone through twenty-two editions, has been dramatized by Mrs. Harry B. Smith for Mr. Herbert Kelcey and Miss Shannon. It is said that the automobile will have an important part in the play.

MRS. FRANCES SQUIRE POTTER

Mrs. Frances Squire Potter, whose first book, "The Ballingtons," is one of the best novels of the season, is spending the year in Cambridge, England, studying sixteenth and seventeenth-century English. She is on a leave of absence from the University of Minnesota, where she is Assistant Professor of English. With her three children she is keeping house, and is at work on a volume of essays, the preparation of which will be as careful as that of her novel, upon which she worked for seven years at varying intervals. After the essays she plans to write a play.

⚘

Mr. Heinrich Conried's plan for a National Theatre is interesting, but I regret to say that it does not seem to me altogether satisfactory. As far as announcements have been made it looks as though the so-called National Theatre was to be rather a feeder to the Metropolitan Opera House than an independent national institution. In Mr. Conried's plan, as I have seen it stated, and as I believe it to be from his own letters on the subject, is for the forming of a school of fashion rather than a school of art. Carried out on the lines laid down, I cannot see that the American playwright will be any more encouraged than by the present system. The success or failure of a National Theatre depends entirely upon the management. Mr. Conried made a great success as the manager of a German theatre, and he has made a success as the manager of German opera. But to manage an American theatre is another thing. In his German theatre Mr. Conried gave plays that had already been tried and proved successful in Germany. As the manager of the Metropolitan Opera House he has given us operas that have long been proved worthy. But why should we believe from this that he should be a good judge of untried plays? It is one thing to produce a success; it is another to discover a success.

⚘

The loud trumpeting of Mr. Conried's plan has knocked on the head another scheme that was on foot for a National Theatre, which to my mind seemed much more what such an institution should be than that of Mr. Conried. The money had already been subscribed and the scheme was in good shape when Mr. Conried threw his bomb into the arena. Whether the people who are interested in the other plan will retire from it altogether, or will only hold back until they see what Mr. Conried is actually going to do, I

cannot say. I can only hope that their retirement is merely temporary.

⚘

Miss Susan Strong, who is about to return to America, her native country, for a season, has made a great success in England. She is a pupil of Francis Korbay, the well-known Hungarian composer and teacher, whose departure from New York some years ago caused genuine sorrow to all lovers of good music. The London *Times* describes her as one of the most interesting singers of the day. Miss Strong is not a singer of grand opera, but rather confines herself to song recitals, interpreting many of the best if least sung masters. I take pleasure in presenting this portrait of Miss Strong, reproduced from a crayon sketch by Mr. John S. Sargent.

⚘

I wonder if Mr. E. J. Hornung is not going to overdo "Raffles" as a hero of fiction. He has already published two "Raffles" books, and now Messrs. Scribner announce "A Thief in the Night: Further Adventures of A. J. Raffles, Cricketer and Cracksman." Sir Conan Doyle has come to the end of his Sherlock Holmes stories as far as the public is concerned. They no longer thrill as they did. There may be publishers willing to pay him a dollar a word for the resuscitation of the great detective, but it is generally admitted by those who admire Sir Arthur's work most that Sherlock Holmes has been overdone. The same fate will befall "Raffles." He was virtually brought back from death for his second appearance upon the scene, but the corpse having once been revived, Mr. Hornung probably thinks he can live as long as Mr. Rider Haggard's "She."

⚘

Mr. Robert Hichens has chosen a startling title, "The Call of the Blood," for his next novel. By the side of this name, "The Call of the Wild" is tame. Mr. Hichens has taken Sicily for the scene of his new story. The scene of "The Garden of Allah," which was the

MISS SUSAN STRONG

From a drawing by Mr. John Singer Sargent

N AND THE MOUSE.   ACT 3
Elliston as Shirley Rossmore, Mr. Edmund Breese as Ready Money Ryder

literary sensation of last year, was laid in Egypt. If Mr. Hichens can paint the scenery of Sicily as he painted the scenery of Egypt, another notable book of word painting may be expected. The new story will not appear until the autumn of 1906, which shows that Mr. Hichens is not taking advantage of the great success of "The Garden of Allah."

The indefatigable Dr. S. Weir Mitchell is at work on a new short novel which will appear serially in the *Century Magazine.* Dr. Mitchell seems to grow younger with the years. As for his work, it is just as vigorous to-day as it was when he wrote "Hugh Wynne," and he was not a young man, by the way, when he wrote that story.

After the horror of ghosts last winter, after the tangled witticisms and humorous indecencies of Bernard Shaw this fall, and after the yearly round of psychological clap-trap by lesser playwrights, the New York theatre-goer meets a reward for his patience. At "The Lion and the Mouse," a play by Mr. Charles Klein, the author of the "Music Master," one may sit before a clean, virile drama, dealing with one of the problems of our modern environment, as it centres about a man who has passed the sentimental and romantic age. More, the spectator may here visit a play that though the force of the dramatic qualities of emotion, of suspense, of dry humor, and of movement compels its audience to listen with a willing momentary belief. Finally he may rest thankful that if the author intended to draw a moral he relegated it to its proper place, where the greater part of the audience cannot discover it, though those that insist on finding a meaning beneath the surface may unearth a creed that personal interest rules the world more than any code of principles.

Perhaps the same delvers are convinced that in their search among the characters they have reached traces of Mr. John D. Rockefeller and Miss Ida M. Tarbell. Unfortunately for them the author admits that he wrote the play before the noted articles ever came to light. Nevertheless, Ryder, a type rather than an individual, through his own strength of character masters the stage for three acts. Even if he does not stand calm analysis unshaken, he holds the attention of his audience, especially in his dialogues with Shirley, a girl whom Americans love to think the example of their race, and with "Jef," a young man unfortunately rare among his social companions. In these latter moments more than anywhere else the elder Ryder's remarks show unusual adaptation to the character of their speaker. When the old man wishes to cut short the queries and explanations of "Jef," he says:

"No Tolstoy! He 's a great thinker! You 're not! No, Shaw! He 's funny! You 're not!"

And when the two part company shortly after, the father calls to his son as the young man starts for the door:

"Is that all?"

"Yes, that 's all!"

"Leave your address with your mother!"

To carry out the task set for them the players have worked conscientiously and well, acting with each other for a thorough general effect. Richard Bennett, as "Jef," places in the usually thankless rôle of the son and lover a good-natured charm, removed from the conventional sappy rendering. Mr. Edmund Breese grasps the dynamics of John Burkett Ryder. At times he drops his sentences into a melodramatic tone, but for the most part he remains consistent and virile. As Shirley Rossmore, Miss Grace Elliston looks her part, and acts it capably, despite an unfortunately monotonous delivery. The minor rôles are intelligently cast so that there come no gaps that the audience would wish to see hurried over. Such a production will not be damned or praised on details so long as the best play is regarded as the play that reaches the highest general level. Whatever "The Lion and the Mouse" lacks in logic, or psychology, or delicate construction, it balances in its clean and dignified tone, its sustained interest, and its independence.

✿

Mark Twain's seventieth birthday was celebrated with much enthusiasm at a dinner given by Colonel Harvey on the 5th of last month. THE CRITIC celebrated the fiftieth birthday of Mr. Clemens twenty years ago with letters of congratulation from distinguished authors and a poem contributed for the occasion by Oliver Wendell Holmes, which I reprint for the benefit of those who may have forgotten it and of others who never saw it:

Ah, Clemens, when I saw thee last,
　　We both of us were younger,—
How fondly mumbling o'er the past
　　Is Memory's toothless hunger!

So fifty years have fled, they say,
　　Since first you took to drinking,—
I mean in Nature's milky way,—
　　Of course no ill I 'm thinking.

But while on life's uneven road
　　Your track you 've been pursuing,
What fountains from your wit have flowed,—
　　What drinks you have been brewing!

I know whence all your magic came,—
　　Your secret I 've discovered,—
The source that fed your inward flame,—
　　The dreams that round you hovered:

Before you learned to bite or munch,
　　Still kicking in your cradle,
The Muses mixed a bowl of punch,
　　And Hebe seized the ladle.

Dear babe, whose fiftieth year to-day
　　Your ripe half-century rounded,
Your books the precious draught betray
　　The laughing Nine compounded.

So mixed the sweet, the sharp, the strong,
　　Each finds its faults amended,
The virtues that to each belong
　　In happier union blended.

And what the flavor can surpass
　　Of sugar, spirit, lemons?
So while one health fills every glass
　　Mark Twain for Baby Clemens!

THE CRITIC celebration was a great

surprise to Mr. Clemens, as expressed in this little note of acknowledgment:

MY DEAR CONSPIRATORS : It was the pleasantest surprise I have ever had, and you have my best thanks. It reconciles me to being fifty years old; and it was for you to invent the miracle that could do that—I could never have invented one myself that could do it. May you live to be fifty yourselves, and find a fellow-benefactor in that hour of awful need. Sincerely yours,
　　　　　　　　　　　　S. L. CLEMENS.

I will venture to say that the most appreciated present that Mr. Clemens received on his fiftieth birthday was the manuscript of Dr. Holmes's poem, sent to him with the compliments of THE CRITIC.

✿

Mr. Clemens's seventieth birthday was celebrated in poetry as well as was his fiftieth. It was not a surprise that Dr. Holmes should put into verse the praises of his fellow-humorist, but it was a surprise that Mr. W. D. Howells should burst forth into song on this occasion. Mr. Howells's contributions to poetry have been few and far between, which shows that the seventieth anniversary of his friend's birth was unusually inspiring. Here is what Mr. Howells said:

A traveller from the Old World, just escaped
　　Our customs with his life had found his way
To a place uptown, where a Colossus shaped
　　Itself, skyscraper high, against the day.
A vast smile, dawning from its mighty lips,
　　Like sunshine on its visage seemed to brood ;
One eye winked in perpetual eclipse,
　　In the other a huge tear of pity stood.
Wisdom in chunks about its temples shone ;
　　Its measureless bulk grotesque exultant rose ;
And while Titanic puissance clothed it on,
　　Patience with foreigners was in its pose.
So that, " What art thou ? " the emboldened traveller
　　　　spoke,
And it replied, " I am the American joke.

" I am the joke that laughs the proud to scorn ;
　　I mock at cruelty, I banish care,
I cheer the lowly, chipper the forlorn,
　　I bid the oppressor and hypocrite beware.
I tell the tale that makes men cry for joy ;
　　I bring the laugh that has no hate in it ;
In the heart of age I wake the undying boy ;
　　My big stick blossoms with a thornless wit.

The lame dance with delight in me ; my mirth
Reaches the deaf untrumpeted ; the blind
My point can see. I jolly the whole earth,
But most I love to jolly my own kind.
Joke of a people great, gay, bold, and free,
I type their master mood. Mark Twain made me."

Of course Mr. Clemens's own speech was the speech of the evening. He was never in better form, which means that he was never more amusing. The most of his address was devoted to instructing his hearers how to live to be seventy:

We have no permanent habits until we are forty. Then they begin to harden, presently they petrify, then business begins. Since forty I have been regular about going to bed and getting up—and that is one of the main things. I have made it a rule to go to bed when there was n't anybody left to sit up with, and I have made it a rule to get up when I had to. This has resulted in an unswerving regularity of irregularity. It has saved me sound, but it would injure another person.

In the matter of diet—which is another main thing—I have been persistently strict in sticking to the things which did n't agree with me until one or the other of us got the best of it. Until lately I got the best of it myself. But last spring I stopped frolicking with mince pie after midnight ; up to then I had always believed it was n't loaded.

And I wish to urge upon you this—which I think is wisdom—that if you find you can't make seventy by any but an uncomfortable road, don't you go. When they take off the Pullman and retire you to the rancid smoker, put on your things, count your checks, and get out at the first way station where there 's a cemetery.

I have made it a rule never to smoke more than one cigar at a time. I have no other restriction as regards smoking. I do not know just when I began to smoke, I only know that it was in my father's lifetime, and that I was discreet. He passed from this life early in 1847, when I was a shade past eleven ; ever since then I have smoked publicly.

To-day it is all of sixty years since I began to smoke the limit. I have never bought cigars with life-belts around them. I early found that those were too expensive for me. I have always bought cheap cigars—reasonably cheap, at any rate. Sixty years ago they cost me $4 a barrel, but my taste has improved latterly, and I pay $7 now.

As for drinking, I have no rule about that. When the others drink I like to help, otherwise I remain dry, by habit and preference. This dryness does not hurt me, but it could easily hurt you, because you are different. You let it alone.

I have never taken any exercise except sleeping and resting, and I never intend to take any. Exercise is loathsome. And it cannot be any benefit when you are tired ; I was always tired. But let another person try my way and see where he will come out.

I desire now to repeat and emphasize that maxim: We can't reach old age by another man's road. My habits protect my life, but they would assassinate you.

All of this goes to show that Mark Twain is still himself. Long may he wave!

Books of To=day and Books of To=morrow

LONDON, December, 1905.
DEAR BELINDA,—

After writing the word "December" at the heading of this letter I feel that I should follow it up by writing you upon some such subject as "How to have a good time." But, then, every one's idea of "a good time" is different, so it is n't any good my attempting to please you or any one else in such matters. Then I might attempt an essay on the subject of Christmas and Christmas customs, and read up the subject so as to appropriately quote all the old carols and interlard my sentences with barn-door flights of learning upon pageants, revels, and wassail bowls, and encourage you to keep up Christmas in the good old way. Last year a well-known Baronet told me that he had been keeping Christmas in the old-fashioned way, but that it had made him and all his Christmas party so very ill that he never would attempt it again. No, the work I have to do this month is strictly businesslike, the fact being that books are now given more than ever as presents, and there being a wilderness of new books around us at the present time, I propose, as usual at this time of the year, to try to assist you in this matter of choosing books as Christmas gifts. With so much to do, I am disposed to divide all the volumes which are before me into two, and to call one lot big books and the other lot little books, and the idea, as I think about it, does n't seem bad, because when you make up your list of friends to receive presents there are always a number of people to whom you must send a big book and others who are good as gold for a whole year —in fact, until next Christmas—if you only remember them with just a trifle. This year there do not appear to be as many big books as in former years. I am disposed to think that the day of really big books is passing away. Publishers find that a big picture book for "grown-ups" is a very short-lived thing, and so I suppose we shall get fewer and fewer of this kind each year.

Messrs. Goupil, whose taste and judgment are almost always above reproach, this year have added to their fine quarto illustrated series a book upon the Duchesse de Berry, who flourished in the early years of the nineteenth century. Perhaps a better subject might have been found, and one wonders often why Messrs. Goupil, with all their facilities and their enterprise, have never yet added to their series a volume upon Madame du Barry. The majority would prefer Du Barry to De Berry. Mrs. Steuart Erskine comes next with a fine book upon "Beautiful Women"— historical ladies of a past day around whom cling romance, gossip, and scandal. This book has delightful portraits reproduced by the skill of Mr. Hyatt. There are no garden books so far this autumn, though one hears that some great ladies are busy with books about their own homes and gardens. "Garden Color," a volume issued last spring, holds the field as the best garden book of the year, and the fine pair of volumes upon "Italian Gardens" issued some months ago makes a good gift. Miss Du Cane also, who is so well known as a very clever artist of gardens, has illustrated with gorgeous colored sketches Mr. Bagot's book upon the Italian Lakes,

and this makes a very pretty volume, uniform with Menpes's "Japan." I was saying how much the big book has decreased in numbers the past few years, and this is in part owing, no doubt, to the success of the colored book initiated by Messrs. Black with the volume upon "Japan" to which I have just alluded. There is now in this series at least thirty volumes (each published at a sovereign) from which a choice may be made of books both handsome and readable. This series deserves all the success it has met with. And in this same *format* there has just been added a most delightful "Life of Kate Greenaway," written by Mr. Spielmann and Mr. Layard. It is crammed full of specimens of Kate Greenaway's work, all chosen with good judgment and good taste — such a fascinating record of one of the very few first-class decorative book artists England can boast of. And there are heaps of letters to the artist from Ruskin, Frederick Locker, and others. To turn the pages over and just look at the pictures is a joy. This year there are a great many good biographies and memoirs. Unfortunately at the time I write this letter only a few of those promised are really published. The first favourite is Mr. Wilkins's "Memoirs of Mrs. Fitzherbert and George IV." For very many years it has been known that there was a box at Messrs. Coutts's containing vindications of Mrs. Fitzherbert, her marriage certificate, etc., and from time to time endeavors have been made to publish these papers, but unsuccessfully. When Lord Holland published his memoirs of the Whig Party in 1854, there were statements therein which were supposed to be injurious to Mrs. Fitzherberts' reputation, and one relative endeavored in a partial biography to justify Mrs. Fitzherbert, but he failed to make use of these papers, at any rate fully, and it has been left to Mr. Wilkins to negotiate their publication. Mrs. Fitzherbert was twice a widow before George IV., then Prince of Wales (1785), fell, or thought he fell, in love with her. He was badly taken with the malady, and on one occasion attempted to stab himself in despair for her sake. They were married in a drawing-room, and everything went well until Charles Fox stated in the House that he didn't believe they were married at all. This was a real bomb, and the Prince went off to Mrs. Fitzherbert and said, "What do you think, Maria? Charles declared in the House last night that you and I were not man and wife." However, this was soon hushed up by the skill of Sheridan, and all went well for many years afterwards. Another biography which has already attracted a lot of notice is Mr. Sichel's "Life of Lady Hamilton." Mr. Sichel has been fortunate in securing the co-operation of Mrs. Morrison, the owner of the priceless Nelson-Hamilton correspondence. The book is a fuller and better written life than hitherto has appeared of Lady Hamilton, a subject ever dear and ever fresh to the reading public, and particularly opportune this year, when everything relating to Nelson is being read. The authoritative "Life of Marie Antoinette," written a year or so ago by M. de Nolhac, has just been issued in a new form. Hitherto the book has been accompanied by a number of prints, which have made it a high-priced book, but now the whole of the historical narrative can be purchased in a remarkably well printed and attractive-looking book—a very handy, inexpensive, and a very readable account of the reign and tragic end of this unfortunate Queen. Two political biographies are promised, those of Sir James Graham and Sidney Herbert. Mr. Justin McCarthy brings up the "History of our Own Times" to the accession of King Edward. "Mrs. Brookfield and Her Circle," by Charles and Frances Brookfield, will attract much attention. It seems but the other day that Mrs. Brookfield was about, looking as handsome as ever in her old age. Mrs. Brookfield was the original of "Lady Castlewood" in "Esmond," and moved in the centre of the brilliant world which included Thackeray, Tennyson, the Hallams, the Lytteltons, and Dean Stanley. Two other biographies of social celebrities which every one hopes soon to see are Sir Algernon West's "Life of Admiral Keppel" and Mr. Herbert Paul's "Life of Froude." Both books are bound to add much to what we know already about two magnetic personalities. The "Holman Hunt Memoirs of the Preraphaelite Brotherhood" will surely be another favorite. I would have liked to say much about Mr. Romilly's "Letters to Ivy from Lord Dudley," but I have no space, for I must now scamper through the titles of the children's books. The new Golliwogg book is "The Golliwoggs' Fox-hunt," which, after a spirited chase, ended in the fox getting down a hollow tree, and though he lost his brush he preserved his mask, and lived to be hunted another day. Mr. Walter Emanuel has successfully done "The Zoo: a Scamper," plentifully interspersed with some of his excellent jokes. Lady Ridley has a new book, "The Sparrow with One White Feather"; and the Duchess of Buckingham has written a very entertaining volume called "Willy Wind and Jock and the Cheeses." "Told to the Children Series" is a successful series of inexpensive story-books based upon the old heroic tales, well printed and well illustrated. Seton Thompson's new book is "Monarch, the Big Bear," with heaps of pretty illustrations. Other excellent story-books are Mr. Lucas's "Old-Fashioned Tales," Mr. Hudson's "Little Boy Lost," Miss Evelyn Sharp's "Micky," and Miss Gilder's "Autobiography of a Tomboy." Needless to say, Mr. Strang is to the front with two capital stories for big boys, well worthy of the Henty traditions which Mr. Strang has already proved he worthily sustains. "Maitland Major and Minor," by Charles Turley, and "The Head of Kay's," by P. G. Wodehouse, may be singled out from the great mass of children's literature which comes upon us every Christmas season.

I wanted to finish up by saying a good deal about the smaller but none the less important books which every one will require. I think if the choice were to be given to me of selecting half-a-dozen inexpensive presents of taste, I should choose first the new book by the author of "Elizabeth and her German Garden." It is called "The Princess Priscilla's Fortnight." Next I would choose De Goncourt's "Love in the Eighteenth Century," a charming little essay about France and French ways at a time about which every one wishes to know as much as he can. Then there is a new and much better printed edition of Maeterlinck's great book, "The Treasure of the Humble." No book of modern times has touched a higher note than this. The fourth book I shall name is Mr. Birrell's new volume of essays, "In the Name of the Bodleian." Mr. Birrell has never written a dull line, and I am sure never made a dull speech, or told a story which was not well worth telling. His new book is full of learning, but it lies lightly upon Mr. Birrell's shoulders. He is always brilliant, always to the point, and delightfully epigrammatic. The fifth volume of these six elect is Lady Lindsay's "Godfrey's Quest," a fantastic and charming poem written in the gifted manner which has marked all Lady Lindsay's works. As far as I am aware, Lady Lindsay's volume is the only distinguished volume of poetry this Christmas. Last I shall name Mr. Lucas's volume, "The Friendly Town," a fitting companion to his successful "Open Road."

Your friend,
ARTHUR PENDENYS.

English "Estranged"

By WILLIAM ARCHER

MY eye has just fallen upon a paragraph in the London *Daily Chronicle* which has aroused in me such burning indignation that I must give it vent without a moment's delay. The peccant paper is already, no doubt, on its way across the Atlantic, and it is important that a disclaimer should follow it as quickly as possible. Questions of language are not the trifles they appear, and I am quite serious in holding that people who write in the tone of the *Chronicle* paragraphist not only fly in the face of common-sense, but do grievous international mischief. Without further preamble, I present to the reader's most unfavorable consideration the offending paragraph:

In an English book just published occur two turns of phrase : " I concluded to stay," and " lung-trouble." It is certain that no one within the four seas uses these words without deliberation or by inadvertence. The Englishman who says " lung-trouble " or " conclude " (for " decide ") does so for the express purpose of enriching the English language from the stores of America. We ask him not to take the task upon himself. If we must set ourselves to borrow, let it be from the other tongues, not from our own estranged. Some lendings from France we always need, as does France from us.

The writer then goes on to remark that while we have borrowed "poseur" from France, the French have borrowed "snob" from us, and misapplied it, to express the same idea. I am not sure that the French "snob" is the exact equivalent of the English "poseur"; but for an example of linguistic snobbishness in the home-made British sense of the word, commend me to the *Chronicle* paragraph.

It is really time that people who want to turn up their noses at Americanisms should learn, in common prudence, to turn up their dictionaries first. How many hundreds of so-called American barbarisms have proved to be good, sound, classical English! Over "conclude" the paragraphist puts his foot in it conspicuously. He may, perhaps, have heard of a play called "Julius Cæsar," composed by a Midland Englishman, wholly untainted (for the best of reasons) with Americanism, in which occurs the phrase:

. . . the Senate have concluded
To give this day a crown to mighty Cæsar.

And again, the same writer, in one of his poems, says, "They did conclude to bear dead Lucrece thence." Does the *Chronicle* demand better authority? Or will it tell us that Shakespeare was perversely bent on "enriching the English language from the stores of America"? The *Chronicle* man may conceivably seek a loop-hole for escape in pointing out that both the Shake-spearian phrases refer to a decision arrived at by several persons—in other words, to the "conclusion" of some sort of debate—whereas the phrase he reprobates refers to the determination of a single person. But is a mental debate a thing undreamt of in his psychology? Does he never stand "this way and that dividing the swift mind," and finally "conclude" for or against some project? The next time he wants to sneer at an Americanism, I think he had better "conclude" to make certain first that it was not familiar to Chaucer a hundred years before Columbus was born. As for "lung-trouble," I was not aware that America could claim credit for the expression, nor am I inclined to concede it to her on the paragraphist's authority. But if he should prove to be right in this instance, the expression is a distinct "enrichment" of the English language, and a feather in America's cap. How often do we want to say that there is something amiss with some portion of our physical economy, without being able or willing to give a definite name to the disease? And, in such an instance, how can we put the matter more briefly, or more in consonance with the genius and tradition of the English language, than by speaking of lung-trouble, heart-trouble, or brain-trouble, as the case may be? It is really difficult to write with patience of the folly which would thus paralyze the language, and at the same time raise a barrier of pedantry between us and our cousins of the West. Indeed, I am not sure that I have succeeded in discussing the matter with that judicial calm which usually characterizes my utterances. I confess to feeling a distinct "pain in my temper"—or an attack of temper-trouble, if the *Chronicle* will permit me to say so.

Not that I profess an indiscriminating admiration for every locution that comes from America. There are objectionable Americanisms, just as there are detestable Anglicisms. For instance, on 1 July, 1904, I read in the *Daily Chronicle*, of all papers, a dispatch "From Our War Correspondent" in the Far East, containing the following expressions:

It is up to the honor and sense of justice and of right of the peoples of the entire civilized world to see her [Japan] through. . . . I have interviewed not a few of the sense-carriers of the nation, and found there was quite a strange unanimity of opinion.

Neither "it is up to" nor "sense-carriers" seems to me a valuable addition to the common stock of our speech. "It is the duty of" and "representative men" are good enough for me. I should never use, nor encourage others to use, these unnecessary and (as it seems to me) ungraceful neologisms. At the same time, my voice in the matter is only one among many millions. The phrases are, so to speak, put up for election into the English language. For my part, I blackball them; I "have no use for them"; but I frankly admit the right of America to propose phrases for election, and gratefully acknowledge the substantial value of hundreds of the phrases proposed by her and elected by acclaim. It is quite possible that, a generation hence, "it is up to" and "sense-carriers" may have proved their right to survive—by surviving. They may fulfil some function which I cannot divine, and gradually establish themselves in the language. On the other hand—and I think more probably—they may be nothing but ephemeral turns of phrase, of which every year produces its crop in every living language. What is the meaning of a living language if it be not one that can take on and cast off new expressions, according as they prove or do not prove adapted to its uses? It is extraordinary what pains some people will take to convince themselves that it is vulgar for a language to be alive, and that it ought in decency to pretend to be as dead as a door-nail.

"But," my adversary may object, "if you claim the right to blackball 'sense-carriers,' why should you be so angry if I exercise the same right in the case of 'lung-trouble'?" The right is unquestioned; what exasperates me is the exceeding and elaborate badness of the reason alleged. No attempt is made to show that "lung-trouble" is ungraceful, illogical, or superfluous — that some more expressive phrase (for instance, "pulmonary affection") meets all our requirements. No — the sole defect of the phrase is its (alleged) American origin. The principle of its rejection is formulated in these memorable terms: "If we must borrow, let it be from the other tongues, not from our own estranged." In other words, instead of accepting with gratitude the natural enrichment of our speech due to the nimble Transatlantic brain, let us interlard the language of Shakespeare and Milton and Bunyan, of Dryden and Swift and Defoe, of Emerson and Hawthorne and Lincoln, with lumbering German vocables and modish tags of French! A more perversely nonsensical doctrine was surely never enunciated. It is unhappily true that there are a few French terms (such as "naïf" and "tête-à-tête") for which our language has as yet evolved no satisfactory equivalent. The self-respecting writer will do all he can to avoid even these, and use them only when it would be, so to speak, an affectation to refrain. But the vile practice of flying to a French word whenever an English one was in the least difficult to find has long been abandoned by all educated people; nor is there much danger that the exhortations of the *Chronicle* will revive it. I, for my part, am all for accepting foreign expressions that can be Anglicized without difficulty or grotesqueness. For instance, I regard "overman" and "hinterland" as legitimate English words. That, however, is a matter of opinion, and is not what the *Chronicle*-man has in view. His principle is that you show respect for the English language when you call a man a "poseur," disrespect when you say that he has "lung-trouble." Was there ever a quainter inversion of reason!

·————

Oriental Definitions

Jagannatha

By MARGUERITE MERINGTON

The idol rides (we cry), rides forth in state ;
Vishnu (we cry) seeks victims by the road—
And we whom Brahma framed, precipitate,
Hurtle ourselves beneath the deadly load !

Our feet that Brahma fashioned for the dance,
Halt, maimed (we cry), through life must bear their mar,
Crushed by the adverse wheels of circumstance—
And yet who reared the idol, built the car !

JAGANNATHA

Willis and Poe: A Retrospect

By ANNIE RUSSELL MARBLE

FENIMORE COOPER said through one of his characters, "To an American, *always* means just eighteen months." Happily we have outgrown some of the braggart traits which called forth such extreme sarcasm but do we not seem still precocious occasionally, anxious to appear older than we are in history and letters? The day of the American literary centenary is at hand and with patriotic zeal the celebrations have begun. That an author is read, or even is popular, one hundred years after his birth is scarcely sufficient ground, however, for proclaiming him among the immortals of literature. Reading some of the lavish tributes heaped upon Emerson and Hawthorne one felt assured that the men, reserved and sincere, would have deplored such extravagance. On the other hand, there is a feeling of satisfaction at the coming of these centenaries, if they are observed with taste and discrimination. Such is the fitting time to disprove false statements and uproot prejudices, to collect bits of personalia from the surviving family and few acquaintances of the author, or to record in an effective form a special message which the author has brought to some individual reader. It is the occasion for registering the present rank of the author in comparison with earlier popularity or neglect; it is not the occasion for glowing prophecies.

Perhaps it is fortunate, as a means of emphasizing the true significance of the centenary, that the present month in America recalls the birth of a minor almost forgotten, writer. Following the revival of interest in seer and in romancer, and preceding the acclaims which will soon greet the three favorite New England poets, is this centennial year of Willis, once the most successful of earlier American writers, if success be gauged by popularity and financial returns. With new force recurs the truism, "Time! the corrector where our judgments err." Fifty years ago Willis ranked, abroad as well as in America, with Irving and Longfellow in general favor, surpassing Bryant, Hawthorne, and Poe. He outlived his own prestige, and his star of fame, once so conspicuous, has lost its radiance until there is not even a glimmer of revival. Justice seems now to be done his memory by recalling such phrases of characterization as "the graceful trifler," "the prince of paragraphists," or

The topmost bright bubble on the Wave of the Town.

Occasionally some reader of authority rescues a few of his stanzas from the mass of buried verses and prose ephemera. Colonel Higginson has recently instanced "the sweet, dying cadences" of "The Belfry Pigeon." With kindly judgment, tinctured by boyhood's memories, he finds evidence "to atone for all of Willis' coxcombry and to show that, in spite of the English applauses that spoiled him, he was a poet at heart," in the melodious lines,

Whatever tale in the bell is heard,
He broods on his folded feet unstirr'd,
Or, rising half in his rounded nest,
He takes the time to smooth his breast,
Then drops again with filmèd eyes,
And sleeps as the last vibration dies.

Poe's relation to Willis was that of a just, intuitive critic and a warm, often dependent, friend. Spurning the bulk of his writings that gained the ear of the social world, Poe delighted in those simple stanzas by Willis, beginning, "The shadows lay along Broadway."

In this pictorial study of two women, attended by the "Unseen Spirits" of hauteur and repentance, Poe admired the "grace, dignity, and pathos," and asserted that here was "a true imagination," a verdict accepted by latter-day critics. Poe was really our first critic with intuition to pierce through the film of popularity and with courage to affirm that Longfellow was overrated as a poet of originality, that the obscure Hawthorne was "a man of extraordinary genius," and that Willis's fame was largely due to his temperament, with its versatility and energy, and to the effective "display of his wares." In spite of such detraction he regarded Willis as a sincere friend, with far-reaching, helpful influence.

With frank acknowledgment that Willis's own work was of only passing value, it may be worth while to record that he had qualities of mind and heart which, joined to his potential popularity, enabled him to do many a service for struggling authors, then almost unheeded but now among the few American writers who are candidates for lasting fame. Through his *Athenæum* sketches and his editorial columns in the *Mirror* and the *Home Journal*, he introduced, or, in turn, defended from unjust attacks, Bryant, Halleck, Cooper, Hawthorne, Poe, and Longfellow. His columns were kindly and encouraging in tone, even if they sometimes lacked keenness, in those days when newspaper notices generally savored of hyperbole or invective. In Poe's letters one may find many iterations of his indebtedness to Willis. Writing Griswold he said, "Willis, whose good opinion I value highly, and of whose good word I have a right to be proud, has done me the honor to speak very pointedly in praise of 'The Raven.'" Again, with more than formal or politic thanks, he wrote Willis, "I have not forgotten how 'a good word in season' from you *made* 'The Raven' and *made* 'Ulalume.'" Both these poems, which now rank high on the list of native poetry, were first printed anonymously in inferior journals with meagre circulation and might have been buried there, had not Willis

reprinted them in his popular columns with notes of sure approval and adroit inquiry as to the author, thus challenging public curiosity. His comment on "The Raven" as "the most effective single example of fugitive poetry ever published in this country," and his more effusive praise of the phonetic merit of "Ulalume" were almost the first pronounced words of recognition of Poe as poet.

Willis did more than stand sponsor for the first-fruits of genius of his less fortunate friend. He gave him employment, with strong support and opportunity, and came to his defence in print on two noteworthy occasions. When the poverty of the Poe family was unfolded to the public by a kind but indiscreet woman, Willis not only sent inquiries of friendship and practical aid, but, yet more, he wrote a judicious statement of the case in his *Home Journal,*—"kind and manly comments," said Poe in a letter of thanks. Through the intimacy established while Poe was assisting Willis as editor of the *New Mirror* in 1844 and 1845, the latter was able to answer with force and dignity some of Griswold's insinuations in his famous obituary of Poe in the *Tribune.* Against the charge of erratic and violent temper Willis testified:

With the highest admiration for his genius, and a willingness to let it atone for more than ordinary irregularity, we were led to expect, by common report, a very capricious attention to his duties, and occasionally a scene of violence and difficulty. Time went on, however, and he was invariably punctual and industrious—a patient, industrious, and most gentlemanly person, commanding the utmost respect and good feeling by his unvarying deportment and ability.

Willis was the first commentator to explain the fearful effects of a few grains of alcohol on Poe's brain, and to appeal for a kindlier judgment for the man in his sanity and for the poet gifted far beyond the common knowledge.

Without recalling in detail other services to American authors of half a century ago, amid the words of disparagement which are his due and the yet more scathing censure of silence, one may pause for a word of appreciation of Willis, the friend, and may find reason for Professor Richardson's affirmation that Willis "was a power not to be ignored in the development of letters in New York."

Twelfth Night

By CHARLES J. BAYNE

LAST of the wassail nights,
  Wholesomely merry,
Still on the mistletoe
  Clings the white berry;
Still are the apples red,
  Brown is the ale:
Feast of our Saxon sires,
  Hail and all hail!

Bring forth the boar's head,
  Bring forth the Rhenish;
Tankards that melt away,
  Haste to replenish;
Lift on the stoutest log;
  Loud be the laughter,
Until the sound of mirth
  Shake wall and rafter.

Call back the sturdy days
  When hearts of oak
Beat to the lilting strains
  We now invoke;
Call back the hearty days
  When squire and yeoman
Feasted the home-returned
  Pikemen and bowmen.

Masques in the Temple hall,
  Staged for the benchers,
Wait while the turning-spit
  Heaps up the trenchers—
Wait while the venison,
  Basted with spices,
Smokes as the richest
  Of Yule's sacrifices.

Now Merry Andrew comes,
  Fresh from the morris;
Now rustic Corydon
  Trips it with Chloris:
Let the soft virginals
  Answer the tabor;
After this wassail night
  Come days of labor.

Such were the old delights,
  Rounding the Yule;
Where sleeps His Majesty,
  Lord of Misrule?
Still are the apples red,
  Brown is the ale:
Feast of our Saxon sires,
  Hail and all hail!

The Lambs*

By H. W. BOYNTON

MR. LUCAS'S Life of Charles and Mary Lamb (as it might well have been called, though only the brother's name appears upon the title-page) fitly complements his admirable edition of their Works and Letters. One must regret that the book-loving pair could not, through the paltry accident of mor-

CHARLES LAMB (AGED 50)
From the etching by Brook Pulham. (First state)

tality, see themselves arrayed in these costly glories of paper, typography, and illustration, and glossed with so

full and sympathetic a commentary. It would really seem that for once a publisher has not claimed too much in postulating the finality of his version. Yet we know that other editions are to come—it is a part of our faith in the permanence of that cherished fame—and we may find it in our hearts, without belittling the present acquisition, to hope that finality will in this instance prove to be a relative term. Other data, we trust, remain to be unearthed; other Lamb enthusiasts, doubtless, are to find fresh reward for their assiduity.

Mr. Lucas has of course drawn largely upon Talfourd for his facts; but has also come into possession of some important new material. Upon two points he has certainly thrown fresh light: upon the fact of Lamb's recurrent but never confirmed intemperance, and upon the hitherto obscure episode of his second and serious love-affair. Of those too frequent alcoholic lapses we had perhaps heard enough for our comfort. Lamb himself was sufficiently frank in speaking of them; far more frank than men of less achievement and equal frailty find it possible to be to-day. Not that he was unashamed, but that prudery had not then begun to prescribe reticence in that connection. The line had not yet come to be sharply drawn, in theory, between the victim of "rum," whose home was in the gutter, and the total abstainer. Lamb was, socially, at his best after a glass or two; and it is no marvel if, now and then, he passed the bounds of decent exhilaration. Drunkard (despite the unmistakable autobiographical, note in those feeling "Confessions") he never was. Yes, we may venture to quote— so much it breathes of human contrition, so wholesomely short it comes of mawkish self-abasement—one of the good man's own comments upon such a lapse:

I protest I know not in what words to invest my sense of the shameful violation of hospitality which

* The illustrations in this article are taken by permission from a "Life of Charles Lamb" by E. V. Lucas. G. P. Putnam's Sons.

I was guilty of on that fatal Wednesday. Let it be blotted from the calendar. Had it been committed at a layman's house, say a merchant's or manufacturer's, a cheesemonger's or greengrocer's, or, to go higher, a barrister's, a member of Parliament's, a rich banker's, I should have felt alleviation, a drop of self-pity. But to be seen deliberately to go out of the house of a clergyman drunk! a clergyman of the Church of England, too! . . . And, then, from what a house! Not a common glebe or vicarage (which yet had been shameful), but from a kingly repository of sciences, human and divine, with the primate of England for its guardian, arrayed in public majesty, from which the profane vulgar are bid fly. Could all those volumes have taught me nothing better?

The bibulatory excess in question occurred, it should have been said, at the rooms of Mr. Cary, of the British Museum.

Of Lamb's mature attachment for the popular and accomplished actress, Fanny Kelly, we are tempted to speak with some fulness. The brief correspondence which makes the affair intelligible is not here first published; but it here takes its proper place in a general view of Elia's life and character. It consists in but three letters, the first containing a rather formal profession of love and proposal of marriage, the second Miss Kelly's womanly but decided refusal, and the last Lamb's quiet and half-humorous submission to her reasonable will. Mr. Lucas does not make too much of the episode; indeed, it seems to me that he hardly attaches enough importance to it. We had known in a vague way that Lamb was at one time an ardent admirer of Fanny Kelly, and were familiar with the rumor of his offer of marriage; here impression and rumor are crystallized into unmistakable fact. There is no getting away from this clean and compact record; there is no denying that it brings to a focus more than one aspect of Lamb's character and of his sister's. A Lamb intent upon sacrificing his vaunted bachelorhood, an Elia turning his thoughts away from Cousin Bridget: surely there must have been more, or less, in this man than one has suspected: more or less in Bridget herself. In the light of this suspicion we are tempted to trace once more the not

unfamiliar events of that double career, and shall be surprised if we do not find them in some respects more intelligible than heretofore.

We may pass over Lamb's childish and Bluecoat days, and the few years which followed. Even the early romantic attachment for Alice " W.," with its ensuing sonnets, need not delay us long: that also belonged to a preliminary phase of experience. No doubt Lamb felt as sincerely as other boys of nineteen; and like them was inclined to take it for granted that all the Graces had blue eyes of a certain tinge and shape, and all the Primal Truths were hidden under a certain tangible mass of yellow hair. He continued for some time to look back upon her, or upon his notion of her, with tenderness, but without passion. He seems to have connected the experience, at the time, with his single attack of madness. In May, 1796, he writes to Coleridge that he has just spent six weeks " very agreeably in a madhouse near Hoxton "; and that " my head ran on you in my madness, as much almost as on another Person, who I am inclined to think was the more immediate cause of my temporary frenzy."

In September of the same year took place what we must call the first really great event in Lamb's experience; an event which made a man of him, and largely determined the course of his subsequent life. The letter in which Lamb tells Coleridge of it is one of the most moving in the language, partly because it is not a mere piteous outcry, but the utterance of a spirit which feels its power to withstand.

. . . My poor dear dearest sister in a fit of insanity has been the death of her own mother. I was at hand only time enough to snatch the knife out of her grasp. She is at present at a madhouse, from which I fear she must be moved to an hospital. God has preserved to me my senses,—I eat and drink and sleep, and have my judgment, I believe, very sound. My poor father was slightly wounded, and I am left to take care of him and my aunt. Mr. Norris of the Bluecoat school has been very, very kind to us, and we have no other friend, but, thank God, I am very calm and composed, and able to do the best that remains to do. Write—as

THE GRAVE OF CHARLES AND MARY LAMB IN EDMONTON CHURCHYARD

religious a letter as possible—but no mention of what is gone and done with.

There is a touch of momentary morbidness in the postscript: he wishes Coleridge not to speak of poetry to him. He has "destroyed every vestige of past vanities of that kind." A kind of penance, clearly; a sacrifice of cherished treasures wrung from the sensitiveness of a mourning son and brother. That mood quickly passed; a few leaves had been blighted, but his nature was sturdier than ever at the root. The mother could not be restored, but the sister was to become to him, through the very fires of that horror, more beloved, more necessary than ever. The love of David and Jonathan has its parallels, but where shall we find a parallel for the love of Charles and Mary Lamb?

Well, it is remarkable, it is perhaps a sign of depravity, how little satisfaction we take in these unusual kinds of devotion. Are we really delighted and exalted, as the persons involved were, with Montaigne's passion of friendship for La Boétie, or Shakespeare's for "W. H."? Do we really care for exhibitions of parental and filial piety? Are we not inclined to feel that marriage, or what Mr. Bernard Shaw might consistently call "super-marriage," affords the only legitimate material for approbation, where strong human feeling is concerned? How we commiserate the "old maid" who chances to love her father, or her work, more than the first or second man who comes along; or the bachelor whom labor and friendship deplorably suffice. Reluctantly we own to a share in this hopelessly common prejudice. We like to see people married and happy, or married and unhappy, taking their chance with the rest of us, and, if need be, their mischance. Then we know where they are; for the experience of matrimony, with all its variety, is a game of which, we flatter ourselves, we know the rules. We do not so much care why a man does marry; the main question is, Why does n't he? We have wondered somewhat in our youth over the relation between Elia and his Cousin Bridget. Did Lamb intend that we should wonder a little? Did he discern an engaging piquancy in the title of cousin which the title of sister lacks? It should be our revenge upon him then that we discern a kind of infidelity in his advances to the divine plain Miss Kelly,—and his consolation that we like and understand him all the better for it. He was, after all, a man like other men, capable of staking his utmost upon the greatest of all games of chance. To know this is to double our satisfaction in what we can but consider the fortunate defeat of his hopes: there was no room for him at the table, and presently he ceased to be troubled by the call of the blind, winged croupier.

The first love experience belonged, as we have seen, to Lamb's salad days, and need not be taken too seriously. It is creditable to him, it shows that he is alive, and we are rejoiced that it comes to nothing. The later experience is, not to be irreverent, a horse of another color. Lamb was now forty-four years old, his sister fifty-nine,

Fanny Kelly twenty-nine. Lamb had suffered no recurrence of his derangement, but Mary had spent weeks, sometimes months of every year in retirement. These attacks affected Charles acutely; partly because he suffered for her, partly because he missed her. At such times he showed a somewhat feverish desire for society, at such times his potations were most likely to end disastrously. At the time of the proposal of marriage, the play-going Lambs had long admired Miss Kelly on the stage, and had for some time known her intimately in private life. Lamb had seen a quarter-century's service in the East India Company, and, with a salary of six hundred pounds and what he got by writing, was in a position to marry.

What, then, is the substance of this correspondence of which we are making so much?

Would to God [says Lamb in his first letter] you were released from this way of life; that you could bring your mind to consent to take your lot with us, and throw off for ever the whole burden of your Profession. . . . I am not so foolish as not to know that I am a most unworthy match for such a one as you, but you have for years been a principal object in my mind. In many a sweet assumed character I have learned to love you, but simply as F. M. Kelly I love you better than them all. Can you quit these shadows of existence, and come and be a reality to us? can you leave off harassing yourself to please a thankless multitude, who know nothing of you, and begin at last to live to yourself and your friends?

As plainly and frankly as I have heard you give or refuse assent in some feigned scene, so frankly do me the justice to answer me. It is impossible that I should feel injured or aggrieved by your telling me at once that the proposal does not suit you. It is impossible that I should ever think of molesting you with idle importunity and persecution after your mind is once firmly spoken—but happier, far happier, could I have leave to hope a time might come, when our friends should be your friends; our interests yours; our book-knowledge, if in that inconsiderable particular we have any advantage, might impart something to you, which you would every day have it in your power to repay by added cheerfulness and joy which you could not fail to bring as a dowry into whatever family should have the honor and happiness of receiving you, the most welcome accession which could be made to it. . . .

The letter has several interesting aspects. In style, to begin with, it is altogether unlike Lamb; we find nothing which resembles it in the course of the whole published correspondence. This is rather a proof of the stress under which it was composed than anything else. The tone and substance of the letter are undoubtedly characteristic,—not always ingratiatingly characteristic, one might think, in the eyes to wish her to be his own was to wish her to be not the public's. Nor is the allusion to what she might gain from her husband's and sister-in-law's book-learning altogether a propitious one. However, there is no evidence that Miss Kelly, being, as we have said, a sensible woman, took offence at any of these awkwardnesses, unlike Lamb as they indeed were. She knew her suitor, and herself; and her reply seems to

JOHN LAMB'S PETITION FOR CHARLES LAMB'S ENTRY INTO CHRIST'S HOSPITAL

of the sensible woman to whom it was addressed. The use of the plural pronoun might convey a warning—"be a reality to us," "our" friends, "our" interests, "our" book-knowledge: such phrases might well seem ominous to a putative bride, however fond she might be of the third person involved. Desire to be an additional member of an existing "we" is not a common incentive to wedlock. Here also is an ingenuous slighting of the recipient's profession which might not have been palatable. The probability is that fond of the theatre as Lamb was, and greatly as he admired Miss Kelly as an actress, have been no less sincere than final. It was of a nature hardly likely to tempt more indiscreet persons than Lamb to "importunity and persecution": her heart had long been hopelessly engaged. Lamb replies in whimsical vein; and the incident is closed. All three letters have the same date. Ten days later Lamb writes an unsigned criticism of a play in which Miss Kelly was appearing, and says of her:

She is in truth not framed to tease or torment even in jest, but to utter a hearty yes or no; to yield or refuse assent with a noble sincerity. We

Skirting her own bright hair they rove,
And to the Sunny add more Sun:
Now on that aged Face they fix,
Streaming from the Crucifix;
The flesh-clogg'd Spirit disabusing,
Death-disarming sleeps infusing,
Intuitions, foretastes high,
And equal thoughts to Live or Die.

Gardener bright from Eden's Bowers,
Tend with care that Lily Flower;
To its root thy leaves infuse
Heaven's sunshine, Heavens dews;
Tis the type, & tis the pledge,
Of a Crowning Privilege.
Careful as that Lily Flower,
This maid must keep her precious dowery
Live a Sainted Maid, or die
Martyr to Virginity.

    Virtuous Poor ones, sleep, sleep on,
    And waking find your labours done.
          autograph   C. Lamb

A POEM IN LAMB'S HANDWRITING FOR WILLIAM AYRTON

IN LEIGH HUNT'S STUDY
From a hitherto unpublished drawing from memory, by Thornton Leigh Hunt
Reproduced by permission of Mrs. Shelley Leigh Hunt

have not the pleasure of being acquainted with her, but we have been told that she carries the same cordial manners into private life.

A something magnanimous tribute from a rejected wooer; Miss Kelly remained on friendly terms with the Lambs, and long outlived them, dying unmarried at the age of ninety-two.

We do not know how much Lamb may have concealed, but he would appear to have been rather disappointed than deeply grieved, at the outcome of this episode. It was not so much untoward as unwished-for. The last fifteen years of his life he spent pretty contentedly in that comfortable estate of mitigated bachelorhood which his Bridget made possible. For her he had a very strong devotion, though he seems to have included her, as well as the woman he wished to marry, in one of his favorite denunciations of clever women. The utterance, taken literally, is extraordinary indeed: it is to the effect that women only make themselves absurd and contemptible when they try to write; that "a female poet, or female author of any kind, ranks *below an actress.*" But it is not probable that Lamb looked on his sister as a particularly clever woman, or that he would have classed her as a "female author" at all; certainly not in the company of the persons who moved his outburst, blue ladies, then generally adored, such as Mrs. Barbauld, and "L. E. L."

How, then, are we to picture Mary Lamb herself, this writer who was not an author, this helpmeet who was not a wife, this person under a cloud of mental infirmity, this matricide whom all

CHARLES LAMB
After a model by H. Weekes
From Tilt's " Authors of England," 1837

the world loved? Briefly, she seems to us one of the most remarkable persons of whom we have any record. It is one thing to kill your mother and be locked up in a madhouse; it is another to come hopeful and smiling out of the experience, without a tinge of morbid self-reproach, or of morbid fear for the future. Nine tenths of the time, the quality for which Mary Lamb would have been chiefly marked was her sanity, her admirable mental and moral poise. It would seem that her fits of derangement served her somewhat as the periodical "spree" serves one kind of physical constitution: as if to the end of clearing the mind, the fancy, the entire nervous system, of the perilous stuff which but for these occasional evacuations might have poisoned the whole body. Apart from these periods, Charles was clearly the less sane of the two. Once in so often the too familiar warning would come, and the pair would go, hand-in-hand, and in tears, to the private retreat in the neighboring suburb. After a time she would return, cheerful as ever, to take care of her brother and to let him think that he was taking care of her; probably the best possible working arrangement between man and woman. Mary Lamb certainly thought so, and there is hardly a better passage in her correspondence than that in which she formulates her canny theory of the case:

> I make a point of conscience never to interfere or cross my brother in the humor he happens to be in. It always appears to me to be a vexatious kind of Tyranny, that women have no business to exercise over men, which, merely because *they having a better judgment*, they have the power to do. Let *men* alone, and at last they come round to the right way, which *we*, with a kind of intuition, perceive at once. But better, far better, that we should let them often do wrong than that they should have the torment of a Monitor always at their elbows.

Almost superhuman, that last sentence — certainly super-feminine. Mary Lamb held quaint views about the sphere of woman to which in this day a considerable number, perhaps a majority, of her sex would find it impossible to subscribe. We do not venture to assert that they were right; we only envy the man who had the advantage of them.

> In how many ways [she writes in *The British Lady's Magazine*] is a good woman employed, in thought and action, through the day, that her *good man* may be enabled to feel his leisure hours *real substantial holyday*, and perfect respite from the cares of business! Not the least part to be done to accomplish this end is to fit herself to become a conversational companion: that is to say, she has to study and understand the subjects on which he loves to talk. . . . To make a man's home so desirable a place as to preclude his having to wish to pass his leisure hours at any fireside in preference to his own, I should humbly take to be the sum and substance of woman's domestic ambition.

The passage concludes with the demure remark that British ladies who had fulfilled this ambition must have found it "attended with enough of *mental* exertion, at least, to incline them to the opinion that women may be more properly ranked among the contributors to than the partakers of the undisturbed relaxation of man." We do not choose to read too much irony into the observation. Certainly she succeeded in the

task, such as it was. At twenty-one Lamb says she is all he can wish in a companion. Ten years later, during one of Mary's attacks, he confesses how necessary to him in every way she has become. He is reasonably assured that her loss is only temporary, yet

> . . . Meantime she is dead to me, and I miss a prop. All my strength is gone, and I am like a fool, bereft of her coöperation. I dare not think, lest I should think wrong; so used am I to look up to her in the least and biggest perplexity. To say all that I know of her could be more than I think anybody could believe or understand; and when I hope to have her well again with me it would be sinning against her feelings to go about to praise her; for I can conceal nothing that I do from her. She is older, and wiser, and better than me, and all my wretched imperfections I cover to myself by resolutely thinking on her goodness. She would share life and death, heaven and hell, with me. She lives but for me. . . .

MARY AND CHARLES LAMB
From the painting by F. S. Cary in 1834

And what was Mary Lamb's attitude toward the possible marriage of this man to whom she stood as mother, sister, and cherished companion? It is certain that she would have wished it if she could have seen happiness for him in it. As early as 1803 she had contemplated the possibility with cheerfulness, and with her usual good sense.

You will smile [she writes] when I tell you I think myself the only woman in the world who could live with a brother's wife, and make a real friend of her, partly from early observation . . . and partly from a knack I know I have of looking

JOHN LAMB
The father of Charles Lamb

into people's real character, and never expecting them to act out of it—never expecting another to do as I would in the same case.

It is impossible to suppose that she did

not know, and approve of, Lamb's purpose with regard to Miss Kelly or that she may not have felt his disappointment almost, yes, quite as keenly as himself.

Yet perfect as she might have proved herself in the sisterly-in-law relation, we cannot help being glad, for the sake of all concerned, that her powers were not put to the test. Lamb would have been an affectionate and well-meaning husband; but that is, for some reason, a far less tolerable kind of domestic being than an affectionate and well-meaning brother. A Miss Kelly, however good-tempered and unexacting, might have found it hard to put up with some of Lamb's bachelor ways. She might have found it impossible to accustom herself, as Mary Lamb had done, to be a "contributor rather than partaker of the undisturbed relaxation of man."

"The story of the lives of Charles and Mary Lamb," wrote Talfourd half a century ago, "is now told; nothing more remains to be learned respecting it." Yet Talfourd believed Lamb's celibacy to be an estate of deliberate self-sacrifice for the sake of his sister. We are glad it was neither that nor a result of insensibility; he wished to marry, and he could not manage it; and for both facts we should be sincerely grateful.

With Mary Lamb the case is somehow different. Her life, with all its shadows, we can but feel to have been rounded and complete. We suppose it true that it is more to a woman to be a mother than to be a wife. Mary Lamb's maternal instinct brooded over not only her brother but his friends—over Hazlitt and Martin Burney, and, above all, Coleridge. She outlived Lamb many years, dying in 1847, a very old woman. Her body was laid above that of her brother. What noise did she make in the world, what did she write? That is something for us to talk of, if at all, at another time. Whether she was a "female poet" or "female author" of any considerable kind does not concern us at the moment. Both she and her brother belong to that small company of persons who, having achieved something in art, are yet principally cherished in memory for what they were; not for their supernal virtues, but for their sweet and wholesome humanity. This is what Thackeray was paying tribute to when, with tears, he called Lamb "Saint Charles"; this is the generous quality for which, with something like a personal pang of affection, we call to mind the gentle features, firm, yet smiling, of his sister—surely the best of sisters.

REDUCED FACSIMILE OF LETTER FROM LAMB TO WILLIAM WORDSWORTH
From the original in the possession of Mr. Gordon Wordsworth

CHILDREN FLYING KITES
From a painting by Charles C. Curran

Charles Courtney Curran

CHARLES COURTNEY CURRAN possesses the rare faculty of painting for the sake of a simple artistic pleasure in the expression of his subject quite without reference to that demand upon memory or responsive thought so usual in this day of "illustrations" and "story telling" pictures. He enacts the doctrine that the truest appeal of oil and canvas should be almost as abstract as that of musical sounds. So, though sometimes his results tender charming meanings, as in the "Sirens," most frequently he places little stress in this direction compared to the emphasis he bestows on the manner of presenting and of conveying his sentiment. To that latter end his work bears the stamp of realism, for he arouses in the minds of his public a sense of true unqualified emotion through an effect of an impression gained by an instant-long vivid glance at a well-known region. Nevertheless the result does not halt with the passionless photographic aspect of a mere copy so often found in such attempts. A fair proportion of men and women, painters or otherwise, gain artistic conceptions of everyday situations that remain moderately well limited by truth to facts. Yet through superficiality, or other faults, comparatively few in any measure express such ideas in those harmonies of drawing and color that arouse in their neighbors the desired feelings, whether of pleasure or of sorrow. Mr. Curran, however, not only knows and appreciates what he paints, but he understands how to communicate that acquaintance to others. Sometimes the scene may be one such as the "Children Flying Kites," or a pasture with the mist of the hills driving across the seed-grass, and out-crops, and mullenstalks, or a view from a bare ridge of rifted clouds breaking to show glimpses of valleys, or, perhaps, an interior where a girl sits at her piano in the afternoon light. He treats these records of local and yet general truths without pretension and without affectation beyond his strength, retaining, the

while, a modern and individual rendering that pays all deference to tradition. He neither lays an undue emphasis on drawing nor on elaborate or super-refined coloring, though clean and well controlled in the former direction, and clear and, as a rule, full of sunlight in the latter. He disposes the proper mass in the proper place with a grasp of the slow gradations of values —the relative strength of light and dark of every part of the canvas. Especially when out-of-doors painting modulations of blue-gray or mellow light he sounds the depth of moving atmosphere. He composes his lines with a quiet sureness that lacks visible formula. As a result the "Children Flying Kites" or his companion subjects arouse no movement of curiosity or of reminiscence, no historical interest, no desire to look before or after, no thought that could be better satisfied in words. Rather he controls and marks his painting with the needed sentiment of peace and relish in man and nature. He allures the eye and the heart and the brain not so much by a suggestion of a tale as by a composition of graceful forms. It is Mr. Curran's art that holds the spectator's gaze.

————

Charles Courtney Curran was born in Hartford, Kentucky, in 1861, He began to study art at the Cincinnati School of Design. From there he attended the Art Students' League in New York until he made a trip to Paris in 1888. In 1900 he became a member of the American Arts Commission at the Paris Exposition, and he returned to America as Assistant Director of Fine Arts at the Pan-American Exposition. He has taught at the Pratt Institute and at the Art Students' League. He is a member of the Society of American Artists, and other art associations. His work has been represented by his power to win the Carnegie prize and the first Corcoran prize for 1905.

H. ST. G.

BENJAMIN FRANKLIN
From the miniature by Thuron

A Few Things Recalled by the Franklin Bicentenary

By LE ROY B. RUGGLES

THE revival of interest in the life and works of Benjamin Franklin has caused many a long-forgotten and dust-covered volume to be brought down from the top shelf and reread with old-time enjoyment. At the public libraries and the book-shops the call is constant for later writings on the remarkable career of this many-sided man. The supply of literature on the subject is quite equal to the demand, for Doctor Franklin, in his growth from a humble beginning to one of the most highly-honored and best-beloved characters of two continents, provided material which made him the darling of biographers and historians.

Two hundred years ago, in the city of Boston, a son was welcomed to the family circle of Josiah Franklin, "tallow-chandler and sope-boiler." Although Benjamin was the fifteenth child to bless this home there is no reason to believe that his coming was not fraught with as much pleasure as the advent of his older brothers and sisters. Two more children followed Benjamin, but of this large family only one was to receive the applause of the world which the proud parents probably hoped each would win.

The leader in the man may easily be traced back to the boy. His companions naturally looked to Benjamin to take the initiative in all their sports and deviltries, and it is safe to say that he fought all the battles and played all the tricks of the typical boy. He was, however, at the same time, studious,

BENJAMIN FRANKLIN
From C. W. Peale's copy of the portrait by David Martin

and although his school-days were very limited he made the most of his opportunities.

In a large family in comparatively poor circumstances, it is easy to imagine that occupations for the boys was a subject of much thought and solicitude with the parents. In this case, Mrs. Franklin—a pious soul—planned and looked forward to the time when Benjamin should become a clergyman. The father thought of a number of trades for his son, and finally decided he should help him make candles.

When the would-be sailor was twelve years of age his brother James, a printer, found himself in need of an apprentice, and the lad was "bound out" to him until he should reach the age of twenty-one. While acquiring a proficiency in the "art preservative of all arts," young Franklin also devoted much time to reading all the books that came in his way. Locke on "Human Understanding" and Xenophon's "Memorabilia" were devoured with the avidity some of the youths of to-day give to "Diamond Dick, the Avenger."

FRANKLIN FOUND BY DIOGENES
From an old French engraving

Benjamin had ideas of his own; *he* wanted to be a sailor. But

The best laid schemes o' mice and men
Gang aft a-gley.

About this time he was inspired, or, rather, thought he was inspired, to write poetry. These effusions, which he hawked about the streets of Boston,

BENJAMIN FRANKLIN
From a painting by Mason Chamberlain, R. A.

he later acknowledged to be "wretched stuff, in the Grub-street ballad style," and added, "but my father discouraged me by ridiculing my performances, and telling me that verse-makers were usu-

It is almost needless to add that James made it rather warm for his younger brother when the real author was discovered. In fact he made it warm for him for many real and fancied

BENJAMIN FRANKLIN IN 1779
From an oil painting in possession of the Historical Society of Pennsylvania

ally beggars; so I escaped being a poet."

He next turned his attention to writing short articles for publication in Brother James's paper, but evidently Brother James had a poor opinion of Benjamin's qualifications as a writer, for he summarily refused to print these articles. However, the young apprentice, by secretly passing anonymous literary productions under the office door, not only had the satisfaction of seeing them in print but also of hearing them commended by his brother and his brother's cronies, and ascribed to various prominent personages.

misdemeanors. Franklin himself says: "I fancy his harsh and tyrannical treatment of me might be a means of impressing me with that aversion to arbitrary power that has stuck to me through my whole life."

At any rate this treatment decided seventeen-year-old Benjamin Franklin to hie himself elsewhere. Accordingly, without asking "by your leave" of his master, he boarded a ship and soon found himself in New York, "without the least recommendation to, or knowledge of, any person in the place, and with very little money in my pocket."

It did not take the youth long to

make a tour of the printing-offices in New York, nor longer to find that his services were not necessary to their welfare. A prospect of work in Philadelphia induced him to go thither, and the first picture we have of him there is when he bought, with a three-penny piece,

three great puffy rolls. . . . Having no room in my pockets, walk'd off with a roll under each arm and eating the other. Thus I went up Market-street as far as Fourth-street, passing by the door of Mr. Read, my future wife's father; when she, standing at the door, saw me, and thought I made, as I certainly did, a most awkward, ridiculous appearance.

In fact Miss Deborah laughed at him. Probably she blushed and denied it when accused by Benjamin during the courtship which began a few months later, but after they "exchanged promises" perhaps she confessed and was forgiven.

In a remarkably short time, considering his youth, Franklin gained for himself many and influential friends in Pennsylvania. One of them, Governor Keith, was the cause of sending him on a wild-goose chase to England. Keith gave him the expectation that money would be furnished there to purchase supplies necessary for starting a print-shop in Philadelphia. However, the money did not materialize, and the young man made the best of the situation by working at his trade in London.

During the two years spent in England on this occasion, he appears to have enjoyed himself to the utmost, and without giving much thought to the choice of his pleasures. Therefore into this period of his life crept considerable "errata," as he called his questionable actions. On the return voyage to America, however, he evidently found some difficulty in satisfying his conscience, for he formed a set of rules as a guide for his future conduct through life, and committed them to memory. A long sea voyage is frequently prescribed for the benefit of one's health. Perhaps it is also a good thing for one's morals.

Meanwhile, Miss Read, who had received but two letters from him during his absence, doubtless came to the conclusion that Franklin was a fickle lover, for on his return to Philadelphia he found that she had married a potter named Rogers. Biographers endeavor to excuse her by claiming this marriage was greatly forwarded by Mrs. Read, who did not take much stock in the absent Benjamin and his promises. If this is the truth, she soon had reason to regret her interference, for in a short time Mrs. Rogers went "home to mother" and her husband disappeared from the scene forever. What became of him is not exactly known, but a rumor of his death reached Philadelphia, and this was enough to determine Franklin and his former sweetheart to carry out their original plan, and they were accordingly married.

At this time Franklin was working at his trade in the printing-office of Samuel Keimer, but he soon decided to start a newspaper. Keimer, hearing of the plan, immediately set to work to publish one himself and thus circumvent his rival. Telling of this transaction in his "Autobiography," Franklin says that "after carrying it on for three-quarters of a year, with at most only ninety subscribers, he [Keimer] offered it to me for a trifle; and I, having been ready some time to go on with it, took it in hand directly; and it prov'd in a few years extremely profitable to me."

To many people Franklin is perhaps best known through the sayings of "Poor Richard" and, as a humorous after-dinner speaker recently said, as the "inventor of lightning." *Poor Richard's Almanac* first appeared in 1732, and was continued by Franklin for nearly twenty-five years. About ten thousand copies, a remarkable number for that time, were sold annually. We glean something of Franklin's purpose in publishing this almanac from his own words:

Observing that it was generally read, scarce any neighborhood in the province being without it, I considered it as a proper vehicle for conveying instruction among the common people, who bought scarcely any other books; I therefore filled all the little spaces that occurr'd between the remarkable days in the calender with proverbial sentences, chiefly such as inculcated industry and frugality, as the means of procuring wealth, and thereby securing virtue; it being more difficult for a man in want to act always honestly, as, to use here one of those proverbs, *it is hard for an empty sack to stand upright.*

Through his writings in the *Pennsylvania Gazette* and short tracts on many subjects, Franklin soon became widely known as a profound thinker and as the advocate of new ideas for the welfare of his fellow-citizens. It was largely through his efforts that America's first public library was created in Philadelphia in 1731. In 1736 he organized the "Union Fire Company," Philadelphia's first fire department. In 1744 the American Philosophical Society was established, the outgrowth of a small club he had formed. In 1749 he organized a board of trustees and raised $2000 by subscription for the establishment of an academy. From this "Academy and Charitable School" we have the University of Pennsylvania of to-day. No new undertaking of a local nature was ever started without first enlisting Franklin's counsel and activities.

This man possessed a remarkable genius for bringing others to his way of thinking. His arguments were the embodiment of pure common-sense. By a most simple yet thorough process he dissected knotty problems and presented them anew in a light easily understood by all. This admirable system of philosophy was greatly enhanced by his humble manner in the advocacy of his opinions:

I made it a rule to forbear all direct contradiction to the sentiments of others, and all positive assertion of my own. I even forbid myself . . . the use of every word or expression in the language that imported a fix'd opinion, such as *certainly,* *undoubtedly,* etc., and I adopted instead of them, *I conceive, I apprehend,* or *I imagine* a thing to be so or so; or it *so appears to me at present.* . . . I soon found the advantage of this change in my manner; the conversations I engag'd in went on more pleasantly. The modest way in which I propos'd my opinions procur'd them a readier reception and less contradiction; I had less mortification when I was found to be in the wrong, and I more easily prevailed with others to give up their mistakes and join with me when I happened to be in the right.

During this period, and in the spare moments of the busy years which followed, Franklin's keen and logical mind was occupied with various scientific questions and in conducting experiments to prove his theories. It was in 1749 that his greatest discovery was made — that lightning is electricity. When the learned Royal Society of London heard of these simple kite-flying experiments it ridiculed both the theory and its originator. However, Franklin later had the satisfaction of being elected an honorary member of this society and full amends were made for its former treatment of him.

It was not to be expected that a man of Franklin's character and abilities would be overlooked by his fellow-citizens in their choice of public servants. From 1736, when he was elected clerk of the General Assembly of the Province of Pennsylvania, until 1787, when he was a member of the Convention called to frame a Constitution for the new confederacy of the United States of America, he was constantly in the public service. During this period of over fifty years he served in many capacities both at home and abroad, his attainments winning respect for him in whatever position he found himself. His political rise and the growing confidence of the people is clearly shown in the varied character and increasing importance of his employments.

For ten years he was a member of the Pennsylvania Assembly. In 1737 he was appointed Deputy Postmaster-General for the Colonies of America. In 1757 he was sent to England in the interest of the colonies. He was occupied for five years on this mission, and during this time made many friends, among them such men as Adam Smith, Hume, and Robertson.

In 1764 Franklin was again sent to England to present a petition for a change of government for Pennsylvania

Great faithful. and beloved Friends and Ally,

The Principles of Equality and Reciprocity on which you have entered into Treaties with us, give you an additional Security for that good Faith with which we shall observe them from motives of Honor and of Affection to Your Majesty.

The distinguished part you have taken in the support of the Liberties and Independence of these States cannot but inspire them with the most ardent wishes for the Interest and the Glory of France.

We have nominated Benjamin Franklin Esquire to reside at your Court, in quality of our Minister Plenipotentiary, that he may give you more particular assurances of the grateful Sentiments which you have excited in us and in each of the United States. We beseech you to give entire Credit to every thing which he shall deliver on our Part, especially when he shall assure you of the Permanency of our Friendship and we pray God that he will keep Your Majesty our great, faithful and beloved Friend and Ally in his most holy Protection.

Done at Philadelphia the twenty first day of October 1778.

By the Congress of the United States of North America your good Friends and Allies

Attest Cha Thomson Secy.

To
our Great, faithful and beloved Friend and Ally
Louis the Sixteenth, King of France and Navarre.

FRANKLIN'S CREDENTIALS AS MINISTER TO FRANCE
Photographed by the permission of the Historical Society of Pennsylvania

and to look after the interests of that province. Matters of grave importance continually arising, a supposed short visit extended to ten years. The heroic efforts he exerted during this period to avert the impending conflict between the colonies and the mother country were of no avail.

The morning after his return to America he was elected a delegate to the Continental Congress. He was then made one of a committee of three to journey to Canada, where an unsuccessful attempt was made to persuade the Canadians to join the new union. On his return, he was one of the committee of five to whom the duty of drawing up the Declaration of Independence was assigned.

In September, 1776, with John Adams and Arthur Lee, he was sent to France to solicit the aid of Louis XVI. At this time Dr. Franklin (for honorary degrees had long since been conferred upon him by several universities) was seventy years old and not in the best of health. On mentioning to his friend, Dr. Cooper, of Boston, that he had been ordered to France, he observed that the public, having eaten of his flesh, now seemed resolved to pick his bones. "Ah," replied his friend, "I approve their taste, for the nearer the bone the sweeter the meat."

This, in truth, seems to have been the case, for the most important work of Benjamin Franklin's life was accomplished during the nine years he remained in France. At the time of his arrival his writings on scientific subjects and his public services had made him one of the best known men in the world. He was a member of every important scientific· and literary society in Europe, and immediately found himself much sought after by the foremost men of the country. He also became the popular idol of the French people: engravings of his venerable face were hung in shop windows, snuff-boxes were embellished with his likeness, and numerous medallions were struck off in his honor.

A good story is told at the expense of his knowledge of the French language. It appears that he could read French very well, but found some difficulty in writing or speaking it, or in following a lengthy address. At a session of the French Academy of Sciences, finding it somewhat difficult to follow the exercises, yet not wishing to seem less appreciative than the rest of the audience, he said he would applaud every time he saw Madame de Boufflers give signs of approbation. It thus happened that he applauded loudest at his own praises.

But he was in France on the business of his country, and did not neglect it. He aroused an immense enthusiasm for the cause of the struggling American colonies, then at war with one of the most powerful nations of the world, and convinced the French government that it was to its own best interest to give aid.

In 1778 he was commissioned sole plenipotentiary at the French Court by the American Congress. France at this time was having troubles of her own. She not only had a war on her hands, but was nearly bankrupt. Yet Dr. Franklin, through his mastery of the art of diplomacy, borrowed no less than twenty-six million francs from that country to help carry on the war against England.

In 1781 Franklin asked Congress to accept his resignation, as his infirmities were increasing. Instead of doing this, Congress sent him a commission, jointly with John Adams and John Jay, to negotiate peace with England.

During his stay in France he was applied to for aid by an American in financial distress. The applicant was apparently known to the Minister as an honest man. On sending him a sum of money sufficient for his immediate wants, Franklin stipulated that the money was not to be returned, but that (after the applicant should again be financially established) a like sum should be given to the first deserving person who might apply for assistance, imposing a like stipulation in turn. In this manner he thought a little charity might go a long way, and hoped "it might pass through many hands before reaching a knave that would stop its progress."

Soon after his return to America, in 1785, he was elected President of Pennsylvania, with but one dissenting vote besides his own (his own being cast ''as a matter of modesty ''), and was afterwards twice unanimously re-elected.

M. T. CICERO's

CATO MAJOR,

OR HIS

DISCOURSE

OF

OLD-AGE

With Explanatory NOTES.

PHILADELPHIA:

Printed and Sold by B. FRANKLIN,
MDCCXLIV.

After retiring from the public service, the remaining two years of Dr. Franklin's life were by no means idle ones, although most of the time was passed in intense pain. Writing to his niece in November, 1788, he says, in speaking of his health:

When I consider how many more terrible maladies the human body is liable to, I think myself well off that I have only three incurable ones, the gout, the stone, and old age: and these notwithstanding, I enjoy many comfortable intervals, in which I forget my ills and amuse myself in reading

or writing, or in conversation with friends, joking, laughing, and telling merry stories, as when you first knew me, a young man about fifty.

During these last years he interested himself in local affairs and wrote on various scientific subjects. It has been regretted by many that he did not devote more of his time to his ''Autobiography,'' which had been commenced long before, but which, unfortunately, was brought down only to the year 1757. In this book we learn much of the influences and events which helped to shape his character. It is written in a simple and charming vein, and the lessons he draws therein for our guidance makes its reading as full of profit as pleasure. He does not preach sermons, but writes in a common-sense, yet jovial, way, and keeps us good-natured while pointing out our faults.

On the 17th of April, 1790, then in his eighty-fifth year, this great and good man passed to the land of his fathers; but his works and worth will ever remain with us.

Admire Benjamin Franklin's genius and abilities as we may, it is as a *man* he must appeal to us in the strongest sense. The letters written by him to his friends show him at his best. They are filled with wit and wisdom, love and sympathy, advice and encouragement; he is happy when his friends meet with success, or sincerely sorrowful when misfortune overtakes them.

To follow his steps in their devious course is to learn a great lesson in industry, frugality, honesty, patriotism, and charity. Nothing undertaken by Dr. Franklin was carried on in a perfunctory manner. All his thought and all his genius was enlisted to gain a complete mastery, to the most minute detail, of the subject before him. The result of this labor, study, and genius, and the practical application of it for the benefit of his country and of mankind, entitle him to all the honor we can bestow.

Benjamin Franklin*

By JOSEPH H. CHOATE

EDUCATION is now in all civilized countries the question of the hour, and the unsolved problems of secondary, technical, and university education are engaging universal attention. As a diversion from this general discussion, it may not be uninteresting to study the lives of those great and rare men who, without any of these extraneous aids, achieve undying fame and confer priceless blessings on mankind. For them schools, colleges, and universities are of little account, and are not required for their development. The world is their school, and necessity is often their only teacher, but their lives are the world's treasures. It is in this view that I ask your attention for a brief hour to the life, character, and achievements of Benjamin Franklin of Philadelphia.

His whole career has been summed up by the great French statesman who was one of his personal friends and correspondents in six words, Latin words of course:

"*Eripuit cœlo fulmen, sceptrumque tyrannis,*" which, unfortunately for our language, cannot be translated into English in less than twelve:
"He snatched the lightning from the skies, and the sceptre from tyrants."

Surely the briefest and most brilliant biography ever written. He enlarged the boundaries of human knowledge by discovering laws and facts of Nature unknown before, and applying them to the use and service of man, and that entitles him to lasting fame. But his other service to mankind differed from this only in kind, and was quite equal in degree. For he stands second only to Washington in the list of heroic patriots who on both sides of the Atlantic stood for those fundamental principles of English liberty, which culminated in the independence of the United States, and have ever since been shared

by the English-speaking race the world over.

You must all be familiar with the principal facts in Franklin's life. He was born a British subject at Boston, in Massachusetts, then a village of about 12,000 inhabitants, in 1706, the year in which Marlborough won the battle of Ramillies and made every New Englander very proud of being a subject of Queen Anne. He was the fifteenth child in a family of seventeen, a rate of multiplication enough to frighten the life out of Malthus, and more than sufficient to satisfy the extreme demands of President Roosevelt. His father, born at Ecton in Northamptonshire, came of that ancient and sturdy Saxon yeomanry which has done so much for the making of England. Having followed the trade of a dyer for some years at Banbury, he emigrated in 1685 to Boston, where, finding little encouragement for his old trade, he engaged in the business of tallow-chandler and soap-boiler. The boy could never remember when he learned to read and write, and at eight years old he was sent to the Boston Grammar School, one of those free common schools then and ever since the pride of the Colony and the State. But in two years, at the age of ten, his school days were over forever. His father finding that with the heavy burden of his great family he could afford him no more education, took the child home to assist in his business, and the next two years the future philosopher and diplomatist spent in cutting candle wicks, filling moulds, tending the shop, and running errands.

That he highly valued the little schooling that he had, meagre as it must have been, appears from his last will made sixty-two years afterwards, in which he says that he owed his first instruction in literature to the free grammar schools of his native town of Boston, and leaves to the town one hundred pounds sterling, the annual

* Inaugural Address of Joseph H. Choate, American Ambassador, October 23, 1903, as President of the Birmingham and Midland Institute. Published in full here for the first time. By permission of Mr. Choate.

interest to be laid out in silver medals to be distributed as honorary rewards in those schools, and to this day the Franklin Medals are striven for and valued as the most honorable prize that a Boston boy can win.

But how did this particular boy, without an hour's tuition of any kind after he was ten years old, come to be the most famous American of his time, and win his place in the front rank of the world's scientists, diplomatists, statesmen, men of letters, and men of affairs? It was by sheer force of brains, character, severe self-discipline, untiring industry, and mother-wit. His predominant trait was practical common sense amounting to genius. God gave him the sound mind in the sound body, and he did the rest himself. He soon revolted at the vulgar duties of his father's business, and at the age of thirteen was apprenticed till his majority to his elder brother, who was a printer and bookseller, and the publisher of the *New England Courant*, one of the earliest newspapers in the Colonies.

From this time forward the printing-office was his school and his university, and probably did more for him than Oxford or Harvard could then have done. With a raging thirst for knowledge he developed a keen and unfailing observation of things and of men, and, above all, a constant study of himself, of which he was a very rare example. He denied himself every pleasure but reading, and robbed his body of food and sleep that he might find time and food for his mind, reading every good book on which he could lay his hands. He soon mastered the art of printing as it was then known, and very early developed a faculty for the use of his pen which gave his brain a vent. He began with two ballads—"The Lighthouse Tragedy" and "Blackbeard the Pirate"—and hawked them about the town. The first, he says, sold wonderfully, but his father discouraged him by ridiculing his performances, and telling him verse makers were generally beggars, and "So," he says, "I escaped being a poet; most probably a very bad one."

So precocious was his literary faculty that very soon he began contributing leading articles to the *Courant*, and when he was sixteen, his brother having been placed under an interdict for criticising the authorities, he became himself the publisher and editor, and of course the circulation increased. But he was still only an apprentice, and his manly and independent spirit found it as hard to brook the indignities and blows to which his master, though he was his brother, subjected him, as he had found it before to ladle the tallow and fill the moulds in his father's shop, and so at seventeen he took to his heels, shook the dust of Boston from his feet, and ran away to Philadelphia.

He landed in the Quaker City with but one dollar in his pocket, and as he had often dined on bread, he bought three rolls, and marched up Market Street, his pockets stuffed with shirts and stockings, eating one roll and with another under each arm. His future wife saw him in this guise as he passed her father's door, and thought he presented a ridiculous appearance, as he certainly did. But he had thoroughly learned his trade, and soon found employment as a journeyman printer. He would have gone on very well had he not been sent to London by the Governor of the Province on a promise of business which totally failed. He found himself in that great city without a friend, and with little money in his pocket. But he soon found employment at good wages in the best printing offices at thirty shillings a week, lodged in Little Britain at three and sixpence, and so managed to keep his head above water for eighteen months, but lived an aimless and somewhat irregular life.

However, he worked hard at his trade, and made some ingenious acquaintances, among them Sir Hans Sloane, the founder of the British Museum, and Sir William Wyndham, once Chancellor of the Exchequer — the former by selling him a curiosity which he had brought from America; the latter by his skill in swimming, in which he had from boyhood been a great expert. His own account of this last acquaintance is not a little diverting. He had visited Chelsea with a party of friends, and on the return by water was induced to give them an exhibition of his skill in this manly art. He swam all the way from Chelsea to Blackfriars, performing many feats of agility both upon and under water that surprised and pleased the spectators. Sir William, hearing of this, sent for him, and offered if he would teach his two sons to swim to set him up in that business, and so he might have spent his life in London as the head of a swimming-school, and never have lived to snatch the lightning from the clouds or the sceptre from tyrants, or to change the map of the world.

Before leaving London he accepted from a reputable merchant who was returning to Philadelphia an offer of a clerkship, and in a few months he learned much of the business, but was thrown out of it by the death of his employer, and by a terrible illness, from which he barely recovered. Referring to this illness he wrote his own epitaph, which, fortunately for the world, there was no occasion to use:

THE BODY
of

BENJAMIN FRANKLIN

(Like the cover of an old book,
Its contents torn out
and stripped of its lettering and binding)
Lies here, food for worms.
Yet the work itself shall not be lost,
For it will, as he believed, appear once more
In a new
And more beautiful Edition,
Corrected and Amended
By
The Author.

Soon after this illness he turned over a new leaf, with firm resolve to train himself for a successful and honorable life by the practice of every virtue. He returned to his old business of printing, which for twenty years he followed with the utmost diligence, and became very prosperous.

About this time he conceived the bold and arduous project of arriving at moral perfection, and rigidly schooled himself in the virtues of temperance, order, resolution, frugality, industry, sincerity, moderation, and cleanliness. By constant reading, study, and observation he made the very best of the great mental capacity with which he had been endowed by Nature. He set to work deliberately and with conscientious fidelity to improve to the best advantage all his faculties, not for his own good and happiness only, but for the benefit of the community to which he belonged. From an odd volume of the *Spectator* which fell into his hands he modelled his style, training himself more rigorously than any school could have trained him, and thus acquired very early in life that power of clear and lucid expression which made all his subsequent writings so effective.

A brilliant modern writer, Hugh Black, has said that

culture is the conscious training in which a man makes use of every educational means within his reach, feeding his inner life by every vital force in history and experience, and so adjusting himself to his environment that he shall absorb the best products of the life of his time, thus making his personality rich and deep.

It was this self-culture that Franklin sought to attain, and he never lost sight of his object. Self-control, once achieved, enabled him in large measure to control others. No wonder, then, that in Philadelphia, at that time already a large city, he not only rapidly achieved success in his business, but became before long a marked figure in Pennsylvania and throughout the thirteen Colonies. He never wasted time, and so time never wasted him, and at the age of forty-two he was able to withdraw from the active management of his business, and to devote himself to public affairs and to scientific studies in which his soul delighted.

In the meantime, and always in the way of business, he had engaged in two literary ventures, which at the same time exercised his active brains, and extended his reputation very widely. He purchased the *Pennsylvania Gazette*, when it was on the verge of ruin and collapse, and it became under his editorship the best newspaper in America, and by means of it he exercised vast power and influence throughout the Colonies. And *Poor Richard's Almanac*, which he started when he was twenty-six years old, and continued to publish for twenty-five years, proved to be a splendid vehicle for the exercise of his wonderful common sense, lively wit, and keen interest in all sorts of affairs. He was very human, and nothing human escaped his searching interest. It was an almanac designed for the general diffusion of knowledge among the people. Where there were few or no books, it found its way with the Bible into every household in the land. Every number was full of worldly wisdom, proverbial philosophy, inculcating the practice of all the homely virtues, such as honesty, frugality, industry, temperance, and thrift as the sure guides to success and happiness, and with all this a generous sprinkling of the liveliest wit and fun. Its circulation rapidly multiplied, and Poor Richard, as a pseudonym of Benjamin Franklin, made him and his personal traits, which it so fitly displayed, familiar in every household, and the influence which he wielded by it was simply unbounded.

In later years he published "Father Abraham's Speech," which was a comprehensive summing up of all Poor Richard's good things, ransacking all literature for proverbs of wit and wisdom and inventing many of his own, touching the conduct of life at all points, so far as utility and worldly advantage are concerned. The world greedily seized it and still cherishes it, for it may now be read, not in English only, but in French, German, Spanish, Italian, Russian, Dutch, Bohemian, Modern Greek, Gaelic, and Portuguese. Under the title "Science du Bonhomme Richard" it has been thirty times printed in French and twice in Italian, and as "The Way to Wealth" twenty-seven times in English in pamphlet form, and innumerable times as a broadside. It is by far the most famous piece the Colonies ever produced. No wonder, for if any man would follow its precepts as faithfully as Franklin did himself, he was sure to become healthy, wealthy, and wise. A cheerful temperament that was worth millions, and irresistible good humor, pervaded all he wrote. Sydney Smith, another example of the same traits, by way of playful menace, said to his daughter: "I will disinherit you, if you do not admire everything written by Franklin."

From the time that his circumstances permitted him to do anything but work solely for daily bread, Franklin manifested and cultivated a constant interest in public affairs, and his unerring instinct for public service was as keen as if he had been specially trained to that end at Oxford or at Cambridge. His fellow-citizens, recognizing his capacity and efficiency, eagerly availed themselves of his leadership in every public movement. Thus he became the founder or promoter of the first debating society for mutual culture and improvement in Philadelphia, the first subscription library, the first fire club, of the American Philosophical Society, and of what finally became the University of Pennsylvania, which still holds a deservedly high rank among institutions of learning. Under his inspiring lead Philadelphia became better lighted, better paved, better policed, and better read than any other city on the continent. As Clerk, and for many years a Member of the Assembly, Postmaster of Philadelphia, and Deputy Postmaster-General for the Continent, he rendered great service, and came to know the affairs of his own and the other Colonies, and thus became known himself better than any other man in the land.

In 1754 he was the leading spirit in the Convention held at Albany, to form a plan for the common defence of the Colonies and the Empire against the French and Indians. It was Franklin who devised the broad and comprehensive scheme which the Convention adopted, many features of which subsequently appeared in the Constitution of the United States. But it was rejected by the Colonies because it gave too much power to the Crown, and by the British Government because it gave too much power to the Colonies—a sure proof of that wise moderation which always characterized its author. In the following year he rendered great services to General Braddock, who had entered on his ill-fated expedition for the capture of Fort Duquesne without proper supplies or means of transportation, and after his calamitous defeat Franklin actually took the field with a considerable military force, and commanded on the frontier, building stockades and forts, and protecting the panic - stricken Colonists from the threatened onset of the enemy.

Carlyle thus describes Franklin's services to Braddock:

About New Year's Day, 1755, Braddock with his two regiments and completed apparatus got to sea ; arrived 20th February at Williamsburg, Virginia ; found now that this was not the place to arrive at ;—that he would lose six weeks of marching by not having landed in Pennsylvania instead ; found that his stores had been mispacked at Cork ; that this had happened and also that—and, in short, found that chaos had been very considerably prevalent in this adventure of his, and did still in all that now lay round it prevail. Poor Braddock took the Colonial militia regiments ; Colonel Washington, as aide-de-camp, took the Indians and appendages, Colonel Chaos much presiding ; and, after infinite delays and confused hagglings, got on march—2,000 regulars, and of all sorts say 4,000 strong.

Got on march, sprawled and haggled up the Alleghanies—such a commissariat, such a wagon service as was seldom seen before. Poor General and Army, he was like to be starved outright at one time, had not a certain Mr. Franklin come to him with charitable oxen with £500 worth provisions, live and dead, subscribed for at Philadelphia. Mr. Benjamin Franklin, since celebrated over all the world, who did not much admire this iron-tempered general with the pipe-clay brain.

Thus by the time he reached middle life, Franklin had become the best known and most important man in the Colonies; but with all his varied work he had never lost sight of science and its practical application to the service of man, which was really his first love. His vast reading had made him a living encyclopædia, and he had managed to acquire some knowledge of French, Italian, Spanish, and Latin, which then and afterwards stood him in great stead. His inventive genius was called into constant play, and he made from time to time many new and useful inventions, for no one of which would he ever take a patent or any personal advantage to himself, for he said that, as we enjoy great advantages from the inventions of others, we should be glad to give the world the benefit of our own.

But his discoveries and inventions finally culminated in his studies and experiments in electricity, and their startling and marvellous result made him as famous in all other countries as he already was in his own, and placed him in the very front rank of living men. The story of Franklin and his kite drawing the lightning from the clouds, and making positive practical proof of its identity with electricity, had been too often told to need to be repeated here. It was no lucky àccident. It was seven years since the Leyden Jar, the first storage battery of electricity, was made, and during the whole interval Franklin and all the other scientists in the world interested in the subject had been studying and experimenting to find out what this mysterious substance was. He had been writing from 1747 to 1751 the results of his investigations to his friend Collinson in London, by whom they were read at the Royal Society, at first, as he says, only to be ignored or laughed at.

In May, 1751, came Franklin's masterly but very modest paper declaring the identity of electricity and lightning, and suggesting how by pointed iron electricity might be actually drawn from a storm cloud, and buildings and ships protected from its danger. It was soon translated into French, German, and Latin, had great sales, and made a tremendous sensation. But Franklin's fame reached the highest point when D'Alibard, a French philosopher, following the suggestions in his pamphlet, constructed an apparatus exactly as Franklin had directed, and made actual demonstration of the truth of his theory, a month before the great discoverer himself flew his kite in his garden in Philadelphia.

Franklin took the universal applause that followed as quietly and modestly as he had put forth his suggestions. It was all fun to him from the beginning. Dr. Priestley says that at the close of the first summer of his experiments, when it grew too hot to continue them, the Philosopher had a party on the banks of the Schuylkill, at which spirits were first fired by a spark sent from side to side through the river, without any other conductor than the water, a turkey was killed for their dinner by the electrical shock, and roasted by the electrical jack, before a fire kindled by the electrified bottle, when the health of all the famous electricians in England, Holland, France, and Germany was drunk in electrified bumpers, under a discharge of guns from the electrical battery. Honors and distinctions now crowded upon him: the Royal Society, as if to make quick amends for its previous neglect, by a unanimous vote made him a member, exempting him from the payment of all dues, and the next year with every circumstance of distinction awarded him the Copley Medal, and Yale and Harvard conferred their honorary degrees upon him.

However much the people of Pennsylvania appreciated and enjoyed his growing fame, they were not willing to give him up to science, but enlisted his services and insisted upon his leadership in every great political question. When the dispute between the Penns as Proprietors and the people of Pennsylvania, on the claim of the former that their estates should be exempt from taxation, reached a crisis in 1756, the Provincial Assembly decided to appeal to the King in Council for a redress of their grievances, and who but Franklin should go to represent them?

This vexatious business, finally ending in a compromise which was on the whole satisfactory to his constituents, detained him in England for upwards of five years—from the summer of 1757 till 1762. Times and the man had changed since the stranded journeyman printer took lodgings in Little Britain at three and sixpence a week, and won his chief distinction by swimming in the Thames from Chelsea to the City. The houses of the great were now thrown wide open to him, and the

modest house in Craven Street, where he took up his residence, and which is still marked by a tablet to commemorate the fact as one of the notable reminiscences of London, was thronged by great scientists to congratulate him on his triumphs, and to witness at his own hands his scientific experiments. Congratulatory letters reached him from all parts of Europe. He made the acquaintance and friendship of such men as Priestley, Fothergill, Garrick, Lord Shelburne, Lord Stanhope, Edmund Burke, Adam Smith, and David Hume, Dr. Robertson, Lord Kames, and David Hartley, with all of whom he enjoyed delightful intercourse. He witnessed the coronation of George the Third, and revelled in the meetings of the Royal Society, where his welcome was very warm. Pitt, who had vastly weightier things upon his mind than Franklin's errand—Pitt, who afterwards as Lord Chatham was, as we shall see, one of his staunchest friends and admirers, he found inaccessible.

At this time Franklin was a most intensely loyal British subject, and gloried in the anticipation of the future greatness and power of the British Empire, of which the Colonies formed no mean part. In this respect, the Colonists whom he represented were all of the same mind. Green, in his "History of the English People," says of them at this time:

From the thought of separation almost every American turned as yet with horror. The Colonists still looked to England as their home. They prided themselves on their loyalty, and they regarded the difficulties which hindered complete sympathy between the settlements and the mother country as obstacles which time and good sense could remove.

He freely lent the aid of his powerful pen while in England to the maintenance of British interests. In his pamphlet, to which great praise was awarded, on the question whether Canada or the sugar islands of Guadaloupe, both of which had been conquered, should be restored to France in the event of peace, and in which he stoutly maintained the retention of Canada, he declared that a union of the

Colonies to rebel against the mother country was impossible.

But [he added] when I say such a union is impossible, I mean without the most grievous tyranny and oppression. People who have property in a country which they may lose, and privileges which they may endanger, are generally disposed to be quiet, and even to bear much rather than to hazard all. While the Government is mild and just, while important civil and religious rights are secure, such subjects will be dutiful and obedient. The waves do not rise but when the winds blow. What such an administration as the Duke of Alva's in the Netherlands might produce I know not, but this I think I have a right to deem impossible.

When Mr. Pratt, afterwards Lord Camden, a stalwart friend of America through all her troubles, said to him, "For all that you Americans say of your loyalty and all that, I know that you will one day throw off your dependence on this country, and notwithstanding your boasted affection for it, you will set up for independence." He answered: "No such idea was ever entertained by the Americans, nor will any such ever enter their heads unless you grossly abuse them." "Very true," replied Pratt, "that is one of the main causes I see will happen, and will produce the event."

But Franklin was more than a staunch loyalist. He was an Imperialist in the most stalwart sense of the word, and on a very broad gauge. His biographer, Parton, truly says:

It was one of Franklin's most cherished opinions that the greatness of England and the happiness of America depended chiefly upon their being cordially united. The "country" which Franklin loved was not England nor America, but the great and glorious Empire which these two united to form.

And Franklin himself wrote to Lord Kames on this visit:

No one can more sincerely rejoice than I do on the reduction of Canada, and this is not merely as I am a Colonist but as I am a Briton. I have long been of opinion that the foundations of the future grandeur and stability of the British Empire lie in America; and though, like other foundations, they are low and little now, they are nevertheless broad and strong enough to support the greatest political structure that human wisdom ever yet erected. I am, therefore, by no means for restoring Canada. If we keep it, all the country from the St. Lawrence to the Mississippi will in another century be filled with British people. Britain itself will become vastly more populous by the immense increase of its commerce; the Atlantic Sea will be covered with your trading ships, and your naval power thence continually increasing will extend your influence round the whole globe and awe the world.

Again he wrote, in 1774:

It has long appeared to me that the only true British policy was that which aimed at the good of the whole British Empire, not that which sought the advantage of one part in the disadvantage of the others; therefore, all measures of procuring gain to the Mother Country arising from loss to her Colonies, and all of gain to the Colonies arising from or occasioning loss to Britain, especially where the gain was small and the loss great . . . I in my own mind condemned as improper, partial, unjust, and mischievous, tending to create dissensions, and weaken that Union on which the strength, solidity, and duration of the Empire greatly depended; and I opposed, as far as my little powers went, all proceedings, either here or in America, that in my opinion had such tendency.

This first protracted stay in England was evidently one of the happiest periods of his long and useful life. For the first time he enjoyed abundant leisure, and the opportunity to indulge to the full among congenial and sympathetic friends his joyous social disposition and love of the best company. He made many delightful country visits, and excursions to Scotland, France, and Holland, and greatly enjoyed the recognition he received in the degrees of LL.D. at Edinburgh, and D.C.L. at Oxford. He sought out the humble birthplace of his father at Ecton, and worshipped in the ancient church around which his rude forefathers slept. In 1762 he returned to America with regret, apparently almost wishing to come back and spend the rest of his days there. For not long after his return he wrote to Mr. Strahan, one of the friends he left behind him: "No friend can wish me more in England than I do myself. But before I go, everything I am concerned in must be so settled here as to make another return to America unnecessary"; and again: " I own that I sometimes suspect my love to England and my friends there seduces me a little, and makes my own reasons for going over appear very good ones."

So there was at least a possibility that he might become a resident of England for the rest of his life, and thus the wheels of Time might have been set back awhile, in fixing the date of the final separation of the American Colonies from Great Britain, which sooner or later was obviously inevitable.

But, wholly unexpectedly to himself, Franklin was destined to spend ten years more in England, years equally momentous to himself, to the Colonies which he represented, and to the Mother Country of which he was so loyal and devoted a son.

Hardly had he reached Philadelphia on his return from his five years' sojourn in England, when there was a new outbreak of the old trouble between the people of the province and the Penns as Proprietaries of Pennsylvania as to their claim to exemption of their property from taxation. Worse still, the ominous news came from London that George Grenville had determined upon the passage of the dreaded Stamp Act, and thereby to impose taxes upon the Colonies by Act of Parliament, in defiance of what they claimed as their immemorial right and usage to pay only such internal taxes as their own provincial governments should impose. They did not dispute or seek to shirk their obligations to grant aid to the King, and make their just contribution to the common cause, but insisted upon their right to do it in what they claimed to be the only constitutional way, by the vote of their own representatives, and that taxation without representation—without their consent — was an injustice to which they would not submit.

No sooner did these dismal tidings reach Pennsylvania, than Franklin was again dispatched to London to do the best he could to prevent the disastrous measure. And what was now of much less importance, to present to the King the petition of the people of Pennsylvania, that he would take the government of that Province into his own

hands, they making such compensation to the Penns as should be just. But of course the question of the injustice of taxation without representation and contrary to ancient usage, which affected all the Colonies alike, swallowed up all local issues. Franklin arrived only in time to find that the immediate passage of the odious measure was inevitable. He joined with the agents of the other Colonies in an appeal to Grenville, but all their efforts were fruitless. "We might," said Franklin, "as well have hindered the sun's setting. Less resistance was made to the Act in the House of Commons than to a common turnpike Bill, and the affair passed with so little noise that in town they scarcely knew the nature of what was doing."

Having done all that he could to prevent the passage of the Act, Franklin was inclined to counsel submission. But public opinion in the Colonies was obstinate, and by unanimous action they refused to obey it, or to take the stamped paper on any terms. To the great disgust of his constituents, by whom he was denounced as a traitor, he went so far, at the request of the Government, as to nominate a stamp distributor under the Act for Pennsylvania. But he and all the other officials under the Act were compelled by the anger of the Colonists to decline or resign. Agreements were signed everywhere not to buy any British goods imported, and English trade fell off to such a degree that the new Administration under Lord Rockingham, who had opposed the Act, very quickly considered its repeal.

One of the most celebrated incidents of Franklin's career was his examination by a Committee of the House of Commons, which was considering the question of repeal. He was summoned before it to give evidence respecting the state of affairs in America—a subject on which he was better informed than any other man in the world.

Without passion, with perfect coolness and absolute knowledge, he demonstrated that the Act was unjust, inexpedient, and impossible of execution, and gave convincing proof that it should be immediately repealed. His testimony is one of the most memorable pieces of evidence in the English language, and some of his answers can never be forgotten. Being asked what was the temper of America towards Great Britain before 1763—(it will be remembered that the Stamp Act was passed in 1765)—he said:

The best in the world. They submitted willingly to the Government of the Crown, and paid in their Courts obedience to the Acts of Parliament. They had not only a respect but an affection for Great Britain, for its laws, its customs, and manners, and even a fondness for its fashions that greatly increased the commerce. Natives of Britain were always treated with partial regard. To be an Old England Man was of itself a character of some respect, and gave a kind of rank among us. . . . They considered the Parliament as the great bulwark of their liberties and privileges, and always spoke of it with the utmost respect and veneration. Arbitrary Ministers, they thought, might possibly at times attempt to oppress them, but they relied on it that Parliament on application would always give redress.

Q. Can anything less than a military force carry the Stamp Act into execution?

A. I do not see how a military force can be applied to that purpose.

Q. Why may it not?

A. Suppose a military force sent into America, they will find nobody in arms. What are they then to do? They cannot force a man to take stamps who chooses to do without them. They will not find a rebellion; they may indeed make one.

Q. If the Act is not repealed, what do you think will be the consequences?

A. A total loss of the respect and affection the people of America bear to this Country, and of all the commerce that depends on that respect and affection.

Q. If the Stamp Act should be repealed, and the Crown should make a requisition upon the Colonies for a sum of money would they grant it?

A. I believe they would.

Q. Why do you think so?

A. I can speak for the Colony I live in. I had it in instruction from the Assembly to assure the Ministry, that as they had always done, so they should always think it their duty to grant such aids to the Crown as were suitable to their circumstances and abilities, whenever called upon for that purpose in the usual constitutional manner.

Q. Would they do this for a British concern, as suppose a war in some part of Europe that did not affect them?

A. Yes, for anything that concerned the general interest. They consider themselves a part of the whole.

Q. Don't you know that there is in the Pennsylvania Charter an express reservation of the right of Parliament to lay taxes there?

A. I know there is a clause in the Charter by which the King grants that he will levy no taxes on the inhabitants unless it be with the consent of the Assembly or by Act of Parliament.

Q. How then could the Assembly of Pennsylvania assert that laying a tax on them by the Stamp Act was an infringement of their right?

A. They understand it thus—By the same Charter and otherwise, *they are entitled to all the privileges and liberties of Englishmen.* They find in the Great Charters and the Petition and Declaration of Rights that one of the privileges of English subjects is that they are not to be taxed but by their common consent. They have, therefore, relied upon it from the first settlement of the Province that the Parliament never would, nor could, by color of that clause in the Charter, assume a right of taxing them till it had qualified itself by admitting representatives from the people to be taxed, who ought to make a part of that common consent.

So clear, convincing, and irresistible was Franklin's testimony, that the repeal of the Stamp Act followed immediately. His evidence before the Committee closed on the 13th of February. On the 21st, General Conway moved for leave to introduce in the House of Commons a Bill to Repeal— which was carried. The bill took its third reading in that House on the 5th of March. It passed the House of Lords on the 17th, and on the 18th of March, only five weeks after Franklin had been heard, the King signed the Bill.

The debates on that critical occasion, which promised for the moment to reconcile England and her Colonies forever, have been but scantily reported, but Pitt, in support of the repeal, in one of his last speeches as the Great Commoner, is said to have surpassed his own great fame; and Burke's renown as a Parliamentary orator was established. Macaulay says:

Two great orators and statesmen belonging to two different generations repeatedly put forth all their powers in defence of the Bill [for repeal]. The House of Commons heard Pitt for the last time and Burke for the first time, and was in doubt to which of them the palm of eloquence should be assigned. It was indeed a splendid sunset and a splendid dawn.

Franklin's own personal way of celebrating the joyous event of the Repeal of the Stamp Act was peculiarly characteristic of that spirit of fun and good humor which pervaded his whole life. He made it the occasion of sending a new gown to his wife. He wrote her:

As the Stamp Act is at length repealed, I am willing you should have a new gown, which you may suppose I did not send sooner, as I knew you would not like to be finer than your neighbors unless in a gown of your own spinning. Had the trade between the two countries totally ceased, it was a comfort to me to recollect, that I had once been clothed from head to foot in woollen and linen of my wife's manufacture, that I never was prouder of any dress in my life, and that she and her daughter might do it again if it was necessary. I told the Parliament, that it was my opinion, before the old clothes of the Americans were worn out, they might have new ones of their own making. I have sent you a fine piece of Pompadour satin, fourteen yards, cost eleven shillings a yard, a silk negligée and petticoat of brocaded lute-string for my dear Sally, with two dozen gloves, four bottles of lavender water, and two little reels. The reels are to screw on the edge of the table when she would wind silk or thread.

The repeal, following so closely as it did on the close of Franklin's examination as its necessary sequence, raised to a very high point his reputation in England, where he already commanded universal respect and esteem, and roused the Colonies to the wildest enthusiasm over his name. His constituents in Philadelphia, quite ashamed of their recent criticism upon him, gave him the whole credit of the great result. Everybody on both sides of the water, except the King and the "household troops," as Burke called them, hoped with him that "that day's danger and honor would have been a bond to hold us all together for ever. But alas! that, with other pleasing visions, is long since vanished."

The attempt to impose taxation by Act of Parliament on the Colonies was almost immediately renewed, and ushered in that long and unhappy controversy which finally resulted in the accumulation of oppressive measures on the one side, and acts of resistance on the other, that brought the Colonists to an appeal to arms in defence of what they deemed to be their rights and liberties.

We will not undertake to rake over the ashes of the memorable contest, to measure out praise or blame to one side or the other.

Historians are now happily agreed that the leaders on both sides in the great struggle were actuated by honest intentions and patriotic motives. It was impossible for them to see in the same light the great questions of right and of policy which divided them, and which nothing but the final separation of the Colonies from the Crown could solve.

It might be claimed with some show of reason that, at the outset at least, it was not a contest between the English people and the American people, but between the King with a submissive Ministry and Parliament here and his subjects beyond the sea, and that a great part of the English people had very little to do with it. If we may accept the statements of your own most approved historians, large portions of the English people were no more represented in the Parliament than the Colonists themselves.

I may be permitted to quote once more in this connection from Green's "History of the English People." He is speaking of Parliament between 1760 and 1767, the very time we have been considering:

Great towns like Manchester and Birmingham remained without a member, while members still sat for boroughs which, like Old Sarum, had actually vanished from the face of the earth. . . . Some boroughs were "the King's boroughs," others obediently returned nominees of the Ministry of the day, others were "close boroughs" in the hands of jobbers like the Duke of Newcastle, who at one time returned a third of all the borough members in the House. . . . Even in the counties the suffrage was ridiculously limited and unequal. Out of a population of eight millions of English people, only a hundred and sixty thousand were electors at all!

What would be thought to-day of great questions of national policy being decided by a House of Commons in which neither Birmingham nor Manchester had a representative, and in the election of whose members only one person out of fifty of the English people had a vote!

At any rate, we may, I think, exchange congratulations to-night, that with our great struggle the good people of Birmingham had literally nothing to do, and at least a considerable portion of the people of England hardly more.

But you get an idea of the vast difficulties with which Franklin, who gallantly remained at his post in London through all those weary years from 1766 to 1775, had to contend, as the representative of the United Colonies, for, besides Pennsylvania, he was presently made the agent of Massachusetts, New Jersey, and Georgia.

His great powers [says John Fiske] were earnestly devoted to preventing a separation between England and America. His methods were eminently conciliatory, but the independence of character with which he told unwelcome truths made him an object of intense dislike to the King and his friends, who regarded him as aiming to undermine the Royal authority in America.

But it is not to be forgotten that Chatham, Burke, Fox, Barre, and Conway, all champions of the cause of the Colonists, were regarded in the same light by the same party.

And strange to say, down to this time Franklin had no suspicion that the obnoxious measures of the Ministry had their origin or chief backing in the Royal closet.

I hope nothing that has happened or may happen [he wrote in the spring of 1769] will diminish in the least our loyalty to our Sovereign, or affection for this nation in general. I can scarcely conceive a King of better dispositions, of more exemplary virtues, or more truly desirous of promoting the welfare of his subjects. The body of this people, too, is of a noble and generous nature, loving and honoring the spirit of liberty, and hating arbitrary power of all sorts. We have many, very many, friends among them.

No doubt, however, he did in the end incur the King's hearty displeasure; and a story that has long been current would seem to indicate that the Royal mind at last opposed even his views on electricity, of which it might have been supposed that Franklin was himself king. The substance of Franklin's discovery was that sharp points of iron would draw electricity from the clouds, and he recommended lightning rods with such sharp points. The story is that in the heat of his animosity against the Americans and Franklin the King insisted, on political grounds, that on Kew Palace they should have blunt knobs instead of sharp points. The question between sharps and blunts became a Court question, the Courtiers siding with the King, their adversaries with Franklin. The King called upon Sir John Pringle, President of the Royal Society, for an opinion on his side in favor of the knobs, but Pringle hinted in reply that the laws of Nature were not changeable at the Royal pleasure. How far the story in detail is true can only now be guessed from a well-known epigram that was actually current:

> While you, great George, for safety hunt,
> And sharp conductors change for blunt,
>   The empire's out of joint.
> Franklin a wiser course pursues,
> And all your thunder fearless views,
>   By keeping to the point.

During these ten years in London Franklin kept up a lively fire of pamphlets and communications to the newspapers, advocating with all the resources of his wisdom, wit, and satire the integrity of the Empire and the cause of the Colonists. Two of these —"Rules for Reducing a Great Empire to a Small One," and "An Edict of the King of Prussia"—had a tremendous circulation, and became, and continued for many years, very famous. He continued his philosophical investigations, and was also the most popular diner-out in London, where the charms of his conversation made him a universal favorite. He maintained his intimate association with the most distinguished men of science and learning, and a most loving and constant correspondence with his wife, daughter, and sister, from whom his protracted separation was to his great and tender heart a source of constant anxiety and privation.

But at last, as the prolonged contest waxed hotter and hotter, as the representative of all the Colonies he became the very storm-centre around which all the elements of discord and growing hatred gathered in full force, and was often the target for the attacks of both sides. In England the Ministry regarded him as too much of an American, and the most ardent patriots at home as too much of an Englishman. He evidently thought that both sides were in fault. Here he constantly exerted all his great powers to justify his countrymen and uphold their cause. To them by every mail he urged patience and moderation, begging them to give the Ministry no ground against them.

As Mr. Parton truly says: "His entire influence and all the resources of his mind were employed from the beginning of the controversy in 1765 to the first conflict in 1775, to the one object of healing the breach and preventing the separation." But at such times, when the air is charged with mutual suspicion and hatred, when forebodings of war are agitating the public mind, what Hamlet says is more true than ever: .

Be thou as chaste as ice, as pure as snow, thou shalt
    not escape calumny.

The Court party professed to regard him as the embodiment of all the alleged sins and offences which they imputed to the entire body of Colonists, and they determined at all hazards to make an end of him. The news was on the way of the famous Boston tea party, in which a body of leading citizens of the New England capital in disguise boarded the ships that brought the tea, on which the obnoxious duty had been imposed, and emptied it all into salt water. The whole harbor of Boston became a seething cauldron of East India Company's tea on which no duty had been paid. Passive resistance was at last breaking out into open rebellion. Probably the frenzy of excitement on both sides had never reached

such fever heat—and in January, 1774, the storm burst on the head of the devoted Franklin.

I shall not attempt to describe the scene in the Cockpit at the meeting of the Committee of Lords of the Privy Council, met to pass upon the Petition of the Assembly of Massachusetts Bay for the removal of the Governor and Lieutenant - Governor. Franklin had transmitted to the Speaker of the Assembly, as in duty bound, their letters showing, as he believed, a studied purpose on the part of the colonial Royal officers to bring down more stringent measures upon the Colonists and to abridge their liberties, and he had sent them, as he was expressly authorized to do, for the avowed purpose of mitigating the wrath of the Colonists against the Government at home which, as they believed, had initiated and was solely responsible for those measures.

The hearing before the Committee of the Privy Council, on the Petition of the people of Massachusetts to remove these officers because of the letters, was made the occasion of a ferocious attack upon Franklin, who had presented the Petition. The Solicitor-General overwhelmed him with vituperation, while the Lords of the Committee applauded with jeers and cheers an attack universally condemned ever since. His calm self-command and unruffled dignity, as he stood for an hour to receive the pitiless storm of calumny, in such marked contrast to the conduct of his assailant and his titled applauders, is striking evidence of his conscious innocence. Upon the canvas of history he stands out from that ignoble scene an heroic figure, bearing silent testimony to the cause of the Colonists for whose sake he suffered—not a muscle moved, not a heart-beat quickened,—and casting into the shade of lasting oblivion all those who joined in the assault upon him. He said to Dr. Priestley next day that

he had never before been sensible of the power of
a good conscience; for that, if he had not considered the thing for which he had been so much
insulted as one of the best actions of his life, and

what he should certainly do again in the same circumstances, he could not have supported it.

An eye-witness who watched him
closely says:

He stood conspicuously erect without the smallest
movement of any part of his body. The muscles
of his face had been previously composed so as to
afford a tranquil expression of countenance, and he
did not suffer the slightest alteration of it to appear
during the continuance of the speech.

He has been blamed by several
writers of high repute, but on what exact ground is not definitely specified.
From whose hands he received the
letters is not known. He did receive
them confidentially "from a gentleman
of character and distinction," but who
he was was a secret which, at any cost
to himself, Franklin was bound to keep,
and he carried it to the grave with him at
the cost of all the dust and obloquy that
have been thrown about the matter.
Having come honorably into possession
of the letters, he could not have withheld the knowledge of them from the
leaders of the Colony to whom he was
responsible for his conduct, without a
breach of trust towards them, and his
countrymen, who justly regarded the
assault upon him as an affront to themselves, accepted his own view and statement of the matter.

There is no doubt that the powerful
invectives of Wedderburn, which were
extremely eloquent and ingenious, and
became the talk of the town, did seriously impair the prestige of Franklin
during the rest of his stay in London.
On the following day he was summarily
dismissed from his office of Deputy
Postmaster-General. But all this did
not deprive him of the respect and
esteem of the distinguished friends
whom his character and commanding
abilities had gathered about him.

I do not find [he wrote a fortnight after the
assault] that I have lost a single friend on the occasion. All have visited me repeatedly with affectionate assurances of their unaltered respect and
affection, and many of distinction, with whom I
had before but slight acquaintance.

In demonstration of his own fidelity
to Franklin, Lord Chatham not long

afterwards, on the occasion of a great
debate on American affairs in the
House of Lords, invited him to attend
in the House, being sure that his presence in that day's debate would be of
more service to America than his own,
and later, in reply to a fling of Lord
Sandwich at Franklin, he took occasion
to declare that

if he were the first Minister of this country, and
had the care of settling this momentous business,
he should not be ashamed of publicly calling
to his assistance a person so perfectly acquainted
with the whole of American affairs as the gentleman
alluded to, and so injuriously reflected on,—one
whom all Europe held in high estimation for his
knowledge and wisdom, and ranked with our
Boyles and Newtons; who was an honor not to
the English nation only, but to human nature.

Franklin continued his efforts at conciliation as long as he remained in
London. He actually advised Massachusetts to pay for the tea which had
been destroyed, for which again he was
rudely blamed by the leaders in Boston. He even offered, without orders
to do so, at his own risk, and without
knowing whether his action would be
sustained at home, to pay the whole
damage of destroying the tea in Boston, provided the Acts against that
Province were repealed, and to his last
hour in London he labored without
ceasing to heal the growing breach.
Hostile critics have insinuated doubts
of his sincerity in all his efforts for
peace and union, but the evidence of
his fidelity is overwhelming.

Speaking of Franklin in London
from 1764 to 1774, the "Encyclopædia
Britannica" says:

He remitted no effort to find some middle ground
of conciliation. . . . With a social influence
never possessed probably by any other American
representative at the English Court he would doubtless have prevented the final alienation of the Colonies, if such a result under the circumstances had
been possible. But it was not.

Let me cite another witness out of a
host that might be called: the *Annual
Register* for 1790 announcing Franklin's
death says: "Previous to this period
[the affair at the Cockpit] it is a testi-

mony to truth and bare justice to his memory to observe that he used his utmost endeavor to prevent a breach between Great Britain and America."

Dr. Priestley, who spent with him the whole of his last day in England, says of the conversation:

The unity of the British Empire in all its parts was a favorite idea of his. He used to compare it to a beautiful china vase, which if ever broken could never be put together again, and so great an admirer was he of the British Constitution that he said he saw no inconvenience from its being extended over a great part of the globe.

Professor Tyler, in his "Literary History of the American Revolution," describes Franklin at the date of the Battle of Lexington as

a man who having been resident in England during the previous ten years had there put all his genius, all his energy of heart and will, all his tact and shrewdness, all his powers of fascination, into the effort to keep the peace between these two kindred peoples, to save from disruption their glorious and already planetary empire, and especially to avert the very appeal to force that had at last been made.

But Franklin's efforts were of no avail. His mission of mediation and conciliation had failed, his dream of an imperial and perpetual union of England and the Colonies, as an Empire, one and inseparable, had vanished. The measures taken on both sides rendered any reconciliation impossible, and in March, 1775, he sailed for home, to throw in his lot with his own countrymen—arriving at Philadelphia two weeks after they had drawn the sword and thrown away the scabbard, and the Battle of Lexington had begun the actual War of Independence.

I have now brought Franklin to the great parting of the ways, to the point where he ceased to be a British subject and became an American citizen, bound now to secure and maintain the cause of the Colonies with all his might, and as loyally as he had thus far sought to reconcile the Colonies and the Mother Country.

I may not on this occasion pursue further the narrative of his life, except

to indicate how clearly it displayed his astounding abilities and capacity for public service, his enlightened patriotism, and his rare devotion to duty. No sooner had he arrived in Philadelphia after his ten years' absence than his fellow-citizens, deeming him more than ever the indispensable man, made him a member of the Continental Congress, where he was one of the Committee of Five appointed by the Congress to prepare the famous Declaration of Independence, the other four members being Jefferson, John Adams, Sherman, and Livingston. The declaration drawn by Jefferson was only slightly amended by Franklin, who signed it with the other members of Congress. It will presently be seen that eleven years afterwards he also signed the Constitution of the United States, which he had a hand in making. To have signed both of these historical instruments is equivalent in American history to the highest patent of nobility, only five others sharing the honor with Franklin.

But, in spite of the Declaration of Independence, the cause of the Colonists was in danger of becoming hardly better than hopeless unless they could secure foreign aid and alliances—and, who again but Franklin, the printer's apprentice, the veteran diplomatist, the scientist of world-wide fame, the accomplished linguist, the one man of letters whose works had been translated into many languages, and the most experienced man of affairs on the Continent, could be chosen for that arduous and delicate service? He was almost immediately dispatched to Paris, for that purpose. Although he had now passed his seventieth year, and was already beginning to feel the infirmities of age, he consented to serve, and there for nine years more of exile he discharged his diplomatic duties with such wisdom, energy, pertinacity, and tact, and such marvellous shrewdness, that the much-needed supplies of money and military stores were from time to time obtained and the Colonists enabled to maintain their footing in the field. After the Battle of Saratoga, which has been justly described as one of the decisive battles of history, the Treaties of Commerce and Alliance were signed which powerfully assisted the Colonists to make good their Declaration.

This brilliant achievement was chiefly due to the skill and sagacity of Franklin, and it was largely aided by his marvellous personal popularity among all classes of the French people. His arrival in Paris was the signal for a tremendous outburst of popular enthusiasm, which met with a hearty response throughout Europe, and it extended at once to the fashionable world and to the philosophers and scholars as well as to the populace.

"His virtues and renown," says Lacretelle, "negotiated for him; and before the second year of his mission had expired no one conceived it possible to refuse fleets and armies to the countrymen of Franklin."

The German, Schlosser, says:

Franklin's appearance in the Paris Salons, even before he began to negotiate, was an event of great importance to the whole of Europe. Paris at that time set the fashion for the civilized world, and the admiration of Franklin, carried to a degree approaching folly, produced a remarkable effect on the fashionable circles of Paris. His dress, the simplicity of his external appearance, the friendly meekness of the old man, and the apparent humility of the Quaker procured for freedom a mass of votaries among the court circles. . . .

Pictures of him appeared in every window, and portraits, busts, medallions, medals, bearing his familiar head, were in every house and every hand.

A French writer of the day, in his description of Franklin at the Court, says:

Franklin appeared at Court in the dress of an American cultivator. His straight, unpowdered hair, his round hat, his brown coat, formed a contrast with the laced and embroidered coats, and the powdered and perfumed heads of the courtiers of Versailles. This novelty turned the enthusiastic heads of the French women. Elegant entertainments were given to Dr. Franklin, who to the reputation of a philosopher added the patriotic virtues which had invested him with the noble character of an Apostle of Liberty. I was present at one of these entertainments when the most beautiful woman of three hundred was selected to place a crown of laurels upon the white head of the American philosopher, and two kisses upon his cheeks.

An American Ambassador of to-day still affects similar simplicity of dress by Act of Congress, but he would hardly know how to take such a reception as was thus accorded to the venerable philosopher.

But all this incense did not turn his head, which he kept level for the important affairs that he had in hand.

The amount and variety of business which fell upon him would have taxed the energies and capacity of the strongest man in middle life, and his health was already beginning to decline. He was obliged to act not only as Ambassador, but in lieu of a Board of War, Board of Treasury, Prize Court, Commissary of Prisoners, Consul, and dealer in cargoes which came from America. When peace happily returned he took an active and important part in negotiating the final Treaty with Great Britain, and no one in the world rejoiced more heartily than he in the restoration of friendly relations between Great Britain and the United States. It would be impossible to describe in anything short of a volume the activity, the brilliancy, and the success of his long years in Paris.

It was exceedingly fortunate for both countries at this time, that, in spite of the intervening contest of so many years, Franklin in his important post of Ambassador in Paris still retained the esteem and friendship of many distinguished Englishmen whose acquaintance he had made during his fifteen years' residence in London. To two of these—Lord Shelburne and David Hartley—are posterity indebted for much of the wisdom, moderation, and statesmanship on the part of Great Britain which contributed so largely to the Treaty of Peace. The first overtures came from Franklin to Lord Shelburne, afterwards the first Marquis of Lansdowne, Minister of the Colonies, who responded by sending a confidential mission to Franklin, with a letter which concluded: "I wish to retain the same simplicity and good faith which subsisted between us in transactions of less importance."

Presently Mr. Fox, as Minister of Foreign Affairs, sent Thomas Grenville over to represent him in the negotiations. Great Britain then had no diplomatic representative at the French Court, and so it came about, as Bancroft says, that Franklin, the Deputy Postmaster-General, who had been dismissed in disgrace in 1774, now as the envoy of the rebel Colonies at the request of Great Britain introduced the son of the author of the Stamp Act to the representative of the Bourbon King.

The final negotiations of the Treaty on the part of England were entrusted to Franklin's lifelong friend, Mr. David Hartley, in whose apartments in the Hôtel de York the definite Treaty was signed. The credit and honor of the negotiation on the American side must be divided between Franklin, Jay, and Adams, to whom, for this great service, their countrymen owe an incalculable debt of gratitude.

At the signing of one of the Treaties in Paris Franklin is said to have worn the same old suit of spotted Manchester velvet which he had last worn on the fatal day at the Cockpit years before, when Wedderburn attacked him, showing how deeply, on that occasion, the iron had entered into his soul.

In view of his fifteen years' service in England and ten in France, of the immense obstacles and difficulties which he had to overcome, of the art and wisdom which he displayed, and the incalculable value to the country of the Treaties which he negotiated, he still stands as by far the greatest of American diplomatists.

In his eightieth year, quite worn out by his labors and infirmities, he returned to his "dear Philadelphia" to spend the brief remnant of his days, as he hoped, in rest and retirement, but that was not to be. He was immediately elected President of Pennsylvania —an office of great responsibility, in which he continued for three years.

I had not firmness enough [he said] to resist the unanimous desire of my country folks; and I find myself harnessed again in their service for another year. They engrossed the prime of my life. They have eaten my flesh, and seem resolved now to pick my bones.

In 1787, at the age of eighty-one, he was a member of that remarkable body of men who met to frame the Constitution of the United States, and it was most fortunate for the nation that he was so. In spite of his great age, he attended all the sessions five hours a day for four months, and took an active part in the discussions and committees. He it was who proposed the amendment by means of which the States came together to form a more perfect union. The small States had been contending most vehemently and persistently for absolute and entire equality. The large States were equally tenacious for a proportional representation. Agreement seemed impossible until Franklin in Committee proposed the simple compromise, which was adopted, and on which the Constitution has thus far safely rested, that in the Senate all States, great and small, should have an equal vote, but in the House of Representatives each State should have a representation proportioned to its population, and that all Bills to raise or expend money must originate there.

He gave close attention to all the great questions discussed in the Convention, which sat in secret session. As he was too infirm to stand and speak he was permitted to write out what he had to say, to be read for him by a fellow-member, and so it came about that his are the only speeches reported entire, and they are very brief and pithy. On one occasion, when there seemed no prospect of any further progress because of hopeless dissensions, he moved that prayer be resorted to at each day's opening of the Convention as the only remedy.

I have lived, Sir, a long time [he said], and the longer I live the more convincing proofs I see of this truth : that God governs in the affairs of men. And if a sparrow cannot fall to the ground without His notice, is it probable that an Empire can rise without His aid? We have been assured, Sir, in the sacred writings that " except the Lord build the house, they labor in vain that build it." I firmly believe this; and I also believe that without His concurring aid we shall succeed in this political building no better than the building of Babel.

When the great Compact of Concessions and Compromises was finished it probably suited no member exactly, so much had each been obliged to yield of his own cherished opinions in the cause of harmony. But Franklin threw the whole weight of his influence in favor of an unconditional signature of the great instrument by all the delegates.

I consent, Sir, to this Constitution [he said] because I expect no better, and because I am not sure that it is not the best. The opinions I have had of its errors I sacrifice to the public good. I have never whispered a syllable of them abroad. Within these walls they were born and here they shall die.

He carried his point and all the members signed.

It can hardly be doubted that it was the combined personal weight and influence of Washington and Franklin that prevailed with the people in all the thirteen States in favor of the adoption of the famous Constitution, which they had done so much to devise and perfect.

He lived to see Washington, who had been his close friend and fellow laborer since the days of the Braddock disaster, elected unanimously the first President of the United States, and to see the new Nation, which he had been so potent to create, fairly launched upon its great career. He lived long enough to see the youthful Hamilton at the age of thirty-two installed as Secretary of the Treasury, and to read the first report of that marvellous genius on the Public Credit of the new-born Nation, whereby, as Webster said: "He smote the rock of the national resources, and abundant streams of revenue gushed forth; he touched the dead corpse of public credit, and it sprang upon its feet." His last public act, only twenty-four days before his death, was a powerful appeal for the abolition of slavery, full of his old wisdom, wit, and satire, and of the spirit which animated the sublime proclamation of Lincoln three-quarters of a century later. And then at last, utterly worn out by his long years of public service, but rejoicing in their grand result, he "wrapped the drapery of his couch about him and lay down to pleasant dreams."

His grateful country honors his memory and cherishes his ever-growing fame as one of its noblest treasures, and transmits from generation to generation the story of his matchless services. His autobiography, written near the end of his wonderful career, is valued by all readers of the English language as one of the most fascinating contributions to its literature. And the lessons of honesty, temperance, thrift, industry, and economy, which he inculcated and practised with such brilliant success in his own person, have been of priceless value to his countrymen, and contributed very largely to their social, material, and intellectual well-being. So that, taking him for all in all, by general consent they class him with Washington and Hamilton and Lincoln in the list of illustrious Americans.

The Philosopher's Joke

By JEROME K. JEROME

Author of "Three Men in a Boat," "Idle Thoughts of an Idle Fellow," "Paul Kelver," etc.

II

.   .   .   .   .   .

It is from the narrative as Armitage told it to me that night in the club smoking-room that I am taking most of my material. It seemed to him that all things began slowly to rise upward, leaving him stationary, but with a great pain as though the inside of him were being torn away—the same sensation greatly exaggerated, so he likened it, as descending in a lift. But around him all the time was silence and darkness unrelieved. After a period that might have been minutes, that might have been years, a faint light crept towards him. It grew stronger, and into the air which now fanned his cheek, there stole the sound of far-off music. The light and the music both increased, and one by one his senses came back to him. He was seated on a low-cushioned bench beneath a group of palms. A young girl was sitting beside him, but her face was turned away from him.

"I did not catch your name," he was saying. "Would you mind telling it to me?".

She turned her face towards him. It was the most spiritually beautiful face he had ever seen. "I am in the same predicament," she laughed. "You had better write yours on my programme, and I will write mine on yours."

So they wrote upon each other's programme, and exchanged again. The name she had written was Alice Blatchley.

He had never seen her before that he could remember. Yet at the back of his mind there dwelt the haunting knowledge of her. Somewhere long ago they had met, talked together. Slowly as one recalls a dream, it came back to him. In some other life, vague, shadowy, he had married this woman. For the first few years they

had loved each other; then the gulf had opened between them—widened. Stern, strong voices had called to him to lay aside his selfish dreams, his boyish ambitions, to take upon his shoulders the yoke of a great duty. When more than ever he had demanded sympathy and help, this woman had fallen away from him. His ideals but irritated her. Only at the cost of daily bitterness had he been able to resist her endeavors to draw him from his path. Another face, with soft eyes full of helpfulness, shone through the mist of his dream—the face of a woman who would one day come to him out of the future with outstretched hands that he would yearn to clasp.

"Shall we not dance?" said the voice beside him. "I really won't sit out a waltz."

They hurried into the ball-room. With his arm about her form, with her wondrous eyes shyly, at rare moments seeking his, then vanishing again behind their drooping lashes, the brain, the mind, the very soul of the young man passed out of his own keeping. She complimented him in her bewitching manner, a delightful blending of condescension and timidity.

"You dance extremely well," she told him. "You may ask me for another later on."

The words flashed out from that dim haunting future: "Your dancing was your chief attraction for me, as likely as not, had I but known?"

All that evening and for many months to come the Present and the Future fought within him. And the experience of Nathaniel Armitage, divinity student, was the experience likewise of Alice Blatchley, who had fallen in love with him at first sight, having found him the divinest dancer she had ever whirled with to the sensuous music of the waltz; of Horatio Camelford, journalist and minor poet, whose journalism earned him a bare income, but at whose minor poetry critics smiled; of Rosalind Dearwood, with her glorious eyes and muddy complexion, and her wild hopeless passion for the big, handsome, ruddy-bearded Dick Everett, who, knowing it, only laughed at her in his kindly, lordly way, telling her with frank brutalness that the woman who was not beautiful had missed her vocation in life; of that scheming, conquering young gentleman himself, who at twenty-five had already made his mark in the city, shrewd, clever, cool-headed as a fox, except where a pretty face and shapely hand or ankle were concerned; of Nellie Fanshawe, then in the pride of her ravishing beauty, who loved none but herself, whose clay-made gods were jewels and fine dresses and rich feasts, the envy of other women and the courtship of all mankind.

That evening of the ball each clung to the hope that this memory of the future was but a dream. They had been introduced to one another; had heard each other's names for the first time with a start of recognition; had avoided one another's eyes; had hastened to plunge into meaningless talk till that moment when young Camelford, stooping to pick up Rosalind's fan, had found that broken fragment of the Rhenish wine-glass. Then it was that conviction refused to be shaken off, that knowledge of the future had to be sadly accepted.

What they had not foreseen was that knowledge of the future in no way affected their emotions of the present. Nathaniel Armitage grew day by day more hopelessly in love with bewitching Alice Blatchley. The thought of her marrying any one else—the long-haired, priggish Camelford in particular—sent the blood boiling through his veins; added to which sweet Alice, with her arms about his neck, would confess to him that life without him would be a misery hardly to be endured, that the thought of him as the husband of another woman—of Nellie Fanshawe in particular—was madness

to her. It was right, perhaps, knowing what they did, that they should say good-bye to one another. She would bring sorrow into his life. Better far that he should put her away from him, that she should die of a broken heart, as she felt sure she would. How could he, a fond lover, inflict this suffering upon her? He ought, of course, to marry Nellie Fanshawe, but he could not bear the girl. Would it not be the height of absurdity to marry a girl he strongly disliked because twenty years hence she might be more suitable to him than the woman he now loved and who loved him?

Nor could Nellie Fanshawe bring herself to discuss without laughter the suggestion of marrying on a hundred and fifty a year a curate that she positively hated. There would come a time when wealth would be indifferent to her, when her exalted spirit would ask but for the satisfaction of self-sacrifice. But that time had not arrived. The emotions it would bring with it she could not in her present state even imagine. Her whole present being craved for the things of this world, the things that were within her grasp. To ask her to forego them now because later on she would not care for them—it was like telling a schoolboy to avoid the tuck shop because, when a man, the thought of stickjaw would be nauseous to him. If her capacity for enjoyment was to be short-lived, all the more reason for grasping joy quickly.

Alice Blatchley, when her lover was not by, gave herself many a headache trying to think the thing out logically. Was it not foolish of her to rush into this marriage with dear Nat? At forty she would wish she had married somebody else. But most women at forty —she judged from conversation round about her—wished they had married somebody else. If every girl at twenty listened to herself at forty there would be no more marriages. At forty she would be a different person altogether. That other elderly person did not interest her. To ask a young girl to spoil her life purely in the interests of this middle-aged party—it did not seem right. Besides, whom else was she to marry? Camelford would not have her; he did not want her then; he was not going to want her at forty. For practical purposes Camelford was out of the question. She might marry somebody else altogether — and fare worse. She might remain a spinster; she hated the mere name of spinster. The inky-fingered woman journalist that, if all went well, she might become—it was not her idea. Was she acting selfishly? Ought she in his own interests, to refuse to marry dear Nat? Nellie—the little cat—who would suit him at forty, would not have him. If to any one but Nellie it might just as well be to her. A bachelor clergyman! It sounded almost improper. Nor was dear Nat the type. If she threw him over it would be into the arms of some designing minx. What was the girl to do?

Camelford at forty, under the influence of favorable criticism, would have persuaded himself he was a heaven-sent prophet, his whole life to be beautifully spent in the saving of mankind. At twenty he felt he wanted to live. Weird-looking Rosalind, with her magnificent eyes veiling mysteries, was of more importance to him than the rest of the species combined. Knowledge of the future in her case only spurred desire. The muddy complexion would grow pink and white, the thin limbs round and shapely; the now scornful eyes would one day light with love at his coming. It was what he had once hoped; it was what he now knew. At forty the artist is stronger than the man; at twenty the man is stronger than the artist.

An uncanny creature, so most folks would have described Rosalind Dearwood. Few would have imagined her developing into the good-natured, easy-going Mrs. Camelford of middle age. The animal, so strong within her at twenty, at thirty had burnt itself out. At eighteen, madly, blindly in love with red-bearded, deep-voiced Dick Everett, she would, had he whistled to her, have flung herself gratefully at his feet, and this in spite of the knowledge forewarning her of the

miserable life he would certainly lead her, at all events until her slowly developing beauty should give her the whip-hand of him—by which time she would have come to despise him. Fortunately, as she told herself, there was no fear of his doing so, the future notwithstanding. Nellie Fanshawe's beauty held him as with chains of steel, and Nellie had no intention of allowing her rich prize to escape her. Her own lover, it was true, irritated her more than any man she had ever met, but at least he would afford her refuge from the bread of charity. Rosalind Dearwood, an orphan, had been brought up by a distant relative. She had not been the child to win affection. Of a silent, brooding nature every thoughtless incivility had been to her an insult, a wrong. Acceptance of young Camelford seemed her only escape from a life that had become to her a martyrdom. At forty-one he would wish he had remained a bachelor; but at thirty-eight that would not trouble her. She would know he was much better off as he was. Meanwhile, she would have come to like him, to respect him. He would be famous: she would be proud of him. Crying into her pillow—she could not help it—for love of handsome Dick, it was still a comfort to reflect that Nellie Fanshawe, as it were, was watching over her, protecting her from herself.

Dick, as he muttered to himself a dozen times a day, ought to marry Rosalind. At thirty-eight she would be his ideal. He looked at her as she was at eighteen and shuddered. Nellie, at thirty, would be plain and uninteresting. But when did consideration of the future ever cry halt to passion; when did a lover ever pause thinking of the morrow? If her beauty was to pass, was not that one reason the more, urging him to possess it while it lasted?

Nellie Fanshawe at forty would be a saint. The prospect did not please her: she hated saints. She would love the tiresome, solemn Nathaniel: of what use was that to her now? He did not desire her; he was in love with Alice, and Alice was in love with him. What would be the sense—even if they all agreed—in the three of them making themselves miserable for all their youth that they might be contented in their old age? Let age fend for itself and leave youth to its own instincts. Let elderly saints suffer,—it was their métier,—and youth drink the cup of life. It was a pity Dick was the only "catch" available, but he was young and handsome. Other girls had to put up with sixty and the gout.

Another point, a very serious point, had been overlooked. All that had arrived to them in that dim future of the past had happened to them as the result of their making the marriages they had made. To what fate other roads would lead, their knowledge could not tell them. Nellie Fanshawe had become at forty a lovely character. Might not the hard life she had led with her husband — a life calling for continual sacrifice, for daily self-control—have helped towards this end? As the wife of a poor curate of high moral principles, would the same result have been secured? The fever that had robbed her of her beauty and turned her thoughts inward had been the result of sitting out on the balcony of the Paris Opera House with an Italian Count on the occasion of a fancy-dress ball. As the wife of an East End clergyman the chances are she would have escaped that fever and its purifying effects. Was there not danger in the alternative: a supremely beautiful young woman, worldly minded, hungry for pleasure, condemned to a life of poverty with a man she did not love? The influence of Alice upon Nathaniel Armitage, during those first years when his character was forming, had been all for good. Could he be sure that, married to Nellie, he might not have deteriorated?

Were Alice Blatchley to marry an artist could she be sure that at forty she would still be in sympathy with artistic ideals? Even as a child had not her desire ever been in the opposite direction to that favored by her nurse? Did not the reading of Conservative journals invariably incline her towards Radicalism, and the steady stream of Radical talk round her husband's table invariably set her seeking argument in favor of the feudal system? Might it not have been her husband's growing Puritanism that had driven her to crave for Bohemianism? Suppose that towards middle age, the wife of a wild artist, she suddenly "took religion," as the saying is. Her last state would be worse than the first.

Camelford was of delicate physique. As an absent-minded bachelor, with no one to give him his meals, no one to see that his things were aired, could he have lived till forty? Could he be sure that home life had not given more to his art than it had taken from him? Rosalind Dearwood, of a nervous, passionate nature, married to a bad husband, might at forty have posed for one of the Furies. Not until her life had become restful had her good looks shown themselves. Hers was the type of beauty that for its development demands tranquillity.

Dick Everett had no delusions concerning himself. That, had he married Rosalind, he could for ten years have remained the faithful husband of a singularly plain wife, he knew to be impossible. But Rosalind would have been no patient Griselda. The extreme probability was that having married her at twenty, for the sake of her beauty at thirty, at twenty-nine at latest she would have divorced him.

Everett was a man of practical ideas. It was he who took the matter in hand. The refreshment contractor admitted that curious goblets of German glass occasionally crept into their stock. One of the waiters, on the understanding that in no case should he be called upon to pay for them, admitted having broken more than one wine-glass on that particular evening: thought it not unlikely he might have attempted to hide the fragments under a convenient palm. The whole thing evidently was a dream. So youth decided at the time, and the three marriages took place within three months of one another.

It was some ten years later that Armitage told me the story that night in the club smoking-room. Mrs. Everett had just recovered from a severe attack of rheumatic fever, contracted the spring before in Paris. Mrs. Camelford, whom previously I had not met, certainly seemed to me one of the handsomest women I have ever seen. Mrs. Armitage — I knew her when she was Alice Blatchley,—I found more charming as a woman than she had been as a girl. What she could have seen in Armitage I never could understand. Camelford made his mark some ten years later; poor fellow, he did not live long to enjoy his fame. Dick Everett has still another six years to work off; but he is well behaved, and there is talk of a petition.

It is a curious story altogether, I admit. As I said at the beginning, I do not myself believe it.

(Conclusion)

STINGS & FLINGS

from

"*The Silly Syclopædia.*"

If we could see ourselves as others see us many of us would wear a mask.

It is a wise son that owes his own father.

Rolling stones gather no moss, but look at the excitement they have.

Consistency is a jewel, but it is n't fashionable to wear it.

Everybody knows that money talks, but nobody notices what kind of grammar it uses.

Every woman loves an ideal man until she marries him—then it's a new deal.

Fair play is a jewel, but so many people can't afford jewelry.

Money cannot buy happiness, but most of us are willing to make the experiment.

Kisses go by favorable circumstances.

It takes a lot of money to teach a Duke how to love an American heiress.

How many people in this world are being coaxed when it's a club they need.

Failures made by other people pave the road to your success.

Charity begins at home, and ruins its health by staying there too much.

Every woman jumps quickly from mice and at conclusions.

If it were impossible to speak anything but truth in this world, how many times a day would we be insulted!

The Day and Hour

By RICHARD WATSON GILDER

I

The Whisperers

New York— 1905

IN the House of State at Albany—in shadowy corridors and corners—the whisperers whispered together.

In sumptuous palaces in the big city men talked intently, with mouth to ear.

Year in and year out they whispered, and talked, and no one heard save those who listened close.

Now in the Hall of the City the whisperers again are whispering, the talkers are talking.

They who once conversed so quietly, secretly, with shrugs and winks and finger laid beside nose—what has happened to their throats?

For speak they never so low, their voices are as the voices of trumpets; whisper they never so close, their words are like alarm bells rung in the night.

Every whisper is a shout, and the noise of their speech goes forth like thunders.

They cry as from the housetops—their voices resound up and down the streets; they echo from city to city and from village to village.

Over prairies and mountains and across the salt sea their whispers go hissing and shouting.

They say the thing they would not say, and quickly the shameful thing clamors back and forth over the round world;

And when they would fain cease their saying, they may not, for a clear-voiced questioner is as the finger of fate and the crack of doom.

What they would hide they reveal, what they would cover they make plain;

What they feared to speak aloud to one another, unwilling they publish to all mankind;

And the people listen with bowed heads, wondering and in grief;

And wise men, and they who love their country, turn pale and ask: "What new shame will come upon us?"

And again they ask, "Are these they in whose keep are the substance and hope of the widow and the fatherless?"

And the poor man, plodding home with his scant earnings from his hard week's work, hears the voices, with bitterness in his soul.

And thieves, lurking in dark places and furtively seizing that which is not their own; and the petty and cowardly briber, and he who is bribed, nudge one another;

And the anarch and the thrower of bombs clap hands together, and cry out: "Behold these our allies!"

73

II

A Woman of Sorrows—Josephine Shaw Lowell *

IT was but yesterday she walked these streets
Making them holier.   How many years
Widowed,—with all her love poured on her kind,—
She ministered unto the abused and stricken,
And all the oppressed and suffering of mankind,—
Herself forgetting, but never those in need;
Her whole, sweet soul lost in her loving work;
Pondering the endless problem of the poor.

In ceaseless labor, swift, unhurriedly,
She sped upon her tireless ministries,
Climbing the stairs of poverty and wrong,
Endeavoring the help that shall not hurt,
Seeking to build in every human heart
A temple of justice—that no brother's burden
Should heavier prove through human selfishness.

In memory I see that brooding face
That now seemed dreaming of the heroic past
When those most dear to her laid loyal lives
On the high altar of freedom; and again
That thinking, inward-lighted countenance
Drooped, saddened by the pain of human kind,
Though resolute to help where help might be,
And with undying faith illuminate.
She was our woman of sorrows, whose pure heart
Was pierced by many woes; sister and saint,
Who to life's darkened passageways brought light,
Who taught the dignity of human service,
Who made the city noble by her life,
And sanctified the very stones her feet
Pressed in their sacred journeys.

Most high God!
This city of mammon, this wide, seething pit
Of avarice and lust, hath known Thy saints,
And yet shall know.   For faith than sin is mightier,

*For portrait of Mrs. Lowell see " Lounger."

And by this faith we live,—that in Thy time,
In Thine own time the good shall crush the ill;
The brute within the human shall die down;
And love and justice reign, where hate prevents,—
That love which in pure hearts reveals Thine own
And lights the world to righteousness and truth.

NEW YORK, December, 1905.

III

To Emma Lazarus—1905 *

DEAR bard and prophet, that thy rest is deep
    Thanks be to God! Not now on thy heart falls
    Rumor intolerable. Sleep, O sleep!
    See not the blood of Israel that crawls,
Warm yet, into the noon and night; that cries
    Even as of old, till all the world stands still
    At rapine that even to Israel's agonies
Seems strange and monstrous, a mad dream of ill.
Thou sleepest! Yea, but as in grief we said:—
    There is a spiritual life unconquerable;
    So, bard of the ancient people, though being dead
Thou speakest, and thy voice we love full well.
    Never thy holy memory forsakes us;
    Thy spirit is the trumpet that awakes us!

IV

A Tragedy of To-day

New York, 1905

I

IN a little theatre, in the Jewry of the New World, I sat among the sad-eyed exiles;

Narrow was the stage and meagrely appointed, and the players gave themselves up utterly to their art;

And, before our eyes, were enacted scenes of a play that scarcely seemed a play.

The place was a city in a wide, unhappy land;

* Read by the author at a memorial meeting in honor of the poet, Emma Lazarus, held at Temple Beth-El, Seventy-Sixth Street and Fifth Avenue, New York, on Sunday evening, November 19, 1905, under the auspices of the New York Section of the Council of Jewish Women.

Even in that empire which drifts to-day like a great ship toward a black and unknown coast;

While men, with blanched faces, cry out: "Unless the tempest abates quickly, behold the mightiest wreck on all the shores of time!"

And the time of the drama was our own time; and the coming and the going; and the people themselves were of our own day and generation;

The people, with strange beards, and look of the immemorial Orient; like those men and women who, alien and melancholy, plod the New-World streets;

Like those who, in slow and pitiful procession, on a fixed day of mourning, with dirges and wailings, poured innumerous into the city's open places.

And, as the play went on, at times the very speech of the actors, in hot debate, crackled and sputtered like the fuse of a Russian bomb.

And there an old man, the preacher of a hunted race and a despised religion, all alone called to his people to follow him, and their God, the God of Israel.

Passionately he proclaimed the faith of the fathers, and the saving word and protecting arm of the Almighty;

He, the voice and prophet of the Lord High God, called aloud to them who strayed:

"Come ye back to your God, and to His Everlasting Word.

"You young men who have forgotten Him, the Unforgetting, and you old men mumbling your prayers, and, cowards! leaving the holy shrine unprotected";

And the young men answered and called the old man the name of them who are dead and have passed away;

And the old men, unheeding, swayed to and fro, mumbling their ancient psalms and ineffectual supplications.

Then, while the noise of the beastly rabble swelled louder and nearer—then did the preacher turn once more to the Lord of Hosts, lifting up his voice in praise and prayer, and faith unquenchable;

Crying to God with a loud voice and saying: "Lead me, Thou Jehovah! in the right way,

"For now has come the great day of the Lord; now, Lord, save Thy people and bless Thy heritage,

"Thou who wert, and art, and ever shalt be! Show now Thy Almightiness, send Thy miracle as lightning from on high."

Nearer and nearer came the curses and shrieks and the wailing lamentations; and men and women fled, wounded, before the infamous and infuriate avengers;

Then the crash of guns and the terror of carnage and rapine unspeakable;

And, in the midst, the voice of an old man crying to heaven, and falling smitten and dead before the shrine of the God of Israel.

And, listening, I heard not only the sounds of the mimic drama — but, louder and more dreadful, the panting of miserable women who welcomed death, the deliverer;

And from Kishineff and Odessa I heard, once more crying to heaven, the outpoured blood of the Jew.

II

And still as I listened and dreamed, the crimson flood widened to a great and lustrous pool,

And looking therein I saw reflected the faces of many known well to my heart and to the hearts of all the world,

For there were the features of mighty warriors and makers of laws and leaders of men; of poets inspired and painters and musicians; and of famous philosophers, and of men and women who loved, and labored for, their kind;

And the faces of preachers and prophets; of those who mightily cursed the unrighteous, and who to a world in darkness brought light everlasting;

And chief of all I saw in that crimson mirror the face of him whose spirit was bowed beneath the eternal agonies of all mankind.*

* " The Whisperers " is reprinted from the N. Y. *Evening Post;* " A Tragedy of To-Day " from the N. Y. *Times.*

PETER PAN'S TERRIBLE FIGHT WITH CAPTAIN HOOK

"Peter Pan"

By HOMER SAINT-GAUDENS

IF you do not believe in Fairies before the end of the third act of Mr. J. M. Barrie's play, "Peter Pan," the boy who would n't grow up, but who longed for a mother to tuck him in bed, then you will surely be the death of the Fairy Tinker Bell, whom you can see only as a dancing light. But if you do believe at once, and take the second turn to the right, and then go on 'till morning, you will come to the Never Never Never Land. There you ought to find hollow-trees, and snowballs, and toad-stools-big-enough-to-sit-on, and a lion-that-lets-his-tail-be-cut-off, and friendly-Indians-with-war-whoops-and-fights, and wolves-that-dare-not-touch-you-if-you-look-at-them-between-your-legs. And there you 'll be sure to come across a Pirate Crew, and a Pirate Ship. It 's a true Pirate Crew that sings "Heave Ho!" and makes captives walk the plank. Their leader, Captain Hook—a mad minded man,—thirsts for the blood of Peter Pan, while terribly

afraid of a crocodile that fortunately swallowed a clock whose ticking warns Captain Hook of his approach. For Peter Pan had cut off Captain Hook's hand, long ago, and had thrown it to the crocodile. That gave the crocodile a taste for Captain Hook. He 's called Captain Hook because of the hook he now carries at the end of his left arm.

You see every first time a baby laughs his laugh becomes a Fairy and lives as long as the baby believes. Of course children can easily learn to fly away with the Fairies. They can come back, too, if their parents keep the nursery window unbarred. So it happened that Peter Pan flew away when he was born, for he heard his parents talking about the prospect of making him President when he grew up, and he wanted always to remain a boy. But he stayed so long that when he tried to return he found the window shut. Then he went to live with the Lost Boys who fall out of perambulators when nurse is away. If they are not claimed within seven days they are sent to the Never Never Never Land.

It is all very clear. You find out at once that Peter Pan is dreadfully fond of stories, for he steals into the room as Peter Pan flies outdoors Nana, the nurse dog, shuts the window so quickly that she cuts off Peter Pans' shadow. Later when the children have gone to sleep Peter Pan comes back to look for the shadow with his Fairy Tinker Bell,

PETER PAN TELLS WENDY OF THE NEVER NEVER NEVER LAND

while Mrs. Darling tells them to her three children. Of course when Peter Pan thinks that Mrs. Darling has seen him he wishes to run away. But just whom you can see only as a dancing light. But after the shadow has been found it won't stick, so while Peter Pan tries to rub it with soap, Wendy, the oldest of the children, opens her eyes, and not being afraid, sews the shadow on Peter Pan again while he tells her about the Never Never Never Land. Then Wendy calls to her brothers to hear more. The Fairy Tinker Bell, whom you can see only as a dancing light, is jealous, but in spite of her Peter Pan teaches the Darling children to fly, so that they all go away together through the window to the Never Never Never Land.

CAPTAIN HOOK STEALS BELOW TO POISON PETER PAN'S MEDICINE

There the Darling children, and the Lost Boys, and Peter Pan build for Wendy a house with a tall hat for a chimney, and windows with babies looking out and roses looking in. Only so as to hide from Captain Hook they all live in rooms under the ground, at the foot of the hollow trees, where they have a bed-for-the-whole-family, and pillows-to-dance-in. After a while the children decide that they ought to go home to their mother. But the Pirates know where the children live, and so, when the Pirates have driven away the friendly Indians that are on guard above, they capture the children as they come out of the hollow-tree-trunks, and then the Pirates chain the children's hands so that they cannot fly, and take them to the Pirate Ship. Meanwhile Peter Pan, who would not go back to Ever Ever Ever Land, falls asleep on the bed-for-the-whole-family, and Captain Hook steals below to poison his medicine. But the Fairy Tinker Bell, whom you can see only as a dancing light, catches Captain Hook in the act, and saves Peter Pan by drinking the poison herself. Then Peter Pan finds out that the Fairy Tinker Bell, whom you can see only as a dancing light, may be kept alive by all the children saying that they believe in Fairies. Of course you yourself, like the other children, truly believe, so you clap your hands and wave your handkerchiefs as Peter Pan wishes, and it is all as it should be.

Then Peter Pan goes to the Pirate Ship. He carries a clock just like the clock the crocodile swallowed. With this time-piece, Peter Pan frightens Captain Hook so badly that he gains one or two minutes in which to arm the boys, and finally to drive overboard the whole Pirate Crew, and Captain Hook. After that of course Peter Pan takes the Darling children home again to their mother. Mrs. Darling tells Peter Pan that she will care for him in the Ever Ever Ever Land. But when Peter Pan finds that some day he still might become President he decides to go back to the Never Never Never Land with his Fairy Tinker Bell, whom you can see only as a dancing light. There they live in their house in the tree-tops where the Fairies, whom you can see only as other dancing lights, flit to and fro. Once a year Wendy, the motherly soul, comes to give the house a spring cleaning. You know what that means.

The story here may seem to be froth, or a comic opera scenario. It is neither. Perhaps you take it for nursery talk, and perhaps you are right. But if you have not retained youth enough to enjoy it you ought to be ashamed of the candles on your next birthday cake. No one but Mr. Barrie would have dared to cast for the stage such an unruled dream. No one but Mr. Barrie could have induced Mr. Frohman to accept the production. No one but Mr. Barrie could have written it in a way to have brought success.

The pure phantasy of this creation of sympathy for the young may not be judged by dramatic standards. Yet Never Never Never Land cannot be so very far away from the island of the admirable Crichton. The author makes us children again willy nilly, by accumulating the detail of childhood, and insisting on the little incidents of childish lives. The father lives for a long time in the kennel of the nurse dog, because he is sorry for having maltreated her. The Pirates make the gentlest of splashes rise above the bulwarks when they are shoved overboard. The Never Never Never Land children play at eating with nothing on the table. This process of whimsical invention keeps true to its sphere where everything remains within the scope of childish imaginings. Here appears no hint of older people re-assuming the young point of view. The actors are merely playing play their parts, just as children would do in such a case. The Pirates are not really pushed into the sea. They hesitate on the rail, and look about them leisurely before they topple out of sight. For all this the author does not force a caricature. Captain Hook leans back in his chair of state on the Pirate Ship and moralizes on fame as a glittering bauble, while sharpening his talons on a neat square of sand-paper. "I have never sat down to afternoon tea," he says. "No woman's lips have ever plucked the roses from my cheeks." Yet somehow he escapes becoming a buffoon.

The company in America has done its work admirably. Its members forward the intangible fancy of the text with an expressive impersonation, up from the lion-that-lets-his-tail-be-cut-off, through Mr. Ernest Lawford, who plays the parts of Mr. Darling and Captain Hook with much taste, to the dainty work of the star herself. Miss Adams admits that her part gives her the greatest pleasure, and that she was only too happy to hear, recently, that Mr. Barrie is writing, for the piece, another scene about the Pirates. On the stage she bears out her words. She becomes Peter Pan to such an extent that her audience forget, even after the play, that she has been acting a part. She can hardly be called a boy when she dances with Tinker Bell, whom you can see only as a dancing light, in the first act, with the pillows in the third act, and when she sings "Sally in Our Alley." That is right, for Peter Pan is not a boy but a boyish thought.

Memoirs and Letters

Reviewed by JEANNETTE L. GILDER

I

A Dentist under the Second Empire

THERE are two most interesting books just published—one the "Memoirs of Dr. Thomas W. Evans,"* the other a new volume of Brookfield papers called "Mrs. Brookfield and Her Circle." Either one of these books is worth a whole letter to itself, but coming at the same time they must share one in common.

The late Dr. Evans, it is well known, was an American dentist who flourished in France during the Second Empire. He not only looked after the teeth of the Emperor and Empress, but he was the close friend of both; and it was he who aided the Empress in her flight from France at the time of the Commune. A chapter from this book, giving an account of the flight of the Empress, the first absolutely authentic account to be printed, was published in the October number of the *Century Magazine*. The rest of the book is entirely new, and is, to use a hackneyed phrase, more interesting than a novel. To my mind, books of recollections, where there is anything to recollect, are always more interesting than novels, but they may not be so, as a rule, to the average reader.

Dr. Evans's "Memoirs" are edited by Edward A. Crane, whose intimacy with the doctor lasted over thirty years; and who was singled out by Dr. Evans to be the editor of his "Memoirs" and manuscript remains. Dr. Evans made no pretension to literary ability, but at the same time, if these "Memoirs" are in his own words, he knew how to express himself in an interesting and picturesque manner. Dr. Evans's close attachment to Napoleon III. and his family, the confidential relations he maintained with other sovereigns and princely houses, and his large and intimate acquaintance among the men and women who, from 1848 to 1870, were the governing powers in Europe, afforded him unusual opportunities of observing the evolution of political ideas and institutions in France, and the conditions and the causes that immediately preceded and determined the fall of the Second Empire as seen from within. No man, moreover, says his literary executor, "was better acquainted than he with what may be termed the moral atmosphere of the several Courts to which, for so many years, he was professionally attached."

In November, 1847, Dr. Evans went to Paris with his wife, he having accepted an invitation from Cyrus S. Brewster, an American dentist of repute then living in Paris, to become his professional associate. Dr. Brewster was the dentist of Napoleon III. when he was Prince Louis. The Prince sent for Dr. Brewster one day, but he was ill and could not go, and Dr. Evans went in his stead. He was kindly received by the Prince, who was then, as President of the French Republic, living in the Élysée Palace. Dr. Evans apparently gave satisfaction, for he was called in the next time the Prince needed a dentist. Not only was he called in professionally, but he was invited to tea on many occasions at a house in the Rue du Cirque, where the Prince was a frequent visitor.

This house [says Dr. Evans], in which Madame H—— lived, was to him easy of access—a gate in the wall, enclosing the garden of the palace, opening on the street close to the house. There, free from the restraint of official surroundings, the Prince-President loved to take a cup of tea, or to sit during the whole evening sipping a cup of coffee, or smoking a cigarette, his black dog, a great favorite with him, sometimes at his feet, and sometimes on his knee.

The relations of the Prince and Madame H—— were the subject of

---

* "Memoirs of Dr. Thomas W. Evans—The Second French Empire." Edited by Edward A. Crane. Illustrated. Appleton. $3.00 net.

censure and even of scandal. The irregularity of the situation he himself recognized; but he "was too kind-hearted to break away from it without some strong and special motive." To use his own words, which Dr. Evans quotes from the Barrot "Memoirs":

Since, up to the present time, my position has prevented me from getting married; since, in the midst of all the cares of the Government, I have, unfortunately, in my country from which I have been so long absent, neither intimate friends nor the attachments of childhood, nor relatives to give me the comforts of a home, I think I can be pardoned an affection that harms no one, and which I have never sought to make public.

Dr. Evans was charmed with the Prince at his first interview. He found him an excellent listener to the conversation of others, and it was with the greatest interest that all listened to him when he chose to speak:

However light the subject, his remarks were never commonplace, but were often weighty, and always bore the impress of originality. There were times when he exhibited rare powers of description, and a delicate but lively appreciation of the humorous side of things; and other times—the subject moving him—when his earnest and kindly words and the sympathetic tones of his voice were irresistibly seductive, and we — hardly knowing why, whether we were captivated by the personality of the speaker, or surprised at the height to which he carried his argument—in wondering admiration sat in silence under the spell of the Charmer.

He talked with freedom of his past life in other countries, of Napoleon and of government in general; but spoke rarely and with more reserve about the French politics of the day. At this time—while President of the Republic—the Prince had few intimate friends, and but very few acquaintances. At times he seemed to be oppressed with a sense of political isolation and loneliness, and more than once was heard to say sadly: "I do not know my friends, and my friends do not know me." Dr. Evans was with the Prince on the morning preceding the night of the *coup d'état*. He writes:

I noticed that his manner and conversation were more than ordinarily affectionate. There were mo-

ments when he appeared to be thoughtful, as if there was something on his mind that he wished to speak about, and yet did not. When I was leaving he went with me to the door of his study, where I had been conversing with him, and then, placing his arm within my own, walked with me through the adjoining room. He knew that great events were about to happen, but this knowledge did not ruffle his serenity, or change in the least the suavity of his voice or the complaisance of his address. That evening there was a reception at the palace, and a crowd of people, his cousin, the Duchess of Hamilton, being present among the rest. No one had the slightest suspicion of the blow that was soon to fall; but just as the Duchess, with whom the Prince was talking, was about to leave, he said to her in the very quietest way, as he gave her his hand, with a kindly smile, "Mary, think of me to-night." Something in the tone of his voice, rather than the words, impressed her strongly. What could he mean? The next morning, when the Duchess awoke, she learned what was in the mind of the Prince when he bade her good-night, and was amazed at his extraordinary self-control, his seeming impassiveness, and the gentleness of his manner, at such a critical, decisive moment in his career.

One great claim upon Dr. Evans's affection was that although he was the Emperor's dentist he did not treat him as a servant.

I was richly repaid in many ways; but more especially by the direct support and encouragement he gave me in the practice of my art, and the social consideration he accorded to me, and, through me, to my profession.

Heretofore if a dentist was sent for to attend a patient he was expected to enter the house by the back-stairs, with the tailor and the butcher-boy; but with the Emperor Dr. Evans held no such position; he was invited to dinners and balls, and not only that, but he was the close friend and adviser of both their Majesties.

Never was a ruler judged more falsely than Napoleon III. [writes Dr. Evans]. He loved mankind, and was always thinking of ways in which he could benefit the people or make some one happy. On one occasion, after he had spoken of the condition of the laboring classes in France, and the measures that ought to be taken to raise the standard of living among the people generally, I ventured to say to him: "Why! your Majesty is almost a Socialist, your sympathies are always with the poor;

their welfare would seem to concern you more than anything else."

" It ought to," he replied. Was he not worthy of the title given to him by the people—" *L'Empereur des Ouvriers* " ?

The Emperor, Dr. Evans assures us, hated to be shut up, and was never so happy as when he could get away from Paris and be in the open air. "He loved the country and country life. I have heard him say that he would have liked nothing better than to be a farmer."

The Emperor, according to Dr. Evans, was a most industrious man. He retired late and rose early. He was fond of writing and took great pleasure in sending to the press communications to be published anonymously. What he wrote was always well written. He needed no help in his literary work.

In writing of the character of the Emperor, Dr. Evans says he was slow to form friendships, but when once made they were lasting.

They were not broken by calumnious stories— these he never cared to listen to. " You have no need to defend yourself," he said one day to one of his friends ; "the more they calumniate you, the more I love you."

The Emperor despised flattery and even the semblance of it. If the Emperor never forgot a kindness he never forgot an injury, and was as sensitive as a woman to personal offence.

If [says Dr. Evans] the ambition of Napoleon III. was equal to that of the first Napoleon, it was less personal and more scrupulous. If ambition led to the downfall of the first Napoleon, pride may have been the cause of his own downfall.

Dr. Evans knew the Empress when she was Comtesse de Teba, long before her marriage to the Emperor; and he says that she was accustomed to come to his office and take her turn with his ordinary patients. After her marriage she sent to him to come to her, and almost apologized for so doing. Eugenie de Montijo was not so dazzled by the splendor of her new position as to forget the companions of her earlier and more simple life. The maid that she had had in her early days remained with her when she was Empress. She was a little woman, not in good health, fretful, irritable, and timid, but her devotion to her mistress was unquestioned.

"Yes " [said the Empress to me one day] " Pepa is timid ; she starts at the rustling of a curtain, and turns pale at the moaning of the wind, and screams at the sight of a mouse, and is in a constant state of terror lest we should all be assassinated ; but let her see or think that I am in any real danger—ah ! then she is no longer afraid, but has the courage of a little lioness."

Of course, the most thrilling chapters in this book are those that describe the flight of the Empress to England at the time of the Commune. Had it not been for the American dentist the Empress Eugenie might have met the fate of Marie Antoinette at the hands of the mob, for it was to him that she went for protection when she found herself in the streets of Paris, alone and helpless.

II

The Delightful Brookfields Again

Any one who thinks that the subject of the Brookfields, and their relations to Thackeray and to literature in general, is exhausted, need but turn to these two large volumes * to find his

* " Mrs. Brookfield and Her Circle." By Charles and Frances Brookfield. Two volumes, illustrated. Scribner. $7.00 Net.

mistake. They are made up of letters written to and by the Brookfields, and are quite as interesting as any other Brookfield volumes that have been published ; and this is paying them the highest compliment. There is, of course, much of Thackeray in these volumes; there is also much of Tennyson and Carlyle and of other contemporary men of letters.

There is not much in the way of notes required in these letters, for they speak for themselves. Here is one to Mrs. Brookfield, written in the spring of 1844. Mr. Brookfield tells of a dinner where he was placed

between a twaddling, benevolent, self-satisfied old Cheeryble, and a pilling surgeon. Lord Palmerston's speeches were amusing to me as exhibiting how a Public Man, thoro'ly accustomed to speak, and not caring the shadow of a fraction of a hang whether he succeeded or not, would handle such flimsy topics. He did not excel, however, nor anybody else. Dickens spoke, shortly and well enough, but it had a cut and dried air, and rather pompous and shapely in its construction and delivered in a rather sonorous deep voice. Not a jot of humor in it. He looks like Milnes, same height and shape, still longer hair, but not his demoniacal good humor of expression.

The season of 1845 was spent by the Brookfields in London, where they had the most delightful sort of a time. They belonged to what Thackeray described as the "set"—a privileged few who passed their time in close and constant intimacy. Thackeray, for instance, was in the habit of breakfasting with the Brookfields every Saturday, but that regular engagement in no way prevented their all meeting at dinners there and in other places that same day as well as on most others. In a letter written by Mr. Brookfield to his mother, who had asked for a leaf from his diary, he tells of a dinner to meet Wordsworth and Tennyson, Gladstone and others. Later on in the summer Mr. Brookfield writes to his wife:

I did nothing in the world yesterday, but travel into the city to get a few good cigars cheap. In returning I asked Tom Taylor and his friend, Albert Smith, to look in and meet Thackeray, but neither came. Thack came at 11½ and sate till 1½—and going home (I find to-day) has sprained his ancle and must be laid up in lavender for some days. I told him it would make a capital advertisement for my Spirit Merchant. "Alarming accident to the Fat Contributor. Yesterday Evening, etc., late or rather early hours, etc., from the cheerful convivialities of a Revd. Gent. not 100 miles from Golden Square."

The next day he looked in upon Thackeray, who "has a box of grouse and bestows a brace upon himself and me at his chambers."

In another letter a dinner given by Tennyson is described by Mrs. Brookfield:

He consulted us as to a dinner he wished to give to a few intimate friends, ourselves amongst the number—my cousin Harry Hallam, also there. The invitations had all been accepted, and the day for the dinner had arrived, when, in the early part of the afternoon, my husband found Alfred Tennyson at his lodging, superintending the dismantling of his bedroom, with workmen taking down his bedstead ; it had occurred to him that there was no drawing-room for the ladies he had invited, and that we should all have to meet together in his one sitting-room and remain there throughout the whole evening. My husband succeeded in persuading him to give up this chivalrous intention, and assured him we should enjoy the novelty of remaining in the dining-room. We had a most agreeable evening, and Alfred's hospitable anxiety on our behalf was entirely relieved, after all his perturbation, by the landlady placing her own private sitting-room at our service for the special occasion. I believe we were all surprised to find how perfectly everything had been arranged for this party of seven or eight guests. The dinner was excellent, the waiting admirable, and we found that Alfred had quietly secured the best possible assistance from outside resources.

The second volume of these letters is, if any thing, more interesting than the first. In one of these letters Mrs. Brookfield describes a dinner given to Miss Brontë, then in London practically for the first time:

There was just then a fashion for wearing a plait of hair across the head, and Miss Brontë, a timid little woman with a firm mouth, did not possess a large enough quantity of hair to enable her to form a plait, so therefore wore a very obvious crown of brown silk. Mr. Thackeray on the way down to dinner addressed her as Currer Bell. She tossed her head, and said "she believed there were books being published by a person named Currer Bell . . . but the person he was talking to was Miss Brontë—and she saw no connection between the two."

I cannot say that all of these letters are worth printing, but most of them are. Here is an amusing one from Mrs. Carlyle to Mr. Brookfield:

You are very absurd,—a great merit, let me tell you, in these sensible times ! But you must not come *to-night!* You must come to-morrow night or Monday night, because, you see, there are two "terrible blockheads" coming to-night by their own appointment, and Mr. C. says he "would n't for any consideration have Brookfield there along with such a pair of Jackasses!" I suggested that the very Jackassness of the people might amuse

you. But he declared, "No! No! such a combination is not to be thought of!"

These two volumes are enlivened by some unusually attractive portraits and sketches, some entirely new to print, others more familiar, but still rare.

The Editor's Clearing-House

A Plea for Old Favorites

THE successful re-publication of Mr. John Hay's "Castilian Days," a far better piece of work than his more widely-known "Pike County Ballads," leads one to the cheering belief that a good book, even though it be an old one, still stands a chance of being read, and that there may be a few discriminating persons who, weary of modern mediocre fiction, turn with pleasure to some of those old favorites which are in most cases only to be found upon the top shelves of old-fashioned libraries.

Novels depicting society are more evanescent in their interest than those portraying character, which makes it all the more surprising that Major L. W. M. Lockhart's "Fair to See" and "Mine Is Thine" should be so enjoyable to us. The life of the Highland gentry of fifty years ago is quite as interesting as those studies of peasant life which have enjoyed such vogue of late.

Recent events in South Africa have demonstrated the fact that there has been little change in the British Army since Braddock's defeat. Perhaps this accounts for the singularly modern flavor of Col. Bruce Hamley's military novel, "Lady Lee's Widowhood," whose humor has stood the test of half a century wonderfully well. This book furnished Lester Wallack with material for "Rosedale," a play that, after forty years, still lives.

Coeval with "Lady Lee's Widowhood" are "Frank Fairleigh" and "Lewis Arundel," by Francis E. Smedley. Mrs. Oliphant, in her "Autobiography," speaks of meeting Smedley on the Continent, and of her surprise at finding that the man who

wrote so much of athletics and sport was so crippled that his limbs were supported by an iron frame. This recalls the fact that Alfred Ollivant, author of the delightful "Bob, Son of Battle," which breathes the very air of the moors, is an invalid who has only taken up writing since his back was injured by a fall from his horse.

Two novels much in vogue in England some forty years ago were "The Semi-Detached House" and "The Semi-Attached Couple." They were written by the Hon. Emily Eden, the daughter of Lord Auckland, and show a skill in character-drawing and a lightness of touch not common among women writers of that day. That they are pleasantly remembered by an older generation of readers is proved by the appearance, every now and then, in the literary columns of magazines, of inquiries as to where they may be obtained.

Fifty years ago few American writers dealt with society, but two books exist by which one can reconstruct the New York of that time. George William Curtis has been so identified with recent American literature that it is hard to realize that one of his most successful books was written in 1853, but "The Potiphar Papers" are still the authority on the parvenu society of that day. "The Upper Ten Thousand," by Charles Astor Bristed, originally appeared in *Fraser's Magazine*, and showed us life in New York when Bleecker Street was the dividing line between business and fashion, and Third Avenue was the speeding ground for trotters. A little later appeared that charming book, "The Sparrowgrass Papers," by Frederic S. Cozzens, a New York merchant, the possession of which in a family argues at least two generations of literary discrimination. These papers were read by the author to his fellow-members of The Sketch Club, a body which afterwards developed into The Century Association. It was the pioneer of books on country life and is written with that appreciation of nature and sympathy with children that have become a marked feature of recent literature. Even "The Child's Garden of Verses" contains nothing more graceful or more truly childlike than the lines which Mr. Sparrowgrass wrote at his little boy's request, for his sweetheart:

> Chocolate-drop of my heart !
> I dare not breathe thy name ;
> Like a peppermint stick I stand apart
> In a sweet, but secret flame.

. . . . .

> And I thought, as I swung on the gate
> In the cold, by myself alone,
> How soon the sweetness of hoarhound dies,
> But the bitter keeps on and on.

"Emily Chester," by a Mrs. Crane of Baltimore, showed ability of no common order. It was one of the first of those psychological novels which have always been liked in this country and which have been pushed to their farthest development in the latest stories of Mr. Henry James. In "Emily Chester" the heroine is beloved by two men, one of whom appeals to her very strongly on her mental and spiritual side, but whose personality is disagreeable to her, while the other, although much inferior to his rival, satisfies her æsthetic sense. The struggle between the two sides of her nature forms the interest of the story and created something of a sensation when such problems were not as often made the theme of fiction as they now are.

It was a real pleasure to read again Mrs. Brush's delightful story, "The Colonel's Opera Cloak," reprinted within the last two years. The shiftless Southern family, planted in a keen New England community, the terrible children, their inefficient mother, and the old darky Pomp, the real hero of the book, are all drawn with a skill and feeling that atone for the slender thread of plot. So far this book has escaped the dramatizer, though it contains the material for a good comedy.

The old-fashioned juvenile book would hardly be popular nowadays. Would the modern child, who demands a "Young Chauffeur Series," or "The Young Trust Breaker," have any patience with Miss Edgeworth's "Harry and Lucy" or "Frank" ? I am afraid not, although most children like "The Parents' Assistant," in spite of its title. But surely "Holiday House," with the immortal Mrs. Crabtree hectoring poor Harry and Laura, would still find readers, for the book is rich in that spirit of childish mischief which is confined to no time or country and pervades "Max und Moritz" as well as "Buster Brown."

To the many distracted elders seeking suitable Christmas books for their young friends, a new edition of "The William Henry Letters," by Mrs. Diaz, would be a godsend. William Henry is a plain average boy who is sent to boarding-school, whence he writes these letters to his family, illustrating them himself. The book contains no melodramatic incidents; only the usual round of schoolboy life, but William Henry, Dorry, and their friends are far better worth knowing than the mawkish Elsies and be-curled Fauntleroys of a later day.

MARY K. FORD.

A Burst of Enthusiasm

It was with a sense of keen disappointment that one of THE CRITIC'S faithful readers, who had been looking forward to the December issue for a satisfying critique on "The House of Mirth," laid down the number after reading the half page which alone was given to the consideration of that novel. It may be that to others beside Miss Dunbar Mrs. Wharton's last book is not a "great novel" but there are certainly those to whom it seems entitled to that rank. I, for one, must take issue with that statement as well as with others made in the criticism referred to. I cannot agree for instance that my interest in the book arose either from "curiosity" or "moral enthusiasm" or a mixture of both. There can be no question as to the supreme excellence of the book as a work of art; its technique, its style, are incomparable: but its chief charm does not after all lie in these. That, it seems to me, is the fact that, while reading it, one has the sense that one is living life, not reading about it, and is n't that the greatest possible test?

Are all "the figures" again, "of one exceedingly unpleasant tone"? Does Gerty Farish fall under that head or Selden or even Rosedale, one of the strongest as he is surely the frankest character in the book? As to the heroine, I find myself utterly at variance with the opinions of the critic. If I ever felt on terms of "real intimacy" with any one in a book it is with Lily Bart; as a matter of fact I feel better acquainted with her than with half of the real women I know. So far from thinking of her as "gloved, veiled, and on her guard," I live, with her, through all her little triumphs and failures, sympathize with her hurt pride, skilfully hid under a calm and smiling exterior, deplore her inconsistencies and changes of purpose, feel sorry for her faults and mistakes, for which she is honest enough to take the blame herself, and glory in her ultimate triumph. I use the word advisedly. Think to what depths she, with her inherited tendencies and in the midst of that artificial environment, might have fallen and how, after all, in every crisis of temptation, she did hold on to the best that was in her, sacrificing wealth, position, a life of ease—all that she had

been taught to think of as of the most worth—so to do. Not one "unlovely thing" about or in her has been suppressed, never was author more honest with her readers than Mrs. Wharton has been in this regard; you see right into the heart, mind, and soul of this woman, and what do you read at the end? Not failure to my mind, but success, not as the world counts it to be sure, but success of the spirit. She keeps her true self, her noblest self, inviolate through all the petty ignominies as well as the great disasters that fall to her lot. To find her equal in fiction one must turn to George Eliot, Thomas Hardy, or George Meredith; no other writers of English have done such justice to their women characters.

If the book as a whole may be regarded as a "castigation of the fast set," it is the most skilfully written sermon yet presented on this text. There is no lecturing, no cant, no tedious or cynical dissertations on its morals or lack of morals. The picture simply is before you, you may look or you may pass it by. I would recommend a perusal of the book to all those on the lower rungs of the ladder whose greatest ambition is to achieve the top.

I cannot, in conclusion, refrain from voicing my admiration for the courage, no less than for the art of Mrs. Wharton's performance,—courage of a high order, for what she attempted demanded not only great skill but genius, for if she had failed not only her position in letters but in society would have been hazardous—but she has not failed.

ALICE MAY BOUTELL.

The Book-Buyer's Guide

ART

Cram—Impressions of Japanese Architecture and the Allied Arts. By Ralph Adams Cram. Illus. Baker Taylor. $2.00 net.
The general reader as well as students of this subject will find Mr. Cram's book interesting and instructive.

Dick—Arts and Crafts of Old Japan. By Stewart Dick. McClurg. $1.20.
After the scores of books on Japanese art and art industry, and by men who on the ground have studied the art of Nippon, this book seems shallow and of slight value. It scarcely penetrates the surface and is but a primer for belated beginners. Nevertheless, being illustrated and written in straightforward style, it may serve a good purpose in opening some eyes. Unlike the author, who apparently thinks that more fresh air and a world-wide outlook "gave the death-blow to Japanese art," we believe that this manifestation of the deathless spirit of Yamato may yet have a grander expansion while taking a higher flight. As matter of fact, apart from the auction mart Japanese art is handsomely holding its own even if its more recent manifestations abide at home and do not go globe-trotting for the delectation of aliens.

Henderson—Constable. By M. Sturge Henderson. Scribner. $2.00 net.
This volume, one of a long series on the art of the many ages, deals adequately with its subject, "Constable." The author not only indulges in restrained criticism, but presents the actions and interests of the artist in a vivid and chronological manner. The half-tones are carefully made and of sufficient size.

Hill—Pisanello. By G. F. Hill. Scribner. $2.00 net.
This book is a companion to that on "Constable" in manner of treatment and in form as one of the series of Lives of Artists. Pisanello, the painter and the medallist, together with his brother workers upon the little reliefs, have been comprehended here in a distinct and lucid manner.

Leech—Pictures of Life and Character. By John Leech. Putnam. $1.50.
"There is far more fun, good drawing, more good sense, more beauty in John Leech's *Punch* pictures than in all the Art Union illustrations, engravings, statuettes, &c., put together," said Dr. John Brown, and any one who is fortunate enough to possess this handy little volume of Leech's inimitable contributions to *Punch* will surely agree with him. It is a book full of enjoyment.

Parsons—Catalogue of the Gardiner Greene Hubbard Collection of Engravings. Compiled by Arthur Jeffrey Parsons. Government Printing Office.
A most carefully studied and printed book on this very detailed subject.

Ransom—Couches and Beds of the Greeks, Etruscans, and Romans. By Caroline L. Ransom. University of Chicago Press. $4.50 net.
Though this book was begun as an archæological study it should appeal to any lay reader at all interested in such a subject. The work contains not only a chronological survey of the various forms, but, in another portion, longer discussions of details. The whole has been unusually well illustrated with many carefully made half-tones and line cuts.

BELLES-LETTRES

Alexander—Il Libro D'Oro. Translated by Francis Alexander. Little, Brown. $2.00.
A very unusual collection of more than one hundred and twenty miracle stories and sacred legends written by fathers of the church and published in Italy, in the XVIth, XVIIth, and XVIIIth centuries.

Bronson—English Essays. Selected and edited by Walter C. Bronson. Holt. $1.25.
A book intended for use with college classes in literature, and containing some of the best specimens of the essay from Elizabethan days down to the present time—from Bacon and Milton to Pater and Stevenson. These fill 360 pages, to which 40 of critical and explanatory notes are appended. The book is well suited to its special purpose, and should also be welcome to the general reader who is interested in this line of literature.

Cadogan—Makers of Modern History. By Edward Cadogan. Pott. $2.25 net.
Three essays of moderate compass on Louis Napoleon, Cavour, and Bismarck, three men who were eminently "makers of history" in three countries and, indeed, in all Europe. Their biographies written at full length would be a complete history of the period in which they lived, and these scholarly studies of their work, and their influence, though not in any sense a substitute for histories properly so-called, are well suited to stimulate interest in the study of such literature.

Coudert—Addresses by Frederic R. Coudert. Putnam. $2.50.
This lawyer made an unusual name for himself at the New York bar. Those of his speeches that seemed most popular, most serious, most worth publishing have been included in this volume. Arbitration and International Law, History and Biography, Morals and Social Problems and Social Organizations, all are dealt with in his strong, and clear-headed manner.

Dawson—The Makers of English Fiction. By W. J. Dawson. Revell. $1.50 net.
These direct, clear, simple, literary criticisms

of seventeen of the first names in the history of English fiction plus three more general chapters must take their place among the best literature of their class. The author refrains from wild theories or strange deductions, and is exempt from bias towards any especial domain of letters. Mr. Dawson uses his common-sense to guide himself and his followers to the true value of books.

Dickinson—A Modern Symposium. By G. Lowes Dickinson. McClure. $1.00.

A series of political and sociological reflections presented in the form of discussions between imaginary speakers. A suggestive little volume, well-worth reading.

Dunn—Cicero in Maine. By Martha Baker Dunn. Houghton. $1.25.

A collection of essays on not unusual topics, rather too self-consciously light and airy in tone. Most of the papers are personal and reminiscent, and all seem untouched by imagination and unsubdued by reflection. Mrs. Dunn has hardly the temper of an essayist. The fluency, humor, and homely wisdom which these papers show might be employed at better advantage, one would suppose, in writing fiction. Many of the essays have been published in the *Atlantic*.

James—The Question of Our Speech. The Lesson of Balzac. By Henry James. Houghton. $1.00 net.

There is no doubt whatever that we—even the best educated of us—are far from accurate in our speech. Of course, conversation has its permitted liberties, and it is not desirable that a copy-book correctness should rule. But there is a distinction between ease and slovenliness. Mr. James is evidently inclined to believe that this distinction is less well observed by Americans than by Englishmen; and coming here after so long an absence he ought to be a good judge. At all events, his criticisms are reasonable and his advice is salutary. In the same volume is printed the paper on Balzac recently published in the *Atlantic Monthly*. The French novelist has had an influence upon Mr. James so potent that his assumption that his methods are the last word in the novelist's art is not surprising. But a saner view, perhaps, is that, great as Balzac was, and close as was his analysis of life as he saw it, he still falls a little short of that humanizing touch which raises genius to the first degree of power. His admirers can never make the world in general believe that he holds the supreme place which Mr. James would give him.

Lecky—Washington. By W. E. H. Lecky. Century. 75 cts.

An essay upon the character of Washington from "A History of England in the Eighteenth Century," by W. E. H. Lecky, now placed in the Thumb Nail Series, a volume of pocket size.

Marvin—The Companionship of Books. By Frederic Rowland Marvin. Putnam. $1.25.

These are very brief and modest essays, whose author seems to prefer throwing out suggestions to developing them showily. A very great number of topics are covered in its volume, and the curious reader will find a charm in its miscellaneousness. There is no little suggestiveness in these sincere fragments of literature.

Pais—Ancient Legends of Roman History. By Ettore Pais. Dodd, Mead. $4.00 net.

From a number of lectures chiefly given at the Lowell Institute of Boston the author has constructed an exhaustive volume on the very early Roman legends which formed the substratum of later political and social development. Professor Pais has made deep researches on his subject in Italy and Sicily and goes extensively into much dubious and detailed ground. The book is a scholarly one, essentially for the scholar.

Platt—Bacon Cryptograms in Shakespeare. By Isaac Hull Platt. Small, Maynard. $1.00.

Sundry old fooleries in the "cipher" line, with a few new ones of the same sort, set forth in better typography than such stuff deserves.

Sheldon—A Study of the Divine Comedy of Dante. By Walter Sheldon. Weston. 50 cts.

Four lectures intended for beginners in the study of Dante, but treating the subject mainly from an ethical point of view.

Stevenson—Edinburgh. By Robert Louis Stevenson. Lippincott. $1.00.

A pleasant re-edition of a charming essay by a master of style.

Trent—Greatness in Literature. By W. P. Trent. Crowell. $1.30 net.

Professor Trent has in the main high ideals of culture, and in these papers there is pleasant discourse about the masters of literature, the methods of literary study, and the relations of literature and science. He is not here addressing critics, but students, and much that seems elementary is consequently appropriate enough. His protest against impressionism in criticism and his plea for standards of "greatness" are well judged. But the distinctions he makes between the "supremely great," the "very great," the "great," the "important," and the "minor" writers are rather mechanical. It is difficult to appraise literature in such a fashion. No one will deny that Shakespeare belongs in the first class; but it is not so certain that Lucretius is superior to Horace or Wordsworth inferior to Spenser. Such labels sometimes refuse to stick. Professor Trent's practice is indeed better than his precept, for he has a good word to say for the *dii minores* who, with all their faults, may still touch a sympathetic chord in us. His views of the way literature should be taught are in the main sound. Neither philological analysis nor "chatter about Harriet" is calculated to impart the sense of literary values.

Wagner—Justice. By Charles Wagner. McClure. $1.00 net.

How little effect popular education has had upon popular culture is illustrated by the success of the books of Pastor Wagner. In this volume, as in "The Simple Life," the obvious is set forth in the most obvious manner. Much that is said is sensible enough; but surely there needs no ghost come from the grave to tell it us. "Justice" is a pretty little volume which will satisfy certain modest ideas of a Christmas gift. It would be ridiculous, were it less painful, to reflect that its author has been hailed in this country as an apostle of a new and wonderful gospel.

BIOGRAPHY

Bielschowsky—The Life of Goethe. By Albert Bielschowsky. Putnam. Vol. I. $3.50. To be reviewed at length later.

Boswell—Life of Johnson. By James Boswell. Frowde. $1.00.

A reprint of the third edition of this famous biography edited under the superintendence of Edmund Malone, in 1799.

Browne—A Bibliography of Nathaniel Hawthorne. Compiled by Nina E. Browne. Houghton. $3.00.

This book begins a series of bibliographies of authors prominent in fiction. They are to be brought out in special editions where great attention will be given to material, arrangement, and general display.

De Wertheimer—The Duke of Reichstadt. By Edward de Wertheimer. Lane. $5.00.

Though numbering only twenty-one years, the life of Napoleon's son fills a large volume, by reason of the intrigues of which he was the centre throughout his tragic and pathetic existence. The great Emperor's second marriage, his downfall and captivity, the despicable weakness of Marie Louise, and the anxiety through all Europe to obliterate remembrance of Napoleon by coercion, and almost imprisonment of his son, give interest to a volume for which a searching inquiry has been made in State and private archives. No pains have been spared to give a fair account of the Duke of Reichstadt's life, and all associated with it. Numerous illustrations adorn the book.

Gosse—Sir Thomas Browne. By Edmund Gosse. Macmillan. 75 cts. net.

Sir Thomas has been fortunate in his biographers and editors, but there was none the less room for a compact account of his life and work like this latest addition to the "English Men of Letters" series. It has been prepared with excellent taste and judgment, as we might expect from Mr. Gosse.

Margoliouth—Mohammed and the Rise of Islam. By D. S. Margoliouth. Putnam. $1.35 net.

The fortieth volume in the "Heroes of the Nations," a series notable for the uniformly high character of its successive issues, and every way deserving the general favor it has won among the best class of readers. The series should be in every home and school library, as of course it is sure to be in all public libraries.

North—Old Greek: An Old-time Professor in an Old-fashioned College. A Memoir of Edward North. By S. N. D. North. McClure. $3.50.

It would hardly seem possible that the life of a teacher in a small college, quite unknown outside of his limited local surroundings, could have any special interest except for his old students; but the book is a delightful picture of the man and the teacher, his influence on all who were associated with him; and incidentally a striking illustration of the educational value of the small college as distinguished from the great universities. The selections from his lectures and other writings show that he was not merely an "Old Greek," of the best type, but a man of the broadest culture and the widest literary and social sympathies.

Page—The Chief American Poets: Selected Poems. Edited by Curtis Hidden Page. Houghton. $1.75 net.

Like his "British Poets," this is not a comprehensive anthology, but deals, as its title indicates, with a select few. Here in a single volume we have what the editor believes to be all of the best work of the nine American poets whom he regards as "chief." These are Bryant, Poe, Emerson, Longfellow, Whittier, Holmes, Lowell, Whitman, and Lanier. Here are nearly 45,000 lines of verse, over 12,000 of which are Longfellow's. The selections have been made with good taste and judgment and the notes are ample and to the point.

Skae—The Life of Mary Queen of Scots. By Hilda T. Skae. Lippincott. $1.25 net.

It cannot be said that Miss Skae sheds any new light on Mary's history. The old story is merely retold, all the romantic facts being presented, and the question of Mary's guilt or innocence remaining as great an enigma as ever.

Sorrel—Recollections of a Confederate Staff Officer. By Gen. G. M. Sorrel. Neale. $2.00.

One of the best of the recent books on the Civil War as seen from the Southern side, giving an inside view of camp life from the general's quarters, and military movements and experiences from the same point of view, with graphic sketches of many of the leading Confederate commanders.

Trollope—Autobiography of Anthony Trollope.
Dodd, Mead. $1.25.
A new edition of an already well-known and entertaining autobiography.

BOOKS FOR THE YOUNG

Gerould—Sir Guy of Warwick. By Gordon
Hall Gerould. McNally. $1.00.
A simply retold tale of a knight whose fame was the heritage of two nations. Many would find it tedious to read of the hero's one love and many adventures in the unfamiliar tongues of the old romances, and to these the present author has brought a portion of by-gone flavor qualified of necessity by the modern form of the text. The woodcut illustrations are adapted to the nature of the subject.

Harrison—The Moon Princess. By Edith
Ogden Harrison. McClurg. $1.25 net.
With a simple, unaffected style the writer has narrated a child's story of lively interest. The pictures in color and line are unusual for such a work.

Mabie—Myths Every Child Should Know.
Selected and edited by Hamilton W. Mabie. Doubleday, Page. 90 cts. net.
The matter is taken from Hawthorne, Church (Homeric Stories), Kingsley (Greek Heroes), and other standard sources; and the book is well suited for both home and school reading.

**St. John—The Face in the Pool. A Faerie
Tale.** By J. Allen St. John. McClurg. $1.50.
This Faery tale with text and illustrations by the same hand shows that Mr. St. John is a better writer than illustrator. The story possesses charm of imagination, and the volume has been edited as a holiday book with several colored half-tones as well as line cuts.

FICTION

Barry—Our Best Society. By John D. Barry.
Putnam. $1.50.
A sprightly and acute narrative of the social and literary adventures of a young dramatist and his wife, first published as a serial in THE CRITIC. The tragi-comedies of such an existence have been capably realized by the anonymous author and relentlessly put forth. Most observers of the social phenomena of contemporary New York are already familiar with the type of that ingenuous young couple, Mr. and Mrs. Edward Foster, who are pictured here. From first to last, the book touches upon a remarkable variety of social phases and is undoubtedly a valuable document of certain manners and points of view of our day and section. Considered as a novel, the book lacks conventional structure and plot, but so does the life it discriminatingly portrays.

Beaconsfield—Coningsby. By the Earl of
Beaconsfield. Lane. 75 cts.
A small and new edition of a novel famous in 1844.

Cabell—The Line of Love. By James Branch
Cabell. Harper. $2.00.
Seven mediæval love-stories, told with much grace and spirit. They have throughout a distinct and agreeable flavor and are embellished with illustrations in color by Howard Pyle. An interesting contribution to romantic literature, not beyond popular understanding and enjoyment. The book is elaborately issued in a holiday edition.

Connolly—The Deep Sea's Toll. By James B.
Connolly. Scribner. $1.50.
These short stories tell of the lives of the Gloucester fisherman, and are full of tragedy, pathos, and human nature. They are written with a good deal of spirit, and while much that they contain is incomprehensible to the ordinary land-lubber, there is enough left to reach the hearts of most ordinary mortals.

Gardiner—The Heart of a Girl. By Ruth
Kimball Gardiner. Barnes. $1.50.
This contribution to child psychology is not meant for children, although the title will undoubtedly induce parents to buy it for that purpose. All of Mrs. Gardiner's gifts of intuition, memory, imagination, and observation have been marshalled in the depiction of Margaret Carlin, and her years of training in the art of writing stand her in good stead. The picture is of a clever child. not particularly lovable, but attractive, nevertheless. The games, the superstitions, the habits of thought of an active-minded girl are here surprisingly related. The precise nature of all the details perhaps makes the length of the story somewhat of an obstacle, but the rare quality of charm which made "Richard Practicing," one of the best short stories of the year when it appeared in the *Century Magazine* is here present also, even if in more diluted quantity.

Mills—Caroline of Courtlandt Street. By
Weymer J. Mills. Putnam. $2.00 net.
A romantic tale of New York City in the olden time (but good for any other latitude) which would be attractive in plain every-day dress, but is peculiarly so in its novel and charming holiday garb, with delicate and dainty borders of exquisite tint on every page and full-page artistically colored illustrations.

Phillips—The Social Secretary. By David
Graham Phillips. With eleven illustrations by Clarence F. Underwood. Decorations by Ralph Fletcher Seymour. Bobbs-Merrill. $1.00.
An entertaining, breezy story, written from a woman's point of view, evidently by a man, even though it were anonymous, and (evidently) by a Yale man (see page 33). A Washington society girl of diminished fortune but undisputed position pilots a Western Senator and his wife through the perils of a winter in the Capital. He had piled up a fortune and bought his way into the Senate. She possessed "bottled" hair and a lovable

disposition. There is a son—but that is the same old story. The insight into political life is entertaining. Western writers would give us greater cause for appreciation, however, if they would only rectify the provincialism "all afternoon." Mr. Underwood's illustrations add to the book. The styles in women's clothes are not recent to be sure, but they are graceful. And a "real lady" does not hold her hand-bag by the chain.

Phillpotts—Knock at a Venture. By Eden Phillpotts. Macmillan. $1.50.
Though Mr. Phillpotts writes almost entirely of Dartmoor, he never permits his readers to wish that he might change his theme. He is, in fact, always at his best when dealing with the Devonshire peasant, and with each new book that comes from his pen is renewed in us wonder that he can give such variety to types that are essentially the same. The beautiful descriptions of scenery and weather that he has made familiar abound in these short stories, but it is to be regretted that his tendency to botanize shows no diminution. In his sincere love and knowledge of Nature, Mr. Phillpotts forgets that the average reader cannot follow him, and does not even know the names of most of the flowers that he so minutely describes as to suggest a botanists' calendar to the uninitiated. But his peasants are inimitable. The stories are of many kinds, though the tragic note prevails, the tragedy of primeval natures. The human knowledge is still here, the insight into woman's complex nature, and the humor. The dialogue between the two old men at the burial of Amos Thorn, in "Jonas and Dinah," is itself sufficient to convince us that Mr. Phillpotts's hand has in no wise lost its cunning.

Sterling—Shakespeare's Sweetheart. By Sara Hawks Sterling. Jacobs. $2.50.
Here the reader is led to believe that Ben Jonson asked Anne Hathaway to tell her love story and then to file it away in a London vault where it was recently discovered. The tale has been told in a quaint, old-fashioned atmosphere that cannot but be pleasing. Miss C. E. Peck, the illustrator, with her drawings in color and marginal decorations, proves herself a woman of unusual talent for her task with a sentiment to conceive and a power of drawing to execute.

Thackeray—The History of Henry Esmond. By William Makepeace Thackeray. Ginn. $1.50.
An edition of the classic novel especially adapted to meet the needs of high-school classes with unusually helpful notes.

HISTORY AND TRAVEL

Atkinson—The Philippine Islands. By Fred W. Atkinson. Ginn. $3.00.
Rising like a solid pyramid out of the readable and shallow, and the pragmatic, official, and unreadable mass of articles and publications on the Philippines, is this book of the first

general superintendent of American education in the Dewey archipelago. He is a stalwart for the continuance of the policy of the administration as inaugurated by McKinley and carried out under Roosevelt and Taft. Here we have something definite and clear, yet comprehensive, with copious illustration of the text by half-tone reproductions of photographs. Literary proportion is well observed. One third of the matter treats of geography, history, and of the factors which slowly working during ages have made the Filipino what he is. Analyzing the humanity, the author believes in him, the average islander, as an improvable specimen of the race and his enthusiasm is contagious. This is a wholesome, stimulating, enjoyable book, the ripe fruit of an earnest worker, a lover of ideals, yet a master of facts. It is a real illuminator of the theme treated.

Curtis—Egypt, Burma, and British Malaysia. By William Eleroy Curtis. Revell. $2.00.
Far apart and to the American eye unconnected in alien thought or mutual interests, at first sight, seem these lands described by the Chicago *Herald-Record's* argus-eyed correspondent. In reality, the Nile land, the sapphire country, and the federated Malay States are all one in their illustration of the British genius for governing various races and of substantial success in practice. Not that Mr. Curtis approves, either in snap judgment or reflection after near-at-hand examination and wide experience of observation, of all that John Bull does. He is at times as severe, and perhaps as far "off" as are Mr. Alleyne Ireland's amazingly English interpretations of American colonial administration. Yet Mr. Curtis is usually very fair and generously appreciative. Apart from his judgments, his descriptions are vivid, rich in color, and while his eyes are as restless as a Tartar's, his pen—pardon, we mean his type-writer key—makes reading as pleasant as it is easy. This is the latest and best literary photograph of the contemporary British protectorates here so agreeably treated.

Healy—The Valerian Persecution. By Patrick J. Healy, D.D. Houghton. $1.50.
It tends to prejudice a fair-minded student, who inquires for science, to find ecclesiastic permission to print given in Latin on the fly-leaf. The more "authority" the less truth—perhaps. In fact, however, Dr. Healy's book is a genuine contribution to a study of the relations of Church and State in the Roman Empire of the third century. The data of actual martyrdom seem scanty as compared with the copiousness of official documents on the Government's side. It may be that a more thorough acquaintance with the facts of later persecutions may show that Dr. Healy possibly exaggerates the relative severity of the first general onslaught of force against conscience. However, it may be that the scholarly work before us is of the highest value and timeliness. The same questions which the author handles with such

scholarly insight and patient detail have emerged in Japan within our memory, while in China this is the question of questions to the missionary and teacher. Chinese orthodoxy and State religion, besides being one, are, in historic view if not to prophetic insight, as cruel, bloody, and uncompromising as was that of old Rome, though few but the scholar of native text and record realize this. A hearty welcome to such books which, buried at birth to the crowd, are beacon lights to the statesman and thinker. Christianity and Paganism are opposed systems, hence their collision, while persecution may arise from patriotism rather than despotic malice or fanatical hatred. Both in acuteness and erudition this book is a leader.

Hulbert—Washington and the West. Edited by Archer B. Hulbert. Century. $2.00 net.

A careful reprint of Washington's Diary of September, 1784, kept during his journey into the Ohio Basin, in the interest of a commercial union between the Great Lakes and the Potomac; with a scholarly commentary thereupon by Mr. Hulbert, who is well-known by his "Historic Highways of America." The Diary richly deserves reproduction, and the commentary is in appropriate keeping. The book is illustrated with maps, a view of Washington's Mill, etc.

Lowery—The Spanish Settlements within the Present Limits of the United States: Florida, 1562–1574. By Woodbury Lowery. Putnam. $2.50 net.

A continuation of the author's previous volume, which covered the Spanish settlements from 1513 to 1561; and one of the most valuable and interesting of recent works on the early discovery and settlement of our national territory. Besides what strictly pertains to the settlement of Florida, it reviews the relations of Spanish policy with French aggression in North America, and tells the story of the French missions in the region north of Florida as well as in that colony.

Mignet—Histoire de la Révolution Française. By François A. M. Mignet. Clarendon Press. 75c.

Mignet's classic is edited and annotated by M. A. Dupuis, B.A. The portion given begins with the opening of the States-General, and ends with the death of Louis XVI. No better selection could have been made for students who desire to acquire a literary knowledge of the French language.

Nitobé—Bushido: the Soul of Japan. By Inazo Nitobé. Putnam. $1.25.

A revised and enlarged edition of a book the peculiar charm of which has been widely recognized. "Bushido" is the Japanese feudal equivalent of "chivalry"; and it embodies "the maxims of educational training brought to bear on the Samurai, or warrior class" of the nation. It is a timely publication just now, when everything connected with Japan

is attracting universal attention. An introduction by William Elliott Griffis, author of "The Religion of Japan," adds materially to its value and interest.

Outram—In the Heart of the Canadian Rockies. By James Outram. Macmillan. $3.00.

An interesting account of a climbing trip through the Canadian Rockies with maps and good illustrations from photographs.

Reinsch—Colonial Administration. By Paul S. Reinsch. Macmillan. $1 50.

This volume distinctly meets the demands of early students of political evolution, but, quite as distinctly, deals with its subject in too dry a manner to appeal to the reader with only a vague desire for an understanding of the question. Education, colonial finance, banking, currency, commerce, agriculture, labor, and land are taken up, and minutely examined with a care and exactness that requires application to follow.

Thayer—A Short History of Venice. By W. R. Thayer. Macmillan. $1.25.

This condensed, straightforward volume should meet with the demands of anyone looking for a "first book," on the subject. It would set his mind free from misconceptions of the history of the city of islands, from the time of the invasion of Attila till its subjection by the House of Hapsburg.

MISCELLANEOUS

Allen—American Book-Plates. By Charles Dexter Allen. Macmillan. $2.50.

Charles Dexter Allen's useful "American Book-Plates," originally published in 1894, has been reprinted. It is still the only book on the subject and serves its purpose well as an indispensable book of reference. Of course, designers—such as J. W. Spencely and Sidney L. Smith—have come into prominence since 1894, and the bibliography of the subject has been increased during the last ten years by monographs such as Lemperly's catalogue of the works of E. D. French, and considerable magazine literature. Death has taken off some noted collectors here mentioned, such as S. P. Avery and E. H. Bierstadt. All of this does not impair the usefulness of this book for the long period which it covers. The varied interest inherent in *ex-libris* is emphasized by chapters on "mottoes," "armorial book-plates," "allegorical plates," "early American engravers," etc. The index is satisfactory, although it might have been well to include the illustrations in the same.

Ames—Matrimonial Primer. By V. B. Ames; with a pictorial Matrimonial Mathematics. Decorations by Gordon Ross. Paul Elder. $1.50.

A collection of maxims alphabetically arranged, and specially designed for the married. "M." for instance, "is for Money and Mothers-in-law," etc., and the advice to the wife is,

"When your husband seems willing that all the economy shall be at the home end, insist upon laundering his shirts yourself." This sort of thing goes through the alphabet.

Anonymous—The Long Day. The Story of a New York Working Girl as told by Herself. Century. $1.20.

Upon reading this record of a working girl's life in New York, one unconsciously marvels that such experiences could have been endured by the refined, sensitive, educated woman indicated by the style of the narrative. Why did she not return to her Pennsylvania home rather than continue to face the evils of the city? Unlike most present writers upon sociological subjects, she did not descend from her proper rank in the city to live in the conditions and thus describe them. She was a country school-teacher who came to the city to make her way.

That she saw underpaid life in many of its worst forms there is no doubt: as a laborer in a sweat-shop, in lining jewel-boxes, as a "shaker" in a steam laundry, and as an inmate of a working-girl's home. The sordid detail and squalor are described with painful minuteness. The Epilogue is the most valuable part of the book to the reformer, for the author puts her finger upon the evils of workaday life for New York girls: most of them have not learned to work, therefore they fail and turn to the easiest life for maintenance. The average working girl, she believes, is even more poorly equipped for right living and thinking than she is for intelligent industrial effort. Obscene stories are listened to because they cannot be avoided. She deplores the absence of trades-unions such as exist in Chicago and other Western cities. She advocates free kindergartens and working-girls' hotels, which should be non-sectarian and without rules except of decent conduct, where there is a "parlor" to keep girls off the street and avoid the necessity of using their bedrooms for callers. She advocates greater interest in the workwoman on the part of the Church, and the dissemination of better literature—not of the Shakespeare, Ruskin, and Pater type. The whole pathetic little tale recalls the recent masterly piece of fiction by "O. Henry," in which the girl is saved from a step downward by a rude chromo of Lord Kitchener, who seemed to look displeasure as she was dressing to spend an evening with her tempter. As a human document this is an important piece of work.

Bryce—Constitutions. By James Bryce. Oxford University Press. $1.50.

A reprint virtually in its original form of an already famous volume.

Clute—The Fern Allies, of North America North of Mexico. By Willard Nelson Clute. Stokes. $2.00.

The wild flowers and ferns have received ample attention, but heretofore the fern-allies have been treated only in so technical a manner as to discourage the novice. This volume aims to describe all this species of plant carefully and correctly, with the aid of more than one hundred and fifty illustrations, and in a manner to encourage the beginner in this study.

Dixon—The Life Worth Living. By Thomas Dixon, Jr. Doubleday, Page. $1.25.

An ingenious volume, setting forth the beauty, the comfort, and the cost of Mr. Dixon's home at Tidewater, Virginia. Numerous photographs display interiors and exteriors of the house as well as bits of landscape; and represent Mr. Dixon's children engaged in various sports. Mr. Dixon does not tell the city-bound, whom he loudly pities, how they may escape from bondage; so the recital of his own contentment may be found of no particular philanthropic value.

Goodhue—Good Things and Graces. By Isabel Goodhue. Paul Elder. 50 cts.

This little book of amusing epigrams cast in the mould of cooking recipes has a flavor that escapes many a more pretentious effort of its class.

Heilprin—A Complete Pronouncing Gazetteer or Geographical Dictionary of the World. Edited by Angelo Heilprin and Louis Heilprin. Lippincott.

With the year 1905 Lippincott's pronouncing gazetteer celebrates its semi-centennial, its first edition having been printed in 1855. The book as it stands to-day after many editions is a monument to editors and publishers alike. It has proved its reliability through the ages and is invaluable as a book of reference. The latest changes in geographical conditions are to be found in this new edition.

Henry—Lodgings in Town. By Arthur Henry. Barnes. $1.50.

The fifteen reproductions from photographs of New York and Mr. Everett Shinn's frontispiece of Trinity Church on New Year's Eve (which should be in color) would make this little book valuable as a souvenir of New York, even though the style of the text were not as engagingly frank and direct as it is. A wave of sentiment seizes the reader even in the dedication "To an optimistic Country and 'Little old New York,'" and if he happens to live within sight of Diana on the Tower, the Flatiron, and the ceaselessly plashing fountain seen through the autumn haze in Madison Square, he feels the grip of all that the book describes, for he is near enough one of the pulses of the city to throb with all the life that centres there.

Johnson—An Old Man's Idyl. By Wolcott Johnson. McClurg. $1.00 net.

A simple record of an uneventful married life of some thirty years, including a honeymoon in Europe and happy home life with wife and children; bearing internal evidence of being founded upon actual experience, and appealing to readers whose domestic history has been of the same character. Others, who have not "been there," may think it dull and common-place, or possibly over-sentimental.

Lankester—Extinct Animals. By E. Ray Lankester. Holt. $1.75.

A boy or girl at all interested in natural history will find Professor Lankester's "Extinct Animals" a delight. Externally, there is little to suggest that it is designed for young people, but from decorous cover to cover the book is filled with photographs and drawings of the curious "reconstructed" creatures. Though of scientific importance, these grotesque and astonishing forms are fascinating to a child, and their charms have too long been the exclusive property of paleontologists. The book is no "first steps in paleontology," it is simply a portrait gallery with a brief description of each subject. That the lucid, comprehensible text is, being Professor Lankester's, scholarly in its accuracy rather than capsuled in romance, should prove no deterrent to any healthy-minded child—or even grown person.

Racster—Chats on Violins. By Olga Racster. Lippincott. $1.25 net.

The eight hundred years of evolution which preceded the fully developed Stradivarius violin has been studied with remarkable care and consistency in this little volume. The author admits the vagueness of her field, and accordingly refrains from formulating rash conclusions. Space hardly permits detailed examination, but what she does present in the way of history and theory she sets forth clearly and in a form well adapted to meet the approval of the casual reader upon such a subject.

Riordon.—Plunkitt of Tammany Hall. By William L. Riordon. McClure. $1.25.

A series of interviews with a "practical politician," published in the New York *Evening Post*, *Sun*, *World*, and the Boston *Transcript*. He discourses upon honest and dishonest graft, the dangers of the dress-suit in politics, municipal ownership, and numerous other subjects valuable to the student of local affairs. The gentleman's portrait taken on a bootblack stand is prefixed to the volume, and the seal of respectability is placed upon the work by a prefatory tribute from the pen of Mr. Charles F. Murphy.

Wellford—The Lynching of Jesus. By E. T. Wellford. The Franklin Co. 50c. net.

The author of this striking little book, a Presbyterian pastor, deals with the legal aspects of the Trial of Christ. He has dropped religious and sentimental methods,

brought forward a clear statement of what the customary Jewish legal procedure should have been in a case of this kind, and then shown wherein the people of Jerusalem departed from the paths of the law. To those interested in the history of Christ the work must prove of unusual interest.

POETRY AND VERSE

Benson—Peace and Other Poems. By Arthur Christopher Benson. Lane. $1.50.

The Peace which gives title to Mr. Benson's book is not that which has lately fallen with benediction upon the warring world-powers; but is that which the scholar, whose thought is as it were, habited in the guise of *Il Penseroso*, ever seeks in "some still removèd place." We pass, with Mr. Benson and the dove-brood of his gentle meditations, even amidst the brownest shades of his scholarly musings.

Cheney—Poems. By John Vance Cheney. Houghton, Mifflin. $1.50.

This latest contribution from the muse of an ever-welcome singer gives everywhere evidence of that tender and gracious perception of the natural world, to which we have been accustomed in Mr. Cheney's previous work. But the poet has other notes to which it is well and timely to hearken; and these are sounded with no doubtful stress in such vigorous exhortation as we find in "Great is To-Day," and in "A Trilogy for This Time"; which latter is a true, brief sermon in the Gospel of Humanity, and one which raises again the pertinent question many are asking at this moment, with regard to civic freedom in its highest ethical significance.

Songs and Lyrics from the Dramatists. Scribner. $1.25.

One of the latest of the "Pocket Classics," edition that holds many good selections of the verse of the play-writers from Nicholas Udall to Phineas Fletcher.

Tozer—Dante's Divina Commedia Translated into English Prose. By H. F. Tozer. Clarendon Press. $1.00.

This prose version is primarily intended for readers not acquainted with Italian, but it will also be helpful to students of the original text who have only a limited knowledge of the language. To both classes the concise footnotes will be very useful. The translation is close but fairly readable.

(*For list of Books Received see the third page following.*)

Photo by Elliott & Fry

THE RT. HON. JOHN MORLEY
(See page 144)

THE CRITIC

Vol. XLVIII   FEBRUARY, 1906   No. 2

The Lounger

MR. ST. LOE STRACHEY, editor of the London *Spectator*, has interested himself in artistic homes for the English poor. Not only artistic but inexpensive. They cost as little as $750.00 and have conveniences that the average English laborer's cottage usually lacks. It would be a good thing if some of our wealthy manufacturers took a hint from "The Book of Cheap Cottages" in building for their employees. Anything more hideous than the usual American laborer's cottage could hardly be imagined. It is simply an unattractive box. One thing is to be noticed among English laborers, or perhaps I should say English laborers' wives,—and that is their love of flowers. The humblest cottage in England is ornamented with vines, and the humblest garden gay with flowers. The dearth of flower gardens in this country —that is, among the poor, or even the well-to-do, is one of the first things to strike a foreigner. You can travel for miles through the New England farm countries, for example, and it is very rarely that you see a flower garden. There may be shrubs or trees but few flowers.

When Sidney Lanier died he left a widow and three or four sons. He died poor, as he had lived poor, but his widow by heroic efforts educated her young family, and they are now, all who are old enough, successful business men. Charles D. is the president of the Review of Reviews Company, Henry W. is a partner of Doubleday, Page, & Company, and the editor of *Country Life in America*, while a younger brother is with the *Review of Reviews*.

Speaking of Mr. Lanier reminds me that for the first time there is an adequate life of his father, the late Sidney Lanier, the poet. This life tells the story of the struggle of Lanier for recognition. Though he has a much wider circle of admirers to-day than he had at any time during his life, he is still "caviare to the general." During her lifetime, Charlotte Cushman did more than any one else to attract the attention of the public to Lanier. Since his death he has been written about a great deal, but I doubt if outside of a cultivated few his name, much less his work, is known. His biographer, Mr. Edwin Mims, thinks it is still too soon to give Lanier his proper place among American or English poets.

COPYRIGHT 1906, BY THE CRITIC COMPANY.
ENTERED AT NEW ROCHELLE, N. Y., POST OFFICE AS SECOND CLASS MATTER.

One of the most important biographies of the season is the "Life of James Anthony Froude," by Herbert Paul, of which Messrs. Scribner are the publishers. A large amount of new and interesting material in regard to Froude's life and career has been brought together, and this fact, together with Mr. Paul's gifts as a writer,

MRS. ELIZABETH W. CHAMPNEY
From a pastel by J. Wells Champney

should not only make an interesting but an entertaining biography. Mr. Paul has been assisted in the preparation of the book by Miss Froude and Mr. Ashley Froude, the historian's only son. I understand that there will be no allusion to the unpleasant features of the Carlyle controversy, for which we cannot be too grateful.

Mrs. Elizabeth W. Champney, a reproduction of whose portrait by her lamented husband is given herewith, has achieved a pleasant reputation as the author of "Romance of the French Abbeys." Mrs. Champney during the lifetime of her husband spent most of her summers in France, where she collected material for her books.

It is interesting to note the number of writers who are buying farms in Connecticut. Up around New Hartford, which is in the northern part of the State, several well-known writers have bought abandoned farms, and also in Fairfield County, which is nearer New York. Mr. Albert Bigelow Paine has bought an old house, a brook, and some thirty acres in the township of Redding, while within the last week or two Miss Ida M. Tarbell, who has made herself famous by her "History of the Standard Oil Company" and her attacks upon Mr. John D. Rockefeller, has bought a beautiful old farm in the same township. There was a time when the writing fraternity hovered around the confines of Grub Street, but now it is breaking away from the city and buying farms among the hills of New England. The pioneer in this direction was Miss Kate Sanborn, who wrote a most interesting book about her experiences as an abandoned farmer.

Among the women writers who have bought farms in New England is Miss Helen M. Winslow, who nearly four years ago bought the De Horte mansion at Shirley, Mass. Miss Winslow finds that she can do a great deal more work, and better work, in the quiet of the country. A recent story, "Spinster Farm," is founded on some of her own experiences.

The most lively contribution to our magazine pages is "The Commercialization of Literature" by Mr. Henry Holt, the well-known publisher, which was published in the *Atlantic Monthly*. Mr. Holt answers categorically a recently published volume of "Publish-

Schillings's remarkable book, "Flashlights in the Jungle," is published by Messrs. Doubleday, Page, & Co. The photographs in this book, numbering 320, were secured by Dr. Schillings in the heart of Africa. They show for the first time the wild beast in his na-

THE OLD DE HORTE MANSION AT SHIRLEY, MASS.
The Residence of Miss Helen M. Winslow

er's Confessions," and says many true and many amusing things. While the article will be particularly enjoyed by publishers and authors, it still furnishes much interesting reading for the general public. Mr. Holt's vigorous personality stands out in every line of this article. It would be most interesting to hear an author's confessions—particularly one of the several authors at whom Mr. Holt's shafts of sarcasm are aimed.

Messrs. Brentano make the interesting announcement of a complete and uniform edition, the first time in English, of the writings of Prosper Merimée, translated from the French by Mr. George Saintsbury, Professor of English Literature in the University of Edinburgh. This shows not only enterprise but excellent taste on the part of Messrs. Bretano.

The authorized edition of Dr. C. B.

tive haunts. Dr. Schillings played "Peeping Tom" to the lions, tigers, zebras, hyenas, giraffes, and other native animals, and snapped his camera and flashed his flashlight on them while they were off their guard. Messrs. Doubleday, Page, & Co. paid many thousand dollars for the original photographs and for the rights to publish the book in this country. As the book was not originally copyrighted here they have only the "courtesies of the trade" to protect them. It was of the author of this book that President Roosevelt said: "The man who wrote that book shares the true spirit of a sportsman, and is just what I want a sportsman and hunter to be."

There seems to be an effort nowadays among authors to get strange titles for their books. Sometime ago Mr. Ridgely Torrence published a little book called "The House of a Hundred

Photo by F. Hollyer, London

THE LATE MR. HENRY HARLAND

Lights." Now Mr. Meredith Nicholson goes him several better with a new novel called "The House of a Thousand Candles." By the side of a thousand candles a hundred lights would make little showing in the dark. Now let us have "The House of Five Thousand Electric Lights."

⁂

Mrs. Craigie (John Oliver Hobbes) has recently finished a new novel in which a nonconformist is the hero. The hero is in strong contrast to the character of Robert Orange, the Roman Catholic, about whom there has been so much discussion. Mrs. Craigie is herself a Roman Catholic, but her father, Mr. John Morgan Richards, is not only a Protestant but he is a nonconformist, and was a leading light in the Dr. Parker's City Temple. Arrangements have just been made, by the way, for the publication of Mr. Richards's book—"With John Bull and Jonathan"—by Messrs. Appleton. Mr. Richards has just returned to England. His book, the story of his experiences rather than a novel, contains a frontispiece portrait of himself, with pictures of Mrs. Craigie at various ages.

⁂

In this Mr. Richards gives this interesting picture of his gifted daughter, in her childhood:

The dramatic instinct was so strong that she entreated me to buy a toy theatre for her, with pasteboard figures representing the characters; and she would invent the story to fit the drama, making little speeches for each character as she pushed them onto the stage. This love of the theatre, I should confess, she may have inherited from me.

A governess at the school she attended told my wife in great alarm that Pearl was in the habit of sitting on a table, with the girls around her crying with laughter at her imitations of the men and women she had met in the street.

⁂

The recent death of Henry Harland, at San Remo, Italy, recalls many memories. Mr. Harland was a *protégé* of Edmund Clarence Stedman, and it was through Mr. Stedman that his first book, "As It Is Written," was published. I was literary adviser of the American branch of Cassell & Company at the time, and the manuscript was given me to read without any mention of Mr. Stedman's name or that of the author. It was signed with the penname "Sidney Luska." It was written in the author's hand, not typewritten, but it was as easy to read as print. Not being a very long story, I read it in an evening and strongly advised its publication. It was published, and with success. After that the same firm published other of Mr. Harland's Jewish stories, for, curiously enough, his first three books dealt with Jewish life in New York, and so cleverly that no one thought for a moment that the author was not a Hebrew. After Mr. Harland went to England and got in with the set that made the "Yellow Book" possible, his style changed, and in some respects for the better; though "The Cardinal's Snuff-Box," which he wrote two years ago, was the best thing that he ever did,

MR. JOHN MORGAN RICHARDS AS PRESIDENT OF THE SPHINX CLUB; A HITHERTO UNPUBLISHED CARTOON BY MR. F. C. GOULD
From " With John Bull and Jonathan "

and gave him a place among contemporary writers that nothing that he had written before could possibly have done, clever as those early books were.

It seems to be the fashion to write in epigrams nowadays. Some time ago John Oliver Hobbes was the only person who made a specialty of the epigram, but now they all do it. Some of the most amusing are to be found in "The Secret Kingdom," by Frank Richardson:

No woman ever discovers that she was married at sixteen until she is well advanced in her decadence.

When all is said and done, a woman is as young as a man can make her feel.

Fashion is never funny. It may be beautiful, or it may be ugly ; but it is always serious.

In a man optimism is the result of love, pessimism the result of liver.

Mr. Richardson has the usual English idea of the American girl, which is that she is the daughter of a self-made, and not very well-made father; that her name is "Mame"; that she chews gum, and talks in a slang that was never heard on land or sea.

Photo by Russell & Son

MR. SIDNEY LEE

Author of " A Life of William Shakespeare," &c.

Miss Mary MacLeod is fortunate in having her Shakespeare story-book introduced by so distinguished a Shake-

spearian student as Mr. Sidney Lee. That Mr. Lee recommends this book is sufficient to insure its success if that success were not assured by its own qualities.

The dramatization of his novel, "The Clansman," by Mr. Thomas Dixon, Jr., has proved so successful in the South that it is to be produced at the Liberty Theatre in this city early in the present month. Of all the novels that Mr. Dixon has written, "The Clansman" is the one that lends itself the best to dramatization.

In a volume of recollections with the striking name "Fifty Years of Failure" there is an interesting anecdote:

A painter friend and I went into the club one day, and found a member thereof sitting on the table in the morning room. There was an air of mystery about the whole proceedings. To this member entered James McNeill Whistler ; the member got off the table, and expressed his intention of giving Whistler a thrashing. Then the row began. Whistler was not a big man, but it ended in his opponent going down the stairs very much more quickly than he would have done by his own volition.

The title, "Fifty Years of Failure," suggests that of the late Rev. Mortley D. Babcock's little book, "The Success of Defeat." Both of these books, while they chronicle failure, are optimistic in their outlook.

An enterprising London publisher, who inaugurated the successful First Novel Series, has now supplemented his scheme by a Last Novel Series. I would suggest that some American publisher take up this idea, and I could also suggest to him the names of several authors still writing whom I would like to see in the series.

Mr. W. W. Story, the American sculptor and poet, has come to America, and will take a studio in New York, intending to divide his time hereafter between that city and Rome, where he has for so many years made his home.

Some years ago Mr. Story published a most delightful volume of recollections. He has lived such a full life, however, since then that he could easily write another volume of equal interest. Mr. Story's most famous contribution to literature is his poem, "Cleopatra," which has been recited as often as Longfellow's "Building of the Ship."

⁂

The first volume of the much-talked-of "Memoirs" of Sir Wemyss Reid is published by Cassell & Co. When the second volume will be published no one knows. Sir Wemyss Reid was a journalist and a man of affairs, a member of many clubs, and a man with a large circle of friends, including Gladstone in politics and every one in literature. The first volume extends from 1842 to 1885, and in it he records his impressions of men and events up to the latter year. The second volume carries the "Memoirs" down to within a few weeks of Sir Wemyss Reid's death, and is withheld because it contains political revelations which cannot yet be published. There is a good deal about Lord Roseberry in this second volume, and it is said that his lordship is quite willing to have it published; but the author's literary executors doubt the advisability, notwithstanding Lord Roseberry's assurance, and no one knows when it will be published.

⁂

Mrs. Margaret Deland, who has not written a novel for several years, has just finished one which has successfully begun its serial publication in *Harper's Magazine*. The publishers kept dark as to the subject-matter of this novel, but they are banking heavily on its success. Mrs. Deland is to be complimented on her literary reticence. It is unusual in these days for a successful novelist to allow several years to elapse between novels.

⁂

"Trilby" as a book may be gathering dust on the library shelves, but as a play it is going on its successful career, with the original Svengali, Mr. Wilton Lackaye, to the fore.

If there is anything in getting a word of commendation from the President, Mr. Madison J. Cawein's new volume,

Photo by Bangs

MR. WILTON LACKAYE AS SVENGALI

"The Vale of the Temple," should attract more attention than poetry usually does. Mr. Cawein has long been known to readers of verse as a poet with a charming talent, not very great, but genuine. It was of Mr. Cawein that the late H. C. Bunner wrote many years ago in *Puck* some verses lamenting that any man should turn his attention to poetry. I cannot recall a whole stanza of this "poem," but I remember that it ended with the line that "Madison J. Cawein has a hard row to hoe." Mr. Bunner did not mean Mr. Cawein alone, but any man who hoped to gain recognition through the medium of verse.

In the new edition of Miss Agnes Repplier's "In Our Convent Days," will be a frontispiece portrait of Miss Repplier and Mrs. Elizabeth Robins Pennell taken when they were school-girls together.

Our magazine editors apparently believe that reminiscences, biographies, autobiographies, diaries, letters, and such like are quite as interesting to their readers as fiction. The sum, $50,000, paid by the *Century Magazine* for the Hay-Nicolay "Life of Lincoln" in serial form is twice as much as was ever paid for any novel; and I am told that *McClure's Magazine* has paid even more for the serial rights of Carl Schurz's, "Memoirs" now running through its columns. The Waddington papers were among the most interesting published in *Scribner's*, and now diaries and letters of George Bancroft, the famous American historian, are to be published in that magazine. Mr. Bancroft was a very old man at the time of his death, and had known during the course of his interesting life such famous men as Byron, Lafayette, Goethe, Humboldt, Lamartine, Guizot, Bismarck, and Moltke.

The Rev. Percy Grant, of the Church of the Ascension, whose sermons are distinguished for their contemporaneous human interest, has just published a volume of poems—"Ad Matrem"—through the Cheltenham Press. The Cheltenham Press, by the way, is Mr. Ingalls Kimball, an original member of the firm of Stone & Kimball, which was organized and doing a good business while its two members were Harvard undergraduates.

In reply to many inquiries I beg to state that Miss Elisabeth Luther Cary's "Studies" of George Meredith's novels will be published in book form before long.

For the benefit of those who do not know the tricks of English pronunciation, I may say that the name of the hero of Mrs. Humphry Ward's novel, "Fenwick's Career," is pronounced as though there were no "w" in it—Fen'ick. There is a foundation of fact in this story as well as in most of those written by Mrs. Ward. This author does not pretend to follow the lives of her originals absolutely; she simply takes them as the foundation. The "Fenwick" of her new story is apparently the painter Romney. There is a guess that the heroine is Lady Hamilton, but I have heard this emphatically denied by those who ought to know best.

Mrs. Carter Harrison, the wife of Chicago's ex-Mayor, has a new fairy-book ready, "The Moon Princess." One would not suppose that the thoughts of the wife of a Chicago Mayor would turn to fairyland, but apparently they do.

It is pleasant to know that a book of such gentle qualities as Mr. Charles Warren Stoddard's "The Island of Tranquil Delights" is in its third edition. In these days the very title of the book is restful after so much of the strenuous life in prose and poetry.

A platform partnership has been formed between Mr. Jerome K. Jerome and Mr. Charles Battell Loomis. This mixture of English and American humor ought to be interesting.

It is not alone members of the theatrical profession who have press agents. Certain authors seem to find them harmless necessary adjuncts to their profession. I am in receipt of a note sent out by an agent in which his author is described as a "well-known society leader," and later on in the paragraph as "the representative of one of the oldest and most distinguished families of Boston." Still farther on in the paragraph it is announced that "he enjoys the distinction of being one of two unofficial Americans presented by the

Copyright by Vander Weyde, 1905

MR. JEROME K. JEROME

American Ambassador to King Edward VII. at the first levee held in St. James's Palace by a King of England since the reign of William IV." Just what bearing this has upon his ability as a writer is not made quite clear.

The character of Mr. Winston Churchill's new novel may be inferred from the fact that it is to be illustrated by Mrs. Florence Scovel Shinn. Mrs. Shinn's illustrations it is well known are of the humorous sort, and have done much to enliven even such lively pages as those of "Mrs. Wiggs" and "Susan Clegg."

Speaking of poetry, the John Lane Company has just published a new

Photo by Beresford

THE LATE LAURENCE HOPE

volume of verse by the late Laurence Hope. I have spoken before of "The Garden of Kama: An Indian Love," and "Stars of the Desert," by this author, and with praise. Laurence Hope, who in private life was Violet Nicolson, was a woman of tremendous passions. How much of the poems that she has printed were translations, how much her own, it would be hard to say; but I imagine if they are translations that the author put as much of herself into them as FitzGerald did into his translations of the "Rubaiyat." This new volume, "Indian Love," is the last that we will get from Laurence Hope, for, quite in character with her writings and temperament, she committed suicide, through grief over the death of her husband, only a few months ago. The poems in "Stars of the Desert" were the finest of this writer, but there are separate poems in other volumes that are quite up to the best of these. From the present volume I quote this beautiful lyric called "My Desire":

Fate has given me many a gift
    To which men must aspire,
Lovely, precious, and costly things,
    But not my heart's desire.

Many a man has a secret dream
    Of where his soul would be ;
Mine is a low, verandahed house,
    In a tope beside the sea.

Over the roof tall palms should wave,
    Swaying from side to side,
Every night we should fall asleep
    To the rhythm of the tide.

The dawn should be gay with songs of birds,
    And the stir of fluttering wings ;
Surely the joy of life is hid
    In simple and tender things !

At eve the waves would shimmer with gold
    In the rosy sunset rays,
Emerald velvet flats of rice
    Would rest the landward gaze.

A boat must rock at the laterite steps
    In a reef-protected pool,
For we should sail through the starlit night
    When the winds were calm and cool.

I am so tired of all this world,
    Its folly and fret and care,
Find me a little scented home
    Amongst thy loosened hair.

Many a man has a secret dream
    Of where his life might be ;
Mine is a lovely, lonely place
    With sunshine and the sea.

❧

I have been at some pains to get this portrait of the late Laurence Hope, whose death by her own hand has already been chronicled in this magazine. Her posthumous volume, "Indian Love," is reviewed by Miss Edith M. Thomas on another page. The well-known English critic Richard Garnett, writing of her in the London *Bookman*, says:

Had Laurence Hope, like George Sand, been capable of transferring her emotional enthusiasm to historical romance, or social politics, or the idyll of country life, she might have won a great name, but emotion with her was absorbed by a single passion; like that other Hope of Mr. Watts's canvas, she had but one string to her lyre.

But that one string, I may add, was capable of sounding heights and depths of passion that few poets of this day and generation have reached.

❧

Mr. Vaughan Kester, whose story of life in the Mississippi Valley during the middle part of the last century, "The Fortunes of the Landrays," wrote most of his book at the historic Woodlawn

ARGILL CASTLE: RESIDENCE OF MR. PAUL KESTER

Give me a soft and secret place
    Against thine amber breast,
Where, hidden away from all mankind,
    My soul may come to rest.

Mansion in Virginia of which his brother, Paul Kester, the dramatist, up to a year ago, was the owner. Woodlawn Mansion is intimately as-

MR. JOHN LUTHER LONG

sociated with the memory of George Washington, for it was the portion of his estate that he cut off from the home plantation by his will to become the residence of his adopted daughter, Nellie Custis. When the Kester brothers first acquired the property it was in a sadly neglected state, but during the four years of their ownership they restored it and developed it, until it is now one of the most beautiful properties in Virginia. Mr. Kester owns now an even more interesting residence, Argill Castle, in Westmoreland County, England, which he purchased last spring and took his family to last summer. Argill Castle, while not of the oldest, is still one of the most picturesque of its kind in England, and is filled with historic and romantic associations.

⚑

Those who think that the American playwright is a poorly paid individual have only to look at this picture of Mr. Kester's castle to change their minds, at least as far as he is concerned. Curiously enough, Mr. Kester had never crossed the ocean until he sailed for England to occupy his picturesque castle in the Lake country.

⚑

I am glad to be able to present this new photograph of Mr. John Luther Long. Up to the present time the only picture of Mr. Long that has been published shows him to be a rather sentimental-looking young man with a hat pushed away back on his head. The present picture is a much better portrait, and shows the serious writer—the man who created "Madame Butterfly"—which charming story, by the way, has recently been made the subject of an opera and sung with success in Italy.

⚑

A book of the maxims of Lord Beaconsfield has recently been published in London. The Earl's cynicism is exemplified in two quotations taken at random:

Mrs. Darlington Vere was a most successful woman, lucky in everything—lucky even in her husband, for he died.

Most marriages turn out unhappy. Among the lower orders, if we may judge from the newspapers, they are always killing their wives, and in our class we get rid of them in a more polished way, or they get rid of us.

There is nothing personal in these remarks, for the marriage of Lord Beaconsfield was known to have been an unusually happy one.

⚑

Mr. E. Gordon Craig, the talented son of Miss Ellen Terry, has sent me a copy of his pamphlet on "The Art of the Theatre," illustrated from his own designs of stage setting. While I find these designs interesting I cannot think

that they would be very effective behind the footlights.

⚑

When we think of the National Conservatory of Music we can hardly remember when it was not with us: but according to a recently published circular it is only twenty years old. The National Conservatory was founded by Mrs. Jeannette M. Thurber, whose untiring enthusiasm has held it together through stormy times. If the Conservatory had never done anything else than the bringing of Dvořák to this country, it would have proved its excuse for being.

⚑

A distinguished American author, whose novels I may say have the largest sale in England of any of his fellow-countrymen, was amused recently by the receipt of this letter from a London publisher, whose name, by the way, he tells me he had never heard:

It has occurred to me you may feel disposed to publish under my auspices, and if you have a new novel ready or in preparation of the regulation 6/- length I shall be glad if you will kindly bear me in mind. Terms cash down on acceptance within a week of the receipt of the MS. for world volume rights only, or, if you prefer, publication on a royalty.

The Art of the Theatre

E.GORDON CRAIG
1 9 0 5

Trusting I may have the pleasure of doing business and hoping to hear from you soon, faithfully yours.

If it were as easy as this publisher seems to think to get world volume rights of the most popular American writers on his list, the publishing business would not offer as many knotty problems to those who follow it as it does at the present time.

tice" Mr. Wagner takes up in the genial, human, and simple way, which by this time must be familiar to nearly every reading person in the United States, the essentials of right and duty towards oneself and towards others. "The Gospel of Life" is a volume of

REV. CHARLES WAGNER

Charles Wagner has not yet ceased to be an influence with us. His impressions of President Roosevelt, in the form of an account of his visit to the White House when he was in America last year on a lecture-tour, have recently appeared in *McClure's Magazine*, and there are announced two new books from his pen, "Justice" and "The Gospel of Life." In "Jus-

sermons interpreting the Gospel in terms of real life. Mr. Wagner has practically completed his impressions of America, which are now appearing in a French magazine, and will probably be brought out serially in America, · later to be produced in book form. While in this country Pastor Wagner lived the strenuous rather than the simple life. He was on the go from early morn till dewy eve, with *fêtes* and feasts thrown in.

By permission of the publishers, The John Lane Company, we reproduce the original manuscript of William Wat-

COLUMBUS

From his adventurous prime
He dreamed the dream sublime;
Over his wandering youth
It hung, a beckoning star.
At last the vision fled,

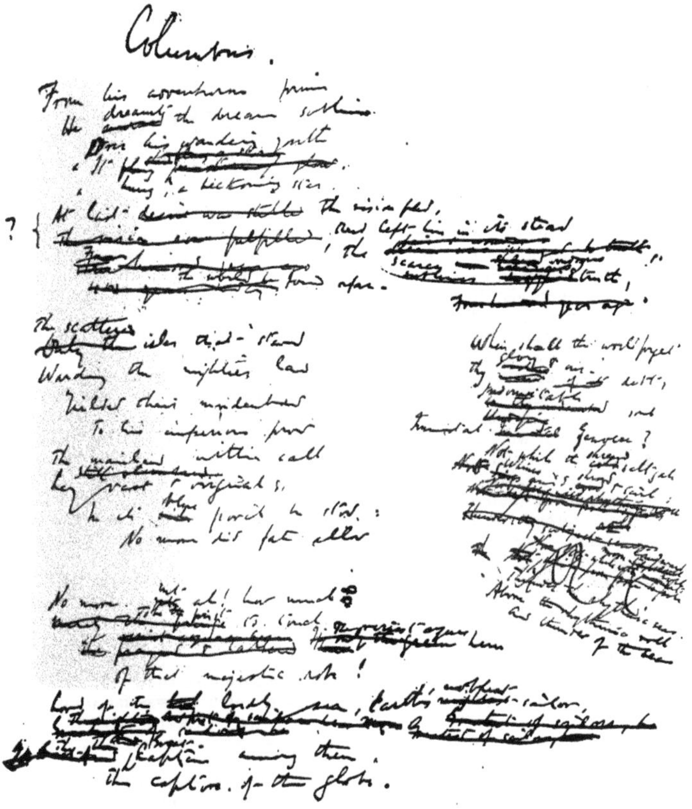

FACSIMILE OF THE ORIGINAL MANUSCRIPT OF "COLUMBUS" BY MR. WILLIAM WATSON

son's poem on "Columbus," which was given to the Congressional Library, at Washington, at the suggestion of the late Hon. John Hay. As it is almost impossible to read Mr. Watson's manuscript, we give an interpretation of it in plain type.

And left him in its stead
The scarce sublimer truth,
The world he found afar.

The scattered isles that stand
Warding the mightier land
Yielded their maidenhood
To his imperious prow.

The mainland within call
Lay vast and virginal ;
In its blue porch he stood :
No more did fate allow.

No more ! but ah, how much,
To be the first to touch
The veriest azure hem
Of that majestic robe !
Lord of the lordly sea,
Earth's mightiest sailor he :

Great Captain among them,
The captors of the globe.

When shall the world forget
Thy glory and our debt,
Indomitable soul,
Immortal Genoese ?
Not while the shrewd salt gale
Whines amid shroud and sail,
Above the rhythmic roll
And thunder of the seas.

Three Generations of Romances

By ANNE WARNER

I

GRANDMOTHER was tatting in the mullioned window. Her kerchief was modestly crossed on her alabaster neck. Her ankles were also crossed. She had on a skimpy gown that was twenty-four inches round the waist and forty-four round the hem. Grandmother's hair was tied up in a snood. A sampler hung on the wall. Some posset boiled on the hob. A pair of snuffers lay across a pair of wool-cards.

Grandmother sighed as she tatted. Then her soft azure eyes gazed modestly out of the mullions. A blush at once overspread the lily-white of her complexion. Her brooch heaved rapidly up and down.

In sooth it was Edward Merton who was approaching. Grandmother was terrible agitated ; her very instep shook like an aspen. The blush yielded to a becoming pallor. She looked out of the window again.

Edward Merton was still approaching.

Grandmother's brooch nearly burst with maidenly emotion. Her taper fingers let the tatting cease to tat. It fell to the floor unheeded and the next instant Grandmother nearly fell on it.

For Edward Merton was approached — aye — he was even knocking — was even lifting the latch—was within !

How can my pen describe Edward Merton's appearance as he tripped over the cat, demolished a spinning-wheel, and brought up against Grandmother's father's "Grandfather's Clock"? You

see I am seventy years too early for the vernacular which would simply say that he had been on a terrible tear and was a sight. But I will do my best with what 1840 provides for the circumstances.

Edward Merton was distinguished-looking; he came of virtuous and highly respected parents, but alas!—

Edward's hair and cravat were black and both spread over a stock that was much disordered. His eyeballs were black also, and seemed to be turning around and around in his flushed and fevered brain. The Wine Cup and its Curse were printed all over his waist-coat, and also all over the rest of him. Alas! Alas!—

You cannot wonder that when he started to embrace Grandmother she averted her face and waved him away, while a pearly tear coursed unbidden over her ivory profile. He was forced to go back to the clock and to feign an ease which he was far from experiencing, for Edward Merton's impulses were good,—it was only that he was —Alas!

Grandmother stayed averted and waving for quite a while, and then wiped away the tell-tale tear, murmuring,

"What, Merton,—again!"

The words were simple but shocking as live wires. Edward hung his head. He had good reason to be overcome by so deserved yet merciful a reproach. Its current seemed to catch him corner-ways. He was evidently touched.

Grandmother perceived her advantage even though she failed to perceive that he was standing on the tatting.

She spoke with energy:

"Why, Merton, will you thus break my heart? Why will you persist in such evil courses? Why do you not sign the Pledge?"

Edward looked at her. The light of eloquence flooded her. She seemed like some goddess earth-born. His worse than wasted life rose up before him. Manly resolve kindled his bosom, hope dashed high on every breaking rock. He lifted up his head. He was resolved.

"For Thee, oh Best and Fairest,"— he cried, clasping Grandmother to his ruffled bosom, — "for thee I would promise to do all things possible or impossible."

A soft radiance bathed Grandmother in celestial joy.

"You will sign the Pledge?" she cried in ecstasy.

"I will sign," said Edward Merton firmly.

He signed.

He married Grandmother.

Alas!—

II

Mamma sat in a bower, working red roses and white beads into a three-corner shelf-mat. Her hoop-skirt was two yards across, she had ringlets on each side. Although frail as a lily the Soul of Mamma was lofty and noble, —as you will see.

After carefully outlining a green thorn and sewing a bead dew-drop on the extreme end, Mamma suddenly jumped.

It was Clement — her childhood's play-fellow—who had come up behind her unperceived with a real thorn.

"Industrious, — ever industrious," he exclaimed teasingly, picking up her left-hand bunch of ringlets and pressing them to his lips. "Is that red rose so absorbing that I am altogether forgot?"

Mamma looked earnestly around over her shoulder.

"No, Clement," she said gravely, "you are not forgotten, but in this hour of Peril other voices should outweigh mine."

"I hear no voice but yours at present," said Clement, striving to speak carelessly. Nevertheless, a close observer may have easily observed that he suddenly became extremely pale.

Mamma stuck in her needle, put aside her work, and rose to her feet. Softness and emotion strove for mastery in the glowing splendor of her raven eye.

"Clement," she said, extending one hand north and the other south like a Demosthenes, or a weather-cock, "if the cannon of Fort Sumter found you deaf, strive to recall the echo from Bull Run. If you were not in on the March to the Sea get out and steal some other march. If the shrieks of the dead and dying have not touched you surely the buying of substitutes has. Clement—" Mamma's voice faltered, she gathered all her strength—"Clement, if no other call has been heard by you — hear mine now. I beseech—nay—I implore!"

She was irresistible. Clement was fired.

"I will go!" he cried with enthusiasm.

Mamma sank down exhausted.

"I have given a soldier to my country," she said, and allowed Clement to cut a ringlet for a souvenir.

He cut it all wrong and the short hair showed.

"Too bad," said Mamma, thoughtfully, when she saw herself in the mirror next time,—"but if Clement goes to the war I shall have peace and Augustus won't mind the loss of one curl if he has not to be tormented by jealousy. . . ."

(Mamma married Frederick in the end.)

III

I stood in the boat-house doing Physical Culture Exercises. After my two-mile swim and six-mile scull each morning I invariably do exercises for an hour. It preserves mental poise, regulates the distribution of oxygen and builds up the knee-pans.

Just as I was putting myself through a hoop according to the diagram in last Sunday's paper Jack came rushing in. Jack is as tanned as I am, only half-a-head shorter, and holds the championship for hopping on the left leg.

"My dear girl," he cried (we have known each other a fortnight and more)—"do be careful,—you might so easily break the hoop."

"What did you come here for?" I asked, tossing the hoop away and picking up a broomstick with which to commit further prodigies.

"I came"—said Jack—"to tell you that Port Arthur has fallen."

I dropped the broomstick. I was as near to staggered as a post-graduate in heliocentrics could possibly be.

"Fallen?" I shrieked.

"Fallen," repeated Jack.

Then I remembered.

"Oh, well, I don't care," I said, spinning an oar on my thumb, "it flustered me a bit on account of a bet that I'd made, but after all—"

"What bet?" interrupted Jack, lighting a cigarette without permission (Jack is thoroughly up to date).

"A bet with little To-ko who keeps the Jap Store," I said lightly.

"What did you bet?"

"My hand against that gold-embroidered kimono that hangs in the window."

"What ever made you bet your hand?" Jack asked.

"I'm neither an heiress nor a typewriter, so I had nothing else to bet."

Jack laughed.

"Of course you'll treat it as a joke now?" he said.

I drew myself up.

"Of course I will *not*," I said, "am I not an American girl?"

He turned white behind his tan.

"Girl—girl—" he stammered, "of course you're an American girl and of course honor is all right and a fine thing in its way—but in a case like this—"

"Honor! Who spoke of honor?" I interrupted haughtily.

"I — you —" he stumbled, — then stopped.

"It isn't a question of honor at all" —(I was fairly a-scorch with indignation!)—"don't you know that little To-ko is only keeping a store so as to learn colloquial English, and that in his own land he is——"

"Is what?" Jack gasped.

"A marquis!" I said, triumphantly.

The Making of Books

By FRANCIS GRIERSON

GOOD books have but one purpose: to comfort the heart and stimulate the mind. Books that we love play the part of invisible friends. We get from them a continuous current of sympathy which acts and reacts in various ways on our own mind and the minds of others. It is through sympathy that the magic current is created. A book is valued not so much for what it reveals in the realm of pure intellect as for what it reveals of the secret sentiments and feelings of the reader. In books we see ourselves in the author and become acquainted with our own double, so to speak, as a second person. The best writers, like the best poets, "hold the mirror up to nature." We admire most in every writer not that which we do not understand, but that which we have long felt but never expressed, the sentiments which we have never been able to formulate in words, the emotions that seemed too deep to be brought to the surface, the dreams that seemed too vague and distant for rhyme or reason. As we are attracted to the persons we love best not because some one else tells us to love them, so are we attracted to the books which suit best our age, temper, and experience. We are not influenced by praise or blame in these things; the attraction comes from within. For every category of thought and experience there is a corresponding class of books; for every temperament, some other mind whose mission it is to perform the service of self-revealment. There is a secret attraction which leads us to certain books little read by the public, perhaps unknown to the public. In youth we enjoy most the books of action, because action is the thing we most desire; when we begin to think we become interested in ideas, and eventually we prefer the writers whose sentiments and experiences approach nearest our own. No one can appropriate the wisdom of another mind; we can only appropriate the consolation offered by another. Intuition is inherited knowledge; but the world is the distillery of wisdom. Drop by drop sagacity is distilled from experience and the liquor of life put away in the memory to mature with age. A mushroom comes up suddenly and soon withers; but the oak grows slowly and lives long. Fleeting things give confused impressions; the mind has no time to centre on the cause of fleeting phenomena. We gravitate to certain books as to certain people; and, as no system of education succeeds in giving us intellectual sensations and poetic emotions of which we are not capable, so no school of art or literature has ever succeeded in weaning the mind from the thing which suits it best. As for real feeling and sentiment, if you would make others weep, you must, as Horace says, begin by weeping yourself.

While it is true that many are carried away by the literary fashions of the time because of the influence of passing modes, underneath these things there is a force which compels people to prefer one book to another.

As for books of criticism, an abyss separates the critical spirit of 1890 from that of 1902, and it is not too much to say that in another decade the narrow and insular customs and teachings of the latter part of the nineteenth century will appear as vagaries enacted in another world and will have as little influence on serious minds as the strange old fashions of 1860 now have upon us. The truth is that the force which some people persist in ignoring is the force which has brought about the recent rapid changes in thought and criticism. That force is science. It is a cold, material thing to look at, but it has both soul and spirit, it assumes a sort of personality. It was the engineer who made a visit from New York to London a mere matter of a six-days pleasure-excursion, put Paris within seven hours of London, and made it possible for dramatic and art critics to attend first nights and the opening of exhibitions in Berlin, Vienna, and Rome, and be back again in London within a period of a few days. The telegraph and the steam-engine have accomplished a universal miracle. The telegraph alone brings the opinions of people living at the ends of the earth into our homes every morning, and we are made to see and feel what insularity really means. Art and science force the most obtuse to bow before a power superior to mere sentiment and book-learning. A ship-load of excursionists visit a foreign land for the first time. They start out brimming over with prejudice and haughty with national conceit, but the instant they land on a foreign shore they find themselves surrounded by people and things which set a cold-blooded defiance to every prejudice, every gesture, every thought and feeling which they bring with them. It is useless to complain. If they do not understand the language, so much the worse; if they do not like the cooking, again so much the worse; at any rate they must eat to live and make gestures to be understood. It is the only deaf and dumb exercise some people ever get. But even this small experience is something. They now begin to understand the meaning of the word "travel."

To many minds the first experience in a foreign country is nothing short of an intellectual revelation. Here, on the soil of London, Paris, Berlin, or Rome, books of travel begin to be judged for exactly what they are—some good, and many very bad. The intelligent mind begins to imbibe, as if by magic, new truths culled from the garden of cosmopolitan experience. Without quite knowing how or why, the wide-awake traveller has attained a certain knowledge of people and things which books were powerless to bestow, and he returns home wiser, more critical, with a great deal of his provincial prejudice worn off. A long sojourn abroad finishes the all-important education and the critical mind is forever freed from old-fashioned prejudice and cock-sure judgments. And so we are prevented from repeating the old, sentimental error that books, philosophy, and latter-day schools of thought have wrought the great intellectual change which the world has lately seen. The railroad and the steamship are the miracle workers. What will the changes not be in another twenty years! Books of critical and philosophical thought not based on the new order will at once be cast aside as worthless. Every critical work which gives the least sign of the insular and provincial spirit will be ignored as worse than useless. It will be found impossible to sit in London, Paris, or New York, as Carlyle sat in Chelsea, and produce acceptable judgments on anything or anybody. To deal with foreign questions without having moved about in the world, even now, means contradiction and refutation at the hands of any observing sailor, soldier, or commercial traveller who may care to take up the pen and write. The universal rule now is: experience first, then analysis and judgment. Bacon was right: books must follow science.

There has been much waste of time and energy in the making of modern books. Writers like Hugo, Balzac, Tolstoy, make one think of a locomotive with the steam kept at high-pressure. Carlyle put into "Sartor Resartus" psychological pressure sufficient to found a colony or build a dozen retreats for aged working men. The fault of "Sartor Resartus" lies in its size. It is a book instead of an essay. What energy was expended here to little or no purpose! Preaching nullifies itself when it passes a certain point. Many great writers spend three or four times more dynamic power than is needed in the work they have to do. True, if the engineer did not let off the steam

there would be an explosion. But that is another matter. All superfluous work is old-fashioned the moment it is printed. When we say of a serious work it has no *raison d'être* we admit its inutility; and the lack of clarity and precision in the manner of composition in any work is sufficient to nullify the whole. But in considering books like "Sartor Resartus" we have to consider two things combined in one: the manner and the subject. If Carlyle had reduced this mass of eloquence and energy to one compact essay of fifteen pages how different would have been the result. People need suggestive writing far more than the didactic and the philosophical. Again, consider the time and energy wasted in writing the "History of Frederick the Great" in ten volumes! Is there any one in our day, excepting a professional historian, willing to give up whole weeks to the reading of such a work?

Balzac wore himself out in writing scores of novels which no one reads now. He left three or four masterpieces, and died before he had time either to see or enjoy life. In "Peace and War" and "Anna Karenina" much energy is wasted. Long works are too often like long sermons which end in fatigue. There are laws which defy even the forces of genius to render void. There is something painful in the thought of Victor Hugo sitting down in the cold and cheerless room of a Brussels hotel, with bread and water before him, there to scribble as fast as the pen can be made to move all day and half the night, like an automaton without sense or sensibility. There is in such work much of the garrulous spirit, little of the soul of inspiration. And the futility of it is appalling. Balzac, who sat in his garret all day and night writing novels which found little favor even in his own day, may have thought such books absolutely necessary, but we know now for a certainty that they were not. And, somehow, we do not sympathize with an author who writes for twenty-four hours without intermission. Georges Sand seated herself at her writing-desk and began work much as a type-writer would begin to copy. When she had filled a sheet of paper she let it fall on the carpet; when the carpet all about her was covered with manuscript she would cease writing. Zola, in his turn, wrote six pages every morning. We can hardly blame some people for considering genius to be automatic and believing that it writes without knowing how or why.

It is impossible that a book which contains neither scientific analysis nor literary inspiration can long hold a serious place in the intellectual world. There are no supreme works written in the ordinary moods. Chateaubriand, Flaubert, and Renan meditated for months, and sometimes years, before beginning a work. They waited for the inspiration. With them, thought was like a conscience; a mood, something sacred; an inspiration like an eternal benediction. They were artists in the sense in which Goethe speaks of art. Chateaubriand died in 1848, and Balzac in 1850; the first was thirty years writing his "Memoirs," the second wrote scores of novels which no one reads; and while Georges Sand was daily covering her carpet with manuscript, her friend Gustave Flaubert was waiting for the idea, taking notes, meditating, correcting.

Adventure and romance come to every one who moves about in the world. The more people travel the less interest they take in certain books. When we read Gibbon we are held by the personal style of the writer and the relation of romantic facts. He tells us of real people. We move on and on with the historian, feeling that we are walking the earth and meeting its denizens in* flesh and blood. We are brought face to face with human passions, ambitions, follies, adventures; we pass from one epoch to another by a natural process. This is why Gibbon is great. But Chateaubriand is still greater, for the reason that he himself is telling us what he saw, what he heard, what he felt. History, therefore, is of two kinds: what is related from documentary evidence as actual reality, and what is related as personal experience. But personal experience will always take the first place in the minds and the hearts of people who think. "Vanity Fair" is certainly the work of a master; but the difference between "Vanity Fair" and De Quincey's "Confessions" is that the first entertains us by fictional scenes and circumstances, while the second entertains and instructs us on a basis of actual fact, and compels us to descend or rise with the author through scene after scene of personal hope and despair, physical suffering, and mental anguish, altogether individual, experienced, and real. De Quincey's "Confessions" cause us to live through a period of psychological and physical experience worth more than all the sermons ever preached against the evils of opium eating. For we get a moral without preaching and art without artifice. And for this reason the "Confessions" will live when "Vanity Fair" has passed away.

In works of fiction we imagine we know; in personal works we feel that we know. For the imagination leaves the mind in doubt and the result is often negative. A personal narrative contains, first of all, the advantage of the psychological effect of actual experience; secondly, the indelible impression created by the knowledge of that experience. In drama the assumption of sincerity weakens the impression; one gesture too much, one movement in the wrong place is enough to dissipate the illusion of reality. The greatest sorrows are the most silent; and the personal feeling is one of the secrets of supreme work. The minds who have risen above ephemeral states and passions, who have attained a plane superior to the noises of the world, are the ones who hold the most authority and the most charm. In the race of genius they win in a canter. It is the sententious and sensitive "I" which gives the essays of Montaigne their wonderful vitality. He never thinks until he begins to write, and the spirit that moves him is, to a certain extent, garrulous; but the narrative of personal hopes, fears, doubts, and daily impressions, told with candor, and serenity, makes the book immortal. In the

"Essais" we are not only thinking, but living with a human being. It is philosophy mingled with human experience. Montaigne holds us by his personal gossip, his natural manner, and a rare gift of penetration and common-sense. No wonder Madame de Sévigné cried: "Ah! l'aimable homme que Montaigne! qu'il est de bonne compagnie! c'est mon ami; mais à force d'être ancien il m'est nouveau. Mon Dieu! que ce livre est plein de bon sens!"

The writers who assume an authority by preaching it are never the ones who wholly succeed. The real authorities are too serious to take the world seriously. The greatest content themselves with transcribing impressions, recording events, portraying persons, spiritual states, and material conditions in the simplest manner possible. They possess too much common-sense to become fanatical, and too much discretion to sermonize. Montaigne, Bacon, Gibbon, Chateaubriand, Goethe, Flaubert, Renan, were egoists in the highest and most philosophical meaning of the word. The true authoritative mood is instinctive; it is not put on as a warrior would don a coat of mail. Bacon writes with the force of an eternal edict; Gibbon with the pomp of a Roman triumph; Flaubert with a kind of philological magic intended only for his equals; Renan with the placidity of a human sphinx who never winks or winces; Chateaubriand with something like the quality of an elegiac symphony whose movements include the heroic and the pastoral.

Every perfect thing passes beyond the limit of the definable. The contour and expression of the highest personal beauty, the fragrance of the rarest flowers, the suggestive melodies in the most inspired music, the atmospheric influence of a perfect day or a moonlight night — these and other things possess an element and an influence which evade analysis. Everything that can be described with precision falls below the level of supreme attainment. It is easy to analyze the fabric of the loom, but the gossamer web which imagination and sentiment weave from the souvenirs and sensations of life eludes precise definition. Mere power can never create an atmosphere in any art. The psycho-artistic atmosphere constitutes the creative charm. Works like "L'Assommoir" make us feel the reality of the author's power without poetic distinction. No athletic grace is required in the wielding of a mallet or a battle-axe. And there is a marked difference between the egoism of power and the egoism of intellect. Powerful writers are never happy unless they are manifesting their power. It would be too much to ask them to desist for a period long enough to distinguish and discriminate. But the finer egoism of the intellect is not content with the writing of six pages every morning; it is inspired by a feeling of selection, a sense of the economy of moods and emotions. Between personal power and personal charm there is a great gulf fixed. The author of "L'Assommoir" forces the reader along, for the reader does not always desire to go. The author of "Sylvestre Bonnard" persuades, creates an atmosphere, and charms. With him we are glad to go.

M. Anatole France has tact, taste, and philosophical insight. He is full of the common-sense which accompanies the highest critical faculty. While Zola expended a vast amount of power in depicting and stating the obvious, M. Anatole France uses the obvious as a frame in which to set a fine picture. He knows how to be witty and wise for divers minds — Zola for a much larger class with limited minds. The energy displayed in "L'Assommoir" is that of the thunder-storm. We know exactly where we are going before we read many chapters: the clouds are black, the atmosphere sultry, and we look for thunder and lightning. In the beginning of the book we witness a terrific battle between washerwomen who have muscles like prize-fighters. The sensitive reader feels like holding his head between his hands and shouting, like Macbeth: "I 'll see no more!" We move on steadily after this into an element of blind passion and delirium tremens. Now, in depicting scenes of pugilism and delirium tremens the one thing needed is puissance; the things which are not needed are delicacy, poetic nuance, a high standard of taste. Emile Zola expresses physical energy, Anatole France intellectual force. And it would be idle to deny that a two-column newspaper dialogue of M. Bergeret produces a better effect on the minds of critical readers than a whole book by M. Zola. Such is the difference between these two authors, living in the same city and writing in the same language.

Art is common-sense made beautiful. The miracle of the idealization of the revolting has not yet been produced. Anatole France expresses with the pen what the great artists express with the brush and the chisel; and if the Marquise de Sévigné were living now she would certainly exclaim: "Ah! l'aimable homme que Monsieur Bergeret!"

In the making of books it is necessary to consider the two principal kinds of books which attain success: the works which are written in and for a certain city or country, and those which rise above the local idea. The former are the first to be neglected in the march of time. The local environment changes much more rapidly than the national; the national more rapidly than the universal. So rapidly do local conditions and appearances change in our age that it is possible for a successful book to become old-fashioned in the space of five years. Is there, indeed, a popular work of to-day which will be read a hundred years hence? There will be ten times as many good books written about persons and events of the time which people will be compelled to read, and the want of time will prevent scores of good books from being talked about. But if the ordinary changes of scene and sentiment were not enough to kill thousands of books the changes created by science would do so. When every one can have plenty of adventure in cheap and easy travel, think and speak in two or three languages, see and hear by personal experience, much reading can be dispensed with. Experience will put an end to the superfluous in literature. When the world opens before the masses like a panorama, ever varying, and palpitating with vivid scenes and pleasant emotions, when millions of people can go from one end of the globe to another in a few days, provincial prejudice will give place to a sentiment of broad and cosmopolitan culture.

Out=of=Doors from Labrador to Africa

By DALLAS LORE SHARP

HERE is a collection of five new nature-books—animal romances, three of them, of wild life as the nature-novelist imagines it. The other two are books of exploration, observation, and camera-hunting—wild life as the trained naturalist sees it. The three romances trust to their style and prefaces for their interest—falling back rather hard upon the preface, it must be said, as if somebody had been lying. "Truth is stranger than fiction," they each begin, "and all the fiction in this volume is solemn truth."

Happily, only conscientious, literal people heed prefaces nowadays, so that most readers of "Animal Heroes," * "Red Fox," † and "Northern Trails" ‡ will get the stories untroubled by any thought of fact and reality.

And they are worth getting, for they are good stories, all of them—charmingly told, beautifully illustrated, and very unlike—as the artist-author, professor, and preacher are unlike. Yet the amazing thing about the three romances is their sameness. The dif-

* "Animal Heroes." By Ernest Thompson Seton. Illustrated by the Author. Scribners. $2.00.
† "Red Fox." By Charles G. D. Roberts. Illustrated by Charles L. Bull. L. C. Page & Co. 75c.
‡ "Northern Trails." By William J. Long. Illustrated by Charles Copeland. Ginn & Co. $1.50.

ference is largely one of style, of vocabulary, I had almost said—the difference between "kindreds" and "folk." You read the same preface in all; and you start off with the same story. In "Animal Heroes" it is an old slum cat and her kittens in a cracker-box. The one extraordinary kitten of "pronounced color" survives and comes to glory. In "Red Fox" it is a pair of foxes and their cubs in a hole among the hills. The one extraordinary cubby, "more finely colored," survives and comes to glory. In "Northern Trails" it is a pair of wolves and their pups in a cave among the rocks. The one extraordinary puppy, "larger than the others," survives and comes to more glory than the cub or the kitten of the other tales.

Of course, there is variety in all of these — cats, foxes, wolves — kittens, cubs, puppies. It is in the extraordinary puppy that they are alike. And this extraordinary pup has been done so many times since the days of "Wild Animals I Have Known," that three more extraordinary pups (or cubs or kittens) one after the other make the critic long for a pup that is just ordinary dog.

It is only the critic, however, that would be likely to read the books one after the other, and only he, also, who would, perhaps, lament this overworked *cum laude* pup.

Individually, these books are interesting. Mr. Seton, in "Animal Heroes," is still master, as he is the pioneer, in this field. No one has matched his "Wild Animals I Have Known." "Animal Heroes" is a good second; but it suffers, like a younger son, by coming later. Mr. Seton has invented just one plan for his best stories, and it served well in the first volume; but this last is the fourth, at least, made after the plan, to say nothing of those by other writers who have copied it. That plan should have been patented.

Except for the reindeer story, Mr. Seton has made certain advances here even over his first work. He shows greater variety of treatment, more flexibility of style, and less strain. He

is nearer reality because he is here a straightaway story-teller, and enjoys the freedom. Out of not commonplace, but certainly very *real*, material, he now writes the capital story of "Arnaux."

Mr. Long is at his best, too, in "Northern Trails." The book would have been much better without the first story—for the plan is not original; it is "written down" and it lacks reality in spite of the author's efforts. But as for the rest, even Mr. Burroughs will find little in the natural history to object to, and certainly no one can hold out against the story interest of the chapters, nor the grace and charm of the style. We could only wish that Mr. Long did n't see quite so much with his own eyes, for many of us live the year around in the woods, and—well—most of our animals must have gone over into Mr. Long's woods. The publishers show the same lack of taste in over-illustrating this book as in Mr. Long's other recent volumes. It is a pity, too, for Mr. Copeland has excelled himself— and most of his rivals—in "Northern Trails."

Mr. Roberts has gone them all one better in "Red Fox"—a volume to the adventures of this individual! But it is n't a sincere piece of work. Mr. Roberts knows the thing cannot be done to last over night. There is n't enough to a fox; his psychology, his interests, his daily round is too limited to sustain him throughout a volume. The author has tried to meet the lack of substance with style. The fox makes raids on barnyards in "violet sunsets," he fights woodchucks in "rose-lit grass"—atmosphere this, purple patches, that do not convince, but only emphasize the smallness of Red Fox and the largeness of the story. Not a page of it comes from the woods direct. Of the incidents, to quote the preface, "there is authentic record of them all in accounts of careful observers"—of Red Fox playing dead, running the sheep's backs, and jumping into a cart (the climax of the story) to escape the dogs,—these records are in our nursery-books. What we have n't read before we cannot quite believe — the bees, for instance, driving Red Fox from his fetid den to go into the honey business there! But all this we could take, for we are boys enough to like the fighting (there is a deal of this, for there is a fight on every page), were it not for the anthropomorphizing of the beast — as extreme and unreal as the rose-lit treatment of the grass.

"With Flashlight and Rifle," * by C. G. Skillings, we have no romancing at all, no imagination, no poetry, no purple patches. The author goes into the wilds of Africa to shoot and to photograph real beasts. The volume is the unadorned account of his killings —wanton slaughter it often seems— and the album for his startling photographs. Never has the jungle before been so photographed. There is an uncanny realism about the book, such an uncovering of savage forms by the flashlight as to make one afraid of his own tame dark.

"Two Bird-Lovers in Mexico," * by C. William Beebe (the second lover is Mrs. Beebe), is more real nature— Mexican out-of-doors done into a book with so simple a style, so genuine an enthusiasm, and illustrated with such excellent photographs, that it is bound to take a host of other bird-lovers, and lovers of travel into the mesquite wilderness and about the magic pools of Mexico—where, in the dead of winter, one lives a wild, free life in camp! and "feels how good a thing it is to be alive, to be hungry and to eat, to be weary and to sleep." The lovers have a honeymoon of a time. They have made one of the most delightful of nature-books.

* "With Flashlight and Rifle." By C. G. Skillings. Translated by Henry Zick. Harper & Brothers. $2.00.

* "Two Bird-Lovers in Mexico." By C. William Beebe. Houghton, Mifflin, & Co. $3.00.

The Beginnings of James McNeill Whistler

By A. J. BLOOR

To THE CRITIC for September, 1903, Mr. Bloor contributed an article on Whistler's boyhood, which derived a special interest from the inclusion of a number of letters written by the artist when a lad. Since then Whistler's fame has been both tested and increased by the exhibition in London of a collection of his works under the auspices of the International Society of Artists, of which he was the President—an event that drew thousands of art lovers to the New Gallery in Regent Street; and interest in his genius has been augmented by the announcement that to the Smithsonian Institution in Washington Mr. Charles L. Freer, of Detroit, has given his remarkable collection of works of art, which is particularly rich in Whistlers, and includes the decorations of the famous "peacock room" from Mr. Leyland's house in London—a collection hereafter to be seen in a building to be erected in Washington at Mr. Freer's expense.

The following letter from Whistler to his mother bears (*more suo*) neither date nor place of writing; but as his visit to Venice lasted from September, 1879, to November, 1880, it must have been written toward the close of the latter year:

MY OWN DEAREST MOTHER : I have been so grieved to hear of your being ill again—and now I am delighted to hear better news of you. Do not let any anxiety for me at all interfere with your rapidly getting quite well—for I am happy to tell you that my own health is capital and the weather alone in all its uncertainties retards my work—which, however, is now very nearly complete—so that I look forward to being with you soon. It has been wofully cold here. The bitterest winter I fancy that I ever experienced, and the people of Venice say that nothing of the kind has been known for quite a century. Mrs. Bronson was telling me —by the way you will be pleased to hear that they have returned from their wanderings, and are now settled in their palace on the Grand Canal—well, she told me that since it was known that she was here, her many pensioners have called to welcome her back, and all said to her the same thing:

"Look, Signora," they said, pointing to their white hair, "look, I am old, and yet I have never seen such a winter, and I only wonder that I have lived through it to tell the Signora!"

At last the ice and snow have left us, and now the rain is pouring down upon us. To-day reminds me of our stay long ago at Black Gang Chyne! After all, though, this evening the weather softened slightly, and perhaps to-morrow may be fine—and then Venice will be simply glorious, as now and then I have seen it. After the wet, the colors upon the walls and their reflections in the canals are more gorgeous than ever, and with sun shining upon the polished marble mingled with rich-toned bricks and plaster, this amazing city of palaces becomes really a fairyland,—created, one would think, especially for the painter. The people with their gay gowns and handkerchiefs, and the many tinted buildings for them to lounge against or pose before, seem to exist especially for one's pictures—and to have no other reason for being! One could certainly spend years here and never lose the freshness that pervades the place!

But I must come back to you all now, though, even if I return afterwards. Yes, I hope now in a couple of weeks or so to pack all my work and see how the long-hoped-for etchings will look in London. Also you know, for I daresay Nellie has told you, that I have fifty pastels! So you see, Mother dear, that I have not been idle—though I have found my labors terribly trying. It will be pleasant to talk them all over with you when I come back. I shall have plenty to tell you of all the beautiful things I have seen, and I hope you will like some of the pastels I have done—Nellie must tell you about them. They are much admired here —and I think rather well of them myself—though sometimes I get a little despondent.

My kind friend, Mr. Graham [Lorimer Graham, probably], whom you remember my writing to you about, has been away for some weeks in Rome—returning only the other day. I was glad to see

him, for he had been most courteous and persistent in his good services to me. He brought Mr. Bronson with him a couple of mornings ago, and very jolly was our meeting, for I always liked him—he is most original and amusing. I have dined at the Bronsons since, and they are most amiable and nice. Mrs. Bronson, who is the most generous woman possible, has been so kind to a poor gondolier I was painting, and who fell ill with dreadful cough and fever. I told her all about him, and she at once had all sorts of nice things made for him, and Miss Chapman, who is staying with the Bronsons, has been herself to call on poor Giovanni. He is getting well now I hope, and will soon be able again to pose for his picture. Mrs. Harris, the wife of the American Consul, has been very charming—always asking me to her house and presenting me to all her best acquaintances. She is a dear old lady, and I know you would like her. So you see I have not been without friends, Mother, and, notwithstanding the fearful climate, not absolutely forlorn and cheerless. I am so glad to hear that everything is happily arranged for Annie's future—give my love and congratulations to her when you see her, or send them through Sis. And now good-bye, my darling Mother—I do hope you will be quite well and strong again directly now—for I hear accounts from England saying that the sun is shining upon all there, and that everything is warm and delightful! You asked once about Susie Livermore's etchings—doubtless she has had them all before now—for they were left out purposely for her—ready in their frames. I received your nice Christmas card, mama dear, and meant to have written at once to tell you how gratified I was—but it is the same old story, my dear Mother. I am at my work the first thing at dawn and the last thing at night, and loving you all the while though not writing to tell you. Remember me to Mrs. [illegible], and give my love to all.

Your fond son,

JIMMIE.

This letter, written at forty-six years of age, may serve as an introduction to the completely developed man Whistler, and to some estimate of that man's work of brush, burin, chalk, and pen—with reference to the ethics of art procedure and its relations to human brotherhood and higher civilization. This may perhaps be done without trenching on the ground claimed as his own by the real or supposed or merely *soi-disant* critic, whose only or main interest in an artist is so often confined to the latter's relations to the technique of art. Such critics do not include an artist's literary work in their summaries of his output, and Whistler himself professed the same scorn for literary quality in art as he did for the schools. Yet no artist ever owed as much to his own literary faculty—naturally one of real though elusive distinction—as Whistler. The letter to his mother, given above, however punctuationless, shows him at his best; but his pen was almost invariably either venomous or inconsequent. The epigrams he so carefully prepared for use at the first subsequent opportunity were sometimes sufficiently bright, even witty, as, for instance, when pointing to one of Leighton's pieces among a crowd of others on exhibition, he likens it to "a diamond in the *sty*" —and when, in the case of a worthy but somewhat strait-laced Academician's objection to a certain nude, he paraphrased the motto of the order of the Garter and the English Arms into "*Horsley soit qui mal y pense.*"

His own pen did as much for his position in the world of art as his brush, and not even the most industrious, jewel-losing actress, more carefully, if with apparent unconsciousness, cultivated the personal eccentricities which excite the pens of others—of journalistic and sensation-hunting onlookers—to the comment and gossip that make for the notoriety of their subject.

But if some geniality or wisdom occasionally lurks in his *jeux d'esprit* they are much more often charged with revenge or detraction and filled, even if he were not always conscious of it, with the unscrupulousness of the egomaniac; nor does all his persiflage and thin pretence of courtesy hide their frequent brutality. It is, indeed, quite questionable whether the art-world of the future will not charge him with having brought more suspicion on art and really wrought more evil to it by his tongue and pen than he has achieved good for it by pencil and needle.

Whistler seems, in fact, all through his adult life, to have deserved the picture drawn of him under the name of Joe Sibley by his early *confrère*, du Maurier, in his first edition of "Trilby."

"He was a monotheist, and had but one god. Sibley was the god of Joe's worship and none other; and he would hear of no other genius in the world!" No amount of adulation from follower or admirer was too much for him, but one whisper of criticism, the slightest thwarting of his selfish demands, or questioning of his inordinate claim of originality turned him into an implacable foe. So Swinburne, who had so warmly and so usefully taken him up —this poet of front rank, for telling the truth, that Reynolds had long before said what Whistler repeated in his "Ten O'Clock,"—Swinburne became "one Algernon Swinburne" and an "outsider of Putney." He remained "friends" with his successive acquaintance only so long as he was not yet prepared to "shake" them for fresh victims to his self-worship, and one is tempted to believe that his unscrupulous jocularity toward others, while utterly refusing to take a joke on himself, was sometimes deliberately resorted to for the purpose of provoking a quarrel and so disrupting hitherto good relations.

Not long after the beginning of his professional success he rewarded Leyland (of the Peacock Room), his lavish patron and promoter, with whom he had, of course, finally picked a quarrel, by depicting him, life-size, as the devil with his hoofs and horns. Ingratitude and contumely to those who had most served him became finally his habit.

There are, however, few vices—some moralists say there are none—which do not have their root in a norm of good. Channing, from his pure point of view, necessarily thought Napoleon a very bad man. But, doubtless recognizing that he was a consummate administrator as well as a self-seeking and merciless warrior, the critic says that the destroyer of kings and maker of empires "extorts admiration." And one feels that, in a world of greater or lesser Philistines, the exceptional artist who preserves an utter independence ought to have much to his credit, even if he makes a most objectionable caricature of his rôle.

The last enemy of all flesh Whistler

met — outwardly, at least — with the characteristic jauntiness displayed to all his previous foes, the making of which he declared—did he say it sincerely, or simply in defiance?—was his "only joy." But he returned to his old Chelsea haunts from the continent well realizing, doubtless, that it was to die, notwithstanding that his last letter from The Hague to one of the London newspapers, charged with his habitual mock politeness and subtle insolence, but really calling it to task for publishing a premature report of his death, was meant to convey the impression to the world that much more work might be expected from him. Then straightway he delivers his characteristic deathbed injunctions for the puzzling and baffling, even beyond the grave, of not alone the public, but those few who still cling to him as friends. We must certainly admire the pluck in such a course, even if we don't admire other elements that led to it.

So, too, though the peculiar nomenclature he adopted for the output of his brush and needle inevitably, in its novelty, excited ridicule and censure, and was surely adopted, just as his hirsutial oriflamme was carefully cultivated, mainly as an advertisement to attract the custom of the hunter after art-novelties and art-bargains, even as his wand and flat-brimmed hat were assumed to mark him out to "the man in the street," there is no little to be said in favor of such nomenclature by those who recognize the sisterhood of the various fine arts. Whistler's early days, as we have seen, were passed in an atmosphere of music, and apart from the masterful craving of erratic genius for novelty, and his appreciation, on reaching manhood and looking forth on the world, of the value of new processes in systematic self-advertising, it was therefore not unnatural that he should use musical terminology in giving titles to the output of his work in graphic art. Why should he not speak of that work as symphonies or harmonies in white, in green, in blue, in gray, or what not? Why should the word "arrangement" be confined to musical notes? Is not what is perhaps

his masterpiece, his mother's portrait, really and truly, as children say, an "arrangement" in black and gray?

Some one has said that Whistler first disclosed the poetry in a London fog, which is hardly true, even of the Occidental field of art, for Cazin and Turner, to say nothing of preceding painters, did the like, while the rain and mist effects are admirable in some of the high-class Japanese output, much influenced Whistler, generally, but not invariably, for good. But some of Whistler's night-effects certainly originated in the main with himself, though he may have received some hint therefor from "The Milky Way" of his favorite master Tintoretto. Why, then, should not his exquisite renderings, in dry point, of night-effects, be named, one a "Nocturne in Blue and Silver," another a "Nocturne in Black and Gold," even at the risk of contributing to offend Ruskin?—that inspired man, who, though he perhaps never visited the Cremorne Gardens at night, and is to be read not at all for the guidance of the tyro in art-technique (in defining which he makes frequent mistakes, often foolish and sometimes grotesque), will ever stand, *facile princeps*, among those who have led the Anglo-Saxon world to fruitful communion with the spirit of art. For Ruskin, whatever his shortcomings or his over-statements where art appliance in the concrete is concerned, did more to induce, among our not over-sensitive English-speaking race throughout the globe, a respect for the graphic and plastic fine arts than any other man in the annals of that race; just as Prince Albert, by his initiatory World's Exposition, did more for art-application in the Occidental world, and for art-interchange among all races, than any other man. It was his Crystal Palace Exhibition of 1851 that really disclosed Oriental art to the whole Western world, though a century and a half before, in one corner of it, Louis XIV. had, in his latter years, tried to set the fashion to his court for Japanese bronzes and lacquers, and, in another, Sir William Chambers had published, later in the eighteenth century, his opinion that Chinese architecture, originating in the tent form, might advantageously be utilized in rural holdings. (Which reminds me that I once heard General Sherman, at an architectural dinner, give it as his opinion that tent life was much more wholesome than house life. And army surgeons unite in preferring tent hospitals to any other kind.)

The fact that certain terms have hitherto been held specific for only the tonal field of the fine arts, seems no sufficient reason why their aptness should not be extended to other fields. If Whistler were not so insistent in the expression of his contempt for any variety of his art outside of his own rendering of it, one might be inclined to give him credit for adopting this musical nomenclature—for forging this link, visible even to the generally half-blind multitude, between those two of the fine arts most in evidence before them. For a general comprehension of the indubitable fact that all the fine arts have in reality one source of inspiration, and one spring of action, would go far toward the better understanding and the better treatment of all those arts, and of all their professors, by the art-loving public—and, indeed, by the masses,—and thus toward the surer well-being of the art-executant, and the advancement of a finer civilization than that of the present. "*Etenim omnes artes quæ ad humanitatem pertinent, habent quoddam commune vinculum, et quasi cognatione quâdam inter se continentur,*" Cicero said two thousand years ago, and with every fresh manifestation of civilization this truth has become more apparent.

Catalogues and chronological tables of the not meagre professional output, though mainly etchings, of Whistler have long since been given to the artistic public by Thomas, Wedmore, and others, as also have all sorts of criticism on it, running through the gamut, customary where real originality appears, of arrested observation, incredulity, misapprehension, ridicule, defence, the championship and detraction of opposing partisans, and, in due sequence, the cumulative admiration

which ends in the general adoption of a new master and, unfortunately in the end for art, in a non-judicial attitude on the part of his disciples, impelling them to ascribe the same value to all that comes or has come from his hand, good, bad, or indifferent, and the worst with the best. Ruskin might better, perhaps, have not taken a leaf from Whistler's own well-thumbed book of contempt and invective when characterizing a special output of the latter in black and gold, and may himself have been far from his best mood for appreciation as to the picture's intrinsic merits; but he was entirely justified in his non-acceptance of an artist's egotistical assumption that all his work is equally worthy,—though, indeed, the claim is in most instances made by his enthusiastic but not always sagacious followers rather than by himself—whereas some temporary eclipse of his creative power may have resulted in a really inferior example.

Here are some early judgments of critics controlling journalistic or other serial art columns. Whistler is a mere "*amateur prodige.*" "Whistler is eminently" (another says "uncompromisingly") "vulgar." Another: he is "full of foppish airs and affectations." The same man who was subsequently to "stand up" with him at his wedding, Labouchere, in his *Truth*, characterizes one of his exhibitions as "another crop of Whistler's little jokes"; and the Attorney-General, in the Ruskin-Whistler libel suit, obviously agreed with "Labby" when he announced that the plaintiff had largely "increased the gaiety" of at least one nation. The *Daily Telegraph*, however, put its finger on what Whistler was undoubtedly frequently guilty of (like so many others, particularly of the so-called impressionist school), when it warned him not to "attempt to palm off his deficiencies as manifestations of power"—which was merely another way of putting a previous critic's statement that "He is really building up art out of his own imperfections." And that is certainly what not a few artists try to do, though it is the part of charity—which Bacon says we can never have in excess—to suppose that they don't themselves realize it.

Such contemptuous criticisms as the few I have adduced from the multitude were so frequently expressed, and in such similar terms, that one can't help recognizing that habit of "follow my leader," from which only the saving remnant of the literary cliques (so abhorred of Mazzini) and, perhaps not least, the art-literary cliques of whatever passing day, seem readily to emerge. But all the same had not Burne-Jones considerable grounds for his opinion that Whistler carefully evaded the difficulties of painting because of a temperament not sufficiently robust and insistent for a habit of overcoming them? The Frenchman Anquetin, whose reputation as an authority in technique is, I believe, acknowledged in the art-world to be among the highest, accuses him of the same thing, and is still more severe in his judgment, classing him among extremely clever tricksters and jugglers ("*escamoteurs*"). He it is also, if my memory serves me, who characterizes much of Whistler's output as fragile, slight, and evanescent.

In these latter days the critical tune is quite changed, though the old game of "follow my leader" is just as much played as in the inappreciative, faultfinding days. Here, selected from many others, is a recent Rhadamanthian utterance—an American one—and a good type of what for a few years past, and particularly since our artist's death, it has been "the thing" to say:

Mr. Whistler has long since demonstrated his right to leadership, his superiority being quite unquestioned. . . . Since Rembrandt, no one has succeeded quite so well as Whistler in making the stroke tell for so much, in securing, by the artistic arrangement of light and shade, splendid results, and in suggesting in every way picturesque compositions. [Whistler's own brother-in-law, Haden, long ago compared him to the same prodigy in Dutch art.] All is assuredly the work of a master, of a man grandly endowed, sensitive to all the possibilities of the needle on copper. His lightest touch is full of genius, and he performs the seemingly impossible with this limited medium. Whether

in the figure or landscape, in marine or architecture, these etchings seem to have been just the proper means of expression, suiting the man's temperament exactly.

The present writer would like, in view of this laudation, to hint, for the benefit of the architectural student, that albeit architecture (that is, on its merely structural, not on its high art level—though in Venice, one of our artist's stamping-grounds, most buildings may be classed as art-architecture) is much in evidence as one of Whistler's vehicles, and fits admirably into his often superfine methods and dreamlike effects, the tyro in that art will gain very much more instruction, and not seldom more inspiration, from Prout's unsurpassed renderings of architectural exterior than from Whistler's. Necessarily so, because Prout's outcome is meant to be nothing else than a rendering of selected architecture, the selections, of course, being based on an appreciation of their value as architecture *per se;* while Whistler's inclusions, as adjuncts to his portrayal of examples of the building art, mainly occur when they happen to be present in those general collocations of foregreater degree than Whistler's, they are apt to include more of non-architectural accessories than are Prout's.

But to return to Whistler's critics, our present-day one—he is speaking of a Whistler collection of etchings and dry points—adds: "It is all very entrancing and is worth not one but many visits to look at leisurely in the ground, middle distance, and background, of water and atmosphere, of twilight, moonlight, darkness, which best afford the master an opportunity to depict physical facts as they appeal to his very sensitive and alert organization, and his rare temperament. Piranesi's masterly, if somewhat coarse, etchings of Roman architectural remains, as they appeared about a century and a half ago, may also be classed among good studies for the acquirement of proficiency in portraying existing results of the building art, though with some reservation; for, though specifically architectural in much true spirit, reverently, and to come away full of the joy of having seen, if not of absolute possession."

Surely, however, neither indiscriminate censoriousness nor hysterical laudation should induce us to support the pigments he lays on his canvas. We have, indeed, his own word for it that a so-called picture from his hand, accidentally placed on the wall in an exhibition of some of his finished output —a simple study, or rather, in fact, a

WHISTLER AND HIS YOUNGER BROTHER

fallacy that because Whistler deserves, by reason of his best work, the rank finally accorded him in France, where, more than elsewhere, the chiefs of graphic and plastic art speak with authority, it follows that his worst work—done perhaps with his powers at low ebb, or in self-indulgent, happy-go-lucky mood—may not be as valueless, *per se*, and apart from the market value of his mere name, as the average work of the tyro or of the disappointed senior, who cannot, being destitute of the *vivida vis animi*, work it, along with his conscientiousness, into the mere memorandum—was "not worth the canvas it was painted on," though he caught two of his indiscriminating followers raving over it. This self-depreciatory dictum of our artist seems quite at variance with his other oracle that "the master's work is finished with the first stroke of his brush on the canvas"; but the difference is more apparent than real, for some artists of a certain temperament do not lay hands on their implements—brush, pen, chisel, burin, or what not—till their impending deliverance is so thoroughly formulated in their own brain that their work is, to their own perception, finished. Moreover, such an unusual note of humility reminds us of the little colloquy between Whistler, hand, for the diminutive proportions of the ordinary palette by no means suited our artist's conception of his surpassing endowments—did he not, in

WHISTLER'S MOTHER

as teacher, and his class of devout students. *Question :* "Do you know what I mean when I say tone, value, light and shade, quality, movement, construction, etc.?" Pious *Answer* in chorus: "Oh, yes! Mr. Whistler." Cynical—but may we opine semi-truthful ?—*Rejoinder :* "I'm glad, for it's more than I do myself."

In short, did Whistler seriously believe that he was the demigod in graphic art his nimble tongue and his facile pen, as an almost constant rule, proclaimed? Did he not, palette in hand —or, I should say, table under his fact, play a long game of bluff rather to secure incense for the man Whistler than appreciation worth earning for the artist? He knew, of course, that the early Christians among the gentiles adopted the butterfly as an emblem of immortality; but did not the same symbol secretly commend itself to his acute fancy as representative of the combined quickness, grace, and irresponsibility he recognized in himself, and as something as far as possible removed from the "heavy weight" qualities rightly demanded by the world in its leaders, and in which he recognized himself as lacking? This, of course, is rank heresy to his disciples, but the independent observer and analyzer need trouble himself but little with those to whom Whistler is the only painter and etcher, and the one original at all points. For instance, they quote, as something the like of which was never heard before, his remark at the Eden trial to the presiding judge who thought his charge of a thousand guineas for a portrait an excessive one: "It is true, I painted

It was substantially what most professional men, before attaining the eminence which commands the employment before-time anxiously awaited— or indirectly, sometimes directly, solicited, or fished for with more or less pulling of secret wires—have every now and then, under the law of self-preservation, or the sentiment of self-respect, had to say or to hint to their paymasters. Even the lawyer who protects the layman's property-interests, or the physician or surgeon who pro-

WHISTLER'S FATHER

that portrait in two sittings; but I did so with the experience of my whole life." That was a good retort, because it was true and was entirely apt to the occasion, unlike many of the speaker's *jeux d'esprit*.

But it was not in the least original.

tects his health and life, have occasion to resort to it when encountering an ignorant or stingy client or patient. How much more the laborer in any field of art, whose output, from the Philistinistic point of view, is mere play and self-indulgence, not solid, marketable product. One recalls the hint Rubens gave his imperial patron —his picture of the monarch's hand shaking an empty purse over the artist's outstretched palm. I have many times

product from the question of time expended and money invested in it.

If one agrees that any masterly reproduction in art of objects or conditions in nature worthy of selection and

WHISTLER'S MATERNAL AUNT
(From the first drawing made by Whistler)

had occasion to note the substance of Whistler's retort from the lips or pen of the architect. It is, in fact, difficult for the often but superficially cultured man, who has achieved pecuniary success in the channels of trade or manufacture, to separate the value of any

permanent record and rangement is entitled to its proper, if almost infinitesimal, share of the reverence due to the Supreme Designer and Creator of the gift of expression, as of all other gifts, and if one, being of much observation and long memory, contrasts the

slowly cumulating consensus of laudatory opinion, culminating in this
sentiment of reverence, with earlier
inappreciation, non-recognition, disparagement, neglect, and privation,
one can hardly fail to make much
allowance for the external souring of a
nature that has been the object of such
contrary estimate, while all along, or
at least quite soon, the possessor of
the gift must have been conscious of
his own value, and probably at no time
disposed to underrate himself or it.
Inopportune conditions of earlier manhood, unfortunately too common with
the practitioners of any of the fine
arts, were doubtless, too, in Whistler's
case, intensified to his highstrung
organization by his memories of the
well-sheltered boyhood, disclosed in
my extracts from his mother's journal,
and by some contact, more or less
close, but everything being seen
through very sharp young eyes, with
court life. One is, therefore, much
inclined to take a quite indulgent view
of his course. Yet in the interest of
art itself and of that future and higher
civilization toward which art, with its
all-illumining and unquenchable torch,
leads, at the same time that it beauti-
fies, the way, it may be quite necessary
for some one to attempt to indicate the
injury which accrues to the progress of
civilization from the shortcomings and
mistakes of the professors of art. It
is my belief that Whistler should be
presented to the rising generation of
artists who adopt graphic rendering as
their specialty, not only as a shining
example, but as a warning.

It is quite true that the man of
genius, before it is recognized by the
multitude, is often impelled, through
the mere instinct of self-preservation,
to become more or less of a recluse;
but if his social instincts be strong, or
if circumstances compel him to mix
much and continuously with average
or inferior men, he is apt to wear some
sort of armor, or at least a slight mask,
but not infrequently his panoply of
protection and defence takes the form
of irony and his mask of persiflage or
buffoonery. When, however, through
the medium of the competent critic—

of course, as in the case of all other
vocations, the opinion of most professional critics is accepted as final only
by the masses of onlookers — when
through the competent art critic (sometimes, indeed, mainly through the
competent art dealer), the artist has
gained his rightful reputation, the excuse for flamboyant and spectacular
self-advertisement no longer exists.
But what is to be said in the case of
the artist who, after being recognized
at his top-level, objects to being, as a
colorist, classed on the lower level
which is all his inordinate self-apprecia-
tion, or his game of bluff, assigns to
Velasquez, and who doubtless also regarded himself, as a limner and etcher,
superior to Rembrandt?—of the artist
who, among a gallery hung with pictures of the Royal Academicians, likens
one painting by Leighton to "a diamond in the sty," which compliment,
paid only because it affords opportunity
for wholesale detraction of all the other
artists represented, does not prevent
his jealous, sour sneer, "Paints too, I
believe," after hearing a eulogy on
Leighton's versatility and rare accom-
plishments? How must those who
think that ethics as well as art have
their place in the world, characterize
his treatment of Leyland in the matter
of the peacock room? What is to be
said of the one-sided, sharp-bargaining
egoist who, in his diamond-cut-diamond
duel with Sir William Eden, lauds his
own "thoughtless kind feeling and exquisite taste," and tells him it is "impossible" for himself, Whistler, to
"write a rude letter," just as if the
grossest rudeness may not be varnished
with extreme politeness? "*Grattez le
baronnet,*" he says, "*et vous trouverez
le boutiquier.*" But it is as plain as
noonday that the animus leading to
the suit (which, luckily for Whistler,
was determined in France) was, on the
Butterfly's side at least as much as on
the Baronet's, the merest "tradesman's
and huckster's" attempt to get as
much as possible for as little as possible — "something for nothing."
What is to be said of his refusal in
several instances, after being paid his
own price in advance, to give up to

their owners the portraits of them he had finished to his own satisfaction? His unreasoning apologists attribute such practice to "supreme devotion to his art." Those who regard the golden rule as the paramount one for the conduct of life view it as the fruit of a self-worship that did not halt at—however he may have deluded or compromised with his conscience—sheer dishonesty, and as a direct blow at the fair repute and good name of artists—the confraternity to which, as a member thereof, he owed something—in the lay community that sustains them.

Whistler's sign manual, the butterfly, may have commended itself to the self-gauging artist no less than to the early Christians, as an emblem of the immortality he deemed, or pretended to deem, his due—of the glorious ascent from the tomb that ended an ignoble period of crawling on the earth's surface. But perhaps also, feeling the need of a mask, yet realizing

WHISTLER'S GRANDFATHER

that even the lightest would be too rigid and burdensome for his mobile features, he adopted, in preference, an airy, graceful, gay-hued go-between, whose light-winged flutterings should ward off the annoyance of the too-familiar gaze of the exoteric multitude from his own superfine lineaments. He waxes wroth that Ruskin should be "undismayed by the presence of the Masters with whose names he is sacrilegiously familiar." *Mirabile visu!* The impious self-seeker Ruskin pilloried by the saintly altruist Whistler! And what are all the other masters in comparison with the superior of Velasquez? Is he not the man who, like the royal critic of Spain, feels sure that if he had had the making of the world he would have put together a much better one than the Lord did? Is not he, Whistler, the last and greatest of the masters, who, while condescendingly allowing that "God is always good," thinks Him "sometimes careless," and that the Nature on which He has placed His stamp is "usually wrong"; that it gives only "slovenly suggestions," that it "seldom succeeds in producing a picture," and that "unlimited admiration is given to very foolish sunsets"? Every thinking person realizes that the Creator has endowed His chief work with faculties for discrimination, selection, alteration in dealing with Nature's output, and every designer of partly factitious landscape knows that insignificant details —as compared with the masses in Nature's layout—of terrene structure and of vegetation may be advantageously handled for the attainment of some desired specific effect. But our meek Whistler thinks nothing of arraigning the Almighty for not trimming and posing the last detail for the artist's immediate behoof in front of his canvas, and for making his sunsets so resplendent and luminous that all Whistler's pigments and deftness of finger fall immeasurably short of the glorified tints and subtle blendings so foolishly spread over the western sky. But, after all, he is not wholly pessimistic as regards the future of Nature. He admits that she may improve and perhaps "creep up to" himself.

Before leaving the butterfly mark, one need hardly be accused of an unbalanced imagination if one connects its varieties of expression, on the artist's etchings, with the varying moods of a highly sensitive temperament. The delicate lines, diminutive as is the space allowed them, are as full of varying expressions as are the curves and incisions of a tiny Japanese carving in ivory. Generally a human grin is traceable in the few strokes on its central white background, and this is intensified when the butterfly's chevelure-like wings are dark and well defined. Sometimes there is a suggestion of the nude human body with limbs of wire. It was probably in pessimistic moods that the insect was given a forked proboscis or a forked tail, and, in a specially venomous access of feeling, two forked tails. In one instance the forked tail is curled far above the head and stretches beyond an astral nebula. In such a sphere the artist's fancy had doubtless often disported itself. In at least one of the river-etchings the butterfly looks like a human head submerged to the lips and still sinking. In "The Baronet and the Butterfly"—as complete an example, probably, of self-glorification, studied insolence, and special pleading, as is extant, even in the autobiographical inscriptions of Egyptian or Assyrian sovereigns—the far-soaring insect has hitched itself, like Emerson's wagon, to a star, and, overpassing the flood and the commercial features squat on its brink, ascends, "*rayonnant de gloire*," through the clouds, *ad astra*. The butterfly signature to Whistler's resumé of the legal findings in this *cause célèbre* of a lady's outpainted portrait in brown and gold is evidently meant for himself, winged and fork-tailed, capering in a closing dance of triumph, after some prefatory high-kicking, as displayed on the title-page.

It is worth mentioning that the butterfly emblem, which some say had its origin as a free paraphrase of the artist's monogram, was not used by the artist in his first etchings, the Thames series, of the early sixties. After the publication of that series there was an intermission of a good

many years before he returned to the dry point and needle. This he did at the instigation of Mr. Avery, on the

WHISTLER'S GRANDMOTHER

latter showing him the collection he had gathered (much more complete than that possessed by the artist himself), some time in the late seventies or early eighties. It was only then that he adopted the butterfly signature, trademark, or "marginal remark," whichever he may have preferred to have it considered; though, if the first, it is often a pleonasm alongside of his manuscript signature; if the second it is surely *infra dig.* for one "chosen of the gods" to stand behind a bargain counter; and if the last it is as surely violative of his own dictum that "marginal remarks are odious." However that may be, the butterfly became finally his recognized signature, on bank cheque no less than on picture.

A GIRL CROCHETING
From a painting by Edmund C. Tarbell

Edmund C. Tarbell

EDMUND C. TARBELL creates in his paintings a nucleus of objects and thoughts so fused that through the aspect of the visible the spectator comes to feel the sentiment of the intangible. The artist's grasp of such a combination, the result of felicitous selection and presentation, has reached its highest level in his most recent production, the "Girl Crocheting." Before the first exhibition of the canvas Mr. Tarbell held his reputation chiefly through his interest in open-air studies of landscapes and figure compositions. However, with this last effort, in treating a room and its occupant, he has turned towards a new field, one that recalls the Dutch indoor scenes of women about their household duties, so typical of Terborch and the men of his class. In the present instance a girl, wearing a conventional modern shirtwaist and skirt, sits tranquilly beside a mahogany table, where she bends over her crocheting in silent absorption. The light, from the window behind her, falls softly upon her hair and back, upon the rough surface of the wall, across a copy of a Velasquez, and some Japanese prints that fade into the mellow shadows, and over the highly polished table-top. The attitude of the figure remains both natural and realistic. The room certainly displays nothing uncommon. It should be a matter of comparative ease for Mr. Tarbell, with his thorough technical training and original sense of beauty, to create, by an anecdotal category of details, a simple likeness of such an unsophisticated young woman, and such frank surroundings. His unusual qualities, in this case, lie in a capacity to associate with the forms at his command thoughts and feelings that are tranquil. For, by means of his insight into the possibilities of warm, modified lights, and by means of his ability to deal with semi-opaque shadows and reflected color he has infiltrated hum drum, every-day situation with a poetical atmosphere strangely devoid of the usual accompanying mystery. Perhaps much of the charm of his search for the thought in unaffected objects may be credited to his apparent dislike of over-subtile but always-to-be-discovered tricks, employed to reveal dexterity on the part of the artist rather than graciousness or strength on the part of the art. Mr. Tarbell draws with a lovable touch that never fails to remain in keeping with his clearly chosen shades and accents of light. He fills with breadth his delicate regard for color. In his treatment of actual surfaces he exhibits a definite understanding and skill in dealing with various textures, as when he succeeds in the unusual task of contrasting the clear reflected light of the girl's shirtwaist against the dull, luminous glow of the wall. Again and again he repeats his faculty of spreading suggestiveness and individuality of character without mannerisms. Yet that he may more completely raise himself above the level of an imitator to the position where he may bind feeling and fact into a comprehensive whole, he works cleverly and sympathetically at his calling, that by nature must be one of deception. Nevertheless, he sees to it that the deception remains plausible, and in this plausibility he hides and yet expresses what he feels by what he sees.

———

Edmund C. Tarbell was born in West Groton, Massachusetts, in 1862. He first studied painting at the Boston Museum of Fine Arts, where he remained until he went to Paris. There, with Eugene Benson, also a Boston painter, he worked under Daunat, Boulanger, Lefebvre; and in the Académie Julien. Since his return he has devoted himself almost entirely to New England, painting what he found first at hand, and teaching in the Boston Museum of Fine Arts. He is a member of the National Academy of Design. His work has received numerous prizes both abroad at Paris and at home, as in the case of the Shaw fund at the Society of American Artists.

H. ST. G.

A Portrait of Coleridge by Washington Allston

By ANNIE NATHAN MEYER

THE original of this portrait of Coleridge is at present on exhibition at the Boston Museum, loaned by the owner, Mr. Richard H. Dana, a great-nephew of the artist. The fact that Allston painted two different portraits of the poet at an interval of eight years has been the cause of no little confusion. Indeed, the two portraits are so different—more so than is accounted for by the mere difference in age—that to have the one picture in mind while reading a description of the other naturally led to the most rasping of arguments on the part of otherwise highly estimable persons.

This portrait, which is, I believe, reproduced for the first time, was painted in 1805, when Coleridge was in Rome. Although but thirty-three years of age, his best work was already done, and he had left England in the vain hope of regaining his lost health. While in Rome, Coleridge's chief intimates were the two Americans, Allston, then twenty-six years old, and Washington Irving, the brilliant young law clerk who had not yet begun his literary career with the Salmagundi papers. It was the charm and fellowship of these days in Rome that caused Irving's short-lived determination to throw up the study of the law and become a painter. We may thank our stars that later he saw that the sudden resolution was due rather to his admiration of Allston and the glamour of the Italian landscape, than to any real talent for art. After all, we should miss Washington Irving from our literature rather more than Washington Allston from our art.

The three congenial young men certainly enjoyed rare times in the glorious old-world capital. As Allston painted, Coleridge would hold forth in the wonderful way we have heard so much about, on every subject under the sun. And not only do we hear of these talks in the studio, but also as they took place during the long walks which the trio indulged in about the city. Allston, looking back on it all, said humorously: "Coleridge used to call Rome 'the silent city,' but I could never think of it as such while with him, for meet him when and where I would, the fountain of his mind was never dry, but, like the far-reaching aqueducts that once supplied this mistress of the world, its living stream seemed specially to flow for every classic ruin over which we wandered."

Of the quality of this flow of language, Allston has given us this high praise: "When I recall some of our walks," he says, "under the pines of the Villa Borghese, I am almost tempted to dream that I have once listened to Plato in the groves of the Academy."

When we remember, not only the universal eulogies of Coleridge's powers of conversation, but also those that were showered on the social and intellectual charm of both Allston and Irving, we may well regret the loss to the world of the permanent record which Coleridge had prepared. These papers were among those which the panic-stricken sea-captain forced him to throw overboard when followed by the spies of Buonaparte.

We are given here and there in the correspondence of Allston an inkling of some of the conversations. Evidently at least once there was waged a heated discussion over the comparative merits of the Greek and Gothic architecture. Coleridge is quoted as declaring that while "Grecian architecture is a thing, Gothic architecture is an idea," and then followed the delicious boast that he *"could make a Greek temple of two brickbats and a cocked hat !"*

The friendship between the poet and the painter lasted for more than twenty-five years. Allston once de-

COLERIDGE
From a painting by Washington Allston in the possession of Mr. Richard H Dana

clared, "to no other man do I owe so much intellectually as to Mr. Coleridge," and Coleridge wrote Allston: "Had I not known the Wordsworths, I should have esteemed and loved you first and most, and as it is, next to them I love and honor you."

When Allston was seriously ill in Bristol in 1813, Coleridge rushed to him and nursed him devotedly. It was during Allston's convalescence that he painted the second portrait of the poet, which now hangs at the National Portrait Gallery in London, and of which Wordsworth said: "It is the only likeness that ever gave me any pleasure; it is incomparably the finest likeness taken of Coleridge."

The Bristol portrait was painted for a friend and admirer of Coleridge, Mr. Wade, who valued it so highly that, although apparently agreeing with Wordsworth that the picture should hang in some public gallery, nevertheless on his death willed it to a relative with the injunction not to part with it. In some way, years after, largely, it is said, through the efforts of Wordsworth, the portrait was finally secured for the National Portrait Gallery. When, in 1854, this portrait was for the first time placed in the hands of an engraver, the London *Guardian* said of it:

It is by far the finest portrait of Coleridge in existence, and much more recalls the power and intellect of the face than any other we ever saw. He is sitting in a room which has something of an antique cast about it, with his hand upon a book, looking upward; the portliness and white hair of middle life have come upon him, but the expression of his face is very refined and beautiful, and the form of his head grand and noble.

Allston himself said:

So far as I can judge of my own production, the likeness of Coleridge is a true one, but it is Coleridge in repose; and though not unstirred by the perpetual ground-swell of his ever-working intellect, and shadowing forth something of the deep philosopher, it is not Coleridge in his highest mood, the poetic state, when the divine afflatus possessed him.

When in that state [he goes on to say] no face I ever saw was like his : it seemed almost spirit made

visible without a shadow of the physical upon it. Could I then have fixed it upon canvas ! but it was beyond the reach of my art.

I wonder if Allston realized that in the earlier and unfinished portrait his art had reached higher, that he had caught more of that "divine afflatus," more of the fire and intrepidity of genius. His biographer says of it, "it is extremely interesting, and though far from finished, does not disappoint the admirers of Coleridge"! This is lukewarm praise, indeed, it would seem to me, for I am of the opinion that this unfinished portrait, taken just as it was left by the artist, is more interesting and satisfactory as a portrait than any of the "finished" ones I have seen, and this includes the one by Leslie, as well as that of the very young poet painted by Vandyke.* And not only do I hold this earlier Allston portrait of Coleridge above all the others, but as the best canvas I have seen from the hand of Allston. The charm of the picture lies not alone in the subject; it is handled with great vigor and certainty; there is a dash and spirit about it that is exceptional, perhaps, in any age, certainly in the age in which it was painted. Here is the inspiration red-hot, before it has been pressed into the mould of conventionality, according to the strait-laced rules of "historical painting," which had their influence even when the subject was a contemporary.

Wherein lies the oft-felt but never explained charm of some unfinished paintings? That some have thought the charm consists merely in the lack of finish has proved the undoing of many a modern artist. To leave a poor picture unfinished adds neither to its charm nor value. In so far as anything so intangible as charm may permit of analysis, I should say the truth lies approximately here: A picture may possess a certain indescribably subtle quality, which lends fascination to it; this quality once achieved, there is danger that it escape while the artist is trying to give it the

* Of this later Vandyke, Cunningham quaintly says, "he was allied more in name than talent with him of the days of Charles I."

quality of permanence. A great artist knows how to be master of his genius without making it wilt and sicken under obvious bonds. Spontaneity, life, freshness of statement, directness of means employed, subordination of

It may be interesting to end with Allston's own remarks in his Lectures on Art upon unfinished paintings:

I may here notice [he says] a false notion which is current among artists, that some parts of a pic-

ANOTHER NEW PORTRAIT OF COLERIDGE

A contemporary portrait, hitherto unpublished, of the poet Coleridge; the work of R. Dawe, R.A., and an illustration in Lord Coleridge's history of this famous Devonshire family. London, Fisher Unwin; New York, Charles Scribner's Sons

the unessential,—all these are qualities that in a painting make for charm, and they are as elusive as the will-o'-the-wisp! One moment the charm is there, the next it is not. It happens, for instance, that it is felt supremely in the unfinished "Athenæum portraits" of Washington and his wife and in the delightful unfinished portrait of Mrs. Perey Morton, of Gilbert Stuart, as it is felt in this unfinished portrait of Allston. Let us not attempt further to break the butterfly on the wheel; let us simply be grateful!

ture should be left unfinished. The very statement betrays its unsoundness, for that which is unfinished must necessarily be imperfect; so that, according to this rule, imperfection is made essential to perfection.

Of course, in one way he is quite right: one cannot catch a will-o'-the-wisp with a yard-stick! But I have a notion that Allston would scarcely approve of my holding his unfinished "Coleridge" in as high esteem as I do. All of which goes to show that a painter may paint better than his theories!

The Young Pretender

By J. SANFORD SALTUS

THE next King of France! Who will he be? A question often asked by the adherents of the Duc de Orléans, Don Carlos, Victor Napoleon, and Jean de Bourbon, the youngest of the "Pretenders," whose claim to the throne of Louis XVI. rests upon the assumption that he is his great-grandson and grandson of Louis XVII.* ("Naundorff"), the Dauphin (?) who according to popular rumor died in prison June 8, 1795, and was buried at night

AUGUSTE-JEAN-CHARLES-EMMANUEL DE BOURBON (JEAN III.), 1905, GRANDSON OF "NAUNDORFF" (LOUIS XVII.)

in an unmarked grave by the wall of the churchyard of Ste.-Marguerite † in an obscure quarter of Paris. That the

Dauphin did not die in prison, but that with the assistance of friends he made his "escape" therefrom—a sick child being left in his stead,— is now the almost universally accepted belief of historians. It is also thought that his "escape" was known to Fouché and assisted by Josephine Beauharnais, and that beside the sick child several other children, whose names are said to have been Tardif, Leminger, de Jarjages, and Gornhaut, were used as "blinds," while the real Louis XVII. was being helped out of the country by the Royalists. But at present it is not my purpose to write about Louis XVII., but to tell a little about Auguste-Jean-Charles-Emmanuel de Bourbon and his antecedents, or Jean III. as he is known to his followers and supporters, now rapidly increasing in numbers and influence.

At Delft, August 10, 1845, ended the strange, adventurous life of the exile Charles William Naundorff,* whose grave in the old cemetery (at Delft) soon after his interment bore, by official permission, the following inscription:

Ici Repose

LOUIS XVII:

Roi de France et de Navarre
Charles Louis Duc de Normandie
Né à Versailles le 27 Mars 1785
Décédé à Delft le 10 Août 1845

June 8, 1904, the remains of "Naundorff" were exhumed and re-interred in the new cemetery at Delft, and once more by official permission the old inscription appears upon the tombstone. King William II., King William III., Queen Wilhelmina, have allowed this inscription to remain unmolested. Why?

On the coming of age of the "Naundorffs" the Dutch government grants to them the legal right to the name de Bourbon.

---

* "Correspondance et Intimé et Louis XVII.," by Otto Friedrichs, Paris, 1904, is a most scholarly and interesting work on "Naundorff" and his claims
† See the publication, "Ville de Paris, 1904, Commission du Vieux Paris, l'ancien Cimetière Paroissial de Sainte-Marguerite, Historique Inhumation du Dauphin Disparition prochaine (1624-1904) Annexe au Procès Verbal de la Séance du Février, 1904"; and "Le Cimetière du Sainte-Marguerite et la Sépulture de Louis XVII.," par Lucien Lambeaux, Paris, 1905.

* At Versailles, in the presence of Bismarck, Jules Favre signed the armistice, and he sealed it with a ring he wore. The ring was a present to him from Naundorff!

In 1818 "Naundorff" married Jeanne-Frederique Einert, and while it is thought that he resembled Marie-Antoinette more than Louis XVI., two at least of his eight children, the late Charles-Louis (Charles XI.), and Marie-Thérèse, born in 1835 and still living, are pure Bourbon types. The profile of Marie-Thérèse, as shown in a recent photograph, is almost identical with that of Louis XVI.

The late Charles-Edmond, "Naundorff's" fifth child, was the father of Jean de Bourbon, who was born at Maëstricht, November 6, 1872, and married February 7, 1898, Mlle. Cuillé. Their only child, Henri-Charles-Louis (the Dauphin), was born November 27, 1899.

In their pleasant home on the Faubourg St.-Honore, every Wednesday afternoon "Prince and Princess" de Bourbon hold an informal reception, where their "party," and scholars interested in "The question," meet and talk of what France was in the past, of what France may be in the future, and perhaps glance at the latest number of *La Légitimité*, the recognized organ of the "Naundorffists," now in its twenty-third year, or one of the books on Louis XVII., of which quite a number have been published during the last six months.

The bust of "Naundorff" stands in the corner, and while the features of "Prince Jean" show a resemblance, in the young man the Bourbon nose is more pronounced and in the long thin eyebrows there is a most startling reminder of Marie-Antoinette.

Two little incidents will serve to show how strongly the marks of heredity are noticeable in the face of "Prince Jean." A domestic saw him in the

" NAUNDORFF " LOUIS XVII.
Taken soon after his death in Delft in 1845

hall of the hotel where I was stopping and soon after, on seeing a picture of "Naundorff" on my writing table, remarked, "I saw a gentleman in the hall to-day—I don't know who he was, but he looked like this picture." On the Rue de Rivoli I purchased a postcard on which was the head of Marie-Antoinette, evidently a reproduction from an old picture. I showed it to a friend, and instantly came the exclamation: "I only saw him once, but what a wonderful likeness to Jean de Bourbon!"

The Great Commonplaces of Reading*

By JOHN MORLEY

THERE are those who have misgivings lest the multiplication of public libraries and means of access to books should have the effect of slackening the native energy of the mind, dulling the edge of the will, and numbing mother wit. That is the view of some, and there may be danger of the kind. We have not yet had experience to know, but I cannot conceive how these effects can come from a judicious use of the knowledge and stimulation books alone can supply. For people who have free access to all forms of literature it would be selfishness to grudge the opening of these treasures to other people less favorably placed than themselves. A library may be the means of quickening the intelligence, of opening new paths to young men and women, who without it would not have known their own faculties, or have been stimulated to make the best use of their gifts. We waste many things, time, and money; but no waste is so dreadful to think of as the waste of human character and the brain above the average of a man's fellows, through not giving access to those agencies and instruments that develop the exceptional brain or larger heart to full available capacity and service.

The object of reading is not to dip into everything that even wise men have ever written. In the words of one of the most winning writers of English that ever existed — Cardinal Newman — the object of literature in education is to open the mind, to correct it, to refine it, to enable it to comprehend and digest its knowledge, to give it power over its own faculties, application, flexibility, method, critical exactness, sagacity, address, and expression. These are the objects of that intellectual perfection which a literary education is destined to give.

Literature consists of all the books—

and they are not so many—where moral truth and human passion are touched with a certain largeness, sanity, and attraction of form. My notion of a literary student is one who through books explores the strange voyages of man's moral reason, the impulses of the human heart, the chances and changes that have overtaken human ideals of virtue and happiness, of conduct and manners, and the shifting fortunes of great conceptions of truth and virtue. Poets, dramatists, humorists, satirists, masters of fiction, the great preachers, the character-writers, the maxim-writers, the great political orators—they are all literature in so far as they teach us to know man and to know human nature. This is what makes literature, rightly sifted and selected and rightly studied, not the mere elegant trifling that it is so often and so erroneously supposed to be, but a proper instrument for a systematic training of the imagination and sympathies, and of a genial and varied moral sensibility.

What is needed is the historic sense of the progress through the ages. This is of more importance than all the events got out of the three-decker volumes of history. What should be known is the progress of the world as a whole, and its effects on the human heart in all its variations. These are the important matters, and it is as much the object of a library to give a key to this general interest and knowledge as to provide special information. Every good library is in itself a book. As a collection of books it has abundant value; but, more than that, it represents the thoughts, the feelings, the motives, the impulses of men of all ages. All the leading facts of life are there; all the differences between man and man; all the differences between the ages are there — the tears, the laughter, the labors of mankind are in a library; the efforts, the failures, the glories, the idle dreams and their mis-

* This paper is composed of several extemporaneous addresses on books and reading, and has been revised for this publication by Mr. Morley.—EDITOR CRITIC.

chiefs—the whole overwhelming drama of humanity is there. To be sensible of this there must be what some one has called the "feel" of a library. I agree with a friend who tells me that when, at night, he puts out his library lamp, and turns the key in the door, leaving all the procession of saints, sages, warriors, and martyrs, the champions of freedom, truth, and justice, those who had been trampled down and failed, and those who have succeeded and been torchbearers to truth, leaving them all in a sort of sublime solitude and darkness, it is then he feels, more than in the working day, the true pathos of mankind, the deep mystery of time.

No sensible person can suppose for a single moment that everybody is born with the ability for using books, for reading and studying literature. Certainly not everybody is born with the capacity of being a great scholar. All people are no more born great scholars, like Gibbon and Bentley, than they are all born great musicians, like Handel and Beethoven. What is much worse than that, many come into the world with the incapacity of reading, just as they come into it with the incapacity of distinguishing one tune from another. To them I have nothing to say. Even the morning paper is too much for them. They can only skim the surface even of that. I go farther, and frankly admit that the habit and power of reading with reflection, comprehension, and memory all alert and awake, does not come at once to the natural man any more than many other sovereign virtues come to that interesting creature.

What I do venture to press upon you is that it requires no preterhuman force of will in any young man or woman—unless household circumstances are more than usually vexatious and unfavorable—to get at least half-an-hour out of a solid busy day for good and disinterested reading. Some will say that this is too much to expect, and the first persons to say it, I venture to predict, will be those who waste their time most. At any rate, if I cannot get half-an-hour, I will be content with a quarter. Now, in half-an-hour I fancy you can read fifteen or twenty pages of Burke; or you can read one of Wordsworth's masterpieces—say, the lines on Tintern; or, say, one-third—if a scholar, in the original, and if not, in a translation—of a book of the "Iliad" or the "Æneid." I do not think that I am filling the half-hour too full. But try for yourselves what you can read in half-an-hour. Then multiply the half-hour by 365, and consider what treasures you might have laid by at the end of the year, and what happiness, fortitude, and wisdom they would have en you during all the days of your life.

You may have often heard from others, or may have found out, how good it is to have on your shelves, however scantily furnished they may be, three or four of those books to which it is well to give ten minutes every morning, before going down into the battle and choking dust of the day. Men will name these books for themselves. One will choose the Bible, another Goethe, one the "Imitation of Christ," another Wordsworth. Perhaps it matters little what it may be so long as your writer has cheerful seriousness, elevation, calm, and, above all, a sense of size and strength, which shall open out the day before you, and bestow gifts of fortitude and mastery.

The possession of some books is a real necessity for all. I have had in my time in perambulating England, for political orations or other purposes, to mingle much among what are called the upper middle classes—I hate these distinctions of classes, but my meaning will be understood—and I was constantly appalled at the shocking trumpery I found on the shelves of those who were kind enough to entertain me on those occasions. Much talk there is of Shakespeare, of Milton, of Bacon, of Locke, and so forth; but how many copies of these authors, not to mention Burke and others, but of authors whose names are continually on our lips, are to be found in private houses? Not a quarter as many as might be expected. Of course, everybody who is able to possess anything beyond bread and cheese, clothing, and the wherewithal to keep a roof over his head, ought to possess some three, four, or five books: it is surprising how very few of the volumes are that contain the root of the matter in literature, the gems and pearls and fine gold of literature. It is a great mistake to think you cannot understand or enjoy the pleasures of literature unless you possess a library: a very few books will serve, if rightly chosen. It is a great thing to know such books, so that the world, past, present, and future, shall not be all cloud and chaos to the mind, without order, system, or significance. Those who know very little of the past and care very little for the future will make but a sorry business of the present. The present, or what Goethe called "this portion of eternity," concerns us most; but we shall not understand the present, nor have the means to deal with its problems and duties, unless we have some notion of the general order of the past and experience for the future. For the past you must know history.

The greatest lesson of history is the fact of its oneness; of the inter-dependence of all the elements that have in the course of long ages made the European of to-day what we see him to be. It is, no doubt, necessary for clear and definite understanding and comprehension to isolate your phenomenon, and to follow the stream of our history separately. But that cannot be enough. We must also see that this stream is the effluent of a far broader and mightier flood—whose springs and sources and great tributaries lay higher up in the history of mankind.

We are learning [says Mr. Freeman, whose little book on the " Unity of History " I cannot be wrong in warmly recommending even to the busiest] that European history, even from its first glimmerings to our own day, is one unbroken drama, no part of which can be rightly understood without reference to the other parts which come before and after it. We are learning that of this great drama Rome is the centre, the point to which all roads lead, and from which all roads lead no less. The world of independent Greece stands on one side of it; the world of modern Europe stands on another. But the history alike of the great centre itself, and of

its satellites on either side, can never be fully grasped except from a point of view wide enough to take in the whole group, and to mark the relations of each of its members to the centre and to one another.

Now, the counsel which our learned historian thus urges upon the scholar and the leisured student equally represents the point of view which is proper for the more numerous classes. The scale will have to be reduced; all save the very broadest aspects of things will have to be left out; none save the highest ranges and the streams of most copious volume will find a place in that map. Small as is the scale, and many as are its omissions, yet if a man has intelligently followed the very shortest course of universal history, it will be the fault of his teacher if he has not acquired an impressive conception, which will never be effaced, of the destinies of man upon the earth; of the mighty confluence of forces working on from age to age, which have their meeting in every one of us; of the order in which each state of society has followed its foregoer, according to great and changeless laws "embracing all things and all times"; of the thousand faithful hands that have, one after another, each in their several degrees, orders, and capacities, trimmed the silver lamp of knowledge, and kept its sacred flame bright, from generation to generation and age to age, now in one land and now in another, from its early spark among far-off dim Chaldeans down to Goethe and Faraday and Darwin, and all the other good workers of our day.

The shortest course of universal history will let him see how he owes to the Greek civilization, on the shores of the Mediterranean two thousand years back, a debt extending from the architectural forms of our buildings to some of the most systematic operations of his own mind; will let him see the forum of Rome, its roads and its gates—

What conflux issuing forth or entering in,
Prætors, Proconsuls to their provinces
Hasting or on return, in robes of state—

all busily welding an empire together in a marvellous framework of citizen-

ship, manners, and laws, that laid assured foundations for a still higher
civilization that was to come after.
He will learn how when the Roman
Empire declined, then at Damascus
and Bagdad and Seville the Mahòmetan
conquerors took up the torch of science
and learning, and handed it on to
Western Europe when the new generations were ready. He will learn how
in the meantime, during ages which we
both wrongly and ungratefully call
dark, from Rome again, that other
great organization, the mediæval
Church, had arisen, which, amid many
imperfections, and some crimes, did a
work that no glory of physical science
can equal, and no instrument of physical science can compass, in purifying
men's appetites, in setting discipline
and direction on their lives, and in
offering to humanity new types of
moral obligation and fairer ideals of
saintly perfection, whose light still
shines like a star to guide our own
poor voyages. It is only by this contemplation of the life of our race as a
whole that men see the beginnings and
the ends of things; learn not to be
near-sighted in history, but to look
before and after; see their own part
and lot in the rising up and going down
of empires and faiths since first recorded
time began; and what I am contending
for is that, even if you can go no farther
than the mere vestibule of this ancient
and ever venerable Temple of many
marvels, you will have opened the way
to a kind of knowledge that not only
enlightens the understanding, but en-
riches the character—which is a higher
thing than mere intellect—and makes
it constantly alive with the spirit of
beneficence.

I know it is said that such a view of
collective history is true, but that you
will never get plain people to respond
to it; it is a thing for intellectual dilet-
tanti and moralizing virtuosi. Well,
we do not know, because we have
never yet honestly tried, what the
commonest people will or will not respond to. When Sir Richard Wallace's
pictures were being exhibited at Beth-
nal Green, after people had said that
the workers had no souls for art, and

would not appreciate its treasures, a
story is told of a female in very poor
clothes gazing intently at a picture of
the Infant Jesus in the arms of His
Mother, and then exclaiming: "*Who
would not try to be a good woman who
had such a child as that?*" We have
never yet, I say, tried the height and
pitch to which our people are capable
of rising.

If a man is despondent about his
work, the best remedy that I can prescribe to him is to turn to a good
biography; there he will find that
other men before him have known the
dreary reaction that follows long-sus-
tained effort, and he will find that one
of the differences between the first-rate
man and the fifth-rate lies in the vigor
with which the first-rate man recovers
from this reaction, and crushes it down,
and again flings himself once more
upon the breach. I remember the
wisest and most virtuous man I have
ever known, or am ever likely to know
—Mr. Mill—once saying to me that,
whenever he had written anything, he
always felt profoundly dissatisfied with
it, and it was only by reflecting that he
had felt the same about other pieces,
of which the world had thought well,
that he could bring himself to send the
new production to the printer. The
heroism of the scholar and the truth-
seeker is not less admirable than the
heroism of the man-at-arms.

I understand that in the library at
Woolwich, which has been open for
three years, the proportion of books
issued is something like—fiction, 65
per cent.; history and biography, 15
per cent.; poetry, 7 per cent.; travel
and topography, 7½ per cent.; natural
science, 6 per cent.; and useful arts—
well, the rest. That is, using the word
in its technical sense, but under certain
circumstances I would call poetry useful, and even for the 65 per cent. of
fiction there is something to be said—
not, of course, for the trash which too
often takes the honored name of fiction.
I might justify the claim of poetry and
fiction to be classed among the books
called useful, as rousing and stirring
the imagination. Our prosaic lives
need all the stir and imagination poetry

and fiction can give. Can any one say
that it is a deplorable thing that so
much attention should be given to
Walter Scott, Dickens, Dumas, Thackeray, George Eliot, Jane Austen, Mrs.
Gaskell, and other admirable story-
tellers, not to mention living authors,
which might seem invidious? If fiction
takes a large place in a library, I do
not care so far as it promotes cheerfulness and good humor, for that is
wanted. Information is, of course, the
object of everybody, but cheerfulness
and good humor are as important as
any information, except information on
our own special calling. Of course, it
may seem deplorable that drama and
poetry should be in the proportion of
260 volumes to 3300 of fiction in a
public library, but it does not surprise
nor discourage me.

Characters in fiction live with us, and
are as much part of our lives as our
friends in our own street. Some of
the characters in fiction are as real to
us as the great characters in history.
Of course, our comparisons of men of
action with men of literature are idle
and meaningless: and when we are
told the world of books is peopled with
shadows, in a sense it is true—we are
all shadows. But the figures in books,
through which great ideas have been
launched into the world, characters
who exhibit human nature in large and
striking aspects, creations of poetry
and fiction—they are not shadows:
they are substance. Would any man
say that Napoleon Bonaparte is the
substance, but Goethe and Byron, his
contemporaries, mere transient shadows; or that Pitt, Fox, Canning, and
Castlereagh are substances, but Scott,
Shelley, and Wordsworth mere phan-
toms? It would be wrong to say any
such thing. These men are the directors of thought into the grooves in
which it moves: their books contain
substance; and there is far more that
is shadowy in the events of the lives of
great actors, to whom we rashly give
the name of reality and real history.
The great Duke of Marlborough said
that he had learnt all the history he
ever knew out of Shakespeare's historical plays. I have long thought that if

we persuaded those classes who have
to fight their own little Battles of
Blenheim for bread every day, to make
such a beginning of history as is furnished by Shakespeare's plays and
Scott's novels, we should have done
more to imbue them with a real interest in the past of mankind than if we
had taken them through a course of
Hume and Smollett, or Hallam on the
English Constitution, or even the
dazzling Macaulay.

A taste for poetry is not given to
everybody, but anybody who does not
enjoy poetry, who is not refreshed,
exhilarated, stirred by it, leads but a
mutilated existence. *I* would advise
that in looking for poets—of course,
after Shakespeare—you should follow
the rule of allowing preferences, but no
exclusion. I have heard people talk
of the claim of poets as of a contested
election; but one poet will appeal to a
man's mind where another will not.
Here I will say something which may
perhaps bring upon me a storm of
criticism from some of my friends. If
I were asked upon what poet should a
reader begin I would say Byron. He
was not the greatest of poets, but he
had daring, energy, and the historic
sense, with a loathing for cant in all its
forms. At the beginning of last century he was the great central inspiring
force of democracy on the Continent
of Europe; and when democracy extends its reading, and applies itself for
inspiration to poetry, apart from the
facts, needs, and demands of the day,
then Byron, I think, will once more
have his day.

. . . . . .

Knowledge is worth little until you
have made it so perfectly your own
as to be capable of reproducing it in
precise and definite form. Goethe said
that in the end we only retain of our
studies, after all, what we practically
employ of them. And it is at least
well that in our serious studies we
should have the possibility of practically turning them to a definite
destination clearly before our eyes.
Nobody can be sure that he has got
clear ideas on a subject unless he has

tried to put them down on a piece of paper in independent words of his own.

Various mechanical contrivances and aids to successful study are not to be despised by those who would extract the most from books. Many people think of knowledge as of money: they would like knowledge, but cannot face the perseverance and self-denial that go to the acquisition of it. The wise student will do most of his reading with a pen or pencil in his hand. He will not shrink from the useful toil of making abstracts and summaries of what he is reading. Sir William Hamilton was a strong advocate for underscoring books of study.

Intelligent underlining [he said] gave a kind of abstract of an important work, and by the use of different colored inks to mark a difference of contents, and discriminate the doctrinal from the historical or illustrative elements of an argument or exposition, the abstract became an analysis very serviceable for ready reference.

This assumes, as Hamilton said, that the book to be operated on is your own, and, perhaps, is rather too elaborate a counsel of perfection for most of us. Again, some great men—Gibbon was one, and Daniel Webster was another, and the great Lord Strafford was a third—always before reading a book made a short, rough analysis of the questions which they expected to be answered in it, the additions to be made to their knowledge, and whither it would take them.

After glancing my eye [says Gibbon] over the design and order of a new book, I suspended the perusal until I had finished the task of self-examination; till I had revolved in a solitary walk all that I knew or believed or had thought on the subject of the whole work or of some particular chapter: I was then qualified to discern how much the author added to my original stock; and if I was sometimes satisfied by the agreement, I was sometimes armed by the opposition, of our ideas.

I have sometimes tried that way of steadying and guiding attention; and I commend it to you.

Such practices keep us from reading with the eye only, gliding vaguely over the page; and they help us to *place* our new acquisitions in relation with what we knew before. It is almost always worth while to recall a thing twice over, to make sure that nothing has been missed or dropped on the way, or wrongly conceived or interpreted. And if the subject be serious, it is often well to let an interval elapse. Ideas, relations, statements of fact, are not to be taken by storm. We have to steep them in the mind, in the hope of thus extracting their inmost essence and significance. If one lets an interval pass, and then returns, it is surprising how clear and ripe that has become, which, when we left it, seemed crude, obscure, full of perplexity.

I need not tell you that you will find that most books worth reading once are worth reading twice, and—what is most important of all—the masterpieces of literature are worth reading a thousand times. It is a great mistake to think that because you have read a masterpiece once or twice, or ten times, therefore you have done with it. Because it is a masterpiece, you ought to live with it, and make it part of your daily life.

Another practice is that of keeping a commonplace book, and transcribing into it what is striking and interesting and suggestive. And if you keep it wisely, as Locke has taught us, you will put every entry under a head, division, or subdivision.* This is an excellent practice for concentrating your thought on the passage, and making you alive to its real point and significance. Here, however, the high authority of Gibbon is against us. He refuses "strenuously to recommend."

The action of the pen [he says] will, doubtless, imprint an idea on the mind as well as on the paper; but I much question whether the benefits of this laborious method are adequate to the waste of time; and I must agree with Dr. Johnson that "what is twice read is commonly better remembered than what is transcribed."

All this takes trouble, no doubt; but, then, it will not do to deal with

* "If I would put anything in my commonplace book, I find out a head to which I may refer it. Each head ought to be some important and essential word to the matter in hand" (Locke's "Works," iii., 308, ed. 1801). This is for indexing purposes, but it is worth while to go farther, and make a title for the passage extracted, indicating its pith and purport.

ideas that we find in books or else-where as a certain bird does with its eggs—leave them in the sand for the sun to hatch and chance to rear. People who follow this plan possess nothing better than ideas half hatched, and convictions reared by accident. They are like a man who should pace up and down the world in the delusion that he is clad in sumptuous robes of purple and velvet, when in truth he is only half covered by the rags and tatters of other people's cast-off clothes.

Apart from such mechanical devices as these I have mentioned, there are habits and customary attitudes of mind which a conscientious reader will practise if he desires to get out of a book still greater benefits than the writer of it may have designed or thought of. For example, he should never be content with mere aggressive and negatory criticism of the page before him. The page may be open to such criticism, and in that case it is natural to indulge in it; but the reader will often find an unexpected profit by asking himself: What does this error teach me? How comes that fallacy to be here? How came the writer to fall into this defect of taste? To ask such questions gives a reader a far healthier tone of mind in the long run, more seriousness, more depth, more moderation of judgment, more insight into other men's ways of thinking as well as into his own, than any amount of impatient condemnation and hasty denial, even when both condemnation and denial may be in their place.

Again, let us not be too ready to detect an inconsistency in our author, but rather let us teach ourselves to distinguish between inconsistency and having two sides to an opinion. "Before I admit that two and two are four," some one said, "I must first know to what use you are going to put the proposition." That is to say, even the plainest proposition needs to be stated with a view to the drift of the discussion in hand, or with a view to some special part of the discussion. When the turn of some other part of the matter comes, it will be convenient, and often necessary, to bring out into full light another side of your opinion, not contradictory, but complementary; and the great distinction of a candid disputant, or of a reader of good faith, is his willingness to take pains to see the points of reconciliation among different aspects and different expressions of what is substantially the same judgment.

Let me pass to another topic. We are often asked whether it is best to study subjects or authors or books. Well, I think that is like most of the stock questions with which the perverse ingenuity of mankind torments itself. There is no universal and exclusive answer. My own answer is a very plain one. It is sometimes best to study books, sometimes authors, and sometimes subjects; but at all times it is best to study authors, subjects, and books in connection with one another. Whether you make your first approach from interest in an author or in a book, the fruit will be only half gathered if you leave off without new ideas and clearer lights both on the man and the matter. One of the noblest master-pieces in the literature of civil and political wisdom is to be found in Burke's three performances on the American war—his speech on Taxation in 1774, on Conciliation in 1775, and his letter to the Sheriffs of Bristol in 1777. I can only repeat what I have been saying in print and out of it for a good many years, and what I believe more firmly as observation is enlarged by time and occasion, that these three pieces are the most perfect manual in all literature for the study of great affairs, whether for the purpose of knowledge or action.

They are an example, [as I have said before now], an example without fault of all the qualities which the critic, whether a theorist or an actor, of great political situations should strive by night and by day to possess. If their subject were as remote as the quarrel between the Corinthians and Corcyra, or the war between Rome and the Allies, instead of a conflict to which the world owes the opportunity of one of the most important of political experiments, we should still have everything to learn from the author's treatment : the vigorous grasp of masses of compressed detail, the wide illumination from great principles of human experience, the

strong and masculine feeling for the two great political ends of Justice and Freedom, the large and
generous interpretation of expediency, the morality,
the vision, the noble temper.

No student worthy of the name will lay aside these pieces, so admirable in their literary expression, so important for history, so rich in the lessons of civil wisdom, until he has found out something from other sources as to the circumstances from which such writings arose, and as to the man whose resplendent genius inspired them. There are great personalities, like Burke, who march through history with voices like a clarion trumpet, and something like the glitter of swords in their hands. They are as interesting as their work. Contact with them warms and kindles the mind. You will not be content, after reading one of these pieces, without knowing the character and personality of the man who conceived it, and until you have spent an hour or two —and an hour or two will go a long way with Burke still fresh in your mind —over other compositions in political literature, over Bacon's civil pieces, or Machiavelli's ''Prince,'' and others in the same order of thought.

From this point of view let me remind you that books are not the products of accident and caprice. As Goethe said, if you would understand an author, you must understand his age. The same thing is just as true of a book. If you would fully comprehend it, you must know the age. There is an order; there are causes and relations between great compositions and the societies in which they have emerged. Just as the naturalist strives to understand and to explain the distribution of plants and animals over the surface of the globe, to connect their presence or their absence with the great geological, climatic, and oceanic changes, so the student of literature, if he be wise, undertakes an ordered and connected survey of ideas, of tastes, of sentiments, of imagination, of humor, of invention, as they affect and as they are affected by the ever-changing experiences of human nature and the manifold variations that time and circumstances are incessantly working in human society.

We are constantly asked whether desultory reading is among things lawful and permitted. May we browse at large in a library, as Johnson said, or is it forbidden to open a book without a definite aim and fixed expectations? I am for a compromise. If a man has once got his general point of view, if he has striven with success to place himself at the centre, what follows is of less consequence. If he has got in his head a good map of the country, he may ramble at large with impunity. If he has once well and truly laid the foundations of a methodical, systematic habit of mind, what he reads will find its way to its proper place. If his intellect is in good order, he will find in every quarter something to assimilate and something that will nourish.

.   .   .   .   .   .

Literature does not end with knowledge of forms, with inventories of books and authors, with finding the key of rhythm, with the varying measure of the stanza, or the changes from the involved and sonorous periods of the seventeenth century down to the *staccato* of the nineteenth, or all the rest of the technicalities of scholarship. Do not think I contemn these. They are all good things to know, but they are not ends in themselves. The intelligent man, says Plato, will prize those studies which result in his soul getting soberness, righteousness, and wisdom, and he will less value the others. Literature is one of the instruments, and one of the most powerful instruments, for forming character, for giving us men and women armed with reason, braced by knowledge, clothed with steadfastness and courage, and inspired by that public spirit and public virtue of which it has been well said that they are the brightest ornaments of the mind of man. Bacon is right, as he generally is, when he bids us read not to contradict and refute, nor to believe and take for granted, nor to find talk and discourse, but to weigh and to consider. Yes; let us read to weigh and to consider. In the times before us that promise or threaten deep political, economical, and social controversy, what we need to do is to induce our people to weigh and consider. We want them to cultivate energy without impatience, activity without restlessness, inflexibility without ill-humor. I am not going to preach any artificial stoicism. I am not going to preach any indifference to money, or to the pleasures of social intercourse, or to the esteem and good will of neighbors, or to any other of the consolations and necessities of life. But, after all, the thing that matters most, both for happiness and for duty, is that we should strive habitually to live with wise thoughts and right feeling.

Oriental Definitions

Yogi

By MARGUERITE MERINGTON

A Yogi
Is a sort of holy fogy
That does not wash or shave :
His ways are rather logy
From living in a cave.

He dines off water, dates,
Cheese-parings, plaintain-rind,
Then sits and demonstrates
The Universal Mind !

YOGI

A Concord Note=Book

SIXTH PAPER

The Women of Concord—I.

By F. B. SANBORN

IN this part of my notes and recollections mention will be made of Mrs. Dr. Ripley, the grandmother of Emerson, and her daughter-in-law, Mrs. Samuel Ripley; of Miss Mary Emerson, the aunt, and Mrs. Lidian Emerson, the wife, of Waldo Emerson; of Mrs. Asa Dunbar, the grandmother of Thoreau, his mother, Mrs. Cynthia Thoreau, and his sister Sophia; of Mrs. Mary Wilder White and her friends, intimate at Dr. Ripley's Old Manse; of Mrs. Samuel Hoar, mother of the Senator, and her daughter, Miss Elizabeth Hoar; of Mrs. Bronson Alcott and her daughters Louisa and May; and of Margaret Fuller, the friend of most of these Concord families, although she never lived in Concord. Of these ladies, fourteen in all, I knew all but four,—the two grandmothers, Mrs. White, and Miss Fuller,—and of those I heard so much that I seem to have known them, although all four died before I ever set foot in Concord,—which, for the first time, was in April, 1851, while I was studying for Harvard College at Exeter, N. H. They represent three generations of active life in the little town which the genius of Emerson, Hawthorne, Thoreau, and Alcott has made so famous; they were all distinguished in their several ways, and half a dozen of them have been the subject of biographies, longer or shorter. Most of them lie buried in the village cemeteries of Concord, though but few of them were born there.

Madam Ripley (whose first husband was Emerson's grandfather, and who was Phebe Bliss, the daughter of Phebe Walker and Rev. Daniel Bliss, who preceded Rev. William Emerson in the Concord pulpit) was one of a family whose members were divided by the Revolution,—her brother, Daniel Bliss, having taken the English side in that contest, and another brother, Theodore Bliss, having been an officer in the Revolutionary army. She was born in what was then the Parsonage of the town (now the oldest house in the village), in 1741; the Old Manse was built for her in 1769, after she married her father's successor in the parish; at Rev. William Emerson's death, in 1776, she continued to occupy the New Manse; and there, in 1780, she married Rev. Ezra Ripley, her husband's successor; there, too, she died in 1825. Her second husband was ten years younger than herself; by both husbands she had eight children, of whom three were sons, and two of these were clergymen.

She therefore may be said to have belonged to the clergy herself—as, indeed, was sometimes claimed by her daughter, Mary Moody Emerson, who was born in the New Manse, now the Old one, in 1774, and lived to be almost ninety. Madam Ripley was a stately and cultivated lady, who saw much affliction in the separations and bereavements of her family. Her brother was exiled and his Concord property confiscated for his Toryism; her youngest son, named for his uncle, Daniel Bliss Ripley, who graduated at Harvard in 1805, and began law-practice in Boston, was involved in a duel, and left New England, never to return. He lived for some years at St. Stephens, in Alabama, and corresponded with his family at Concord. Her daughter, Sarah Ripley, often mentioned in the correspondence of her friend, Mrs. White, seems to have been wooed by Henry Wilder, who died young in the West Indies; Sarah remained unwedded, and did not long outlive her mother and brother. What I believe is the first mention of the

Old Manse in literature occurs in a letter from Mrs. Van Schalkwych (Mary Wilder), of the year 1803, apparently, in which she said:

"I passed last Thursday night at the Parsonage. Sarah Ripley and I remained in the west parlor two hours after the family had retired for repose. The night was remarkably fine, the air clear, and the heavens serene. The river had overflowed its banks, and presented a little sea to our view; its clear surface reflected every surrounding object softened by moonlight. You recollect the peculiar beauty of that prospect, especially when the river is swollen by rains. After contemplating it some time with still rapture, mine eye settled on the Balm-of-Gilead opposite the window. Perhaps you do not remember that tree; 't is not remarkable for its beauty or majesty, nevertheless it is to me one of the most interesting of inanimate objects; for under it I passed an hour the last evening I spent in Concord with my brother. Henry, Sarah, and myself, after strolling on the banks of the river, returned, and standing beneath the branches of the tree, Henry carved our names on its trunk. 'Before they are obliterated,' said he, 'we shall meet and renew them.' May you, my friend, never have the agony of believing that a being, dear beyond expression, was sacrificed for you."

This meeting of the three was in the summer of 1801, after Mary Wilder's first marriage, at the age of twenty, to a handsome and wealthy French planter of Guadaloupe, who died there, soon after her brother, in the winter of 1801-2, leaving his young widow in the midst of insurrection and disease. She returned to Concord a year after leaving it, and lived at her mother's house, which had been the Parsonage of Rev. Daniel Bliss, until her second marriage, to Judge White of Salem, in 1807. In the interval of her absence, her friend Samuel Hoar, the father of the Senator, had graduated at Harvard, with his classmates, Frisbie and Rockwood, for whom he named two of his sons, and had gone to Virginia as a tutor of the sons of Colonel Tayloe

of Mt. Airy, near Richmond. Her stepfather, Dr. Isaac Hurd, was the chief physician of Concord, and, after her period of mourning was over, Mrs. Van Schalkwych became the belle of the village. Judge Hoar, in his memoir of Dr. Hurd, says:

"Before her first marriage, and during her widowhood, she was the most distinguished of all the young ladies of Concord for beauty, grace, and sprightliness. The fascination of her manners and conversation made the hospitable mansion of Dr. Hurd a most attractive place to the young men of that day; and it has come down as a beautiful tradition to later times."

Among her friends and suitors were Frisbie and Rockwood, graduates of 1802, but she married White, a graduate of 1797, and lived with him at Newburyport till her death in 1811. But among her many female friends, none was more important than Mary Emerson, the elder half-sister of Sarah Ripley at the Manse. Their friendship began in 1803, and two years later this ardent and eccentric woman was described by Mary Wilder as the best sick-nurse in the world,—a character in which her later friends could hardly recognize her. She wrote:

"There are few offices so delicate and so difficult to discharge as that of *garde-malade*. Mary Emerson possesses just the firm decision, the patient vigilance, the animating faith, and the enlivening vivacity of mind and manner that fit her for it. I would describe the influence of religion on the mind, the temper, and the life of this uncommon woman,—but I despair of doing justice to it. . . . My dear Mary writes too much like other great people to be always legible; and she will not be surprised when I acknowledge I have not enjoyed the whole of her valuable manuscript."

It was not till after Mrs. White's death that Mary Emerson, then living in Boston, and taking some care of her young nephews, orphaned by their father's death, made the acquaintance and secured the devotion of Miss Sarah Bradford, who afterward became the wife of Rev. Samuel Ripley. This was in 1809. Long afterward, in 1844, Mrs. Ripley said:

"Mary Emerson, a sister of my husband, heard of me when I was sixteen, as a person devoted to books and a sick mother; sought me out in my garret, without any introduction, and though received at first with sufficient coldness, did not give up until she had enchained me entirely in her magic circle. She was then but thirty-five, she is now seventy, and still retains all the oddities and enthusiasms of her youth. A person at war with society as to all its decorums, she eats and drinks what others do not, and when they do not; dresses in a white robe these October days, enters into conversation with everybody, and talks on every subject; is sharp as a razor in her satire, and sees you through and through in a moment. She has read all her life in the most miscellaneous way, and her appetite for metaphysics is insatiable. Alas for the victim in whose intellect she sees any promise! Descartes and his vortices, Leibnitz and his monads, Spinoza and his *Unica Substantia* will prove it to the core. Notwithstanding all this, her power over the minds of her young friends was once almost despotic."

When this acquaintance was formed, in 1809, Miss Bradford, at sixteen, was already versed in Latin, had read Homer in Greek, and was venturing on Italian and French. To one of her schoolmates, the daughter of Rev. Dr. Allyn, the witty minister of Duxbury, she thus described her new friend: "Miss Emerson is a pious and sensible woman between thirty and forty years of age,—a sister of our minister. She was so kind as to make the first advances by calling on me; and from her society I expect to derive the greatest advantages; she appears extremely intersted in the religious improvement of the young." To Mary Emerson herself she used a more enthusiastic style, "With every rising dawn your idea is associated. The day no longer presents in prospect an unvaried tasteless round of domestic duties. Bright gleams of hope illumine the dull perspective." This enthusiasm was often

chilled by the harshness of her new friend's censure. I know of few mild answers more touching than this, after one of these occasions of censure:

"Dear Mary, the severity of your remarks drew a few tears, and shed a temporary gloom over meditation. But you will accuse me of pride again when I tell you an emotion succeeded somewhat like resignation for the loss of earthly friendship, at the recollection of being amenable alone to a higher tribunal,—though just and holy, yet infinitely merciful, — where an unguarded expression will not condemn. Have I led you to believe I consider myself faultless? I am daily conscious of much offence in thought, word, and deed; but I have not thought it necessary to pain or disgust you by the recital of defects I live only in the hope of amending. Dearest friend, remember that language of reproof much less harsh would find its way to the heart and conscience of your affectionate Sarah."

When I came to know both these remarkable women (Mrs. Ripley intimately), as I did in 1855, Mary Emerson was eighty-one and her friend Sarah was sixty-two; but they had retained unchanged their earlier characteristics. The younger, white-haired but still blooming in complexion, and youthful in all her sentiments, bore her weight of learning—far beyond that of Margaret Fuller, or any other of her sex in New England—with the modesty of a school-girl; while her ripened judgments, formed in the companionship of what was most thoughtful, advanced, and excellent in a very wide circle of friends, were those of experienced age. The elder woman had passed into some of the deformities of age, and did not quite merit that vivid description of her which her adopted niece, Miss Hoar, gave many years after: "She was a little, fair, blue-eyed woman, her face never wrinkled, and with a delicate pink color when past eighty (she was eighty-nine when she left this world), —a blue flash in her eyes like the gleam of steel,—yellow hair, which, however, was cut close, and covered up with a black band and a mob-cap." I should add to this that the band was apt to be awry, the expression of her features seldom genial, even when she took you into favor (as she did Thoreau, actively, and myself with more reserve), and what Miss Hoar calls "the eccentricities and necessities of old age" displeased at the first impression. But all this could not efface, nor much disguise, the singular activity of her unique mind, the vivacity of her conversation, or, when she chose to write well, the admirable vigor and point of her epistolary style. Her nephew Emerson, at whose house I first saw her, told me more than once that, in her prime, she was "the best writer in Massachusetts," —the Massachusetts, be it remembered, of Channing and Everett, of Bryant, Dana, and the *North American Review*. He added in his written sketch of her, only published after his death: "Her wit was so fertile, and only used to strike, that she never used it for display, any more than a wasp would parade his sting."

Nothing could be more descriptive of this side of her genius. Combined with what Emerson called his "fatal gift of perception," which was equally bestowed upon this aunt, and was an Emerson trait, handed down for generations, she was anything but an agreeable companion and housemate to those she did not affect. In a parable her nephew declares this, while asserting, as he well could, the high, erratic wisdom of her counsels:

"It is frivolous to ask, 'And was she ever a Christian in practice?' Cassandra uttered to a frivolous, skeptical time, the arcana of the gods; but it is easy to believe that Cassandra, domesticated in a lady's house, would have proved a troublesome boarder. Is it the less desirable to have the lofty abstractions, because the abstractionist is nervous and irritable?"

Acting on this disguised wisdom, with that prudence in secular matters which so distinguished him, Emerson, though he loved and venerated this aunt, and sometimes had her for a visitor, did usually, while I knew her, give her a fine room in the old ante-Revolutionary farmhouse, now the Antiquarian Museum, fifty rods from his own hospitable door,— to which, also, he often retreated for writing when the press of society became too great, and to which he sent the heroic John Brown of Osawatomie in 1857, when entertaining him at his table, for conversation. It was in this room that the celebrated conversation occurred with Mrs. Thoreau, of which Emerson makes mention, and which I heard reported at the time by Sophia Thoreau, in her mother's smiling presence. The regard Mary Emerson then (1856–57) had for the genius and the paradoxes of Henry Thoreau—so like and so unlike her own—was so marked, and was so reciprocated, that Mrs. Thoreau, who had known Miss Emerson all her Concord days, and sometimes had this Cassandra for a boarder, thought it proper to call on the lady in her farm-house parlor. At that time Mrs. Thoreau, who was hard upon sixty, had newly set up a cap with long yellow ribbons, which were matched by still longer bonnet-ribbons. Donning this headgear, and accompanied by Sophia, less showily attired, she walked to the Deacon Brown house, then managed by Mrs. Julia Clark, and was shown into the ground-floor room where Mary Emerson sat at her book of philosophy or religion. As they entered and saluted, Miss Emerson rose to her full height of four feet three inches, responded to the salutation, but closed her eyes. The call lasted the proper ten minutes, and Henry Thoreau was largely the theme. As his womankind rose to go, Miss E. also rose, and said: "Mrs. Thoreau, you may have noticed that while we were speaking of your admirable son I kept my eyes shut."—"Yes, Madam, I have noticed it."—"It was because I did not wish to look upon those ribbons of yours, so unsuitable at your time of life and to a person of your serious character." She then bade them farewell.

It was in this room that I called on her, and received from her a philosophical book then in vogue, by Morell, which she had read with pleasure, and had insisted that Thoreau should read and give her his opinion of it. She expected the same thing of me. Meeting her at Mrs. Emerson's tea-table soon after, where I was accompanied by my sister Sarah (to whom, some years after, I was indebted for a fortunate rescue from the hands of kidnappers), I asked how long I might keep her book. At the same time she criticised to my sister, and quite justly, if rather severely, the manners of a retired *sous-lieutenant* of Louis Philippe's army, who gave lessons in French and fencing to myself and some of my pupils. In course of the next day, I received from her this note, dated only "Friday noon," but probably late in 1856, which I retain as a sample of her handwriting at the age of eighty-two:

"SIR,—Keep the book as long as is requisite for your full acquaintance. My love to your sister, and tell her I regret sadly the imprudence I was guilty of, thro' a strange stupidity, in speaking of the French Instructor, respecting his manners. I know not the *least harm of his practice.* I beg her to forget what I complained of in his manners; it was a foolish gossip, for which I am willing to make full confession. And can trust her honor to conceal it.

"With good wishes I am yours,
"M. M. E.
"*Mr. Sandburn.*"

I was present in December, 1858, at a conversation of Bronson Alcott's in Mrs. Emerson's parlor (Emerson himself being absent, I think, on one of his lecturing tours, but represented in his own house, as he often was, by Thoreau), when Mary Emerson distinguished herself. Henry James, father of the novelist, two of whose sons were pupils of mine, was present. Not understanding the law of an Alcottian conversation, he began and continued to show his own wit by perplexing the subject with some of his questions and witty paradoxes,— much as if, at a parlor-wedding, some lively damsel should thrust herself into the place of the blushing bride. Alcott

fell into polite silence, and Thoreau, while contesting some of James's assumptions, could not check the flow of the semi-Hibernian rhetoric,—in which, as Thoreau said afterwards, James uttered "*quasi* philanthropic doctrines in a metaphysic dress, but for all practical purposes very crude,—charging society with all the crime committed, and praising the criminal for committing it." Miss Emerson heard this with rising wrath; but when, finally, James spoke repeatedly and scornfully of the Moral Law, her patience gave way. Rising from her chair at the west side of the room, and turning her oddly-garnished head toward the south side, where the offender smilingly sat, she clasped her little wrinkled hands and raised them toward the black band over her left temple (a habit she had when deeply moved), and began her answer to these doctrines of Satan, as she thought them. She expressed her amazement that any man should denounce the Moral Law,—the only tie of society, except religion, to which, she saw, the speaker made no claim. She referred him to his Bible and to Dr. Adam Clarke (one of her great authorities from childhood), and she denounced him personally in the most racy terms. She did not cross the room and shake him, as some author, not an eye-witness, has fancied,—but she retained her position, sat down quietly when she had finished, and was complimented by the smiling James, who then perhaps for the first time had felt the force of her untaught rhetoric.

Reading her letters in 1864, the year following her death, Emerson said in his journal (as he afterward said to me): "Aunt Mary is a genius always new, subtle, frolicsome, unpredictable. All your learning, Platonistic, Calvinistic, English, or Chinese, would never enable you to anticipate one thought or expression; she is embarrassed by no Moses or Paul or Shakespeare, after whose type she is to fashion her speech. Her wit is the wild horse of the desert." "Ah," she said, "what a poet Byron would have been, if he had been born and bred a Calvinist!"—as she had been. The first Mrs. Emerson, Ellen

Tucker, was a favorite of hers, and she was appreciated by her in turn. In the spring of 1829, soon after Emerson was installed in his Boston pulpit, Miss Tucker went South for the benefit of her delicate health, and on the way she seems to have been joined by Aunt Mary, then probably boarding with Rev. Dr. Howard at Springfield. In her journal, after mentioning Hartford, Miss Tucker wrote:

> We must leave [there] one who seems
> Like a vision in our dreams;
> She will dwell upon our mind.
> Flesh and blood so well refined,
> That one questions whether death,
> Wasted form, or loss of breath
> Will be in her path to Heaven,—
> All her body seems to glow
> With her spirit's action so.

I quote this from Dr. Emerson's notes (in the Centenary edition) to his father's Essay on Mary Emerson. Of the same year, 1829, but later in the season, was this letter of Waldo Emerson to his aunt, which was found by me long ago in the mass of family papers at the Old Manse, after I had ceased to live or visit there much, since the death of Mrs. Ripley and the dispersion of her household:

"BOSTON, Friday, July 31, 1829.

"MY DEAR AUNT:

"Pray tell me in letter whether yet you are in Concord, and how long you will stay, that I may peradventure snatch a day and come up. I read, with something more of profit than you might approve, the almanacs. [These were her diaries.] Before you charged me not to transcribe, I had copied off thus much, which I send. William [an elder brother] comes on August 15. You must surely stay, that you may have seen the whole generation.

"Ellen [Tucker] writes me every other day. She says she mends, but decides that I shall not come to see her till her mother comes and returns. And her mother stays, having been sick. I threaten to rebel and go, maugre the nurses.

"I am striving hard to-day to establish the sovereignty and self-existent

excellence of the Moral Law, in popular argument, and slay the Utility swine, —and so must run.

"Yours affectionately,

"R. W. E."

In other words, the young minister in Boston was writing his next Sunday's sermon, which was to maintain the sovereignty of Ethics, and scatter the forces of the Utilitarians, at the time very boisterous in England, and perhaps in Boston, which then always sneezed when England caught cold. When Alcott first heard him in Boston, the year before, the subject was the Universality of the Notion of Deity, such general topics being much in Emerson's line as preacher. Miss Tucker was still at the South, and it was then that Emerson addressed to her those fanciful lines, beginning,

> The green grass is bowing,
>   The morning wind is in it;
> 'T is a tune worth thy knowing,
>   Though it change every minute:
> 'T is a tune of the spring,
>   Every year plays it over;
> To the robin on the wing,
>   And to the pausing lover.

The wedding came in September, 1829, and in a little more than two years after, Ellen was dead. Emerson gave up his pulpit, went abroad for nearly a year, and there made the acquaintance and secured the lifelong friendship of Carlyle. His aunt rather frowned on this intimacy, and much distrusted Transcendentalism. In October, 1835, when she had been listening to Alcott's exposition of his new system of education, based largely on the early guidance of children into a knowledge of their own minds, she said it needed, to understand it, "a more composed head than mine, which was less composed than usual." She asked Alcott to make it plainer to her. "While the form dazzled,—while the speaker inspired confidence,—the foundation of the — the superstructure, gilded and golden, was in depths of, —I will tell you plainly what, when I am furnished more with terms as well as principles. No marvel that Age is at a loss to express itself about a system, theory, or whatever, which is proposed for Infancy." Yet she took great pride in her Transcendentalist nephew, even while repudiating his principles.

Mary Emerson was not thought at first to look with much favor on Miss Jackson of Plymouth, who in 1835 became the second Mrs. Emerson. Soon after the marriage she said to her, with the acid sweetness that she sometimes affected. "You know, Dear, that we think you are among us, but not of us." In truth, Mrs. Emerson held a position in religion midway between the gloomy but fading Calvinism of Mary Emerson, and the intuitive, ideal Theism of her nephew. She valued ancient forms, while she welcomed the newer and broader light beginning to shine through them. She was a stately, devoted, independent person, with something the air, when I knew her (the last forty years of her long life), of a lady abbess, relieved of the care of her cloister, and given up to her garden, her reforms, and her unceasing hospitalities. She had that regard for social observances which Mary Emerson scorned or forgot,—but she could free her mind in dissent or reproof with an energy that equalled Aunt Mary's, though without leaving a barb in the wound inflicted. Bronson Alcott, whom she knew well, and did not always spare in her infrequent censures,—for, like all generous natures, she preferred to praise or be silent rather than to blame in public,—drew her picture in this point very well, among those portraying Sonnets in which so many of his friends appear "vively limned," as old Marston says. After complimenting her for noble companionship, and native piety,

Embosomed in the soul that smiles on Fate,
Fountain of youth, still sparkling o'er the brim,—

Alcott goes on:

Then I recall thy salient quick wit,
 Its arrowy quiver and its supple bow,—
Huntress of wrong ! right well thy arrows hit,
 Though from the wound thou seest the red drops
  flow : .
I much admire that dexterous archery,
And pray that *sinners* may thy target be.

With many months and even years of invalidism, Mrs. Emerson, who was born in Plymouth a few months before her illustrious husband in Boston, outlived him by ten years, and saw her ninetieth birthday before she died, in November, 1892. She was a woman of excellent New England culture, and much practical good sense, for which she did not always get full credit ; of high aims and outflowing goodness of heart, showing itself in mercy towards all animate things ; and of a certain susceptibility on the side of the supernatural, which might be misunderstood by those who knew her but casually. She made no claims for herself, though strenuous for the causes she espoused ; but she went on her own intellectual and spiritual way, but slightly affected by the views of those about her, even of such as she loved,—and she hated no one. The tribute paid her by Thoreau, after living long under her friendly roof, was sincere and deserved. He said : "I thank you for your influence for two years. I was fortunate to be subjected to it, and am now to remember it. It is the noblest gift we can make ; what signify all others that can be bestowed ? You have helped to keep my life 'on loft,' as Chaucer says of Griselda,—and in a better sense. You always seemed to look down at me as from some elevation,—some of your high humilities,—and I was the better for having to look up." Along with this unassuming loftiness there went the considerate and the playful qualities ; and I have often been her partner at whist, which I dare say her poet-philosopher never was.

The Venality of Talleyrand

By JOSEPH McCABE

WHEN, a few years ago, it was gravely claimed in a serious American magazine that Prince Talleyrand was born and bred in Maine, and the son of an American fisher-girl, a few readers may have suspected at length the appallingly mythical character of many of the stories about him. His mother, a daughter of the Marquis d'Antigny, was not only a very well-known figure amongst the nobility of Paris, both before and after the Revolution, but was receiving a pension of sixty thousand francs a year from Talleyrand for some time before her death. His father was one of the most reputable and distinguished nobles of the court of Louis XVI.; his uncle one of the most venerable among the clergy of the Emigration and the Restoration. Not even Chateaubriand, the most venomous of his royalist enemies, ever breathed a suspicion about his title to the historic name of Périgord. Yet an American writer of repute has feverishly implored history to "purge itself" of Talleyrand's claim to high and purely French parentage by means of the idle chatter of a group of Maine fishermen of a hundred years ago.

The truth is that no distinguished actor in modern history has been so recklessly mythified as the great diplomatist. The biography of Talleyrand has generally been constructed on peculiar lines, and historians and literary men have fallen headlong into the snare. Professor Sloane, for instance, tells us that Talleyrand was, in his early clerical days, "a friend of the infamous Mme. du Barry, and owed his promotion to her." He has a facile justification in the fact that almost every biographer of Talleyrand, including Lady Blennerhasset, gives without reserve the story of his encounter with that lady. He is made to reply, when Mme. du Barry rallies him on his pensiveness, that "il est plus aisé d'avoir des femmes que des abbayes à Paris"; and Louis XV. is said to have rewarded

him at once with a Rheims *abbaye.* But the date of this conferment, as any inquirer could find in the *Gazette,* is September, 1775, or sixteen months after the death of Louis XV. and the disappearance of Mme. du Barry. The locality of the *abbaye* points obviously to the influence of Talleyrand's uncle, who was coadjutor to the Archbishop of Rheims. The story is a clear fabrication, and the acquaintance with Mme. du Barry wildly improbable.

With such lack of discrimination has the conventional picture of Talleyrand been pieced together. His whole career has been thickly overlaid with myths. This is largely due to the number and inventiveness of his enemies. Not only the groups of politicians that he left behind him when he passed from the old *régime* to the Revolution, from the Directorate to Napoleon, from the Empire to the Restoration, and from the Bourbons to the Orleanists, but rival diplomatists, embittered clerics, discarded subordinates, and others, have contributed to the mosaic. It is partly due, also, to the tradition of mystification which he somehow left behind him. In England and America this was not unnatural. When he visited London in 1792 and America in 1794, he was preceded by a reputation. One of the gayest figures of pre-revolutionary days, and hot from the crater of the volcano, he was expected to dance and gesticulate and emit electric phrases. Our grandfathers were not a little surprised when they were introduced to a pale, sedate, stolid-looking man, who returned their courtesies very briefly, and then fell into an almost impenetrable silence. It was known that he thawed somewhat in Fox's drawing-room, or in the little parlor of Moreau-St. Mery's book-shop at Philadelphia, but his general composure, his puffy rounded face and full figure, and his deep, deliberate, sententious speech disconcerted people. A myth of duality grew up about him, and it became the custom to accept without question all that was said of this quiet, grave, impassive man with the reputation for wit and license.

Whatever later research has done in the way of illumining the general character of Talleyrand, it is usually believed that the tradition of his singular venality has been established. This was one of the features that the general historian, and especially the Napoleonist, felt justified in regarding as beyond question. "Never was greed more dishonest than his," says Professor Sloane. Now, the judicious biographer would, if he felt compelled to use the word "greed" at all, rather put that there was never greed more honest than his. It is true that the historian might fall back on Sainte-Beuve. "La vénalité est la plaie de Talleyrand," says Sainte-Beuve, "une plaie hideuse, un chancre rongeur et qui envahit le fond." But he would discover on careful inquiry that Sainte-Beuve professed to have a "terrible doubt" about Talleyrand's complicity in the death of Mirabeau (one of the most frivolous charges ever raised) and other matters of the same weight. In this case Sainte-Beuve had positive documents to produce, a rare opportunity. These papers are the letters that the American Government published in 1797, and that constitute the chief ground of the accusation of venality. "They show," says Professor Sloane, that the French foreign minister attempted to "extort a bribe" from the American agents. I do not know how one extorts "bribes"—in England the language is opposed to it whether the law is or no—but will briefly examine the American documents.

The facts are that Adams sent three envoys to Paris in 1797 to adjust differences with the French Government. They were refused an audience, but were visited by three men, who were undoubtedly Talleyrand's agents, and who told them that the doors of the Foreign Ministry would be opened if they would pay $250,000 "for the Directors" and induce their country to lend France $6,000,000 on certain bad Dutch securities. After some nego-

tiation on this basis the American President recalled his envoys and published their despatches. Even these plain facts are sometimes twisted in the usual way. The recent Cambridge (England) history of the French Revolution puts it that the agents demanded $250,000 for Talleyrand and the $6,000,000 for the Directors!

Let us keep to the documents. As is well known, Talleyrand was at that time despotically controlled by Barras, the strongest and most corrupt of the five Directors. It is certain the bulk of the "bribe" would go to Barras; probable that he fixed the sum. However, I do not stress that. Talleyrand would certainly share the money. The more important and constantly overlooked circumstance is that the Americans were quite willing to pay the $250,000, and neither then nor afterwards expressed any resentment of it. This is made perfectly plain in their report. They wrote home that it was "according to diplomatic usage," and said they "might not so much regard a little money, such as he stated to be useful." They say, again, that it was "completely understood on all sides to be required for the officers of Government, and therefore needing no further explanation." There is not a whisper of moral indignation so far. It was the larger sum, of which Talleyrand would not have touched a cent, that roused America. This was regarded as a real extortion, a "tribute" to France, and was met with even warlike preparations.

It is needless here to discuss Talleyrand's (supposing that the blunder was his and not Barras's) unwisdom in trying to make this audacious bargain for his country. It is enough to note that the whole of the resentment was directed against a proposal which meant no profit to himself. Later writers have confounded the two, as some did in France at the time. But so little serious notice was taken of the matter at Paris that when Talleyrand resigned (on quite other grounds) in the following year, and wrote the only apologia of his life, he dismissed this subject in two lines. Professor Sloane thinks he was forced to resign "in consequence of his scandalous attempt to extort a bribe from the American envoys." He might have quoted Napoleon as his authority—his only authority—but he probably recollected that the ex-emperor's charges against people at St. Helena are not weighty. The resignation came long after the affair, and had no connection with it. Half the rhetoric expended on it would have been arrested by a patient reading of the official American version.

This affair is almost the only one in which we have authentic evidence of an attempt to extort money on the part of Talleyrand. It does not exhibit his character in an attractive light, but we may keep some sense of proportion, and not speak of "hideous sores" and "devouring cancers." Apart from the peculiar circumstances in which Talleyrand then was, he saw money offered and accepted on all sides. He had seen Mirabeau and Danton in the pay of the Court. He was to see Sieyès, who was so admirably indignant with him, take 400,000 francs from Napoleon on the 18th Brumaire. He was himself to pay out money to foreign ministers under the empire, and see Joseph Bonaparte bring bags of diamonds from Portugal. He had seen Pitt willing to give a secret commission of 10,500,000 francs during the Lille negotiations, but express moral indignation when a much larger sum was asked. Malmesbury had tried on his own account to buy the note of one of the Directors. Commissions were then common and were commonly exaggerated. Talleyrand was exceptional mainly in his opportunities; and in the fact that, as Baron von Gogern indulgently says, "he preferred to be paid in coin rather than with the usual presents and brilliants." And we must remember that it is quite unknown how far he was acting under the instructions of Barras. There is no other case in which he is known to have exacted beforehand, or stipulated for, a sum of money for a service to be done. In such an exceptional case we have a right to suspect the action of Barras.

The second serious authority that

Sainte-Beuve appeals to is Count von Senfft. The Saxon envoy at Paris was a friend and admirer of Talleyrand, so that his testimony is impartial. But here again Talleyrand's critics snap up the first word of accusation too eagerly. Senfft says that his Government gave Talleyrand a million francs in 1807 (at the same time giving half a million to a minor French official), and there is no need to doubt this. He also says, however, that Talleyrand made a good deal out of the Rhine Confederation, and used Baron von Gogern "in his financial relations with the German princes." Here we have another instance of the mere retailing of gossip. We turn to Von Gogern ("Mein Antheil an der Politik"), and we find him solemnly assuring us that, though he believes Talleyrand did make a lot of money somehow, "not a single bargain, or condition, or offer was made, either directly or indirectly, in regard to the Nassau and the many other princes that he admitted into the Rhine Confederation." Such are the foundations of this charge of phenomenally "dishonest greed."

For, after the American letters and the statements of Senfft, Sainte-Beuve has nothing but *on-dits* to offer in justification of his violent language. To quote Chateaubriand is hardly more scholarly than to quote the exiled Napoleon. When a friend gave Talleyrand a long account of the plot of *Les Martyrs*, ending with the remark that the heroes were eventually cast *aux bêtes*, Talleyrand promptly ejaculated: *Comme l'ouvrage*. Chateaubriand smarted under many such quips, besides his bitter resentment of Talleyrand's political versatility. He is hardly likely to have been scrupulous in reproducing the rumors that were current in Royalist circles. Sainte-Beuve tells us that Talleyrand himself estimated at sixty millions the sum he had made in commissions during his diplomatic career. He does not tell us when and where the admission was made. It may have been in one of the spurious letters with which discharged secretaries entertained an unexacting public. Finally, when Sainte-Beuve adduces Governor Morris as an authority he is trifling with us. Morris merely mentions the persistent rumor of Talleyrand's heavy gambling to dismiss it as "greatly exaggerated, if not false."

The case does not grow much stronger when we go from Sainte-Beuve to Bastide, another favorite of the critics. Bastide's work (one of the earliest biographies of Talleyrand) is an amusingly reckless tissue of gallant adventures and dark crimes. When he comes to deal with Talleyrand's venality, he quotes especially from a pseudonymous document of 1799, which ends with the charge that Talleyrand has by his immorality "outraged the morals of Republican France." Those who are acquainted with the morals of Paris under the Directorate will appreciate the indignation. From this judicious source Bastide gathers a number of definite charges of corruption. He has said that Talleyrand made thirty millions during the Directorate, but his specific charges only amount in all to fourteen millions and a half. And the list is too absurd for words. It includes $1,500,000 made by speculation on the Bourse during the Lille negotiations, and $2,000,000 as a share in the spoiling of neutral vessels by French pirates. The latter item may have grown out of the fact that during the American War of Independence, Talleyrand had, like most other Frenchmen with money, fitted out a privateer to raid British ships; but it does not appear that he made any profit. The list further includes $1,000,000 received from Austria for securing the secret articles in the Treaty of Campo Formio (with which Talleyrand had absolutely nothing to do) and $1,000,-000 for betraying these to Prussia. There may be some truth in a few of Bastide's smaller items, but from so tainted a source no responsible biographer would attempt to derive information.

A third and much more respectable biographer is Michaud, the most imposing of Talleyrand's critics. Like Sainte-Beuve, Michaud makes no attempt to conceal his intense dislike of the diplomatist, and is betrayed over and over again into the admission of stories that we now know to be anachronistic or otherwise disproved. Lady Blennerhassett has shown the incredibility of his statement (on no authority whatever) that Talleyrand concealed from Spain the fact of Napoleon having reduced its subsidy, and pocketed the difference (12,000,000 francs) for two years. In fact, Michaud contradicts himself, saying later on that the fact was only concealed for a few months. The whole story is grossly improbable, and entirely without support from the Spanish side. It is, as usual, a blank *on-dit*. Michaud also quotes one of Napoleon's angry allusions to Talleyrand at St. Helena, in which the Minister is said to have received $400,000 from the merchants of Genoa. The whole passage is a string of untruths and distortions. It opens with a denunciation of Talleyrand's marriage as "a triumph of immorality." The marriage had only been performed under compulsion from Napoleon himself. Talleyrand was theologian enough to know that the fact of the Pope secularizing him did *not* make free to marry. Moreover, Napoleon must have known well that Mme. Grand was not a wife, but a *divorcée*. Any evidence has been thought good enough to hang Talleyrand on. Michaud's other stories do not prove that Talleyrand received a cent.

Thus we find ourselves floating amongst a mass of contradictory and elusive rumors the moment we attempt to analyze the evidence for Talleyrand's "corruption." Specific charges take Protean shapes and slip away from us. One writer affirms dogmatically that Talleyrand made $3,000,000 out of the treaty with Portugal; the eager Bastide reduces the sum to $1,200,000; and Michaud is merely sure that Talleyrand made something out of that transaction. Senfft refers us to Gogern for an account of the sums he made out of the Rhine Confederation; Gogern denies that any money passed between Talleyrand and himself, but knows that

the diplomatist made money somewhere. Professor Sloane opines that
Talleyrand was in the pay of Napoleon
from the first; Lady Blennerhassett
finds that, when Napoleon sailed for
Egypt, Talleyrand *gave him* 100,000
francs. The contradictions are enormous.

Are we to suppose, then, that there
was little or no ground for the charge
of venality? By no means. The private fortune of Talleyrand would be
unintelligible unless we assume that he
received large sums of money in addition to his official salary. He returned
from America in 1796 almost penniless.
He held office under the impoverished
Directorate for one year, was again idle
for a year, and resumed the foreign
ministry under Napoleon at the end of
1799. He told the Prussian ambassador that he intended to make money.
He had a large establishment to keep
up, and was habitually generous with
money. One remembers the story of
his curling a young lady's hair at the
foreign office with thousand - franc
notes. He was foreign minister under
Napoleon for seven years only, yet
contrived to entertain on the most
splendid scale at his hotel and at
Neuilly. It is true that he spent or
gave away all he got. The loss of a
million francs in 1812 forced him to
sell his hotel and its furniture. He
sent money to emigrant clergy (who
had violently denounced him), provided generously for friends and relatives, gave his mother a yearly pension
of 60,000 francs. However, on the
whole, we must agree with Lytton that
his expenditure was far beyond his
ordinary income. In the treaties and
negotiations with which he followed up
the victories of Napoleon he probably
received generous *cadeaux*. Consider
his extraordinary opportunities! After
Marengo he had to negotiate treaties
with Austria, England, Prussia, Turkey, Bavaria, and Tunis, and give constitutions to Lucca, Genoa, Piedmont,
Switzerland, and Elba. After Austerlitz he had an even larger mass of
negotiations; his hotel was besieged
with the representatives of fifteen
sovereigns, and even the ambassadors

of Prussia and Austria were noticed
playing with his adopted daughter and
her lap-dog. At Vienna he was the
acknowledged champion of the smaller
states against the larger ones that were
ready to devour them.

There can be no doubt that he received money, a vast amount of money
in all, from the states that profited by
his diplomatic arrangements. But let
us be just to him. He was never
known to sell the interest of France or
any humane cause. "He could never
be induced," says Senfft, "even from the
most powerful motives of interest, to
favor plans that he regarded as pre-
judicial to the peace of Europe." At
one time the Poles put four million
florins in the hands of his friend, Baron
Dalberg. Talleyrand refused to further
their cause on the ground that it en-
dangered the peace of Europe, and returned the money. Senfft also points
out that his opposition to Napoleon's
schemes at the height of his power is a
proof of something very different from
what we usually call venality. "The
opinion he pronounced on the Spanish
business, bringing a fresh disgrace upon
him, will give him a glorious place in
history for ever." Baron von Gogern
says: "He sought first the honor and
glory of France and after that the
peace of the earth." As to his commissions the baron caustically observes
that "die Magnaten eines Eroberers
werden wahrscheinlich immer so den-
ken." He tells, too, how at Warsaw
Talleyrand once privately saved a German house from the vengeance of Napoleon, and refused to take a franc for
his action. After the Hundred Days
he gave away 459,000 francs, and pass-
ports to all who asked, so that Na-
poleonists might get away. Napoleon
had rewarded him with the principality
of Benevento. Here was an opportunity for a corrupt and greedy man.
But it is clear from Demaria's "Benevento sotto il Principe Talleyrand"
that his rule was one prolonged and
unselfish effort at reform through a
wisely chosen representative.

Talleyrand did not know what devotion to a personality, or a cause embodied in a personality, was. The

scandalous neglect of him by his family in early years on account of his lameness, their forcing him into the ecclesiastical sphere against which he had a natural repugnance, and his experience of the eighteenth-century Church from within, had brought about an atrophy of that faculty. Let us remember, too, that the personalities he was accused of deserting were Louis XVI., Barras, Napoleon, and Charles X. It is amply proved to-day that he was a sincere and enlightened liberal statesman a sincere patriot, and a sincere humanitarian. He deserted Napoleon deliberately in the hour of triumph on humanitarian and patriotic grounds. It is true that he sought to make money out of his position as minister of his country, in a degree that betrays some cynicism. It is equally certain that he was never bought, or bribed, or corrupted to betray the just interest of his country or wantonly to sacrifice the peace of any nation. He took in each case the diplomatic course that it was his duty to take; and *then* he claimed or received money from any state or individual that benefited by his course. He was not a great man. But he was something very different from the caricature that is still apt to disfigure the pages of historians.

Journalism the Destroyer of Literature

By JULIAN HAWTHORNE

THE interest we feel in wealth, as wealth merely, seems to have been increasing of late years; in every part of civilized life it is more or less manifest. Immense fortunes are still something of a novelty, and are managed awkwardly; and in various ways they create social unrest. The dollar is an unhuman thing, unindividual, unspiritual; it bestows power upon whomsoever has it, without regard to his personal virtues or frailties, gifts or vices; it gives ability to do and get things, but not to enjoy them. It may bring you death or life, and yet nothing could be more material. If we covet it overmuch, we incur a loss which no amount of dollars can liquidate.

Oliver Wendell Holmes, speaking through the mouth of his "Autocrat," utters playfully a philosophic truth when he says that the House of Man is built in several stories, each of which, in different moods and seasons, the man occupies. There is the material story, or plane of existence, the intellectual, the spiritual. Each has its indispensable function; but if we dwell exclusively in the lower, the higher become closed against us; the right order, which alone keeps all open and active, is to live from the higher through the lower; the reverse way proves impracticable. These several planes are not continuous, like greater or less, but are distinct, like cause and effect,—the mental impulse, for example, which causes a capitalist to corner a stock, sends a bullet through the brain of a man ruined thereby. Evidently, so far as society seeks wealth above other things, it shuts itself up in the lower planes, and shuts out the higher, or spiritual.

Wherever society abides, it uses a mode of speech proper to its state; and the mode of speech of the material plane is the newspaper. The characteristic utterance of the spiritual plane, on the other hand, is literature. But, owing to our unspirituality, literature for the time being languishes. Journalism, the lower voice, attempts to counterfeit the tones of the higher, but the result is counterfeit. So long as journalism attends to its own (material) business, it is not only harmless, but useful; but as soon as it would usurp what is organically above it, it becomes hurtful; not only because it does not give us what it pretends to give, but because the plausibility of that pretence may lead us to accept it as genuine, and thus atrophy the faculties whereby literature, the true voice of the spiritual, is apprehended. Let us· more closely examine this predicament in which we find ourselves.

The newspaper is splendidly officered, sagaciously managed, admirably done. It properly aims to tell the daily story of the material side of life. Never had it more influence than now; but this influence is no longer due—as in the old times of the London *Times*, and of Horace Greeley, and others—to editorial comment upon or interpretation of news, but to the news-columns themselves. The effect upon readers of this chronicle of our material condition and activities is insensible, or subconscious; but it leaves its trace on every aspect of civilized existence. And reciprocally, the reading community affects the tone of the thing it reads; we would not have such newspapers were we not such a public, any more than we could be such a public did we not have such newspapers. We are devoted to industry, commerce, trade, finance, and their corollaries; our government betrays a tendency to become one of the people, by and for capitalists. Our practical measure of a man is the degree of his material success; and it is accordingly the tale of success and failure, and of the conditions thereto appertaining, that the newspaper mainly imparts. Its spell is in the thing told, not in·the manner of its telling, which—save for the perfunctory accentuations of political partisanship and the dribblings of sentimentality—are presented as naked facts, and nothing more. For the newspaper, as a business enterprise, must avoid antagonisms with its vast and mixed audience; impassioned newspapers, however virtuous, being short-lived and of restricted circulation. The news—adorned with what photographs and head-lines you will—but the news free from dogmatism, bias, and the personal equation, is what the reader wants; and so arranged that he may readily pick out what happens chiefly to concern him, and skip the rest.

Now all this, useful in its own degree as it is, obviously involves no appeal to the spiritual affiliations of man,—carries no message to his soul. Yet so general and profuse is the distribution of the newspaper that a large part of the public reads nothing else, or what else it does read is (as we shall presently see) infected with the newspaper principle. The persistent reflection of the lower side of life, which the newspaper's mirror shows, gradually induces the reader to accept it as the whole of life,—prone as at best we are to ignore our higher selves,—with the result that heart and soul are atrophied, as aforesaid, and we are landed in a blank materialism.

But is not the newspaper an educational force?—does it not broaden a man, remove his prejudice, and abate his provincialism?—is it not a sort of university of general knowledge? If we catechize a graduate of this university, the result is not reassuring. The area of his available information is, indeed, unrestricted; but he is also free to select from it only what he fancies, and these are items which tend to inflame, rather than to dissipate, his provincialism and prejudices. Finding, too, so many things apparently incompatible offered for his belief, he ends by drifting into scepticism; while his sympathies are bankrupted by the very multitude of the appeals to them. Thus he acquires an indifferentism which is rather that of impotence than of philosophy; for the indifference of the philosopher is due either to faith in a state of being purer than the earthly, or else to a noble superiority to destiny; whereas the mind of the newspaper graduate has simply lost virility. Instead of mastery of marshalled truths, he exhibits a dim agglomeration of half-remembered or mis-remembered facts; and because the things he cares to read in his newspaper are few compared with those he skips, he has lost the faculty of fixing his full attention upon anything. His moral stamina has been assailed by the endless procession of crimes and criminals that deploys before him, often in attractive guise; and as for ideals, he may choose between those of the stock exchange, and of State legislatures.

Our Harvards and Yales may have their shortcomings, but they need not fear the rivalry of Newspaper-Row.

Yet we may admit that the chief danger of the newspaper to the public mind is its technical excellence. Its stories of a day are not only well printed and illustrated, but they are well written,—terse, clear, strong, and to the point; and not only have men grounded in journalism written good books, but in two recent instances at least a journalist has risen to the highest rank in literature. On the other hand, men of established literary standing contribute special articles to newspapers; and war correspondents have won a niche in the temple of fame, nor is it any fault of theirs that Manchuria has not brightened their renown. But if, by such means, waifs of literature be occasionally dragged neck-and-heels into a place where they do not belong, so much the worse for literature, and for the community thereby led to accept this abnormal miscegenation for a legitimate marriage.

Consider for a moment that literature is writing which is as readable and valuable to-day as it was a hundred or a thousand years ago,—a longevity which it owes to a quality just the opposite of that essential to journalism; that is, it lives not by reason of what it says, so much as of the manner of the saying. It is nature and life passed through a human mind and tinged with his mood and personality. It is warmed by his emotion and modified by his limitations. The emotion, while catholic and sympathetic, is also always individual; no one else ever felt or could feel precisely as this writer feels, though no reader but recognizes the feeling. Personal, likewise, are the limitations, due to the make and circumstance of his intellect and to the nature of the report to him of his senses. Any given work of literature is therefore unique, and, implicitly, sincere. It is a product not simple, but complex; not crudely put forth, but digested, assimilated, made part of the writer, given his stamp, signature, history, and heredity; not till then does it appear on his page. Like nature and

man, consequently, literature has an inward beneath the outward—a spirit within the letter; when you have read the words for the first time and seized their obvious meaning, you have not exhausted their message, or received the best part of it. Returning to it after an interval, you discover something that had at first escaped you; as your mood or degree of insight varies, so will fresh secrets disclose themselves. There ·are recesses within recesses, secret springs, something alive; and withal there is unity—the wholeness and symmetry of art.

The highest literature is that of imagination, though much true literature is not strictly imaginative,—Aristotle and Huxley, though not on Homer's or Shakespeare's level, wrote literature. Imagination is of all gifts the most human and mysterious; being in touch with the infinite in finite man, it is creative. Fact is transfigured by it, and truth humanized; though it is not so much as based upon invention, fancy may be its forerunner. Like all creative impulses, it is suffused with emotion,— with passion even,— but under control; the soul is at the helm. Imagination moulds and launches a new world, but its laws are the same as those of the world we know; it presents scenes of enchantment earth cannot rival, but laid in truth and wrought in reason,—transcending, but not contradicting what we call reality. The writer of imagination questions not whether his writing be true,—he knows its truth with a certainty transcending argument, feels himself the very instrument of verity, marches with nature and revelation at once, rhymes with them, and is conscious of the weight, might, and lift of their forces. He is as sure of his subject as of his own being, and never more keenly than when his sensible toil and pain are greatest, does he know the creative delight which is of the soul only. But the endowment is rare; implying independence or privacy of mind, a self-confidence that for the moment fears no criticism, and rises into oblivion of outward things. Moreover, works of true imagination often show a beautiful provincialism, as of one dwelling remote from the knowingness and commonness of current experience, who eschews the roaring market-place of multitudinous information, and withdraws to solitudes where appear to him the pure and vital sources only of life. These, after his own fashion, he pores over and uses, not conformably with vulgar sagacity, but under the light of his own wisdom. Thus we often find a wondrous simplicity and naïveté in the greatest imaginative work,—a sort of village flavor; which brings home to us humiliatingly but salutarily the tinkle and tinsel of our super-serviceable civilization.

Not all of these qualities are always present even in good literature, but the personal and the emotional always are, abiding even in the noble edifice of Bacon's "Essays," and in the quiet seriousness of Darwin's walk. On the other hand, though intelligence constantly shines on its path, not even the highest specific achievement of intellect can of itself be literature, since the greater the purity of intellect, the less is it individual, and its finest attainments are, as time passes, discounted or modified. Literature has its playgrounds, too, where it disports itself lightsomely as a child, but a child whose eyes sparkle with divinity that may at any moment bring to our own tears as well as laughter. Or it may seem preoccupied with sober descriptions of people and things; but in the midst of them we find ourselves subtly drawn toward magic casements, wherefrom, beyond boundaries of mortal vision, we behold the lights and shadows, the music and the mystery of fairy-land.

In all this, what is there congenial with bright, hard, impersonal, business-like, matter-of-fact journalism? Of course, it is physically possible to print in a newspaper (on the page which nobody looks at till after all the rest of them have been sampled) Keats's "Ode to a Nightingale," or a reprint, by kind permission of the publishers, of, let us say, Kipling's "They." It is physically possible thereupon to open our mouths and affirm, "The newspaper is a 'literary medium,' as well as a news-purveyor; and what more do we need?" Yes, we may go through the motions of harnessing Pegasus to a market-garden cart, and call the result a team; but Pegasus will not stay harnessed; out sweep those mighty pinions of his, and yonder he plunges into that fleecy cloud, aloft in the blue. He does not belong on the market-garden plane, and was not really there even when we were fastening the traces. Keats's Nightingale cannot be made to sing cheek by jowl with a soap advertisement, in the gas-light glare of Miss Makeup's Advice to the Love-lorn. Violently to bring these things together is not to unite them, though it *is* profanation; and the fate of the profaner is to lose his power of ever seeing the sunlit summits of the Delectable Mountains at all. In his spiritually blind state, it is given him to enjoy as supernal truths the artfully painted frescoes on the walls and ceiling of his St. Regis palm-room. They are hand-painted, and they cost money.

No; what lives in literature, dies in journalism,—the individual touch, the deeps of feeling, the second sight. But if not in newspapers, can we not find in magazines and weeklies the benediction of true literature? This brings me back to what I was saying just now about reading-matter which, though not journalism, has been infected by it.

The original magazine was what its name implies—a place for the storing of treasure—in this case, of a literary sort. Such were the English *Gentleman's*, *Chambers's*, *Bentley's*, and our own *Graham's*, *Putnam's*, and *Harper's*. The editing of these periodicals consisted merely in collecting and binding together a number of papers, stories and essays, of such goodness or badness as might be obtainable, and with no pretence of sorting them or harmonizing them into anything like a coherent organism. They were innocent of illustrations and of advertisements; there was not much money in them, or paid out by them; even Dickens's magazines would have been considered niggardly nowadays. But they did afford a mouthpiece for real writers, and not a few real literary treasures have first seen the light in their pages. But the modern conception of magazine editing began, perhaps, with the *Atlantic*, and rose to what it is to-day. It is a conception of a complex sort.

The editor has to keep before his mind the following things,—his readers, his illustrators, his writers, his advertisers. The first make the mare go; the second co-operate with the first, and are really the occasion of them; the third give the first encouragement in their good work, and appease the indifference which the second may feel toward the efforts of the fourth, who bring up the rear as handsomely as they may. There is nothing artificial in this situation; if the magazine was to exist, thus must the elements arrange themselves. The humor of the thing is that the writers, who actually come last in consideration, are theoretically first, and illustrators, readers, advertisers, editor, and magazine altogether, dance attendance upon them. Certainly, without their contributions the magazine could not exist except as the avowed picture-book, which, practically, it now is. The editor and the readers, again, are obviously created by the prior existence of reading-matter; while the advertiser advertises because the sale of the reading-matter (with illustrations) enables him, by its circulation, to reach buyers. It may also be true that many persons buy magazines mainly for the pleasure and profit which they derive from the advertisements; but that is a side-issue. And the fact remains, that an article which can serve as a pretext for illustrations has a better chance of being seen by the world than one which cannot; in other words, literature, *quâ* literature, is not, from the point of view of the business-office, and, implicitly, of the editor, the feature of the periodical most vital to its success. And if it be objected that this cannot be the case in magazines which are not illustrated, we are brought to another of the complications which modern editing involves.

The editor, with respect to his liter-ary material, must consider two things; the first being whether any given contribution is up to the literary standard (whatever it may be) of the particular magazine for which he is responsible. This standard is, of course, fixed by the taste of the class of readers which the magazine is supposed to address; the article must not be either above or below their heads, or alien from their sympathies, or offensive to their moral or other prejudices,—and there are other considerations too obvious to mention. But, having made the best guess he can on these points, the editor cannot wholly ignore his individual preferences; or even should he succeed in so doing in some special instance, yet in the long run his personal equation will betray its influence.

But this is not the only or the chief element in the case; for, in the second place, the editor must determine whether the article, being otherwise satisfactory, will harmonize with the other contents of the issue of the magazine in which it is to appear. His assumption is—and has to be—that the magazine will be read through by its purchaser from the first page to the last; and his artistic instinct, as an editor, demands that there shall be in its pages such a compromise between variety and unity as shall produce upon the reader's mind an effect at once stimulating and satisfying. This is necessarily a matter in which no technical merit in a volunteer contribution can have weight. Suppose the contribution to be a signal work of genius, and therefore intrinsically most desirable,—its very brilliance will make the rest of the magazine look like blank pages, and the editor must consequently reject it. And the better—the more conscientious—the editor is, the more will he feel bound to turn back what is good, because it happens not to be the kind or the degree of good that matches with the rest of his product. In the interest of the artistic proportions of the magazine, he shuts his door against the artistic excellence of the writer. Of course this difficulty may be avoided if the editor have ordered from the writer the kind of article he wants; and this is often done; but there remains the drawback that an ordered article is apt not to turn out to be literature. Every other merit may be preserved; but the literary touch—that, somehow, has vanished. The Muse would not come to terms.

Even in an un-illustrated magazine, therefore, literature cannot count upon a welcome. No doubt there comes now and then a genius, favored both by nature and by destiny, who overrides all rules, and introduces a new era; but we must regard the average lot. And there is still another stumbling-block in literature's path, which brings us round once more to the influence upon literature of the newspaper.

The newspaper is the characteristic voice of the age; and the age cannot have two characteristic voices. And the success of the newspaper, its enterprise, its dashing invasion of fields beyond its legitimate sphere, have compelled the magazines, each in a greater or less degree, so to modify their contents as to meet this novel rivalry. They try to handle "timely" subjects, to treat topics of the day, to discuss burning questions. Such things are impossible to the literary spirit; but writers are not lacking, and their work is often masterly—on its own plane, which is that of the newspaper. Important uses are served; but they are not literary uses. Fiction does not escape the infection; the class of stories which is upon the whole most acceptable in magazines has to do with current domestic and social problems, and with the dramas and intrigues of business. The interest is sustained, the detail is vividly realistic, the characters are such as you meet everywhere, the whole handling is alert, smart, telling, up-to-date;—but where are the personal touch, the atmosphere, the deep beneath deep of feeling, the second sight, the light that never was, on sea or land, the consecration, and the poet's dream? What has literature to do with these clever stories? You may read the entire contents of a magazine, and all the articles seem to have been the work of the same hand, with slight variations of mood; and next week,

how many of them all remain distinct in your memory? The market-garden cart has come to market, drawn by neat and serviceable nags; but Pegasus is aloft yonder above the clouds, where he belongs. Everybody can write nowadays; but the literary geniuses are as rare as ever, and never before had such difficulty in getting a hearing. The newspaper spirit has banished them, and has closed above us the gates of the spiritual plane.

The reason we are not producing literature is that we are preoccupied with other matters, and do not want it. But whether or not we want it, we need it profoundly; and the inevitable swing of the pendulum will bring it back in due season. There are already symptoms, if one will give heed to them, of discontent with the dollar as the arbiter of human life, of weariness of wars of traders, both on the floor of 'change, where the dead are suicides, and on the field of battle, where Japanese and Russian peasants kill one another in behalf of rival pawnbrokers. There is a longing to re-establish humanity among human beings, both in their private and their public relations; to turn from the illusion of frescoed and electric-lighted palm-rooms, and to open our eyes again to the Delectable Mountains, with their sun and moon and stars. The premonitions of such a change are perceptible; and, along with them, a timid putting forth, here and there, like early spring buds upon the bare boughs of winter, of essays, sometimes in fiction, sometimes otherwise, which possess quite a fresh aroma of the spiritual genius. Some of them arrive from over seas, some are of native culture. They are at the polar extreme from the newspaper fashion, and for that reason the more significant. They have a strange, gentle power, which many feel without understanding it, and love they know not why. These may be the harbingers of a new and pure literature, free and unprecedented, emancipated both from the traditions of the past and from the imprisonment of the present. Man cannot help himself, but is succored from above.

Women and the Unpleasant Novel

By GERALDINE BONNER
Author of "The Pioneer," etc.

A SHORT time ago a writer in the literary department of a London paper made the bold assertion that "the most unpleasant books were written by women and their readers were principally among women."

It was an accusation that possessed enough of truthfulness to give it sting. The vitriolic quality bit sufficiently deep to call out a retort here and there, denials from one of the accused or an anonymous partisan, and assent from those who, though they thought the matter written by lady novelists was often of a hectic and unconventional nature, had evidently carefully perused it. They recalled to mind Dr. Johnson's reply to the lady who said she was so sorry to see he had put all the wicked and improper words in his dictionary—"And I am sorry to see, Madam, that you have been looking for them."

This is not the first time such a charge has been brought against the Lady Novelist. It is an old story. She has been the object of this particular reproach since she first took to writing. And one cannot deny that for such a tender and delicate being, whose influence upon the coarser male of the species leads him upward and onward, she has a curious predilection for subjects which are morbid, unpleasant, or of a sultry, equatorial warmth. George Sand, in her long series of novels of hysterical sentiment and lawless passion, was not merely giving expression to her own untrammelled temperament, — she was acting the pioneer in that particular field of emotional exposition where the woman's talent seems to run,—she was blazing the trail.

When Byron wrote about love being an episode with a man while it was "woman's whole existence," he was probably making his deductions from his own personal observations. To love Byron was doubtless an engrossing experience, and even if the *grande passion* were not to last to the confines of eternity, its victim said that it was and evidently believed she was telling the truth. What Byron probably did not think of was that his aphorism was equally applicable to women in other departments than simply as an adorer of himself or some other beloved male object.

Love, in some form or other, is beyond doubt "woman's whole existence." It may be as the adoration for one especial, segregated being, or it may be for several of them advancing into her life and passing through it in detached Indian file. It may be as a mother, the absorbing, life-filling love of offspring that goes on through progressive stages of evolution strengthening as it advances. It may be as a sister, as a child to a parent, as a friend. But except in rare cases, it is present in some form, an influencing, directing, obsessing preoccupation. The self-sufficing woman is a rarity, a deviation from accepted standards, what in botany is called "a sport." The normal female finds the fulfilment of her being in the cultivation of and relinquishment to some absorbing affection. Nature created her for it, and if Fate has diverted her from it she will try to make up for the loss in futile, pathetic ways—take to pet dogs, or adopt orphans.

Naturally the woman writer's talent turns to the exploitation of this dominant characteristic, follows the line of least resistance. She is not only drawn to the regions of sentiment and passion by observation and experience, but by an instinctive sympathy with, an intuitional knowledge of, the complications that arise there. It is her sphere, the place where she feels herself at home among comprehended, familiar things. She has a subtle, understanding insight into the romances, hidden or expressed, of the feminine life—the peaceful, legitimate ones of home, husband, and children, the wild, storm-shaken ones of those who are a law unto themselves.

She is indifferent to the great outside questions of the epoch. The commercial developments of recent years—looming into such huge predominance in the life of to-day—are matters of inferior moment. Women do not write convincingly or with authority of financial matters, of politics, of business. If they treat of such a momentous happening as a strike it is as it comes against or effects the indoor, feminine existence. A collapse on the stock market, which has its own romance, will not draw from them words of such eloquent sincerity as the refusal of the lover or the betrayal of the maid. A bank failure, unless its reaction upon some one can be shown in the intimacy of a domestic drama, will be a matter of far less flurried consequence than the birth of a baby. Politics—the game of kings—is in their eyes as nothing compared to the game of love. The Boss, with his tenebrous power, is a figure of no vital import compared to the lover who comes sparking in the dusk.

It is true that there have been strong, adventurous women who have tried to extend their spheres and intrude into the men's territory. They write about stocks and strikes and politics and they write cleverly, with an affectation of bluff, manly hardness, a sort of swagger, which gives one a mental vision of them with their hands in their breeches pockets and silk hats on the backs of their heads. But this assumption of masculine knowingness is only a clever *pastiche*. It does not sound genuine and is not conducive to the creation of interesting narrative. Has any woman ever written a good novel—that is, one that the reader peruses with unflagging attention—the pivot of which was a great political intrigue, or a great financial transaction? There is matter for romances in both these departments of modern life, but not sentimental romances, not the romances that arise from the bestowing of hearts and hands.

Even such strong, original spirits as George Eliot and Charlotte Brontë,

women who had a virile force of intellect and power of expression, weakened when they came to the "male" part of their books. The political side of "Janet's Repentance" is dull; one wants to skip; and so it is with "Middlemarch." In "Adam Bede" it is the story of Hetty and the tongue of Mrs. Poyser that charm us. In "Daniel Deronda" it is Gwendolen and her fate. It is to the feminine and passional element in each novel that we give, not so much our admiration, as our interest, our avid eagerness of attention. So with Charlotte Brontë. The earlier part of "Shirley," where the difficulties with the mill hands and owners are so clearly set forth, has not that same gripping power which distinguishes everything that has to do with the heroine. It is Shirley, and particularly Shirley and her love affairs, that absorbs us. We read rapidly on to get to her, glance ahead to see when she is coming on the stage again, and bear with the quarrelling curates and the long-winded mill owners to hear something more of a young girl and the men who are her swains.

The domestic environment to which women are thus restricted for their material is an unfortunately circumscribed area. With indefatigable industry they have worked it in every direction; no field was ever more thoroughly cultivated. Every situation that can develop in the Home Circle and on the Domestic Hearth they have studied and treated. No complication rising from the course of true love has escaped their diligence. They have chronicled the life of the virtuous and well meaning, from the palace where worthy royalties reign to the hovel where peasants lead a poor but honest existence. In this *milieu* there are no secrets hidden from the Lady Novelist. She has plucked out the heart of its mystery and studied it under a magnifying glass.

The result is not only that respectable domestic life, as a background for fiction, has been worn threadbare, but its exploiters have lost all illusions as to its romantic and glamorous properties. They have revolted against it as dull, *banale*, philistine. It represents to the English mind Clapham and Sunday tea, and to the American suburban flats, commutation tickets, and the servants' Sunday out. We all know that genius can transmute the dun web of every-day life into an airy, prism-shot fabric beautiful as the Lady of Shalott's web; but then a genius does not happen very often. Even among the Lady Novelist's they are rare. And to these artificers in sentiment, expositors of the inner life of the most highstrung of created beings, every-day existence with its well-stocked larder, its well-filled purse, its untempted virtue, its unpicturesquely sound digestion, and sane satisfaction with this best possible of worlds, is not the stuff of which dreams are made—the splendid, rainbow dreams to which the ardent imagination of the Lady Novelist seriously inclines.

It is outside the home corral, beyond the walls of the Queens Gardens, that the wide, mysterious world lies where things happen that are not always perfectly pleasing and proper. Here hearts are sometimes ill-regulated organs, courtship is not invariably carried on in parlors with a chaperon in the next room, and married ladies have been known to prefer other than their rightful lords. Here are the people who make romances, who "strut and fret their hour upon the stage" as players in a drama where the tension is high, the action sensational and spirited. Here there is "many a weed, and plenty of passions run to seed." Here is the *Pays du Tendre*, the Sea Coast of Bohemia, and all the other strange, beguiling places, inhabited by delightful, unconventional beings who are everything but humdrum, and whose lives, whatever else they may be, are never dull.

And it is here that the Lady Novelist seems to find her best material—or let us say the material that she finds best suited to her mental structure and her point of view. She is romantic and here there are romances. They are the sort of romances with which she is sympathetic; not those of modern business life. The heroine is

not the daughter of the heartless Monopolist, nor the hero the proud, young Socialist destined to conquer him. Montague and Capulet may lead roaring factions, but they are not the heads of rival political parties. The battles that take place are not the giant combats of Trust Magnates. It is a place where the woman's life is much more to the fore than it is anywhere else in the world, even in modern America. All that pertains to heroines—what makes them sad and what makes them happy—is set forward in a foreground which is somewhat out of focus. The rustle of their skirts is always in the air, and sometimes the scent of perfumery is almost too heavy and gives to the surroundings a suggestion of something unaired and artificial.

That the material the Lady Novelist finds here is often morbid, frequently unpleasant, and sometimes improper, is only too true. With her temperamental bias toward the feverishly intense and her endeavor to escape from the familiar flatness of the purely domestic, she goes to the other extreme and chooses subjects that frequently surprise and occasionally shock her readers. Men do not seem to understand the reason for this deviation and accuse the woman writer of a natural predilection for matter of the "Speckled Peaches" variety, and the woman reader of aiding and abetting her in her breach of good taste. What the man does not see is that the majority of such subjects have a vital bearing on the lives of women. The authoress chooses them as something of real tragic import, the reader devours them as bearing on questions that are of close and intimate reality. Such dramas of the female life as Sara Grand treated in "The Heavenly Twins" seem febrile and unhealthy to the man's less restricted and more open-air experience. But he does not grasp the deadly significance of such a situation to the woman, who, in close proximity, too helpless or too timid to escape, has every detail of its obnoxiousness forced upon her observation and ground into her consciousness.

These subjects have a deathless,

vital interest to women. They have burned scars into their lives for centuries. They have the force of old grievances, long-endured wrongs. That a woman should write and other women should read such a book as "Pigs in Clover" shows the extent of this interest and its capacity to dull all squeamishness and delicacy of taste when the subject deals with amatory, feminine complications. A book like "The Daughter of the Vine," the story of which is the downfall through drink of a woman, is the last note of morbid repulsiveness. Its author has selected one of the most unpleasant of themes and "written it up" with a grim, deliberate functuousness of detail. But women have read it, not for its attractiveness, but as a grewsome picture of a dreadful doom that has wrecked lives known to them and sometimes dear to them. In "The Maternity of Harriott Wicken" Mrs. Dudeney showed the vagaries of the maternal instinct, roused from apathy by the realization of a child's infirmity. To women the unpleasantness of this book is balanced by its insight into a situation of the profoundest importance. The relation of mother and child, written of with understanding and sympathy, redeems it of all taint of unwholesomeness. It is a world-old subject; the last word will never be said of it.

No one can deny that the readers of books of this kind are women; as the writers of them are women. But it must be remembered that they read them, not as men do for recreation and diversion, but seriously as matter which bears on their own immediate affairs. They read them somewhat as they read cook-books, and fashion papers, and magazines for mothers, with almost the reluctant respect that is given to educative literature.

They are not lightly or casually interested in them, but absorb them with gravity, giving a profound mental consideration to their morbid psychology, their close, unaired view of life. Not only the choice of feminine subjects, but the feminine point of view from which the subjects are treated, gives them the grasping charm of the known and familiar. Women have written them from their own experiences and observations. They have bubbled or dripped out of female hearts, and to female hearts their message goes. No wonder the man feels himself an embarrassed outsider when he intrudes into this symposium of feminism. These Eleusinian Mysteries are not for his profane and uncomprehending comments, his unenlightened and ignorant derision. He has no place there. Clodius at the festival of the Bona Dea was not more awkwardly *de trop*.

By the Hill of Dan

By CLINTON SCOLLARD

MARIE, I wonder if you recall,
  Conning the past like a written scroll,
That day, the goldenest day of all,
  And the long rest under the giant bole
  Where the singing Banias waters roll?

Over the bough-tops the blue of noon—
  A Syrian sapphire shot with gold—
Quivered and burned; and a lyric rune
  Stirred in the leaves, and the bulbul told
  Its pleading, passionate love-tale old.

On a curious web of Kermanshah
  Our tempting mid-day feast was spread;—
Figs from the dale of Derdera,
  The white rice cakes and the barley bread,
  And the Lebanon vintage amber-red.

Then afterward, in the plane-tree shade,
  How we sat and talked of the coming years,
While the carelessly tethered horses strayed
  Afar through the thicket of bamboo spears,
  And the dragoman stormed at the muleteers!

We have followed fate, and we meet no more,
  And I know not whither your footsteps fall;
But when spring returns, and the swallows soar,
  I often wonder if you recall
  That day, the goldenest day of all.

What We Read to Children

By ADÈLE MARIE SHAW

Way out yonder
Is the land of Wonder-Wander.

THE days when Puritan babies died of too much religion and too few flannels are now so far in the remote that we reproduce them only for the tragedy of contrast, since, however the carper may be justified of his carping, it is safer to over-amuse the babies of to-day than to let them "perish in prayer and praise" from a world of discipline that tempts none of them to stay.

Not that creed or climate ever killed the art of story-telling. Many there be who hold that Mother Goose was a Bostonian, and in frozen Finland no less than under Porto Rican palms stories have been told to little children.

Now that these tales, old and new, have been gathered into books, they seem to overflow the world. Variously printed and pictured they heap themselves upon department-store counters and stare from the book-shop windows for the confounding of well - meaning aunts and prowling uncles. They are "classic" and trashy, painful and pretty, good, bad, and commonplace, and the most remarkable of all are those intended to be read to the child before he can read to himself.

Even in days before their numbers were so great, what resources things read to us provided for reminiscence! Pictures stamped on linen pages of Father Tuck, colored prints whose gorgeousness crayons could not rival, have outlasted in memory greater works. Maturer classics have faded from mind before the tragic idyl where "In the barn a little mousie ran to and fro" till kitty "caught the little mousie, long time ago."

Perhaps the grown-up's first thrill of real poetry came from

Little white lily
Sat by a stone,
Drooping and waiting
Till the sun shone.

He had to stand on tiptoe to follow the lines with the book laid flat upon his mother's knee. Afterward, although it had no picture, he could find the place and "read" it himself, from the big letters at the top to the dab of small print that stopped it, a little way down the right-hand page. It sang itself in his head, always with the sound of his mother's voice.

If he be a certain kind of grown-up his first memories of Mother Goose return to him in songs sung by that same voice with "Bobby Shafto's Gone to Sea," "Billy Boy," "The Old Crow," "Cockoo-Cucko-oo," and "Hush, my child, lie still and slumber."

The love of rhyme and verse comes into being with the first breath and outlasts mumps and measles, cold days and wet. The companion demand to "Wead it," which is always "Sing it," persists unwearied through many seasons. The supply is beginning to meet that demand. Stevenson and Eugene Field have both been given melodies, and this is well, for if there were no notes ready for their words, then, in every enlightened household, airs not so good would have to be made to order. Lydia Avery Coonley's "Singing Verses for Children" makes a home richer, and Weedon's "Bandanna Ballads" are a charm for keeping the restless spirit laid when sleepy time brings no sleep.

Whether it be "Tell Aunt Rhoda" or a song more modern, some verse and some melody a child should have. The "April Baby's Book of Tunes" contains both, and a good story to boot. It combines with much seduction the song and the story, the old and the new, and it must be read or read and sung from cover to cover with great frequency. There should be a large and obliging family of adults wherever it appears. That the real April baby's comment on the tale is said to have been "What silly babies and what a silly mummy!" does not matter in the least.

In song or story the responsibility of the grown-up is not light. It is not necessary to go back to Cotton Mather and his idea of a children's book ("Some Examples of Children in whom the Fear of God was remarkably Budding before they died: in several parts of New England") to discover a deal of infant literature worth expurgating or forgetting. The worst of many of even the good stories is that one must forever adapt, omit, or change as one reads. Bad English one can amend. " ' *Will* I bring it to Mama?' asked Georgie, picking up the *teeny* shell," or even "*Was* you ever in the beautiful mountains?" may occur in an otherwise "pretty story" and the skill of the reader is not greatly tested, but an evil moral is quite as frequent and not so easily amended. The Jack-the-Giant-Killer heroes who win by lying only, the dreary commonplace of much of Hans Andersen, will bear cutting or cheerful comment. Kipling's butterfly who wins by falsehood, the nine hundred and ninty-nine imprisoned wives denied even the diversion of scolding, the legendary precedent for the stoning of cats, require delicate handling.

But not the handling of a prig. A child must have legends, fairies, marvels. All the worse for him if he must take the husk with the corn, if he belong to a race of imbeciles who never "skip" but march straight from frontispiece to finis, "conscientious " and unenlightened.

Such people have neither wisdom nor humor. Without humor it is perhaps impossible to be wise. The true sense of humor comes late to most, never to many, though seldom in the history of man has there existed a person who suspected he had n't it. We all think we appreciate subtlety in humor, just as we all know we are "gentlemen." So humor exists in "traces" only within the didactic covers of the older stories, and it is found none too often in the newer ones. It is a happy baby that hears "The Walloping Window Blind" as a lullaby. Vague comprehensions steal upon him early and fit him for an appreciation of Chip's dogs (which he takes to at an incredibly infantile

period) and for "Alice in Wonderland." The full bliss of Oliver Herford is not for babes. The rhyme of the ant,

Let Fido chase his tail all day,
    Let kitty play at tag.
She has no time to throw away ;
    She has no tail to wag,

tickles the elect of childhood, but leaves the mighty average like Marjorie's bereaved fowl who "was more than usual cäm."

But Alice assuages grief and kills indifference, makes the languid vigorous and inspires the lively. "Alice" is worn and grimy even unto the last and most elaborate edition, and whether the real and only Tenniel or the wonderful Peter Newell bodies her forth, to the whole world of children there is a kind of shining in the very name. No one but a fiend would keep them waiting for Alice and the White Kitten till they could read. Nothing more vigorously stimulates imagination, the faculty that alone shows us made in the image of the Creator. Nothing better encourages that sense of humor which is its twin. These things it is good for the Olympian to remember when his flesh rebels at the hundredth repetition of "Through the Looking-Glass."

A sense of humor can be cultivated. Any normal city child will smile at this:

When our boys and girls are cross, then what shall
    we do ?
Where, when little heads they toss, shall we send
    them to ?
We 'll send them where the naughtiest, crossest
    children are,
We 'll send them off to Cross Town on a Cross
    Town car.

Arthur Macy, who wrote it, has the touch that calls humor into being where it never existed before.

If you polish your mind you 'll certainly find
    How little, how little you know,

may be beyond the normal child, but he is charmed into wiggleless silence by "The Boston Cats."

To all children the charm of rhythm is to be matched only by the charm of infinite detail. The maddening reiteration of "Arabella picked a daisy, Araminta picked a daisy, Arabella picked a daisy," through an endless page gives Janie and Jamie all the delight of a raid on the daisy field. That charm is what has insured the survival of the Franconia stories, the "Phonny Books" of three generations. It is a question whether or not they should be left to the child's own reading. (Even if they were, could anything bring to him the wilding flavor of that hour of discovery when, treasure trove among unmeaning rubbish of "Ministering Children" and "Advice to Parents," they came forth for us from a loose-hinged garret chest!)

The new edition has wisely preserved the red cover and the enticing headings set between the title and the printed page:

The Alcove.   The Curtains.   Malleville Tries to
                    Speak to Phonny.

Where in the world is a better fairy than the White Mountain nymph of Beechnut's "embellished" story! Games, picnics, the storm, the sick-room, are all endowed with curious and vivid reality. Physical comfort pervades every tale,—and children are all sybarites—always an easy-chair, a couch, apples roasting on the hearth. Woods and water, fires in the open air, Beechnut's "shop," where to this day we could find in the dark the ladder that led to the "loft" above, all are full of fascination.

To many a grown-up the word "country" means the land of "Phonny" who said "Hoh" and followed about after Beechnut. If you wandered in that land, if you set the white stone and the dark stones for the mosaic of Mary Bell's grotto; if you wrote letters to Agnes the fairy, or sang "Come and see me, Mary Ann," you will always be a little in the enchanted realm, though you may never again "go all the way." And if you can find two people who knew Ellen Linn and Mary Bell, Wallace and Mary Erskine, though an instant ago they were complete and willing strangers, they will fall to upon the discovery of that mu-

tual remembrance with gleaming eyes and loosened tongues, while the waves of dawn and of dewy remembrance flood their "illumined being."

The Franconia stories are more interesting than were Rollo and the improving "Mr. George," because they contain less information and more life. "Information," unless it come as a spirit with wings, is dangerous. When it appears naturally, out of past or present, it finds, even among the "littlest," a greedy audience. They like to "know." Church's "Story of the Odyssey," "Royal Children of English History," "Ten Boys who Lived on the Road to Long Ago," and "Seven Little Sisters" give a kind of pleasure due partly to the sense of acquirement.

This acquirement is, of course, necessary; one must have facts. If one can have them, as in these books, made attractive and stimulating so much the better. But character is dependent upon imagination. Cruelty, selfishness, oftenest exist for lack of power to put one's self in the other man's place. Nothing in literature civilizes and teaches better than the right kind of nature and animal books.

To a literal-minded infant one might read "The Elephant's Child" in "Just So Stories." When his eyes begin to widen, try him with Chambers's "Outdoorland." The elephant legend leads naturally to the finer meaning of the Outdoorland story that takes away the artificial fears with which too many nurses, governesses, and even mothers surround the outside world. Reginald Birch's illustrations are real poetry and real country, and there is the best kind of information between the pictured covers.

Another book that spurs a drowsy mind is "Mother Nature's Children." No one, of course, is ever too young to love Lobo, Rag, and Vixen ("Wild Animals I Have Known"), no one too undeveloped to have a soft spot for Johnny Bear.

All these tales are good art and good English. Character is handicapped where it finds the English language a reluctant medium. Apart from any question of morals or religion, it does not need a Ruskin to tell us that the child who is familiar with the English Bible and the best of the English hymns will be better equipped for self-expression than the child who has not responded at a plastic age to the antiphonal measure of the psalms nor heard the poetry of Isaiah. Complete comprehension is not necessary.

In days when "Aunt Louisa's Sunday Picture Book" was the rarest of diversions (its "rocks," very lofty, scrubbed a fine yellow; its "conies," very wee, dabbed a gay vermilion) one might have guessed, when children listened to grown-up reading, that they were driven by a dearth of literature of their own to books of their elders. But they find to-day the same attraction in what is not intended for their understanding. Poetry, prose poetry, the pageantry of words, catch and hold their vigorous attention. The normally book-loving girl or boy gets a pleasure beyond our conceding from what he does not comprehend, and with his pleasure is often mixed a shrewd inkling, clear as his clairvoyance for grown-up conversations.

Absorbed and contented, one four-year-old listened to "Hiawatha," and though as a man he had never opened the book again, knew more of it than the other grown-ups. Years ago a child stood, an interested audience, between her father's knees while he read her the trial scene from "The Merchant of Venice." That play has ever since had to her a peculiar reality. Not long ago two grave Olympians sat down to read "The Reign of Law" in a room where a very small person was striping the dictionary zebra in pink and purple. Through all the long rhapsody on the growing hemp he sat without painting a stroke, and for days to come teased for "more hemp."

Let them listen, when and where they will, even if what they hear make but a "sweet jargoning" in their ears.

"I have read to Howard [nine years old] 'The Song of Life,' " said a wise mother. "It told him in the right way all the things that I was afraid he would learn from other children in wrong ways." And when she repeated his questions and her answers the friends to whom she spoke thought, "Fortunate child! the world will be a cleaner place to him all his life for his mother's courageous forethought." In conduct or in books it is not only the spoken word or the printed page, the song notes or the picture, but the medium through which these reach the child's life that make him what he is.

For those who feel too profoundly the danger of such power there is a hint of admirable import on the final page of Goops:

> When you practise virtue
> Do it with a laugh.

To the Lamp=Bearers

By EDEN PHILLPOTTS

CURIOUS it is to note what images will strike the mind before impressions that themselves bear no reference to the thing suggested. Memory links these diverse ideas and sense connects them for us, so that joy or sorrow may lurk in a scent, darkness or light in a sound.

My *Calystegia pubescens* climbing in the arms of a large *Araucaria imbricata*, or monkey puzzle, always reminds me of De Quincey's attack on Goethe. There is the same display of energy, beauty, and futility in each case; for as well may the convolvulus seek to strangle this giant conifer from Chili in fleeting bonds and fret of flowers, as De Quincey, with magic of style and adornments of rhetoric, attempt to ridicule or discredit one so much mightier than himself. To watch him and know Goethe is to see a wave broken into liquid dust against the fore-head of some ocean-facing cliff. There is a gleam of rainbows and the wave has vanished. Now happily has that biography so petty, so narrow, so unworthy of the great pen that wrote it, vanished from the pages of the "Encyclopædia Britannica" and given place to a juster and saner appreciation. One reads De Quincey's biographies less and less as the years pass; but there is much of pure scholarship and poetry that is imperishable, and the style remains a miracle as of yore. It is subject for mourning that to this rare spirit the rational thinker should always be anathema: under a curse. Dogged and inveterate is his bitterness; for free thought his sharpest arrow was ever at the string; and yet constant service blunted it and robbed its point of the venom there. De Quincey had an unvarying argument against those who thought not as he thought and looked with larger tolerance upon the world of religious ideas. Such things were always mad. They must be mad to differ from those dogmas that De Quincey held. Lucretius, Goethe, Shelley—all who stood outside his fold—suffered from actual insanity, or the near threat and terror of it. Lucretius is "the first of demoniacs" laboring under "the frenzy of an earth-born or a hell-born inspiration." Shelley is "a lunatic angel" whose intellect was "already ruined before the light of manhood had cleansed its darkness." As if the light of manhood were not that light of lights, the light of reason. Goethe, indeed, he dares not denominate insane; but his escape is an accident; had Goethe been called upon to face tribulation and grief, he must surely have repeated "the mixed and moody character of his father." His natural mind was "corrupted and clouded"; and this because he regarded his Maker not with awe but curiosity. Strange amalgam of piety and venom mixed is this impotent assault; yet an utterance to study and from which to learn. In phrases that mingle like the classic figures from a frieze, or the interlacing of lovely foliage, he says these vain things. The rationalist—whether poet, philosopher, or artist—must endure his jewelled scourge; and it is interesting to mark how other inspired stylists have displayed a like intolerance. Milton, De Quincey, Ruskin—what remembered music haunts their names; yet who shall say that even in their gardens are not fruits of dust and flowers without sweetness. Milton may truly be forgiven, for he lived at a time when faith demanded blind allegiance to slay the rot at a nation's heart; but for Ruskin I conceive no excuse. His page is blotted with the narrow bitterness of personal disappointment and the unreasoning wrath of fanaticism. When he speaks of Science and the august name of Darwin, again I see the little convolvulus—a frail and fleeting shadow against the deep-rooted strength of forest trees.

De Quincey was my familiar friend through boyhood and beyond it. How often have I slept with him beneath my pillow! And I can grasp a little of his morbid suffering in the eternal struggle for perfection of utterance; I can share a part of his æsthetic torment over cacophony, redundance, obscurity, and all the thousand minute delicacies and subtleties of resonance and dissonance, accent and cæsura that only a De Quincey's ear appreciates and seeks to achieve or evade. How many care for these fine things to-day? How many are concerned if De Quincey uses a word with the long "a" sound, or spends a sleepless night in his endeavor to find another with the short "a," that shall at once answer his purpose and crown his sentence with harmony? Who lovingly examine the great artist's methods now, dip into the secret of his mystery, and weigh verb against adjective, vowel against consonant, that they may a little understand the unique splendor of this prose? And who, when an artist is the matter, attempt to measure his hopes as well as his attainments or praise a noble ambition perhaps shining through faulty attempt? How many, even among those who write, have fathomed the toil and suffering, the continence and self-denial of our great artists in words? This rises in a measure from the common confusion of thought that puts prose and poetry in antithesis, whereas it is a mere platitude to say that poetry is not a form, but an element common to prose and verse alike. We forget that some of the greatest prose in the language is poetry, and while we shrewdly examine the measure and plan of verse, too often overlook the workmanship of great prose, too often underestimate the cost to the artist.

Oh, "average reader," would that I could waken you into a higher ambition and a truer perception touching the business of art. If, for example, before tumbling through your next box of story-books from Mudie's, you would take Aristotle from his dark corner, shake him, dust him, open him, and ponder the "Poetics"! There are, indeed, those who hold that this master-spirit cannot be proved to contain all the truth, and that upon high art

and its infinite horizons he is no longer the paramount sum; but he will more than suffice your purpose and the purposes of those who write for you. Consider a moment what he requires and determine with yourself that you also need these qualities and must obtain them. You probably dislike tragedy. You choose rather that everything shall end happily in your story-books, "because in real life everything does not do so." Too well I know your dreadful arguments! But why do you, who are a truthful soul in your life and in your relations with your kind, tell me to lie to you and weave the thing that is not, because in your hour of leisure you refuse to look upon the thing that is? Do you, readers of the magazines, perceive the insult you put on those who write them? No, no, you neither perceive nor understand. But just for this one evening, to oblige me, wrestle with the great Greek and try to comprehend. Consider what a tragedy means. He will tell you. His six essentials in that sort are Plot, Character, and Diction, Thought, Scenery, and Song. They go to every great story now as then; now as then it is necessary, if a man dare profess and call himself artist, that he shall fight and toil to weld these ingredients in one balanced, perfect unity, so that from his revelation of life there shall spring like a dawn within the reader's soul that salutary *katharsis*—the solemn, purifying principle wrought of pity and of fear. That is man's work! And it is for you to demand it from the story-tellers who call themselves men. Comedy likewise may well be called to bear these six essentials, and had the mighty mind of Aristotle thrown light on that art also, he had perchance demanded not only those qualities, but also shown how, instead of fear and pity, our high comedy in its supreme expression must touch the human heart to tolerance, lift it to love, and warm it with great, sane laughter, such as Rabelais and Cervantes awakened in the world.

Now, "average reader," your work is cut out for you if you are going to apply one poor span of the Aristotelian standard to your modern fiction either of the stage or bookstall; and I warn you to be patient. We who write your tales cannot meet you in a moment with better art. Expect no immediate masterpieces from us; look for no Greek grandeur, Latin beauty, Elizabethan humanity in the autumn lists of 1905, because they will not be there; but develop a desire in yourself towards these things; survey your own contemptible requirements and cease to be content; observe that your abject taste in fiction redounds neither to your credit nor to the advancement of high art —nor any sort of art at all.

Lastly, be short and sharp with those who guide you in this matter; explain to the critics that they too must seek their prototypes in the company of the bygone great and call for a loftier note and nobler ideals; that they must shake us from our slumber and blow Aristotle's trumpet in our ears; that they must put a period to the ceaseless, thin rattle of their unconsidered praise and henceforth pay our mediocrity with the scorn of silence. Be swift, or surely our self-respect must perish.

And then—think of it! you are an "average reader" no more; and they are "average critics" no more; and we shall need swiftly to mend our ways, or follow our feeble stories and vulgar puppets, our mean diction, sentimentality, and nebulous thinking down into the dust of oblivion, where such offences properly belong.

But as well may De Quincey, with his foam of fine phrasing, endeavor to splash the marble front of Goethe; as well may my little convolvulus attempt to strangle the life out of the tree that carries her aloft, as any word of mine seek to teach our "average reader" that real story-telling is toil for strong men and women, not a tawdry burlesque of life spun by mental weaklings to help him through a leisure hour, to assist his digestion after dinner or kill his time in the train. No, it is vain to appeal to his understanding until we have educated it. We must teach him; he cannot help us; and to lift him it is necessary first that we lift ourselves. To despise him is folly; to chide him is unreasonable. Deny his hungry demand for trash—that is the wiser way. Elect a Parliament of Letters and suffer nothing calling itself a novel to reach our "average reader" until authority has passed it! Give him what is better far than the rubbish he cries for. Look to it that he shall have from you what your other children have: the thing they need, not the thing they want; and that you may the better judge for him, stand back a little from the rush and hurry; scan the old roads; keep higher literary company yourself; adjust your self-estimates and your perspective by study of the great of yesterday, not comparison with the small of to-day.

For we stand at a significant point in time. The dawn of a new age of thought is flushing the sky; the older order fades, the old faith, creatress of so much glorious work, now dies the natural death of all faiths that have strengthened the feet and lifted the hearts of men through their appointed centuries. Truth is crowned, and the trumpets of her ministers, Science and Reason, proclaim her. In these high moments of change let the lamp-bearers cling close to their sacred torches; cherish the flame against storm and tempest, and keep clear their ancient altar fires even though they cannot keep them bright. Then the great unborn —those who follow to expand their genius in conditions of culture, tolerance, and knowledge we know not— shall say, even of this our time, that despite perishing principles and decaying conventions, despite false teaching, false triumphs, and false taste, there were yet those who strove for the immemorial grandeur of their calling, who pandered to no temptation from without or from within, who followed none of the great world-voices, were dazzled by none of the great world-lights, and used their gift as stepping-stone to no meaner life; but clear-eyed and patient, neither elated nor cast down, still lifted the lamp as high as their powers allowed, still pursued art singly for her own immortal sake.

Two Books of Song

By EDITH M. THOMAS

MORE than once has occasion been taken by us to lament, that modern priestesshood at the altar of Eros has, for the most part, uttered itself only in strains of a banal and shallow eroticism, —fit subject for grief, for anger, for caustic reprehension. On the precinct of this perilous theme the votaress would do well to recall the successive legends read by Britomart on the doors of approach to Busyrane's enchanted *penetralia:* "Be bold, be bold, and, everywhere, be bold"—but, also, upon a third iron door,—"Be not too bold." This is, perhaps, but to say, the votaress of Eros in song too often lacks inner delicate discretion, while fully equipped as to valor—"in the gross!" In receiving these "Last Poems," * we have the mournful pleasure of indicating one who, as lover and as woman of genius, most nearly fulfilled the measure of requisitions needful in serving at the altar before mentioned. For, so it seems to us, the flame leaped upon that altar in clear corroboration of her vocation, whatever phase in the drama of woman's love-experience was touched upon by the art of Laurence Hope. Here, we may claim, if anywhere in our modern day, was the true inheritor of the Sapphic fervor, of the Sapphic song,—and, shall we not add, of the Sapphic catastrophe! Indeed, this last event (but lately of tragic accomplishment), we may regard as clearly foreshadowed in the pathetic "Dedication" to that love of a lifetime, without whom life proved a burden too heavy to be born. Wrung from the heart of this passionate singer in "Vishnu Land," are these sobbing yet prophetic words:

Small joy was I to thee; before we met
　Sorrow had left thee all too sad to save.
Useless my love—as vain as this regret
　That pours my helpless life across thy grave.

As in a "book of hours," may one read the varying moods and forms of devotion (recorded by this now-silenced priestess of the altar), wherein a woman's heart may spend itself upon the object beloved. Its concentrated brevity permits us to cite the following example—yet it is but one among many of like gems scattered through these pages:

Talk not, my Lord, of unrequited love,
　Since love requites itself most royally.
Do we not live but by the sun above,
　And takes he any heed of thee or me?
Though in my firmament thou wilt not shine,
　Thy glory as a Star is none the less.
Oh, Rose, though all unplucked by hand of mine,
　Still am I debtor to thy loveliness.

Mr. Routh has, so it seems to us, made the proverbial "move in the right direction," in his choice of theme,—the theme being drawn from our own Occident, the Mexico of pre-European time, shimmering in the distance of Aztec mythological antiquity. The author of "The Fall of Tollan" * displays considerable aptitude in his wielding of blank verse, and a fair degree of the ability to "visualize" the scene which he has set, in this "prickly garden," as it were, of a lapsed civilization in our mid-continent. He is, thus, able, at times, to make us possess, with him a "storied moment"—yet not at *all* times! He has achieved this, for example, in such a bit of description as the following, where the slaves serving the feast in "Great Tollan," are seen like "flashes of radiant-plumed birds," as they appear and vanish,

Bearing upon their shoulders swart great bowls
Of checkered clay, smoking with forest game,
And figured silver flagons in which foamed
Brown beaten chocolate and Maguey wine.

But he has sadly missed the desired impressiveness—in such figures as the following, "The timid evening star *trips* softly forth," and "A crafty, dim, and dangerous *basilisk* smile."

* "Last Poems. Translations from the Book of Indian Love." By Laurence Hope. John Lane Co.

* "The Fall of Tollan." By James Edward Routh, Jr. Boston: Richard G. Badger. $1.00.

The Editor's Clearing-House

On the Decay of Honor

Although nobody would deny the charge if properly attacked, it is a truism that only you may call yourself a liar with impunity. This is essentially the same position assumed by a table-companion of mine who, when loudly so proclaimed by a neighbor, used to hush him up with the deft, flattering observation that there were only a few in the secret. So long as the recording angels—our immediate relatives—are kept too busy to talk over affairs with the rest of the guild, we are complacent and lofty observers of this absurd world. We do not care for honor, we care for reputation; and when love of the semblance has supplanted the love of the thing itself, people become shadow-shapes and life a sham.

The false estimate put on the value of the objects of our aim is responsible for most of the misery of our modern, artificial life. From the vulgar desire always to occupy the orchestra stall when the proper place for us would be a flight higher if we consulted our real not our actual purse, to the more deceptive desire always to be seen with "nice" people, one can ring all the changes leading from folly to knavery. Mere display amuses us who are prudent and color-blind; but are we so superior who are silently trembling lest Mrs. Hoax discover that we, too, have not read the novel which evokes our complete sympathy with her ardor? We excuse our ambition for high esteem by the plea that we do not wish to hurt the feelings of others; thus is much Christianity put to the secret blush. Where, now, lies the capital fallacy? In believing that the most obvious and human form of honor—honesty—is a matter of gift not of cultivation. The commonest and severest comment on the morals of the rest of us is the fact that an honest man is always a "crank," "freak," or "traitor." We generally regard the man who tells the truth as a born fool; we shake our heads dolefully and with large, com-

passionate eyes question heaven why he was allowed to find the light of day. We join the crowd and heap the outcast with abusive pity and think ourselves magnanimous that we allow him "well-meaning!" We are slaves to numbers. Democracy has infatuated us with our own sufficiency. Evil itself has been reasoned away until that which distinguishes the "mass of citizens," whose prophet is the public print, is *per se* desirable. Life to-day is so comfortable, so seductive, so conducive to non-resistance that we do not wish to starve following the lone voice of honesty crying in the wilderness of cities.

We are dishonest by choice. In the abstract, *i. e.*, on Sundays, we are formidable champions of righteousness. At the safe distance of centuries we laud and love Savonarola or Luther or Milton; but let a man openly swear at the church and press of our day, fagots are on their way from San Francisco and New Orleans, express prepaid. Such is the fact of private experience. Low as are private morals, those of assemblies are notoriously lower. Nobody doubts that there is not one legislature in the length and breadth of the land which is not corrupt. But just announce what any corporation manager will tell you and what a storm of indignation becomes articulate. Or if you feel that you have insulted the State by doubting the veracity of knaves, will you be consoled at the spectacle of the workingman? The uplifted arm that fails to fall because the whistle has sounded "Time!" might well be the symbol of labor's honor. The job well done, the contract carefully executed are the exception. Ask a workingman why and how he does a given portion of your veranda; tools are dropped and the boss consulted as to whether the work ought to go on.

Already the blighting effect of this indifference of adults to honor is having its way with the youngster. You may win over, but you cannot convince a pupil that it is dishonest to copy another's paper or accept his prompting. The boy knows how his mother has read as her own before her Investigating Club a learned address written by a more fortunate neighbor. A textbook in common use recently in our high schools treats with relish of the humor of the situation the fact that Washington Irving was wont to write compositions for lads who did his sums. And few are the mature men of to-day who have not a large stock of stories over which, to their everlasting dishonor, they linger with open delight. Who of us is ignorant that the crib is the cradle of the classics? If a fellow passes his examination, he gloats over the vindication of his honor!

Just here lies the secret of the whole matter. We are too prone to judge by results. Success is our touchstone of morals. Montaigne tells of the Persian's answer to those who marvelled that so wise a man's counsels should meet with such ill results: the master of his counsels was himself, but of the results, fortune. We are not very different from that marvelling Persian crowd. We have simply carried the wonderment to its logical conclusion. Because results are in the hands of chance, because people ask what we have done or acquired, not how, we become careless about the means and sacrifice honor to glory. We have not merely discounted the old adage that honesty is the best policy; America disproves it daily. And yet we ought not to regret the passing of so commercial a motto.

PHILIP BECKER GOETZ.

What He Craved

"G. G. A.," a contributor to *Good Housekeeping*, writes a story called "A Young Wife's Confession," which needs renaming. It should be called "A Young Bachelor's Obsession." This G. G. A. is by no means a wife, young or old, nor even a husband, but some lad unacquainted with the details of household work, and imbued with the ideals of the eighteenth century. Here we have "a sensitive, high-spirited woman of twenty-five," "drawing a salary of fifteen hundred dollars a year,

dressing and living well," who presently marries "a clerk whose hours were long and whose income was fifteen dollars a week," of which he paid half for rent of a five-room flat. This person is described as being "a man good and true as steel, who would have made a splendid husband for the right woman"; and it becomes presently apparent that the right woman for him was a Dutch housemaid, a two-hundred-and-sixty-dollar-a-year woman —"and found." He "craved a little well-cared-for corner which would be a home in every sense of the word, presided over by a systematic, cheerful, and contented little woman who would have made it and him her pride. Such a woman would have been his queen *and would have been treated as one.*" The italics are mine. The word "queen" must have a weird connotation in this man's mind. A female systematically cheerful and content in housework for two and the society of one man may be called "a treasure" in the sense of an invaluable servant— but is scarcely regal.

If Prince Albert, on marrying Queen Victoria, had been able to confine her labors, interests, and "pride" to housework and to him he might by some intellectual acrobatics have still considered her as "his queen"; but could hardly have persuaded himself—or her—that she was treated as such. The sinful heroine of this masterly tale seems to regret giving up $1500 a year, work she liked, association, and general respect, for half of $780 and solitary confinement to a two-hundred-and-sixty-dollar-woman job.

In order to add to his black picture this callow youth describes a practical and experienced business woman of twenty-five as going around "with hair uncombed, shoes unbuttoned, and clad in a wrapper none too clean." Just why the brisk neatness essential to years of business success should have thus sunk to shame is not explained— why be too precise in one's psychology on a subject one knows nothing about?

This angel of unselfishness, who had cheerfully allowed the woman who loved him to give up $1110 a year and undertake distasteful labor for his personal service (subtract half of $780 from $1500 for above loss), is remarkably patient under her evil behavior.

He was unfailing in his cheerful kiss at going and coming, never complained of her errors and omissions, helped wash the dishes at night, and on Sundays turned to and cleaned the flat. After a long time of this voiceless virtue the worm turned one day, and went so far as to suggest that this offensive woman clean her teeth (one wonders in vain why she had discontinued this bit of personal hygiene), comb her hair, and put on a fresh wrapper. This was his first criticism in two years. For two years this unusually able woman (for not every working girl can command her previous salary) had spent every day and all day in a dirty wrapper, doing nothing but read novels. Stung to the quick by this comment on his part, she first weeps from 7.45 till nearly 11 A.M., at the same time planning her campaign. And it was a campaign. We now see something of the dormant capacity once worth $1500. No mere charwoman, no housemaid, no ordinary wife—or queen—could accomplish what she did when really aroused. Here is the campaign:

I cleaned the ceiling, the walls, the floors ; and washed the windows, put up fresh curtains, and blacked the range, scoured the sink and the ice-box, rearranged the pantries, put clean linen on the table, and did what I had never done before— sewed a button on the band of his shirt and darned a pair of socks.

By this time, says this guileless pretender of "A Young Wife," "it was late." Late! It would have been late next day. Does this man really imagine that housework is a kind of witchcraft, requiring only " a little wife well-willed" and it is done? Has he no faintest conception of the hours of time and foot-pounds of strength required to do a piece of house-cleaning like that— even by an expert? And here is this limp sloven, rising in a burst of genius after two years' solid idleness, and doing this miracle between 11 A.M. and —"late"! She still has time to bathe, comb her hair, clean her teeth and nails

(the previous condition of this whilom successful business woman is revolting to think of), put on the dress he liked best and a clean white apron. Then she prepared the daintiest supper she knew how.

But alas! Her supernatural energy deserted her when it was all over and he had come home — so proud and pleased that the queen had got to work at last !—and she was cross.

Time passes. Presently two babies arrive, and the husband getting "a raise" of "just double his former salary," which is about what she got before, they move into the suburbs. He remains an angel—never a vice appears—no touch of temper or criticism; he simply took himself off evenings, and after eight years this "clever and brainy woman" " noticed the growing indifference and began to realize that his love for me was dying."

This person's previous position must have been that of companion to an idiot. No—it says she was employed by "one of the most prominent corporations in the United States,"—and there is no syndicate of Insane Asylums yet, that I know of.

Having grasped this astonishing fact, our intelligent friend "spent the most of a day trying to grasp Walter's idea of the ideal wife and mother."

It does seem as if she could have got hold of it sooner. It was by no means abstruse. All the man "craved," as he repeatedly said, was cleanliness and quiet, and,— yes, cheerfulness. He was not ambitious—not in the least exacting. If he had only had a little more money he would have been perfectly satisfied with a Chinaman. Chinese help is clean, quiet, and cheerful — economical, too, and does not mind monotony.

The good man is really to be pitied for his inability to compass so simple an ideal. On fifteen dollars a week one can hardly afford to give even three dollars for a servant, board two, pay rent, and all the rest. No—he was poor, and he must have a wife or no servant at all. Why he should have selected one so expensive and inexpert is the only mystery—he was surely thoughtless in his choice. Having made it he stuck to it manfully; and after eight years his patience was rewarded. She reformed. She grasped, after an all-day effort, this great Ideal, and strove to attain it. And, in course of time she did. After earnest and prolonged effort she learned to clean her teeth, to comb her hair, to wear clean clothes—even to decorate a little occasionally.

She learned, being "a clever and brainy woman," to sweep and dust and wash and iron and cook and sew and take care of the children. "Every move became a labor of love," she says proudly—not moving the household goods to another domicile, but just moving around in the house.

The ever-virtuous husband responded with ardor, and they proceeded to enjoy an interrupted honeymoon; but, as the young wife wisely says, it would not be safe to put most men to so long a test.

There are two ways in which all this painful difficulty might have been avoided. One is for the noble-minded young man who wanted a queen to have gone to the nearest intelligence office and hired one on trial. If, as it appears, he could not have afforded this, he should have chanced it and married one outright—he could hardly have slipped up on it worse than he did. Or he could have got a job as an iceman and satisfied himself as to royal capacity in many a kitchen before he committed himself.

The other way is so simple that we wonder neither this unselfish and devoted husband nor the uncommonly able woman thought of it.

She should have kept her job. Then they would have had $2280 a year. A five-dollar servant, with three dollars a week more allowed for her board and room, and five dollars a month more for rent, would have raised their expenses from his $780 to $1256. They would thus have had a clear $1024 a year to lay up against the coming of the babies. With a contribution like this to the family funds perhaps the young wife would have preserved her self-respect, worn something other than a wrapper, and cleaned her teeth with gratifying regularity.

But this ideal husband did not want an able coadjutor. He wanted a— queen!

CHARLOTTE PERKINS GILMAN.

Irving

By O. C. AURINGER

THE New World's first great humorist and the best,
   Irving, sleeps out his slow half-century—
   Our arch-retainer of humanity,
Lord of the courts of laughter in the West.
Now England's Minster gathers to her breast
   The English Irving;—last and greatest he
   Of such as ruled the realm of tragedy,
In that long line to mimic art addressed.
What bonds then broke!—what laughter and what tears
   That hour ran mingling on the unseen shore
    When Irving Irving met!—oh dream not so;
But know them, full revealed, among their peers,
   Stripped of the masks that here in time they wore,
    Heart-sweet and whole in Heaven's unclouded glow.

The Book=Buyer's Guide

BELLES LETTRES

**Birrell—In the Name of the Bodleian, and
Other Essays.** By Augustine Birrell.
Scribner, $1.00.

The title essay in this graceful little bundle by
the author of "Obiter Dicta" is by no means
the easy chief of the lot. While doing justice
to Sir Thomas Bodley, there is not that loving, affectionate intimacy with the library itself
which would show that the writer had ever
been among the faithful haunters of the dusty,
musty place. Yet that is an apt suggestion
of his, that a new benefactor could do as excellent service to this "glorious foundation"
as did Sir Thomas Bodley. Very complete,
too, is Mr. Birrell's picture of that public-
spirited gentleman, and his deft manner of
handling his theme, in brief yet with justice
to the subject, ought to induce some one to
hearken to the statement that fresh gifts
would be very timely. Not long ago a reader
from this side the sea, impressed by the hospitality and by the poverty of the Bodelian,
wrote from its own recesses to the greatest
giver of libraries that the world has ever seen,
begging him to turn his thoughts for a moment
from the reading public to this treasure house
of the English-speaking race. Into the mists
of Scotland the bold petition travelled, and
no response ever journeyed back again. Perhaps a kind Fate may cause that library-
lover's hand to open this volume and Mr.
Birrell's words may strike home.

Pleasant are the sketches in some of the
other essays, based, as a rule, on some event
or other. But even when written as book
reviews there is a note that promises longer
life to the words than that of mere criticism.
Arthur Young, for example, has here a re-
introduction to the public, who may read this
without taking the whole autobiography that
inspired it and it will perhaps be wise enough
for his purpose. So with the others. They
are very illuminating.

**Brewster — Representative Essays on the
Theory of Style.** Chosen and Edited by
William T. Brewster. Macmillan. $1.10.

A collection of essays, lectures, etc., in which
the subject of literary style is discussed by
certain of its masters—Newman, De Quincey,
Spencer, Lewes, Stevenson, Pater, and Frederic Harrison. The book is intended primarily for students of rhetoric, but there are few
professional writers whose work might not be
the better for a careful reading of any one of
these papers.

Crosland—The Wild Irishman. By T. W. H.
Crosland. Appleton. $1.50.

The author of this book is of those who come
to scoff and remain to pray. One expects of
him bitter sarcasm and finds on the whole
kindly appreciation. The Irishman is apparently a more decent fellow than the Scotsman
in Mr. Crosland's opinion. Ireland needs, in
fact, to get rid of the Scots who have settled
there. Then there would be a chance for
Irish virtues to develop. These virtues are
precisely the reverse of those with which the
race has usually been credited. As a dealer
in paradox Mr. Crosland can do no less than
say this. There is some truth in paradox,
and when we are told that excess of morality
in one direction may mean excess of crimin-
ality in another, we are willing to believe it.
Similarly Irish humor may have been over-
estimated. Mr. Crosland's satiric comments
upon the Neo-Celtic movement are timely and
salutary. A country afflicted with that is
surely "most distressful."

Howells—London Films. By W. D. Howells.
Illustrated. Harper. $2.25 net.

These are not mere snapshots at scenes in the
greatest of the world's great cities, for Mr.
Howells is very much at home in London, and
what he sees there to-day is colored more or
less vividly by his recollections of what he
observed on his first visit and later ones. He
by no means disdains to treat of hackneyed
themes, and a large majority of his readers
will enjoy the book none the less for this
reason. It is the obvious and familiar, not
the recondite, that charms most people so-
journing in London; and the greater number
of these films record sights that are more or
less vividly impressed on the retina of almost
every American visitor to the City of Cities.
The author's style, here as elsewhere, is lucidity itself; and for this reason, as for others,
it is interesting to compare these impressions
of a distinguished American novelist revisit-
ing England, with those of another eminent
American fiction writer who is now recording
the effect upon his mind of a brief sojourn
here after long residence abroad.

Symons—Spiritual Adventures. By Arthur
Symons. Dutton. $2.50 net.

In reviewing an English book, the American
critic is in a dilemma which is not readily
overcome. He must needs revert his mind
to the greater literary traditions of the mother
country, and an English volume, irrespective
of its merit, trailing ever so faint a light of
the national glory, necessarily throws a little
dust in the somewhat critical eye of the bookman. But in the volume before us we have
rather less difficulty, as these stories, half a
dozen in all, belong to a school rather than a
country: the school of the Decadents, unfortunately. It is Mr. Symons's simple and forceful style, with its delicate psychic touches,
combined with his really great gift for the
vital story, which disarms our criticism of his
philosophy. "Esther Kahn" is perhaps the
most wholesome of these haunting stories,
having a definite culmination in the creation
of the artist through suffering. But, on the
whole, "The Death of Peter Waydelin" is the
achievement of the book, in the tragedy and
realistic horror of its setting. Mr. Symons

has fulfilled his genius in this style of work. His attitude towards the gentler sex is best expressed by himself in these lines from his "Christian Trevalga." "To live with a woman, thought Christian, in the same house, the same room with her, is as if the keeper were condemned to live by day and sleep by night in the wild beast's cage. It is to be on one's guard every minute, to apprehend always the claws behind the caressing softness of their padded coverings, to be continually ready to amuse one's dangerous slave with one's life for the forfeit. The strain of it, the trial to the nerves, the temper! it was not to be thought of calmly. He looked around him and saw all the other keepers of these ferocious, uncertain creatures, wearing out their lives in the exciting companionship: and a dread of women took the place of his luxurious indifference." One is tempted to quote more of Mr. Symons because of the fascination of the style, and a certain truthfulness in the theme, but it must be admitted that we hope for him in the future a broader and cheerier philosophy when he has reinforced his knowledge of the sensual woman with a deeper knowledge of the spiritual woman.

BIOGRAPHY

Macfall—Whistler: Butterfly, Wasp, Wit, etc. By Haldane Macfall. Edinburgh: T. N. Foulis. 6d., 1s., 2s. 6d.

A biographical and critical essay of ten thousand words or less, set off with half-tone reproductions of etchings of this "Londoner to the bone."

Vignaud—Vie de Colomb. Par Henri Vignaud. Paris: H. Welter; New York: Lemcke & Buchner. $3.00.

An octavo of over 500 pages, consisting of essays on the origins of the discoverer's family, the date of his birth, his voyage to the North, his settlement in Portugal, his marriage, and other topics more or less closely related to these. The learned Secretary of the American Embassy in Paris has long been known as a high authority on all matters pertaining to the personality and the achievements of Columbus, and his reputation will be greatly strengthened by the publication of this volume.

FICTION

Chamblin—Lady Bobs, Her Brother, and I. A Romance of the Azores. By Jean Chamblin. Putnam. $1.25.

"An obscure actress," without "talent enough for success, or vanity enough for failure," seeking rest and a place where she can "fight it out with herself," finds herself embarked, at Brooklyn, on the *Dona Maria*—her destination the Azores. To her friend Nora she writes a series of letters briefly describing the voyage, and telling at greater length of what she sees and experiences in a little visited but most picturesque corner of the globe. Unless the actress were a born writer, the publication of her correspondence would interest no one but herself and Nora. As it happens, however, she has a facile and humorous pen, and her letters are literature. Her voyage to the Portuguese islands, her sightseeing trips when she reaches them, and her unforeseen meeting with Lady Bobs's brother (an old flame), and its romantic sequel—these furnish the material for a very fresh and entertaining story. There is a fanciful frontispiece in color and half-tone photographs confirm the author's well-sketched verbal pictures of a romantic and unhackneyed region.

Goodloe—At the Foot of the Rockies. By Carter Goodloe. Scribner. $1.50.

A group of capital stories of life at a military post in the Northwest Territories—a Mounted Police detachment in Alberta. English (and colonial-English) soldiers and civilians, including women and children, and a sprinkling —or rather more than a sprinkling—of red Indians, are the *dramatis persona* of these tales. Good as the stories are in themselves, they have gained much in the telling; for Miss Goodloe has just the right dramatic and artistic touch, knowing as well what to omit as what to include, in treating the episodes that furnish the material for her sketches.

Harrison—The Carlyles. By Mrs. Burton Harrison. Appleton. $1.50.

In her latest novel, Mrs. Harrison has not given us an "international romance" in the sense in which that phrase is understood nowadays—though there is more or less in it about the Confederate colony in Paris after the Civil War. It is, instead, a story of North and South immediately after the Rebellion, the scene opening in Richmond on the day the Unionist forces entered the burning city. The Carlyles are old-line Southerners, whose patriotism is none the less pure and ardent for being sectional; and one feels that the hero and the heroine's father—Carlyles both—are sketched from life. Having made which remark, one has a moment's misgivings as to whether "Mona" Carlyle and her gallant cousin "Lance" are the heroine and hero after all, rather than Cecil Dare and Donald Lyndsay. However this may be, there is no doubt as to the charm of the book and the accuracy of the picture it presents of certain aspects of post-bellum life in Dixie.

Mott—Jules of the Great Heart. By Lawrence Mott. Century. $1.50.

A striking story of a French-Canadian trapper of a century or so agone, who makes a long and on the whole a losing fight with the factors and trappers of the Hudson Bay Company in the far Northwest. Jules Verbaux is a man of great strength and courage and adroitness, not free from human passions, but kindly and magnanimous. His wife has been stolen away from him, and this is the story, with "incidental divertissements," of his weary but at last successful search for her. It is strong, imaginative, and picturesque, and as the first work of a very young writer deserves to be specially noted. The dialect—a *mélange* of French-English and English-

French—is about the thorniest we have ever had to cope withal, and is likely to discourage many readers. We miss the striking illustrations of Schoonover that accompanied such of the chapters of the book as appeared in *The Century*, though one of them serves as a frontispiece.

Wright—Where Copper was King. By James North Wright. Small, Maynard. $1.50.

In the guise of a novel, a former Superintendent of the Calumet and Hecla mine describes the life of the mining folk who did such fruitful pioneer work in the upper peninsula of Michigan some forty years ago. The total amount paid in by original holders of the stock of this copper-mining company was $12 per share, the value of each of its shares is now about $700, and it has paid out over $90,000,000 in dividends. These facts have given the property an extraordinary reputation, and will attract attention to a book about the mine by one of the directors of the company. It should be said, however, that the story is not, in any sense, an advertisement. The real name of the mine is not used, and the figures given above are not derived from this source.

HISTORY AND TRAVEL

Bigelow—The German Struggle for Liberty. By Poultney Bigelow. Harper. $2.25. Vol. IV.

The fourth volume on the attempts to obtain constitutional liberty in Germany covers the period of the Revolution of 1848. It contains the same slap-dash miscellaneous kind of matter as do its three predecessors, and does not deserve, any more than they, to be ranked as history according to any established canon, nor as literature if grace of style and a clear thread of consecutive narrative are to be regarded as necessary. The book may be described as a series of composite photographs of certain participants in the mid-nineteenth-century events based on any radical opinion that could be caught in various haphazard snapshots.

It could hardly be understood without reference to other books if the reader were new to the subject, so that it can be of little use to a new generation by itself if they would gain a comprehension of the part played by the characters herein depicted with a slashing journalistic pencil. Readable as parts of Mr. Bigelow's "history" are, the whole cannot be regarded as a serious contribution to the literature on Germany.

Curtis—India. By William Eleroy Curtis. Revell. $2.00.

The modern maker of descriptive books of observation does not travel like Cæsar, who swam to shore with his manuscript in his mouth. It is in Pullman palace-car or luxurious "Wagon-Lit," or on ocean greyhound, that this owner and daily user of a typewriting machine lives, moves, and has his being. From observation to keyboard he arrives before the evening meal. He posts his letter to Chicago before Lyra has passed zen-

ith. Then, on native *terra-firma*, he revises, reads proof; and, behold, a book! But, as hot cakes and syrup are relishable, so we confess to enjoying Mr. Curtis's quick, photographic style. Besides, he tells us much that most books leave out. He helps us to adjust traditional notions to present-day reality. Jewelled India, with the various courses and strata in its civilization, its "varieties of religious experience," its jungles of dogma, its forests of idols, with the show and throng of the bazar, are all here on his pages, indeed, but Mr. Curtis is also an inquiring Yankee. He goes beyond the mirror. He reveals. He criticises. We admire things American, especially American women, more than ever. Our patriotism warms. Yet he tells us also that native princes are not mere puppets. They not only rule, but govern. They care for their people. With much to criticise in the past, British administration is noble, practical, successful, and worthy of study by American statesmen. Which of Asiatic lands would most fascinate the scholar and tempt to long residence the man who loves to solve problems? Egypt, India, China, Japan? After reading Mr. Curtis's book we answer without faltering, "India." It is the London among countries.

Humphrey—The Indian Dispossessed. By Seth K. Humphrey. Little, Brown. $1.50 net.

In effect a sequel, or supplement, to the late Helen Jackson's "A Century of Dishonor." The fact that public attention cannot be effectually drawn to the evils here attacked, save in the form of fiction, is responsible for Mrs. Jackson's having followed up her book of facts with the highly popular novel "Ramona." The present work is illustrated with sixteen photographic portraits.

Joubert—The Truth about the Tsar and the Present State of Russia. By Carl Joubert. Lippincott. $2.00.

It is not Russia that has gone mad but Tsardom. As autocratic sovereigns, the hours of the Romanoffs are numbered. A constitutional monarchy or the United States of Russia are the only alternatives possible. Such are the opinions of Carl Joubert—who claims to know both the land and the ruler, and who reiterates in this volume the ideas he promulgated in "Russia as It Really Is." Though he acknowledges ignorance among the people, he still accredits clear, well-defined theories of what Russia needs to all classes, educated and uneducated alike. He claims that the great Revolutionary party in Russia is working quietly and steadily toward its goal and accumulating treasures against the day when they will be needed. But this claim was made some months ago. Already the prophecy is a back number, for events have marched fast in the land. Joubert speaks of an explosion like the French Revolution. Already many more victims have fallen in Russia than in the whole period of the French Terror, and the end is not yet.

Much of the Tsar's policy is the fault of the

Dowager, reactionary in the extreme and wholly sympathetic with the measures adopted by Plehve, who, in our author's opinion, met a deserved death. Not pleasant is this picture of mother and son, nor indeed that of the whole realm riddled with treasonable thought and plots against the monarch,—a monarch who refused to avert the dire catastrophe menacing his dynasty. Journalistic in style, the book is interesting because at this moment everything connected with the subject attracts attention. Even if only half its statements are true, it is still worth reading,—now when the fate of the weak, dreaming monarch is still in the balance, and when it is still a question whether the moujiks are fitted for self-government as the author thinks.

Reed—The Brother's War. By John C. Reed. Little, Brown, & Co. $2.00.
Certain subjects have fallen into accepted lines, and phrases used in their regard have become merely conventional signs indicating the speaker's point of view without rousing new thoughts to activity in auditors of the same way of thinking. Discussions on the Civil War reveal many such phrases ready for use, often the heritage of those who use them, because the latter were born after the great national experience of the fifties and sixties, but born nevertheless into fixed grooves of opinion. Celebrations like the Garrison Centennial bring out, moreover, reminiscences of anti-slavery agitation, and give the present generation whiffs from an atmosphere of the past and a past with which they are familiar from the literature they have been fed upon. Now to the host of volumes from the Northern point of view is added a new one from the Southern, yet claiming to be wholly dispassionate in its survey of the causes leading up to the Civil War. And this claim must be allowed. Member of a slave-holding family, Mr. Reed fought through the war as a devoted son of Georgia, an ardent believer in the Confederacy, and convinced from theory and from experience that the negroes were an inferior race, suited only to a life of dependence upon Caucasians. Furthermore, he held that the Africans were most fortunate in their forced immigration to America. With a record that might easily rank him among the unreconstructed, he certainly gives honor to both sides with marvellous impartiality. It is a very honest book, and the reader cannot help admiring the writer for his justice toward his late foes in a conflict still vivid to his memory. But his words springing from his

point of view remind us that it is an alien one to all our traditions. Appreciation for the Ku-Klux Klan, for example, has a strangely unfamiliar sound, as have, too, his phrases in regard to slavery. The author does not confine himself to the causes of the war, causes wherein the actors, to his mind, were moved by much higher than the apparent reasons. His last chapters are devoted to the present, and his conclusions are (1) that both sides were right in the war; (2) that slavery was a curse to the slaveholders and a blessing to the slaves; (3) that the condition of the negroes in the South at the present, excepting the few thousands lifted by Tuskegee and Hampton, is deplorable and menacing to the whole social organism; (4) that the one solution possible, to redeem the error of giving the franchise to the negroes, is to establish the whole race in a state of their own, giving them first territorial government and letting them gradually become equal to other States.

It is a bold proposition, and should, perhaps, receive consideration. Certainly the book deserves attention, whether the proposed solution does or not. It is not exactly well written, but it is distinctly impressionist and first-hand. And in these days of book-making that alone is a pass to the gentle reader.

Munk—Arizona Sketches. By J. A. Munk, M.D. Grafton Press. $2.00 net.
Nearly twenty-two years ago the author of this book went to Arizona, where, in 1883, his brother had located a cattle ranch for their joint occupation. The southeastern part of the territory is especially familiar to him, his recollections covering the period of the last Indian raid, under Geronimo, in 1885. Since then the Apaches have been no less peaceful than the Pueblos themselves. Dr. Munk's style is wholly lacking in literary finish, but his account of ranch life and other matters in the southwestern corner of the United States teems with interesting facts and photographs.

MISCELLANEOUS

Pulitzer—A Cynic's Meditations. By Walter Pulitzer. Dodge. $.75
These meditations of an amiable cynic are all in the approved apothegmatic form. "In marriage he who hesitates is bossed." "If woman makes all the trouble in life, it's woman who makes life worth all the trouble." Illustrations and decorative borders make the booklet attractive to the eye.

(For list of books received see third page following)

Photo by Van der Weyde   DR. EDWARD EVERETT HALE IN HIS EIGHTY-FIFTH YEAR

THE CRITIC

Vol. XLVIII   MARCH, 1906   No. 3

The Lounger

HERE is dear old Dr. Edward Everett Hale, eighty-four years old, hard at work as usual and happy in his work. Take him away from his books and his writing pad and he would be miserable. *Lend a Hand* is the name of his magazine, and "Lend a Hand" is his motto. He is always ready, always interested, and he is as interested and eager to-day in his great work as he has been since he was a young man. Dr. Hale's career records no failures. He has, like a number of contemporaneous periodicals, been "a success from the start." There has never been a time when the world has not followed his pen or listened to his voice. No writer to-day has a wider circle of friends and none better deserves them.

Speaking of young old men, who could be younger than the Hon. John Bigelow, editor and author. Although he has celebrated his eighty-eighth birthday, there is no more vigorous man of half his years in New York, and a good many young men might envy him his vitality. Perhaps one reason why Mr. Bigelow is so young and strong in his eighty-eighth year is that he has always lived a simple life. He has lived a busy life, but that hurts no one. He has not, however, burned his candle at both ends. He has always followed the rule of early to bed, early to rise, and he has lived on simple food,—no sauces, no pastries, for him. And the consequence is that notwithstanding his years he is hale and hearty.

There have been any number of novels that have sold more than Mrs. Wharton's "The House of Mirth," although that has to the present time reached a sale, I am told, of one hundred and twenty thousand copies; but there has been no novel that has been as much written about and as much discussed. Not only have the regular critics reviewed it in due course, but it seems as though all its readers wanted to write reviews of it; and every periodical that publishes criticisms has been deluged by reviews of Mrs. Wharton's story. I have known books that have reached a sale of from one hundred to two hundred thousand copies, but I have never known any one who has read them. On the other hand, every one I know is reading "The House of Mirth." I hear it discussed wherever I go. Not everybody who has read it thinks that it is as great a novel as do its more enthusiastic admirers; but all agree that it is a fine performance and better than anything that we have had from an American author in a long time.

COPYRIGHT 1906, BY THE CRITIC COMPANY.
ENTERED AT NEW ROCHELLE, N. Y., POST OFFICE AS SECOND CLASS MATTER.

It is no harder to sell expensive books in this country than it is cheap ones. A book of illustrations reproduced from a rare Italian manuscript, customed to regard Mrs. Brookfield as the important member of the family, but in this book we see that Mr. Brookfield was no figurehead. He now

DRAWING ON A WOODBLOCK OF MR. AND MRS. BROOKFIELD BY W. M. THACKERAY
INTRODUCING HIS OWN PORTRAIT

of which a limited edition is published at $600 a volume, was subscribed to the moment it was seen by New York collectors. Only six hundred copies of the book were printed at all, and less than one hundred allowed for the United States. *Apropos* of limited editions, Messrs. Scribner have just prepared a limited edition of 260 copies of President Roosevelt's "Outdoor Pastimes of an American Hunter." Each copy of this edition, of which there are only a few left, has been signed by the author. The text is printed by De Vinne on hand-made Ruisdael paper; the illustrations are printed on special paper that has been ironed as for an etching; the binding is half pigskin, with stamped title and khaki paper sides.

By permission of Messrs. Scribner I am allowed to reproduce these three cuts from the latest volume of Brookfield letters—a book about which it would be difficult to say too much in praise. Heretofore we have been ac-

comes before the footlights to receive the applause that he deserves. How many of us would add years to our ages to have belonged to "the set" of which the Brookfields and Thackeray were the star members. The drawings here reproduced are published in "Mrs. Brookfield and Her Circle."

Mrs. Burton Harrison has recently finished a new novel which is said to be the best thing she has done since "The Anglomaniacs." The heroine is a Southern "Daisy Miller"—that is, a "Daisy Miller" up to date. Mrs. Burton Harrison, Mrs. Wharton, Miss Dauer, are not the only "society ladies" writing novels. There is Miss Frances Davidge, whose recent story "The Game and the Candle," is attracting flattering attention.

At the time of his death Sir Wemyss Reid was the literary adviser, or editor as it is called in England, of Cassell & Company. He has been succeeded by Mr. Arthur Spurgeon, who recently made a visit to this country to learn some of the American ways of running the publishing business.

ᔗ

Anne Warner, the creator of "Mrs. Clegg" and other humorous characters, will in a measure depart from her early manner in her new story which will ap-

author does not know what her characters are going to say from page to page, and that she is as much amused by their humorous sayings as are her readers.

ᔗ

The Baroness Orczy, author of "The Scarlet Pimpernel," which has been successful as a novel and even more

WILLIAM HENRY BROOKFIELD AT THE AGE OF 23

pear serially in *The Century*. In this she recounts her experiences during a recent trip through France. The story is told in the form of letters, and is, like everything that Mrs. French writes, in a humorous vein. I am told that this

successful as a play, having been produced by Arthur Terry and Julia Neilson, will be out with a new novel in the new year. It is called "A Son of the People," and the scene is laid in the author's native Hungary.

A recent list of literary men in politics, all as office-holders, includes George Bancroft, John Bigelow, John Lothrop Motley, Bayard Taylor, Washington Irving, Lowell, Hay, Hawthorne, Howells, Booth Tarkington, and Winston Churchill. But it omits the late Richard Henry Stoddard, who served for many years in the New York Custom House; Bret Harte, who was U. S. Consul at Glasgow; William Henry Bishop, who is still serving his country in Italy; Edward Arlington Robinson, whose verses recently received enthusiastic, if belated, praise from President Roosevelt and a position in the New York Custom House.

✧

I believe that Mrs. Craigie (John Oliver Hobbes) is going to put the case of her play, also her novel, "The Flute of Pan," into the hands of a lawyer. It seems that "The Flute of

where it was produced by Miss Olga Nethersole. The book, however, is a success. The author does not like to have it compared with "Graustark" or "The Prisoner of Zenda." It is not an imitation of either of these two stories, but I should say that as far as plot goes it belongs to the "Zenda" class. The Princess of Wales, who is a friend of Mrs. Craigie, has written her a letter about the book, in which she says that she read it with delight because it is the only book that she ever read that gave an accurate picture of court life. If "The Flute of Pan" gives an accurate picture of court life we cannot but be glad that we live in a republic and are not courtiers.

✧

The Rev. William Mottram, a first cousin of George Eliot, has written a book on "The True Story of George Eliot in Relation to Adam Bede." In this the author shows how the chief

MRS. BROOKFIELD
From a drawing by W. M. Thackeray

Pan" and "The Prince Consort" are as much alike as two peas, and as Mrs. Craigie's play was produced before "The Prince Consort" she is going to see just where she stands in the matter. Her play was not a success in London,

characters in the novel were drawn from George Eliot's nearest relatives: "Adam Bede" was her father; "Dinah Morris" her aunt; "Bartle Hassey" her schoolmaster; "Mrs. Poyser" her mother; "Seth Bede" her uncle; and

Photo by Knox, N. Y.

MRS. CRAIGIE

"Hetty Sorrel" an unhappy girl in whose tragic fate George Eliot was deeply interested. It has generally been supposed that there was more truth than fiction in "Adam Bede," but the actual placing of the characters, perhaps, has never before been given with absolute authority.

Signora Serao's book, "In the Country of Jesus," has been translated from the Italian and will be published in America before long. In less than two years "Nel Paese di Gesu" has gone through thirty editions, which would seem to prove that the English and American publishers have been napping. A book of this sort that has gone through thirty editions one might have supposed would have been published in England before this. Signora Serao, who is a fervent Roman Catholic, made a journey to Palestine to visit the places where Christ lived, worked, and died. As she puts it, "to seek out the soul of that Blessed Lord."

One is safe in saying that Mrs. Francis Alexander, of Florence, is one of the oldest women, if not the oldest, writing to-day. Mrs. Alexander is in her ninety-third year, and has just translated from the Italian more than 120 miracle stories and sacred legends, which will be published by Messrs. Little, Brown & Company with the title "Il Libro d' Oro." Mrs. Alexander was an intimate friend of Ruskin, who, in a preface to "The Story of Ida," introduced her daughter, Miss Francesca Alexander, to the reading world. Few little books, slim in plot, small in size, have ever attracted the attention of this charming story. Although the author of only one book, and that not remarkable for anything but charm, the name of Francesca Alexander is known to every one who keeps in touch with the literature of the day.

Brentanos have published as a separate book George Bernard Shaw's preface to the London edition of "Mrs. Warren's Profession." Mr.

Shaw calls it "The Author's Apology." He should, however, call it "The Author's Defence," for there is nothing very apologetic in what this playwright says.

It is a great pleasure to lay before the readers of THE CRITIC this admirable portrait of the Rev. Dr. Samuel M. Crothers, author of "The Gentle Reader" and "The Pardoner's Wallet," and one among the galaxy of stars that have been discovered by the telescopic eye of the editor of the *Atlantic Monthly*. Dr. Crothers lives in Cambridge. under the very shadow of Harvard University and the homes of Longfellow and Lowell. He is naturally saturated with all that is rich and rare in American letters. The Doctor's first book to attract attention was made up from his essays in the *Atlantic*, and appeared over the attractive title of "The Gentle Reader." No book of its class since "The Autocrat" has delighted so wide an audience. "The Pardoner's Wallet "—not so good a title, perhaps, as that of the first book —is of the same kind, and a delightful kind it is. That these books by Dr. Crothers should be so popular shows that this age is not given up entirely to novel - reading or to living the strenuous life.

Dr. Crothers began preaching when he was nineteen years old and has kept it up ever since—for about five years as a Presbyterian and since then as a Unitarian. Until the last seven years such things as he had published were sermons and articles in religious journals. His first magazine article was published in 1898 or 1899 in the *Atlantic Monthly*. In 1902 Messrs. Houghton, Mifflin & Co. published a little story by him called "Miss Muffet's Christmas Party." Dr. Crother's life has been taken up with the duties of his profession to which he has always given the first place. He has never written his sermons, and he objects to "essays " in the pulpit, but he has always been in the habit of writing for his own amusement.

Photo by Purdy, Boston
THE REV. S. M. CROTHERS, AUTHOR OF "THE GENTLE READER," ETC.

It is authoritatively announced by Dr. Robertson Nicoll, and he ought to know, that Mr. Swinburne is engaged in preparing a new book. "Love's Cross Currents," recently published by Messrs. Harper, was not a new book, having been written more than thirty years ago. Dr. Nicoll does not hesitate to say that Swinburne's *magnum opus* as a prose writer is the book that is still to come. The chapters that make the foundation of this book were begun more than a quarter of a century ago. Mr. Swinburne then determined to write an exhaustive book upon the Elizabethan dramatists, and to this end saturated himself with their writings. The first instalment of the book came out in the *Fortnightly Review* when Mr. Morley was the editor. From time to time chapters appeared, each dealing with one dramatist. Then the continuation of the essays was taken up by the *Nineteenth Century*, and ran through that magazine during several years. Later Mr. Swinburne contributed chapters of the same book to *Harper's*

reading to be done in the British Museum and Swinburne disliked to go there. Finally he was persuaded, and after a quarter of a century was "seen there again bending over Rowley quartos and making extracts." An interesting incident connected with this story is that he should have allowed a mass of work, to which he had given a consider-

Photo by Elliott & Fry

MR. ALGERNON CHARLES SWINBURNE

Magazine. The book, Dr. Nicoll tells us, has been close upon completion for years. It was virtually finished several years ago, but there was some

able portion of his life, to remain scattered and lost in magazines for the sake of about ten pages. "This shows two things," says Dr. Nicoll: "an amazing strength of the artistic conscience, and an amazing faith that time would allow *him* to take nearly forty years over *a book.''*

D. Appleton & Company in the series designed by Mr. Ripley Hitchcock called ''Stories of the West.'' Mr. Hough took the cowboy for his subject

MR. EMERSON HOUGH

This is not a very good portrait of Mr. Swinburne, but it is the best that has been taken in recent years. It represents him as a little more robust-looking than he is at the present day. There is a striking contrast between this massive dome, all-seeing eye, and large, clear-cut nose, and the dreamy portrait painted by the late G. F. Watts when the poet was in the first flush of his success.

❧

Mr. Emerson Hough is very much to the fore as a writer of fiction. The periodical press is publishing serials by him and publishers are rushing out books from his pen. Mr. Hough, as this picture proves, is a young man, and he is capable of a lot more work than he has done. His first book that I remember was published by Messrs.

and treated him so picturesquely that the book was as entertaining reading for the average reader as a novel.

❧

Mr. Edgar Saltus, who has not published a novel since 1903, has brought out through the A. Wessels Company a new story called ''The Perfume of Eros: A Fifth Avenue Incident.'' One need not go any farther than the title to understand the character of the book. Mr. Saltus is one of the cleverest of the younger generation of American writers, but he has not yet made the place for himself that his talent should command. Somebody in England recently made up a volume of his epigrams and aphorisms, and it was one of the wittiest books of the year.

THE HOUSE OF JULIET, SHOWING THE PIAZZA DELLE ERBE

That the writing gift may be hereditary is proved in the case of two daughters of Mrs. Julia Ward Howe. Mrs. Richards has long been known as the writer of unusually popular children's books, while Maud Howe Elliott has written novels and other books. Her "Roma Beata," which was published a year ago, was most delightful reading. She has followed this by another volume, "Two in Italy," which is illustrated with full-page drawings by the author's husband, Mr. John Elliott. The Elliotts, by the way, have taken a studio in New York for the winter. They spent their summer in the literary and artistic colony that has builded its home on the hills around Windsor, Vermont.

The town of Verona, Italy, having recently acquired the tomb of Juliet, it is interesting to see what that tomb used to look like and what it looks like to-day; and it is also interesting to know that the house of Juliet still stands. It is the one in the picture with the tablet set into the wall over the arch. Apparently it is now occupied by a hatter, if we may judge from the sign that swings under the windows.

"A Levantine Log-Book," by Jerome Hart, the clever editor of the San Francisco *Argonaut*, is announced by Longmans, Green & Company. The book consists of a series of sketches based on a stay of two seasons in the Levant. Mr. Hart, although a busy editor, finds time to travel. He has already written a book of his travels in Spain and through America. He has a good journalistic style and his books are decidedly readable.

Miss Ellen Glasgow's new novel, "The Wheel of Life," is one of the first to usher in the new year. Miss Glasgow, who won her spurs as a writer of Southern stories, has laid the scene of her new novel in New York City and made its hero a literary man. Miss Glasgow's first novel, which was published in her callow youth, but which gave great promise, was called "The Descendant." Its hero was a journalist and the scene was laid in New York; so New York is not a new background for Miss Glasgow's stories.

The Countess of Strafford has edited a fourth and final volume of "Leaves from the Diary of Henry Greville," which will be published in this country by Messrs. Scribner. The time covered is from 1861 till 1871. The Countess brings the journals down to 1871, though they were carried on for a little while beyond that year; but after that they are of too private a nature for publication.

Among the new recruits from royalty into the realm of letters is the Crown Princess of Saxony, who early in the new year will publish a book called "Confessions of a Princess." The book is an autobiography, and if it really gives us the true autobiography, and not a fictitious one, it will be well worth reading.

In Captain Harry Graham's new book, "More Representative Men," he has this amusing but good-natured fling at Mr. Carnegie's library-giving habit:

> And now his private hobby 't is
> To meet a starving people's need
> By making gifts of libraries
> To those who never learnt to read ;
> Rich mental banquets he provides
> For folks with famishing insides.

The author of "The Trident and the Net," who is also the author of "The Martyrdom of an Empress," has baffled the curiosity of those who would penetrate her anonymity. It is known, however, that she was really a maid of honor to the martyred Empress of Germany; that she married a member of the English diplomatic corps in Vienna, and that she now lives in this country and has lived here for a number of years. Her family consists of her husband and one son. Her husband is an editor and writer; the son is busy with his education. Their home is within easy reach of New York, and is an old-fashioned house surrounded by large grounds—some twenty-five or thirty acres. The author of "The Martyrdom of an Empress," as she is always described, has not been off these grounds in four years. She lives there winter and summer, and amuses herself with her garden, her dogs, and her writing.

Amelie Rives—the Princess Troubetzkoy—has recently returned from Italy and gone to her home in Virginia to devote her time to her literary work. Her most notable work was done at the old homestead, and she has gone back there for further inspiration.

Mr. Volney Streamer, who will be pleasantly remembered as the literary adviser of Brentano's, and as the author and compiler of a number of books, has just accepted the position of librarian of The Players, for which he is eminently fitted.

Unless the owner of the recently discovered letters of Charles Lamb, which are to be published in the *Atlantic Monthly*, permits of their publication in an edition of Lamb's Works, no edition of "the gentle Elia" will be complete. It is very irritating to English biographers to find so much literary material owned in America, and by those who guard their treasures with a jealous eye.

Mr. Herbert Paul, in his "Life of Froude," does not prove that this fascinating historian stuck to facts. Apparently he never attached any great importance to the truth. He worked for effect—to make a picture—rather than for historic accuracy.

Mrs. John Lane, an American woman married to an English publisher, has written a book called "The Forbidden Fruit." It is not, however, a novel, but is a treatise on the shaddock or grape fruit, which is one of the institutions of the American dinner table, but very little known in England. Mrs. Lane, by the way, is called an American woman, though she was born in Switzerland. She was, however, educated in Boston and spent most of her life there, and her first husband was a Boston man.

The late Edward Atkinson was not only a statistician and economist, but he was the inventor of a stove,—a curious construction that burned very little fuel but cooked slowly. If I remember rightly, the food could be put in at night and would be ready for the morning meal, and not more than ready. Mr. Atkinson's contention was that it was not only a saver of fuel, but that it was the best possible cooker of food, as it cooked slowly and every particle was done to a turn. After hearing him describe this stove I came very near buying one. I did not do so, however, but a friend of mine did, and I profited by her experience.

Mr. M. M. Dawson's book, "The Business of Life Insurance," has reached a second edition, which is not surprising considering the amount of attention that the life-insurance business is attracting. Our insurance companies would do well if they would only take as their motto, and live up to it, the saying of Poor Richard, "Honesty is the best policy."

Apropos of the late John Bartlett, the compiler of that invaluable book "Familiar Quotations," a woman was heard to say not very long ago that Bartlett was her favorite author; that he wrote the best poetry and the best epigrammatic prose of any modern writer. Which reminds me of the woman who liked the dictionary because it was written in such short sentences.

THE TOMB OF JULIET AS IT WAS

THE TOMB OF JULIET AS IT IS TO-DAY

A series of papers on "The Negro and the Nation," published by Mr. George B. Merriam in the Springfield *Republican*, have been collected and will be published in book form by Messrs. Henry Holt & Co.

It is interesting to watch the changes that are going on in out-of-door magazines. A few years ago we had but one country-life paper. That was *Country Life in America*. It was, as the legend goes, "a success from the start." Mr. J. Horace McFarland, of Harrisburg, Pa., was the printer of this magazine, and his work helped largely to give it its reputation. The publishers, however, Messrs. Doubleday, Page, & Company, when they set up their own printing establishment in New York, took over the printing of their two magazines. Mr. McFarland's occupation, so far as a country-life periodical was concerned, seemed to be gone—but only for a time. The Review of Reviews Company started *The Country Calendar*, and Mr. McFarland was one of its editors as well as its printer. It was a beautiful publication, but its days were short and it was soon absorbed by *Country Life in America*. Now comes the "important announcement" from Boston that Mr. J. Horace McFarland, who "has been one of America's foremost exponents of country living," is to be the printer and associate editor of *Suburban Life*, a periodical published at the "Hub," and with rather a local than a general circulation. It is announced that more pages will be added, and that the covers will be printed in color, and, in other words, that it will look as much like *Country Life in America* as it is possible to make it.

There are two thousand more biographies in "Who's Who" this year than there were last,—not American, but English, to which are added many American names. Not only does the book contain all these new biographies, but it records the number of the sons and daughters of the Who's Who as well as the number of his motor car.

So when you walk the streets of London and see a car dashing by you with a number dangling from its back you will know at once who is riding in it. It is now up to the American "Who's Who" to add sons and daughters and motor-car numbers to its new edition.

The publishers tell us that "The Divine Fire" is spreading; that they have already sent eleven editions of the book to the press and twenty-three editions of "The Lightning Conductor." Now the question is, Was "The Lightning Conductor" the cause of "The Divine Fire"?

The book of the holiday season was Mr. Marion Crawford's "Salve Venetia," with its 220 illustrations by Mr. Joseph Pennell. The book was published in two volumes, and the large edition prepared for the holidays was entirely exhausted. Those who secured this delightful book in time for the Christmas stocking were fortunate. In Mr. Crawford we have the brilliant as well as the accurate historian. When a novelist of his gifts turns his pen to the writing of history his audience follows him, for his histories have all the charm of romance. And why not? He writes only of the most romantic countries and times.

Messrs. Putnam have two romantic-sounding names on their list of authors —Myrtle Reed and Olive Green. The former writes sentimental stories; the latter tells us what to have for breakfast. One plays upon our heart-strings, the other caters to our baser appetites. Miss Green tells the story that she was recently trapped into a studio party where every one was expected to do parlor tricks. She happened to see a chafing-dish, and caught at it like the proverbial straw. When her time came, she proposed making pork-chops with spaghetti sauce. One of the men was despatched for the chops, and Miss Green's turn was pronounced the star act of the evening.

Another book is soon to be announced with Lord Byron as the hero. It is frankly called "The Maid of Athens." It is written by Miss Lafayette McLaws, and will be published by Messrs. Little, Brown, & Company. There have been three or four books with Byron as the hero, but none of them has suggested this in their titles. The latest, "The Marriage of William Ashe," of course, gave no sign that Byron was meant in the character of Geoffrey Cliffe, but it was not hard to recognize. Miss McLaws wrote her Byron story long before any of the others, appeared, and had serious thoughts of never printing it when she saw how many were published written around this theme; but she has been persuaded by her publishers, and the book will soon appear.

Mrs. St. Leger Harrison, better known by her pen-name, "Lucas Malet," has just finished a new novel. It is four years since her story, "Sir Richard Calmady," appeared, so no one can accuse her of over-production.

M. Jusserand has just finished the new volume of his literary history of the English people. He writes in French, then has a translation made for the English edition, and himself revises this translation. M. Jusserand speaks English perfectly, for he was a member of the French Embassy in London long before he became French Ambassador to this country.

It is gratifying to know that new editions of the late Mrs. Helen Jackson's "Ramona" are being printed every year. Mrs. Jackson wrote this story almost under inspiration. It was her first and her last novel, and though she published volumes of poetry of a very high order it is as the author of "Ramona" that she will be known in the literary history of this country.

Mr. Francis Wilson, the actor and musical-comedy singer, is known to be a great lover of books, not the ordinary every-day book, but rare books and fine editions. He would rather spend an hour in his library than an hour on the stage, and he has collected with so much skill that his books are known to all bibliophiles the country round. Occasionally Mr. Wilson takes his pen in hand and writes. He has written of his friend, the late Eugene Field, and now he is going to write of another dead friend, the late Joseph Jefferson, in a series of papers that will appear in *Scribner's Magazine*. The first paper appeared in the February number and dealt with "Rip Van Winkle." In it Mr. Wilson describes how the play was developed from the story, and how from the first Mr. Jefferson believed in its ultimate success. Of course the story is not new; Mr. Jefferson has told it in his inimitable way in his autobiography—but it is a poor story that will not bear retelling.

The amusing Mr. Edward S. Martin discourses on Riches in a recent number of the *Atlantic Monthly*. Mr. Martin apparently would be content with something less than a million a year.

Our good friend with a million dollars a year [he writes] cannot eat much more or better food, or drink much more or better drinks than we can. If he does, he will be sorry. We have the better of him in having the daily excitement and discipline of making a living. It is a great game—that game of making a living—full of chances and hazards, hopes, surprises, thrills, disappointments, and satisfactions. Our million-a-year friend misses that.

A million a year is too much money for any man unless he be generous enough to divide up with his friends; and there are such.

Mrs. Richardson, an English lady who has written a book on Japanese military hospitals, tells this amusing anecdote:

Said one English lady to another: "My husband has quite lost his appetite; I wish I could find something to do him good." Said the other: "You had better get him to try jiu-jitsu; it will probably cure him in a short time." Said the first lady: "I never heard of it before; how do you cook it?"

It is extraordinary the number of new things that are discovered about people long since dead. We are always having our attention called to unpublished letters of great men when we had supposed that everything concerning those men had been published. As, for instance, the Thoreau diaries, recently printed; all new material, and yet we have had volumes of Thoreau from time to time. I wonder what Thoreau would think if he were alive to-day and could see the Manuscript Edition of his complete writings, illustrated with one hundred photogravures from nature, in twenty volumes, and limited to six hundred signed sets, each containing a page of original manuscript. The illustrations are from photographs of the woods and fields about his forest hut. When Thoreau was alive no one bought his books. He describes in his diary the editions of unsold copies that were stored in his rooms — editions that now bring their weight in gold.

It was a happy thought on the part of Messrs. McClurg & Company to publish an edition of George Eliot's "Romola" in Italian. The work of the translation and editing is being done by Dr. Guido Biagi. Dr. Biagi writes to his American publishers:

The work is more important than I imagined. I have unexpectedly stumbled upon valuable material which throws great light upon Eliot's sources of information. I have found the original cards of all the books studied by George Eliot, here in the National Library, for " Romola." These books, with their ancient views of Florence, gave to her the first idea of the scenes of the novel. I have reproduced the cards signed by Lewes studying with her. I can now furnish more than 120 illustrations, and give documentary evidence of the historical materials utilized by the great novelist for her book.

Mr. Putnam Weale's book, "The Reshaping of the Far East," is illustrated with photographs taken by Japanese officers during the actions described, and were supplied for the work by the Japanese Government.

A new novel by Maarten Maartens, the Dutch novelist who writes in English, is called "The Healers."

Mr. Hall Caine before retiring to his castle on the Isle of Man stopped awhile in London to recover from the fatigues of his American journey. I am told that Mr. Caine has found a subject for his next novel and has very nearly found a title. He always finds his titles, I believe, before he begins his work, considering them a very important part of the book.

Mr. W. D. Howells's " London Films" has made a hit among London readers. They like his snapshots of them, taken, as one of their critics describes, by "pressing a button on the brain."

A new and sumptuous life of Mary Stuart is announced by Messrs. Scribner. One of its special attractions is the photogravure reproductions of every portrait of Scotland's famous Queen that has ever been made.

Mr. William J. Long has not been discouraged from writing books about animals because of the severe criticism of his work by John Burroughs. Mr. Burroughs had a good deal of fun with Mr. Long some time ago as well as with Mr. Thompson Seton; but neither of these writers seems to have been deterred by Mr. Burroughs's criticism. Mr. Long is out with a new book, and Mr. Thompson Seton is out with one or two new books. Some of Mr. Long's critics say that his animals are not human beings. This is a sly dig at Mr. Thompson Seton, whose animals are given all the qualities of human beings. Nature books are a good thing, but they are a better thing when they are real nature and not the nature of the author's imagination.

The Things of the Spirit

By EDWARD FULLER

PURELY materialistic theories of the universe are probably less common now than they were a generation ago. Nor at any time have they sufficed to explain the mystery of human life. Glorify brute force as we will, the story of the race cannot be properly told except in spiritual terms. The things of the spirit are the things which are eternal. It is this truth which Mr. George Edward Woodberry endeavors to enforce. "The Torch" * is a volume of lectures on "race power" originally delivered before the Lowell Institute of Boston. Mr. Woodberry's thesis may best be stated in his own words.

In one part or another of time and place, and from causes within and without, the race, coming to its best, flowers in some creative hope, ripens in some shaping thought, glows in some resistless enthusiasm. Each of these in its own time holds an age in its grasp. . . . These ideas, moods, energies, have mysterious potency; they seem to possess an independent being; though, like all the phenomena of life-energy, they are self-limited, the period of their growth, culmination, and decline extends through generations and centuries; they seem less the brood of man's mind than higher powers that feed on men. . . . Though they proceed from the human spirit, they rule it; and in life they are spiritual presences which are most closely unveiled to the apprehension, devotion, and love of men.

Such a theory of the history of the world is at least intelligible. It is essentially the theory of the Christian Church, and it explains so far as may be what is perhaps in the last analysis unexplainable. But one can hardly help feeling that Mr. Woodberry is occasionally a little fanciful in developing it. One may at least reasonably doubt whether the life of the race is so far an exact parallel to the life of the individual that the race, like the individual, finds its life by losing it—that is to say, that a nation by decay "wears the seal of God's election in history."

Such an idea is certainly carried to extravagant lengths when the author adds: "Nay, if the aristocracy of the whole white race is so to melt in a world of the colored races of the earth, I for one should only rejoice in such a divine triumph of the sacrificial idea in history; for it would mean the humanization of mankind." There seems to be a *non sequitur* here. Somewhat fanciful, too, is the emphasis placed upon the Titan myth as one of the corner-stones in man's interpretation of life. Mr. Woodberry has possibly read into the poets, ancient and modern, more than they intended to say. In dealing with the four whom he selects as the most conspicuous examples among Englishmen of race power — Spenser, Milton, Wordsworth, and Shelley,— he shows his finely critical sense, although some of his dicta are open to disagreement. It is difficult to see in Spenser a mind of transcendent power or to understand why he should be compared to Vergil. Nor can one think that the influence of Shelley has been as great upon the race in general as upon Mr. Woodberry.

The forces which govern conduct are spiritual forces. But in "The Children of Good Fortune" * Dr. Henderson takes a rather materialistic view of moral obligations. To him at least Goethe's doctrine—*Entbehren sollst du, sollst entbehren*—makes no appeal. He denies that the welfare of the race and the welfare of the individual can be at odds; right and wrong, he says, are purely matters of human opinion. The highest good is to get the most out of life for oneself. This is essentially the Nicomachean ethics. Dr. Henderson regards self-sacrifice as immoral. It was a view natural to the hard pagan world, where "deep weariness and sated lust" had "made human life a hell," and where the philanthropies which Christianity produced were

* "The Torch." By George Edward Woodberry. New York: McClure, Phillips, & Co. $1.25.

* "The Children of Good Fortune." By Dr. C. Hanford Henderson. Boston: Houghton, Mifflin, & Co. $1.30.

unknown; in these days there is a certain moral callousness about it. Praise of "efficiency" leads to a similar disregard of the ethical office of failure. It is more important for a man to do his best than to achieve his best. "Was the end gained or was it not?" This is the question which the author would make the test. "Saints and sinners, ascetics and sensualists, patriots and traitors, are, to that extent, moral or immoral in just the measure of their success. Moral condemnation falls upon conduct which does not carry out its own purpose." Elsewhere it is said that "morality, as a science, is unemotional." That is one reason why "scientific" methods of morality fail. Conduct cannot be divorced from feeling; we do not do right simply because we know it is right. Naturally "unemotional" morality leaves no place for religion. One feels disposed to say that Dr. Henderson has written a most immoral book about morality.

It was, perhaps, a certain absence of moral feeling which made that movement of the human mind known as the Renaissance too often seem a degradation rather than an elevation of life. The old ideal which it supplanted, the ideal of human brotherhood as embodied in a universal Church and a universal State, has had hard measure from modern critics; but there is still something to say for it. In his interesting volume of "Renascence Portraits,"* Dr. Paul Van Dyke deals with three men whose careers illustrated, in greater or less degree, the darker side of the revolt against tradition. These three are Pietro Aretino, Thomas Cromwell, and Maximilian I. They differ widely, to be sure, but they are not without some kinship of spirit. The Emperor Maximilian was the best one morally, not only pious but (which did not always follow) decent in life and speech. And although he was orthodox he was not indifferent to the New Learning. Dr. Van Dyke says that "his love for art centred around his dominant passions," but he adds: "Few men have served the muses for

* "Renascence Portraits." By Paul Van Dyke, D.D. New York: Charles Scribner's Sons. $2.00.

naught." As a politician he was singularly impractical, and his allies found him fickle and weak. The vices as well as the virtues of the "Renascence" —as Dr. Van Dyke prefers to say—are better shown in the singular career of Aretino. This pornographic blackmailer has usually been written down a knave; and truly it is hard to reconcile his brutal immorality with his interest in religion. But to label him "a blatant hypocrite" is, as Dr. Van Dyke points out, to evade the problem which his character presents. It is nearer to the truth to regard him as the child of his time alike in its good and its evil. A similar test may be applied to Thomas Cromwell. Dr. Van Dyke is an apologist for Wolsey's *protégé* and successor. While he does not paint him as "a Protestant hero" and says truly enough that his attitude towards the Church was dictated by political considerations, he believes that he was "a statesman working hard to give England an efficient government and to guide her safely through the difficult transition from the mediæval to the modern state." No doubt Cromwell has been unjustly accused of many delinquencies; and the testimony of Pole, which is here ably analyzed, must be taken with several grains of salt. But the unfavorable view of his character, which Dr. Van Dyke attempts to refute, does not depend upon the testimony of Pole. It may be amply justified by the admitted facts of his career. That he was a man who could be genial when he was in the mood, that he was not incapable of kindness, is perfectly true. But lack of real principle made him cruel to those within his power, and subservient to the King. His correspondence with the Princess Mary alone suggests the applicability to him of the phrase once applied to Bacon—"the meanest of mankind." The best answer to Dr. Van Dyke's defence is the wellnigh universal hatred with which he was regarded by the English people. No man ever more richly deserved his fate. His bloody end was at least in some sense an expiation for the murders of More and Fisher. Dr. Van Dyke thinks that he would have saved these; but it was he who brought them into danger of their lives. Probably he was not without some compunctious visitings of nature when he was brought face to face with the results of his intrigues. But of genuine moral scrupulousness he does not seem to have had a trace. In this respect he was a fairly typical example of the baser side of the Renaissance. And because he represented its material and not its spiritual ideals his life ended in the only kind of failure that counts—moral failure.

How far we have travelled from the moral ideals of the Renaissance, how far we have returned to the moral ideals of the Middle Ages, are curiously illustrated in Dr. Gladden's little book on "Christianity and Socialism."* It has been the fashion to regard what we call with patronizing contempt mediævalism as the synonym of all that is unintelligent and reactionary. But that conception of a universal Church and a universal State which was its essence is a noble conception; and in our revolt from individualism and nationalism we are returning to it. Dr. Gladden says truly that the teaching of Christ is addressed to the individual; but its effect is to bring the individual to a renewed social consciousness. There are those who assume that the doctrine of the brotherhood of man is a new doctrine, that its discovery has been left to modern philanthropy. But the great monastic movement of the Middle Ages was based upon nothing less. We are apt in these days to plume ourselves upon our industrialism and to believe that the type of civilization illustrated by the trolley car has finally solved the painful riddle of the world. Yet there

never was a time when the gulf between rich and poor was deeper or the sum of human misery more startling. There is every reason to believe that labor was much better off, comparatively speaking, in the thirteenth century than it is to day. A more modest estimate of the achievements of applied science would therefore seem to be in order. Dr. Gladden's appeal for the application, not of science, but of Christianity, to the problems of life is justified by the facts, although he himself apparently does not recognize the historic reason for making it. His book is none the less full of good advice to both employers and employed, and he endeavors to reconcile their differences in a truly irenic spirit.

It is curious to note how in "The Essentials of Spirituality" * an advocate of "ethical culture" like Dr. Felix Adler lays marked emphasis upon individualism. He observes, for example, that Savonarola was "too passionate" to possess true spirituality. "The spiritual life is unperturbed and serene." And yet it is still true that he who loses his life shall find it. The old ascetic ideal, which drove men into the African desert, failed to conquer the world. The man who makes the thought of perfection his constant inner companion is not likely to be a conqueror. And in fact Dr. Adler does not mean quite what he says. His theory followed logically would lead us all into a moral Nirvana. But if we are to regard the welfare of others "as much our concern as our own," then we must take up social duties and learn that the things of the spirit are the things of the life around us.

* "Christianity and Socialism." By Washington Gladden. New York: Eaton & Mains. $1.00.

* "The Essentials of Spirituality." By Felix Adler. New York: James Pott. $1.00.

The Self-Hypnosis of Authors

By MORGAN ROBERTSON

BEING a literary worker, and having drawn the deductions embraced in the following argument from his own experience and observation, the writer may, perhaps, be excused the rather cocksure tone of the specialist rendered necessary by his subject; but, being anything but a specialist, a psychologist, he will make no assertions and deal in no abstractions not based upon the now generally accepted "working hypothesis" of the late Professor Hudson — that is, that the subconscious mind (subjective brain, subliminal self, "immortal soul") is constantly amenable to suggestion and is unable to reason inductively.

Hypnosis, say the psychologists, is induced sleep, of exactly the same nature as natural sleep, and they adduce as proof the well-known suggestibility of the somnambulist, who will always go back to bed if so ordered to by a familiar voice. But what the psychologists do not say is that hypnosis is but the visible, spectacular phase of a vast mind state extending from simple preoccupation through the stages of absent-mindedness, reverie, stupidity, drowsiness, drunkenness, somnambulism, sleep, stupor or lethargy, to coma and death; and that we are all of us— all who think, and work, and worry,— according to our habits of life, in one of these stages, and in each stage amenable to suggestion in a degree proportional to the depths of our slumber. It is said that we are absent-minded, or queer, or drunk, or crazy, or that we are down with nervous prostration, but never that we are hypnotized, even though the word has been used so often to express its exact, though hidden meaning, that it has become ironical slang. "He had me hypnotized," we hear a yarn-spinner say, telling a story on himself, and not realizing that it was his amenability to suggestion or his inability to reason inductively that made the story possible.

Hypnosis, we are told again, is fatigued consciousness, plus a dominant idea. Granted, but we are not told the rest—that it makes little difference whether the consciousness is fatigued first, or whether the dominant idea comes first; whether the consciousness is fatigued suddenly, as in the presence of some overpowering personality, or as the result of shock, or is wearied by years of mental effort; whether the dominant idea is born of the victim's own life and environment, or is projected telepathically from the subconscious mind of the person nearest to, or with the strongest influence over, the subject of the hypnosis. Yet these are iron-hard facts—except that in the latter case the dominant idea can be removed instantly, at any stage of the hypnosis, by intelligent suggestion from the influencing personality.

Now what is this subconscious mind, so amenable to suggestion? There is a theory which appeals to the writer. Consider yourself born without the five senses. You have never in your life seen anything, not even light. You have never heard anything; you have never smelled nor tasted anything; you have never felt anything; you have not known that the food which kept you alive was pumped into your stomach. Yet, if you were jostled and massaged enough to keep your blood circulating, there is no reason why you should not live and grow—that you should not be a human being, though unaware that you were alive. For consciousness is a function of the brain, and the brain is merely a receiving and transmitting station for the five senses — an automatic machine, fitted by evolution to cognize and tabulate the perceptions sent in by the senses, and to send them —"the stream of consciousness"—to the storehouse of the memory, the primordial brain of Nature. This brain is the intelligence that attends to all involuntary bodily functions, such as heart action, digestion, respiration, etc., and kept you alive while your senses were dead. This primordial brain is the race consciousness, the repository of the inherited knowledge known as instinct. And while its limitations cannot be defined, it is certain that it has knowledge of all things in the universe of interest or concern to its owner.

Now, from a healthy, waking consciousness there pours into it a steady stream of perceptions to lodge there as memory, and from it to the waking consciousness there rises nearly as steady a stream of memory pictures, with intuitions and impulses born of its clairvoyant knowledge. When this knowledge is of the workings of another brain, or consciousness, it is called, when proved to be so, telepathy; but at the time, only a trained and studious self-observer can distinguish telepathy from pure intuition.

So much for the theory: the idea is to make clear that this primordial brain, with its store of memories pertaining to the life of its owner, becomes an active, intelligent entity, with powers all but omnipotent, save that it cannot of itself refuse a suggestion, because its function is to receive and store up. Another point which may be touched upon here is that, while in the case of trained trance mediums, mind readers, clairvoyants, and second-sight Scotchmen, this subconscious mind can force its knowledge into the waking consciousness, with the rest of us it can only do so by affirmation of a thought passing through the brain; there will be an uprush of insistent intuition which fixes the thought, and, as we say, we "have something on our minds." This mind state is so common that the law of affirmation behind it deserves illustration, and in its proper place there will be given incidents that prove it.

The subconscious mind (primordial brain plus memory) cares for the individual during sleep, drunkenness, lunacy, or any state or condition in which the waking brain is inhibited from performing its part. It guides homeward the exiled cat, the carrier pigeon, and the horse with a lost and helpless rider (it would guide the rider

were it not for the conflicting auto-suggestions coming from the reasoning, but bewildered, brain still in charge of the body); it takes good care of the hypnotic subject until the compelling suggestions of the operator come into it; and it gives up, as intuition or telepathy (inspiration), its clairvoyant knowledge to the author, or other creative worker, who can by intense concentration of mind upon his *idea* banish from his brain all other form of thought—that is, hypnotize himself, or, as he might say, get into the mood for work.

There is a time, or rather a mind state, between sleeping and waking—in this abstraction of creative thought, in the frenzy of the poet, or the indolent mood of the dreamer—when one mind is going off duty and the other coming on, that the two are in close touch or communication, and the far-seeing powers of the subjective will be given to the working machine of the objective mind — the brain; and the thought that evolved and the work that is performed through this merging of consciousness will be superior in quality to any that the waking consciousness itself can produce at its best. It will be inspired.

And so Joseph Conrad, a Pole, gets the wonderful mastery of the English language, which, according to report, he cannot speak correctly. And thus did Victor Hugo, a fairly prosperous and comfortable gentleman who never saw much of the world, reach out into the subliminal realm and sense from suffering fellow-men the acme of mental agony that he put into his books. And in the same manner did our latter-day Kipling, a twenty-six-year-old boy at the time, grasp and all but comprehend the realistic picture of life that others lived, and put it into "The Light That Failed"—only, being young, with limited outlets in his objective life, he did not get the whole. He scamped the explanation of the Maisie that he saw—the missing character in the story, the invisible lover, or protector, of the girl. Had Kipling waited a few years, he might have seen that man,

So far—good. So we get our inspiration—all of us who create. But let this be continued though the years; let the self-hypnosis become easier from practice, the auto-suggestions (ideas) scarcer from the drain upon them, and the brain, the suggesting machine, designed only for the *uninspired* work of human existence, become worn and weary from the strain of giving articulate expression to intuitive thought foreign to the life of the thinker, then the self-hypnosis will become chronic; the sluggish brain cannot recover and protect the helpless subliminal self until the next imperative conception (idea) comes along to engage its attention, and there will be an influx of telepathy of all kinds—uninvited, unwanted, unnecessary to the victim's life and work,—which, finding an outlet in the random thoughts that flit through his brain, will rise up and torment him with an insistence and force far exceeding that in the brain that gave it birth—the brain that is suffering the reality, but *knows* the reason of it.

The victim will think it emotion of his own. He will have moods—will become blue, wretched, despondent, with occasional unexplainable elation; he will be weak of will, and helpless before any suggestion, whether it come in the form of advice, good or bad, or as a sneer, a slur, an insult, or a criticism. In time, unless his physical health breaks down and he goes mad too soon, he will realize that he has what they call nervous prostration, and will seek the remedy—rest and change. But, unless he can trace out and run down to its source every telepathic thought that has afflicted him, every harmful suggestion given him, and offset these influences by intelligent *counter*-suggestions, he will never, in this life, completely recover from the effects of his alleged nervous prostration.

One of the greatest temptations which assail the literary worker is to stimulate the brain with liquor, or rather, to lash it when tired; for liquor will not stimulate: it will only drive the brain along on the level of thought that it started on. Then comes the reaction—shattered nerves. In discussing this matter once with a friend, the writer was told of the following experience:

"Up to the end of my third year of story-writing," the friend said, "I had used whiskey casually, sparingly—for it always nauseated me,—and with no thought of its value as a stimulant to the brain. At this time, almost stupid from overwork, but only realizing that I was a little tired, I complained of my condition in a refined home where I was a visitor, and was offered a glass of whiskey to brighten me up. Sensitive to suggestion though I was, this of itself might not have started me to drinking; but the daughter of the house, a well-bred, well-conducted, intellectual girl, hardly more than a child, claimed the same mental fatigue, and, in the presence of her father and mother, drank a little of the same whiskey. It was the first time I had seen a girl of her class drink whiskey for any reason; the incident went into my soul as a suggestion, and whiskey, as a remedy for brain fag, assumed an importance it could never have attained through the advice or example of men. Thenceforth, through the years that followed, I drank whiskey when tired, and always paid dearly for it in the reaction that followed when the work was done—each indulgence being followed by a deeper prostration and a harder struggle to quit. Then there came a time, at the end of a terrible tussle with a dead brain—which nothing but whiskey had revived and driven to its task,—when I found myself without the will-power to stop. Whiskey had me fast; the days and weeks went on, and with nothing in the way of work on hand to engage my thoughts, and entirely unable to concentrate my mind, I could only save myself from utter and ruinous collapse by continuing the supply. But the subliminal self within me, that had given me the plots for my stories, and had, evidently, prompted me to the study of suggestion and suggestibility years before against the very emergency now threatening, arose to the situation in the nick of time. One morning, as I lay half

awake, it took me back on an introspective tour through the years of
drive, and dream, and drink, to that
all but forgotten incident of a refined
young girl drinking whiskey as a remedy
for mental fatigue. It was long since
I had seen or heard of her; but I met
her soon after on the street—a matured
woman, still· refined, well-bred, and
well-conducted. The remedy for brain
fag had not affected *her*. As coherently
as I could I explained the terrible potency of suggestion, and asked her to
experiment with a counter-suggestion.
She had forgotten the first, and denied
any responsibility for my downfall;
then, laughingly, and yet with a note
of earnestness, as though she half-be-
lieved me, delivered the command:
'Don't drink whiskey,' and at the end
of our talk repeated it. I had taken
several drinks that day; but when I
thought of the next there came to me
the old nausea. I have not tasted it
since, nor thought of it without that
sickened feeling. There was no nervous trouble from the sudden depriva-
tion; she had purged my soul and body
of whiskey as quickly and as thoroughly as she would have cleaned a
slate with a sponge."

"All humbug," some will say. "An
effort of will is just as effective." Then
why are churches and temperance societies maintained, and eloquent men
paid high salaries to talk and "suggest," if sinners and drunkards may
save themselves?

Down in the hidden recesses of that
man's soul, buried under the memories
of the years that had passed, lurked
the almost forgotten suggestion that
whiskey was good for mental fatigue.
By reconstructing his soul he himself
might have reached it: the words of
the woman, backed by her personality,
went straight to the spot. And the
psychologist will say that it was *auto-
suggestion* after all. Of course. But
the woman was needed, as are the
preacher, the lecturer, and the Sunday-
school.

Another friend, a gray, wise man
from whom the writer has received
much light on these puzzling psychic
problems, told of a harmful suggestion

given him when very young, from
which he never recovered. He was writing short stories at the time, and the
usual mental fatigue had come to him.

"I was never able to trace it," he
said—"indeed, I only remember the
spoken words from the derisive tone
in which they were uttered, and which
fixed them in my memory long after
the speaker was forgotten. And I
only gave the speech its place as a suggestion after a close study of myself
and the reason of a certain bent of mind
—not peculiar to myself, for I know
that others are so hampered—which
prevented me from beginning a new
story until my pockets were empty and
I had reached the limit of personal
credit. I could write long articles and
long explanatory letters, could attend
to matters of business with my accustomed energy, and felt no inhibition
on my mental powers when directed
toward any of the problems of life not
connected with fiction-writing. I was
rested from the brain fatigue from
which I had suffered; my inventiveness
was not at fault, for I could turn readily
to mechanical contrivances; and, in
short, I was in good mental and physical health. But plots would not come
to me until the nose of the wolf was
under my door, and the reason was
that some one—some man, woman, or
child—had said to me when I was sick
and suggestible, possibly in answer to
my complaint of brain fag, that all
that ailed me was that I was lazy—too
lazy to get to work at a story until
compelled to. As a statement, it was
a lie; as a suggestion it became a
vital truth; for since then, until I quit
story-writing, I obeyed it, except for a
short time during which the curse was
annulled by counter-suggestion given
me during induced hypnotic sleep.
For a few months after this operation
I was able to evolve a new story before
finishing the one engaged upon; but
overwork again plunged me into self-
hypnosis, and the first suggestion resumed its sway. Auto-suggestion did
me no good, and I never could find
that person. I would like to, even to-
day, for he or she ruined my literary
career."

Now, in regard to the much-vaunted *auto*-suggestion of the psychologist— plain ordinary will-power, or the giving of direct commands to yourself to do this, or think that, or put the matter from your mind—there is this to say: it is on tap mainly to those who do not need it — to those who are not self-hypnotized. The self-hypnosis of creative effort puts individual will-power out of reach; for the subliminal self that so largely prompts your moods and emotions, being made of memories, is under the telepathic or suggestive influences of the personalities that have furnished the memories, and no effort of will is available unless these personalities are in agreement. Yet they can be forced to agreement. When an author, by intense concentration of mind, compels himself to take up a piece of work—distasteful for the time— he, as we say, conquers himself; but he really masters by telepathy (hypnotizes at a distance) the personalities with whom he is in touch—*en rapport* —and they fall into accord with his mood. But such an effort of will, far greater than that required in personally hypnotizing a single, and non-resisting, subject, leaves the mind nearly wrecked for the time,—certainly unfit to take advantage of the victory and finish the distasteful task. What wonder that authors, poets, and painters wait for the mood, the inspiration—the moment of telepathic sanction!

Harmful suggestion can be safeguarded against by right living, careful choice of associates, and intelligent counter-suggestion; but against harmful telepathy there is no protection unless, by a chain of inductions almost impossible to the tired brain, the source of it can be traced and the remedy applied. And withal, it cannot at the time be identified as telepathy. It may later, when, by collection of facts and a process of elimination, other factors have been cancelled; but when a strong emotion assails you in response to a trivial impingement on one or more of the five senses, you may know that it is a subliminal prompting, but you cannot know its hidden origin —whether it is intuition (direct from your subliminal self), or telepathy (emotion borrowed from the subliminal self of another). When you feel a strong impulse to write a letter, you cannot know at the time whether the impulse is in response to the needs of the case, or is telepathy from the other party. Such telepathy is very common, and explains the frequent crossing of letters; but only by induction can it be determined which brain first felt the impulse, and, according to the law of psychic phenomena, induction is impossible to the subconscious mind that has you in charge.

As the object of this argument is to prove that the mental fatigue of creative workers is the subjective, or a hypnotoid state, and as such often curable by the same means that an operator would employ in waking a hypnotized subject, it will, perhaps, as space is limited, be sufficient to relate a few experiences, two of which, clear cases of mind-reading, illustrate the law of affirmation mentioned in the beginning —that is, that a subliminal prompting, in the lighter stages of hypnosis—the brain fag of the creative worker—can only manifest itself to the consciousness by affirmation of a passing thought. One experience was the writer's, and in view of its strong personal nature it will, perhaps, be best to frankly relate it in the first person.

It was at the end of years of short-story work, and I was under medical treatment for nervous prostration, but with a dim, shadowy idea in my sleepy brain that there was something else the matter with me. Two dear friends were ill at the time. One, whom I will call Jim, I had been estranged from for several years, but in the days of our friendship he had so often talked with me over the telephone that I never heard the bell ring without being reminded of him. Shortly before I had casually heard of his serious illness, but could learn nothing of his whereabouts or actual condition. The other friend, Tom, had occupied my office, or studio, and when convalescent had moved to Brooklyn, whence he had written later that he was quite well. A week or so afterwards, while dressing in the morning, my telephone rang, but I could not make out what the party who called me was saying. It was a faint and confused jumble of sound; and though I did my best to stir up Central, there was no improvement, and at last I hung up the receiver with the disquieting thought in my brain that Jim was dying, and that some one—a friend, nurse, or physician —was trying to tell me so. The thought grew and tormented me. I could not put it away until, fully dressed, I turned to make up my bed. This brought to my mind the friend that had lain so long on that couch, and the thought came to me—driving out the other—that I ought to go over to Brooklyn and see how he was getting on. This idea, like the first, became insistent and tormenting, and I hurried through my breakfast, resolved to put aside everything else that day, and go over to see Tom. Before I started a messenger arrived from Brooklyn with the news that Tom was dying. An unexpected relapse had set in. He died late that day. I was there, and in the afternoon his brother arrived, and told me that early in the morning, forty miles away, he had learned of Tom's danger, and had called me up on the long-distance telephone, telling me to go over to him. He had repeated over and over to me: "Tom is dying. Go over and see him."

Later I learned that Jim was in no danger at the time, so there could have been no telepathy from him. And there is no determining whether that message that came into my brain in two parts was telepathy from the anxious brother, or subconscious knowledge of what the telephone diaphragm was saying. But each part of the subliminal uprush was the affirmation of a passing thought—one, of the sick Jim, suggested by the telephone bell, the other of the convalescent Tom, suggested by the couch. The first was an outlet for the subconscious knowledge of danger and death, the other for the subconscious knowledge of the need of my presence in Brooklyn; but it never entered my head that Tom

was in danger; I only felt that I ought to visit him socially.

In the deeper stage of hypnosis or sleep, the subliminal self can act without the necessity of a passing thought as an outlet or excuse. It impels the somnambulist to rise and wander around, caring for him a while, and taking him back to bed when the investigation is ended. The subliminal self wakened the writer suddenly at daylight not long ago, just in time for him to drive an interloping tramp cat away from his canary birds. It was not the cat that wakened him, for cats stalking birds make no noise; and there was no telepathy in it, unless he read the mind of the cat, or the subliminal selves of the birds, who were sound asleep. The incident proves nothing of self-hypnosis, but illustrates the powers of the subconscious mind.

The author of several books, while in this worn-out, hazy condition, told me of the following experience, which he considered a curious coincidence. He had felt the grind of penury, and had been forced to draw at times on the future, obtaining advances from editors and publishers for work yet to be done. He could always perform his part when so assisted, and was much surprised and hurt when the treasurer of a publishing house that had brought out his best books informed him that in the future, beginning with the first of the coming year, no more money would be advanced to authors. He accepted the dictum, and avoided that house when he was in need. But about a year after, when the grind of the mill was very severe, and he could hardly decide where to turn for money, he conceived the brilliant plan of choosing a title, drafting a short synopsis of a story to fit, and selling the story in embryo to some editor. Then, in casting about in his mind for the editor whom he might impose upon in this manner, he chose one who edited a periodical published by the same house that had closed its heart to the needs of authors. With his title and synopsis in his pocket, away he went to this editor, and actually induced him to refer the matter to the cold-hearted treasurer, while he waited in the sanctum until the editor returned. "The treasurer said No," the latter remarked as he took his chair. "No," he corrected, "he did n't exactly *say* No—he yelled it."

The author went out, in a strange condition of cheerfulness, nodding pleasantly to the iron-clad custodian of the bank account, and no wise cast down by the snubbing. Though without a cent in his pocket, he did no more worrying, slept well that night, and wakened in the morning, not knowing where he would get his breakfast. But his morning's mail brought him a letter from this publishing house, and as he opened it, out rolled a large and generous check, signed by that treasurer, with a statement that the remittance was in payment of royalties earned by one of his books, which he thought dead and buried, but which had been lately rejuvenated.

His mind state is easily understood. Dazed, and in a subjective condition from work and worry, his subliminal self sent him to the place where it knew a check was already made out for him —waiting to be mailed. His synopsis and idea of selling it were but the passing thoughts in his tired brain that served as an outlet. He forgave the treasurer, who, no doubt, had forgotten the check lately signed, because he had not the individuality to resent anything. He was nearly asleep.

Overwork fatigues the consciousness, and fatigued consciousness is hypnosis; and in all hypnosis there is a dominant idea, born of the operator's mind when the hypnosis is induced by him, in the mind of the victim when it is self-induced. An operator, unless a fiend incarnate, always removes the idea, or obsession, before waking the subject; in self-hypnosis the subject must awake as he can, trace the idea to its source, and remove it, or have it removed—

just how, he must decide for himself.

Every author knows the difficulty— in some cases the impossibility — of dropping a story until it is finished. He is under control of the *idea*, and can remove the obsession only by finishing the story. Then he awakes, or partly awakes, for a time—until the next *idea* comes along.

But the next *idea* may be one not available for fiction—one which cannot be removed in this manner; yet it will seize him with a force commensurate with the depth of his hypnosis, and if he is far enough gone, will torture him along the road to the borderland of madness. Rest, change of scene, and change of air will do him but little good. The *idea* has become part of his soul, and he takes his soul with him. Yet there *is* escape for him.

Phosphatic food will work wonders; and if, added to this, strong contrary *auto*-suggestion, delivered in spoken commands to the inner self at bedtime, do not clear the head, the same end may be attained by suggestion from a strong and sympathetic hypnotist who, when the sufferer is asleep, delivers the commands straight to the suggestible subconscious mind. This failing, the *idea* is a real obsession, a living, tormenting fact that has emanated from the mind of another; and in such case it must be traced to that mind and removed.

The incidents in our lives that will best prove to us this terrible law of psychology are usually so bound up in the most sacred relations and obligations that no man would care to give them out. But enough have been quoted, I believe, to prove the existence of the law to any thinking person, and perhaps to make some think who are not in the habit of it. The asylums are filled by such, as the world is filled with writers who have tried, and failed, and are left with their last *idea*.

Hearn's Stories of Old Japan

Reviewed by W. E. GRIFFIS

THE work on earth of the great interpreter of Japanese fancy is over, and here gathered up are the final fragments of the feast. A sympathetic biographical sketch, as clean-cut and expressive as a cameo medallion, signed F. G., is the appropriate preface. This, with the *Atlantic Monthly* article on "Lafcadio Hearn the Man," by Mr. Nobushige Amenomori (a former pupil in Fukui of the writer of this review), to whom Mr. Hearn dedicated one of his books and wrote about "an Oriental conservative," with the volume of Mr. Hearn's letters, to be collected and published, will make us fairly well acquainted with one who consecrated himself to a great and noble work. Surely the task of helping the East and West, Asia and Europe, to understand and appreciate each other, is one of the most praiseworthy. By his heredity, from a Greek mother and an Irish father, Hearn was especially fitted, by his love of beauty and keen emotional susceptibility, to understand the most emotional—and most self-mastered—of Asiatic peoples. His training in Latin scholarship for the priesthood—from which he broke away — added doubtless to the subtlety of his intelligence, while he admired and ever sought to obtain that element of strength which is characteristic of Northern tongues. One great secret of his success in interpreting the Japanese mind and temperament lay in his patience in seeking out and studying minutely the little things of a people said to be great in such. As Amenomori says of Hearn's mind, it "called forth life and poetry out of dust."

Of Mr. Hearn's very pronounced limitations—especially in studying the science of religion, in which his only teacher seemed to be Herbert Spencer —we may not here speak. Suffice it now to say that this little volume *—

duly bound to represent the silk stitching and pasteboard covers of a Japanese book, or rather fasciculus in a series— contains much that will please the admirers of Yakumo Koizumi (which, without having the Chinese characters before me, I take to mean Eight-fold Cloud Little Fountain).

"The Romance of the Milky Way" tells of the Chinese legend of the "River of Heaven," the court festival instituted in Japan A.D. 755, and of the old classic poems inspired by "Heaven's Silver Stream." The falling dew is the spray from the Herdsman's oar. From "Goblin Poetry" we learn how and why a strange wife brought to the village is called a "horse-bone." Two or three of the other papers tell of native conceits, and show what good copy for editors this faithful husband and father of subjects of the Mikado made of matter that fills the note-books of most students of Japanese lore. "A Letter from Japan" pictures the people of the little country playing with their war toys at home, while the conscripts are facing Russians on sea and beyond in Manchuria. In treating "Ultimate Questions," this ardent disciple of Spencer shows how all his adult life he was under the terrors of the conception of infinite cold, darkness, and space. Mr. Hearn seemed to be without the brace and comfort of certain ideas which lie outside the world of science, but his grasp of the notions of one whom he counted "the world's greatest thinker" is that of a trained mental athlete.

Very suggestive is the final page of this book in picturing in a sentence the elements educative of the people who dwell in "a land of cataclysms." The seer speaks truly in his farewell word, "The capacities of Japan remain unguessed."

*" The Romance of the Milky Way, and Other Studies and Stories." By Lafcadio Hearn.

Sayonara !

222

The Paris of "The Human Comedy"

By W. H. HELM

THE idea is very commonly entertained, even among those who are frequent visitors to *la ville lumière*, and indeed among residents in the more expensive quarters of the town, that the Paris of fifty years ago has almost entirely disappeared, and, if we regard Paris as a city whose boundaries are marked on the north by the Opéra, on the south by the Bon Marché, on the east by the Hôtel de Ville, and on the west by the Arc de Triomphe, the idea is sufficiently near the truth to be accepted as a fair generalization. To another Paris, quite as extensive, if less easily defined, the generalization scarcely applies at all. It may be doubted whether there is any city of equal size which contains so many unrestored houses of far more than centenarian age. Within a few yards of the Boulevard de Sebastopol, and parallel, to the east and the west, with that particularly modern thoroughfare, lie the Rues Saint-Martin and Saint-Denis, and throughout the greater part of their lengths these narrow streets belong to the old Paris rather than the new. Their tall, irregular, bulging houses, their rambling tiled roofs and dormer windows, are of the age when oil-lamps were hung by ropes across the street, and in the mind's eye of the student of history they are peopled with busy crowds whose bustling ceased some centuries ago.

South of the Seine, in and around the venerable Rue Saint-Jacques — along which Gauls and Romans journeyed to and from Lutetia,—there are scores of streets wherein the modern buildings are less in evidence than those which were already old when Napoleon turned the First Republic into the First Empire. The genius of Haussmann, who destroyed so much that was picturesque and created so much that was magnificent, laid his hands but lightly on the Latin Quarter, and spared many of the groves of the Mount Parnassus of Paris.

The truth of such reflections as these will specially impress any lover of Balzac who, his memory charged with the incidents and familiar with the characters of " The Human Comedy," seeks out the streets and houses so elaborately described by the novelist. He will be charmed on discovering that in many instances it is still possible to see what Balzac saw, and to find as real a background for events born of his fecund imagination as we see when we wander in the Katskills with Rip Van Winkle, in Notre-Dame with Quasimodo, or in the Grassmarket of Edinburgh with Old Mortality.

It is the triumph of Balzac that his characters live, and that to the reader well acquainted with even but two or three novels of the "Comédie Humaine" the men and women whose thoughts, words, and deeds are so minutely described are just as much realities as any historical figures of their period.

The Paris of Balzac may be said to cover an irregular area of about three miles round, at the heart of which stands the great Church of Saint-Eustache. Occasionally he invites us outside of that region, to Passy, or to Père-la-Chaise, but with very few exceptions all his Parisian characters dwell within its limits.

It is possible to present some of the local habitations, as they may actually be seen to-day, of Balzac's creations, and to make these material souvenirs take their places in the illustration of incidents of which he made them the scenes. He was possessed by the spirit of locality to an extent rare among imaginative writers. Not even the Kent of Dickens, or the California of Bret Harte, was more deeply bitten into the soul of the writer than Paris into the soul of Balzac.

The majority of those who know "The Human Comedy " at all, know it best from "Père Goriot," and however much critics may differ as to the relative merits of the fifty or so of novels and the many tales which make up the acknowledged life-work of the author, there is assuredly no more vivid analysis of many of the darker and a few of the lovelier aspects of human nature than this story of the old vermicelli-maker, his ungrateful daughters, and the various companions of his shabby existence in the boarding-house of Madame Vauquer.

"No quarter of Paris is less known," wrote Balzac himself of the particular region where lies that Rue Neuve-Sainte-Geneviève of which the Maison Vauquer is one of the most characteristic features, and it is one of the quietest quarters to-day. The street has been renamed (though the old name still remains on a slab of stone at one corner, and there is no Madame Vauquer now. At present the house is occupied by families of cane-chair-menders, mattress-stuffers, and others whose occupations can be carried on at home. The little garden, so carefully described in the novel, forms a convenient and pleasant *atelier* for a chair-mender, while woolcombing and mattress-stuffing can be performed with comfort and despatch in the courtyard, where the well is a picturesque but no longer a useful object, having been stopped-up on account of its danger to children and perhaps to the general health of the tenants.

As we sit on a stone bench in the rough-paved *allée* which runs along the front of the house, and look through the gateway into the sunlit street beyond, we hear again, if we know the story as we ought, the tramp of the soldiers and gendarmes who are coming to arrest the redoubtable Jacques Collin (familiar to his fellow-criminals as Trompe-la-Mort, and to his fellow boarders as M. Vautrin), the escaped convict who at last, through the treachery of another desperado, has been tracked down by the police. His faithless and mercenary comrade in crime having revealed his probable abode, the wizened old maid Mademoiselle Michonneau, who boards with Madame Vauquer, has been offered a thousand francs to drug him and to

ascertain, whilst he is insensible, that he bears the fatal brand upon his shoulder. She has duly performed her odious task. The police arrive, Vautrin's wig is knocked off, and an officer comes forward to seize him. Then the great enemy of society sees that, for the time being, his game is up, and he also sees, by the cowering appearance of the old maid, what part she has played in the catastrophe. Furious for the moment, he calms himself with an effort when he sees the pistols of the police, who would welcome resistance as an excuse for killing him. He draws himself up, and telling them that he understands their desire, he holds out his hands for the manacles. Then he turns his piercing eyes full on the livid face of "La Michonneau," whose own eyes are half-hidden beneath the green shade which she habitually wears. She shrinks back against the wall, and the convict turns to speak to the young provincial Eugène Rastignac, whose ambitious hopes he has penetrated. The rest of the boarders stand around watching the strange scene with mingled astonishment and curiosity. The convict is led away and, as he passes out of sight beneath the archway, the fat cook Sylvie, with just a touch of contempt for the company in general, cries, "Ah, well, he was a *man*, all the same."

Almost beneath the shadow of Notre-Dame, on the island which was for centuries the heart of Paris, and whereon, in far-off ages, the whole city stood, meanders a street of houses ancient in Balzac's days, and some of which were almost certainly there when the few historical events recalled in Victor Hugo's novel occurred. In the time of the Bourbon restoration, when the venerable heroine of Balzac's "Madame de la Chanterie" lived there, the Rue Chanoinesse must have appeared almost exactly as it does to-day. This beautiful old lady, whose life had been doubly wrecked in the storms of an unhappy marriage and of the Revolution, and who had seen her only child dragged to the guillotine, had settled in a quiet house in this peaceful thoroughfare, to devote her remaining years and the

salvage of her fortune to benevolence.   Aided by a few
admirable men who lodged with her, and by a priest of the
neighboring Cathedral, she sent forth material help and
the hope of a happier future to many brought low by misfortune.   When
to-day, as we
pass through this
p i c t u r e s q u e
street, we see—
as we may at any
hour between the
Cathedral   ser-
vices — a white-
haired ecclesias-
tic come out from
a *porte-cochère* on
to the time-worn
cobbles, we can-
not but remem-
ber the devoted
Abbé de Vèze
and the secret
b o u n t i e s of
Madame de la
Chanterie a n d
her friends.

Lovely char-
acters such as
Madame de la
Chanterie, lovely
in soul, and not
merely in t h e
physical envel-
ope of humanity,
do not abound in
the novels of Bal-
zac.   But there
are some who
come as near
to perfection as
men can hope to
arrive in this im-
perfect world.
None is more ex-
quisite in well-
doing than Bour-
geat, the poor
water-carrier of
the Rue des Qua-
tre-Vents.   This
sturdy native of
Auvergne, whose
earnings from his

PONS AND SCHMUCKE IN THE RUE DE NORMANDIE
("Le Cousin Pons")

laborious trade are as a rule barely   and his humble fare, is saving every
sufficient to pay for his garret   sou he can spare to obtain enough

money for the purchase of a horse and a water-cart. At length his little hoard has almost reached the desired sum, and he is looking forward to his horse and cart with far keener pleasure than did ever a *bourgeoise* to the carriage which her prospering husband had promised to buy for her. Just before the cart can be got, however, Bourgeat discovers that his fellow-lodger in the attics is a half-starved medical student, so nearly destitute that he cannot scrape together the fees for his examinations. The lonely water-carrier takes pity on the student, and lends him, on no security but gratitude and talents, the hoard so painfully put by.

More than this, he increases his daily toil, and shares his food with the lad, who at length passes out of the schools, and begins to earn something on his own account. As soon as he can make enough, the young doctor will pay back all that his generous, uncultured friend-in-need has spent for him, and will buy the long-desired horse and cart. But alas! the water-carrier succumbs to the strain to which more work and less food have subjected his once powerful constitution, and in spite of all the devotion that his much-loved and deeply grateful friend can give him, Bourgeat dies in the arms of the youth for whom he has sacrificed his life. That youth becomes rich and famous. He is Desplein, the fashionable surgeon of his time. His faith is dead, but in memory of the simple, loving Christian to whom he owes everything save his own talent, he goes secretly four times a year to the Church of Saint-Sulpice, and there kneels before the altar while the priest says a mass for the pure soul of the peasant whose charity and affection are such bitter-sweet memories for the great doctor. Scoffer though he is, he realizes, as he bows his head before the holy table, that there are more things in Heaven and Earth than are dreamt of in his materialistic creed. He would, as he declares with a rare emotion to a friend in whom he trusts, give all he possesses if the faith of Bourgeat could enter into his own brain.

Sylvain Pons, the elderly musician, is a character less pathetic than Jean Joachim Goriot, since the self-sacrificing love of Goriot for his selfish children is largely replaced in Pons by a selfish, if not wholly unamiable passion for the pictures, and china, and snuff-boxes which he collects so assiduously and with so keen an eye to a bargain. Goriot, moreover, is content with the wretched fare provided at Madame Vauquer's table, whereas Pons is ready to sacrifice his self-respect, so preciously guarded in other directions, in return for a costly dinner with his rich connections, whose flunkeys do not conceal

THE ARREST OF VAUTRIN

"À NOUS DEUX"

Rastignac at Père-la-Chaise in " Le Père Goriot"

their contempt for the ridiculously ugly old bachelor in his out-of-date clothes.

Yet there is still a pathetic side to the story of Sylvain Pons, and it is shown in his affection for his fellow-musician, the German pianist Schmucke. These two quaint *artistes* shared the floor of a house in the Rue de Normandie, in that quarter of Paris still known as the Marais, shared it rather unequally, because Pons filled the best of the rooms with his extensive collections. Schmucke's tastes needed no material objects for their gratification. Whilst Pons was haggling over a Sèvres tea-cup, Schmucke would dream of a *motif* of Mozart, and trace it to its origin in the world of sentiment. Pons was conductor of the orchestra at a boulevard theatre, and his friend was employed under him; Pons wrote the music for the lyrics, and Schmucke the orchestral parts. They used to sally forth together in the morning to give lessons at girls' schools, where their ugliness was as much a recommendation to the principals as their knowledge of music, and in the evening they walked together to the theatre. The idlers of the neighborhood called them "the two nut-crackers." They died within a month of each other, and were buried side by side.

Strolling through the Rue de Normandie we can picture the two old friends starting out to their work, Pons wearing his antiquated cape, his faded greenish coat, his black trousers, and his gaiters, and with his hat on the back of his head, Schmucke in garments a little less ancient in cut perhaps, but if anything more threadbare.

Yes, there they come. Schmucke is savoring a melody from "Il Barbière," Pons is chuckling to himself over his purchase this afternoon, somewhere in the neighboring Rue St.-Antoine, of a bronze statuette which he knows to be worth three hundred francs but for which he has given forty. They are ugly indeed, but there is that about them which arouses a kindly feeling, and we do not wonder that these strange-looking fogies, who could never have made love with success, are by far the best-loved of all in their little world at the theatre.

Balzac, so many of whose creations were laid to rest in the old cemetery of Père-la-Chaise, lies there himself, on the top of the hill whence his worldly hero, Rastignac, looked out, after the sorry funeral of poor old Goriot, over the Paris which he was beginning to understand. It is a wonderful panorama that one sees from this lofty hill, less extensive than the view from the top of the Eiffel Tower, less intimate even than that from the terrace of the great basilica of Montmartre, less picturesque than that from the heights of Saint-Cloud, whence Paris is seen with the green expanse of the Bois de Boulogne in the foreground.

But there is more of the history of the city in the view from Père-la-Chaise. One gazes out over the quarter of Saint-Antoine, where, at the foot of the hill, the Revolution began with the destruction of the Bastille. As we stand where Rastignac stood, we are surrounded by the bones of hundreds of the men who have given France her splendid place in literature, art, and science. Just below us is the willow that grows above Alfred de Musset's grave, and behind us is the stone bearing on its face that one word "Balzac," which speaks so eloquently to those who know the man in his works. The penniless Rastignac, his innocency sapped by the poison of social ambition, his heart torn between contempt for the daughter who left her father to die in a garret, and love for the woman who could offer him a road to wealth and power, turned from the grave of the weak, devoted old man and looked out over Paris, to the quarter between the gilded dome of the Invalides and the Arc de Triomphe, wherein, in those days, the luxury of the city centred. He had drunk of the bitterness of poverty and obscurity, he had tasted the sparkling wine of worldly success. He knew that the life opening before him was selfish, hard, mercenary, but he would conquer society with its own weapons.

"The struggle is between us two," he cried. And then, descending the

LA RUE CHANOINESSE AND THE ABBÉ DE VÈZE
in " Madame de la Chanterie "

whose father's burial he and the garçon of the Maison Vauquer had been the only followers.

The last of the material souvenirs of Balzac which we recall here is of the novelist himself rather than of his novels. In the year 1848 or thereabouts, being worried by duns in Paris, he took lodgings in Passy, then a village in the environs, at a house in the Rue Basse. There is little remarkable about the front of the house; it is just a plain, white, two-storied French dwelling of a hundred years ago, or of to-day, for that matter. But at the back is a garden, and at the bottom of the garden is a doorway leading into one of the oldest lanes in the world, from the look of it. Truly this *ruelle*, with its crumbling walls of stone and plaster, its ivy, and its shade of overhanging trees, is as happily devoid of suggestions of modern "improvements" as anything to be found within the girdle of the fortifications. By means of this byway, Balzac, when insistent voices from within the house reached his ears as he worked in his little pavilion at the end of the garden, could avoid the unpleasantness of an interview with any holder of the overdue bills which throughout his life were the only tangible results of his experiments as a printer and typefounder. It needs but little imagination to see him hurry off down the lane, hatless and in slippers, to await events, whilst he dreams of exploiting the jewels of Golconda or the silver mines of the New World. It was M. Rodin, by the way, the creator of that wonderful statue of Balzac which will some day "come to its own," who reminded us of the house at Passy. The great French artist of to-day admires the great French novelist of the past intensely, and it is a delight to listen to his reflections on the scenes and personages of the "Comédie Humaine."

hill with rapid strides, he went off to dine with Delphine de Nucingen, at

BALZAC AT PASSY.

COMMERCE

One of a series of eight lunettes on the Progress of Civilization
in the Rotunda of the Iowa State Capitol

Copyright, 1906,
by De W. C. Ward, N. Y.

Kenyon Cox

KENYON COX prospers in his art largely through his skill at drawing. He takes rank not as an interpreter of life, nor as an exploiter of ideas, but as a maker of pictures with an understanding of selection, of elimination, and of insistence in combination of colors, in premeditated balance, and in largeness of mass and line. He evolves results that attract attention through mastery and appreciation of formal rules rather than through quirks or idiosyncrasies. Of late years he has spent much time on wall decorations where he couples his thorough sympathy for present accessories to an understanding of academic traditions. With his clarity of perception he admires the attributes of classical antiquity; he analyzes the Renaissance method of coloring and of grouping figures, with heed to the scale on which they were drawn to conform to their architecture; he studies the details that bind them to their local wants. Then by the application of these results of the past to present-day requirements he creates mural decorations that for once are not easel pictures in heavy frames; he poses his men and women both for their own graciousness and for their share of the patterns and big tones of color that influence the general scheme of composition and that co-operate with the surrounding architecture. Besides, his desire for carrying power and proper accent and proportion in the result when in place leads him to seek both simplicity of composition and breadth and directness of treatment. Therefore he handles his medium of canvas and oil much after the fashion of fresco painters. First he completes fully rendered sketches of the whole composition with studies of the arrangement of drapery which help to solve the problem of design and space filling. Then he places upon his canvas a painstaking and minute drawing in black and brown. Lastly he applies his thin wash of paint sparing in outlines or local color or detail, with as a result an absence of the muddy or overworked effects brought by the loading of solid color. A series of eight lunettes on the Progress of Civilization in the Rotunda of the Iowa State Capitol well represent his latest efforts. Here, as the architecture demands more than usual prominence of the compositions, he gives vent to considerable decorative license in introducing landscapes and animals theoretically at variance with his canons, though all the while restraining himself to a treatment that forbids undue stress upon perspective. Again as the Rotunda benefits by an exceptional number of windows, he paints in a high key with considerable light and shade lest the shadows produce dark or spotty effects. In his "Commerce," which typifies the qualities of the series, he confines himself to simple and few colors with flat surfaces that remain sure in values. Here, too, the influence of his Venetian studies appears strongly in the white and gold drapery of the reclining girl, in the magenta of the tips of the wings upon her head, and in the blue of the horizon. Yet his decorative understanding guides him clear of jarring notes, and fills the whole with a gravity quite the antithesis of much of the modern "Music Hall" order of work. In more than any other way, however, he impresses his public with an ability to draw, and with a charm and classic strength in laying down the fundamental needs of his art.

Kenyon Cox was born in Warren, Ohio, in 1856. He studied at his art, while still quite young, in Cincinnati and Philadelphia until at the age of twenty-one he went to Paris for five years' work under Carolus Duran and Gérôme. His pictures were principally portraits and figure pieces until he took his first step towards mural work by painting two decorations for the library of Congress. He has also made a name for himself as an art critic through his ability to write clearly and forcibly of what he actually knows. Since 1882 he has been a member of the Society of American Artists and of other societies of the class.

H. ST. G.

DR. R. OGDEN DOREMUS.

Edwin Booth and Ole Bull

By DR. R. OGDEN DOREMUS

DURING a social call paid by Mr. Edwin Booth and his devoted friend, Dr. Fordyce Barker, at my house in Union Place (Fourth Avenue above 18th Street), New York, in September, 1868, I asked the eminent tragedian if he would read Byron's "Manfred" for the Philharmonic Society, while its orchestra of one hundred members and the Liederkranz Singing Society rendered Schumann's symphony. He replied: "I am going to Cincinnati to-night, but will read the poem, and write you my decision." He kept his promise, and here is his letter.

BURNET HOUSE, CINCINNATI,
Sept. 14th, 1868.

MY DEAR DOCTOR:

In a hurry! I have had Byron's "Manfred" copied (extracts from it), and herewith send you to ascertain if your musical accompaniment, choruses, etc., etc., can be arranged in accordance with it. If so, I will read it for you, some of these days and nights. But you know not what you do! You are dealing with a *Wampire!* I axes more nor what I gives, as you will surely find to your cost some day.

To return to our mutton pie. If these extracts can be used, or any part of them (draw a pen through the surplus ones), I think I can manage it, and feel pretty confident that I can furnish spirits

224

(though I be a temperance man) for the occasion. But you know I will be very busy after my shop in 23d Street is open, and I do not see just yet exactly how I can steal a night off. Will see.

While in Pittsburg I did go to the cemetery, as Mrs. Doremus advised me to do, and saw the splendid monument, the statue of her uncle; it is really very fine. The cemetery itself is, I think, in point of scenery and natural advantages, the finest in this country.

Please remember me kindly to Mrs. Doremus and to my dear Dr. Barker. Pardon my haste, and believe me,

Very truly yours,
EDWIN BOOTH.

P. S. Can you return the MS. I send with this? No! on second thoughts you had better retain it until we meet.

Till then, Adieu!

A fortnight later came a second, and longer letter, written in the same jocose style:

TOLEDO, Sept. 27th, 1868.

MY DEAR SIR:

As for the "*tout ensemble* of the whole," all I can say is, first, I will read "Manfred" according to Byron, if it can be arranged, provided my professional duties during the coming winter will permit, on condition that, should my first attempt prove a failure, you will give me an honorable discharge. Secondly, " I can call spirits from the vasty deep," but I am not quite positive that they will come, or speak when I do call them.

The "raps" are very feeble at present, but by my courageous example I may possibly succeed in winning over to the good cause a "dainty spirit" of the "Ariel" type.

Thirdly and lastly, I must know the object of this institution. If it be charitable, ye greenback is no consideration; on the other hand, ditto.

The successful performance of so novel a rôle (if I should succeed) will be sufficient remuneration, for it will be the means of opening a new rich field for future harvesting.

But to conclude (*à la* Dogberry), I may ask a favor of the "Society" one day, and to you as its worthy head and ears I will whisper my intent,— sh-sh-h! I have seriously thought of "doing" (as we say in the "green-room") "Manfred" at my theatre, and, to give it proper effect, I'll need the aid of those who sing and play a little. You may guess the rest. A subject for future consideration.

I know Byron is d—ning me above the clouds (if he be in that direction), for he hated actors, shows, and fairs, and *booths* (*vide* his letters con-

cerning Faliero), but it's a good thing and a Xtian's duty to refine and elevate the "Gods" and "Groundlings" of a playhouse; besides, it would be a "trump card." You see I do *not* ignore those quaintly symboled bits of paper.

You see, my dear Doctor, I have never been bold enough to "chisel" the dear *pub*. in this quiet, easy way. I've always given 'em my sweat in return for their "stamps," and I hesitate lest my first attempt at "reading" should "squelch" me.

Therefore, if at the last rehearsal my wits or voice should fail me, I'll claim the privilege of "throwing up the sponge." Thus you have the whole thing in a nut-shell; I'll do my best, and charge you less than any other notoriety you might light upon.

I hope all will terminate serenely, so that this may lead me into doing that which, I know, will be a great service to me.

With kindest regards,
I am yrs.,
EDWIN BOOTH.

In due course the Philharmonic Society announced Mr. Booth's reading of "Manfred" in its prospectus for the season's public rehearsals and concerts.

About a month before the date of the performance, I called on Mr. Booth at his beautiful theatre at 23d Street and Sixth Avenue (which should never have been destroyed to give place to a business structure), and was taken to his spacious and ornately decorated dressing-room. The celebrated actress Miss McVicker, who was then performing with him, and whom he afterwards married, was present. When I stated the object of my visit, she exclaimed: "Please don't ask Edwin to read 'Manfred.' He is already so overtaxed by the labors of the theatre,—superintending the costumes, about which he is very particular, and the working of the complicated scenes, etc., that he cannot get the sleep he needs."

This I knew, for Dr. Barker had informed me that he only slept four hours a night. I said that neither I nor the Philharmonic Society would consent to Mr. Booth's injuring his health, but that we had announced his reading of "Manfred," and had sold season tickets on the understanding that he was to do so. We were consequently placed in a predicament.

"Get Edwin Adams to read it," said Mr. Booth; "he will do it better than I can. In my paint and feathers, on my own stage, I can do anything; but in a dress-suit, white cravat, and white kid gloves, holding a book in my hand, I don't know where I should be." When I told him I did not know Edwin Adams, he volunteered to give me a letter to him. But I was loath to give up the idea of Mr. Booth reading for us. "I will have the poem printed in such large type that you can place the book on a music stand, and occasionally turn a leaf." I did so, and I have a copy of the book to this day.

"Besides I have another object in view," I added. "There are thousands of people opposed to theatres, who would not attend one of your Shakespearian performances, but would like

EDWIN BOOTH

to hear you *read* Shakespeare, as Mrs. Fanny Kemble Butler is doing. You need not memorize 'Manfred,' but only read it."

Mr. Booth was standing with Byron's poem in his hand, and, glancing at it, said, "I will do it."

The Evening Mail.

CHARLES H. SWEETSER,

EDITOR AND PROPRIETOR,

Office, 229 Broadway, cor. Barclay Street.

WEDNESDAY EVENING, SEPTEMBER 25.

—Last evening Dr. Doremus was serenaded at his residence on Fourth avenue by the Philharmonic Society, under the leadership of Carl Bergman, the recently elected president of the society. The following selections were admirably performed:

Fackeltanz....................Meyerbeer.
Overture, Rienzi................Wagner.
Serenade ....Schubert.
Overture, Merry Wives of Windsor . ....Nicolay.

After the music had ceased Dr. Doremus appeared and thanked, in a very happy speech, the society for the compliment. The company was invited into the house, where a bountiful collation was served. At the table speeches were made by Drs. Sands, Flint, Bill, and others. The occasion was a very enjoyable one.

"You are not announced for the next rehearsal and concert," I said, "for Mr. Ole Bull is to perform on his violin, with the orchestra."

At this Mr. Booth brightened up, exclaiming: "Please give me a letter of introduction to him. I have a special reason for wishing to meet him. After one of my performances of 'Hamlet,' a lawyer presented me with one of the most beautiful emerald rings I ever saw, saying that Ole Bull had given it to him. This lawyer has since died, and having doubts of his rightful ownership of the ring, I have always kept it in a safe-deposit vault, and now wish to return it to its real owner."

I told him this could best be done at my house, at dinner with our friends, or at a supper after one of his performances. As he was unable to appoint a time before the Ole Bull concert, I sent one of my sons to Booth's Theatre, during the last public (matinée) rehearsal of the Philharmonic Society, when the soloist always appeared, to ask Mr. Booth to come with him to Mr. Cutting's box at the Academy of Music, and present the ring to Mr. Ole Bull, in the presence of some friends. Unhappily, he was in the midst of a rehearsal. That evening (it was a Friday) Mr. Booth sent me the ring with a request to give it and an accompanying letter to Mr. Ole Bull, after the Saturday evening concert.

At the close of the performance, and in the presence of the orchestra and a group of mutual friends, I presented to the renowned violinist the gift of the Philharmonic Society—a piece of silver. I then handed him the ring—a large

to an entertainment at the house of a Grand Duke, to meet certain distinguished ladies. (His princely presence was always an attraction to the fair sex.) Late in the evening, wearied from the labor and excitement of the concert, with its repeated encores, and the animated conversation at the house of the Grand Duke, he had sat down to snatch a moment's repose. His head nodded; but almost immediately he was aroused by his host's touching his shoulder and offering him a glass of liqueur. On raising his hand to take the proffered glass, he found that this ring had been slipped upon his finger.

FRANK LESLIE'S ILLUSTRATED NEWSPAPER.

NEW YORK, OCTOBER 19, 1867.

SERENADE TO DR. DOREMUS BY THE MEMBERS OF THE N. Y. PHILHARMONIC SOCIETY, ON TUESDAY EVENING, SEPT. 24TH, AT HIS RESIDENCE, FOURTH AVENUE

emerald surrounded by diamonds,— with Mr. Booth's letter. His astonishment was great, and the cause of it appeared when we learned how he had come to own the ring, and to lose it.

Aft r one of his concerts in St. Petersburg, he said, he had been invited

We learned the sequel afterwards, from Mrs. Ole Bull. The lawyer referred to was one who had robbed her husband of much money, $25,000 of which Mr. Edward M. Stoughton had subsequently recovered from him. On one occasion he had said to Ole Bull,

Mrs R. Ogden Doremus with infinite
respect from her most grateful servant

A. C. Ball

New York April 29th 1870

who had the ring on his finger: "My wife is extravagantly fond of jewels, especially emeralds; won't you allow me to show her this exquisite gem?" In his usual courtly manner, the artist consented, taking the request as a compliment. This was the last time he had laid eyes upon it, until I handed it back to him with Mr. Booth's compliments.

Very early the next morning, there were vigorous pulls at our door-bell. I said, "That's Ole Bull." It was; and in a very excited manner he asked, "How would it do for me to offer to play for Mr. Booth at his theatre?"— imitating a performance on his violin. "Of course he would be delighted," I replied. But to resume the story of Booth's reading.

read. The overture commences the symphony, and the vocal music consists of choruses, solos, and quartettes. Mr. Booth was not quick at taking a musical cue. Herr Bergmann would play a passage on the piano, and then say, "Now read, Mr. Booth." This was repeated several times. Then another passage was played, followed by the reading. Many times were these drills repeated,—to my great regret, for it was a tax on the actor's valuable time which I had not anticipated. Then we had a rehearsal at the rooms of the Liederkranz Society, with the Philharmonic orchestra and chorus. This was a great success.

On returning from this rehearsal with Mr. Booth, who took advantage of the drive to smoke a cigar, I asked if he

THE DOREMUS HOUSE
Fourth Avenue and Nineteenth Street, where the Parker Building now stands

Mr. Booth met the Philharmonic conductor, Herr Carl Bergmann, at my house, to learn in what part of Schumann's "Manfred" he was to

was not satisfied. He made no reply. I said: "I know you are not, but you shall be. I will have the orchestra play for you at the Academy of Music, while

PROLOGUE.

Saddened, the gentle spirit disappeared.—
Manfred, defiant to the last, repels
Every approach of friendship. 'Tis his fate,
Love to requite with hatred.—There remains
To him one last resource—to " call the dead,"
" And ask them what it is we dread to be."
He will evoke Astarte, his beloved,
And question her; and he who ne'er before
Knew fear, now shudders, as, with this intent,
He seeks the halls where Arimanes dwells,
Grim Sovereign of the powers invisible.

HYMN OF THE SPIRITS IN THE HALL OF ARIMANES.

Hail to our Master!—Prince of Earth and Air!
  Who walks the clouds and waters—in his hand
The sceptre of the elements, which tear
  Themselves to chaos at his high command!
He breatheth—and a tempest shakes the sea;
  He speaketh—and the clouds reply in thunder;
He gazeth—from his glance the sunbeams flee;
  He moveth—earthquakes rend the world asunder.
Beneath his footsteps the volcanoes rise;
  His shadow is the Pestilence; his path
The comets herald through the crackling skies;
  And planets turn to ashes at his wrath.
To him War offers daily sacrifice;
  To him Death pays his tribute; Life is his,
With all its infinite of agonies—
  And his the spirit of whatever is!

PROLOGUE.

As Manfred enters, with defiant mien,
The hall where Arimanes sits enthroned,

FACSIMILE OF AN ESPECIALLY PREPARED EDITION OF " MANFRED "
FOR MR. BOOTH TO READ FROM

you stand on the stage and read, next Wednesday afternoon." This was done, and he seemed gratified.

Just before the concert, I invited the orchestra into the large "green-room" of the Academy of Music, and said: "Gentlemen, you have authorized me to purchase an elegant silver vase, to be presented to Mr. Booth, but it does not sufficiently express your indebtedness to him." After referring to his frequent rehearsals with Herr Bergmann, I said, "I ask one of you to offer a motion that this music be performed at his theatre." The motion was promptly made, seconded, and unanimously carried.

At the close of the concert, which was in every way successful, I presented Mr. Booth with the silver vase, and informed him of the resolution of the Society to repeat the performance at his theatre. A Wednesday matinée was chosen. Recalling the offer of Mr. Ole Bull referred to, I thought this a fitting occasion for him to play. Learning that he was in Cincinnati, I telegraphed him there, and received a reply from his *impresario* that he was on a concert tour in the West, and would not return for two months. An hour later, I received a telegram signed by Ole Bull himself, saying "I will be there!"

He broke up his tour and played at this matinée in Booth's Theatre! A beautiful illustration of his generous nature and artistic sympathy!

Mr. Booth called to consult with me as to the sort of present he should make to Mr. Bergmann for his repeated private rehearsals. We considered many things. Finally I proposed a baton, made of one of the light metals —magnesium or aluminum,—which were a novelty in those days. He asked if it would be too much trouble for me to go with him to Tiffany's. I went with him, and there we met Mr. Whitehouse, the skilled artist of that firm. He suggested that the baton be made of aluminum "matted" (this metal was then twice as expensive as sliver); that a spiral gold band should be wound around it, engraved with a

few bars from Bach, Beethoven, and Mendelssohn, that it should be surmounted with a Greek cross of gold, and that there should be a large amethyst, marked "B. B." (Booth–Bergmann) at the other end. This unique baton Mr. Booth presented to the great conductor, after the matinée performance at his theatre.

Mr. Ole Bull's appearance was a surprise to him, and he said, "Had I known it in time, I would have had a *golden violin* made for him!"

With Mr. Booth on his own stage, thoroughly familiar with the music, and not reading, but reciting, Byron's poem (for his memory was marvellous), I anticipated a great treat, and went to the gallery, so as not to be annoyed by the turning of programmes, or other disturbance. At the close of the performance, on going towards the stage I met Mr. Booth in a passageway. Grasping his hand I expressed my delight, and said that at certain passages tears had run down my cheeks. Pressing my hand tightly, he said, "They did down *mine!*" When next you read "Manfred," think of Edwin Booth in his prime, and with his rich, full, pathetic voice, reciting it, and moved to tears!

A large silk flag, surrounded with silken tassels, and having a polished staff, was not completed at the time of Mr. Ole Bull's second concert (January 9, 1870), hence its formal presentation was deferred until the day of his departure for his native land. In the "Memoirs" published by his widow the following account of the ceremony is quoted from an April number of the New York *Tribune :*

"*Herr Ole Bull*, from the *N. Y. Philharmonic Society*," was the inscription upon a beautiful silken flag presented to the great violinist yesterday on the deck of the United States revenue cutter, which conveyed him from the Barge Office at the Battery to the steamship *Russia*. (Dodworth's unrivalled cornet band played appropriate music.) The flag was the Norwegian colors, with the Star-Spangled Banner inserted in the upper staff of the section.

The Committee of Presentation were Prof. R. O. Doremus (President), Mr. U. C. Hill (Vice-President), and Mr. D. Schaad (Secretary). Ole Bull

FACSIMILE OF A LETTER WRITTEN BY EDWIN BOOTH TO R. OGDEN DOREMUS in return for their stamps; and I hesitate lest my first attempt at 'reading' should 'squelch' me. Therefore, if at the 1st rehearsal my wits or voice sh? fail me I'll claim the privilege of 'throwing up the sponge'. Thus you have the whole thing in a nut-shell. I'll do my best, and change in any other matters you might light upon. I hope all will terminate serenely & that this may lead me into doing that which, I think, will be of great service to me.

With kindest regards I am yours ever.

was accompanied on board the steamer by quite a large number of friends, among whom were Miss Adelaide Phillips, Miss Alida Topp, Mrs. Belknap and sister, Dr. and Mrs. Doremus, General Banks, Senator Roscoe Conkling, Mr. F. S. Appleton, and others.

Dr. Doremus's presentation speech, happily conceived, was responded to in the warm-hearted and impulsive manner peculiar to the artist, whose impulsiveness has ever characterized the products of his genius, and whose warm-heartedness is known to hundreds who have blessed him for his generosity.

Senator Conkling and General Banks also made appropriate speeches. As the cutter left the steamer, the company waved together their regrets and their farewells; and the form of the fine old gentleman, bareheaded and swinging his hat, was seen as long as forms could be distinguished in the distance.

This beautiful flag, according to Ole Bull's promise on its acceptance, was always carried in the 17th of May procession in Bergen, and floated on the 4th of July. A beautiful silver vase presented by the Philharmonic Society, a piece of silver plate given by the Young Men's Christian Association of New York, for whom he had played, and a gold crown given him in San Francisco, were among the other mementos he carried to his home in Norway.

Shortly before Mr. Booth's fatal illness, I called upon him at his home in Gramercy Park, which he had generously presented to his fellow-members of the Players Club. As we walked around the little park, I recalled to him incidents in the brilliant career of Mr. Ole Bull in Europe and the United States. I alluded to his unbounded generosity, his ardent patriotism, the devotion of a large part of his wealth to erecting a national theatre in Bergen, etc. Once, on a visit to one of our Northwestern cities, his compatriots had greeted him on his arrival, had carried him on their shoulders to his hotel, and had subsequently erected his statue in bronze; in Bergen also a statue was raised in his honor.

In his last illness Ole Bull said to his wife: "I will wind my watch as long as I can. When I can do so no longer, I wish you to wind it and give it to my friend Dr. Doremus; to be bequeathed, when he has done with it, to my spark, his little son Clarie, whom I taught to play the violin."

When she told me this after his death, I wrote that I could not accept the precious gift,—that it should go to some member of her husband's family. Her answer was: "They all wish you to wear it as near your heart as he bore you near his own."

I need not say that I have worn it ever since.

At his death, all Norway was prostrated with grief. The steamer that bore his remains from Lyso, his island home, to Bergen was draped in mourning, and a convoy of sixteen steamships similarly clad followed in the procession. Guns were fired from the fort and answered by the steamers, and church bells were tolled. The long quay, covered with green juniper, looked like a mossy bed; and for three miles evergreens covered the road that led to the mountain cemetery, where a place, originally designed for the King, received his precious remains, and "found a King!"

A band, preceding the casket, raised on a high catafalque, had played his music; young girls dressed in black had borne his trophies; and distinguished men carried his golden crown and other princely gifts. Fifty thousand mourners, flocking from all parts of Norway, assembled on the mountain sides to witness the last sad ceremonies, and listen to an address by the poet Björnsen.

I recalled that once when I was dining with Ole Bull at the home of Mr. and Mrs. Stoughton, our host had said: "Doctor, *I* don't think much of Ole Bull's fiddling. You know what I mean,—I don't think much of his fiddling, as compared with his great heart."

Mr. Booth stopped walking, dropped my arm, and exclaimed, with a dramatic gesture, "Ole Bull was n't a man,—he was a god!"

The Future for Americans

A Caustic Letter from an English Author

I HAVE asked and obtained permission of the writer of this letter, a well-known English author, to publish it in these columns; not because of its flattering words concerning THE CRITIC, but because of the cordial spirit it voices for American literature. Coming at the dawning of the new year, it is particularly welcome, and I sincerely hope that it is prophetic of a better appreciation of American writers by their English cousins. [Editor, CRITIC.]

"I congratulate you on your timely remarks concerning 'Criticism'; they were much needed. But I think I am even more pleased to see that you have said the dignified word, in the right place, concerning the literary calling. It is well to let the world know that the thing called literature is no joke, or speculation, or fad, but a solemn reality and the most *satisfying*. I call it a predestined election, the highest calling in the world. I think your position is just as great and triumphant as that of any writer who devotes the whole time to creative work, seeing that THE CRITIC is edited to perfection; I know of no other magazine to place beside it except the *Atlantic Monthly*. There is nothing here to compare it with; neither have we the writers to place beside yours. Only the other day I was looking over some old CRITICS I have here and I found myself obliged to read on and on all the articles I had read two years ago!

"There are no writers like the American writers, as there is no country like America; let the unregenerate Cockney say what he pleases. We all know the depth of the bitter envy and jealousy that lurks in the Cockney mind when he has to deal with an American writer or novelist. I have only seen two appreciative notices of THE CRITIC here, and one was by a Scotchman, editing in London, and the other by an Irishman, editing here. Scratch a competent English critic and you will usually find a Scotch or Irish Celt. Who is A. B. Walkley? I asked when he introduced my first volume of essays to his London readers; his name is English, but his wit and logic and penetration are not English but French. How comes that? I asked. The answer came: 'He is the most brilliant Oxford graduate of his year.' But, I said, that means nothing; it will not give him style and logic and make him write like a Frenchman. At last I made the discovery that his mother was a Frenchwoman. It is curious that with all their envy the English cannot do without this foreign talent. Mr. Walkley is the leading writer on the *Times*, and is, in spite of his rapier logic and Gallic wit, the recognized leader of the London critics. And so it goes. I do not believe the Americans are acquainted with these important facts. They should always be taken into consideration when it is a question of English criticism of anything American.

"One thing more: an Englishman thinks he is a cosmopolitan when he has made two trips to Paris or made a flying tour through Canada. A New Yorker is a born cosmopolitan. Sheer ignorance is at the bottom of much of the English envy. A true cosmopolitan cannot feel envious. But if English art and literature are decadent the native talent of Americans is all the greater by contrast, and it may well cause a spirit of honest pride in the American breast. Indeed, at no time in any day has the outlook presented so much to be thankful for. I feel as you do, and I would not change places with any millionaire living. I used to think when I was a musical prodigy that nothing in the world could equal the magic of music for the opening of doors; but the magic of literature surpasses it. I have seen what can be done by a single printed poem, essay, or little book; the marvels a single printed page can produce, and the

instant respect that real literary production calls forth in every cultured
community from Saint Petersburg to
San Francisco. But Americans ought
to feel thankful that the future is practically for them, and I am more than
pleased to see that in New York editors
as well as writers feel proud of their
own, of their high position, of their influence.

" I am sorry to see that Mr. James
has not done American novelists anything like justice. Something ails him.
He says himself that his style has become an exaggeration, but how is it
that he cannot see the marvellous freshness, originality, and power of the
real American novel, of the American
short story, especially the dialect
stories? Of course I don't know how
Mr. James has been answered, as I see
no American newspapers, but to answer
him effectively the writer would require
to possess not only a cosmopolitan
mind, but a cosmopolitan experience,
and I feel I am competent not only to

attack his position in the matter but to
leave him without a crutch to stand
on. Of course I am well aware that
no novice, no matter how brilliant the
talent, could do it, but for me the
thing would not be difficult. I am
only afraid some sensitive authors in
America would feel discouraged at
such a pronouncement.

" What a grave error it is to under-
value any book because the great
public buys it in hundreds of thousands! I have taken particular pains
to read the big-selling novels to see
exactly what it is the great public *do*
appreciate, and in every instance coming under my notice, from "David
Harum" to "Eben Holden," the
books deserve all the success they
gained. If the public took to Meredith
and James, snobbery would become
universal, art and life would be things
of no account. Words would take the
place of nature and truth. I am on
the side of the great American public
in this matter. From that position
nothing can move me.''

Oriental Definitions

Suttee

By MARGUERITE MERINGTON

" Oh, not for man to live alone
'T were good," the new-made widow-said ;
"And so my flame shall make us one
And heap live coals upon his head !"

But he who dreamed enfranchised, free
To roam the groves of regions higher,
Sighed, looking down on his suttee,
" Oh, now the fat is in the fire !"

SUTTEE

The Clay and the Potter

By LOUISE DRISCOLL

WHAT is the end, O Potter, what to be
The shape, design, and color planned for me?
Seems I would help could I foresee the thing
Thou meanest to complete by this slow fashioning.
Might I not haste thee to the ultimate
By knowing what it is thou wouldst create?

> *Coherent power taking inert clay,*
> *Selecting and omitting with sure play*
> *Of steady fingers ; skilful, not to be*
> *Resisted or evaded ; patiently*
> *As one who knows the end the Potter stands*
> *And guides, or fast, or slow, the wheel with his wise hands.*

I have but this, O Potter, for my own:
I know that I was senseless, overgrown
As other clods lie; impotent, without
Slow stirring hope or feeble throbbing doubt,
Until thou touched me—separated, broke—
And I began to wonder and awoke.

Some animals come into being blind,
I know not why thou chose to lift and bind
Upon thy wheel the clay thou mightst have passed.
I do not know what power holds me fast.
I do not know what service shall be mine.
I do not know my meaning nor design.

> *Deliberate action touches each man's soul,*
> *Controlling and compelling, giving dole*
> *Of light that is half darkness, making wise*
> *Only the simple-minded.   He who tries*
> *To shape himself is grotesque.   Who lies still*
> *Comes out the image of the Potter's will.*

I may not cease my questions, they come fast
Upon each other, warring at the last.
I know I am who was not, and I know
Thou art, O Potter, who hast made me so.
But whence and whither who shall answer me?
And why and what the end of it shall be?

> *Silent, inscrutable, the Potter stands*
> *And guides his wheel with careful, skilful hands;*
> *Selects and sets aside, makes great or small,*
> *And tells his plan to no one, and hears all,*
> *And takes insensate clay and gives it fire*
> *Of interest and question and desire.*

Two Studies in Luxury

By MARY K. FORD

IN a recent article on "The Integrity of the American Character," ex-President Cleveland points out that what is most to be dreaded is such a deterioration in the moral fibre of a nation that there will be "nothing left to build repair upon." At the same time in an article on "The Decay of Self-Control," in one of the English monthlies, Dr. William Barry, the well-known Roman Catholic writer, is quoted as ascribing it, among other causes, to the multiplication of pleasures in life.

Through the far-reaching medium of fiction Mrs. Wharton has enforced this same lesson, and what she has done for American life in "The House of Mirth" Mr. Howard Sturgis, with as skilful a touch, has accomplished for the more significant society of London in his remarkably interesting· novel, "Belchamber."

It is rather striking that two such books should have appeared within six months of each other, for without being alike they have many points in common. Both describe life in the rich and self-indulgent society which many suppose to be the most desirable that either country has to offer. Each book traces the career of a young person brought up in the midst of great luxury—the one a man richly endowed by the accident of birth, the other a woman greatly gifted by nature—and both, alike victims of their environment, are left at the end of the story: the one, his hopes blighted, his aspirations crushed, with the rest of his life stretching drearily before him; the other, the more fortunate one, lying in her desolate room in a forlorn boarding-house, the peace of death upon her face.

No one can follow the fortunes of Lily Bart without realizing the deteriorating effect of a luxurious life upon the moral fibre of human beings; and the utterances of President Roosevelt upon the merits of a life of en-

deavor gain new force from Mrs. Wharton's brilliant social satire. Lily recognizes the best in people, and so far appreciates it that she refrains from many acts that others of her set consider permissible; but her standards are constantly being lowered, and she is continually skirting the edge of shady transactions so that finally, when by no fault of her own she finds herself in a very unpleasant predicament, she has really herself to thank for it. Her moral fibre has been so undermined by her self-indulgent way of life that she has neither the courage nor the decision to grasp the best when it is within reach. Even Selden, the nearest approach to a hero that the book contains, is infected by this same fatal vacillation, and only realizes when too late what he and Lily might have been to each other. The same indecision of character is the weakness of Sainty, the hero of "Belchamber." He allows himself to become the prey of a scheming mother and her worthless daughter, and, in spite of the tremendous advantage of his wealth and position, and a strong desire to benefit his fellow-men, he never accomplishes anything. He and Lily are the victims of their surroundings, with this difference—Lily is a willing one, while Sainty makes a few ineffectual struggles before the waters of adverse circumstance close over him. As we read of these unfortunates we begin to understand those lines of Browning's which have provoked so much criticism from moralists:

> Let a man contend to the uttermost
> For his life's set prize, be what it will !
>
> .   .   .   .   .   .
>
> And the sin I impute to each frustrate ghost
> Was, the unlit lamp and the ungirt loin,
> Though the end in sight was a crime, I say.

Both books are extremely well written, showing marked skill in the delineation of character. In their complete lack of any lovable character both books recall "Lady Rose's Daughter." Most of the men and women described are hard and grasping if not distinctly vicious, and yet the variety shown is endless. It is discouraging to see how many kinds of objectionable people there are in the world.

That keen observer Mr. James Bryce, in his "American Commonwealth," comments upon the pleasantness of social life in this country and considers that it arises in great measure from the absence of a caste system. He is undoubtedly right, but while this lack is a boon to our society it is a drawback to our fiction. The social inequalities of an aristocratic society add to a story a picturesque element which is entirely lacking in a democratic community and which gives the novel of English life an advantage to start with. Mrs. Wharton has as skilful a touch as Mr. Sturgis and is even wittier, but his superiority in constructive skill, joined to his advantage in *locale*, makes his book the more interesting of the two. As studies in contemporary manners they are matchless and of equal value. To carry conviction to the minds of

their readers, writers must speak with authority, and no one can read either of these books without feeling its veracity. There is no guesswork here, and the lesson that they teach is all the stronger from the fact that there is no preaching, no solemn arraignment of society; the characters speak for themselves, depicting in a most lifelike way the society which women strain every nerve to enter and for which they are ready to sacrifice their happiness and that of their families. "The House of Mirth" contains nothing sadder than the glimpse we get of Lily's early home, her extravagant mother, her overworked father—a home of which her own miserable death is the legitimate outcome.

And what a lesson the book teaches! It is not for nothing that Mrs. Wharton has taken her title from the Book of Ecclesiastes, that cry of satiety that has come down the ages to us with its burden of "Vanity of vanities! all is vanity!"—a cry even more significant now than when it was uttered nearly three thousand years ago by the wisdom-sated monarch who in these words summed up his experience of life.

The Sundering Flood

By HATTIE TYNG GRISWOLD

How shall I bear me in the hour to be,
  When Thy great Sundering Flood comes rushing down,
And I shall feel the coldness of that sea
  In which all mortal men shall one day drown?

Shall I be glad who have been sad so long,
  So weary of life's ceaseless care and fret?
Shall I be blithe and sing a joyous song,
  When with that icy foam my feet are wet?

Or will the sweetness of the happy earth
  Sweep over me, and friends hold me in chain,
And shall I feel that love has had new birth,
  And every rose of life will bloom again?

God knows I have been brave up to this hour,
  No coward drop in all my languid blood;
Bid me not part from courage, O Thou Power
  That hold'st in leash e'en Thy great Sundering Flood!

A Concord Note=Book

The Women of Concord—Margaret Fuller and Her Friends—II.

SEVENTH PAPER

By F. B. SANBORN

AND now I come to Margaret Fuller, whom it was never my good fortune to know; but of whom I have precious reminiscences, placed in my hands for publication by Mrs. Marcus Spring of Los Angeles, the cousin of my good old friend, Dr. Earle, and the most intimate in Margaret's circle of later years. They came together from opposite poles of American society,—Margaret from the exclusive and rather elated Cambridge and Boston circles, to which of her own wilfulness she had conjoined the unpopular purlieus of Transcendentalism; and Rebecca Buffum from the quiet, practical, self-repressing influences of Quakerism. Probably Horace Greeley, representing still another unlike *outré Manche* province of American life, with his exasperatingly pretty and half-insane wife, brought Margaret and Rebecca together in New York, when the Sibyl of New England went in 1844 to help edit the New York *Tribune*. It was the suggestion of Mrs. Greeley in the first instance, and at her invitation Margaret went to live at the house of the Greeleys on the river bank, a long way from the *Tribune* office, which, in that first winter of 1844-45, burned down. Ellery Channing, who had married Ellen Fuller, the younger sister of Margaret, was also in the *Tribune* office as a sub-editor at that time, and was sent up to his house by Mr. Greeley that eventful night of the fire, to quiet the anxieties of the household.

Much earlier than this had Margaret Fuller found her way from Cambridge and Groton to Concord, attracted, as were Alcott, Hawthorne, Ellery Channing, and others, by the starlit radiance of Emerson's genius. As he frankly said in that memoir of Margaret which he contributed to the friendly life of her in 1852 (now too little read), Emerson was not at first prepossessed in her favor, and she did not contribute to a better appreciation by a rather marked disregard of Mrs. Emerson's position as hostess. But all this yielded finally (as it did not in Hawthorne's case) to the influence of her genius and her real magnanimity, flavored, as they were, by certain self-conscious traits of the Fuller family. She went to Boston in 1836 and took some part in the instruction at Mr. Alcott's Temple School, then at its height, and not yet persecuted by the Philistinism of Cambridge and Boston which afterward ruined it. Margaret easily saw the defects in this noble system of education, and thus noted them down in her journal:

"Preacher, you make three mistakes: you do not understand the nature of Genius, or creative power; you do not understand the reaction of matter on spirit; you are too impatient of the complex, and, not enjoying variety in unity, you become lost in abstractions, and cannot illustrate your principles."

Margaret did understand "the reaction of matter on spirit," and suffered from it in after years. Of her at the same period (1836-37) Alcott gave this character in his diary: "She is clearly a person of liberal and varied acquirements and given to the boldest speculation. Not wanting in imaginative power, she has a rare good sense and discretion. She adopts the Spiritual Philosophy, and has the subtlest perception of its bearings; takes large and generous views of all subjects, and in disposition is singularly catholic. The blending of sentiment and wisdom in her is most remarkable. I think her the most brilliant talker of the day,— with a quick and comprehensive wit, firm command of her thoughts, and a speech to win the ear of the most cultivated." This is a close portrayal. In the Alcott Sonnets, written thirty years after her shipwreck, Margaret's whole existence is briefly pictured:

Thou Sibyl rapt! whose sympathetic soul
Infused the mysteries thy tongue failed to tell,
Though from thy lips the marvellous accents fell,
And weird wise meanings o'er the senses stole
Through those rare cadences, with winsome spell:
Yet, even in such refrainings of thy voice,
There struggled up a wailing undertone,
That spoke thee victim of the Sisters' choice,—
Charming all others,—dwelling still alone.
They left thee thus disconsolate to roam,
And scorned thy dear, devoted life to spare;
Around the storm-tost vessel sinking there
The wild waves chant thy dirge and welcome home.
Survives alone thy sex's valiant plea,
And the great heart that loved the brave and free.

Margaret was invited by the Springs to make the tour of Europe with them, and in their company she did visit England, Scotland, France, and Italy. They sailed from Boston in the *Cambria*, August 1, 1846, and met in England, Scotland, and France, Wordsworth, Carlyle, De Quincey, Mazzini, George Sand, and other world-renowned persons, who are described in Margaret's letters published in her biography and works. Mrs. Spring says:

"In Paris Adam Mickiewicz, the handsome Polish poet, there living in exile, came often to see Margaret, and sometimes dined with us. He kept alive in his heart the hope of sometime seeing his dear Poland freed from Russian rule. Afterwards, in letters, he encouraged Margaret to marry Ossoli, visited her in Rome after the marriage, and had our American artist, Thomas Hicks, make a portrait of her for him. Margaret and Ossoli asked Mickiewicz to be godfather to their child, born at Rieti in January, 1848."

In 1847 the Springs, who had parted from Margaret in Italy, returned home. She remained to pass through those experiences, public and private, which glorified and saddened her last three years; writing often to her friends, but not communicating the facts concerning her marriage and her child till long afterward. In the last year of her life she wrote thus to Mrs. Spring, and these letters, I think, have not before been printed.

Some Last Letters of Margaret Fuller Ossoli

"FLORENCE, December 12, 1849.
"DEAR MARCUS AND REBECCA:
"A letter from Mr. Dougherty, a notice in the *Tribune* of Miss Bremer's visit to the North American Phalanx, doubtless made in company with you, bring you so forcibly to mind that I must e'en devote the last two hours, and the best and quietest of the twenty-four, to answering your letters. For I have actually two letters from you to answer,—and excellent ones likewise.

"Your letter, my dear Rebecca, was written in your noblest and most womanly spirit. I thank you warmly for your sympathy about my little boy. What he is to me even *you* can hardly dream; you who have three, and in whom the natural thirst of the heart was earlier satisfied, can scarcely know what my one ewe lamb is to me. That he may live, that I may find bread for him, that I may not spoil him by overweening love, that I may daily grow better for his sake,—are the ever-recurring thoughts, say prayers, that give their hue to all the current of my life. Yet in answer to what you say, that it is still better to give the world this living soul, than a part of my life in a book,—it is true: and yet,—and yet, —of my book I could know whether it would be of any worth; of my child I must wait to see what his worth will be. I play with him, my ever-growing mystery,—but from the solemnity of the thoughts he brings there is refuge only in God. Was I worthy to be the parent of a soul, with its immense capabilities of weal and woe? God be merciful to me, a sinner! comes so naturally to the mother's heart, I think. . . ."

"FLORENCE, February 5, 1850.
"You have no doubt received ere this a letter from me, written, I think, in December; but I must suddenly write again to thank you for the New Year's letter. It was a sweet impulse that led you to write together, and had

its full reward in the pleasure it gave. I am glad it entered into the heart of Evelyn Story to write that letter: it was in the spirit of that tender and generous friendship both she and her husband always showed me. I trust the tie formed between us will last as long as our lives. It was also pleasant that it was the Lowells who took pains to show the letter. As to its subject-matter,— I have written as little as possible about Ossoli, wishing my friends to form their own impressions when they saw us together.

"I have expected that those who cared for me simply for my activity of intellect would not care for him; but that those in whom the moral nature predominates would gladly learn to love and admire him, and see what a treasure his affection must be to me. But that would be only gradually; for it is by acts not words that one so simple, true, delicate, and retiring can be known. For me,—while some of my friends have thought me exacting, I may say Ossoli has always outgone my expectation in the disinterested-ness, the uncompromising bounty, of his every act. He was the same to his father as to me. His affections are few, but profound and thoroughly car-ried out; his permanent affections few, but his heart is always open to the humble, suffering, heavily laden ones. His little habitual acts of kindness rose to the height of the occasion,— and stayed there. His enthusiasm was quiet, but unsleeping. He is very un-like most Italians, but very unlike most Americans too. I do not expect all who care for me to care for him, nor is it important to him; he is wholly with-out vanity. He is too truly the gen-tleman not to be respected by all persons of refinement.

"For the rest, if my life is free and not too much troubled; if he can enjoy his domestic affections, and fulfil his duties in his own way, he will be con-tent. Can we find this in bustling America for the next three or four years? I know not, but think we shall come and try. I wish much to see you all, and exchange the kiss of peace; there will, I trust, be peace within if

not without. I thank you warmly for your gift; be assured it will turn to great profit. I have learned to be a willing adept in economy, by my love for my little boy. I cannot bear to see him suffer any want. I have looked happily to the time when we could in-troduce the babies to each other. I hope that may be yet, and that I shall find little Marcus well. My little Nino, as we call him for house and pet name, is now in perfect health. I wash and dress and care for him, and think I see a great deal more of his little cunning ways, and shall know him better, for doing all for him; though it is incon-venient and fatiguing at times. He is very gay and laughing,— sometimes violent, for he has come to the age when he wants everything in his own hands,—but on the whole sweet and very fond of me. He says *kiss* in pref-erence to the Italian word *basia*. I don't cherish sanguine visions about him; I shall try to do my best by him and enjoy the present moment.

"MARGARET."

And now comes the last letter, posted at Gibraltar as their ill-fated ship lay off the Rock there, after a tragic event that might well have been ominous of the fate of the voyage which began so ill.

"SHIP 'ELIZABETH,' OFF GIBRALTAR,
"June 3, 1850.

"MY DEAR MARCUS:

"You will, I trust, long ere receiving this, have received my letter from Flor-ence, dated 19th May, enclosing one to my mother, informing you under what circumstances I had drawn on you through Fienzi and Hall, and mentioning how I wished the bill to be met, in case of any accident to me on my homeward course. That course has, as regards weather, been thus far not unpleasant; but the disaster that *has* befallen us is such as I never dreamed of. I had taken passage with Captain S. L. Hasty,—one who seemed to me among the best and most high-minded of our American men. He showed the kindest interest in me; his wife, an excellent woman, was with him. I thought, during the voyage, if safe and my child well, to have as much respite from care and pain as seasickness might permit. But scarce was that enemy in some measure quelled, when the Captain fell sick.

"At first his disease presented the symptoms of nervous fever. I was with him a great deal; indeed, whenever I could relieve his wife from a ministry softened by great love and the heroism of womanly courage, but in the last days truly terrible with disgusts and fatigues. For he died, we suppose (no physician has been allowed to come on board to see the body), of confluent small-pox. I have seen since we parted much suffering, but nothing physical to be compared to this,—where the once fair and expressive mould of man was lost in corruption before life had fled. He died yesterday morning, and was buried in deep water,—the American consul's barge, about six o'clock, towing out one from this ship which bore the body. It was Sunday; a divinely calm, soft, glowing afternoon had succeeded a morning of bleak cold wind. You cannot think how beautiful the whole thing was,—the decent array and sad reverence of the sailors, the many ships with their banners flying, the stern Pillars of Hercules, all veiled in roseate vapor; the little angel-white sails diving into the blue depths with the solemn spoil of the poor good man, now still, who had been so agonized and gasping as the last sun stooped. Yes, it was beautiful,—but how dear a price do we pay for the poems of this world!

"We shall lie now in quarantine for a week, no person permitted to come on board, till it is seen whether disease may break out in other cases. I have no good reason to think it will *not*, yet do not feel afraid. Ossoli has had it, so is safe. The baby is, of course, subject to injury. In the earlier days, before I suspected small-pox, I carried him twice into the sick-room, at the request of the Captain, who was becoming fond of him. He laughed and pointed; he did not discern danger, but only thought it odd to see the old friend there in bed.

"It is vain by prudence to seek to evade the stern assaults of destiny. I submit. Should all end well, you see we shall be in New York later than I expected; but keep a lookout! Should we arrive safe, I should like to see a friendly face. Commend me to dear William and other dear friends, especially Jane. And Marcus, Rebecca, Eddie,—with most affectionate wishes that joy and peace may continue to dwell in your house. Adieu,—and love as you can your friend,

"MARGARET."

"When this letter came, it had been slashed and fumigated, and there was a strong odor of sulphur; but we did not lose hope. In expectation of the arrival of sick persons, we sent the children and their nurse to the country, and offered the servants their choice to leave us or stay. They all stayed, and we were waiting anxiously when the fearful storm came in July, and after it news of the loss of the ship *Elizabeth*. We soon received this letter from Mr. Emerson:"

"CONCORD, 23d July, 1850.

"MY DEAR SIR:

"The morning papers add no syllable to the fatal paragraphs of last night concerning Margaret Fuller; no contradiction and no explanation. At first I thought I would go myself and see if I could help in the inquiries at the wrecking ground, and act for the friends. But I have prevailed on my friend, Mr. Henry D. Thoreau, to go for me and all the friends. Mr. Thoreau is the most competent person that could be selected; and in the dispersion of the Fuller family, and our uncertainty how to communicate with them, he is authorized by Mr. Ellery Channing to act for them all.

"I fear the chances of recovering manuscript and other property, after five or six days, are small, and diminishing every hour. Yet Margaret would have every record of her history for the last three or four years; and whatever is found by any one would easily be yielded up to a diligent seeker. Mr. Thoreau is prepared to spend a number of days in this object, if necessary, and you must give him any guidance or help you can. If his money does not hold out, I shall gladly pay any drafts he may make on you in my name. And I shall cordially unite with you in any expense that this painful calamity shall make necessary.

"Yours faithfully,
"R. W. EMERSON.
" MARCUS SPRING, ESQ."

"Henry Thoreau came on; Margaret's mother, sister, and brothers came to us, and also Charles Sumner, whose brother Horace was lost in the ship. We had known him pleasantly in Paris, and probably he had taken passage to be with the Ossolis. Mr. Spring, Mr. Sumner, Mr. Thoreau; and some of the Fuller family went to Fire Island. The sister did, by a strong appeal, get some of Margaret's things from a wrecker's wife. But the only papers saved were some love-letters of Margaret and Ossoli."

So far Mrs. Spring, recalling the memories of more than half a century. Thoreau reported to Emerson in a letter from Fire Island Beach, July 25th, at the house of Mr. Oakes, within a mile of the wreck. W. H. Channing was with him, and Charles Sumner and Marcus Spring had been there on the 24th. "At flood tide, about half-past three P.M., when the ship broke up entirely (July 19th), Margaret sat with her back to the foremast,—her husband and child already drowned. A great wave came and washed her aft. . . . Four bodies remain to be found; the two Ossolis, Horace Sumner, and a sailor. I have visited the child's grave.

"We got here yesterday noon. Arthur Fuller has this moment reached the house of Mr. Oakes; he got to the beach last night. Mrs. Oakes dried the papers that were in the trunk; they appeared to be of different kinds. Some were tied up. . . . I expect to go to Patchogue, whence the pilferers must have chiefly come, and advertise." Thus far Thoreau, who brought away a button from Ossoli's coat,—the only memento of him except the few

letters among the papers saved by Mrs. Oakes, that reached Margaret's friends in America.

Mrs. Spring goes on: "Margaret's mother sat like a stone in our house,— she shed no tears, she even smiled when we spoke to her, but she neither ate nor slept; it was pitiful. I sat down on a low seat before her and told her stories of our life and our travels together. Suddenly tears came into her eyes; she laid her hand on my head and said 'You make me think of my child alive.' The stony, dead silence was broken; they had been fearing for her life and her reason. A long time after this our son Edward Spring was visiting Emerson in Concord, and, noticing an engraving hanging on the wall, he said: 'Why, Mr. Emerson, where did you get this? It was Margaret Fuller's.' Mr. Emerson came forward quickly and said: 'Tell me about it. It was picked up on the shore at Fire Island after the wreck, and given to me as probably belonging to her.'

"For years afterward, if I went to the seashore, I would dream of Margaret, always pleasantly. In my dream she always seemed happy; it may be that the requiem of the winds and waves was the best for her,"—alluding to Alcott's lines in the sonnet quoted. "She believed in the higher education of women, and in equal rights for them as citizens. She would have rejoiced in the wonderful progress they have made in these things since her time. Let our sex never forget Margaret Fuller."

I have spoken of Margaret among Concord women, although she never lived in the town. About the beginning of 1840, when the *Dial*, which she edited, was in preparation, Emerson and Thoreau made much effort to find a suitable house for her and her mother in Concord, without success. After her sister, Mrs. Channing, went to reside there, in April, 1843, Margaret was often a visitor in three or four houses of her friends. With Hawthorne at the Old Manse, as at Brook Farm, she was never intimate, and in a paper left behind by him, and posthumously printed, he spoke ungenerously of her. The poet Lowell had also spoken ill of her in his "Fable for Critics,"—and this was why she took pleasure in having "the Lowells" give currency to Mrs. William Story's friendly letter concerning Margaret's private marriage.

I now turn to a group of women living in Concord who were in many respects unlike those already mentioned, yet striking examples of their type,—the grandmother and aunts of Henry Thoreau. Mary Jones, the mother of Mrs. John Thoreau, was a contemporary of Phebe Bliss, who married William Emerson and Dr. Ripley,—but her life and fortunes were dissimilar. She was the only daughter of Colonel Jones, of Weston, seven miles southeast of Concord, a prosperous citizen with fourteen sons, many of whom, like their father, took the British side in the Revolution of 1775. The Colonel died the year before, about the time Mary Emerson was born in the Old Manse, and escaped the worst of the conflict. One of his sons (Simeon, I think) undertook, after the Concord Fight, and while the British troops were besieged in Boston, to carry in supplies to them by sea, of which the British navy had control then. He was captured by the patriots and imprisoned, with a companion, in the old blockhouse jail at Concord, where in the next year Sir Archibald Campbell was imprisoned, much complaining to Washington of the hardships of his confinement. The Jones family, according to tradition among the Dunbars and Thoreaus, undertook to supply young Jones with better food than his prison fare, and Mary, his sister, carried him some on the 17th of June, while the cannon of Bunker Hill were roaring. In this way, during some weeks, they furnished him from Weston with knives, etc., with which he and his comrade made saws, and escaped through the barred window of the prison, taking refuge in the Jones cider-mill at Weston, where they were fed for a day or two by the alert sister Mary. She then captured a horse from one of the great pastures,

harnessed him in the Colonel's chaise, and contrived to send the two fugitives off in that conveyance, toward "the Eastward,"—that is, Maine. At Portland they stabled the borrowed horse, and sent word to the owner that he might have him by paying charges; they in the meanwhile going on into King George's country.

At this time Asa Dunbar, a young parson who had graduated at Harvard in 1767, gave up the parish in Salem, where he had been "settled," after preaching as a candidate in Bedford, near Concord, and retired into rural Worcester County, to study law with another Tory gentleman. He was in love with Mary Jones, whom in due time he married, and began law-practice in Keene, N. H., where he flourished as lawyer and Freemason for some ten years, and where his son Charles and three daughters were born. Cynthia, the youngest, who afterward married John Thoreau, was born a little after her father's death in 1787. Mrs. Dunbar, his widow, remained in Keene awhile, then took her children and went to visit her brothers in Maine and New Brunswick, narrowly escaping shipwreck on the voyage back to Boston. Finally, she went to Concord and married for her second husband Captain Jonas Minott, a prosperous farmer, who owned lands in the New Hampshire wilderness, at Kearsarge Gore, now Wilmot. Driving up there with her husband, in a two-wheeled chaise, which none of the pioneers at the Gore had ever seen, she created a sensation, to which she never seems to have been averse; but before she said farewell, she had taught the natives how to make coffee,—a new art in that region. By and by her second husband died, and she continued to live on his farm near Bedford, but in Concord, where her literary grandson, Henry Thoreau, was born in 1817,—the third child of Cynthia Dunbar.

It will be seen by this sketch of Mary Jones's career that she had vivacity, energy, and resource; true New England traits, but not of the highest type. Her daughters resembled her in this, though differing from each other.

Mrs. Thoreau had all the resource and vivacity of her mother; was full of energy and of conversation, a reformer of evils, and a friend of the poor; but alas! a gossip, and with more or less of the village quarrels on her mind and her busy hands. She was well-taught and well-read, a notable housewife, who could "do her own work" and often did; but entertained much company, and was herself very entertaining in her endless discourse about matters high and low. Her dearest theme was her own children, and especially Henry when I knew her,—for John, the elder son, had died long before. Her sister, Louisa Dunbar, had been a belle and a successful teacher; an early friend of Daniel Webster, when he studied law in Boscawen, and, as she told me once, was "converted," or turned to serious thoughts of the Calvinistic religion, by the conversation of young Webster. She remained true to the Trinitarian Church, as did the aunts of Henry on the Thoreau side; indeed, they were among the leaders in the Trinitarian secession from Dr. Ripley's ancient parish, eighty years ago, and did much to sustain the dissenting ministers, among the first of whom was Rev. John Wilder, the grandfather of Mrs. Todd, of Amherst. The family of John Thoreau divided on the religious issue; Helen and Sophia, the two daughters, becoming Episcopalians, as their ancestors in the Island of Jersey had been; John and Henry disconnecting themselves from all churches, and the father and mother equally friendly to Unitarian or Trinitarian Congregationalists, although, under the influence of Garrison and Parker Pillsbury, they were ranked as "Comeouters" in the anti-slavery contests. When the Women's Anti-Slavery Society was formed in Concord, before 1840, all these Thoreau and Dunbar ladies, with their close friends, Mrs. Mary Merrick Brooks, wife of one of the leading lawyers, and Miss Prudence Ward, daughter of a Revolutionary Colonel, Joseph Ward, became ardent and active members. At their houses fugitive slaves and anti-slavery orators could often be found; and it was they (particularly Mrs. Brooks) who persuaded Emerson to give his address on Emancipation in 1844, and made the arrangements for it.

Reminiscences of a Franco=American

No. I—Jules Lemaître

By JEANNE MAIRET (Madame Charles Bigôt)

The art of the critic is essentially easy, insinuating, ever-moving, all-embracing. It is a wide, clear, and winding river that bathes rocks, fortresses, vine-clad hills, or fertile valleys. While each object remains in its place, ignoring all the others; while the feudal tower disdains the vale, and the valley knows not the hill, the river flows on from one to the other, embraces it without harming it, refreshes all with its clear waters, understands them, reflects them. When a traveller is interested in all these varied sites, he steps into a boat, and the river carries him gently forward, so that he may see the ever-changing spectacle.

These words of Sainte-Beuve, the prince of critics, may well serve to introduce M. Jules Lemaître. The volumes entitled "Les Contemporains," in which our author has gathered the studies written during ten or fifteen years, contain certain portraits, certain essays, which it is a pure delight to read and read again. In this kind of criticism, which breaks away from rules and formulas, the writer feels perfectly at ease with himself and his readers; he does not hesitate, while reviewing a book, to talk—and how agreeably!—of himself, to relate an anecdote or develop a theory. And, if one is sometimes a little astonished, the surprise soon merges into pleasure. When M. Lemaître changes his mind, and burns what he once adored, he does not hesitate to say so, and we accept these fluctuations as quite natural.

To quote Sainte-Beuve once more:

Each day I change. Years roll on; my predelictions of the past season are no longer those of the present; my friendships themselves fade and are replaced by others. Before the final disappearance of the changeful being known by my name, how many men have died in me! . . .

And Alfred de Musset, borrowing this thought from the great critic, wrote:

Il se trouve, en un mot, chez les trois quarts des hommes,
Un poète, mort jeune, à qui l'homme survit.

As M. Lemaître confessed with ingenuousness, or pseudo-ingenuousness, to his fleeting thoughts, to his changeful ethics, he was by many looked upon as an unsafe guide, as a frivolous person. M. Brunetière, whom he called "the most imperious of our critics," took him to task, as an austere schoolmaster might scold an unruly pupil. But M. Lemaître was no schoolboy, and he replied thus:

I could as well as other men judge by rule and not by impressions. I am accused of being an unstable spirit. I could fix my ideas if I chose. I am quite capable of judging books instead of analyzing the impressions they make on me; of adopting immutable principles; in one word, of being a real critic—mediocre, perhaps—but a critic.

Only, then, I should not be sincere. I should say things of which I am not sure; whereas, of my impressions, I am quite sure. . . .

M. Brunetière is apparently incapable of considering a work otherwise than in its relation to other works, as belonging to this or that group. The philosophy of literary lore, a system of ethics underlie each of his judgments. What a wonderful gift! While he reads a book he thinks of all the books written since the beginning of the world. The works he analyzes are classified, and for all eternity. I humbly admire the majesty of such criticism. . . . Yet how sad never to open a volume without thinking of all its forerunners and comparing it with them! . . to judge eternally—never to enjoy! Were M. Brunetière to read "for pleasure," his conscience would not be at peace; he would consider himself as sinning, or as consenting to be a dupe. As to us, when we make a mistake, we do not greatly trouble ourselves about it; we are quite resigned to retract our verdict, to replace our admirations of to-day by our admirations of to-morrow. If by some evil chance M. Brunetière should make a mistake, how terrible that would be! A single error would destroy his whole system. . . .

And do not believe that impressionistic criticism is necessarily empty and frivolous. To read a book and to enjoy it does not imply that all classic literature is forgotten. Our memory, like that of others, is peopled with many images. After all, what constitutes the charm of reading new books is the way in which they evoke these images. Our sympathy with what is beautiful in art is a great mystery; it arises out of time and space, and the origin of each new impression is lost in an infinity of causes stretching back into the misty past.

And again:

The imperious and singularly living writer who represents in our midst the class of severe critics, said to a brother worker suspected of indolent epicurism: "You praise what pleases you. I never do." What a hard fate! . . . Let me add that this ascetic and reasoning method, so difficult to handle after a really superior fashion, can yet be acquired, to a certain extent, by men of honorable mediocrity.

What M. Lemaître did not say in so many words, though he let it be understood, was that his easy, nonchalant criticism rested on a very sure basis of solid learning and of impeccable taste. No one among his contemporaries went deeper (when he chose to do so) into the soul of a writer or dissected with a more pitiless scalpel an overrated talent than did M. Jules Lemaître.

And now, who and what is M. Jules Lemaître?

I always recall him as he used to appear at some great first representation at the Comédie Française. He was at one time dramatic critic of the *Débats*, having taken the place of that exquisite writer and erratic genius J. J. Weiss.

He was of middle height, with bent shoulders, head carried forward, near-sighted and awkward; the evening dress hung ungracefully, as though its pockets were stuffed with books and papers; no one would have taken him for anything but what he was, a man of study, perhaps a professor. He stumbled over those awful stools or cushions the *ouvreuses* put under one's feet, and murmured, "Pardon—Madame—pardon," as he strove to gain his seat. And people whispered: "Lemaître . . . Jules Lemaître . . ."

In those days he was about thirty-five and looked almost fifty. His hair inclined to curl, early turned gray, then white, leaving him a little bald. This added to the height of his forehead, and made the rather insignificant features appear a little lacking in space, as though the face had been of India-rubber and pressed too hard. The expression, the glint of the blue eyes, soon forced one to forget his rather unsatisfactory physique. When he spoke, he let his words drop with a sort of careless grace, with a little hesitation too; the voice was gentle and rather high-pitched. When he lectured, that soft voice swelled and carried to the very extremity of a large theatre, and all hesitation disappeared.

Jules Lemaître was born in that "garden of France," the Touraine, the birthplace of Rabelais, the chosen refuge of Balzac, where even peasants speak classic French, where the climate is soft, the horizons far spreading, and where the wide, lazy Loire shows amid its waters great patches of golden sand. His first teachers were priests: their influence, even in his days of unbelief, was still active. Over and over again, in his essays, in his exquisite little stories, in his conversations, priests and nuns, Christian martyrs, church ceremonies, are alluded to and always with a sort of tenderness.

He loved the things appertaining to religious ceremonies: the swelling harmonies of the organ, the discreet shuffling of feet, the faint odor of incense, the lights and the flowers of the altar. He had been admitted to convent parlors, for visits to some relative; and the hushed peace of the place, even the stiff chairs against the walls, and the abominable pious chromos or painted statues which served as decoration to the room appealed to him. The waving of trees in the garden, seen through the rarely opened windows, evoked the vision of young girls with their teachers strolling along trim gravelled walks, stopping in distant corners, where grottoes harbored statues. And these things, lovely or puerile, silently peaceful, changed the man of the world, the successful critic, the political combatant, once more into the ardently pious little boy who once knelt in his village church.

It was under this influence that he wrote "Myrrha, vierge et martyre," "La Mère Sainte Agathe," "Lilith," "Serenus," "L'Imagier," and other delightful stories and sketches, wherein he displays not only the charm of his infinitely subtle talent, but a delicacy one is surprised to find in a man who passes—and who wishes to pass—for a sceptic and an ironist.

Not that irony is absent from these stories: in "Serenus" it is very keen. "Serenus" is the story of a man of the world under Nero, who singularly resembles some dilettante of the Third French Republic, a man of exquisite tastes, who has known every pleasure, and wearied of all. Through curiosity, through sympathy for a little sister, he frequents the Christians, is implicated with them in one of the periodical persecutions, disdains to separate his cause from that of these chance brethren, whose faith he has never adopted, is imprisoned, and takes poison. Before dying, he writes his confession and puts the papyrus in a metal case. This small metal box, hidden in his garments, is buried with him in the crypt, where his body is venerated with those of the other martyrs. In due time his bones are removed to some church and perform miracles. A scholar, to whom the mysterious case is given, deciphers the manuscript, not without much difficulty, and concludes to keep a discreet silence. The miracles continue.

"Myrrha, vierge et martyre," one of the most delicate of all these sketches, is the story of a little Christian girl, born of freed slaves. From her infancy she has heard of Nero, the bad Emperor, and she pities him, knowing that he must be unhappy. She endeavors to see him, she thinks of him unceasingly, she prays that she may give her life that he may repent of his evil ways. One day, with many others, she is thrown to the wild beasts. Fearlessly, while the lions, dazed by the light and the crowd, cringe before springing on their prey, Myrrha walks toward the imperial box and looks at Nero, all her unconscious love, all her sweet human pity, showing in her beautiful eyes. The tyrant, bending forward, makes the gesture of pardon; but the priest, who watches jealously over the girl, pushes her toward the famished lion.

Lilith is the daughter of Herod, and she is full of compassion for the doomed children of the land. She hears about the Messiah, the Child born, according to the popular faith, to be ruler and to dethrone her father. Though she shrinks at the thought of his downthrow, though she dreads for herself the loss of her accustomed luxuries, a secret power impels her to go to the Child and bid its mother flee.

M. Lemaître says of Renan:

The imagination of this philosopher has remained catholic. He still loves what he denies. He is still a priest. Even his negations assume a mystical turn. His brain is a disaffected cathedral. Hay is stored away in it ; lectures are given in it ; it is yet a church . .

A disaffected cathedral. . . . When he wrote those words did M. Jules Lemaître think only of the great philosopher? They apply so well to himself! Elsewhere, he says:

M. Anatole France spent his childhood in an ecclesiastical school, which, to my mind, is a great advantage. Religious exercises make the soul more gentle and tender. When, in after life, faith departs, one is yet capable of understanding and of loving it in others ; one is more equitable and more intelligent.

In the course of time the priests' pupil entered the École Normale, whence come so many of France's choicest spirits. Here he was the comrade of M. Louis Ganderax, who founded the *Revue de Paris*, of M. Maurice Albert, son of Paul Albert, of M. Georges Duruy, son of the historian,— "Normaliens," sons of "Normaliens." Then, after his three years of study, M. Lemaître began his career as professor, taking his duties to heart, scarcely dreaming, probably, of any other fate. He was sent to Algiers, and later to Havre. But his class did not take up all his time; he wrote some poems, which he published under the title of "Médaillons." Nearly all writers whose prose is peculiarly melodious have begun by rhyming.

While he was at Havre, M. Lemaître sent a short essay to my husband, who was then on the staff of the *XIX*ᵉ

Siècle. The young professor, quite unknown, had only his title of "Normalien" to recommend him to his older comrade. The article was inserted and was followed by others.

One of our good friends, in those distant days, was Eugène Yung, who had founded the *Revue Bleue.* He wrote to my husband, saying: "A young man, a Maître or Lemaître, has been recommended to me. Do you know anything about him? Should you advise me to try him?" The answer was: "Secure his services for the *Revue* if you can."

Very soon after this, a long study on Renan appeared in the *Revue Bleue.* The next day, the name of Jules Lemaître was in all men's mouths.

Renan, like Victor Hugo, had, while still living, entered into immortality. He was a sort of demi-god, whom all revered, and none ventured to attack.

Suddenly, an audacious young man, whom no one knew, fresh from the provinces, dared to look the great writer straight in the eyes, to describe the shape of his large nose, to count the wrinkles and warts of his heavy cheeks; to listen to the learned Sorbonne lectures not in order to be instructed as to how the Bible sprang into life, but to note, pencil in hand, the familiar idioms, the abbreviated words, the "ohs!" and "ahs!" the "allons donc!" the "jamais de la vie!" which disfigured the phrase. Renan as a writer was impeccable; his French a model of purity, of charm, of musical rhythm. As a speaker, he gave himself great license —less, however, that M. Lemaître pretended. This young man was indulging in the perverse joy of attacking an idol: he was in the frame of mind of the Gallic soldiers, pulling beards in the Roman Forum.

Then, when he had allowed his malice to exhaust itself, the critic's tone changed. He asked:

"Is M. Renan gay? . . . Can he be gay?

And then the whole philosophy of the great man was brought to the bar:

"This man has spent twenty years of his life in studying how religions are formed; he has looked into the depths of the human conscience; he has understood the misery of man who conceived such dreams, and who found consolation in them . . . and yet he can be gay!"

Renan was seriously affected by this attack. Knowing full well the power of his personal charm, he asked to see his young critic. Lemaître went to him at once, and, naturally, was entirely won over by the elder man. He could not retract his written words, but whenever Lemaître again had occasion to speak of Renan, it was after a much more respectful fashion, but with much less brilliancy.

On one occasion, he said:

No writer has ever seemed more uncertain than M. Renan, more impalpable; to none have more under-currents of thought, more inextricable or more diabolical imaginings been attributed. I myself, to my shame be it said, once thought him wanting in simple good faith. I am now convinced that the best way to approach this great writer is to read him in all simplicity, and not to seek for more than he wishes us to grasp. If M. Renan seems to us very complicated, it is that the elements of which his genius is composed are numerous, diversified, and sometimes contradictory. If he appears to be wanting in candor, it is perhaps from very excess of candor.

And again:

Can one expect merely simple books from a poet who is as learned as a Benedictine, of a philosopher who once was a seminarist? If his mind is full of contradictions, it is because of its marvellous richness. . . .

When M. Yung called the young professor to him, all thought of teaching was abandoned. The agile pen ran over the paper: essays, stories, sketches, were sown broadcast. All was not equally good, equally worthy of M. Lemaître's very great talent. Certain short stories, published in the *Figaro* and elsewhere, ought never to have seen the light. In his volume of poems, later in his prose sketches, indiscreet reminiscences peeped out, as did allusions, incomprehensible to the mass of his readers, but terribly clear to others. This was the transition epoch, during which he was a little intoxicated by his sudden success; when, also, after years of comparative poverty, he was enjoying his facility for earning a great deal of money.

This very natural, very human delight did not last long. No man ever tired more quickly of assured success than did M. Jules Lemaître. His unquiet spirit was forever stretching out toward something new, something untried.

As literary critic of the *Revue Bleue*, he acquired not only the fame of a witty iconoclast, but he quickly established his right to be regarded as an authority. His studies on Lamartine, on Anatole France, on Daudet, on Sarcey—on how many others!—were not only delightful reading, examples of the purest, most fluid, most harmonious prose; they were also full of substantial matter, of original and forcible thought. But he loved best to strike hard, to cause a stir, to hurl down idols.

His article on M. Georges Ohnet aroused a storm of indignation on one side, of malicious delight on the other. It begins thus:

In this *Review* I usually speak on literary subjects. I beg my readers to bear with me if, to-day, I treat of M. Georges Ohnet's novels. I shall lighten the conscience of many clear-sighted but timorous persons by saying aloud what they think. Then, if these novels are outside of literature, they yet have to do with the history of literature. Their prodigious success challenges attention.

And so on, through some twenty pages or more. It was a terrible diatribe, a pitiless execution, unjust as a whole, as all such executions must be.

I ventured to say this to him, and he defended himself characteristically: "*Que voulez-vous!* . . . That man sets all my nerves tingling. . . ."

Ah, no! a man whose nerves were so easily set tingling could never be an impersonal, loftily impartial critic of the Brunetière school. And therein, perhaps, lies his great charm. We can never read a page of his without feeling his presence, without recognizing in the printed words the sound of his softly modulated voice, without seeing the sparkle of his eye. For the time being, at least, we love what he loves;

we hate what he hates. He carries us away with him, and it is a delight to allow ourselves thus to be carried away.

But M. Lemaître refused to be looked upon merely as a critic. He proved that he could create as well as judge. His exquisite, dainty stories were never as popular as they deserved to be; the irony was too delicate, the charm too subtle for the general public, and of this he conceived some chagrin. A dramatic critic, Mr. Jules Lemaître sat in judgment over so many plays of superior or inferior merit that he was tempted to write plays himself. These were acted, and generally well received. They did not, however, attain to lasting fame. Certain scenes were admirable; the dialogue was crisp, witty, written in the purest French. That did not suffice. To carry a dramatic work well through five, or even three acts, it requires great power of passion, perhaps also a rather coarser and broader sort of talent than Lemaître possessed. It was as though a delicate painter of cabinet pictures had attempted to decorate the walls of some great hall.

And this comparative failure was very bitter to M. Jules Lemaître.

The first in date of these plays is called "Révoltée." Here the author remembered his past, for the husband of his *révoltée*, a far more interesting personage than the discontented, ambitious heroine herself, is a professor, who half kills himself with work, as his modest salary does not suffice to pay for the luxury of his loved and unloving wife.

In the "Député Leveau," political life is portrayed with pitiless satire.

Several of M. Lemaître's plays are founded on his short stories; they do not always improve on them, though "L'Aînée," the story of an eldest sister, always sacrificed to the younger members of the family, is perhaps the most dramatic of his theatrical ventures.

"Mariage blanc," singularly touching and discreet in its original form, a sketch of a few pages only, becomes unpleasant on the stage. More distressing still is the "Pardon." These two plays were admirably acted at the Comédie Française.

Meanwhile, the great critic, the charming writer, was received as member of the Académie Française. If, somewhere about 1877, some gypsy had foretold such a fortune to the obscure professor of rhetoric, doubtless he would have smiled incredulously. Yet, in spite of all, he was not content.

If many beneficent fairies had assisted at the baby boy's birth, one evil-minded one came and tarnished the gifts bestowed upon him; a spirit of discontent, a reckless seeking after the impossible—such was the gift of the "Fée Carabosse."

For a number of years now, M. Jules Lemaître, weary of pure literature, dissatisfied with his work as a critic, angered or saddened by what he deems his failure as an author, has turned his attention exclusively to politics, of which he understands but little, at which he looks through distorting glasses. He is lost to us, who so loved his great talent, who recognized under his light, charming, smiling satire so much real thought, so much also of unswerving literary honesty—to us who reread his "Contemporains" with ever increasing delight—to us who would call him from beneath his tent, where, discontented and silent, he has retired. . . . The pity of it!

Count me Thy Soldier, Love, To-day

By C. H. CRANDALL

COUNT me thy soldier, Love, to-day.
  Give me thy spotless shield,
And send me on thine errantry
  Forth to the fateful field.
Give me thy banner, pure and bright,
  A sword that shall not fail,
And lead me in thy glorious fight
  Till all thy foes shall quail.

The battle-ground lies far and wide,
  The hosts no man can tell;
But here at hand I make a stand,
  One life to dearly sell.
The laurel wreath may not be mine,
  Nor plaudits greet my ear,
But in this place, a little space,
  For Love I couch a spear.

The triumph over dark and wrong,
  The victory for the light,
Waits but each single soldier's stroke
  To put the foe to flight.
Oh, do not doubt that far away
  Your comrades' cheers arise!
Faith, and the blow that proves the faith,
  Shall win the peerless prize.

Count me thy soldier, Love, to-day,
  And when the fight is won,
Then come and walk the battle-field
  At setting of the sun.
And let me join the glad hurrah,
  Or, on my grass-green bed,
Let me but dream I see thee smile
  Above thy soldier dead.

Feeling and Intellect

By FRANCIS GRIERSON

Great thoughts come from the heart.
VAUVENARGUES.

IN vain do we place scientific inventions on a level with the sentiments that spring from the heart and soul; in vain do we try to believe that men work hard for the sake of mere business. There is more force in the social instinct than there is in intellectual detachment. Many men who appear heartless are secretly working for someone else. If the callous were placed in power all government would come to an end; relations and friends would count for nothing; the world would return to barbarism. Men would be contented with a gourd and a goatskin, a cave to sleep in, and a wilderness to wander about in. The deeper men feel the more harmonious does civilization become. All inspiration springs from the heart. Art without emotion and passion is a dead thing, and so is science. Newton and Darwin were great because of the depth of their feeling. Scientific inventions and discoveries, in themselves, are trivial; they are of real value the moment they become useful; and they are useful the moment they make life more tolerable. The telegraph is of value because it makes absent ones appear less distant and the world less cold and formal. So, directly or indirectly, every great thought springs from the heart. The higher a man goes in the regions of the purely intellectual, the less useful he becomes; the more detached, the less sociable. In one word, the farther we go from the human, the more attenuated do our ideas become.

Superficial sentiment is without vital influence. The secret of power lies in the intensity of emotion; but especially so in poetry, art, and literature. By no hocus-pocus can artists and writers adequately depict what they do not feel. There should be a thermometer of temperament as well as for temperature; feeling and emotion have their degrees. We are serene when our feelings are in the temperate zone, indignant when we pass eighty-three, furious when we reach blood-heat, mad at boiling point. When feeling falls below fifty we become indifferent, and when it reaches freezing point we are heartless. An emotion that does not attain the seventy-sixth degree is hardly worth recording. At summer heat the rarest flowers begin to bloom, and nature becomes poetic. While the temperate is the proper sphere for pure reason and scientific observation, it is rarely, if ever, proper for the highest achievement in any art. In the world of art, imagination and feeling are not content with a serenity that touches the borders of indifference. The creative instinct is never effective unless at a certain pitch of enthusiasm. It is the sharp, clear, brilliant current of thought that electrifies the brain. But an idea is worthless unless we can find a form to hold it. In the best work idea, form, and feeling appear to the beholder as one. An electric bolt seems a cold thing, yet a stroke of lightning will consume more at one flash than an ordinary fire would consume in an hour.

To the superficial some of the greatest aphorisms seem like platitudes because they look so simple; but some sayings that appear easy are the most difficult owing to the extraordinary depth required to discover them. Vauvenargues, who declared that great thoughts come from the heart, knew very well what he was saying, and why. Writers of platitudes never have any abiding influence, a platitude being the utterance of a person who is incapable of feeling profoundly. And a man's impressions are not necessarily his thoughts. If Vauvenargues had scribbled mere impressions his aphorisms might have passed for platitudes; but he arrived at his convictions through something more than indefinable impressions. The longer I live the less I esteem work that is purely intellectual. In the history of great writers and artists the head has been the servant of the heart. Take any man or woman known to the public, in any capacity, from playing a violin to preaching a sermon, and then judge between the power of intellect and the power of feeling. Take any art, from sculpture to poetry, music, painting, oratory, and story-telling, compare the work of one man with that of another, and then judge. Put your finger blindly on any of the arts, and choose a subject—for it matters not where you may begin. Is it poetry? Everyone must know why Virgil and Dante hold their own after the lapse of ages. Is it music? Competent judges know why Mozart, Beethoven, and Wagner are preferred to composers like Brahms. Is it novel-writing? Dickens has had, and is still having, more influence than Thackeray, in spite of the latter's keen wit and original power. As for Charlotte Brontë, emotional energy made her a unique personality among novelists, as the same energy has made Signora Duse a unique personality among the figures of the stage. Never, perhaps, has spontaneity and feeling, in the actor's art, been put to such a crucial test as when Signora Duse made her first bow before a Parisian audience. She appeared before the spectators in the simplicity of her own personality—unaided by the academical arts of elocution and traditional convention—as one who had come to pay an indifferent visit, simple beyond all theatrical custom, with an expression that made her look unconcerned with the people about her. But she was being scrutinized by an audience composed of actors, critics, and the leaders of the titled and fashionable world—an audience representing the most critical and fastidious portion of the most intellectual society of Europe: habitués who remembered Rachel, dramatic critics who saw the début of Bernhardt, artists who had painted the portraits of geniuses, poets acquainted with the deepest emotions of the soul, psychologists who had dissected the heart in novels and romances, and, last of all, the women of fashion, supposed to be proof against the impulses of feeling. What could a simple

actress like this do here? The critics felt uneasy, the fashionable women began to feel bored. But, as the play proceeded, Duse rose from her seat; she engaged in a dialogue: it was like someone speaking, not from a written text, but in actual life. For this woman was representing, not a school of art, but the soul of art; not a method of acting, but her own mood; not a dramatic pose, but a living passion. As the critical moment approaches, surprise changes to anxious wonder: the amateurish actress has been transformed—a thrill passes over the audience, it sweeps through nerve and heart as the autumn winds through the oak and elm, stripping them of the last dry leaves of semblance and illusion. Her acting was like a resurrection of the heart from the tomb of dramatic conventionality. It came as dew in the stifling atmosphere of classicism, as warm blood in the formal body of pedantry.

In any form of literature, imagination, without deep feeling, brings us into the clouds. Some writers seem to have long and narrow brains, giving them narrow views about everything. Others seem to have broad and deep brains, and their sentiments and views are large and profound. Others, again, inhabit the seventh floor of intellect—we never walk in to see them, we take an elevator and go up; we visit them by a process of mechanics and metaphysics—but we are glad to get back, even by sliding down the balustrade. Some men live with the world, some in it but not of it, and some on it but not for it. But all great writers have, by some process, known the world. The secret of Sir Walter Scott's power lies in three things: imagination, knowledge, and feeling. But without feeling, imagination and knowledge would have left him a novelist of the second or third order. All the greatest writers owe their power to the concentration of energy in feeling. Milton says that imagination and passion constitute the poet; the same definition holds good for the others. Scott, Balzac, Flaubert, Hawthorne, Meredith, Hardy, George Eliot, and twenty others, prove to us how futile would have been their imagination without deep, emotional power. In vain do pedantic writers try to draw a line between the best prose and the best poetry, for the line exists only by rule, and the feelings recognize none.

If such a thing were possible to invent, a psychometer would be a useful thing for measuring the height and depth of thought and feeling. As in the science of meteorology the weather expert has to consider more than one atmospheric condition before he makes a prediction, so it is of vital interest to know how far above and how far beneath the surface a writer or a speaker can go. In every sphere of art the things most essential are altitude for vision and depth for emotion. Sometimes the speaker or writer attains both height and depth in a few periods: the eye, the ear, and the soul are affected as by the passing of a procession of

heroes, with the sound of a great bell and the thunder of distant cannon. The words and phrases assume the character of a guard of honor that conducts the mind to a seat among the immortals. Once in a long while an occasion presents itself when it requires a child of nature to speak for nature, once in an age the occasion and the orator arise as one. Lincoln, at Gettysburg, unified thought and feeling in a single embrace; by a few simple gestures he conciliated defeat and victory, evoking in a brief space the mysterious harmonies that dwell on the borders of life and death; by an exalted union of heart and intellect he spread the mantle of glory over the dead and the memory of genius over the living. Here, the rail-splitter of the prairies took his place beside Shakespeare the actor and Burns the ploughman. These names are typical examples of the heights and depths attained by Nature left to herself.

The Tyranny of Local Color, or Parochialism in Fiction

By R. BRIMLEY JOHNSON

No observer of recent tendencies in novel-writing can fail, I think, to have observed an evil influence which gained a hold upon that art through certain notable achievements in popularity, and which, although perhaps more rampant a few years ago than to-day, is unfortunately still with us. This phase of illegitimate realism — for as such it must undoubtedly be denied — was brought into prominence by the Kailyard school, and upheld by photographers of the London Streets like the author of "No. 5 John Street" and of Society like Mr. E. F. Benson or Mr. Robert Hichens.

It will not be difficult to distinguish between the methods of work adopted by such writers and those of the legitimate historical novelist, Sir Walter Scott, or of Thackeray, the Society satirist, and Dickens, the artist of low

life. There are living writers, no doubt, equally effective for comparison; but it is more convenient, and less invidious, to agree from the favorites of an earlier generation, of whose standing there can be no question.

Our charge against the "parochial" character of certain English fiction, remarked of late years by a distinguished French critic, need not involve any restatement of the old controversy between realist and romancist, on which Robert Louis Stevenson has written the last word:

The observer (poor soul, with his documents!) is all abroad. For to look at a man is but to court deception. We shall see the trunk from which he draws his nourishment; but he himself is above and abroad in the green dome of foliage, hummed through by winds and rested in by nightingales. And the true realism is that of the poets, to climb up after him like a squirrel, and catch some glimpse of the heaven for which he lives. And the true realism, always and everywhere, is that of the poets: to find out where joy resides; and give it a voice far beyond singing.

We do not condemn local color, as inartistically manipulated, so much for its over-minuteness in detail as for its triumphant tyranny alike over the divine gifts of telling a story and drawing a character. The "costumes" in Scott, Thackeray, or Dickens are as elaborate as those of the writers herein condemned; but they are subordinate to plot and passion. The "scenery" of fiction, whether historical or contemporary, may be as sumptuous as you will without obscuring the men and women it should illuminate.

Nevertheless the fact remains that many widely read modern novelists have permitted these most useful and ornamental instruments of their craft to master them; and by overzealous attention to the accidental elements of their art have fallen to neglect of the essential.

The novel proper is a composition in character, and its legitimate field is the illustration of human life. The novelist's ideal must be to create actual beings, of unmistakable, indestructible individuality; who act and feel according to the law of their own natures, whose experiences may be tested by the most universal philosophy. In other words his *dramatis personæ* must be persons and not types, his method must be portraiture and not photography, his circumstances must be subsidiary and not dominant.

Fiction is one of many mediums for the expression of ideas; and the prose story, like the humanity it represents, consists of two elements which are equally essential to its verisimilitude and its vitality—the one spiritual and permanent, the other material and accidental. Those who allow their costumes or events to form their whole subject-matter produce only the "study in local color," a freak of the artistic imagination.

Now the writers of the Kailyard school offend most grievously against this established canon. They are the slaves of dialect. Their accuracy is un-

impeachable. But characters are not built upon intonation, and the passions outlive short pipes. One has only to recall the glorious gallery of men and women fresh in the memory from Scott's pages, and the creations of these laborious scene-painters will vanish away into thin air. Our shelves are filled indeed with ingenious phonograph-records of idiom and manners beyond the Tweed; but what do we know, at least from such a source, of Highlander or Lowlander—his inheritance from history, his grasp of life. They have given us no romance to stir the blood, no angel visitant to the land of memory.

Charles Dickens again, though no wizard, must be admitted superior to his modern rivals, because with him London is illustrative of character— with them character is illustrative of London. Our old friend Boz put his heart into his heroes, his heroines, his "funny men," and his villains. He cared supremely that the public should love or hate the men and women of the piece, should feel a thrill of honest human pleasure at the triumph of injured innocence and the punishment of sin—commonplace topics, perhaps, but the staff of daily life. The use of copious detail, resulting from keen observation, was, no doubt, prominent in his effects; but, as a rule, it was subordinated to its proper position of a means and not an end.

In books of which Mr. Whiteing's "No. 5 John Street" may be accepted as typical, the normal relation of form and substance is inverted. They are inspired, apparently, by the desire to exhibit an intimate acquaintance with the manners and customs of particular districts, to pursue us into our studies with the hoarse cry of the itinerant news vendor and the shrill laughter of the flower-girl. They are redolent of gas-lamps, underground railways, and tram-cars—cockney to the finger-tips. How well they know their London! and, alas, how little they know life!

Those who scribble of the Smart Set might well have contributed their "revelations" to the columns of a Society paper. To Thackeray the denizens of "Vanity Fair" were more vital than the booths round which they dance and weep; their emotions and their misfortunes were individual, and therefore universal — their personal growth formed unquestionably the whole text and fibre of the design. The ambition of Mr. E. F. Benson, at least in his most popular works, is apparently satisfied by a brilliant and daring presentation of his intimacy with certain "persons of importance in their own day," and Mr. Robert Hichens seeks only to please by a polished veneer of realism in rapid and crowded "living pictures" from the clubs, the drawing-rooms, and the music-halls of the Metropolis. They are quite at home in town at the height of the season; but thought and feeling scarcely concern them. They forget that character is living to us, not by virtue of its environment, but for its acceptance or conquest of circumstances, and in this distinction lies the root of the matter.

It may be contended, I am well aware, that the besetting sin of the critic is to limit art by an attempt to codify artistic laws; and that no production may be justly condemned for not being what its author never intended it to be. But the tyranny of local color is more a positive than a negative evil; its votaries sin by commission, not omission. To make a false picture of life is no less than treachery to art and to humanity, and a novel written for the set purpose of exhibiting certain phases of civilization must be essentially false.

In fiction, certainly, an absolute definiteness of outline is imperative. Every item of correct detail in the drawing of externals is so much clear gain to the picture. The characters must lose by the slightest suspicion of hesitation or vagueness in time, place, and circumstance. As in drama, the appeal is by concrete personal examples, and the more minutely each example can be differentiated from others, the more clearly the actual situation can be isolated, the more forcible is the appeal. Local color as an auxiliary is most justifiable, most effective.

The governing impulse must not, therefore, be lost sight of: the creation of individual human beings, whose fortunes shall passionately absorb their creator. The novelist who may set aside his high calling, and elect to stand or fall by the brilliant correctness of his furniture-painting, is lending a dangerous grace to the most prominent and the most fatal heresy of our time— the worship of materialism.

A History of the Library of Congress

By ANNE HOLLINGSWORTH WHARTON

THE publication of a history of the Library of Congress * is timely to-day, as few persons of intelligence enter the spacious library building in Washington without wishing to know something of the inception of an institution whose influence has been so important.

Whether or not an interest in libraries, in their foundation, organization, and history, is indicative of the intellectuality of a nation, it is a rather significant fact that this most practical and material age is one which may well be known in the future history of the country as the library era. Small and unimportant collections of books, in many of our cities and towns, have in the last twenty or thirty years received endowments that have enabled them to take their places as well-equipped libraries. In line with this interest in the founding and enlarging of libraries, we find the small cramped quarters of the Congressional Library extended into one of the most spacious and magnificent repositories for books in the world.

No patriotic citizen who visits the national capital and passes through the marble halls of the Library of Congress, or enjoys the advantages of its harmonious and admirably arranged reading-room, can fail to be glad and proud that so much time, money, and artistic ability should have been expended upon the preparation of this home for the nation's books—books which more than anything else represent the intellectual and spiritual life of a people.

Mr. Johnston's history of the Library of Congress from 1800 to 1864 is a valuable contribution to the. political and literary history of the Republic as well as to its bibliography. Many pages of this volume are naturally devoted to details of the administration of the library, its bibliographical policy, routine, methods, and plans, which, important as they may be, are interesting only to librarians. On the other hand, this book is much more than a detailed report of ways and means, as the writer has enlivened his pages with anecdotes and expressions of contemporaneous opinion which throw light upon the literary tastes and habits of American statesmen in the first half of the last century. Upon one point there can be no doubt,—that the public men of that time had a genuine love for books, and felt as Mr. Elbridge Gerry said in his report to Congress, "that a library for the use of its members was a necessity, as they should otherwise be obliged at every session to transport to the seat of the General Government a considerable portion of their libraries." In view of the bad roads and difficulties of transportation in those days, we may well believe that Mr. Gerry's practical argument proved to be an eloquent one.

Mr. Johnston in his history takes us back to the early years of the Republic when Congress met in New York and Philadelphia, in which latter city its members enjoyed the advantages of a collection of valuable books, known then as it is to-day under the title of the Library Company of Philadelphia. This company, through its secretary, William Rawle, Esq., tendered to the President and Congress the free use of their books and manuscripts in as full and ample a manner as if they were members of the association. This friendly offer on the part of the Library Company of Philadelphia was accepted with due form and ceremony by President Washington, through his secretary, Tobias Lear. There is every reason to believe that the statesmen gathered in the Quaker City refreshed and strengthened their minds at this fount of learning, which owed its existence to James Logan, Benjamin Franklin, and other worthies of colonial days.

Interesting chapters of this volume are those which treat of the destruction

* "History of the Library of Congress, 1800-1864." By William Dawson Johnston of the Library of Congress. Washington: Government Printing Office, 1904.

of the library by the invading British in 1812, and of the bickerings and discussions incident to the purchase of Mr. Jefferson's valuable collection of books. Many of the arguments against the acquisition of the library of the Virginia statesman may be taken as a fair example of the narrowness of certain public men of the day, while with others the question was made a political issue.

Mr. King of Massachusetts, whom Mr. Johnston characterizes as "a sincere and not uninformed gentleman," exhibited a fine combination of illiberality and partisanship when he urged against the purchase that

it might be inferred, from the character of the man who collected it, and France, where the collection was made, that the library contained irreligious and immoral books, works of the French philosophers, who caused and influenced the volcano of the French Revolution which had desolated Europe and extended to this country.

The Massachusetts statesmen and others in the opposition advocated a careful pruning out of such books as were not suited to the sensitive congressional mind, especially of the works of Voltaire, Rousseau, and other writings of a philosophical nature. The newspapers of the time entered with spirit into this war of words. The Petersburg *Courier* was pleased to make merry at the expense of the literary censors of Congress:

What can be a greater stigma upon the members of our National Legislature than to assert that books of a philosophical description are improper for their perusal? Were Mr. Oakley, Mr. Reed, and Mr. Grosvenor the literary censors of the United States, the works of Newton, Locke, Simpson, Stewart, and all others of equal merit, would doubtless be committed to the flames, and their places supplied perhaps by the "Tales of Wonder," the "Tales of Horror," and the "Arabian Nights Entertainment."

The *Intelligencer* spoke of the Jefferson Library as a collection whose value could scarcely be computed, it being one which could not be bought in the ordinary mode in which books are purchased, while the Washington correspondent of the Boston *Gazette*, trimming its sails to suit the New England breezes of that day, wrote: "The grand Library of Mr. Jefferson will undoubtedly be purchased with all its finery and philosophical nonsense."

In the face of all opposition there were enough liberal-minded and intelligent men in Congress to effect the purchase of the Virginia scholar's unique collection. A bill passed both Houses authorizing the library committee to buy Mr. Jefferson's library for the amount at which it was valued by Joseph Milligan, a Georgetown bookseller, $23,950. This collection of 6500 books became the nucleus of the present library of over a million and a quarter of volumes. The chapter upon the sale of the Jefferson collection would in itself render Mr. Johnston's history worthy · of a place upon the shelves of private as well as of public libraries.

Other interesting chapters are those which refer to the different quarters occupied by the collections of the Library of Congress, to the development of the plans of Mr. Alexandre Vattemare for international exchanges, and to a detailed history of the administration and policy of its several librarians from the early days of John Beckley and Patrick Magruder to the distinguished and important services of Ainsworth Rand Spofford. Succeeding volumes will treat of the building of the spacious new library and of its later policy under the present librarian, Mr. Herbert Putnam.

A Group of Poets

By EDITH M. THOMAS

MR. ARTHUR UPSON has achieved a most creditable piece of work in this, his "Poem-Drama," * builded upon the exceedingly verisimilar foundations of an old ecclesiastical legend of the fourth century. The theme is drawn from the account given by Eusebius Pamphili, who relates that the king of Edessa, being grievously ill, sends by his trusty messenger, Ananias, an entreaty to "Jesus the good Saviour," at Jerusalem, that the latter shall leave the city of persecution, and shall make his residence in the king's own city; undertaking, likewise, the cure of the royal sufferer. The old text contains, also, the reputed reply of Jesus; all which material Mr. Upson has woven most judiciously, with firmness and with delicacy, into his drama, the personages of which live, move, and have individual being to quite an unusual degree, in these days of oft-attempted but seldom vital revival from the "chronicles of wasted times." Mr. Upson has notable lines,—notable both for substance and for manner, as in the following,—the apology of the messenger for his seeming failure:

> My love counts not its duties ; nor, I think,
> Is love summed up in all its victories :
> *'Tis larger and includes defeat.*

Or, take the following dialogue between Cleonis, the Queen, and Ananias who has just been describing the last act in Jerusalem:

ANANIAS: The hoarse mob's laughter down the blazing street,
Making us glad to quit the fearful city.
CLEONIS: Oh, let them never leave their quiet hills,—
These prophets that dream well for all the world !

.   .   .   .

They are of other worlds and strangers here :
Let them remain in mountains—or in gardens !
ANANIAS : Ay, but we need such in this world of men.

CLEONIS : Ye need them as the tiger needeth blood,
Come, show me one great soul that taught you good,
Whom your wild world would have ; one bold emprise,
Without Protesilaus at the prow ?

"Octaves in an Oxford Garden" and some twenty-five sonnets further maintain Mr. Upson's excellent workmanship in this volume. Of the latter, "Thought of Stevenson" and "Sultan's Bread" are admirable examples.

In one of the songs in this shadow-haunted volume of verse,† there is one that tells of the rising of Persephone:

> At length she daunts the tyrannous year,
> Her little laugh usurped the tear,
> Her little song she dares to fling
> Against the black stars, merrily.

Sad—"sad as night,"—sad, even in whatever joy comes with the gift and use of singing; but sad, withal, with an underlying adolescent vitality of sadness, are almost all these "Sonnets and Songs,"—the work of a very true and tender poet,—a singing Persephone who seems to send her heart to us out of the shrouding darkness where the Muse habitually dwells. We have said that this sadness, however, breathes of an adolescent vitality. Does not the Muse herself acknowledge as much in these words, "Youth and its pensive agonies!" Somehow, we are loath to believe that our gifted young *débutante* (though this is her second volume of verse) has put to proof in her own experience the truth of the heart-piercing lyric cry :

> Life is a world that breaks the thing it frees.

But ever, here and there, along her lines, the hopeful tang of youth tempers the impassioned melancholy of the singer. It is present in certain Marlowe-like exuberancies,—in proud fancies of "fighting the stars for glory,"

* "The City, and Other Poems." By Arthur Upson. Macmillan. $1.00.

† "Sonnets and Songs." By Helen Hay Whitney. Harper. $1.20 net.

271

in tender fancies of the world parcelled out as the momentary exultant inheritance of lovers; as in the following:

We'd catch the wind and twine
  The evening stars,—a chaplet musical,—
To crown our folly, lure the nightingale
To sing the bliss your lips should teach to mine.

The keynote of Mrs. Whitney's poetic *Stimmung* is struck (so it seems to us) in one line of her opening sonnet, "Ave atque Vale," where she declares, "I play with Beauty, which is kin to Art." It *is* Beauty that rules in her song-world, and that rules despite the often despairful theme and mood. For instance, in "Flowers of Ice," it is the instinct for Beauty that moves her to find an iridescent parallel, amidst the "North's white sanctity," to express the idea of that arrest of all emotion which results in the "frozen heart and tearless eyes." This is the parallel:

The lights within the ice-floes are our flowers,
Lily, and daffodil, and violet.
Beneath these monstrous suns that never set
Tremble soft rainbows, young as Earth's first
    hours,
Ancient as Time.

We should like to quote, as being most characteristic of the general tenor of Mrs. Whitney's "Sonnets and Songs," this happy-hearted spring-like lyric, "Good-bye, Sorrow":

Day that began with a tear,
  Will you end with a sigh?
Stay! See the blossoming year,
  Laugh up the sky.
Nay, here's a hope for your fear,
  Sweet Sorrow—good-bye!

But the Sonnet diverts us from the Song; and from the ranks of the former, we choose

AMOR MYSTICUS

Not you, nor all the gauds that Fate bestows,
  Can make me swerve so little from my dream.
  Across my veil of mystery you seem
Perhaps a little dearer than the rose,
Perhaps more fair than the long light that flows
  Between the lids of twilight. But the gleam
  Of iris on the breast of wisdom's stream
Is of a radiance that no rival knows.

My heart is not my heart, or it might chance
  To sorrow for the sorrow in your tears;
My soul is locked against all circumstance
Of life or love or death, or heaven or hell;
  I have no place for laughter in my years,
No room where little, little love might dwell.

In reading the "Hymn on the Nativity," who has not felt supremely the richness of fancy — almost of feeling itself—which Milton lavished upon his descriptions of the fleeing divinities of Olympus? Something akin to Miltonic richness meets us in the outset of "Ad Matrem," * in the lines depicting the rout of the Greek godheads, before the Lux Mundi shining over Judean hills. But the poet of "Ad Matrem," even as Milton himself, has other motives than those that dwell with Classic Beauty; though, unlike Milton, this poet of our Transitional Day (Transitional, whether as regards Poetry or Religion) would carry certain questions of the human heart concerning its spiritual faith into the very *adyta* of that faith and to no lesser than its Central Figure:

Art Thou our God and archetypal man?

And, something in the spirit of the "New Mysticism," the poet would answer, to the heart's questionings:

Where love exists all love is in relation.
So in Christ's love and loving ministry
Thou art exalted in my exaltation.

In "Present Day Sonnets," also, is dwelt upon the vitalizing and redemptive principle which pervades a selfless love for humanity. A like gospel, but clothed in Oriental imagery, is repeated in the poems, "Benares," and "At Delphi's Gate." The poet, withal, has a word to say for the joys of the poet's vocation; and this word is to be found in "A Quatrain":

Who sees Apollo feels himself divine.
  Although his life a lowly course must run,
  Yet in his heart he foots it with the sun,
And circles where immortal hours shine.

* "Ad Matrem, and Other Poems." By Percy Stickney Grant. Ingalls Kimball.

Letters of Mme. de Staël to Benjamin Constant, Hitherto Unpublished

Edited by the BARONESS de NOLDE
Great-Granddaughter of Mme. de Constant

Translated by Charlotte Harwood

FIRST PAPER

WHEN Mme. Benjamin Constant died in Paris in 1845, her son by her first marriage, the Baron de Marenholtz, who had hastened to her deathbed, took back with him to Germany her papers and other portable possessions. For years these manuscripts have lain buried in the family archives of the Marenholtz family, but the Baron's granddaughter, Charlotte de Constant's great-granddaughter, the Countess de Nolde, has lately examined the papers, and from among them has chosen the hitherto unpublished letters of Mme. de Staël to Benjamin Constant, which we now present to our readers.

It is not known how Mme. de Staël's letters came into Mme. de Constant's possession, but Mme. de Nolde thinks that some light is thrown on the subject in a letter from Benjamin Constant to Mme. Récamier, written in 1828. He says:

"Before my return to Paris in 1817, I took the liberty of asking you to remove some papers from a trunk, something that I had written *at a time when I was very unhappy*, and that I did not want others to see. You were so kind as to do this. In this trunk were some letters from our friend* that ought not to be seen by any one. Did I not ask you to remove them also? The fact is I have not found them. I have wanted these letters to show parts of them to the Duc de Broglie and his wife†; be good enough to tell me if you have them."

The Duchesse de Broglie was Mme. de Staël's daughter, and on her mother's death she made all possible efforts to obtain what remained of her correspondence with Constant. She writes

* Mme. de Staël.
† Albertine, Mme. de Staël's daughter.

on the 17th of January, 1831, to M. Charles de Constant, asking him to send her from Lausanne a box of Benjamin Constant's papers "which contains, perhaps, my mother's letters"; and M. J. H. Menos says, "What the Duchesse de Broglie so anxiously demanded was delivered to her." But it is possible that another series of letters may have been in question, and in any case an order from Mme. de Constant had anticipated the Duchesse's demand, for on January 6, 1831, she writes to Benjamin's cousin Rosalie, at Lausanne, begging her urgently "to retain the care of the box committed to her charge, which contains papers that ought not to fall into any one's hands."

The historian Sismonde wrote that no one really knew Mme. de Staël who had not seen her with Benjamin Constant, and that he was only entirely himself at Coppet. It is fortunate then that a few more letters have been found that can show us, now so far removed from them, two such celebrated persons in their relations to each other. They were written after the final rupture with Mme. de Staël caused by Constant's marriage in 1808. Mme. de Staël had no premonition of this occurrence, and was mortally wounded when Constant, who had gone to meet her on her return from Germany, informed her of his marriage as she was going upstairs. He wished to present his wife to her immediately, but Mme. de Staël insisted on his keeping the marriage secret for a year, to save her pride, and to this Mme. de Constant, the most amiable of souls, consented.

In 1813, Mme. de Staël went to England, and stayed with the Doxats, a family of French refugees, then engaged in business in London.

" 3rd August, 1813, 'Doxaville' [illegible].

" I do not know if you have received my letter; I chance this one by a traveller to Prague. Whatever may follow I my dress for fifteen hundred francs, which is good enough for one that is not in the fashion of the country. You must write to me by Vienna, at the address of M. de Piez* and Mme. Amplainville, care of Mrs. Doxat, provided you love me still. I have not changed;

Anna Luigia Necker Baron: di Stael Holstein

cry peace; those who would travel can do so. Will they do it? What I can say is that in this house talent is much appreciated, and the money spent is a third more than elsewhere; but that is all. I sent you word that I had sold you have robbed me of my happiness, but I do not deny your power. Would

* An almost illegible name, perhaps Piez. There are some sentences that are not very clear. Fear that the letters might be intercepted by the police probably made her choose names and turn her phrases in a manner comprehensible only to Constant.

it be possible to go to Berlin, even through Mad. Olive, she would not think of it but for seeing you again. But who can tell what you want? At least, all that you have imagined, to use as a pretext to yourself, is false. You know it now.

"God bless you. My daughter is well. I doubt if I can establish her here; there are so many women, and so much money. In any case I shall stay here two years. Write to me. Ah! shall I never see you again!"

LETTER FROM MME. DE STAËL TO BENJ. CONSTANT

"30 November [1813].

"At last, after three months of silence, a line from you to my daughter has reached me; it is of 12th September, and I received it yesterday. But, this morning, Schlegel writes me, on the 30th October, that he did not find you at Göttingen. Is it possible that you did not rejoin the Crown Prince?* He esteems you so much, he has such fine views, that conform so well to our ideas!

"Do you do nothing with yourself, with that so superior 'You' that you have taken from me? The only action of your life will have been against me. Certainly, to see you again would be to be reborn; but where, and how? I would ask nothing better than to go to Berlin next spring, but does not your situation make everything difficult? We must see each other again, however, before we die.

"I, and my book, are a great success here, but my heart is always heavy.

"I shall never rest; all is spoiled, all is lost for me, by you, by you! May God forgive you!

"I do not think this country suits my daughter. Poor Albert,† did you not weep for him?

"I do not wish to die without seeing you again, without having again spoken as I used to speak; but I should wish to die after, because you have hurt me to the bottom of my soul, and you will wound me again.

* Bernadotte.
† Her son killed in a duel.

"Adieu, adieu. I am always as I have been, and you can still tell yourself that I have shed tears only on the death of my unfortunate child, and on your letters; the rest is a cloud, but real life is a pain.

"Adieu. Write to me at present in care of M. de Rehausen, Swedish Minister; there is nothing more to fear; I can conceive nothing to prevent your communicating with me, by way of Holland, every week."

About the year 1811, Mme. de Staël married Albert de Rocca, a young Frenchman, twenty-two years her junior. He had had a very remarkable career, and showed such chivalrous devotion to her that Mme. de Staël at last consented to the marriage, and made him a most devoted wife. A son was born in 1812, but her fear of ridicule was so great that the marriage was kept secret until after her death. In the following letter she speaks of him, but, as usual, her chief interest is politics.

LETTER FROM MME. DE STAËL TO BENJ. CONSTANT

"12th December, 1813.
[On a visit to Coombe Wood, probably at Lord Livingstone's.]

"Ah! why is Albert * not with you? I have been much moved at knowing you to be with the Prince†; you read in my preceding letter that such was my desire. Yesterday Lord Liverpool‡ told me that he had read the draught of an address from the Prince to the French, which was the finest thing that he had seen in his life.

"The most difficult thing, nevertheless, remains to be done, for it would be folly to hope that one could overthrow the man, in spite of the nation.

"The opposition here is not contented with the title of Sovereign Prince given to the Stadtholder §; in

* Albert de Rocca, her husband.
† Bernadotte.
‡ Robert Banks Jenkinson, Lord Liverpool, 1770-1828, Prime Minister. A Tory.
§ William Frederick (1772-1843), Hereditary Stadtholder of the Low Countries. Dethroned by Napoleon, he lived for some time in Berlin and in England. He landed at Scheveningen (November, 1813) and at The Hague was named King of the Low Countries and Duke of Luxembourg. He tried in vain to prevent the separation of Holland and Belgium, and resigned in favor of his son in 1840.

fact they persuade him too much that the word Republic is bad company, and Luther's drunken peasant * is very near flinging himself to the other side. Take care that it does not happen to you. *Sic vos non vobis.* .. . .

"Meanwhile this country is admirable; there is a fundamental love of liberty among the ministers, as among the Whigs; every one outside of the court is penetrated by it. I would much like a talk with you, and it seems to me that from Holland you could easily make a trip here. But after all do what suits you, and do not waste your fine talents any longer, that is all that I desire.

"If you wish to have your work on 'Religions' published here, I suggest to you to make an arrangement with the publisher here to print it for you. For the rest, I want nothing more, but to endure all with you. You seem to me like one of those beautiful places in the Kingdom of Naples, undermined by the volcano.

"Although this country is admirable, it seems to me that Albertine will not like it here if we stay very long. We shall go to Berlin, then, when we are able; that is to say, I think in eighteen months.

"Mackintosh wishes to be remembered to you, and you have some college friends in Scotland, he says, who have retained a high opinion of you.

"My message has had an unheard-of success here; what do they say of it in Germany? They have something better to think of, however.

"I have written to [name illegible]

"Remember me to General Lovenjoul."

Napoleon always regarded Mme. de Staël as one of his worst enemies, and during the time of his power she was banished from France. She had at first looked upon him as the savior of France from the tyranny of the Bourbons, or of the Revolution, but later on came to regard him as the greatest tyrant of them all. She urged Constant to use his elo-

* Luther compared politics to a drunken peasant leaning first to one side and then to the other. Twenty days after this letter Constant employed the same simile in writing on politics to Villers.

quence against Napoleon in the Tribunal, and thus brought disgrace upon him, and banishment upon herself. A few days after Constant's famous speech, Bonaparte said to his brother Joseph, during a public reception at the Tuileries: "What are you going to do at Mme. de Staël's? It is a house where one meets only my enemies; none of my family ought to go there." Until the fall of Napoleon, Mme. de Staël's letters abound in allusions to her struggle with him.

LETTER OF MME. DE STAËL TO
BENJ. CONSTANT.

"London, 10th January, 1814."

"(Address me in care of M. de Rehausen,
Swedish Minister.)

"I wrote to you yesterday by a traveller to Holland, so that I will only add a few lines to Albertine's.

"My health is very bad, and I might easily die. You have taught me not to believe that anything lasts in this world, and all is a dream since I no longer understand you or myself, for can it be that such a man scorned such an affection, and that such a woman did not know how to make herself beloved, when she loved to the deepest depths of her being—but enough of that.

"Mackintosh says that in Edinburg you are considered the most extraordinary being in the world; indeed, I think you are, in every sense.

"All that you say of Albertine is true; you see that she has wit and grace, and withal is beautiful, but she is indolent, and I do not know if she will make herself felt by others.

"I send you a letter for the Comte de Munster that Villers will use or not as he chooses. Has he had news of his brother? I am interested in this, and I thought of writing to M. de Budaschaft, Minister of Police in Russia, if possible—and if I could have the necessary information.

"One must try to help oneself in this world before leaving it. Have you no idea of the counter-revolution, and do you think the course of events in this matter will spare me? The men of this party here are very polite to me, but I

REDUCED FACSIMILE OF LETTER WRITTEN BY MME. DE STAËL TO BENJ. CONSTANT.

know myself, and I know them, and if there are not conditions. . . . [illegible] . . . . Lord Russell and Sydney.

"I am astonished that you did not stay with the Prince Royal.* It is he that I would have near William III.†

"You seem to be very isolated in Hanover at such a time. Try to decide what you want to do; then I will arrange to see you somewhere. My idea was to go to Scotland this summer, to have the political life of my father printed next winter, and to start in the spring of 1815 for Berlin, and from there to go to the Midi by Switzerland, if there is no France, but—but—but— Finally, what are you doing? Give the matter some thought."   .

LETTER FROM MME. DE STAËL TO BENJ. CONSTANT

"18th January, 1814, England.

"I cannot conceive why my letters do not reach you. I have written to you ten times by headquarters directly in every way.

"Your book has not arrived at my publisher's, Murray, ‡ in Albemarle Street. He says that if you will give him the manuscript before it appears on the Continent, he will pay much more if it is political, less if philosophical; but would it not be better really to wait on France? They talk of the Restoration so generally here, that whether it pleases me or not, I am preparing for it by living very literarily. One will be undisturbed, I believe; it is best always to put off till that time.

"I shall go to Scotland and Ireland this summer. But I fear that this country offers nothing for Albertine, and I do not wish to stay here. Do you think I should find the right man in Germany? She is not taciturn, but she has been disappointed. There are no heroes of romance here, and the wealth of the country makes us seem poor,

which is disagreeable when one is not accustomed to it.

"Add to that the counter-revolution, which will be, at the utmost, generous to you, and you will understand my feeling sad. Nothing is clear but the trouble caused by that miserable tyrant* who has done harm that will endure long after him.

"My admiration for this country has not diminished. Personally, I am content here, but Albertine is all my life in this world, and I begin to fear that she will not be happy here. Speak to friends for her, if you can. What would she do if I should die to-morrow? And my health is much enfeebled. Good-bye. Ah! you have destroyed our future.

"Here is a letter from Mackintosh for you. He is an excellent man, but gets a little frightened at the Garat." (An allusion that cannot be understood.)

MME. DE STAËL TO BENJ. CONSTANT

"27th February, 1814.

"I wrote you by the last post, and I send you your piece on 'Destiny,' printed in 'L' Ambigu.' 'L' Usurpation' will be published next week, and I will let you know what they say of it.

"I think my son will see you. Send me word of your plans. Mine are, to return to Switzerland in the spring of 1815, and go from there to Italy; but I wish to see you again, wherever I am, and I ask what you are resolved to do in this matter. My health is very bad, and I do not know if I can surmount the difficult period in the lives of women in which I now find myself.

"I should like to see you again if I must die soon, also if I must live; write me, then, what you will do.

"I think that the allies have done wrong in wishing to go to Paris; French hearts are revolted at it, and it has given a semblance of devotion to one who has done nothing except for himself; they have given the air of a conqueror to the conquered. In short, they have acted badly, and it is because they counted on a Bourbon party that they made this mistake.

---

* Of Sweden.
† King of Prussia.
‡ Murray, Lord Byron's publisher, published "L'Allemagne," the most famous of Mme. de Staël's works (with "Corinne"). It appeared in October, 1813, and the first edition was exhausted in three days. Constant sent him "L' Esprit de Conquête et d' Usurpation," which appeared anonymously.

* Napoleon.

"For myself, I can no longer think of anything but France, and she has found herself dependent. Liberty, what blasphemy?—I have taken so much opium to avoid physical suffering this time, that I am in the state I was in when you wounded my soul. It is much easier. Good-bye. Remember me; no one can have loved you as I love you. Good-bye. Albertine loves you ever."

MME. DE STAËL TO BENJ. CONSTANT

"London, 1st April, 1814.*

"I have given your memoir to the Austrian ambassador. He said that it was full of genius, but that he did not quite understand how one could rid oneself of the father while retaining the son. In fact, the means of putting it in execution is lacking. Every one agrees with you about the regency, but the fact is, that once Bonaparte is over thrown, the old government will be re established,—it is better, perhaps, but it is sad.

"Your letter has moved me profoundly by the fancy that it is possible you may come here. But I do not believe it. What I can assure you of is that M. de Rocca will behave to you as he does to M. de Montmorency. Our mutual attachment is formed for life; he helped me in my misfortune with such noble courage and such tenderness of heart, that I shall never forget it. He has become another being, and you will recognize neither his manners nor his conversation. *Do not, then, think of him as a hindrance*, but, on your side, do what the heart tells you to. It is not for a week, but for life, that we should settle in the same place; but will you do it?

"The inconstancy of your resolutions is so great! You are sure of the reception that I will give you,—too sure alas!

"You ask me why Albertine does not like England. Really, the young people in society are so numerous and so quiet that I understand her ennui. In compensation here there is love, or

nothing, and until now it is nothing She prefers Germany. I shall remain here fourteen months longer. On the 1st July I shall start for Scotland. I will do all I can to overcome her moods, and at eighteen I will take her back to France.

"I am often tormented by the fear that all these cares are not what she should have. Ah! the past, the past! You have ruined our lives by the inconstancy of your disposition; we might have been here together, and sustained each other, if you had not been so set against me.

"Good-bye. Be faithful to France and to Liberty. One attains nothing without unity."

(Addressed to Benjamin Constant de Rebecque, Chevalier de Nordstern, in care of M. Dubois, banker, Luttich.)

MME. DE STAËL TO BENJ. CONSTANT

"Monday, 24th April, 1814.

"I am quite of the opinion that one must rally to the Bourbons, and I hope that they will desire the removal of the foreign troops, which appears to be more essential to liberty than all the Senates in the world. I shall again become the most sincere 'white cockade' in the world, and thinking much more of independence than of liberty, of which, in truth, thoughts are but little worthy. For the rest, I have done with politics, and I shall go to Greece and write my poem on the Crusades of Richard.*

"I have written you, as to what concerns me, that my friend † is as far as you from any altercation. He thinks no longer of a jealousy without any motive.

"As to Mme. de Constant, I shall be delighted to receive her here, if it suits her, and I shall in no wise accuse her of what I found it too cruel to accuse you of yourself in former days.

---

* Letter already published by A. Strodtmann, "Dichter-profile."

* Richard Cœur de Lion. The poem was never written. She speaks of it several times in other letters. On the 6th April, 1814, we read in a letter to Villers (published by M. Isler), "I shall go to see you in Göttingen next year. Make me a plan of my journey from Göttingen to Berlin, from Berlin to Switzerland, from Switzerland to Italy, from Italy to Greece, for I must write a poem on the Crusades, and I prepare for it by a pilgrimage."

† Albert de Rocca.

"Your mind and your talents will always be the objects of my admiration, and to talk with you, if you still like my conversation, will always be the greatest of my pleasures."

The letter is continued by her daughter Albertine.

"You have written me a charming letter, my dear friend, for which I thank you with all my heart. What you say of Schlegel is quite just, but at present he loves you tenderly.

"I am quite sad at leaving England, although I have certainly not enjoyed myself much there, but Englishmen are such true and noble beings!

"I hope that they will travel on the Continent, and they will be very agreeable there. Here they are too much alike outwardly, have the same manner; they must hold to a certain political party, and to a certain thing in society whether fashionable or unfashionable; an Englishman tries to make himself part of a certain thing, rather than to be an individuality himself.

"The French imitate others for effect, and the English do it to avoid being noticed.

"I am a little afraid of France, which I do not know; but what I am rejoiced at is that I shall see you, and again enjoy your wit, which is, for me, a souvenir of my country.

"You will find my mother thinner, and feebler in health; but you will see more than ever how admirable a person she is.

"Adieu."

Ibsen Tells the Story of his Life in Letters to his Friends

By JEANNETTE L. GILDER

AT last the correspondence of Henrik Ibsen to his friends is published.

This collection of letters* is to take the place of Ibsen's contemplated autobiography. They extend over a period of more than fifty years, and provide us with a direct presentment of the man during the changing conditions of his life and of his friendships, and are crammed full of biographical and literary interest never before made public. One great charm of the letters is that they were written without any thought whatever of publication; and while there is nothing of a literary character about them, at the same time the letters of a literary man could not be unliterary. They have not, however, the literary polish that they would have had had Ibsen dreamed that they would see the light of print. Indeed it is

* "Letters of Henrik Ibsen." Translated by John Nilsen Laurirk and Mary Morison. Fox, Duffield, & Co. $2.50.

doubtful whether he would have expressed himself so frankly had he known that he was writing for ultimate publication.

While those to whom Ibsen wrote saved his letters, he did not save the letters of those who wrote to him. It has been impossible in this collection to include a single letter written to Ibsen. None are to be found. So that Ibsen is, to use a modern simile, the man at the telephone nearest you; you hear but one side of the conversation. But that in this case is quite sufficient to make an intelligible story.

The introduction to the book and the notes appended to the letters are intended to remedy the defect—if defect it is—resulting from this one-sided correspondence.

In this connection it is worth while to note a few facts in the life of Ibsen. At an early age he left his father's house at Skien. After his confirmation, at the age of fourteen, he was obliged to support himself, as the family fortune, which had once been ample, had been lost. He was taken into the employment of an apothecary at Grimstad, first as apprentice and then as assistant, and remained there for six years. He returned to Skien to spend short holidays; but his connection with his family became less and less as the years passed by. As a grown man he never wrote to his parents. Two reasons are given for this. In the first place, many years passed before he was in a position to be able to help his family, and when he did reach that position he was already "half a stranger" to them. In the second — and here the editor of these letters thinks that we have the chief reason—

he felt that in the course of his development he had acquired a new basis for his spiritual life in a totally different sphere from that in which ideas moved at home; and to him, with his imperious craving for "completeness," a half-understanding was intolerable. In his father's house strict biblical piety reigned, whereas he himself had cast off the yoke of every outward authority, and valued freedom of thought above all else.

There was, however, never any actual breach between Ibsen and his family. He always kept in touch with his sister Hedvig, whom he took as a model for the child-character of the same name in "The Wild Duck." It was to her that he confided his plans for the future, and in his twentieth year told her that his desire was to reach "the highest, most perfect attainable degree of greatness and understanding," and then to die.

These letters, written to Scandinavians, Germans, Englishmen, Frenchmen, show us how his fame and his influence have spread from country to country. The prophetic words which he wrote in 1866—"I will and shall have a victory some day"—have proved true.

In a letter written to his friend, Carl Anker, in 1858, referring to an earlier period, he says:

I have often wondered what opinion you really formed of me at that time; if you did not find me hedged about with a sort of repelling coldness that made any close approach difficult. And yet it was infinitely easier to me to attach myself to you than to any one else, because there was a youthfulness of soul in you, a joy in life, and a chivalrous way of looking at things that did me good. Preserve all this! Believe me, it is not agreeable to see the world from the October standpoint; and yet there was, strange to say, a time when I wished for nothing better. I had a burning desire for, I almost prayed for, a great sorrow which might round out my existence and give life meaning. It was foolish, and I have fought my way out of that phase—and yet, the remembrance of it is never effaced.

In 1860 we find him writing a letter to the King of Norway, in which he "humbly petitions that he be granted a sum of four hundred specie-dollars [$450] out of the fund voted for artists' and scientists' travel abroad, in order that he may spend six months in visiting London, Paris, the larger German cities, Copenhagen, and Stockholm, with the special purpose of studying dramatic art and literature." He then went on to explain to his Government what he had done and what he hoped to do; but his application led to no result. It is only fair to the Norwegian Government to say that later his appeal was listened to, and he was allowed money for travel and research.

Two years later he appealed to the Council of the University of Christiania for a grant of 120 specie-dollars ($135) from the fund set apart for scientific research in Norway, to enable him to travel in his own country, the object being a collection of songs and legends, both ancient and modern, which were still current among the people. This appeal brought a grant of 110 specie-dollars, and on this he made his tour. He made his collection of legends, which he contracted with a publisher to bring out in book form; but the publisher failed and they were never published.

In a letter to Björnstjerne Björnson, in 1865, he laments his impecunious condition. His monthly outlay, $41.37, had given out, and he was obliged to borrow from his friend to carry himself through October. In another letter to Björnson Ibsen writes more about his affairs:

My book will appear in a day or two, I expect. ["Brand" was published in Copenhagen on the 15th of March, 1866.] About my present position —waiting, worn out with anxiety and suspense— looking forward to the appearance of the book and to the possibility of its producing strife and attacks of all sorts—unable in such circumstances to begin something new, which, nevertheless, is already fully developed within me,—about all this I will say no more.

Dear Björnson, it seems to me as if I were separated from both God and men by a great, an infinite void.

Last summer, when I was writing my drama, I was, in spite of all that harassed and perplexed me, indescribably happy. I felt the exaltation of a Crusader, and I don't know anything I should have lacked courage to face: but there is nothing so enervating and exhausting as this hopeless waiting. I dare say this is only a transition period. I will and shall have a victory some day. If the powers that be have shown me so little favor as to place me in this world and make me what I am, the result must be accordingly. But enough of this.

The most interesting letters are those to Georg Brandes, extracts from which were published in THE CRITIC of February, 1905.

Ibsen certainly knew what he was talking about. If any writer has been abused, both for his ideas of the drama and for his political views, it is he. But whether he has been disturbed by these attacks or not the world does not know. He has kept right on and I doubt if he would change places with any living writer to-day. He would be a fool if he did.

The Editor's Clearing=House

Nonsense Rhymes and Literary Magazines

ARE the two compatible? Do they go together with the ease and grace of the timbers of a builder in wood, or do they produce a discordant, not to say incongruous, effect? There has been a steadily growing tendency in our literary magazines during recent years to incorporate nonsense rhymes in their reading pages. Not alone nonsense, but senseless, soulless—almost I would say sentenceless—drivel! Why is it, and who is to blame? for I do not believe any person who reverences pure literature will sanction such a policy. I am not at war with humorists; far from it. But is humorous verse ever literature? I can scarcely believe it is, especially the skits and limericks now so much in vogue. "They make good fillers," some editor will say. So they do. But would not a quatrain embodying some beautiful thought, a brief lyric full of the joy and the gladness and the hope of life, complete that page just as well? Compare the result of your filler and mine. It is presumed that the reader of a standard magazine is possessed of a wholesome, healthy mind. The doggerel may bring a faint smile of insipid amusement, and it may bring a curl of disgust to the lips. Whereas the lines with a definite purpose for good back of them will produce a thrill of pleasure and possibly a new upreaching of the spirit towards the heights.

Serious verse—poetry, if you will, though pure poetry and plain verse are as different as the antipodes—has suffered a decline of late years, and absurd rhymes have usurped its place in the magazines. The editors will give as their reason for this that they are in the hands of the people, and the people want the funny things. Is such a statement altogether true? The mind of the reading world is becoming more and more elevated and enlightened and critical. I contend that the people who take literary magazines do *not* want silly words often made to rhyme absurdly. They can look for this to the funny corner of the penny daily. Such outpourings are out of place when interlarded with sane and serious work. It is the fly in the ointment; the toad in the flower-bed; the one jarring note in the harmony; the one blot on the picture.

I am not an apostle of long-faced piety. I believe in the wholesome leaven of fun in literature as well as in life. But everything in its place. What an effect is produced upon the acutely receptive mind after reading a study of Ibsen, or a description of the charms of some Old-World city, to let the eye drop upon something like this:

> There was once an old Tom-cat,
> Who would not budge at "Scat!"
> But he ran like the devil
> From Bridget's tin shovel :—
> Now what do you think of that?

Yes, what do you think of it! And sedate, learned, dignified men have given, and are giving, just such stuff to their readers, without so much as an apology. O Shakespeare! O Byron! O Burns! Thank God you are dead!
EDWIN CARLILE LITSEY.

A Reply to "A College Girl"

Without returning to the mood of controversy I should like to venture, through THE CRITIC, a plea to college girls for a dispassionate consideration of Miss Marks's comments upon their reading, to be found in the October issue of this magazine. Perhaps half a decade is not too long a time to re-member with the writer of "A Reply" in the November CRITIC "how it felt to be a college girl."

Such a dispassionate reading would, I think, impress upon one these ideas: that the judgment of the student is essentially popular; that the spirit of one or another great age of literature has not been caught from work on masterpieces in preparatory schools; that one cannot teach literature save for love; that a possible "way out" for the college girl is through the truant reading of "Great Little Books."

Is it to these points that the "Re-ply" takes exception? First, of pop-ular judgment—"What other people read is the arbiter." In objection to this Edna Lyall and E. P. Roe are summoned from oblivion as represent-ative popular authors. Had we been confronted with "The Masquerader," "Olive Latham," "The Crisis," "The Divine Fire," books which "other people" not more than college students have read and are reading, the choice would have seemed truer, but the case would have been lost. And with all respect for Dr. Van Dyke, who is, to be sure, widely read among the stu-dents, is he not in quite general popu-lar repute? To me it seems untrue that the average undergraduate *really* enjoys the esotericism of Mr. Yeats and the other Neo-Celts—but after all they are under complete popular sanc-tion just now.

As for poor Launcelot Gobbo, who if he is n't a "knight" has at least been the occasion of a tilt, we may for the moment let him rest, forgotten if necessary. But shall we be content to have forgotten, or not to have lived with, Henry Esmond and Maggie Tul-liver? Must they be filed with the antiquities, although to be sure they "began and ended," if not "a hundred years," at least more than a decade ago?

For the other objection, to "bio-graphical statistics" as "constituting a knowledge of literature . . . ." and this as the end and aim of col-lege courses," it is only necessary to have read Miss Marks's article to realize that, in the first place, she calls for no exact dates — only centuries; in the second place the only inference drawn is that, since all ages seem alike to the student mind, the *spirit* of no age has been felt; that, in the third place, she emphasizes "the primary condition of the work" as "love for it"; and that she has no good word, throughout, for "the mechanical, mul-tiplication-table method" of teaching Literature.
HELEN M. CADY.

The Book=Buyer's Guide

BELLES-LETTRES

Ainger—Lectures and Essays. By Alfred Ainger. 2 vols. Macmillan. $5.00 net.
In these delightful volumes, edited by Canon Beeching, we have, among other enjoyable matter, papers on the "Three Stages of Shakespeare's Art" and "the ethical element" in his works, Euphuism, Swift, Cowper, Burns, Scott, Charles Lamb's Letters, Coleridge's "Ode to Wordsworth," the influence of Chaucer and his successors, Dickens's amateur theatricals, the secret of charm in literature, true and false humor in literature, the art of conversation, the uses of books, etc. That the author had found the secret of charm in literature no one who is familiar with his genial and sympathetic work on Lamb needs to be reminded.

Lang—Oxford. By Andrew Lang. Lippincott. $3.00.
An alluring-looking volume whose contents do not fulfil the promise of the exterior. A sometime fellow of Merton cannot be supposed to write on his own Oxford as a mere subject for book-making. If ever a topic would have appealed to him, surely it would be this. Yet the impression left after perusal is of put-together chapters. There is no picture of a mediæval student, only broken fragments from Anthony Wood telling what such a youth might have done. That is it. It is all telling. Very charming are the illustrations, fifty of them, great and small.

Mallock—The Reconstruction of Religious Belief. By W. H. Mallock. Harper. $1.75.
A few years ago a distinguished British philosopher remarked that there was a distinct revival of philosophic idealism, and that the day of materialism had gone forever. Since his day the current towards idealism has increased in volume, yet few looking at the development of thought from a standpoint outside the arena of controversy would hesitate to pronounce this movement merely a temporary reaction against the extreme claims of scientists of the Haeckel school. Philosophy must be affected by the results of science, and must bring its tenets into accord with the conclusions of science, even though these conclusions be from a philosophical standpoint purely negative. In his most recent book Mr. Mallock completes the negative work accomplished in his "Religion as a Credible Doctrine," and attempts to reconstruct the basis of religious belief. His books are always welcome, for they are to a high degree suggestive even if not fully convincing. His style and general method of presentation are attractive, and as the treatment is not technical, his latest work can be highly recommended to all interested in fundamental questions. The acceptance of his conclusions is to a great degree a matter of temperament, for nothing in the metaphysical world can be proven according to the methods of proof adopted in the world of science. The most interesting part of the book and probably the least convincing is that wherein he attempts to show that the three beliefs—in a deity, in freedom of the will, in immortality—which make up religion, have a *prima-facie* justification in their effects on practical life; "that life, in short, in those forms which civilized men value, would be utterly unable to flourish or persist without them."

Shaw—The Author's Apology. By Bernard Shaw. Brentano. 60c.
This is a reprint of the preface to "Mrs. Warren's Profession," accompanied by a discussion, both of the play and of New York's intolerance in regard to it, by John Corbin, dramatic editor of the *Sun*. The pamphlet is neatly issued.

BIOGRAPHY

Eytinge—The Memories of Rose Eytinge. F. A. Stokes Co. $1.20 net.
The autobiography of a popular actress, who was the personal friend of Edwin Booth, the Wallacks, and many men and women of histrionic fame, with other people notable in the literary and social life of the last fifty years. The book abounds in interesting anecdote, and is illustrated with portraits of the author and of Booth, Davenport, the elder Sothern, Lester Wallack, Augustin Daly, and Dion Boucicault.

Holyoake—Bygones Worth Remembering. By George J. Holyoake. Dutton. $5.00 net.
The past experiences of a man who has attained fame as an honest and able "agitator," or "as a chartered disturber of the unreasoning stupidity of the public conscience," are certainly worth remembering; and his own record of them is no mean contribution to the general history of these latter days. He has steadily fought, as he says, "for equal opportunities for all men, guaranteed by law, and for equitable participation in profit among all who, by toil of hand or brain, contributed to the wealth of the state." He hopes that his reminiscences may "fulfil one condition—that of having instruction or guidance of some kind in them"—and this they surely have. This book is called "Volume I," and we infer that a second is to follow. It is illustrated with portraits of Cobden, the Newmans, Mazzini, Garibaldi, Stuart Mill, and others.

Konkle—The Life and Speeches of Thomas Williams: Orator, Statesman, and Jurist. By Burton A. Konkle. 2 vols. Campion. $6.00 net.
This is one of the most important works on the momentous period before and during the Civil

War. Mr. Williams, as is well known, was a founder of the Whig and Republican parties, and also a lawyer and jurist of eminence. His career and his speeches naturally and necessarily form no insignificant part of the national history, and they are ably and fully described and presented in these volumes, to which Senator Knox of Pennsylvania contributes an introduction.

Krehbiel—Beethoven: the Man and the Artist as Revealed in His Own Words. Compiled and annotated by Friedrich Kerst. Edited and translated by Henry Edward Krehbiel. Huebsch. $1.00.

Expressions of Beethoven's culled from letters, diaries, recorded conversations, are here classified under various heads, such as "On Composing," "On Education," "Art and Artists," "Religion," "Suffering." Doubtless this slender volume will be of interest, and certainly of convenience to students of Beethoven's life; yet, while some of the quotations are of deep interest, many who reverence Beethoven's genius will regret the inevitable baldness and dislocation of the isolated, numbered paragraphs, and question the wisdom of making plainer the obvious fact that words were not the great master's God-given medium of expression.

Krehbiel—Mozart: the Man and the Artist as Revealed in His Own Words. Compiled and annotated by Friedrich Kerst. Edited and translated by Henry Edward Krehbiel. Huebsch. $1.00.

On the same plan as the preceding.

Latrobe—The Journal of Latrobe. Appleton. $3.50 net.

The notes and sketches of Benjamin Henry Latrobe, an architect, naturalist, and traveller in this country from 1796 to 1820. He was a personal friend of Washington and the architect of the national Capitol both before and after its destruction in the War of 1812. The edifice, as now finished, is essentially in accordance with the design of Latrobe, though the dome is larger than he intended it should be, or than some of the best critics entirely approve. The Journal abounds in entertaining observations on his travels and sojournings in city and country, and the interspersed sketches add not a little to its interest. One of these is of Washington at the age of sixty-four. The book is prefaced with a concise biography by Mr. John H. B. Latrobe.

Osborn—John Fletcher Hurst: A Biography. By Albert Osborn. Eaton & Mains. $2.00 net.

The life and work of the distinguished Methodist bishop are here elaborately and sympathetically set forth by one who knew him intimately and whom he desired to be his biographer. The task has been performed with equal loyalty and ability, and the book is every way a fitting memorial of a man of great gifts, high character, and broad influence.

Putnam—Memoir of Dr. James Jackson. By J. Jackson Putnam. Houghton, Mifflin & Co. $2.50 net.

Dr. Jackson belonged to an old Boston family of note, and was connected with others of the same character—the Tracy, Lowell, Quincy, Lee, Cabot, Putnam, etc. Pages 3–156 of the book are devoted to his ancestry, his father, and his brothers. His grandfather, Edward Jackson, married Dorothy Quincy (Holmes's "Dorothy Q."), who died in 1762. Oliver Wendell drew up the inventory of her possessions, the most valuable item in which after "wearing apparel" (£107, 11s., 4d.) was "a negro boy named Andrew," priced at £40, slavery being then legal in Massachusetts. Dr. Holmes was a grandson of Oliver Wendell who married Mary, daughter of "Dorothy Q.," and he himself married Amelia, daughter of Judge Charles Jackson, brother of James, being thus doubly related to the Jackson family.

Pages 157–441 of the book are the Memoir proper. The doctor, as Dr. Samuel L. Greene, the medical historian, says, was "perhaps the most conspicuous character in the medical annals of Massachusetts.... No physician in the State ever exerted so deep and lasting an influence over his professional brethren or his patients." Dr. Holmes remarks: "With his patients he was so perfect at all points that it is hard to overpraise him... His smile was itself a remedy better than the potable gold and the dissolved pearls that comforted the præcordia of medical monarchs.... To visit [patients] with Dr. Jackson was a medical education." The poet wrote several tributes in verse to Jackson, two of which—"A Portrait" and "The Morning Visit"—might not be recognized as referring to him. The book will interest other than medical men. A friend outside that circle told the present writer that, after looking into it casually, he found it hard to lay it down unfinished.

Vetch—Life of Sir Andrew Clarke. Edited by Col. R. H. Vetch. Dutton. $4.00 net.

The biography of a man eminent in British military and civilian life in Van Diemen's Land, New Zealand, Australia, the Gold Coast, the Straits Settlements, India, and at home as Commandant of a school of Military Engineering at Chatham, as Inspector-General of Fortifications, and in other important capacities, and the recipient of many public honors for his many and varied services to the empire. The book is abundantly illustrated with maps, portraits, views of localities and monuments, etc.

DRAMA

Brooke—On Ten Plays of Shakespeare. By Stopford A. Brooke. Holt. $2.25 net.

This book will need no commendation to the large public familiar with the author's volumes on Tennyson and Browning. The plays discussed are "A Midsummer Night's Dream," "Romeo and Juliet," "Richard II.," "Richard

III.," "The Merchant of Venice," "As You Like It," "Macbeth," "Coriolanus," "The Winter's Tale," and "The Tempest." We should judge that the matter was originally prepared for popular lectures, but it is marked throughout by thorough scholarship, keen critical acumen, and refined taste; but this, as we have intimated, "goes without saying" to those who know the author's former work in English literature.

Holbrook—The Farce of Master Pierre Patelin. Englished by Richard Holbrook. Houghton, Mifflin & Co. $2.00 net.

The first English version of a curious drama, written about 1469, and made from the editor's manuscript copy of the only extant exemplar of the Lyons edition, printed about 1486. There is also but one copy known of an edition of about 1489, and the present version is illustrated with facsimiles of the quaint woodcuts in that edition. No earlier sample of these old farces has come down to our day. This play was wonderfully popular, and attained a fame unparalleled in the history of the early stage and seldom equalled since. All students of the drama will be interested in it.

Porter and Clarke—King Lear. Edited by Charlotte Porter and Helen A. Clarke. Crowell. 75 cts

This latest volume of the "First Folio Edition" of Shakespeare is fully up to the high standard of its predecessors. For its accurate presentations of the Folio text, and its scholarly introductions, notes, and other illustrative matter, it will be extremely useful to all teachers in secondary schools for purposes of reference, though of course not suited and not intended as a substitute for the ordinary school editions in the hands of their pupils. For the general reader who is interested in the history of the texts, it is a cheap and satisfactory substitute for the costly facsimiles of the Folio of 1623.

FICTION

Davidge—The Game and the Candle. By Frances Davidge. Appleton. $1.50.

A capably written book, containing not a single original character. The social atmosphere of contemporary New York is described with vividness and confidence; and Emily Blair is an unusually satisfactory incarnation of the woman who waits and suffers while the man she loves marries somebody else as a means of discovering that he loves her in return. The author has perception, deftness, and some wit, and if she allows her imagination somewhat more scope she may write a novel that is worth while.

Hichens—The Black Spaniel. By Robert Hichens. Stokes. $1.50.

These are obviously not new, as they are also not admirable, stories; and it is unfortunate that after his distinguished success with "The Garden of Allah" the author should have allowed them to be published. One of the most interesting and hopeful features of Mr.

Hichens's career is the number of phases through which he has passed; but it must be admitted that these stories belong to the least commendable stage. They have not the epigrammatic flash of his earlier books nor the substantial impressiveness of his latest. "The Black Spaniel" is a creepy and unpleasant but by no means memorable *tour de force*; "The Mission of Mr. Eustace Greyne" is of an almost juvenile exaggeration; and several of the remaining stories are interesting only as more or less frank preliminary studies for "The Garden of Allah."

Hobbes—The Flute of Pan. By John Oliver Hobbes. Appleton. $1.50.

Mrs. Craigie has often proved that it is impossible for her to be dull; but the interest inspired by her newest novel is not, it must be admitted, of a profound nature. "The Flute of Pan" is sprightly, adroit, and full of a reliable sort of sentiment. If there is any one type of story that all kinds of readers can be depended on to enjoy and weep over perennially, it is that of the husband and wife who at their marriage are unaware of each other's love and who realize their mutual devotion only after many trials and prolonged blindness. In this case the wife is a princess and the husband is an artist; and there is a titled mischief-maker who prolongs the misunderstanding between the princess and her consort. This is not realism, nor is it a robust variety of romance; but it is fanciful and ingenious and full of situations that would be effective on the stage. If the characters in this story are not new and vital creations, if the texture is not brilliant or the phrase subtle, that is because Mrs. Craigie has in this case deliberately chosen the narrower canvas and the paler pigment. In her preface, which is no less charming than the story, the author says that she has made of her material a comedy as well as a romance. It should be safe to predict success for the comedy.

Rawson—Charlotte Temple. By Susanna H. Rawson. With an Historical and Biographical Introduction by Francis W. Halsey. Funk & Wagnalls. $1.25.

A corrected reprint of a novel, founded on fact, which had a wonderful popularity in its day—far out of proportion to its literary merit,—with a biography of its author, who wrote many other books now forgotten; also an account of the persons on whose history and relations the story was based, and a bibliography of the editions, portraits and other illustrations.

Tarkington—The Conquest of Canaan. By Booth Tarkington. Harper. $1.50.

The chief beauty of Mr. Tarkington's novel is its intense sincerity. In a tender, indulgent, yet discerning fashion, the author has loved the place he calls Canaan, and his picture of it is drawn with the keenest precision. Nor have we the slightest hesitation in accepting its extraordinary characters. Canaan is precisely the sort of soil where the eccentric flourishes. There is no exaggeration here. If there is also an undeniable lack of charm, that is perhaps a further tribute to the author, an even finer test of his sincerity. Canaan has no natural and characteristic allurements, and its historian has scorned to stoop from the truth in order to invest it with a fanciful one. So, whoever self-indulgently demands that a novel enthrall him would better not read this story. Mr. Tarkington expects that his reader meet him half way, that he be equipped with a patriotic interest in the small " middle western " town for its own sake. Even then it is thoughtful appreciation, not enthusiasm, that is aroused by Joe Louden, the outcast, who ultimately " conquered " Canaan, or by those excellent portraits of Eugene Bantry, Judge Pike, Norbert Flitcroft. Of the two women, however, it may be said that the fluffy Mamie Pike is a type, and the heroine, Ariel Tabor, a symbol. Neither is a distinct individuality. The world is full of Mamie Pikes. Novels are full of Ariel Tabors. But if it is true that the most responsive of us cannot hope to be swept off our feet by these chronicles of Canaan, it is also true that Mr. Tarkington's performance is not one to be belittled, much less ignored. Its value as a historical document is not inconsiderable and there are parts, at least, of the story whose artistic excellence is solid and indisputable. After all, perhaps there is nothing better in the book than such bits of description as that of Mr. Eskew Arp, who was " only seventy-five, but already a thoroughly capable cynic; " or that more ample picture of Judge Pike's "residence," on opposite sides of whose front walk stood "two cast iron deer, painted death gray, twins of the same mould— their bodies in profile to the street, their necks bent, however, so that they gazed upon the passer-by,—yet gazed without emotion."

HISTORY AND TRAVEL

Hart—A Levantine Log-Book. By Jerome Hart. Longmans. $2.00 net.

A lively account of travel in the Mediterranean and its eastern shores, including Malta, Southern Italy, Greece, Constantinople, Asia Minor, and Egypt. The author spent two seasons in those regions, and gives us the results of his keen and humorous observations of men and things, mingled with much matter of a more serious and solid character concerning political, social, and industrial topics—for instance, the irrigation operations of England in the Nile district and the general state of things down to the spring of 1905. There is also a deal of useful information for the tourist; and the illustrations from photographs are numerous and good.

Little—The Far East. By Archibald Little. Henry Frowde. $2.00 net.

Though of the highest vlaue to the student, this book is not for the general reader. Whether there be war, peace, or things phenomenal of any sort in the Far East, this

English gentleman, tea taster, merchant, traveller, explorer, and writer of valuable books has in his mind's eye the man at home who wants to know the basis facts in geology, geography, climate, soil, water courses, and sea possibilities, which make commerce and aid in the development of man. Whatever one wants to know about the various countries included in the vast Chinese Empire, Japan, Siam, Korea, and Annam, can be easily learned in this book, so trustworthy in its general physiographic statements and so rich in maps, sketches, and diagrams, and all well indexed. It is a necessity on the study table. As "geography is half of war," and three fourths of commercial potency, Mr. Little's superbly equipped work is of especial value and timeliness for these days of expected expansion in the trade and internal development of the Far East.

McCarthy—A History of Our Own Times. By Justin McCarthy. Harper. Vols. IV and V. Price $1.40 a volume.

In marked contrast to the casual newspaper style of the account of the revolution of '48, now far enough in the past to deserve more serious treatment, is the continuation of McCarthy's story of the Nineteenth Century. Here is a narrative of his and our own times brought down to a date fresh in the minds of every reader. The time covered in these new volumes, the fourth and fifth, is brief in comparison with the earlier ones. The first volume runs from Victoria's accession to the end of the Crimean War, while these two cover only four years and a brief résumé of the reign. In many of the discussions on these various important crises just past, the writer has taken active part, and if ever an expression of partisanship were to be expected it would be on this period. Therefore the simple fairness of his narrative is especially noteworthy inasmuch as his leanings are often visible through the network of his equable and justice-giving phrases.

In the chapters on the Greece of 1897, for example, there can be no doubt that Mr. McCarthy thought that England over-estimated her duty to the Turk and neglected a righteous opportunity to aid the Cretans to regain their Greek nationality, a nationality to which they had shown their right. Again, in his discussion of the change of relations between the proletariat and the state, there is evident sympathy with the deserved success of men like John Burns, whose highest honors, by the way, came too late for record in this book. In the Boer War and the Hague conference, too, the opinions on the other end of the pen are not disguised. Only an Irish humor could touch on the Hague discussion regarding legitimate missiles with as true a touch. Much of the matter in the whole book will remain of ephemeral rather than of permanent interest. The time is not come for a final judicial history of the period. But for a clear narrative of events that have not yet disappeared, whose perspective is not certain, and yet which cannot be ignored, Mr. McCarthy's last volumes are very delightful, eminently readable, and valuable. Nor does their fairness make them colorless.

Parrish—Historic Illinois. By Randall Parrish. McClurg. $2.50.

Though this portly volume contains much sober history, strictly so-called, the subordinate title, "The Romance of the Earlier Days," better expresses its general character and its main value and merit. Perhaps the author does not go too far in asserting that "no State of the Union surpasses Illinois in the romantic incidents" of its earlier history. He certainly collects an extraordinary amount of this entertaining material, having drawn it "from every known author on Illinois history." The book will interest the general student of our national history as well as the people of Illinois.

Paul—A History of Modern England. By Herbert Paul. Vol. IV. Macmillan. $2.50, net.

A few decades ago no serious historical scholar would have attempted to describe and explain the near past, yet a marked feature of current historical publications is the attention paid to recent events. This can be directly attributed to the keen desire of an essentially practical age to understand the immediate antecedents of existing political problems. Mr. Paul's history of Modern England is one of the best books of this class. It is written in a clear and forcible style of considerable literary merit. Its spirit is remarkably impartial, which is in itself a noteworthy fact, for few Englishmen are able to free themselves from the acute partisanship so characteristic of English political life. On the other hand the work naturally has the defects inevitably inherent in the treatment of an age too close to us to be viewed in its proper perspective. The treatment is necessarily severely chronological, and the underlying broad social and economic movements had perforce to be neglected. The eight years, 1877-1885, covered by this instalment of the work are marked by the predominance in turn of two striking and enigmatic personalities, Disraeli and Gladstone, roughly speaking the statesman of imagination and of non-conventional morality, and the statesman of common-sense and of conventional morality. The events of these years were momentous, including in foreign and colonial affairs the unfortunate Afghan war; the Russo-Turkish war and the Congress of Berlin; the Zulu war, and the uprising of the Boers leading to their subsequent semi-independence in South Africa; the English occupation of Egypt and the tragic fate of Gordon. In internal affairs, the Irish question was predominant in both of its inseparably connected phases, the economic and the political. The famous Irish Land Act of Gladstone and the development of the Home Rule movement naturally demand a good deal of space. So does the extension of the franchise which in 1884 finally made Great Britain a

fully democratic community, in so far as laws can accomplish this result. On all these subjects Mr. Paul writes entertainingly and satisfactorily, and as this information can be found nowhere else, except with great trouble in scattered special treatises or in voluminous biographies, his book will unquestionably be heartily welcomed by a large number of readers.

POETRY AND VERSE

Austin—Tristram and Isoult. By Martha W. Austin. The Poet Lore Co. $1.00.

How like a sweet poison-corolla the enchanted flower of this legend forever draws and entraps the moth-poet! We speak of the legend of Tristram and Isoult, that has once more yielded inspiration to poetic fancy, and received therefrom fresh, interpretative increment; for (and it gives us pleasure to say so) this result obtains through Miss Austin's recasting of the old romantic tale. Her "Foreword," which is modesty itself, tells us that her own spirited version was for a considerable period withheld from publication because she deemed that its publication had been fortuitously forestalled by the work of another poet upon the same theme. But Miss Austin had nothing to fear on this score, so completely has she made the legend her own, infusing distinctive life into each personality entering into the drama produced by her. Indeed so effectively has she done this, following the English rather than the German conception of each character, particularly the character of King Mark, that the finished play appears to us possessed of acting possibilities, beside being liberally endowed with no small measure of beauty in poetic figure and expression. Striking oppositions of character, as those of the two Isoults, the loves of Guinevere and La Belle Isoult,—loves so like in outward guise, so differentiated in the spirit of each,—all these are introduced with excellent dramatic effect; while over all is the driving whip of Fate.

Culbertson—Banjo Talks. By Anne Virginia Culbertson. Bobbs-Merrill. $1.00.

Closely rivalling the popular work of Paul Dunbar, and in the same sunshiny field of Afro-American life and humor, are these dexterous and merry-hearted rhymed chronicles of cabin and plantation days and doings. These include a captivating variety of themes, touched with considerable originality in dialect, idiom, and orthography. The "Banjo-Picker," who cares little or nothing "erbout yo' singin'," but whose "soul gits up an' humps husse'f" at the "talkin'" of his favorite instrument—the "li'l gal wid de cryin' shoes," proudly pacing up the church-aisle—the old "Uncle's" warning account of the "wood-haunts" that "hone for bad chillen,"—these and sundry other, more or less, familiar figures are detailed to offer the reader genuine amusement and pleasure; while the accompanying photographic illustrations lend their own realistic charm.

(*For List of Books Received see third page following*)

Photo by Elliott & Fry

THE LATE WILLIAM SHARP

THE CRITIC

Vol. XLVIII   APRIL, 1906   No. 4

The Lounger

SINCE the death of William Sharp the authoritative announcement that he was "Fiona MacLeod" seems to have caused some agitation in the world of letters. As a matter of fact who should care whether Fiona MacLeod was William Sharp or William Sharp Fiona MacLeod? Neither were epoch-making writers, and just why there should be such a hubbub on the subject seems to me a little extraordinary, particularly as it was pretty well known that William Sharp did write over the feminine pen-name. There was no similarity in the writing of William Sharp as himself and of William Sharp as "Fiona MacLeod." Mr. Sharp was an industrious, if uninspired, journalist, biographer, poet, and essayist. Fiona MacLeod . was a rhapsodist of the Neo-Celtic school. She (he) stood with W. B. Yates for the so-called "Celtic movement." Was it his own self that Mr. Sharp put forth as "Fiona MacLeod"? However this may be, it is as the woman writer that he will go down to fame. As the author of "The Mountain Lovers," "The Sin Eater," "The Washer of the Ford," he has won a place that William Sharp, though much more prolific as a writer, cannot hope to attain. To keep up the illusion that "Fiona MacLeod" was a real person, a biography appears concerning her in the Eng-

lish "Who's Who." It reads just as real as any other biography in the book, calling her "Miss Fiona MacLeod," giving her recreations, "sailing, hill-walks, listening," and her address as care of her publishers, Chapman & Hall, London. Much more space is devoted to William Sharp in the same book, which gives as his recreations "frequent change of scene and environment: in summer roaming, sailing, and swimming." No address, not even that of his publishers, is given. As far as recreations go, Fiona MacLeod and William Sharp seem to be very much in sympathy. It is something new in the annals of literature for a man who already had a reputation as a writer to make a greater reputation as a woman writer, for not only is the name "Fiona MacLeod" that of a woman, and intentionally so, but the writings are essentially feminine.

☺

A correspondent (Mrs. Morgan Dahlgren), noting what the Lounger said some time ago of the late John Hay's slight estimation of his own work as a poet, sends us, to show how wrong was his self-judgment, a copy of his poem, "The Advance Guard," writing it out from memory, as she fails to find it in any edition of the poet's works — and,

COPYRIGHT 1906, BY THE CRITIC COMPANY.
ENTERED AT NEW ROCHELLE, N. Y., POST OFFICE AS SECOND CLASS MATTER.

by an oversight, omitting the seventh stanza. But from the Rev. W. H. Thomas, of South Norwalk, Conn., I have secured two copies of the poem — one as it was printed in *Harper's Weekly*, soon after it was first read by the author, and the other in a pamphlet issued by Messrs. G. W. Carlton & Co., 1872, to preserve a report of the proceedings at the second triennial reunion of the Army of the James (in which army, as it happens, Mr. Thomas served as a chaplain). The poem was written for this occasion, the date being July 19, 1871. As quoted in the pamphlet, it lacks the fourth stanza, as it was thought that mention of the names of Ellsworth, Putnam, Shaw, and Dahlgren only, might be regarded as invidious! The reading by Colonel Hay was prefaced by the following remarks; and, as may be well believed, was succeeded by tumultuous applause:

Soldiers and Fellow-Citizens : When your committee did me the very great honor to summon me before you to-day, I felt a moment of hesitation in accepting an invitation to which I knew I could not do justice ; but I readily yielded to their kind insistence, supported as it was by my own inclination.

Now that I am come, I have nothing to offer you but a handful of wild-flowers—weeds, it may be — which I have come to cast upon the graves of some young friends who were very dear to me.

Among the few names I mention are some you did not know; and of course there are many omitted, whom we all loved and revered ; but that much may be pardoned to my personal friendships. On such occasions, ''each heart recalls a different name''; but you will all join with me in the sentiments of affectionate devotion with which I consecrate these rude rhymes to the blessed and glorious memory of the Advance Guard of our comrades, who have gone before us on '' detached service.''

Here is the poem in full:

In the dream of the Northern poets,
 The brave who in battle die
Fight on in shadowy phalanx
 In the fields of the upper sky ;
And as we read the sounding rhyme,
 The reverent fancy hears
The ghostly ring of the viewless swords
 And the clash of the spectral spears.

We think with imperious questionings
 Of the brothers whom we have lost,
And we try to track in death's mystery
 The flight of each valiant ghost.

The Northern myth comes back to us,
 And we feel through our sorrow's night
That those young souls are striving still
 Somewhere for truth and right.

It was not their time for rest and sleep ;
 Their hearts beat high and strong ;
In their fresh veins the blood of Life
 Was singing his hot, sweet song.
The open heaven bent over them,
 'Mid flowers their lithe feet trod ;
Their lives lay vivid in light, and blest
 By the smiles of women and God.

Again they come ! Again I hear
 The tread of that goodly band ;
I know the flash of Ellsworth's eye,
 And the grasp of his hard, warm hand ;
And Putnam, and Shaw of the lion heart,
 And an eye like a Boston girl's ;
And I see the light of Heaven that shone
 On Ulric Dahlgren's curls.

There is no power in the gloom of hell
 To quench those spirits' fire ;
There is no charm in the bliss of heaven
 To bid them not aspire :
But somewhere in the eternal plan
 That strength, that life survive,
And like the files on Lookout's crest,
 Above Death's clouds they strive.

A chosen corps,—they are marching on
 In a wider field than ours ;
Those bright battalions still fulfil
 The schemes of the heavenly powers ;
And high, brave thoughts float down to us,
 The echoes of that far fight,
Like the gleam of a distant picket's gun
 Through the shades of the severing night.

No fear for them ! In our lower field
 Let us keep our arms unstained,
That at last we be worthy to stand with them
 On the shining heights they 've gained.
We shall meet and greet in closing ranks,
 In Time's declining sun,
When the bugles of God shall sound recall,
 And the Battle of Life be won !

It is bad news that Mr. Thomas Hardy has given up writing novels and is devoting his time to the construction of his elaborate drama, " The Dynasts," which portrays the whole Napoleonic era. Part I. was published a year ago; Part II. is just published. It is a pity that a man with such splendid talents as Mr. Hardy should devote them to writing plays that no one reads and that are un-actable. But if it entertains him we should not complain, for he has enter-

as Mr. Pinero's " The Squire," and this fact led to tiresome litigation. It seems that some woman had sold the same

MR. THOMAS HARDY
(From his most recent photograph)

tained us with his novels for many years and we owe him a debt of gratitude that it would be hard to repay. Though "The Dynasts" will never see the stage, dramatizations of Hardy's novels, not-ably "Tess of the D'Urbervilles," have had great success. As long ago as 1882 Mr. Hardy and Mr. J. W. Comyns Carr dramatized " Far from the Mad-ding Crowd," which had the same plot

plot to Mr. Pinero and to Mr. Hardy without letting either know what she had done. The buying of a plot is not a new thing for a novelist to do, but it is seldom that he is caught as badly as was Mr. Hardy.

Mr. Jeremiah Curtin has outwitted the pirates so far as the present and future writings of Henryk Sienkiewicz are concerned. Mr. Curtin now translates direct from the Polish manuscript before the book is published in any language. English and American editions will be on the market three years before they appear in any other language. The publishers are congratulating themselves that "On the Field of Glory" is so well protected. What a fortune it would have been to all concerned had "Quo Vadis" been protected!

One of THE CRITIC'S Paris readers writes us:

Photo by Cien, Cracovie

MR. HENRYK SIENKIEWICZ
(From his latest photograph)

I notice in a recent number of your interesting periodical a review of Miss Betham - Edwards's "Home Life in France," in which occurs this phrase: "She is an officer of Public Instruction." Almost at the same moment, the New York *Nation*, in its review of the same book, says: "Miss Betham-Edwards is an *officier de l' Instruction publique de France*, a position to which one may suppose Englishwomen are rarely appointed." I wonder what idea these statements convey to the average American reader? That it is a very erroneous one, I am perfectly sure. Let me explain. The French Minister of Public Instruction—he would be called in Washington the Commissioner of Education—has at his disposal two classes of decorations, which twice a year are showered on the deserving and the undeserving alike. That called *officier de l' Instruction Publique*—the one you mention—is considered superior to the other, which is called *officier d' Académie*, but neither is taken very seriously by the really thoughtful in France. District school teachers, minor poets, unknown architects, unsuccessful authors, artists who have not taken medals, in a word, persons who can't get into the Legion of Honor fall back on these two decorations, which no sensible man or woman should accept, and do, actually, often refuse. These decorations are frequently given to foreigners, especially to foreign ladies. In fact, even in France, they are looked upon as "the woman's decoration." It ought to be explained, further, that an officer of Academy has nothing to do with the celebrated French Academy, and an officer of Public Instruction has as little to do with the educational system of the country. It is amusing to see foreigners parade these titles at home, and still funnier to observe the completely mistaken understanding of them held by the fellow-citizens of these same foreigners.

⁂

I take particular pleasure in calling the attention of the readers of THE CRITIC to the letters published on another page written by the late Lafcadio Hearn to Mr. Henry E. Krehbiel, the musical critic of *The Tribune*, who was long associated with him in journalism. These letters will eventually be published in a volume of Hearn's Letters, edited by Mr. Ferris Greenslet, to be published by Messrs. Houghton, Mifflin, & Company.

⁂

Recently, at the Women's University Club, 17 Madison Square, North, Professor Masujiro Honda, teacher of English literature in the Tokio Normal College, introduced by Consul-General Uchida, spoke on "Social Customs of the Women of Japan." In the course of his descriptions of "insect-listening parties" and "cherry-blossom-opening parties" and parties to "view the snow" or to "hunt mushrooms," — toy-like, miniature customs we should call them, —he remarked that Lafcadio Hearn saw Japan with his imagination; that therefore his books are good reading, but untrue to Japanese life. The works of Miss Alice Bacon, on the other hand, are, according to Professor Honda, absolutely faithful pictures of Japan. Moreover, she had the genuine privilege, almost always claimed by writers on Japan but rarely with reason, of meeting the best people of the country. Her opportunities for observation were therefore most favorable.

Professor Honda spoke with amused tolerance of Japanese-American plays, *e. g.*, "Madame Butterfly," "The Darling of the Gods," and "The Geisha"; of the inherent love of his countrymen for the tragic, and of the necessity of resting in tea-houses from their tears during the course of an ordinary drama, from eleven in the morning until nine at night!

⁂

Mr. John Luther Long's new book is called "The Way of the Gods." Mr. Long, it may be remembered, is the author of "The Darling of the Gods." It is one of the curiosities of literature that Mr. Long, who has made his reputation as a writer of Japanese stories, has never visited Japan. Those who know that country say that his stories are not characteristic of it. The Japanese themselves smile amiably when their American acquaintances speak to them of the Japan of Mr. Long. But this is neither here nor there. His stories are charming and that is all that the reader cares for.

⁂

Speaking of Japanese writers, Mr. Okakura-Kakuzo has just finished "The Book of Tea," which will be found to be an absolutely correct interpretation of Japanese life. A chapter from this book, will be published in the May number of THE CRITIC. Mr. Okakura came to this country as a special commissioner of the Japanese Government to examine into American art. He has made such a careful study of this subject during the few years that he has been here that he has recently been appointed to an official position in the Boston Museum of Fine Arts. Mr. Okakura continues to wear his native costume, his sense of the artistic being too great to allow him to don the clothes of European convention.

***

A well informed reader of THE CRITIC living in New York writes:

People here don't seem to know what in Boston is no secret, as I take it, that "Sidney McCall" is Mr. and Mrs. (second) Ernest Fenollosa. He would naturally be able to write about Japan. He (she—they!) wrote "Truth Dexter" and "The Breath of the Gods," which is an Americo-Japanese story.

***

Jennette Lee, the author of "Uncle William," a new story published by the Century Company, is the wife of Mr. Gerald Stanley Lee, a writer of marked individuality, who has had the misfortune to be compared to Emerson. He is not at all like Emerson, nor does he aim to be. Mr. Lee writes essays, but they are not in the Emersonian style. Nothing could be less like Emerson than his "The Lost Art of Reading," one of the most entertaining books of essays published in many a long day. Mrs. Lee writes fiction. Her first novel was called "Kate Wetherell" and while it was not a great pecuniary success it attracted the attention of all thinking readers. The Lees live at Northhampton, Mass., and are, I believe, connected with Smith College.

***

In an article in *The Independent* the Baroness Bertha von Suttner tells how she wrote her famous novel, "Lay Down Your Arms," which won for her the Nobel Peace Prize of $40,000. It was in 1880 that the thought first occurred to her to write a story on the peace question. Her first idea was to write a little story, in which she would describe a young woman who had lost her husband on the battle-field, and by this tragedy was suddenly awakened to a realization of the horrors of war. While she was engaged in research for a novelette her material grew into such proportions that a two-volume novel was the result, there was so much to say and so many facts to base her argument upon. It is interesting to note that this now famous book went the rounds of the publishers before it was accepted. Says the Baroness:

Full of confidence, I sent my manuscript to the Stuttgart editor who had always heretofore accepted what I offered him and who had recently asked me for a fresh one. But it was promptly returned to me with this message: "We regret it, but this novel we cannot use." So I tried other editors, but all declined it with the remark: "This does not interest our public," or "It would offend many of our readers," or "It is impossible to publish this in the present military state of affairs." Such were the opinions of the leading editors of German periodicals.

She next turned to a Dresden publisher, who kept it a long time, then advised her to change the title, which he found too aggressive, and to modify certain passages which he thought would give offence in military and political circles. This she utterly refused to do. Finally, the book was published as it was written and success followed. There are two editions in this country, one published by Messrs McClurg, called "Ground Arms," the other the authorized edition by Messrs. Longmans, called "Lay Down Your Arms."

***

Mrs. J. O. Wright (Mabel Osgood Wright) has just revealed her identity as "The Commuter's Wife." As in the case of Mr. Sharp and Fiona MacLeod, it was pretty generally supposed by those interested in those matters that Mrs. Wright and "The Commuter's Wife" were one and the same person. Mrs. Wright began writing children's books, which were most successful. Her name for this reason seemed to be associated with that class of literature, and for fear that her next book would be considered a child's book she wrote it without signing her name; but anyone who is familiar with her style could readily detect that "The Commuter's Wife" and the author of "The Friendship of Nature" were one and

Vienna 5/10 1905

Courtesy of *The Independent*

THE BARONESS VON SUTTNER
(Author of " Lay Down Your Arms ")

the same person. Mrs. Wright is the daughter of the late Dr. Samuel Osgood, a well-known clergyman of New York.

One of the first articles in the February number of the *North American Review* that the reader will turn to is

Photo by Haley

MABEL OSGOOD WRIGHT IN HER GARDEN AT FAIRFIELD, CONNECTICUT

In the winter she lives in New York, but in the summer she lives at Fairfield, Conn., in the house built by her father many years ago, the grounds around which are famous for the number and variety of their trees and shrubs. Mrs. Wright is devoted to animals, especially dogs, and her favorites among these are hounds, whose intelligence and affection she ranks above that of other canines.

the social notes by Mr. Henry James. After he has turned to it and after he has read it, I wonder if he will know just what it is all about. I quote a paragraph giving the impressions made upon Mr. James by the miscellaneous crowds in Central Park and other public places:

Why should the general " feeling " for the boot,

in the United States, be so mature, so evolved, and the feeling for the hat lag at such a distance behind it? The standard as to that article of dress struck me as, everywhere, of the lowest; governed by no consensus of view, custom, or instinct, no sense of its "vital importance" in the manly aspect. And yet the wearer of any loose improvisation in the way of a head-cover will testify as frankly, in his degree, to the extreme consideration given by the community at large, as I have intimated, to the dental question. The terms in which this evidence is presented are often, among the people, strikingly artless, but they are a marked advance on the omnipresent opposite signs, those of complete unacquaintedness with the admonitory dentist, with which any promiscuous "European" exhibition is apt to bristle.

tongue. She is one of the few clever writers who are also clever talkers. A writer usually is not a good talker. That is one reason why literary people, as a rule, are not particularly interesting; they save their best for their books; they only shine from the printed page. Mrs. Craigie has as many facets as a diamond. Her talks while she was in America were listened to by eager audiences, and since she has gone back to England she has talked entertainingly to large audiences over there. Not only has she talked, but she has been interviewed. What she says about American newspapers is interesting.

HARDY FLOWERS IN MRS. WRIGHT'S GARDEN

If any one can tell me what Mr. James means by this arrangement of words I should be glad to know. Mr. Meredith himself could not write a more confusing paragraph.

ᴥ

It may be said of Mrs. Craigie that she is always entertaining in whatever she says, whether it be with pen or

She remarks on the popularity of personal journalism in America:

What may be called the "abusive" interview has really been dropped, but the public like details; they like reports written in the style of letters between intimate friends. It's the custom of the country; so no one is offended.

Articles in American papers are much shorter than they are—well, in some English papers; and they are often very brilliantly written. Of course, there are many brilliant writers on the English press too. But I do not think the American editor underestimates the national intelligence as many English editors do. That has been the fault in this country, not only of editors, but of theatrical managers, who are now complaining that the public does n't support the theatre.

Mrs. Craigie remarks on the absence of men at luncheons. They are all too busy for this form of entertainment. The little interest that American women take in politics also made a great impression upon her, and she laments that American men do not take their wives into their confidence in their business affairs, as do Frenchmen.

❧

That indefatigable Shakespearian scholar, Dr. W. J. Rolfe, has just prepared an edition of Shakespeare's Sonnets for school use. It is the first thoroughly annotated edition of the Sonnets published in this country, and is also the first edition to give a concise account of the chief theories of the history and interpretation of the Sonnets that has appeared either in this country or abroad for many years. What Dr. Rolfe does not know about Shakespeare is not worth knowing, and he sets forth his knowledge in the most agreeable manner, so that one need not be a member of a Shakespeare Club to understand and appreciate his comments and annotations.

❧

This caricature of Messrs. Pinero and Shaw from *Vanity Fair* would seem to indicate, if it indicates anything, that Mr. Shaw is disappearing from the dramatic firmament and Mr. Pinero coming forward again. There was a time, (when Mr. Pinero wrote "The Wife Without a Smile,") that his friends feared for his reputation; but now he has rehabilitated himself with "His House in Order," which is being played with great success by Mr. George Alexander in London and will soon be seen in New York with Mr. John Drew in the leading part.

❧

It was not so very long ago that

publishers gave as cold a shoulder to published plays as they do now to poetry; but since Mr. Bernard Shaw's plays have been such a success as books the publishers are experimenting along that line. The Macmillan Company are going as deeply into play publishing as did Mr. H. Russell some years ago, when he was about the only publisher who ventured into this field. The former have published a number of Mr. Clyde Fitch's plays, and what has taken even more courage, Mr. Hardy's "The Dynasts"; not but that the latter is much more creditable as literature—indeed it is almost too much literature and not enough play. Mr. Fitch's dramas have not this fault, if fault it be. Now the Macmillans, who are the publishers of Mr. Winston Churchill's novels, are the publishers of his play, "The Title Mart," which is his first venture in playwriting. His books have been dramatized, and have been successful—that is, "The Crisis" was successful as a play. But Mr. Churchill had little or no part in the dramatization of his stories. "The Title Mart" is virtually all his own. Mr. Stephen Phillips's plays have long been published with success by the John Lane Co. later the Macmillan Co.

❧

The Lippincott Company announce a new novel by Edgar Saltus, whom they call the "Bernard Shaw of America." No other country that I know of has this extraordinary habit of calling people the this, that, or the other of somewhere else. Here in America our actresses are the "American Bernhardts" or the "American Duses," our actors are the "American Irvings," our authors the "American Dickenses" or Thackerays or Balzacs, or what not, all of which is perfect nonsense, the comparison doing them much more harm than good. It was America that dubbed Maeterlinck the "Belgian Shakespeare." Anything less like Shakespeare than Maeterlinck could hardly be imagined. The comparison is a most foolish one.

❧

A later number of THE CRITIC will

From Vanity Fair

MR· A. W. PINERO
(Mr. G. B. Shaw in the background)

contain a review of Mr. Horace Traubel's entertaining and valuable book of Whitmaniana. The portrait of Mr. Traubel and the picture of the famous little house on Mickle Street, Camden, New Jersey, are reprinted from the book by the courtesy of the publishers, Messrs. Small, Maynard & Company.

MR. HORACE TRAUBEL.

All London is being amused by a book called "The Beauty Shop," written by a woman who signs herself Daniel Woodroffe. It is on the "Dolly Dialogues" order. There is a Lady Hardross in the book who confesses to a weakness for yellow journalism. She spends her Sunday mornings reading the *Police News:*

"It all helps to pass away the terrible, the inexorable British Sabbath. I don't want gentlemen to mysteriously suicide themselves, but oh! the restful literary half-hour when they have done so."

She even enjoys advertisements for lost relatives:

"Niece Jane would like to hear from Aunt Ann, last seen at Valparaiso twenty years ago." "Dear me, if I had the luck to mislay either of my old aunts at Valparaiso, I think I should not have advertised."

.⁂.

While Stewart Edward White was making ready the stories now running in *McClure's Magazine* under the general title "Arizona Nights" he was engaged in actively blazing another western trail. Here is his account of it taken from a letter written on the spot: "This far it has been a great summer. First of all, at the six thousand foot mark, we found a fine meadow surrounded by enormous sugar pines, firs, and red cedars; with two springs, and a good-sized running stream. The next thing was to get a carpenter to camp out there. We did so, hired men to 'swamp out' a road—save the mark you ought to see it; but a mountain driver can make it. And now under way is a two-roomed cabin 28 x 14, with outdoor shed kitchen, a 'half pitch' roof on account of the heavy snows, cedar bark half-way up and shakes the other half. It stands in a fine grove at the head of a long gentle slope in which lies the very green meadow. The meadow is irregular in shape, like a lake, and is bordered by tremendous and solemn trees. We have aromatic thickets of white and pink azaleas as high as your head, a bottom land of dogwood, acres of Easter lilies. The pine forest surrounds us. A day's ride takes us over the Shut-eye peaks into the big country. From the gap you can see a diameter of an hundred and fifty miles. We have deer, grouse, quail, trout, and an occasional bear. We are three straight up-and-down hours to Northfork—2500 feet—which is in turn sixty miles from the railroad. Have n't seen a cloud in two months."

animal to discover what made the noise. Perhaps the reindeer, like the alligator in "Peter Pan," had swallowed a clock.

WHITMAN'S HOME, MICKLE ST., CAMDEN, N. J.

Mr. Thompson Seton's animals may have more human traits than the animals that Mr. John Burroughs knows, but they are not altogether works of his imagination. Take the story of the white renskalv in Norway, in his recent book. The material for that story was gathered on the spot by Mr. Seton who was accompanied by his wife, who is nearly always his companion even when he is roughing it the most. Mrs. Seton rode over the Norwegian mountains on ponies, with a pad for a saddle and a piece of common twine for a bridle. There are those who think that Mr. Thompson Seton laid the scene of this unusual animal story in Norway to get out of the reach of Mr. Burroughs's critical eye. That Mr. Thompson Seton is a painstaking author no one will deny. It is said that, noticing a certain curious click that accompanied each step of a reindeer, he crawled for a long distance on hands and knees beside the

Punch is to be congratulated upon its new editor, Mr. Owen Seaman. To my mind Mr. Seaman is much more amusing as a writer than the ex-editor, Mr. F. C. Burnand. Burnand's humor is elephantine. Seaman's touch is particularly light. It is curious that Mr. Seaman should be the editor of two periodicals that are the very antipodes of each other—the *Monthly Review* and *Punch*. The *Monthly Review* is staid and conservative, with never a humorous line unless Mr. Seaman contributes some of his verses to it. There are those who think that *Punch* is without humor, but that is a matter of opinion.

From a little book called "The Schoolmaster" I glean some amusing anecdotes.

"What is a widow?" asks the teacher.

Answer from a small girl: "Please, ma'am, a woman what marries the lodger."

"What is a mother?"

Answer from boy of seven: "A mother is a woman what buys a baby and grows it up."

Ladies, please note the following:

"Why is a motor-car called 'she'?"

Answer: "Because it is driven by a man."

The mistress of the infants was admitting a new scholar, and asked his father's name.

"What is your name?" asked the mistress.

"Tommy Jones," answered the three-year-old.

"Yes," said the teacher, "and what is father's name?"

"Mr. Jones."

"Ah, but what is his other name?" asked the patient teacher. "What does mother call him?"

"Ol' Fathead," was the startling answer.

During a Scripture lesson, which was being taken by a clergyman, some boys were asked each to give a text from the Bible. One lad said:

"And Judas went and hanged himself."

"Well," said the reverend gentleman, "that is, hardly a good text," and pointing to another lad asked him to give a text, and the lad said:

"Go thou and do likewise."

⁂

The number of American girls and young women who go to Paris to finish their education increases year by year, and it is sometimes a problem to know just how to meet their needs.

On the 15th of December, in a pretty studio situated at 112 Boulevard Malesherbes, Mr. Charles Wagner, author of "The Simple Life," inaugurated an original sort of college, founded by a young, energetic, and intelligent teacher, Mlle. Alice Kuhn, who at one time was professor at Smith College. It is an intellectual centre more than a college. There are no boarders. Mlle. Kuhn's pupils live in French families, hard by, and assist at the lessons of their young teacher and, twice a week, at lectures given by professors of the Sorbonne and the Collège de France or by well-known writers. As Mr. Wagner said in his pleasant, familiar talk, the aim of this new venture is to make Americans and French people know each other better. He assured his American hearers that, even in Paris, there were hard workers, great thinkers, honest men and women; one had but to be brought into contact with them really to appreciate their qualities—and such

was, said he, the aim and object of the La Fayette College.

⁂

A new book by Mr. and Mrs. Williamson is out on the other side. It is called "Lady Betty across the Water," and tells the experiences and adventures of a young English girl who makes her first visit to America. It is about time that the Williamsons changed the scene of their stories. Up to the present they have gone over pretty much the same ground; but to bring their hero and heroine to America will no doubt prove to be an interesting departure.

⁂

Byron's grandson, the Earl of Lovelace, has just published in England at his own expense a volume called "Astarte: A Fragment of Truth Concerning George Gordon Byron, Sixth Lord Byron, Recorded by his Grandson, Ralph Milbanke, Earl of Lovelace," which is written to substantiate the charges made by Mrs. Harriet Beecher Stowe a quarter of a century or so ago against Byron. Lord Lovelace's book, of which only a limited number of copies are printed, is sold for $15 net, though it only contains 337 pages. The book has not been very widely reviewed in England, but such journals as have mentioned it have done so with disgust. There are other family skeletons revealed in the book, which, on the whole, has fallen flat, and the American publishers who declined it are probably congratulating themselves.

⁂

Miss Clara Driscoll, whose musical play, "Mexicana," is running at the Lyric, is the author of a vivacious story called "The Girl of La Gloria," which was published some time ago. A new book, a volume of short stories, called "In the Shadow of the Alamo," will soon be published.

⁂

Nothing could be more fitting than that Andrew Lang should write a life of

Sir Walter Scott. It is a pity that it is so short a life, but it had to fit a Literary Lives Series, therefore its pages were limited. Mr. Lang has written a good deal about Sir Walter Scott from time to time, but in this biography he has gathered together the best that he has said or thought and given it to us all in one book.

❦

The choice of Mr. F. Marion Crawford to write a life of Pope Leo XIII. was a wise one. Mr. Crawford was *persona grata* at the Vatican, and not only knows Italian as well as he knows English, but he is a Roman Catholic. Apropos, the *Century Magazine* once accepted an article on Rome, by Mr. Crawford. It was an interesting article, but not being particularly timely was side-tracked for twelve years. When it was accepted Mr. Crawford was an unknown writer, and it was accepted on its merits. When it was published he was at the height of his fame. Mr. Crawford is one of three who will write this life of Pope Leo XIII., which is founded on heretofore unpublished documents and will fill four volumes.

❦

It is said that the Macmillan Company paid a cash advance for Mr. Winston Spencer Churchill's life of his father, Lord Randolph Churchill, that some other publishers to whom the book was offered considered prohibitory. It may be that when the representative of Mr. Churchill offered the book to the Macmillan Company he had come down somewhat in his price; but of course this is something upon which I cannot speak with authority. However I do know that this is a thing that frequently happens. I could mention two notable instances where the price first asked was about double that of the one finally taken.

❦

The publishers are all wondering how Mr. Henry Holt, one of the busiest of their fellow-craftsmen, has found the time to write two novels of the length of "Calmire" and "Sturmsee." The length of these books is about twice that of the ordinary novel, and yet Mr. Holt has been able to write them, to attend to a very large publishing business as well, and also to look after other interests, for Mr. Holt has more than one string to his bow. The Macmillan Company were the first publishers of Mr. Holt's novels, but they have recently been taken over by Messrs. Houghton, Mifflin, & Company. The new publishers announce that this change of imprint is due to Mr. Holt's recent appearance in the *Atlantic* as the author of "The Commercialization of Literature," and to Boston's having shown special interest in "Sturmsee" and "Calmire." The Boston Public Library is said to be the only one in the country reporting "Sturmsee" among the books most in demand, and the anonymity of "Calmire" has been the cause of much speculative correspondence in the Boston newspapers. I can imagine how interested and amused Mr. Holt must have been in reading the reviews of these books that were published not only anonymously but without even a pen name. Hardly a review but was complimentary—some of them exceedingly so,—and it is not surprising that Mr. Holt has now come out and acknowledged his own. Mr. Holt usually takes his holiday in winter. He argues that summer is uncomfortable anywhere, and he might as well be at his office; but that winter being a delightful season that is the one in which to loaf and invite his soul. But I fancy that most of his loafing consisted in writing these two novels.

❦

Mr. Hall Caine is on record as saying that he makes more money out of his books than out of his plays. Take "The Prodigal Son," for instance, which was successfully produced in this country and in London. In a recent interview he said that when he takes everything into consideration—the time it took him to write and rehearse the play, and the general disruption of his life which its production caused—he finds that he is more than a thousand pounds out of pocket. I should like to know how Mr. Caine figures this out. He must put down a big round sum to the disruption of his plans. In the case of "The Prodigal Son" he modestly admits that he had " perhaps the largest material success that any dramatist has had for quite a long time. " He has received money for this play from at least half a dozen European capitals where it is being played and is to be played. To quote more fully :

When I count all that up against the time which has been occupied in the writing or re-writing of the piece ; in the rehearsing of it in London and in New York, to which I went specially ; the other travelling required by it, and the general dislocation of my home life for an entire year, which has been caused by its production—why, I find that I am more than a thousand pounds out of pocket, as a consequence of having produced the most successful play of the season ! It is not that I have earned that amount less than I should have done had I been writing a new novel, but that I am really out of pocket over the whole business to that amount, counting the extra expense which, in a score of ways, has fallen upon me.

Mr. Caine, however, admits that all this may be made up to him as the play is still running and likely to run for some time to come.

New York is to be congratulated that it is at last to have a theatre run for art's sake and not for the sake of the almighty dollar. The New Theatre is not the one announced with a flourish of trumpets by Mr. Conried ; that seems to have disappeared from the horizon. The one that we are to have is financed by some of the best known men in New York, and if they succeed in getting the right sort of management the lovers of the drama may hope for the best. At the time of this writing no manager has been secured. I have no doubt that there are hundreds of candidates, Mr. Conried among the number, but the directors, with Mr. Charles T. Barney as president, are going slowly and, I hope, surely. This project is the one that I feared had fallen through on account of the loud trumpeting of the Conried "National" Theatre ; but I am happy to say that no such calamity has befallen us.

Some of my Arizona readers have asked me to join them in their fight against joint Statehood; but THE CRITIC long since made it a rule to avoid political discussions. Otherwise I should be delighted to line up with the inhabitants of this growing territory in their struggle against amalgamation with an alien community. It certainly seems a mistake to try and force half-statehood upon them ; even from a partisan standpoint it would be farther-sighted to humor the people by letting them preserve their present status till they are qualified to ask admission to the Union as a State by themselves. But I must steer clear of a question that has been made a subject of political strife.

It is a pleasure to note the success of volumes of essays or pleasant literary talk in these days when no one is supposed to read anything but the " six best selling books," meaning fiction. The Reverend Dr. Crothers's volumes of essays, of which "The Gentle Reader" was the first, Mr. Mabie's genial talks, Dr. van Dyke's poetical prose, and Mr. Paul E. More's incisive literary studies are cases in point. Now we have two more books of the same sort. They were published originally in the *Cornhill Magazine* the first under the title of " The Upton Letters." Later another series appeared with the name " From a College Window," by the author of "The Upton Letters," who for the time being wished to remain anonymous. But now it is announced that Mr. Arthur C. Benson of King's College, Cambridge, is the author. Mr. Benson is the son of the late Archbishop of Canterbury, and the brother of E. F. Benson, the creator of " Dodo " and other books of clever fiction. The work of Mr. A. C. Benson runs along different lines. He has published two volumes of poetry, a volume of essays, and several volumes of biography, one of the most recent and best of these being a life of Edward

Fitzgerald. "From a College Window" (Putnams) is even a more frank and intimate book than "The Upton Letters," and will be welcomed by all who admire a delightful literary style combined with fine scholarship.

It is rumored that Sir Arthur Conan Doyle will no longer write for *The Strand Magazine*. It was in the columns of *The Strand* that Sherlock Holmes made his bow to the public, and it has been in the columns of *The Strand* that all his stories have appeared. But now it is said that Sir Arthur has severed the alliance of fifteen years and more, and that his stories will hereafter appear in another magazine.

Messrs. E. P. Dutton & Company are fortunate in being the American publishers of Everyman's Library, edited by Ernest Rhys, and invented by the inventive Mr. J. M. Dent. Fifty volumes of classics will be issued at one fell swoop. I have seen several of these books and they are marvels for the price. Each one is introduced by a well-known writer. Augustin Birrell, G. K. Chesterton, Andrew Lang, Arthur Symons, A. C. Swinburne, George Saintsbury, Herbert Paul, Hilaire Belloc, are a few of the names of those who have performed the gentle function of introduction. The first fifty volumes were published in February, the second fifty in March, and it is believed that before long the Library will reach a thousand volumes. It has included among other historical works Grote's "History of Greece" in twelve volumes, and Froude's "History of England."

Mrs. Kate Douglas Wiggin's publishers announce that she and Mrs. Florence Earle Coates, the poet, are among the few American women who "have been invited to become members of that august body known as the Lyceum Club of London." While there are not as many American members of the Lyceum Club of London as there are English members, there are still more than this announcement would lead one to think. The Lyceum Club had thirty Americans among its members at its foundation, and I should think quite as many more names have been added since then. The Club was founded by Miss Constance Smedley, the author of "An April Princess" and other clever books, for the benefit of original workers in literature, journalism, science, art, and music. The Club was successfully financed before it actually existed. It has branches in France and Germany, but not in America. An effort was made to organize a branch in this country, but for some unknown reason it did not succeed. There are many more women's clubs in London than there are in New York, and every one of them seems to be in a flourishing condition.

It is not always good literature that has the largest sales or receives the warmest praise from quarters least expected. That very sensational novel, "When It Was Dark," has sold over 300,000 copies; and the Bishop of London and the Bishop of Truro have praised it enthusiastically from their pulpits. The name of the author on the title-page is Guy Thorne, but his real name is Ranger Gull. One can readily see why the author of a story as impossible as "When It Was Dark" would hesitate to write the name of Gull on its title-page.

Miss Anne Douglas Sedgwick, has given her new novel the somber title, "The Shadow of Life." The trouble with Miss Sedgwick's books is that they are more or less morbid—too morbid to be enjoyed by the average reader. You may say that "The House of Mirth" is morbid. So it is, but it is as full of wit as a nut is of meat; not humor, understand, but wit. Miss Sedgwick is undoubtedly quite as clever a writer as Mrs. Wharton, but she has not yet found her public. Her admirers are enormously enthusiastic, and believe that she will sooner or later find her books among the "six best sellers"; but at present it is only those who are the most appreciative of good

literature who are their admirers. Miss
Sedgwick is still a very young woman,
and there is reason to believe that
she will yet win the place in popular
favor that she has already won among
the discerning.

❧

Miss Frances Powell, the author of
"The House on the Hudson " and of
"The Prisoner of Ornith Farm," does
not live on the banks of the Hudson
River as has been generally supposed.
She lives in a quiet little hamlet on
Long Island, but she was born on the
banks of the Hudson and has a thorough
knowledge of that region. Frances
Powell is only part of the author's real
name. Shyness prevented her declaring herself with her first novel, but her
friends soon guessed the authorship of
the book as the concealment was very
slight. The new story, "the Prisoner
of Ornith Farm," is in the manner of her
first book

❧

Mr. Herman Knickerbocker Viele
may not be a great playwright but he
is certainly a writer of charming fiction.
No more delicious book of its kind than
"The Inn of the Silver Moon" has
been written by an American in many
years. Nothing that Mr. Viele has
written since has quite equalled that
little book for charm, but at the same
time his other books were well worth
writing and well worth reading.

❧

Mrs. John Elliott (Maud Howe) and
her husband have gone to Spain where
they will spend the next two years.
American artists seem to be turning
their attention towards the country of
the Dons. Mr. Charles Dana Gibson
went some time ago, and Miss Cecelia
Beaux sailed last month. Mr. W. M.
Chase has already been, and Spanish art
has no greater admirer than he. Mrs.
Elliott will no doubt have a book ready
on her return as the result of her experiences. If it is as interesting as her
two books on Italy," Roma Beata " and
"Two in Italy," we shall have reason
to be grateful.

Those who are not familiar with
Captain Harry Graham's " More Misrepresentative Men " will be amused by
his verses on Mr. J. M. Barrie, which
allude to two plays well known over
here :

O tiniest of tiny men !
So wise, so whimsical, so witty !
Whose magic little fairy-pen
Is steeped in human pity ;
Whose humor plays so quaint a tune,
From Peter Pan to Pantaloon !

And modern matrons who can find
So little leisure for the Nurs'ry,
Whose interest in babykird
Is eminently curs'ry,
New views on Motherhood acquire
From Alice-sitting-by-the-Fire !

❧

Messrs. Longmans, Green, & Company announce a new and complete
edition of the Works of John Ruskin,
edited with additions from the original
manuscripts by Messrs. E. T. Cook and
Alexander Wedderburn. This is said
to be the only complete edition, and is to
be sold by subscription and not in book
stores. It will be illustrated with 1300
plates and wood-cuts, over 100 drawings
not hitherto reproduced, together with
much unpublished material.

❧

Mr. Stephen Phillips has his eagle eye
on Ireland as a dramatic possibility.
He will first probably write a drama
on "Faust" for Mr. Alexander, and
when that is finished he will take up an
Irish theme. Mr. Phillips, in a recent
interview, is quoted as saying :

" People may say that blank-verse tragedy is not
wanted. I can only point to the fact that my tragedies have succeeded. They have been, I think I
can claim, works of pure and genuine art, and they
have ' made money.' They have not only ' made
money' on the stage. I do not wish to appear
boastful, or to challenge Mr. Hall Caine, but it may
be interesting to remember that, as books, they
have been more profitable than an average novel.
As a matter of fact, I do not think this is merely a
matter of myself. It seems to me that it is but part
of a movement of poetic revival in the drama all
over Europe."

Mr. Phillips is correct as to the revival
of interest in the poetic drama, and he
is not the only poet who is writing
drama for the stage.

Letters of a Poet to a Musician

Lafcadio Hearn to Henry E. Krehbiel

HEARN never dated his letters, but allusions in the following indicate to me that it was written in the fall of 1878. How long before then he had gone to New Orleans, whence this letter was sent, I cannot say with precision. My impression is that it was a little less than a year. At any rate we were still colleagues in Cincinnati in the fall of 1877, he a reporter on the staff of the *Commercial* newspaper, I a reporter and musical critic of the *Gazette*. His first work in New Orleans (here I must correct a statement of Mr. Greenslet's in the sketch of Hearn's life which prefaces "The Romance of the Milky Way") was done on a little paper called *The Daily City Item*, the organ of the labor unions if I mistake not. I well recall the grotesque contrast between Hearn's sketches—"Fantastics" he called them —and the rest of the writing in the paper. Subsequently, I think within a year, he secured a position on the staff of the *Times-Democrat*.

Before Hearn left Cincinnati I had already begun the studies in folk-music which have occupied so much of my attention ever since. Hearn, himself an ardent folk-lorist, took the greatest interest in these studies, and continued it until we drifted apart in New York after his return from his second visit to the French West Indies. This accounts for some of the things in this letter—the remarks about Creole and Negro music, the patois poems of Père Roquette, the folk-songs of Brittany, etc.

In connection with this side of Hearn's intellectual character perhaps I may be pardoned if I relate in Hearn's own words an incident which will explain the mystery which curious inquiry must have always found hanging about the dedication of Hearn's book "Some Chinese Ghosts," published by Roberts Brothers in 1887. Hearn's memory went back ten years when he wrote that

dedicatory page.* I quote from an article which he published in the *Cincinnati Commercial* on October 1, 1877, entitled "A Romantic Episode at the Music Club":

"Mr. H. Edward Krehbiel, of the *Gazette*, has for several years devoted himself to the study of Oriental music and the chants of the ancient people of the East. There are few studies, indeed, so profoundly interesting as that of the early history of music; none, certainly, that offers a wider field of legend to the gleaner of curious traditions. Mr. Krehbiel found the work of research in this direction as fascinating as it was novel, and succeeded in making a very remarkable collection of beautiful melodies — Hebrew, Indian, and Chinese — fragments of chants heard doubtless in the temple of Solomon, and as old, perchance, as the period of bondage in Egypt; tunes played upon sacbuts and shawms before the Babylonian captivity; Vedic hymns ancient as the castes of India; hymns to Krishna and Mahadeva, to Siva and the dark Venus, born from a lotus flower on the Ganges; songs sung by the Parsees to the rising sun, and by the serpent charmers to their hooded cobras; and music known in all the cities of the Chinese Empire ere yet had been heard that strange song Apollo sang —

"When Ilion, like a mist, rose into towers."

And in these romantic researches the journalistic friends of the researcher felt no small interest.

* The dedicatory page in "Some Chinese Ghosts":
To my friend
HENRY EDWARD KREHBIEL,
The Musician,
who, speaking the speech of melody unto the children of Tien-Hia,—
unto the wandering Tsing-Jin, whose skins have the color of gold,—
moved them to make strange sounds upon the serpent-bellied San-hin;
persuaded them to play for me upon the shrieking Yah-hin;
prevailed on them to sing me a song of their native land,—
The song of Muh-li-wha,
The song of the Jasmine Flower.

Then it came to pass, inthe course of preparing a series of essays upon these curious melodies of the East, that Krehbiel conceived the romantic notion of having the music of Cathay actually performed for him upon the *San-heen* and the *Yah-hin*, and other instruments of the most eastern East, not by musicians of the Aryan race, but even, in sooth, by men whose skins were of the color of gold, and who had dwelt beneath the shadow of the Chinese Wall. And he spoke concerning his desire to us and to others imbued with the spirit of Romanticism.

In the course of a prolonged experience in news-seeking about magistrates' offices we remembered having beheld various Chinese instruments of outlandish shape that had been temporarily levied on by a remorseless constable. There was among them a *San-heen*, or banjo, of the Celestial Empire, covered, like the abysmally bass drums of the Aztec priests, with the scaly skin of a serpent. There was also a *Yah-hin*, or shrieking fiddle, immemorially old. And there was likewise a thing called in English a "moon guitar," but in Chinese called by a name unpronounceable and impossible to spell with confidence. It might be *Yah-hwang*. All these we recollected were the goods and chattels of the laundry-man Char-lee; and we found the little Chinese laundry and its owner. The atmosphere was dense and somniferous with the vapor of opium which arose from the pipes of the drowsy laundry-men. They were lying side-by-side upon a wooden table, and a small lamp burned dimly between them. Char-lee spoke a word of greeting, but the other only half raised his opium-heavy eyes, and continued to draw upon his pipestem until the yellow gum cracked upon the bowl, with an agony of spluttering crepitation.

We induced Char-lee to take down his *San-heen*, upon whose hollow body the amber-colored scales of serpent skin shown like inlaid work of barbaric design. And that we might be charmed with its quality of tone he played cunningly upon it, playing after the classic fashion of the ancients, with a small ivory plectrum. Then the *San-heen*

wailed a strange wail, and spoke a foreign sorrow and awakened in us fancies of a heart longing after the sight of pagoda towers, and of tea gardens, of serrated sails, of sluggish junks, and the eternal mourning of the Yang-tse-kiang.

"Char-lee," spoke the musician, "do you know a little Chinese song like this?" And he sang slowly the most ancient melody of *Muh-li-wha*, or the Jasmine Flower, which may be found in Williams's "Middle Kingdom,"

The opium smoker, hitherto so listless, suddenly laid his pipe down and arose to a sitting posture. He commenced to nod his head approvingly in time to the music, and at last burst out into the song in a shrill falsetto voice. Both the Chinese had suddenly become interested to the degree of delight, as their smiling faces bore witness; and the contrasts of the scene were certainly picturesque. On the one hand, the handsome young Aryan flushed with the triumph of his art which had triumphed over the natural and ancient want of sympathy between Mongolian and Caucasian: on the other hand, those yellow-skinned, feminine-featured strangers in a strange land, welcoming an echo of music from their own with an intensity of pleasure that seemed almost abnormal in being so phlegmatic. And he sang the solemn strain that is still sung with the sacred instruments in the pagodas just as it was sung three thousand years ago. They knew it also, and their faces became grave as the chant itself.

"MY DEAR KREHBIEL:

"I received yours, with the kind wishes of Mrs. Krehbiel, which afforded me more pleasure than I can tell you; —also the *Golden Hours* with your instructive article on the history of the piano. It occurs to me that when completed your musical essays would form a delightful little volume, and ought certainly to find a first-class publisher. I hope you will entertain the suggestion, if it has not already occurred to you. I do not know very much about musical literature; but I fancy that no work in the English tongue has been published of a character so admirably suited to give young people a sound knowledge of the romantic history of music instruments as your essays would constitute if shaped into a volume. The closing observations of your essay, markedly original and somewhat startling, were very entertaining. I have not yet returned your manuscript, because Robinson is devouring and digesting that Chinese play. He takes a great interest in what you write.

"I send you, not without some qualms of conscience, a copy of our little journal containing a few personal remarks, written with the idea of making you known here in musical circles. I have several apologies to make in regard to the same. Firstly, the *Item* is only a poor little sheet, in which I am not able to obtain space sufficient to do you or your art labor justice; secondly, I beg of you to remember that if I have spoken too extravagantly from a strictly newspaper standpoint, it will not be taken malicious advantage of by anybody, as the modest *Item* goes no further north than St. Louis.

"The Creole rhymes I sent you were unintelligible chiefly because they were written phonetically after a fashion which I hold to be an abomination. The author, Adrien Rouquette, is the last living Indian missionary of the South,—the last of the black-robe fathers, and is known to the Choctaws by the name of Charitah-Ima. You may find him mentioned in the American Encyclopædia published by the firm of Lippincott & Co. There is nothing very remarkable about his poetry, except its eccentricity. The 'Chant d'un jeune Creole' was simply a personal compliment,—the author gives something of a sketch of his own life in it. It was published in *Le Propagateur*, a French Catholic paper, for the purpose of attracting my attention, as the old man wanted to see me, and thought the paper might fall under my observation. The other, the 'Moqueur-Chanteur,'— as it ought to have been spelled, —or 'Mocking Singer,' otherwise the Mocking-bird, has some pretty bits of onomatopœia. (This dreamy, sunny State, with its mighty forests of cedar and pine, and its groves of giant cypress,

is the natural home of the mocking-bird.) These bits of Creole rhyming were adapted to the airs of some old Creole songs, and the music will, perhaps, be the most interesting part of them.

"I am writing you a detailed account of the Creoles of Louisiana, and their blending with Creole emigrants from the Canaries, Martinique, and San Domingo; but it is a subject of great latitude, and I can only outline it for you. Their characteristics offer an interesting topic, and the bastard offspring of the miscegenated French and African, or Spanish and African, dialects called Creole offer pretty peculiarities worth a volume. I will try to give you an entertaining sketch of the subject. I must tell you, however, that creole music is mostly negro music, although often remodelled by French composers. There could neither have been Creole patois nor Creole melodies but for the French and Spanish-blooded slaves of Louisiana and the Antilles. The melancholy, quavering beauty, and weirdness of the negro chant are lightened by the French influence, or subdued and deepened by the Spanish.

"Yes, I *did* send you that song as something queer. I had only hoped that the music would own the charming naïveté of the words; but I have been disappointed. But you must grant the song is pretty and has a queer simplicity of sentiment. Save it for the words. (Alas! *Melusine*—according to information I have just received from Christern of New York, is dead. Poor, dear, darling, *Melusine!* I sincerely mourn for her with archæological and philological lament.) L'Orient is in Brittany, and the chant is that of a Breton fisher village. That it should be melancholy is not surprising; but that it should be melancholy without weirdness or sweetness is lamentable. *Melusine* for 1877 had a large collection of Breton songs, with music; and I think I shall avail myself of Christern's offer to get it. I want it for the legends; you will want, I am sure, to peep at the music. Your criticism about the resemblance of the melody to the Irish keening wail does not surprise me, although it disappointed me ; for I believe the Breton peasantry are of Celtic origin. Your last letter strengthened a strange fancy that has come to me at intervals since my familiarity with the Chinese physiognomy,—namely, that there are such strong similarities between the Mongolian and certain types of the Irish face that one is inclined to suspect a far-distant origin of the Celts in the East. The Erse and the Gaelic tongues, you know, are very similar in construction, also the modern Welsh. I have heard them all, and met Irish people able to comprehend both Welsh and Gaelic from the resemblance to the Erse. I suppose you have lots of Welsh music, the music of the Bards, some of which is said to have had a Druidic origin. Tell me if you have ever come across any Scandinavian music — the terrible melody of the Berserker songs, and the Runic chants, so awfully potent to charm ; the Raven song of the Sweyn maidens to which they wove the magic banner ; the death song of Ragnar Lodbrok, or the songs of the warlocks and Norse priests ; the many sword songs sung by the Vikings, etc. I suppose you remember Longfellow's adaption of the Heimskringla legend :

> ' Then the Skald took his harp and sang ;
> And loud through the music rang
> The sound of that shining word ;
> And the harpstrings a clangor made
> As if they were struck with the blade
> Of a sword.'

" I am delighted to hear you have got some Finnish music. Nothing in the world can compare in queerness and all manner of grotesqueness to Finnish tradition and characteristic superstition. I see an advertisement of 'Le Chant de Roland,' price $100, splendidly illustrated. Wonder if the original music of the Song of Roland has been preserved. You know the giant Taillefer sang that mighty chant as he hewed down the Saxons at the battle of Hastings.

" With grateful regards to Mrs. Krehbiel, I remain

" Yours <i>à jamais,</i>

" L. H."

(This must have been written from New Orleans in February of 1881, since it refers to the birth of my first child.)

" MY DEAR KREHBIEL :

"A pleasant manner, indeed, of breaking thy silence, vast and vague, illuminating my darkness of doubt! — the vision of a sunny-haired baby-girl, inheriting, I hope, those great, soft, gray eyes of yours, and the artist dream of her artist father. I should think you would feel a sweet and terrible responsibility — like one of those traditional guardian-angels entrusted for the first time with the care of a new life. . . . I have not much to tell you about myself. I am living in a ruined Creole house ; damp brick walls green with age, zig-zag cracks running down the façade, a great yard with torchon plants and cacti in it ; a quixotic horse, four cats, two rabbits, three dogs, five geese, and a seraglio of hens,—all living together in harmony. A fortune-teller occupies the lower floor. She has a fantastic apartment kept dark all day, except for the light of two little tapers burning before two human skulls in one corner of the room. It is a very mysterious house, indeed ; . . . But I am getting very weary of the Creole quarter ; the people are too infernally wicked to live with, and I think I shall pull up stakes and fly to the garden district, where the orange trees are, but where the Latin tongues are not spoken. It is very hard to accustom oneself to live with Americans, however, after one has lived three years among these strange types. If I ever get a chance to write about the Latin people here there will be revelations. I am swindled all the time and I know it, and still I find it hard to summon up resolution to forsake these antiquated streets for the commonplace and practical American district.

The Spanish and French department which I make for the *Democrat* has been so curtailed for a while that I have not thought it worth while to send you any specimens. But I forward you the last, because the Spanish story is musical and I think very pretty, although very simple. Next week I will have a still prettier story.

Very affectionately,
L. HEARN. .

I weigh nearly 150—so you see the climate agrees with me.

(My baby died within ten days, and I find an allusion to that fact in the opening paragraph of the next letter.)

MY DEAR KREHBIEL:

Your letter rises before me as I write like a tablet of white stone bearing a dead náme. I see you standing beside me. I look into your eyes and press your hand and say nothing. . . . Remember me kindly to Mrs. Krehbiel. I am sure you will soon have made a cosy little home in the metropolis. In my last letter I forgot to acknowledge receipt of the musical articles, which do you the greatest credit, and which interested me much, although I know nothing about music further than a narrow theatrical experience and a natural sensibility to its simpler forms of beauty enable me to do. I see your name also in the programme of *The Studio* and hope to see the first number of that periodical containing your opening article. I should like one of these days to talk with you about the possibility of contributing a romantic—not musical—series of little sketches upon the Creole songs and colored Creoles of New Orleans to some New York periodical. Until the summer comes, however, it will be difficult for me to undertake such a thing; the days here are much shorter than they are in your northern latitudes, the weather has been gloomy as Tartarus, and my poor imagination cannot rise on dampened wings in this heavy and murky atmosphere. This has been a hideous winter,—incessant rain, sickening weight of foul air, and a sky gray as the face of Melancholy. The city is half under water. The lake and the bayous have burst their bonds, and the streets are Venetian canals. Boats are moving over the sidewalks, and moccasin snakes swarm in the old

stonework of the gutters. Several children have been bitten.

I am very weary of New Orleans. The first delightful impression it produced has vanished. The city of my dreams, bathed in the gold of eternal summer, and perfumed with the amorous odors of orange flowers, has vanished like one of those phantom cities of Spanish America, swallowed up centuries ago by earthquakes, but reappearing at long intervals to deluded travellers. What remains is something horrible like the tombs here,—material and moral rottenness which no pen can do justice to. You must have read some of those mediæval legends in which an amorous youth finds the beautiful witch he has embraced all through the night crumble into a mass of calcined bones and ashes in the morning. Well, I feel like such a one, and almost regret that, unlike the victims of these diabolical illusions, I do not find my hair whitened and my limbs withered by sudden age; for I enjoy exuberant vitality and still seem to myself like one buried alive or left alone in some city cursed with desolation like that described by Sinbad the sailor. No literary circle here; no jovial coterie of journalists; no associates save those vampire ones of which the less said the better. And the thought—Where must all this end?—may be laughed off in the daytime, but always returns to haunt me like a ghost in the night.

Your friend,
L. HEARN.

(I do not know the date even approximately of the following: Mr. Johnson was a German newspaper colleague in Cincinnati, afterwards U. S. Consul at Hamburg. Hearn was passionately devoted to the sport of swimming.)

DEAR FRIEND KREHBIEL:

I have been away in Florida, in the track of old Ponce de Leon,—bathing in the Fount of Youth,—talking to the palm trees,—swimming in the great Atlantic surf. Charley Johnson and I took the trip together,—or, to be strictly fair, it was he that induced me to go along; and I am not sorry for the expense or the time spent, as I enjoyed my reveries unspeakably. For bathing —sea-bathing—I prefer our own Creole islands in the Gulf to any place in Florida; but for scenery and sunlight and air—air that is a liquid jewel,— Florida seems to me the Garden of Hesperus. I 'll send you what I intend to write about it.

My delay in thanking you for the splendid notice you gave my book will therefore be understood. We reprinted the review. I would have thought your praise too high, but that the New York *Nation* followed suit with a notice very similar in character, and I am beginning to believe that I builded better than I knew.

Charles Dudley Warner, whose acquaintance I made here, strikes me as the nicest literary personage I have yet met. Otherwise I have been rather disappointed in literary people—they seem a selfish type generally, quite unlike the journalists proper, who are generally right good fellows. Gilder of the *Century* was here—a handsome, kindly man, but I only met him for a moment as I was just leaving town when he arrived.

A book which I recently got would greatly interest you, if it has not already done so — Symonds's " Wine, Woman, and Song." I had no idea before meeting this delightful volume, that the twelfth century had its literary renascence, or that in the time of the crusades German students were writing poems worthy of Virgil, of Horace, of Anacreon. The Middle Ages no longer seem so Doresquely black.

Your friend,
LAFCADIO HEARN.

(The next letter must have been written in 1885, as the book alluded to is Hearn's collection of Creole proverbs which he called "Gombo Zhèbes." This I know from a paragraph in the letter which I am compelled to suppress, and which is an answer to a question of mine as to the meaning of one of the proverbs.)

68 GASQUET STREET, NEW ORLEANS.
DEAR KREHBIEL:

I am happy to find my little book amused you. It is marred by some errors, and one case in which I was deceived by Bigelow's spelling of *gambette* instead of *jambetto* (from Arabic *djântrya, poinara*, French through old Spanish) will have to be corrected in Errata I suppose. Still it is very hard to get a first print of this sort free from error. . . . Cable is back here— lying very low, however. The T. D. [*Times-Democrat*] has been making war on him; and Page [Mr. Page Baker, the editor of the *Times-Democrat*] swears he is going to make it dangerous for him to walk the streets. I fancy he will not show himself much in public. He has come down to do some writing. The open falsehoods of his article in the *Century* have got the whole South down on him. It was a good business speculation, however, to advertise himself by thus kicking up a row.

We have had the meanest winter I ever passed. Cold is nothing; but the dampness, the marsh fogs, and the everlasting rains and the extraordinary changes of temperature have been trying. We expect spring in a few days, however. The Exposition has not been a success. There were no Apocalyptic crowds as predicted. The main building contains perhaps five important foreign exhibits—Japan (educational), China, Mexico, and the Central American displays. The real success is the Government and State Building. I want you to keep a lookout in the *Weekly* or *Harper's Bazar* for my notes on Japanese music. I am going to send you the Japanese musician's treatise on the relation of Japanese music to ancient Greek music, and the history thereof. But for the time being I am keeping away from the Exposition. My work for the Harpers is done— brought me something over $200. They have recalled their artist, and state the Exposition is not exciting interest enough to justify further attention. My letters are divided between the *Weekly* and the *Bazar;* and are chiefly devoted to Oriental subjects.

This summer I hope to do some serious work,—a tiny book of purely original sketches. No money from

"Stray Leaves," which Stoddard is stealing and turning into blank verse. The one thousand copies are not yet sold. After my next effort I hope to change this way of work, and obtain a foreign correspondence from some influential literary journal. Saturday work compels me to close.

Hurriedly your aff. friend,

L. H.

I have much popular Persian music. My library is now worth $2000. It is somewhat of a bore, however, in regard to taking care of — especially if one wants to travel.

(The following must have followed hard on the heels of the last.)

68 GASQUET STREET.

DEAR K.:

I was just writing you when your welcome lines reached me. Please tell me whether Hattori sent you that report. I have found it impossible to see him, and he has not yet answered my note. I have a friend helping me to hunt him up. If I can not see him I will forward note to Japanese Ministry of Education. Would have sent you my own copy, were it not bound up with a lot of French pamphlets on anthropology.

I am glad you think I am improving. Henry James says a fine prose writer rarely reveals himself before thirty-five; and I am not quite so old, — so I have some hopes of being able to reveal myself.

Your criticism of Gayarré was just. The cry about negro-marriage which his pamphlet re-echoes, is characteristic of Southern provincialism of the old era; but historically this pamphlet is not without value. Detaching its chaff, you will find some wheat. I did not send it you myself; but when he asked me to furnish a list of papers, I put your name down, as I thought the thing would interest you.

I am very much gratified to see that your prospects as a musical teacher and historian are so bright, — that you are in a fine way to make a national reputation. Do you not think it would be a good plan to prepare each lecture as if it were to form one chapter of a volume? Some of the greatest literary treasures of America have been formed by this process. Selecting and arranging your addresses at the end of a year or two, you might readily produce a volume of uncommon value and interest. I am trying to do something of this kind in a more humble way. Articles on certain subjects are carefully chosen beforehand, and I spend months in preparing and polishing, and though I print them only in a daily paper, I have the satisfaction of feeling that they are shaped to fit into a plan that may be successfully developed — the plan of a purely original book of impressions. When one gains the publishers, then one can eschew the daily papers as a medium of printing; but in the meantime we can try to utilize them after the fashion of *feuilletonistes*.

I may be able to get North this fall, and would like to; but I have some work to do in our Creole archipelago — some sketches to make, and they will require three or four months' work.

Yours very affec.

LAFCADIO.

(I think the sketches made were those which grew into "Chita: A Story of Lost Island." For the musical allusions in this — the waltz which was dancing when the island was overwhelmed — he consulted me, and submitted his descriptions in writing to me for criticism. After the story was completely written he came to New York and was my guest for six weeks. Nearly all of this time he spent on the story, polishing and repolishing phrase after phrase, coming into my study in his peculiar timid way a dozen times in a forenoon, to ask the effect of a change of a single word in some phrase that I had already thought as perfect as it could possibly be made. But Hearn had a genius of patience like Beethoven, who frequently put Horace's *Nonum prematur in annum* to shame.

The next letter is again of earlier date, as I know from the contents, — some time in 1881 or 1882.)

MY DEAR KREHBIEL:

Much as it pleased me to hear from you, I assure you that your letter is shocking. It is shocking to hear of anybody being compelled to work for seventeen hours a day. You have neither time to think, to study, to read, to do your best work, or to make any artistic progress—not to even hint of pleasure — while working seventeen yours a day. Nor is that all; I believe it injures a man's health and capacity for endurance, as well as his style and peace of mind. You have a fine constitution; but if once broken down by overstraining the nervous system you will never get fully over the shock. It is very hard for me to believe that it is really necessary for you to do reportorial work and to write correspondence, unless you have a special financial object to accomplish within a very short space of time. The editorial work touching upon art matters which you are capable of doing for the *Tribune*, might be done in the daytime; but what do you want to waste your brain and time upon reportorial work for? D—n reportorial work and correspondence, and the American disposition to work people to death, and the American delight in getting worked to death! Well, I have nothing more to say except to protest my hope that the seventeen-hours-a-day business is going to stop before long; for the longer it lasts the more difficult will it be for you to accomplish your ultimate purpose. The devil of overworking oneself is that it renders it impossible to get fair and just remuneration for value given,—impossible also to create those opportunities for self-advancements which form the steps of the stairway to the artistic heaven,—impossible to maintain that self-pride and confident sense of worth without which no man, however gifted, can make others fully conscious of it. When you voluntarily convert yourself into a part of the machinery of a great daily newspaper, you must revolve and keep revolving with the wheels; you play the man in the treadmill. The more you involve yourself the more difficult it will be for you to escape. I said I had nothing

further to observe; but I find I must say something more,—not that I imagine for a moment I am telling you anything new, but because I wish to try to impress anew upon you some facts which do not seem to have influenced you as I believe they ought to do.

Under all the levity of Henri Murger's picturesque Bohemianism, there is a serious philosophy apparent which elevates the characters of his romance to heroism. They followed one principle faithfully,—so faithfully that only the strong survived the ordeal,—never to abandon the pursuit of an artistic vocation for any other occupation however lucrative,—not even when she remained apparently deaf and blind to her worshippers. The conditions pictured by Murger have passed away in Paris as elsewhere: the old barriers to ambition have been greatly broken down. But I think the moral remains. So long as one can live and pursue his natural vocation in art, it is a duty with him never to abandon it if he believes that he has within him the elements of final success. Every time he labors at aught that is not of art, he robs the divinity of what belongs to her.

Do you never reflect that within a few years you will no longer be the YOUNG MAN,—and that, like Vesta's fires, the enthusiasm of youth for an art-idea must be well fed with the sacred branches to keep it from dying out? I think you ought really to devote all your time and energies and ability to the cultivation of one subject, so as to make that subject alone repay you for all your pains. And I do not believe that Art is altogether ungrateful in these days: she will repay fidelity to her, and recompense sacrifices. I don't think you have any more right to play reporter than a great sculptor to model fifty-cent plaster figures of idiotic saints for Catholic processions, or certain painters to letter steamboats at so much a letter. In one sense, too, Art is exacting. To acquire real eminence in any one branch of any art, one must study nothing else for a lifetime. A very wide general knowledge may be acquired only at the expense of depth.

But you are certainly right in thinking of the present for other reasons. Still, there is nothing so important, not only to success but to confidence, hope, and happiness, as good health and a strong constitution; and these you must lose if you choose to keep working seventeen hours a day! It is well to be able to do such a thing on a brief stretch, but it is suicide, moral and physical, to keep it up regularly. The rolling-mill hand, or the puddler, or the moulder, or the common brakeman on a railroad cannot keep up at such hours for a great length of time; and you must know that even hard labor is not so exhausting as brain-work. Don't work yourself sick, old friend,—you are in a fair way to do it now.

Your friend,

L. H.

(From the earliest days of our friendship as fellow reporters in Cincinnati, we were in the habit of exchanging suggestions touching topics for study and our special newspaper articles. Among Hearn's first writings on a petty newspaper in New Orleans was a series of fantastic stories based on conceits which were decidedly repugnant to me. I therefore tried to switch him off onto classic subjects with historical backgrounds. He protested vigorously and flayed writers like Ebers and others, whom I had ventured to say were filling a valuable place in literature in that they brought back the antique life in tangible forms, forms intelligible and vital to the mind of the many. Once he sent me a story in triumph in which he said he had carried out one of my suggestions. It was, like most of the things which he wrote at the time, erotic —only this time there was a classic background. That our habit of submitting subjects to each other and asking advice of each other continued till I was pretty deep in my New York period is plain from the following sketch which he sent me in lieu of a letter—of course without date. The story appeared a few months later in *Harper's Bazar*, I think, and was also turned into a poem, if I am not mistaken, by Mr. Stoddard; but in neither

form did it seem to me to possess half the beauty and strength which mark this outline, which may be only one of his paraphrases of the story as he found it in the French.)

(No date.)

(Hasty) Suggestion, from Arabian Legends. Rabiah was the Bayard of Presslannic Arabia.—I make a hurried sketch of the death-scene.

. . . Now, inasmuch as Rabiah had slain all who dared to attack him singly, and the rest were afraid to attack him unitedly, they drew off, permitting the fleeing women to urge their camels a league ahead, and following Rabiah at a distance only— timidly yet tirelessly, as desert vultures follow the failing traveller.

Then came they to the ghastly pass of Ghazal, a gap in the jagged teeth of the desert-rocks; before them, all was dry as bone, and the yellow sand-sea beyond the gap circled heaving to the verge of heaven.

And Rabiah said unto the women, and unto his mother: "Lo! the beasts fail for weariness. But one man may here hold his own against a host; and I shall stay. Ride ye slowly on."

Then stayed he, and suddenly Nubaishah, son of Habib, coming up pierced him unawares with his spear, and drew back the reeking blade between his stallion's ears, and laughed and said: "Thou art wounded to the death, Rabiah, for by the smell of my spear-head I know it."

But Rabiah rode on to his mother, saying: "Give me to drink, lest I perish of thirst." Now she was of the race of eagles, and she said unto him, tearlessly: "Nay, son; for if thou drink now thou diest, and we are taken, and it is the warrior's duty to fight for his women even till the last. Return, therefore, and smite them while thy strength endures; bear thou the thirst for thy mother's sake."

So he went back and smote and slew, and drave them back, and held all the pass against them while the women fled. And the sun was setting behind him; and in the flame of gold he sat upon his mare like a Djinn.

So they feared to approach; for his

arrows pierced their mail, and they stood afar off, and watched. And Rabiah felt his soul going forth. Then, dismounting, he leaned his right hand upon his spear, his left arm upon the shoulder of his mare,—and he whispered in her ear: "Stand thou still, darling,—still as a stone for the love of me," and she stood as an image stands. And the ghost of Rabiah departed from him; yet the man still stood in the pass, and the mare still stood still as a stone for the love of him.

And the men of Sulaim watched and feared in the night,—watched until the moon sank low.

Then murmured a chief unto his best archer: "Shoot, O son, shoot at the mare." And the man shot.

And the mare saw the arrow coming, and she leaped aside; and only then Rabiah fell upon his face, and only then did the men of Sulaim know that he was dead.

But the women had ridden safely unto the tents of their people.

And the chief of the men of Sulaim stared in admiration at the dead man, and thrust his spear into his eye, and cried: "God curse thee—a man who defendeth his women even when he is dead!" But they sepultured him with honor.

And to-day, even after the lapse of two thousand years, the Arab traveller passing the tomb of Rabiah slayeth a camel in his honor; and the brown girls of the desert pray for boys worthy to bear his name, and the poets of the desert sing of him—aye, even the blue-eyed women of the Touraegs, who make their camels dance to the sound of music under the walls of Timbuctoo. . . .

Will write at length about Kalewala and yourself soon. Don't like the Virgilian theme for your project. There is another Orpheus besides Waïnamoïnen in Kalewala. Waïnamoïnen's harp in the Kalewala signifieth the wind— the weird wind whose name wails. When it is played, the goddess of the sea combs out her green hair by the shore—*the breakers.*

The Russian Players

By HOMER SAINT-GAUDENS

SERIOUS, rational talent of a thoroughly appreciated conservative nature has not saved the Orleneff band of Russian players from a struggle with a miserable theatre, and financial difficulties, during the past season had, at times, brought them to the point of actual starvation. For an American the repertoire of the "Lyceum," on East Third Street, naturally contained many plays of scant interest, either because of their distinctly Russian appeal, as in the case of "Vanyushin's Children," by S. Naidyonoff, or because of what the Anglo-Saxon mind deems the undramatic qualities in such plays as Ibsen's "The Master Builder," where long drawn dialogues must be understood in detail to be sanctioned. But in pieces more readily acceptable here, such as Bertono's "Zaza" on the one hand, and Ibsen's "Ghosts" on the other, the average New Yorker should feel ashamed of the reception tendered the talents of Paul Orleneff, and Mme. Alla Nasimoff, backed by their carefully trained company.

Strangely, though felicitously to Broadway eyes, Orleneff has schooled his followers with a naturalistic curb that produces a supple, intense effect, which wholly lacks the more exaggerated methods of our theatre. Before all an American feels grateful for the artistic sincerity which fills their dramatic climaxes with an imagination divorced from brutality of treatment. The principal character never quite visibly uproots itself, and crashes over the foot-lights at the expense of its surroundings. On the contrary, it remains the focus of a well-drilled cast, where minor parts, neither hectic nor vacant, receive a quiescent impersonation that adds vitally to the success of the whole.

As a worker in such a thoroughly conceived line Orleneff takes rank among the strongest men of his profession. He controls a small, wiry, and yet attractive body, a face adaptable to varying demands, and a flexible voice which must delight his Russian listeners. The imagination, and yet restraint of his easy personality may be typified in such a scene as that in the last act of "Ghosts" where Oswald childishly begs his mother for the sun. There the Russian's business, always to the point, with a realism based on naturalism, produces a spiritual quality at variance with the usually dreaded horror of the moment. He grasps the power of acting with deliberation and the strength of keeping still, that shows his craft in never becoming platitudinous. Especially does he prove his capabilities when with such methods he infuses life and force into the dialogues of "The Master Builder," and discriminates between the varying stages of madness of Halvard Solners in a way that holds an audience half of whom are ignorant of his speech.

Orleneff has been devoted to the theatre from his boyhood, when he stole an occasional fifteen cents to buy a seat in the gallery, or spent a day in a dark room for studying Hamlet under his desk. Twenty-one years ago, at the age of sixteen, he left his school and his well-to-do family, to join a Moscow dramatic company. Recognition came quickly, though in a distasteful manner, since he played comic parts steadily for ten years. However, his best gifts manifested themselves when, in 1893, he took the title rôle in "Tzar Feodora," "The Son of Ivan the Terrible," by Tolstoy, for over five hundred nights. Then, at last, his unquestioned success won him a position that permitted him to free himself from the irksome restraint of his managers.

From that time on, though never mingling with Russian politics, Orleneff constantly passed in and out of jail through his troubles with the censor. For his desire to express his conceptions of the advanced modern theatre led him towards such fields as "The Master Builder," when the religious opinions of the pastor were more than unpopular with government officials. He trod his individual path, however, despite many offers from various Royal theatres, holding seriously to his view that art is but a servant to convey the idea of the man that serves a purpose. Indeed, his respect for his work rests so deep that he has restrained himself from his greatest desire, to play Hamlet,— which, by the by, he understands as a nervous character, until after his first scene with the ghost—waiting for a time when he may be well fitted to do justice to the part.

Such an attitude towards his cause soon won Orleneff the friendship of Checkoff, Gorky, and Stanislaus, and brought about his producing "Karamasoff Brothers," and "Crime and Punishment," by Dostorevsky in Stanislaus' art playhouse in Moscow. Soon the four enthusiasts began to plan a national theatre for the people. That they might the more quickly obtain funds for the project Orleneff started to tour Russia with his company, giving "The Chosen People," by Eugene Tchirikov, a play dealing with the plight of the Jews in Russia. But, as the censor quickly made his customary objections, on Gorky's counsel Orleneff took his piece through Europe only a short time before Checkoff died and the massacres broke out. The trip ended in London, where Orleneff gave much-praised performances at the Haymarket theatre. Then Prince Kropotkin and the Russian refugees became interested, and proposed a trip to America at a dinner given to the actors in co-operation with Sir Henry Irving, Beerbohm Tree, Jerome K. Jerome, Lawrence Irving, Ellen Terry and other theatrical folk. The plan ripened so rapidly that in 1905 Orleneff sailed for the United States with the whole of his cast.

Mme. Alla Nasimoff, his leading actress, who has played with him for ten years, accompanied him in this serious undertaking. A handsome woman of a pronounced Slavonic type, she attacks her parts with vigor and color.

Her intelligence, and qualities of patience and hard work have taught her most successfully to couple her poise of mind and gesture. In such rôles as Zaza, as Hilda in "The Master Builder," as Regina in "Ghosts," or as Leah in "The Chosen People," she brings forward her instinct for character, and her subtle power of expression. She becomes convincing, interesting, appealing, as her need requires, yet she never arouses the fear that she will make a clown of herself. She acts without apparent theatricalism, where her dramatic sense never overmasters her common sense.

Mme. Nasimoff, a woman of broad education, though born at Odessa, spent her early life with her prosperous parents at Jalta on the Baltic and in a Roman Catholic school in Switzerland, until at the age of sixteen she went to Moscow to study music. Soon after her arrival there her love of the stage got the upper hand and she began to attend the dramatic school that Orleneff then conducted in addition to his theatre. Her début, however, she made in a minor rôle in Vilna. Success did not come for some time, but, at last, she received permission to compete with three actresses in the rôle of Tzarina in "Tzar Feodora." Then her proficiency brought such immediate recognition that Orleneff promptly asked her to join his company. The choice was the wisest possible, since here in New York, where she has become the virtual stage manager of the company, he has benefited by her training which is infinitely more thorough than that usual with an actress.

Though the Russian players arrived in this city with meagre properties and funds, yet their first efforts met with universal good fortune. Soon after their landing Mr. Alfred Hayman lent them the Herald Square Theatre for a matinée on March 5, 1905. Their production of "The Chosen People" won them sober attention and unquestioned support, not only from their countrymen, but as well from American playgoers. For the next few weeks they performed from time to time at the Adler Theatre, and other East Side

houses, where they found a warm welcome for their work in their repertoire of "The Chosen People," "The Master Builder," "Ghosts," "A Doll's House," "Karamasoff Brothers," "Crime and Punishment," "Tzar Feodora," "Countess Julie," by Strinberg, "Vanyushin's Children," "The Zwee Family" by Piuski, and the like.

At that time every indication pointed to continued good fortune. The Yiddish press accorded them an enviable place in the theatrical world, and the English papers followed suit. Visitors from north of Union Square came to see the distinct art in their work, despite the hopelessly incomprehensible language. During the following summer the Russian settlement in their behalf gathered $2500 and promised $3500 more, while American friends added another $9000. Finally Mme. Nasimoff went to Russia to raise a new company, and returned with several players, among whom were Mme. Rumshina, who has been on the stage forty years, and A. Karataeff, a young actor of twenty-five, whose Tolstoyan views made residence out of Russia desirable.

But during the past winter the troupe has suffered a period filled with misfortunes. Their ignorance of American business methods led them to sign a disadvantageous contract for the East Third Street Theatre, which proved small, noisy from an assembly hall overhead, with a crowded stage and bad ventilation. For obvious reasons the American attendance fell off to an extent. The Russians, as well, became occupied with the disturbances at home and lessened their support. Finally when, after a rumored quarrel with Orleneff, the Yiddish press withdrew its notices, the company found they were losing money at the rate of $3000 a month.

In December, however, aid came to them from a number of Americans interested in their movement, among whom were Mrs. Francis Hellman, Mr. Robert Underwood Johnson, Mr. Ben Greet, the Rev. Percy Grant, and Miss Smaley. A ladies' committee provided immediate funds as the actors were starving. Then a number of influen-

Copyright by Alice Boughton,
New York, 1906

MME. ALLA NASIMOFF

Copyright by Alice Boughton,
New York, 1906

M. PAUL ORLENEFF

tial persons with the aid of Mrs. Whitney arranged a series of matinées at the Criterion Theatre which materially increased the company's returns. Lastly a men's committee with Mr. Owen Johnson as chairman, Mr. Charles Klein, Mr. Ernest Crosby, and Mr. Paul Herzog attempted to settle their affairs on a more firm basis.

Meanwhile Mr. Ben Greet secured the interest of Mr. Daniel Frohman who sent them to play in Chicago and Boston from February 12th to March 20th. The trip to the former city brought out such favorable comment that Mr. Frohman placed them permanently under the management of Mr. Augustus Dunlap after their return from Boston. Mme. Nasimoff, in especial, created such enthusiasm

that she received offers to be taught English, and to play in America under a four-year contract. Whatever way this project turns out, Orleneff and nine of his company will return to Chicago in November and December, and spend the remainder of the 1907 winter in New York. At present the troupe will act at the Berkeley Lyceum for three nights a week under a temporary arrangement. There has been a rumor that they might take the place of the German players who will soon vacate Conried's theatre. Though such a plan seems far too generous for the natural restrictions imposed by the Russian language, yet without doubt their sincere and highly finished work will receive a deserved place while it remains in the New York theatrical world.

The Prayer=Book of Cardinal Grimani

By MAUDE BARROWS DUTTON

THE Holiday season has come to be the gala month in the book-lover's year. Not only are the ripest fruits of the present generation piled before him then in reckless profusion, but above all his old favorites lie in wait to ensnare his fancy with every decoy known in the art of " doing into book form." For there is no man so susceptible and guileless as the book-lover. The feeling of fine parchment between his fingers, the illuminated initial letter, the edition that fits into his vest pocket, the craft of the illustrator, the rich aroma of morocco, act upon his spirit as old wine. There was, therefore, a singular appropriateness that during the last Holiday season there should have been brought to America, and exhibited in New York, a *fac-simile* reproduction of a manuscript that book-lovers have not hesitated to pronounce the most beautiful book in the world,—the " Breviarium Grimani."

Like many a masterpiece of art, this manuscript has for centuries been practically lost to the world, but not as is usually the case, because its keepers were ignorant of its value, but rather

because they knew it too well. For no sacred relic, and no royal jewel have been guarded with greater vigilance than this illuminated prayer-book, the great art treasure of the Library of San Marco, at Venice.

It is a curious fact, however, that a book, whose value has for generations been so highly prized, should have its beginnings enshrouded in mystery, for although the manuscript bears the name of Cardinal Grimani, the fact alone that the feast days of St. Francis are printed in red shows that the book was not ordered for him originally, but rather for some Franciscan brother. This clue when once discovered proved a puzzling one, for what brother belonging to an order whose first vow was poverty would order a Breviarium for his devotions with every one of its more than fifteen hundred pages hand illuminated by the most famous foreign artists of his day? The search for the owner has proved without question that there was but one Franciscan living during the latter part of the fifteenth century who could have placed this commission, and this was Pope Sextus IV.

JANUARY
From the Grimani Calendar

This pope, when a mere child, had taken the robe of St. Francis in fulfilment of a vow made by his parents before his birth, and with his increasing years had passed through the various grades of the order until he became its head, and had then advanced even further to be cardinal and finally pope. A great lover of all the arts, the man who had lived his own life strictly in accordance with the vow repeated by his ignorant child-lips had now an opportunity to gratify in the name of the state the forbidden desires of his own nature. His home had all the bareness, the simplicity, and the severity of a Franciscan monastery, but without in the Eternal City Sextus was paving the streets, erecting churches and roofs of shelter for the many pilgrims who yearly journeyed to Rome, building bridges across the Tiber, and, what was nearest his heart, founding and equipping the Vatican Library. It was, without doubt, for this institution, which during the life of Sextus became renowned as the finest library in the world, that the Breviarium Grimani was ordered.

When we consider, however, what the book comprises,—1268 pages of text, not one of which is without its marvellously designed border of fruits, gems, flowers, birds, and insects, and these pages interspersed with three hundred full-page miniatures portraying in turn scenes to represent the twelve months of the year, the story of the Bible from Adam and Eve to Ascension Day, and then the lives of all the saints, —when we contemplate the amount of labor involved in such a task when each letter must be done by hand we are not surprised to learn that Sextus died before the work was completed. The papal tiara fell now upon the head of a man less endowed with the love of the beautiful, and the prayer-book remained in the studio of the artists who were making it. From the time of the death of Sextus IV., in 1484, until 1521, we have no trace of the history of the Breviarium, but in that year we learn that Cardinal Grimani, of Venice, son of the Doge Antonio Grimani, who was a patron of art and literature, bought the manuscript from a Sicilian artist, Anto-

nio da Messina, for the sum of five hundred ducats. Antonio da Messina, an artist of no small repute at that day, had become interested in an oil painting, one of the first pictures done in that medium, which Jan van Eyke of Bruges had sent to Naples, and he had consequently made his way across Europe to Flanders to look into this secret process. Thus he came into intimate touch with the Flemish artists whose miniature work had already reached a high stage of development, and it was possibly for that reason that he was one of the few Italian painters and illuminators who were selected to collaborate with the Flemish masters, Hans Memling, either Gerard Van den Meire or Gerard Herenbout (critics disagree as to which Gerard of Ghent is meant), Levian Van Latham, and others, in executing the most beautiful prayer-book in existence. Cardinal Grimani was not a Franciscan, but he was a devoted patron of all the *belles arts*, and had already several of Memling's paintings among the art treasures in his palaces at Venice and Rome. Like Sextus, too, he was a patriot, and thus in bequeathing the Breviarium after his death to his nephew Mariano Grimani, did so with the injunction that he, in turn, should leave it with the full rights pertaining thereto to the Republic of Venice.

Mariano, who lived at Rome, now took the book with him to the city for which it was originally destined, and here it remained during his life. Upon his decease, at the urgent request of Giovanni Grimani the latter was allowed to retain it until his death. A few days before this occurred, he summoned to his bedside the Procurator of the Library of San Marco, and gave the manuscript into his hands. In order that it might be the more carefully preserved he had made for it a special ebony shrine set with gems and cameos, and richly ornamented with columns of alabaster and inlaid figures of bronze. The Procurator bore the precious gift back once more to Venice, and before the entire body of the Senate assembled made the presentation, in their name, to the republic for which they stood. The Senate seemed to have had a full realization of the value of the manuscript, for they immediately voted that it be rebound in order to preserve it better, and to mark their gratitude for the magnificent gift. A rich crimson velvet was chosen for the cover and decorated with heavily gilded ornaments. In the centre of the front cover was set a medallion of the Cardinal with his coat of arms beneath, while one of his father, the duke, embellished the back, and round the edges ran a border of palm and laurel, interwoven, significant of a life religious and vigilant, with here and there the figure of a dove, the symbol of simplicity, and the dragon, the emblem of safeguard. The entire work of this elaborate designing was probably entrusted to one Alexander Vittoria, a sculptor of local fame who had recently completed the statues in the entrance to the Library of San Marco.

When the last detail of workmanship on the new binding had been finished, the prayer-book was laid within its shrine and deposited in the treasury of San Marco, where it was shown only to royal visitors. In 1797 it once more changed its dwelling place, and was brought into the great library where it has since remained, guarded more preciously than any other book in the world. And because of this vigilance we look in vain in the works of Vasari and other art historians for some mention of the Breviarium, and its wonderful miniatures. So closely was it protected from all possible chance of injury that even the librarian, Morelli, mentions that in 1783 he had seen it but three times; once when Gustavus Adolphus III., of Sweden, visited Venice, and twice again "for a few moments by candlelight." Later, however, he was permitted to study the book with the intent of writing a treatise upon it, but unfortunately he died before the completion of the plan, leaving only a few notes on the subject. But these alone were sufficient to attract the attention of *savants*, who have with difficulty, at various times since, won permission from the Italian Govern-

ment to look upon the treasured manuscript. The long anticipated visit proves, however, a tantalizing experience, for the spectator is obliged to stand at a prescribed distance from the shrine, with guards on either side of him to prevent his surreptitiously kodaking any picture, while a priest turns over the pages with face averted lest his breath should in any wise despoil the parchment. At the close of a half hour the visit must terminate, and only in very rare instances is it allowed to be renewed for a similar interval on the following day.

About forty years ago the loss by fire of some of the most valuable manuscripts in Europe awoke in the guardians of the Breviarium Grimani the realization that in spite of all precaution, here was one danger from which they could never be entirely safe, and thus it was that a Venetian photographer was allowed to photograph about one hundred of the most beautiful of the pages and issue them in portfolio form, together with a lengthy text, giving the biography of the book and a description of the coloring of the plates. Admirable as this reproduction was at the time, the rapid development of photographic art soon made this worthy effort appear but as a most crude and unsatisfactory copy of the original. It was, however, suggestive, and doubtless assisted in making possible the *fac-simile* reproduction that this year, for the first time, is calling attention to one of the most gorgeous manuscripts of the Middle Ages.

This latest step was taken when Messrs. Sythoff, publishers in Leyden, Holland, long interested in photo reproduction, at last obtained permission to reproduce the Breviarium Grimani in fac-simile.

The work of the miniaturists stands as a transitional stage between religious and secular art. Especially do we note this in the realistic pictures of the calendarium in the prayer-book. These twelve full-page miniatures, which could form a little book complete in itself, must take their place with ancient chronicles as an authentic portrayal of life in Flanders during the fifteenth cen-

APRIL

From the Grimani Calendar

JULY

From the Grimani Calendar

328

tury; but in interest, in color, and charm of conception and presentation it is more fitting that we compare them with old ballads or Chaucerian tales.

The illustrating of a calendar, or year book, had long become customary. It was one of the early Catholic devices to appeal to their masses of illiterate worshippers by marking the feast days in the Church calendar with the symbols of the corresponding saints. In the course of time, these symbols became confused in the unthinking minds of the peasants with the emblems of their every-day activities. We find, for example, in one of the most primitive calendars that the crude drawing of a hand stands beneath St. Thomas's Day, and below in the commentary is written that it is unknown whether this picture was a symbol of the doubting Thomas who wished to put his hand in his Lord's side, or a glove, emblematic of the winter cold. Likewise in the old runic calendars we find the drinking horn below the day of the Feast of the Circumcision, and even some symbols standing for activities in no wise connected with the Church, such as the rake and scythe to announce the haying season; the shears to foretell the sheep-shearing; and the leg crossed with the spindle, vividly suggestive of the duties lying before the housewife as the winter came on. So gradually the Christian calender lost its purely religious significance and became, in the same way as did painting, an effort to represent the various phases of human life and activities as they passed through the cycle of the year.

Thus Memling, when the task of illustrating the calendarium for the Breviarium Grimani fell to his hands, felt himself in no sense restricted by the ecclesiastical canons of the Church. Recalling the subjects of his best-known paintings, *The Shrine of Saint Ursula* (Bruges), the *Seven Joys of Mary* (Munich), and *The Blessed Virgin and Child, with Donors* (Louvre), we are, perhaps, somewhat surprised to see how, in this part of the prayer-book, he turned away absolutely from religious themes. Still if we examine these same pictures, we find that in them which prepares us for this act. It was customary with the forerunners and even the contemporaries of Memling to paint the figures in their pictures, and then leave the background or landscape for some other artist to complete. Memling, however, not only did this portion of the picture with his own hand, but seemed to take a peculiar delight in doing it. If we take, for instance, the *Madonna and Child* in the Louvre, we see with what care and fine sense of proportion the architectural setting is drawn, and with what charm the little scene of the mounted knight, the moat, and the rustic bridge is portrayed through one of the open arches of the church. This little picture within the larger one, and entirely apart from it in subject, is most significant of the painter's own individuality, for doubtless here alone was he allowed to follow his own instincts.

Memlings's birthplace is unknown, but his home was for many years in Bruges, and the atmosphere of this city, one of the wealthiest of the Hansa towns, the home of many of the merchant princes of the day, this Flemish Venice, with its magnificent bridges and fountains, its bronze statues, its houses ornamented with fine carvings and rich-storied glass, was enough to kindle the imagination and fire the blood of any artist. What it called forth in Memling we see in the pictures in the calendar, where there is a sense of spontaneous delight that is so often lacking in religious art.

The Norse calendar opened the year with a rude drawing of a cornucopia, and Memling chose the same motive for his presentation of January. It seems, in this picture, as if he could not satisfy his desire to portray plenteousness. Detail after detail heaps it up before our eyes: the nobleman dining in solitary splendor, the fire behind his back, the host of stewards waiting on either side of him, the gold-mounted vessels on the table, the carved bas-relief over the mantel-piece, the heavy draperies,—and yet there is a Teutonic atmosphere of *Gemüthlichkeit* given the scene by the pages in the foreground feeding the favorite hounds, and, to us, an amusing note of primitiveness in that the nobleman's place is laid with merely a knife, bone-handled and of generous proportions.

For February the artist gives us a charming winter landscape in the country. Through an open doorway we look in upon the good wife busy with her spindle as she sits before the fire, her skirt turned back over her knees with thrifty precaution, but the true interest of the scene is in the dooryard with the hens and roosters, the cat, the snow-birds, the little pig, and the sheep huddled beneath the rough shelter of a penthouse.

In March the agricultural activities commence. The flocks are let loose on the hill-slopes to hunt for the first bits of green; the oxen are yoked to the plough, and the sower follows behind its trail with swinging arm.

Then with the coming of the next month not even the nobles linger longer within doors. April was always considered by the ancients to be the month of love-making, and Memling has held to the tradition and given us a brilliantly colored bridal procession of a lord and lady out under the white blossoming fruit-trees, and with the castle half enveloped in a green haze in the background.

This picture is followed by a May-day fête, a merry revel in the greenwood. Three huntsmen ahead, in green jerkins and red caps from which float long orange-and white plumes, are winding their horns, while the prancing steeds and the jolly riders respond lustily.

Then once more during the summer months we return to the peasant scenes; the life in the hayfield, where men and women are working side by side with pitchforks and scythes curiously like those used in New England to-day; and to the midsummer shearing, where the master himself, his arms crossed upon his stick, watches the process with highly critical mien.

In color and artistic conception, none of the pictures can, perhaps, equal the September vintage. The gray, flam-boyant castle, filling in the entire background, as well as the heavily laden vines, the richness of the purples and greens, all bespeak the copiousness of the harvest season, while the half-ruined gateway to one side adds the touch of melancholy so closely associated with the fall. It prepares us, too, for the industriousness of the October picture. The farmer, astride one of his pair, guides the horses across the field where the winter seed is being planted, while a boy with bow and arrow keeps watch of the marauding crows; the women are washing the household linen in the canal; and two boats are passing by, one being towed from the bank, and the other punted along with poles, just as one sees in rural Holland to-day. But we are scarcely into the heart of the country fall until we turn to the November woodland scene, where two husky swineherds are hurling sticks into the beech-trees to bring down the shower of nuts that shall fatten their swine.

In the last of the calendar pictures, the trees are again sear and brown. The theme is a hunt, that great mediæval festivity, and, as is befitting December, the hounds have set upon the wild boar, and the leader of the chase has raised his bugle to his lips to announce the finish far and wide.

The restricted edition of the book has made its just distribution of no small importance, and led the publishers to decide that a stipulated number of copies be reserved for all the large countries of Europe, and about one hundred set apart for sale in America. The first American sale was to the Congressional Library, and the Metropolitan Art Museum, Columbia University, and the General Seminary of the Episcopal Church were quick to follow this lead so, that now at last Memling and his friends may look down upon us here and congratulate themselves that the results of his labor at last are to be spread not only over the old world but the new.

SEPTEMBER
From the Grimani Calendar

MR. R. H. MUNRO FERGUSON
By Miss Ellen G. Emmet

Ellen G. Emmet

MISS ELLEN G. EMMET has established herself as one of the most capable and distinctive artists in the younger school of American portrait painters. She exercises her qualities of strength and breadth toward results far removed from that often repeated bogie of ill-manipulated brutality. She earns her greatest success with her male sitters, for though her pictures of women set forth many of her most desirable qualities, yet, on the whole, they include as well a suggestion of posturing that rarely impresses their visitor with the rest, the simplicity, the conviction, and the sympathy that she carries through her work upon subjects of the masculine sex. Perhaps the signally opportune as well as the signally prominent qualities in her portraits of men spring from her power to bring to the surface as much of their personality as can be made visible. To this end, and that of the thorough expression of character without idiosyncrasy, she studies the relaxed attitudes of her subjects, and invites their familiarity in a generally felicitous quest for modern unembarrassed non-conventional poses and costumes. The natural gifts of perception, of character grasp, and of sympathy for the mental attitude as displayed in the physical gesture, she couples with the results of a sound training in drawing and composition. Consciously or unconsciously, in her portraits she demonstrates her appreciation of the comparative simplicity of making a good harmony, and the comparative difficulty of making a good contrast. Therefore she takes pains to place her subjects under conditions where she can study them with moderate soft clear colors, warm or cool, as the case requires, but never clashing in tone or sentiment. She understands how to cope with the amount of light adaptable under varying conditions, and so, while employing strong values of light or shade, she sees to it that the eye is not distracted by black holes, or confused by unexpected bright points. On completion, her work shows no trace of haste, and yet escapes the lack of proportion of over-finish. Details do not obtrude themselves, but her surfaces render their feeling of texture through her careful and yet uncramped brush. No flash of feeble or irresolute attempts at the so-called masculine qualities mars the unity of her canvas. Her art rises above straining after sparkling vitality when the subject demands sober characterization. Her choice of normal attitudes perfects her repose and strength. These qualities, with her sense of form and circumspect preference for only vital accessories, bring to a focus the one compact impression of a unified whole; a whole which offers a refreshing relief to the scattered results and slippery execution of the "effect seeker." She has not attempted to startle the world by the unspeakably novel, but to attract it by painting well within the limits of what it considers its best standards.

———

Miss Ellen G. Emmet, though born in San Francisco, came to the Eastern States when only ten years old. Her first studies in art were under Mr. Dennis Bunker, in Boston, Mass. Some time afterwards she began work in New York City, instructed by Mr. William M. Chase and Mr. Robert Reed, until, in 1896, she went to Paris. There and at Girvirny she painted for three years under Mr. Frederick MacMonnies, who at that time had turned his attention to oils instead of clay. Miss Emmet then completed a half-dozen portraits in England and returned to America in 1900. She has recently held an unusually successful exhibition of ninety-four canvases at Copley Hall, Boston.

H. ST. G.

MR. J. M. BARRIE'S LONDON HOUSE
LEINSTER CORNER, BAYSWATER, OPPOSITE KENSINGTON GARDENS

James Matthew Barrie

AMERICAN admirers of Mr. James M. Barrie are always interested when visiting England to have pointed out to them the snug little countryfied house in Lancaster Gate, Bayswater, where the author of " Peter Pan" has his London residence. Even in this city of architectural surprises, the simple low-roofed cottage, with its white paint, green shutters, high walls, and long garden trailing out behind, forms a very quaint corner. It is just the sort of a place you would expect to find on the High Street of some venerable cathedral town, but with Marble Arch, Park Lane, and the roar of Oxford Circus so near, its rural unpretentiousness is wellnigh disconcerting. Indeed when a visitor stands outside the stout wooden door sunk in the garden wall, and listens to the faint tinkle of a distant bell, he is filled with vague surmises as to what his summons may bring forth. Once admitted, however, into the pretty front enclosure, blazing at the moment with the purple, scarlet, and gold of late autumn blossoms, it is easy to see, in the vulgar parlance of the day, that Mr. Barrie has done himself wonderfully well. Comfort, picturesqueness, and even a gay dash of coquetry go to the make-up of an absolutely unconventional home. The immaculate whiteness of the interior supplies an ideal background for the high polish of much good old furniture, for a few distinguished pictures, and always heaps of flowers arranged by an artist's hands. There are also bits of very choice *bric-à-brac* scattered about, but one of the chief attractions of the reposeful rooms is the fine restraint exercised in every kind of adornment.

In the low-ceiled drawing-room which is again reminiscent of the country and might well serve for a vicarage parlor, the very first object to attract the eye is a portrait of Mr. George Meredith occupying the place of honor. It is an excellent piece of painting, and a vigorous likeness of the present high-priest of British fiction. The delicately featured face, with its ardent eyes and keenly intellectual cast, exercises an almost mesmeric charm even on the canvas. Among his friends it is well recognized that Mr. Barrie's attitude towards Meredith is that of a passionately devoted disciple. He regards the creator of "Harry Richmond," of "Richard Feverel," and of "The Egoist" as the absolute and supreme master of English prose, and not merely master of the literature of to-day, but of all time, past as well as present. In fact, when he mentions Mr. Meredith's name, the deep note of feeling in Mr. Barrie's voice is unmistakable. True he does say "the greatest since Shakespeare," but an eloquent pause on the word *since* sets the listener wondering if by substituting *with* he would not more nearly express his true sentiments. And just here it is interesting to remember how fervently Mr. Gilbert Chesterton and Mr. Max Beerbohm proclaim Meredith a co-equal with the divine Elizabethan. Mr. Barrie's attitude toward the sage of Box Hill is a mixture of reverence for a superbly great artist and philosopher, and something of filial love as well for the man who was among the very first to recognize his (Mr. Barrie's) own gift.

One of his friends is even now fond of telling a story of years ago when Mr. Kipling had risen luminous over the literary horizon and when his virile verse and trenchant prose were filling the mouths and minds of men. At that time some one asked Mr. Meredith who, of all the rising generation, seemed to him to give surest promise for the future. The questioner himself never doubted but that the young Anglo-Indian genius would instantly be named. Not so. Without a moment's hesitation, Mr. Meredith said he was confident a certain youngster, a Scotsman, James Barrie, was better qualified to achieve fame than any literary postulant of the day. As at that time there were only a volume or two of fragmentary essays and a couple of light comedies to Mr. Barrie's credit, the prophecy stands as rather a remarkable bit of foresight.

Few men upon whose work public favor has so firmly set its stamp are as fond of discussing his failures as is Mr. Barrie. It is not of his power as a dramatist, nor of his potent charm as a novelist, that he loves to talk, but rather of the blind contrariety of fate in refusing to qualify him for the special labors after which his boyish soul yearned. What he wished and planned to be in the old days of plain living and high thinking at Edinburgh University was a critic and biographer. There was to be no place for the creator in the scheme of life as he laid it down for himself. This most fecund of artists proposed rather to sit in solemn judgment upon the achievements of others. With this end in view, his first serious essay into the paths of literature was to prepare a ponderous study of a certain well-known character, and then after six hard months of stress and strain to consign every single page of manuscript to the flames. For even then fastidious to the last degree he needed no editor's blue pencil to spell failure. His own exacting taste condemned the work and let it die stillborn. But though biographies burn, bread must be earned, and to keep the wolf from becoming too noisy those brief delicious sketches were sent to the *St. James's Gazette*, beginning with "Auld Licht Idylls," whose popularity soon started Mr. Barrie on the road of glittering fortune.

And speaking of fortune reminds one of the extremely rudimentary ideas of business that are entertained by an author who automatically coins money.

When his career was just beginning in London and checks from publishers were the rarest of blessings, Mr. Barrie begged a friend who was also a brother Scot, to take charge of his small earn-

on, when the figures on the checks doubled and trebled in active style, the brother Scot began to worry. He declared the responsibility was getting beyond him, and after infinite coaxing

Photo by S. C. Beresford, London

MR. J. M. BARRIE

ings, and give him money only as he needed it. The big Northerner consented and for a year or more was purse-bearer, safe deposit, and paying teller all in one, to his chum. But a little later

he finally persuaded young Barrie to go to a well-known bank, and at least to try and manage his money in the or-thodox way. Knowing the directors, some of whom were present that morning, the friend introduced the author, who, solemn and round-eyed, obeyed orders but said never a word. He paid in a sheaf of fat drafts, was given a pass book, put through all the formulas and was finally asked in genial fashion by the white-haired bank president if he would not like some money. Barrie nodded, and still under instructions and preternaturally silent, he filled out a check, handed it across the counter, shook his head when offered paper money, and received ten golden sovereigns in return. There were handshakings and good wishes exchanged, then finally the outer door swung to, and Barrie, his face a burst of sunshine, clapped his pocket and exclaimed, "Well, old man, I did them that time!"

"Did who? What on earth are you talking about, Jimmie?" enquired the tall Highlander.

"Why, the way I got into them," was the reply. "I shove the man a mean little scrap of paper, the man gives me a jolly handful of gold. I tell. you it 's great! It 's the easiest way of making money that ever I struck. I say give me a bank, a bank first and. last and always."

But this incident took place a long while ago, and since then the author's financial affairs have passed into as competent hands as any in England. When Mr. Barrie married Miss Mary Ansell, the pretty actress in Mr. Toole's Company, he acquired a helpmate indeed. Though Miss Ansell had made a hit as leading lady in her future husband's first play, entitled "Walker, London," she left the boards without one backward glance of regret. And almost immediately did she lift all the burden of material cares from her husband's shoulders. Even those openhanded institutions the banks, with their fairy-like transubstantiation of paper into gold, knew him no more. Though to-day his yearly income from novels and plays has reached really splendid proportions, he has none of the sordid weight of riches to bear. Country places and motor cars are supplied to him as by magic, for he has merely to wish for such blessings and they are his. Which reminds one that

Mrs. Barrie herself is an artist to her finger-tips with manifestations of the gift in more ways than one. Even flowers take on a new beauty under her graceful touch, and was she not the wife of one of the wealthiest of playwrights, could herself earn a tidy fortune as either a house decorator or designer of art gowns. Both upholstery and dressmaking are small passions in a way, when she is not busy investing money or laying out gardens. In fact Mrs. Barrie actually cuts and makes every costume she wears, and some of them are creations of genuine talent. With a natural eye for stuffs, combinations of color, and the grace of line, she always has a vast deal of sewing and millinery work on hand.

But it was when the Barries were looking for a country place that this lady showed a positive genius for bargains. In a big touring car the novelist and his wife scoured the home counties for a suitable spot. The search was long and arduous, and at last, to the shocked surprise of all their friends, Mrs. Barrie decided upon a residence near Farnham in Surrey, the establishment of a retired draper, as dry-goods merchants are called in England. It was a very abomination of desolation. The interior was plushy to the smothering point, a tangle of fish-net draperies, velvet-covered and fringed stair balustrades, flaming wall-papers, and scrollwork over mantels. And if the house was hideous the grounds were certainly a degree uglier. But, possessing the rare gift of imagination, the lady closed with an offer for the place, and while her husband returned to Lancaster Gate and work she set about transforming their new property. And such marvellous results as were finally achieved! Out of a welter of brummagem vulgarity rose Black Lake Cottage of to-day, one of the most perfect little estates in England. But if the house is charming, the garden is a romantic bit of paradise, with its old-fashioned stocks, gillyflowers, love-in-a-mist, and hollyhocks, that are a positive joy throughout the summer. Some declare that this change from a draper's dream to an artist's inspiration is little short of miraculous, and Black Lake Cottage is the envy of visitors from far and near.

Yet notwithstanding the manifold excellences of his country home, it is doubtful whether it can ever rival the attractions of Kensington Gardens that lie just across the road from Mr. Barrie's town house. For it is under the wide-spreading trees of the royal park that he puts in his best playtime. Positively adoring children, Mr. Barrie has collected a few choice spirits of tender years with whom he foregathers in the gardens every fine afternoon. There they played out the story of "The Little White Bird" long before that delightful novel was ever written. Peter Pan, with his Indians, his underground house, his pirates and darling Tinkle Bell, were old friends of the boys and girls who spent hours with their grown-up playfellow under Kensington's venerable oaks. No question of age ever arises, for the charm of this unique coterie is that every one is on a perfect equality, taking his or her turn in spinning yarns, exchanging confi-

dences, inventing games, and playing make-believes. First-night triumphs pale before the pleasures of these park gatherings, and it is doubtful whether any one really knows Mr. Barrie as well as these small friends of his. They undoubtedly supply many an inspiration for the worker, who prizes as highly as Lewis Carroll used to do the companionship of little folk. Unlike many of his craft, Mr. Barrie seems inexpressibly bored when either his novels or his plays are the subject of conversation. Of course when in process of creation the labor in hand engrosses all his thoughts, but a play once staged and set going, he appears to positively loathe it. The single exception to this eccentric attitude is "The Admirable Crichton," to which he actually went a second time and expressed himself as tolerably satisfied with the result. Again and again has he been taken to task for the last act of "Crichton," but he valiantly insists that in no other way could the stupidities of social classifications be so clearly exposed.   E. M. D.

A Concord Note-Book

The Women of Concord—III.   Louisa Alcott and her Circle.

EIGHTH PAPER

By F. B. SANBORN

THE most famous of all the Concord women, in all parts of the earth, has long been Louisa Alcott, daughter of the philosopher Bronson Alcott, and commemorated by him in his volume of "Octogenarian Sonnets," every one of which was composed after he was eighty and printed in his eighty-third year. Remembering her enthusiasm as a hospital nurse in the second year of the Civil War, and that her experiences in the army hospital at Washington, as published by me in 1863, in the Boston *Commonwealth* newspaper, first made her known and dear to her countrymen, he thus, in 1880, addressed her in verse:

TO MY DAUGHTER LOUISA

When I remember with what buoyant heart,
'Midst war's alarms and woes of civil strife,
In youthful eagerness thou didst depart,
At peril of thy safety, peace, and life,
To nurse the wounded soldier, swathe the dead,—
How piercèd soon by Fever's poisoned dart,
And brought unconscious home, with wildered head,
Thou ever since, 'mid languor and dull pain
(To conquer fortune, cherish kindred dear),
Hast with grave studies vexed a sprightly brain,—
In myriad households kindling love and cheer;
Ne'er from thyself by Fame's loud trump beguiled,
Sounding in this and the farther hemisphere:—
I press thee to my heart as Duty's faithful child.

The death of the father in March,

1888, was followed almost at once by that of the daughter; his funeral in Boston, which she was too ill to attend, had but a few days' space between it and hers; and they were deposited in the same Concord tomb, until the tardy coming of spring would permit their burial, side by side, on the summit of the ridge where Emerson, Hawthorne, Ellery Channing, and Thoreau repose not far off. Mrs. Alcott had died in the Thoreau-Alcott house in 1877, the next year after Sophia Thoreau's death in Bangor; and now all the members of these two friendly households have headstones in the same Sleepy Hollow Cemetery.

Mrs. Alcott was a Bostonian, who, in 1872, at the request of some friend, wrote this brief account of her family and education. It should have been used by Louisa in writing her mother's biography, for which, about 1878, Mr. Alcott copied from his wife's letters and diaries material enough for a considerable volume, which Louisa had never quite the spirits to edit.

Mrs. Alcott's Early Years

"I was born October 8, 1800, christened at King's Chapel, Boston, by Rev. Dr. James Freeman, and named for my grandmother, Abigail May. My father was Col. Joseph May, my mother Dorothy Sewall, and I was the youngest of twelve children. Born sickly, and nursed by a sickly woman, I have survived all my family. My schooling was much interrupted by ill-health; but I danced well, and at the dancing-school (1812–14), remember having for partners some boys who afterward became eminent divines.

"I did not love study, but books were always attractive. In 1819 I went to pass a year with Miss Allyn of Duxbury, daughter of Rev. Dr. Allyn, the parish minister, who assisted me in reviewing my studies. With her I studied French, Latin, botany, read history extensively, and made notes of many books, such as Hume, Gibbon, Hallam's 'Middle Ages,' Robertson's 'Charles V.,' etc. In October, 1825, my mother died. In 1827, while at my brother's in Brook-

lyn, Conn., I met Mr. Alcott, whose views on education were very attractive. I was charmed by his modesty, his earnest desire to promote better advantages for the young. Not an educated man himself, he was determined that the large fund of Connecticut for educational purposes should be used for higher ends than was the case at that time.

"The same year, 1827, Dr. Joseph Tuckerman, with Mrs. Minot, Miss Cabot (afterward Mrs. Follen), my sister Mrs. Greele, and others suggested an infant school in Boston. Mr. Alcott was sent for to organize such a school. This brought him to Boston, and I had further opportunities of becoming acquainted with him."

It was not until 1828 that the Boston school was begun, but an active correspondence sprang up between the young lady from Boston and the Connecticut reformer of schools. In a letter of March, 1828, Miss May said:

"You inquire about my reading. I have read Locke, Stewart, Brown,—the latter twice. But my reading for the last few years has been rather desultory. My health has been so variable, and domestic trials have at times so oppressed my mind, that I have been guided by the taste of the moment as to the choice of a book. We are at present reading 'Napoleon' by Scott. Dr. Channing has reviewed it in his masterly style."

A little later in their friendship, which was soon to end in marriage, Mr. Alcott noted, and mentioned in one of his sonnets, written a few years after her death, how wise her reading was,—in that respect like his and Mrs. Ripley's:

My Lady reads with judgment and good taste
Books not too many, but the wisest, best,
Pregnant with sentiment sincere and chaste,
Rightly conceived were they and aptly dressed;
These wells of learning tastes she at the source,—
Johnson's poised periods, Fénelon's deep sense,
Taylor's mellifluous and sage discourse,
Majestic Milton's epic eloquence;
Nor these alone her thoughts do all engage,
But classic authors of the modern time,
And greater masters of the ancient age,
In prose alike and of the lofty rhyme,—
Montaigne and Cowper, Plutarch's gallery,
Blind Homer's Iliad and his Odyssey.

I quote this to show what a background of sound literature was behind Louisa Alcott, when she, with far less solid reading, but trained by two competent scholars, her father and mother, began early her long career of fiction. She drew her subjects oftenest from her own family and ancestors, and was much nourished on the Boston traditions handed down by her mother. One of these characters in the family was that Dorothy Quincy, an aunt of Mrs. Alcott, who was a contemporary of the grandmothers of Emerson and of Thoreau, and whose first husband was John Hancock of the Declaration. In Mrs. Alcott's time she was "Aunt Scott," having married for love, after Governor Hancock's death, Capt. Charles Scott. When the engagement between Miss May and Mr. Alcott was announced, Mrs Scott invited her niece and the betrothed to dine with her one Sunday in October, 1828, and Mr. Alcott thus portrayed her in his journal:

A Boston Dame of the Revolution

" This old lady is known as the former wife of Governor Hancock, and still considers herself invested with the honors of Revolutionary respect. She is fond of society, even at her advanced years; to enjoy it she is constantly admitting persons of her acquaintance to visit her, being too much absorbed in her own madamism to visit others. Such persons she receives to her august presence as she sits in her chair; their happiness appears to consist in attendance at her house, and in the entertainment she there offers,—herself, her table, the wine, her association with Governor Hancock, whom she speaks of by the familiar name of ' My Mr. Hancock,' still retaining her primary idea of possession. She seems to be a lady of very little force of mind, depending upon the idea of her connection with Mr. Hancock as the basis of her fame and greatness. Her manners are very abrupt, though apparently very sincere, and the sincerity and amiableness of her disposition make her interesting even in her foibles. We were the sole guests on this occasion; seated in her chair she received us familiarly, and with courtly pleasantry rallied myself on the honor of this new alliance with her name. The roast beef was placed upon the table; she would carve herself. ' Mr. Hancock's wrist was lame; she learned to carve when living with him, and had not forgotten how,' etc."

Dressed in this great aunt's brocade, or the finery of her grandmother, Miss Alcott was a stately figure on the amateur stage, where I often acted in private theatricals with her and her sisters before the war. In spite of narrow means and the loss of their modest sister Elizabeth, who died soon after they returned to Concord from New Hampshire in the winter of 1857–58, the Alcotts were a cheerful family, with a fine turn for dramatic parts and for lively society. They had first appeared in Concord in the spring of 1840, when Louisa was seven years old, and took up their abode in the Hosmer cottage, at the extreme west end of the village. May Alcott, the youngest child, was there born in July, 1840, and there the English friends of Mr. Alcott, Charles Lane and Henry Wright, spent with the family the winter of 1842–43, before setting forth for Fruitlands, their little community, in May, 1843. They came back to Concord, disillusioned, late in 1844, and resided for a time with Edmund Hosmer, where about that time George William Curtis and his brother Burrill, fresh from Brook Farm, lived a few months. In 1846, Mrs. Alcott, with some family property, bought the house known now as "The Wayside," since Hawthorne bought and renamed it in 1852. The Alcotts had called it Hillside, and had passed pleasant childish years there. Louisa's story-telling gift was developed here, and in the barn her earliest plays were acted by herself and her sisters and schoolmates. In her earlier years at Concord she had been for a short time a pupil of Henry Thoreau, and still earlier of her father's Boston school; her other education came irregularly from her parents, from a temporary governess, and sometimes from town schools: but she always missed the careful education that most of the Concord girls had, either in public or in private schools.

Miss Robie, a cousin of Mrs. Alcott, wrote from the first Alcott cottage, December 6, 1841, as follows. It was when the family were very poor but very generous.

"As it was time for me to expect a headache, I did not dare to go to Concord without carrying tea and coffee and cayenne pepper, and a small piece of cooked meat, in case my wayward stomach should crave it, which last article was a little piece of *à la mode* beef. Thus provided, I arrived at the Alcott cottage just after dark of a Friday evening. I got into the house before they heard me, and found them seated around their bread and water. I had a most cordial welcome from Mrs. Alcott and the children. She said to me: 'O you dear creature! you are the one I should have picked out of all the good people in Boston. How thankful I am to see you!' I had a comfortable cup of tea in a few minutes, for I did not dare to go without." (They then opened a bundle in which were clothes for the children, sent by Mrs. J. S. of Boston.) "Mr. Alcott sat looking on like a philosopher. 'There,' said he, 'I told you that you need not be anxious about clothing for the children; you see it has come as I said.'

"Mrs. Alcott wanted comfort and counsel; for, though cheerful and uncomplaining, things had got pretty low. Mr. Alcott was evidently not well, and she was quite anxious about him, and expressed some fears that the little sympathy and encouragement he received in regard to his views would depress him beyond what he could bear. However, after a good talk and a good crying-spell, her spirits rallied, and all was bright again. She told me of a miserable poor woman in her neighborhood, who had just lost a drunken husband, and was in a poor hovel with four children, and she had been aiding her in their small way to a little meal, and encouraging her to have a good heart and keep out of the workhouse, and had interested other neighbors in her behalf. She said it seemed as if this poor family had been brought to her notice to show her how much better her own situation was, and to give a change to her feelings by looking about and doing what she could to assist her.

"I went with her one day to see the family. In the course of the visit the woman mentioned Mr. Alcott. 'I did not know he had been to see you.'—'Oh, yes, he was here yesterday and the day before and sawed up some wood that had been sent me. I had engaged Mr. Somebody to saw it for me, and did some sewing for his wife to pay for it.' Said Mrs. Alcott, 'Then Mr. A.'s sawing it did not do you much good?' 'Oh, yes; they said they had as lief give me the money for it, so I had it to buy some meal.'

"Whilst I was at Mrs. Alcott's, of course I saw no meat, nor butter, nor cheese; and only coarse brown sugar, bread, potatoes, apples, squash, and simple puddings; of these materials were the staples for food. I was obliged to have tea occasionally, but except that, I lived as they did, for I could not have the heart or the stomach to take out my beef. Mr. Alcott thought his wife did wrong to prepare the tea for me. The Alcotts had just begun to do with two meals a day, that the children might have the pleasure of carrying once a week a basket of something from their humble savings to the poor family. Now the saving must be made for themselves.

"Mr. Alcott said he could not live with debt burdening them in this way; that they must live simpler still. He started up and said he would go into the woods and chop for his neighbors, and in that way get his fuel. He has since entered upon this work. They said they should give up milk. I persuaded them against this, on account of the baby. Mr. A. thought it would not hurt any of them."

The baby at this time was May, afterwards the artist, who was nearly 18 months old, having been born in that cottage in July, 1840. From this cottage, which still stands, though much changed, and in which the Alcotts received their three English friends in the winter of 1842–43, they removed to Fruitlands in May, 1843,—returning to Concord in 1844, and occupying the present "Wayside" house till 1850. While they were temporarily living in Boston again, the Concord estate was sold to Mr. Hawthorne.

In the summer of 1852, having prospered by the success of his "Scarlet Letter" and "House of Seven Gables," Hawthorne came back to Concord and bought the Alcott place, containing some thirty acres of land and the remodelled house on which, and on the grounds, Mr. Alcott had expended much labor and good taste in decoration, tree-planting, and arbor-building. Considering its present pecuniary value, the price paid was ridiculously low. The note in which Mrs. Alcott's cousin, Samuel Sewall, who had the care of her property and of Louisa's in after years, announced the sale to Hawthorne, is before me. He wrote:

"DEAR COUSIN:

"Mr. Hawthorne called on me a few days ago and offered $1500 for the place in Concord. I wrote Mr. Emerson, who called on me yesterday. I find he agrees to the sale. Mr. Brooks, to whom I also wrote, thinks we had better make the sale. I shall conclude the bargain unless I hear from you to the contrary to-day. I have not had time to call to see you, but I presume, from what you have said, that you will assent to the sale. $500 will be invested, by Mr. Emerson's orders, in trust for Mr. Alcott, and $1,000 for you.

"In haste, yours affectionately,
"S. E. SEWALL."

Mrs. Alcott, as just mentioned, was then residing in Boston, where I called on the family for the first time, with the late Mrs. Ednah Cheney, then Miss Littlehale, in the autumn of that year, 1852. I had entered Harvard College in the July preceding, while Hawthorne was settling himself at the newly purchased "Wayside." About the time I was passing the college examinations, Hawthorne was writing this note to a friend:

"CONCORD, July 15th, '52.

"I passed by the Old Manse a few days ago for the first time in nearly

seven years. Notwithstanding the repairs, it looked very much as of yore, except that a large window had been opened in the roof, through which light and cheerfulness probably shine into the duskiest part of the dim garret of my own time. The trees of the avenue — how many leaves had fallen since I last saw them — had an aspect of new greenness which disappointed me."

A little less than three years after this (in March, 1855), I went from college to live in Concord, and made the acquaintance of the Ripley family, then living at the Manse since 1845. Mrs. Ripley, already mentioned, had been its mistress for nearly ten years; her husband, Rev. Samuel Ripley, had died in the late November of 1847, and her three daughters and a small grandson made their home with her. The new window, of which Hawthorne spoke, was put in to give "light and cheerfulness," to the chamber of the youngest daughter, the blooming Sophia, and the whole house had an air of friendliness and welcome. Finding that Mrs. Ripley, who kept up her readings in four or five languages, wished to go on with the Greek authors she had been studying for half a century, I arranged to read Herodotus, the dramatists, Plato, and some of the poets every week for an evening; and in this way we occupied many weeks for the next ten years, whenever I was at home in Concord. We did not translate, unless some passage required explanation or comment, but I read aloud and she followed the text. These authors were then as familiar to her as the common French or German writers, and she often remarked on the beauty or the fun of passages, as she would have done in reading Shakespeare. In her own house she had much company, and every Fast-day, in April, it was her custom to give a dinner to several of her clerical friends: among them, Dr. Hedge, of Brookline, and Dr. Hill, afterwards president of Harvard. I was a frequent guest on these occasions, when the old Mocha coffee was brought out which her father, Capt. Gamaliel Bradford, had brought home from his sea-voyages in the Mediterranean in the late eighteenth century. On Sunday evenings she was often a caller at the Emerson house, and it was my pleasant task to escort her home, unless Ellery Channing or some other friend did so. Her conversation was lively, no less than learned, and her manners the most agreeable. The Civil War, in which she had friends on both sides, and lost a son and other dear friends, saddened her greatly, and she never quite recovered her good spirits afterward. "Sorrow, not hope," she once wrote, "is the color of old age." There was a charm in her letters, as in her conversation, and had she striven for authorship she would have been one of the most pleasing, as well as actually the most learned. Her learning did not stiffen her epistolary style, and her descriptions had all the merit which she ascribed to her favorite authors. For example, writing, in 1856, to her sister-in-law, Mrs. Bradford, concerning a week spent at her father's old house in Duxbury, near Plymouth, with her Bradford cousins, she drew this idyllic picture:

"You will like to hear about my Duxbury visit; we found them well. We rode to the beach one day and walked to the pond another. The music of past days sighs through the pines. There was my Arcadia. How my heart used to beat with joy when I caught the first glimpse of the old church spire, as it appeared and reappeared through the woods, when I used to be at father's side in the chaise which went semi-annually or quarterly to carry grandfather (old Colonel Bradford) his dividends. The old house with its high stone steps, the barrels on each side filled with morning-glories and nasturtiums, which, entwined, hung over the old door in festoons; the little parlor and old easy chair in which we always found the palsied old man, who received us with tearful embraces; the great pear-tree at the gate, full of orange pears; the ground strewed with golden high-tops, the girl in the corn-barn paring apples to dry; the woods full of huckleberries,— how sadly they blend to connect the past with the present, and contrast with the future. Why is it that we so hold on to the garment that is failing from us, and look behind as we go onward?"

At the death of Thoreau, she wrote in May, 1862: "This fine morning is sad for those of us who sympathize with the friends of Henry Thoreau, the philosopher and the woodman. He had his reason to the last, and talked with his friends pleasantly and arranged his affairs; and at last passed in quiet sleep from this state of duty and responsibility to that which is behind the veil. His funeral service is to be at the church, and Mr. Emerson is to make an address."

At Mrs. Ripley's own death in 1867, her friends, Emerson, Col. Henry Lee, and others, paid their tributes to her memory. Emerson wrote: "She was absolutely without pedantry. She had no ambition to write her name on any book, or plant, or opinion. Her delight in books was not tainted by any wish to shine or any appetite for praise or influence. She seldom and unwillingly used a pen, and only for necessity or affection. She was without appetite for luxury, or display, or influence,— with entire indifference to trifles." Yet this neglect of writing did not prevent her, as the quotations I have made will show, from having a most perfect and natural style, of that elegance which only comes from a nature singularly high and pure. Col. Lee, who had been her pupil, as so many of the students of Harvard College had been, added his generous word:

"There were probably books she had not read, languages and sciences she had not learned,— but she seemed to have explored every region and to have intuitive ideas on every subject of interest. Over all these gifts and acquirements was thrown a veil of modesty so close that only by an impulse of sympathy or enthusiasm was it ever withdrawn. With a simplicity equally amusing and touching, she impressed you so little with her own wonderful powers, and referred so much to your sayings and doings, that you really went away, wondering at your own brilliancy, and doubting how much you had given, how much received. The eloquent lips are silent; the flashing eye is dull; the blush of modesty has faded from the cheek; the cordial smile will never again on this earth welcome the friends, old or young, humble or famous, neighbors or strangers, who sought this inspired presence."

Alluding to the slight touches of melancholy which the anxieties of the Civil War, in which she lost kindred and beloved friends arrayed against each other in battle and siege, my own notice of her closed with these words, which Miss Hoar cited in her too brief biography: "At length there came a time, after many shocks to her health and affections given by bereaving age, when even the unselfish pleasures were denied to this sweetest of human souls. He who drops or withdraws the veil at the gates of mortal life was pleased to make her removal hence after the joys of earth had ceased to touch her with delight, and when the spectacle of her affliction reconciled those about her to the interposition of death. She has carried with her beyond these shores of anguish and doubt, the love of a thousand friends, and the enduring record of well-spent days." On her tombstone are engraved the familiar words of Tacitus commemorating Agricola, which she so often quoted:

"Placide quiescas, . . . nosque te admiratione, et, si natura suppeditet, similitudine decoremus."

I have already mentioned, in my first chapter, Miss Mary Emerson, the half-sister of Mrs. Ripley's husband, Rev. Samuel Ripley. At this period (1855-60), this eccentric lady used to revisit Concord every year, and had formed a friendly intimacy with Henry Thoreau, whose father, mother, and aunts she had long known. In the summer of 1856, then eighty-two years old, she was visiting her nephew, Waldo Emerson, and saw Henry frequently. Before departing for the rural solitude of Goshen, she wrote several notes to the Thoreau family, among them, this to Henry:

"Saturday Noon, July 12, 1856.

"Will my young friend visit me tomorrow early as he can? This evening my Sister Ripley sends word she will come, and go to see Mrs. William Em-

erson, who is in town. I wish for your writings, hoping they will give me a clearer clue to your faith,—its nature, its destination and object. While excited by your original wit and thoughts, I lose sight, perhaps, of the motive and end and infinite responsibility of talent, in any of its endless consequences. To enter the interior of a peculiar organization of mind is desirable to all who think and read in intermitted solitude. They believe, when the novelty of genius opens on their unpractised eye, that the spirit itself must own and feel its natural relations to their God of revelation, where alone every talent can be perfected and bring its additions to the owner; that faith in the discipline towards moral excellence can alone insure an immortal fame,—or even success and happiness here. God bless you, and thus make you useful to your Country and kind, prays "M. E."

No doubt Thoreau complied with this request, and paid his friend a Sunday visit, before she went to the parish church, where her father had so eloquently preached before the Revolution. At the end of the same week, before setting out for western Massachusetts, she thus wrote to Mrs. Thoreau:

"It is a pleasure I have depended on for weeks, to visit you, and was sure last eve, when I returned from the Manse, that I should spend part of this day at your house. But this weather is extremely trying when visiting; and I conclude I must forego the gratification of seeing your son's library, and daughter's drawings, and leaving my good wishes with Mr. Thoreau and family, personally. But they will exist without voice,—that you may all be prepared to meet your friends, and the good of all nations and denominations, in a world delivered from the alternations of woes caused by the passions of undisciplined men and rulers. Affectionately adieu, "M. EMERSON."

"Thursday Eve., July 17, 1856."

The "undisciplined rulers" here glanced at were President Pierce, the friend of Hawthorne, Jefferson Davis, his Secretary of War, and the Federal authorities in Kansas Territory, who were doing what they could that summer to maintain negro slavery as an institution on that virgin soil. The Emersons and Thoreaus were counteracting this effort as best they could, and John Brown, who next year visited them in Concord, was ranging the prairies with his armed band to protect the harassed pioneers of Kansas.

Along with the polite note to the lady whose unsuitable ribbons she had so sharply censured, went this more affectionate epistle to Henry Thoreau:

"DEAR HENRY:

"I expect to set out to-morrow morning for Goshen,—a place where wit and gaiety never come 'that comes to all.' But hope lives, and travels on with the speed of suns and stars; and when there are none but clouds in the sky,

'Its very nakedness has power
To aid the hour,'

says old Sir Walter. However, the 'old Bobbin Woman was steady to her Bible,' where each page unfolded words of comfort and assurance. Yet the memory of intelligence and extensive mentality will never fail to give a vivid pleasure to reflection,—if shaded by the faith of future uncertainties,—'t is well to admit the decrees of unerring rectitude. If you write to M. E. it will brighten the solitude so desired. Had I been detained by nothing but weather! but I must pack up by daylight.

"MARY EMERSON."

The anxiety she felt for the future salvation of her friend mingled anxiously with her delight in his originality and wit,—his "extensive mentality" as she quaintly styled his comprehensive genius.

I have heard it said that Miss Emerson at one time looked on Miss Elizabeth Peabody, eldest sister of Mrs. Hawthorne, as a suitable wife for her nephew Waldo. But Miss Peabody, like Mary Emerson herself, was hardly qualified for the matrimonial state, with all her talent and amiability. She became a resident of Concord for some years after 1856,—sometimes with Mrs. Hawthorne, sometimes with another

sister, Mrs. Horace Mann, or with her brother, Dr. Nathaniel Peabody. She had been a frequent visitor there before and was a member of the inner circle of the Transcendentalists. During the Concord School of Philosophy (1879–1888), she was constantly in attendance, reading lectures and almost daily taking part in the discussions. She brought to these high debates a great wealth of thought, and the treasures of a memory not always exact, but ever entertaining and suggestive. One of the best of Mr. Alcott's sonnets portrays Miss Peabody so well that I quote it.

Daughter of Memory! who her watch doth keep
O'er dark Oblivion's land of shade and dream,
Peers down into the realm of ancient Sleep,
Where Thought uprises with a sudden gleam
And lights the devious path 'twixt Be and Seem;
Mythologist! that dost thy legend steep
Plenteously with opiate and anodyne,
Inweaving fact with fable, line with line,
Entangling anecdote and episode,
Mindful of all that all men meant or said,—
We follow pleased thy labyrinthine road,
By Ariadne's skein and lesson led:
For thou hast wrought so excellently well,
Thou drop'st more casual truth than sages tell.

Like Mr. Alcott's, her life-work was originally education,—now in this form, now in that, but always with the noblest ideal of what education is. She had derived this ideal from the spiritual surroundings of her youth, which fell in Boston at that fortunate period when Channing, Alcott, the Emersons, Dr. Howe, Horace Mann, the Everetts, Eliots, Quincys, Charles Sumner, and so many more, citizens or public teachers, were all in their own way seeking to promote a broader, more profound culture. She joined with enthusiasm in Alcott's school at the Masonic Temple, and wrote its first record for publication. That school failed, but it pointed the way to nearly all the improvement since made in the discipline of young children. Even the Kindergarten, which Miss Peabody did much to introduce in America, is little more than a systematic rendering of Alcott's principles in the Temple School. And Miss Alcott in her years of trial, before she found her place in literature, was a "kindergartner" in one of Miss Peabody's Boston ventures.

Years before, Miss Peabody had been the publisher of the *Dial*, as well as a valued contributor; and in 1843 while Thoreau was editing that quarterly, during a winter's absence of Emerson from Concord on a lecturing tour (for which see the "Familiar Letters" of Thoreau), she wrote him this letter, never before printed.

"Boston, Feb. 26, 1843.

"My Dear Sir:

"I understand you have begun to print the *Dial*, and I am very glad of it on one account, viz., that if it gets out early enough to go to England by the steamer of the first of the month (April) it does not have to wait another month, as was the case with the last number. But I meant to have had as a first article a letter to the 'Friends of the *Dial*,' somewhat like the rough draft I enclose, and was waiting Mr. Emerson's arrival to consult him about the name of it. I have now written to him at New York on the subject and told him my whys and wherefores. The regular income of the *Dial* does not pay the cost of its printing and paper; there are readers enough to support it if they would only subscribe; and they will subscribe if they are convinced that only by doing so can they secure its continuance. He will probably write you on the subject.

"I want to ask a favor of you. It is to forward me a small phial of that black-lead dust which is to be found, as Dr. C. T. Jackson tells me, at a certain lead-pencil manufactory in Concord; and to send it to me by the first opportunity. I want lead in this fine dust to use in a chemical experiment.

"Respectfully yours,
"E. P. Peabody.

"P. S. I hope you have got your money from Bradbury & Soden. I have done all I could about it. Will you drop the enclosed letter for Mrs. Hawthorne into the post-office?

"*Mr. Henry D. Thoreau, Concord.*"

Mrs. Hawthorne was passing her first winter at the Old Manse, and watching her husband skate with Emerson on the winding river near by. The "certain lead-pencil manufactory" was that of John Thoreau & Sons in Concord and Acton, where Henry made thousands of good pencils after 1850 to pay for the printing of his first book, the "Week."

Like her sister Mrs. Mann, Miss Peabody was a true lover of the poor, and seldom have I known persons to whom, as by an instinct, there gravitated whatever was defeated or unfortunate, more certainly than to these sisters. Their neighbors, of whom I was one for several years, had to defend them against the consequences of their own generosity to the afflicted. The same might be said of Mrs. Alcott, who contracted the fever which, when transmitted to her daughter Beth, caused that child's death by a lingering illness, by attendance on the fever of a poor, neglected woman at Walpole, N. H., where the Alcotts were living in 1856–57.

Louisa Alcott, when I first knew her in 1852, was a serious, bashful girl, sensitive and industrious, who had not then found her vocation, and suffered from the mortifications that poverty brings to girls of high spirit. Traces of a certain acerbity due to this cause, and heightened by her ill health in later years, remained with her through life. It sometimes dashed the enjoyment of the deserved good-fortune that finally came to her, and was so dutifully and generously shared with others. But the warm fancy that shines in all her books kept her usually cheerful, and often gay; so that the rather sad impression given by Mrs. Cheney's biography is not quite just to her life as a whole. Her literary success was long in arriving, but was very complete at last, and promises to be permanent. It began with her recognition by a keen-eyed publisher, Thomas Niles (of Roberts Brothers), who saw in the MS. of "Little Women" the promise of a good writer, and so published it under favorable conditions in 1868. From that time forward she was a popular author, and has been far more widely read than any other of the Concord writers, though, of course, not ranking with most of them in genius.

Long before I knew Louisa Alcott she had begun her career as a story-teller,—orally at first,—but she was a lively (if not very correct) writer in 1845, at the age of twelve. In 1851, when her first story was printed in W. W. Clapp's *Saturday Evening Gazette* of Boston, she had twice come and gone as a Concord resident, following the migrations of her family; but was then a Bostonian. She wrote rapidly then, at nineteen, and, as she said, easily turned off a dozen a month. Those accepted for the *Gazette* were printed and paid for by Mr. Clapp, under the impression they were written by a man; when it appeared a girl had sent them, it was proposed to reduce the price. But, as she said long afterward: "The girl had learned the worth of her wares, and would not write for less, and so continued to earn her fair wages, in spite of sex." Very few of these tales have been reprinted, or deserve preservation. It was only when she began to relate her own experiences, or those of her family and dear friends, that she interested the wider public which has continued to read her, one generation after another.

Concord, although a place very dear to her father, and attractive to her by the presence of Emerson and Thoreau, whom she greatly admired from girlhood, was never otherwise a pleasant home to her. It had been associated with the mortifications that poverty and the unpopularity of her father and his friends brought to a sensitive girl; and though she afterwards received and gave much happiness by her joyous relations with the boys and girls who lived near her, or were pupils of my Concord school, she still came to view the town with little satisfaction. She had small talent for general society, and could not well accommodate herself to customs and formalities which she could throw off in the company of her juniors. One of these, then my pupil, but now a distinguished author and art critic, F. P. Stearns, of Medford, in one of his "Concord Sketches," gives this literal account of her evenings in the society of the young:

"At the Orchard House the Alcotts received their friends on Monday evenings; and some favored youths would go there to play whist, make poker sketches, and talk with the ladies. Louisa usually sat by the fire-place, knitting rapidly, with an open book in her lap; if required to make up a whist-table, she would come forward with a quiet look of resignation, and some such remark as 'You know I am not a Sarah Battles.' After a while her love of fun would break forth, and her bright flashes of wit would play about the heads of all in the room. It was in such ways that Louisa acquired that stock of information about young people and their affairs which she made such good use of afterwards. Her characters act unconsciously before us, as if we looked at them through a window."

To this picture of Miss Alcott in the family circle at Concord may be added another of ten years later (October 1, 1873), drawn by her own humorous pen. Mrs. Lucy Stone, head of the Woman Suffrage Society of Massachusetts, of which the Alcotts were members, as they had been of the earlier Anti-Slavery Societies, had written to Miss Alcott for some service to be rendered in that cause. She replied as follows:

"I am so busy proving ' woman's right to labor' that I have no time to help prove ' woman's right to vote.' When I read your note to the family, asking, 'What shall I say to Mrs. Stone?' a voice from the Transcendental mist which usually surrounds my honored father instantly replied: ' Tell her you are ready to follow her as leader, sure that you could not have a better one.' My brave old mother, with the ardor of many unquenchable Mays shining in her face, cried out: ' Tell her I am seventy-three, but I mean to go to the polls before I die,—even if my three daughters have to carry me.' And two Little Men, already mustered in, added the cheering words: ' Go ahead, Aunt Weedy, we will let you vote as much as ever you like.' Such being the temper of the small convention of which I am now President, I cannot hesitate to say that, though I may not be with you in body, I shall be in spirit, and am as ever,

" Hopefully and heartily yours,
" LOUISA MAY ALCOTT."

Four years later Mrs. Alcott died without having had the opportunity to vote; and the family then left the Orchard House, to reside in the Thoreau-Alcott house, nearer the railroad station, wherein I had preceded them as a four-years' tenant of Sophia Thoreau. Louisa bought the house for her sister, Mrs. Pratt, mother of the "Little Men," one of whom now occupies it with his four children. May Alcott died two years after her mother, and is buried in France, near Paris, where she died, leaving her only child, a girl named for Louisa, whose Swiss father took her to his own home in Zurich, after Miss Alcott's death in 1888. Mrs. Pratt died a few years later, at Concord, and is buried beside her husband in the cemetery there, not far from the graves of her father, mother, and sisters, and near the graves of Thoreau, Channing, Hawthorne, and Emerson.

Another of the women of Concord, of whom the world has heard, but knows too little, was Miss Elizabeth Hoar, sister of the Senator and the Judge, an accomplished scholar, and at home in any society, but early thrown into retirement by the death of her brilliant lover, Charles Emerson (the youngest of the brothers of Emerson), just before they were to have married and taken up their home in the Emerson house. She became thus a sister of the poet-philosopher, and was consulted by him in his literary tasks more than any person perhaps. "Elizabeth the Wise," he once styled her; but her wisdom was of the tenderly feminine kind, more of a Muse than a Minerva. An atmosphere of reserve enveloped her, perhaps against her will,—for she often seemed striving to emerge from it. Her life at home with her formal father and active-minded and strong-willed mother, to whom she was devoted, did not give her that scope and felicity in friendship which her nature demanded; something tantalizing and hesitating breathed out from the self-effacing life which she usually led. A younger friend, of genius half-spoiled by caprice, celebrated her in verse, and entertained her by his sallies of sentiment and humor, but could not place himself in clear relations with a nature so unlike his own. He once wrote to her:

"I cannot, for the life of me, tell why I am attracted to you. It is not because you value my talent,—that I know. When you write me notes and tell me I am a genius, I cannot endure you. Your beauty, your talent, your cultivation do not weigh with me a pin's fee. I do not ask your heart; that, I know, is buried. I do not ask your preference, I know who has that,—it is Emerson. It is not friendship; yours is for Emerson; it is not acquaintance; whose acquaintance, pray, do I want? There is no doubt you are the second person to me in the world. I do not reckon you as a friend or a sister. I pity you a little, I think; but that would repel me; I admire you very much; you are yet too much absorbed for romance. I admire your treatment of society, and your eternal reserve; yet, for none of these things are you the second person to me on the earth. You are almost nothing to me, socially. If you were in prison I should see nearly as much of you. The little people you draw around you, and benefit, are your chains,— and your own intolerable humility. I say you are the best person, by far, we have; the finest American woman I have seen, by far. A. W. is coarse and foolish by your side; Margaret Fuller is heavy and tiresome . . . You draw me to you because you never answer my letters; because when Emerson writes (for instance) you never send me his letters, though I send mine at once to you; because you send me no books or poems, while I send you every book, every poem; all I have, all I think, all I know, — send, write, tell it; and you? You hear me and say nothing; you take what I send and say nothing; but I am drawn to you by this. I can tell you anything,—your discretion is so great, your reserve is so strong."

To this, as in a soliloquy, the Muse addressed replied,—but apparently never sent the answer: "Because I cannot; I have nothing that you want. Because you do not care for such letters as Emerson writes to me, and you always say you don't want them, whereas I do want to read yours. Books and poems? I never have any. I would send you plain sewing. You are only too good for my deserts, but not for my gratitude. But I am the most helpless of mortals."

Such as she was thus described by herself and her uneasy friend, Miss Hoar lived for many years her life of noble talents and humble service. At an emergency she was invaluable; many relied on her friendly services, her unfailing sympathy, not always finding its full expression in her words. She was in the small circles of Concord for half a century the type of Goethe's "Ewig Weibliche," such as there are few in the world in any age. With a fine talent for writing, Miss Hoar published nothing except her Memoir of Mrs. Ripley, which might well have been doubled in its chapters. She accompanied her venerable father to South Carolina, when he went thither on an errand of justice and mercy, and when the haughty slaveholders refused to grant either to the oppressed for whom he pleaded, and expelled him from the State. She lived to see this pride humbled, and the institution of slavery destroyed that had been so intolerant; and she had nothing but compassion for the sufferings of those who had oppressed the poor.

Of Mrs. Hawthorne, who left Concord a few years after her husband's death in 1864, and of her daughter Una much might be said. Col. Higginson has done justice to Una Hawthorne in a recent volume. Of Mrs. Hawthorne, Mr. Stearns, above quoted, says in an unpublished sketch: "She belonged to the class of womankind typified by Shakespeare in Ophelia: a tender-hearted, affectionate nature, too sensitive for the rough storms of life, and too innocent to recognize the guile in others. It was united, as often happens, with a fine artistic nature and superior intelligence. Her face and manners both gave the impression of a wide and elevated culture. Although she lived by the wayside, she had been accustomed to enter palaces. No one knew better than she the heroism which each day requires." Both she and her daughter are buried in England.

The art of drawing and painting, in which Mrs. Hawthorne before her marriage began to take lessons and to practise, never reached very far,—any more than it did in the case of her friend Ellery Channing, who, with the strongest artistic temperament, could never subject himself to the discipline which the hand of the artist needs. May Alcott, with the same natural aversion to discipline, did in fact subject herself thereto, by her force of will. Though long in acquiring the trained hand and eye of the accomplished painter, she succeeded at last; first as a copyist of Turner's water-colors, which she reproduced better (as Ruskin thought) than anyone,—and then as a painter in oils. She married and died just as success in her art began to smile upon her. She wrote well, in a lively and instructive manner, but published little. She had the talent for society, and the taste for it which her sisters lacked, but which her father, in spite of his early asceticism, constantly manifested, and for which his graceful and high-bred manners so remarkably qualified him. I can never forget the admiration of Alcott's bearing in society which Thomas Cholmondeley, the English nephew of Bishop Heber, and Scott's friend, Richard Heber, vividly manifested when meeting him for the first time at a Boston dinner. As I walked with Cholmondeley from this dinner to a Boston book-store, where he wished to buy some of the Concord books, he said to me in his high falsetto voice: "What distinguished manners your friend has! He has the manners of a *very great Peer*," (with that touch of awe in his tone which few Englishmen unlearn when speaking of princes and dukes, and especially of the duchesses of their three kingdoms). It must be said that none of Alcott's descendants inherited this manner; it had come to him by long descent from distant ancestors, and had been heightened by association with the plantation lords of Virginia in his youth,—the class which then, in its best examples, had the finest American courtesy, as seen in that Colonel Dabney of Virginia, whose life was coeval with Alcott's and has been well related by his daughter. The opinions of these gentlemen were one thing, their manners quite another.

Other Concord women might be included in these chapters,—Mrs. Jane Goodwin Austin, and her mother, for instance, both excellent writers, and the daughter, (a cousin of Professor Goodwin) a successful novelist and good friend of the Alcotts; Mrs. Brooks, the leader for thirty years of the Anti-Slavery Society of Concord women, upon whose suggestion Emerson wrote his appeal to President Van Buren in 1837, in behalf of the Cherokees, and gave in 1844 his eloquent appeal for emancipation of the American slaves; and Miss Prudence Ward, an inmate of the Thoreau household for years, and the aunt of Ellen Sewall, with whom both John and Henry Thoreau were deeply in love. But these reminiscences and inedited papers have already been extended too far.

Oriental Definitions

Avatar

By MARGUERITE MERINGTON

Speak your goat and camel kindly,
Nor with hand impar
Chastise stubborn mule behindly,
In your barnyard char.
Count each goose ye throttle blindly
Some ancestral lar!

Look on these defenceless creatures
Harnessed to your car ;
Read your kinship in their features,
And e'en as they are
Banned or blessed by your entreatures
Be your avatar!

AVATAR

Biography, Autobiography, and Letters

By JEANNETTE L. GILDER

A Grand Old Man of Science, a Grand Old Man of Politics, and a Poet

I

IN the past year which has been prolific of biographies and autobiographies there has been nothing more important or more entertaining than the autobiography of Dr. Alfred Russel Wallace.* Dr. Wallace was, if I may use a racing expression, the running mate of Darwin. He is the author of "Man's Place in the Universe," "Darwinism," and other scientific books. There was much competition among American publishers—I dare say the same in England—for Dr. Wallace's autobiography, and now that I have it before me I cannot wonder. In a short preface he tells us that these two volumes would not have been written had not the representatives of his English and American publishers assured him that they would probably interest a large number of readers. These representatives were wise men, though it would not take much wisdom, judging from what Dr. Wallace has already written, to predict that his autobiography would be a mine of interest.

Dr. Wallace had promised his son and daughter that he would write some account of his early life for their information, but as he had never kept a diary, except when abroad, nor preserved any of the earlier letters of his friends, he thought that he had no materials for any full record of his life and experiences. But when he set to work in earnest to get together whatever scattered memoranda he could find, the numerous letters he possessed from men of eminence, dating from his return home in 1862, together with a few of his own returned to him by some of his correspondents, he discovered that he had a pretty fair amount of material. Dr. Wallace, having been assured that a true record of his life, especially if sufficiently full to illus-

trate development of character so far as that is due to environment, would be extremely interesting, has kept this point in mind. He confesses that he found it difficult to write such a record, extending to the memories of nearly eighty years, without subjecting himself to the charge of diffuseness or egotism; but he will find those charges made by no one but himself.

Dr. Wallace was the son of "poor but honest parents," and at a very early age he was obliged to work for a living. He began as a surveyor's apprentice, which gave him plenty of out-of-door exercise. Indoors he devoted his time when not at work to reading, and mostly the reading of scientific books. He attended lectures and lost no means to improve his mind. He always had an idea of being a writer, and he gives us in the first volume of this autobiography his maiden literary effort, which was a description of the South Wales farmer, and an interesting description it is too.

In a chapter devoted to his character at twenty-one, Dr. Wallace tells us the characteristics he had and those that he lacked. If he had one distinct mental faculty more prominent than another, it was the power of correct reasoning from a review of the known facts in any case to the causes or laws which produced them, and also in detecting fallacies in the reasoning of other persons. This power naturally greatly helped him in all his writings, especially those on natural history and sociology. The determination of the direction in which he should use these powers was due to his possession in a high degree of the two mental qualities usually termed emotional or moral, an intense appreciation of the beauty, harmony, and variety in nature and in all natural phenomena, and an equally strong passion for justice as between man and man—an abhorrence of all tyr-

* "My Life. A Record of Events and Opinions." By Alfred Russel Wallace. 2 vols. Dodd, Mead & Co. $6.00.

352

anny, all compulsion, all unnecessary interference with the liberty of others.

Among the marked deficiencies in his mental equipment were his inability to perceive the niceties of melody and harmony in music, though he had a fair appreciation of time, expression, and general effect, and was always deeply affected by grand, pathetic, or religious music; and "in the power of rapidly seeing analogies or hidden resemblances and incongruities." The rhythm and pathos, as well as the inimitable puns of Hood, were the delight of his youth, "as are the more recondite and fantastic humor of Mark Twain and Lewis Carroll in my old age." He confesses also to a want of assertiveness and of physical courage, which, "combined with delicacy of the nervous system and of bodily constitution, and a general disinclination to much exertion, physical or mental, have caused that shyness, reticence, and love of solitude, which, though often misunderstood and leading to unpleasant results, have, perhaps, on the whole, been beneficial to me."

The first volume of these memoirs is not as interesting as the second. Dr. Wallace was finding himself through these pages. When we get to the second volume the interest is more general. We meet his distinguished contemporaries — Darwin, Huxley, Spencer, and the rest. Soon after his return to England, in 1862, after his voyage down the Amazon, Darwin invited him to come to Down for a night, and there he had the pleasure of seeing the famous scientist in his own home and in the midst of his family. A year later, writing to Dr. Wallace, Darwin says:

I am glad you like the little orchid book; but it has not been worth the ten months it has cost me; it was a hobby horse, and so beguiled me.

How puzzled you must be to know what to begin at! You will do grand work, I do not doubt. My health is, and always will be, very poor; I am that miserable animal, a regular valetudinarian.

The chief differences of opinion between Darwin and Wallace are on the subject of the theory of natural selec-

tion; but on other points they were pretty thoroughly agreed.

Writing of Spencer Dr. Wallace says:

Among his intimate friends Herbert Spencer was always interesting from the often unexpected way in which he would apply the principles of evolution to the commonest topics of conversation, and he was always ready to take part in any social amusement. He once or twice honored me by coming to informal meetings of friends at my little house in St. Mark's Crescent, and I also met him at Sir John Lubbock's very pleasant week-end visits, and also at Huxley's in St. John's Wood. Once I remember dining informally with Huxley, the only other guests being Tyndall and Herbert Spencer. The latter appeared in a dress-coat, whereupon Huxley and Tyndall chaffed him, as setting a bad example, and of being untrue to his principles, quoting his essay on "Manners and Fashion," but all with the most good-humored banter. Spencer took it in good part, and defended himself well, declaring that the coat was a relic of his early unregenerate days, and where could he wear it out if not at the houses of his best friends? "Besides," he concluded, "you will please to observe that I am true to principle in that I do not wear a white tie!"

Of all the scientific men of his day Wallace was most intimate with Huxley, and yet he does not tell us as much of Huxley as we would like to know. Perhaps he was afraid of being too personal on account of his very intimate friendship.

In the autumn and winter of 1886 Dr. Wallace came to America to deliver lectures at the Lowell Institute of Boston, and while in this country he travelled around with his eyes open. On reaching New York he had his first experience with American prices, and was very much impressed with the fact that he had to pay two dollars for a cab to a hotel a mile off where he spent the night. He drove out to Central Park in company with the late Henry George, who was then candidate for Mayor, and with Mr. George he attended a meeting at which he was called upon to say a few words to an American audience:

"I tried my best to be forcible, praised George, and said a few words about what we were doing in England, but I could see that I did not impress them much."

Dr. Wallace not only lectured in Boston but he travelled through the country from New England to San Francisco, seeing much and being greatly impressed. The climate of America apparently agreed with him, and he seemed to like the food, for he said he had never had a better appetite and never felt better.

II

One of the most important books of the past six months, as well as the most interesting, is the life of Lord Granville, by Lord Edmond Fitzmaurice.* The book has an interest outside of politics, for Lord Granville was in close touch with all the distinguished men and wo-' men of his day, the late Queen Victoria included among the latter. He began his political career before Victoria ascended the throne and ended it only ten years before her death. Lord Granville was born in the Waterloo year. He spent his early boyhood at The Hague and in Paris, and passed through Eton and Christ Church successfully if not with distinction. The number of his pet names attests to his popularity:

"At Eton Granville Leveson-Gower was 'Alcibiades,' at Oxford he was 'Crichton'; among his London friends he was 'Pussy,' a title he never lost; in his own family he was 'Gink,' a term the origin of which is wrapped in mystery."

Much of Lord Granville's early life was spent in Paris at his father's embassy, and there he learned to speak the language with a fluency and an accent not often acquired by Englishmen.

There are a number of letters here printed that were written in confidence at the time; one of them by Granville to the Duke of Argyll in May, 1855:

The siege of Sebastopol has hitherto been a failure. We have generals whom we do not trust, and whom we do not know how to replace. We have an Ambassador at Constantinople, an able man, a

* "The Life of Granville George Leveson-Gower, Second Earl of Granville, K.G., 1815-91." By Lord Edmond Fitzmaurice. 2 vols. Longmans. $10.

cat whom no one cares to bell, whom some think a principal cause of the war, others the cause of some of the calamities which have attended the conduct of the war, and whom we know to have thwarted or neglected many of the objects of his Government. The French generals seem worse than others; the troops before Sebastopol inferior to ours, if not to the Russians. . . . A friend of the Duke of Wellington quoted here the strong opinion which he had heard more than once expressed by the Duke, that Russia was weak abroad, but utterly unassailable at home. . . . If we make peace, we may probably be hooted from our places; but if we continue war, much of the weight will be thrown in the opposite scale.

At the time of the Indian Mutiny, Granville conducted the correspondence, which is printed at length in this book, with his friend Lord Canning, who was Viceroy of India at the time. Granville, with the permission of the Queen, let his friend into the secrets of the Cabinet. From him we learn that as early as 1857 the Prince Consort had suggested that the Queen should have an Indian title—"any title, such as the Great Mogul, which would connect itself with the ancient history of the country." It was left to Disraeli twenty years later to carry out this idea and proclaim Victoria Queen and Empress.

There are a number of letters from the Queen printed in this book as to England's policy regarding Schleswig Holstein, in which she opposed Palmerston and Russell and carried out her own ideas. When Lord Ellenborough attacked the Queen in the House of Lords for her efforts to preserve peace between England, Austria, and Prussia, she was very indignant, and not unnaturally, and wrote to Lord Granville, through her secretary, complaining of "such base and malignant attacks being insinuated against her by Lord Ellenborough," and expressed the wish that "somehow or other Lord Ellenborough may hear what she thinks of him." She also tells Lord Granville that she "has almost quarrelled with the Crown Princess [her daughter] by deprecating the violent counsels Prussia seemed disposed to pursue, and by pointing out the strong feeling against her that had been created in England." Another letter is more personal. It is not written by her own hand but through her secretary:

"Oh, how fearful it is to be suspected —uncheered, unguided, and unadvised —and how alone the poor Queen feels! Her friends must defend her."

And again:

The Queen is completely exhausted by the anxiety and suspense, and misses her beloved husband's help, advice, support, and love in an overwhelming manner. . . . A few days more of this hard work and terrible unsupported and unshared anxiety will quite prostrate her strength. Her Ministers should know how heavy her responsibility is, and should lighten it by pursuing a prudent course, and one which she feels is for the country's interests—as much as any human aid can!

It was Lord Granville who introduced John Bright to the Queen. This was at Osborne in 1868, and he describes in an amusing letter to Gladstone how Bright behaved:

I called for him at dinner-time—his dress was irreproachable after he had readily agreed to take off a pair of bridal white gloves. He was rather pleased, quoted his tailor's approval of tights, and acknowledged he had promised to rehearse his costume before his wife and daughter.

The beginning of dinner was awful—the Queen with a sick headache and shy, Princess Louise whispering unintelligently in my ear. . . . Bright like a war-horse champing his bit, and dying to be at them. At last an allusion to children enabled me to tell Bright to repeat to Her Majesty his brother's observation — "where, considering what charming things children were, all the queer old men came from." This amused the Queen, and all went on merrily. She talked to him for a long time, and the old *roué* evidently touched some feminine chord, for she was much pleased with him, and saw him again next morning.

Lord Granville's descriptions of his contemporaries are unusually vivid. Here is one of Disraeli in 1876:

I had never met Dizzy in a country house before last week [he wrote to Lord Hartington]. He was exceedingly civil to Lady G— and me. He discoursed to Lansdowne and me, conceiving us to be as great aristocrats as —, on the origin of noble English families. He was occasionally clever and amusing, but I do not think him a really good member of society. He seems to lack ease. Whether owing to love for Lady —, or to the complications of the Eastern question, he was very absent. Upon Lady —— blowing him up violently for trumping her best card, he pleaded that during the third rubber he always began to think of the East. Bunny judiciously asked him if he minded Gladstone's attacks. He said: "No, I like it; it is a proof of his angry and bitter envy." He told me that the small number of a Cabinet was invaluable—that it made Ministers so united and so anxious to do their fair share of work.

After the fall of Khartoum Granville wrote to Gladstone:

I have felt great and deep regret, but no remorse, at being one principally responsible for sending out Gordon. Wolseley proposed it to Hartington; Hartington proposed it to me. We agreed that he should collect what Cabinet Ministers he could find in London to meet the next day. I wrote a short account of what was likely to be proposed, and you telegraphed your sanction. The next day I said to Hartington: "We were proud of ourselves yesterday. Are you sure we did not commit a gigantic folly?" He mentioned this to me later as diminishing my responsibility, which, of course, it did not do in the least, and I still think it would have been indefensible to have refused Gordon's offer. His subsequent conduct made it most difficult how to act. I regret that I did not press more strongly my proposal to the Cabinet to recall him at once when he changed his policy.

I am not surprised that the London reviewers describe this book as the most important political biography that has appeared since Morley's "Gladstone." It is not, I may add, too political for the reading of any American who loves to read of the history of his own time in England written so absolutely from the inside as is this.

III

One of the many poets who has sung unheard while he lived except by a choice few is the late Sidney Lanier. The most notable appreciation that Mr. Lanier had during his lifetime was from the famous actress, Charlotte Cushman. She admired the poet and the man and called attention to him among her friends by reading and reciting his verse. She also encouraged his talent for playing the flute, and when he played in her drawing-room she allowed not even a whisper of conversation.

Since his death more has been writ-

ten and said about Sidney Lanier than
was ever written or said about him
during his life.   He is now placed
among the few genuine poets of America, which, considering his slight output, is an especial compliment.   Mr.
Edwin Mims's * biography is the
first complete and adequate life of
Lanier, telling in his own words, as
much as possible, the varied story of
his life as student, lawyer, University
lecturer, poet, and man of letters.

Mr. Mims, in his introduction, says
frankly notwithstanding his admiration for Lanier, that his work as a poet,
even in American to say nothing
of English literature, cannot yet be
fixed.   Some, of the best American
critics, continues Mr. Mims,

men who have a right to speak with authority,
shake their heads in disapproval at what they call
the Lanier cult. Abroad he has no vogue, as have
Emerson and Poe and Walt Whitman. The enthusiastic praise of the *Spectator* has been more
than balanced by the indifference of some English
critics and the sarcasm of others.

Mme. Blanc's article in the *Revue
des Deux Mondes*, setting forth "the
charm of his personality and the excellence of his poetry," roused but little
interest for him in France.   In view of
this divergence of opinion, Mr. Mims
doubts if the time has yet come for
anything approaching a final valuation
of Lanier's work.   In this book he
attempts to give "a reasonably balanced
and critical study of his actual achievement in poetry and criticism."   Such
men as Lanier and Keats (this is Mr.
Mims's coupling of names, not mine)
must be judged, he thinks, by their
actual achievements; but he adds:

there will always attach to their names the glory of
the unfulfilled life, a fame out of all proportion to
the work accomplished.   Poe had completed his

* Sidney Lanier by Edwin Mims. Houghton, Mifflin &
Co. $1.50.

work; limited in its range, it is all but perfect.
Lanier, with his reverence for science, his appreciation of scholarship, his fine feeling for music,
and withal his love of nature and of man, had laid
broad the foundation for a great poet's career.

Mr. Mims, however, does not hesitate
to say that his personality is one of the
rarest and finest we have yet had in
America."   He thinks that the time
has passed for unduly emphasizing the
pathos of Lanier's life.   "He was not
a sorrowful man," says his biographer,
"nor was his life a sad one," though
the general impression is that he was
sorrowful and that his sorrow was induced by a sad life.

While Mr. Lanier was not known to
a wide class of readers during his lifetime, he had a number of close friends
and admirers among critics and men of
letters.   Lanier was poor to the day
of his death; and after his death his
friends were called upon to help his
widow and little children.   I may add
that these same little children are now
grown men and are among the most
successful business men in New York,
one being president of the Review of
Reviews Company, the other a partner
with Doubleday, Page, & Company.
The younger ones, I believe, are in the
publishing business with their brothers.

I quote one of Lanier's best known
lyrics, which was made popular through
its musical setting by Mr. Dudley Buck:

Look off, dear Love, across the shallow sands,
  And mark yon meeting of the sun and sea,
How long they kiss in sight of all the lands.
  Ah! longer, longer, we.

Now in the sea's red vintage melts the sun,
  As Egypt's pearl dissolved in rosy wine.
And Cleopatra night drinks all. 'T is done,
  Love, lay thine hand in mine.

Come forth, sweet stars, and comfort heaven's heart;
  Glimmer, ye waves, round else unlighted sands,
O night! divorce our sun and sky apart,
  Never our lips, our hands.

M. BENJAMIN CONSTANT
Reproduced from a contemporary lithograph

Letters of Mme. de Staël to Benjamin Constant, Hitherto Unpublished

Edited by the BARONESS de NOLDE
Great-Granddaughter of Mme. de Constant

Translated by Charlotte Harwood

SECOND PAPER

THE following letter gives no indication of the time when it was written.

LETTER FROM MME. DE STAËL TO
M. BENJ. CONSTANT

"Why did you not come yesterday? If you think of coming here to-day, remember that I dine at half-past four, so as to go to Brunet.

"It seems to me unbecoming to go to dinner with Mme. Beugnot* to-morrow, as I have had no word. If you dine there, tell her that I did not venture to come, having received no invitation.

"You do not think of your real friends. You neglect what is good. All the same it is ill judged.

"Friday morning.

"The note was written when yours

---

*The Comte de Beugnot (1761-1838) was then Minister of the Interior of the Provisional Government. He had passed through all the metamorphoses of administrative and political life without appearing to be any further on than he was in the beginning. Deputy to the Legislature, imprisoned during the Terror, Prefect under Napoleon, Director-General of Police under Louis XVIII., then Minister of Marine, he died a peer of France. More famous for his wit than for his deeds, one of his bon-mots is always appropriate. At a committee meeting they spoke of putting a crucifix in the *salle des sections electorales*. "I ask something more," said he, "that these words be inscribed beneath: 'My God, forgive them, for they know not what they do.'"

357

reached me. If you will bring St.....
[illegible] for an hour, I shall be delighted, but these are my plans for the
day. I have nothing from Beugnot.
"Thanks for Villers."

During this period Mme. de Staël saw
Constant often in Paris, but he did not
concern himself much about her. He
speaks in his journal of the pleasure he
has experienced in receiving a letter
from his wife, "the gentle, kind, and excellent creature, so noble and indulgent," who was then in Germany, but he
consoled himself for her absence, and
for the void caused by his break with
Mme. de Staël, by falling madly in love
with Mme. Récamier. This unrequited
passion in no wise interfered with the
friendship between Mme. de Staël and
the charming Juliette, between whom
Talleyrand once found himself seated
at table. "Here am I," he said, "between wit and beauty," which earned
him the retort from "wit," "but at this
moment you have neither one nor the
other." "*J'ai dit que Benjamin Constant
faillit aimer tout à fait*," wrote Anatole
France. "*C'est Mme. Récamier avec sa
figure d'ange et de pensionnaire qui fit ce
miracle.*"

LETTER FROM MME. DE STAËL TO M.
BENJ. CONSTANT

"25 August (Coppet, 1814).

"I have read nothing so piquant, nor
so witty as your remarks.*

"The work is a *chef-d'œuvre*, of
happy thoughts and brilliant sayings.
You have done nothing, in my opinion,
as perfect in its way. I read it to Lady
Doray, who is here, and we exclaimed
at every line; for goodness' sake tell me
the effect it has had on friends and
enemies.

"I must also speak to you of something
that gives me much trouble; it is a letter, of which here is a copy made by
Schlegel. I do not know if it is a way
of blackmailing, or if I really have this
horror to fear.

"It would be dangerous to write *one
word* to that address, but if you have a
man sufficiently intelligent to find out

---

* "Observations sur le discours prononcé par S. E. le
Ministre de l'Intérieur en faveur du projet de loi sur la liberté de la presse."

who lives there, and if unfortunately
you must hear this work spoken of, I
beg you to go to Beugnot for me,
and to have it suppressed. You will
feel what harm this can do, and I cannot, in the circumstances, apply to any
one but you. My anxiety is not for
myself, as you can well believe, but for
my daughter. Let me have a word in
reply to the two subjects of this letter.

"I have been much interested in the
notes to your second edition. An English paper, the *Times*, says, 'the admirable little pamphlet of M. B. C. on
the liberty of the press.' Things are
dull in England, so send your pamphlets
to ... [illegible]. In Geneva also they
are not very liberal."

MME. DE STAËL TO M. BENJ. CONSTANT

"(Paris, 1815.)

"M. de Balainvilliers says that M. de
Blacas† has taken my affair to him,
and that I need do no more in the matter. You will do me a great favor by
giving the details of our affair to A ....
[illegible] to-morrow.

"Are you not going to dine with me
to-morrow? When you speak with any
degree of truthfulness, even on what
displeases me, I draw near to your soul.
Till to-morrow then.

"Tuesday, five o'clock."

In March, 1815, Napoleon returned
from Elba, and many heads trembled.
Mme. de Staël, knowing the confusion.
that would ensue, hastened to Coppet.
Benjamin was undecided what to do.
"Great news!" he cries; "Bonaparte has
returned, the disorder is frightful, my
life is in danger. *Vogue la galère!* If
we must perish, let us perish well!" At
last he was influenced by the general
panic, dared not sleep in his own house,
and took refuge with a friend, the
American Minister, feeling himself safer
there.

LETTER FROM MME. DE STAËL TO M.
BENJ. CONSTANT.

"(Coppet, March, 1815.)

"I implore you, by our old love for
each other, to go at once. If you can
go by Switzerland, I shall be very glad,

---

† See the following.

but what I venture to demand is, your departure. Take a passport on which the baptismal name does not appear. "God bless you."

But it was much a question of "the old love." The real question was to stay as near Mme. Récamier as possible. He finally decided to start for Nantes, and wrote her a farewell letter while waiting for his horses. He soon returned to Paris, however, where his *bel ange* had remained, and Napoleon speedily won him to his cause. To console himself for his unrequited passion he plunged into his favorite vice— gambling. Meanwhile, Mme. de Staël was negotiating her daughter's marriage with the Duc de Broglie, and begging Constant to try and recover for her the money that her father had lent to the French Government in the time of Louis XVI. Napoleon had always held this money as a weapon against Mme. de Staël, whom he detested. On one occasion, when one of the Emperor's ministers promised to reward assurances of devotion on her part with pecuniary advantages, she replied: "I knew that a proof of existence was needed, in order to obtain one's interest, but I did not know that a declaration of love was also necessary."

MME. DE STAËL TO M. BENJ. CONSTANT
DE REBECQUE
" Rue Neuve de Berry, No. 6. Fge du Rouille,
Paris, 7th April
(Coppet, 1815).

" How painful it is to see a man like you behave so foolishly through love of play! You know that sooner or later your aunt will disinherit you for this, and you have no fear, at your age, that every one will say you were quite willing. There is no more reason than dignity in this, and God grant that the need of money all your life may not expiate your momentary passion. *Mon Dieu,* how absurd it is! I have seen no one here who can, or will, excuse or approve of you. I would say much more if it could do any good, but you have only one idea in your head, and the passion that dominates you will never pass, because you will never attain its end, and you have never known anything but difficulty in this world. I pity you, and I am irritated, I admit, at the harm your

ruin will do me, when it will be so thoroughly your own fault! Enough of that. When I knew positively that the Emperor had been kind enough to say that he was very pleased at my silence during this year, and at my conduct towards him, and that I could return, I wrote to the Minister of Police and to Prince Joseph* to tell them that my wish was not to return to Paris, but that the title of my annuity be not refused, since my daughter's marriage depends on it. In fact, I believe that he insists on it, since for fifteen days we have not had a word from Victor.† Do not mention this to any one, above all to Madame R.,‡ but send me word of what you know about it. I have not been able to tell her what you would do if I were not paid, and, generally, I should find it sad for so charming a person to be bargained for. If she were not in question I would not speak a word to you on business, for I consider your fortune lost if you continue your Parisian life. Listen to me as to a prophetess, if you no longer believe me as a friend. Do you know that Mme. Cachet lives in Geneva?"

LETTER FROM MME. DE STAËL TO
M. BENJ. CONSTANT
" 16 April (Coppet, 1815).§

" I have received a letter from you in which you do not tell me a word about Victor, but what is still more surprising is the fact that since Auguste's | arrival we have not received a word from him. This is so strange that I cannot account for it.

" I beg you, *in case* this marriage takes place and I do not receive any money, to be so good as to pay 40,000 francs, or an income of 2000 francs.

" Even if I should combine all my means, I could not exceed 100,000 francs, because my losses in Italy are complete, I have undergone some in England, and the total is menaced. Try to find out (without speaking to any one in the world) how it is that Victor behaves in such an unaccount-

* Joseph Bonaparte.
† Duc de Broglie, future son-in-law of Mme. de Staël.
‡ Mme. Récamier, perhaps.
§ Letter already published in German by A. Strodtmann, " Dichterprofile."
| Quoted in derision from the famous article in the *Journal des Débats* of 19th of March.

able manner. Try to talk with him. "I will not speak to you of politics. I should not know how to *stammer out profane words.* * If it is true that you are working on the Constitution, I advise you to think more of the guarantees than of the explanation of rights. Prince Joseph † has written me the kindest letter in the world. He says he does not *doubt* the *success* of my claim. It is the only thing I wish, above all on account of the postponement of this marriage.

"My health does not permit of my staying in Paris, and I need the Midi to live. I do not know, therefore, when we shall see each other again. Ah! if you could be happy and reasonable! It is hard that at our age one can do without the other.

"You must write to me at Geneva so that the letter will reach me sooner."

Address: " M. Benjamin Constant,
      " No. 2 Rue Neuve de Berry,
                          " Paris."

At the time of Constant's marriage and final rupture there had been a great settling of accounts necessitated by fifteen years of life in common. Mme. de Staël had then made a deed settling the income of 80,000 francs on Constant for life, the principal to revert to her children on his death. As the Broglies were poor, Albertine could not be married without a good dowry, and Mme. de Staël appealed to Benjamin to put half of the 80,000 francs at Albertine's disposal, claiming that he had promised to do so. Her indignation at his refusal inspires some of the most interesting of these letters.

LETTER FROM MME. DE STAËL TO
M. BENJ. CONSTANT
      " 17th April (Coppet, 1815).

" You will have seen by my letters by post that I would have preferred you to act differently. You are a better judge than I, but it seems to me that an interval was necessary and that a journey satisfied it. But enough of that. Yesterday I saw Lucien, ‡ who

is still waiting to return to Paris. I will do the same, unless it is necessary on account of business; but, as I am now, politically, like Nicolle in the " Bourgeois gentilhomme," and as I go straight to the point, it seems to me that the Emperor himself must find it best for me not to return until the Constitution is finished, or until he shall have finished with constitutions.

" My interest is my payment. There are a thousand money difficulties that I cannot remove from my marriage. If I am not paid, Auguste will go, and I will go and will do all I can for what my children really need. If all my efforts are vain, I beg of you to put 40,000 francs at Albertine's disposal, with Fourcault, or 2000 francs revenue. My son takes with him the act made between us, and he will give it to you in exchange for your signature.

" I repeat, if I am not paid before Albertine's contract, the sole service you can render me will be to tell the all-powerful that my liquidation is according to law, that a contract is founded on this liquidation, and that it is absolutely the same as the sale of the woods that the Emperor has rectified. There is, besides, no question of expense, but only to have the Minister of Finance put at the bottom: "The liquidation herein mentioned is approved." For the rest, speak to Auguste. I do not reproach myself for asking you to look after Albertine's interests. You know very well that I do not care much for the royalist party. If the Emperor gives liberty, he will be for me the ... [illegible] ... legitimate, but since the ... [illegible] journey to Antibes, however, I do not know who could resist him to his face. I am less capable of it now than formerly; judge, then, of the nation. In short, I think of nothing but my poor Albertine! But the complication of duty, engagements, and feelings is a torture of which you know nothing. I am sorry to accept the sacrifice of 40,000 francs that you will make to my interests, but in truth, if the marriage takes place and my payment is not made, their situation will necessitate it. That *alone* can determine me to ask it of you, as you know.

---

* Quoted in derision from the famous article in the *Journal des Débats* of 19th of March.

† Joseph Bonaparte.

‡ Lucien Bonaparte, Prince of Camuo, younger brother of Napoleon, a great friend of Mme. de Staël (1775-1840).

"May you be happy in your way; I would have wished it to be in mine."

MME. DE STAËL TO M. BENJ. CONSTANT

"Coppet, 17th April. (1815).*

"Why must I write to you first? I begged you, on my departure, and to make it a sort of duty to you, I begged you, besides, to keep me informed of all news concerning my great affair. You have allowed three weeks to elapse without writing a line,—and now you inform me of what they have said to Auguste. That is not all. You write me two pages in the manner of an acquittal of conscience. 'They say that the Duc de Broglie is thinking of your daughter.' She herself is much hurt at this flippancy apropos of such a matter.

"Auguste will probably have told you that. However, I would have given, I cannot say what, for one word more on so important a subject. M. de Broglie is just the man among all others whom I desire for my daughter, and I cannot conceive how one can treat such a subject so lightly. I know that, since you are no longer bored, I am nothing to you. Since the day that you spoke to the Prince of Sweden,† the tone of your letters has changed, though nothing was different then from what it is now, except that I was the beautiful Angelie,‡ and that I am for you now a remorseful conscience that is felt only when one is unhappy. I have the faculty of reading in the depths of the heart. But write me about Albertine, and try to preserve as much feeling as is necessary for your talent.

"Your letter in the *Journal des debats* was almost the same as the one you addressed to me in the last edition; that is to say, when you had to think of something else.

"M. Rocca has received neither your pamphlet § nor his Thucydides.

"I would willingly have the second

* Letter already published by A. Strodtmann, "Dichter-profile."

† Mme. de Staël, a great friend of the Prince of Sweden, might have been useful to him then; he alludes to it himself in his "Journal Intime."

‡ The abandoned lover; an allusion to the heroic opera, "Roland," by Philippe Quinault.

§ A pamphlet of Constant's: "De la liberté des brochures, des pamphlets et des journaux, considéré sous les rapports de l'intérêt du gouvernement" or "Observations sur le discours prononcé por S. E. le Ministre de l'Intérieur en faveur du projet de la loi sur la liberté de la presse."

edition of the "Liberty of the Press" despatched; you could have it ordered for me at Geneva. M. de Montbuissieur Malesherbes' letter has irritated me more than I can say, and you know the feelings that have agitated me on reading it. Thank God, my father will not have to endure such an apology! I have done well to absent myself. When do you advise me to return, and should I choose Clichy, or an apartment in town? Advise me about this. I am in agreeable English society here. I have taken a liking to Coppet, now that I am here of my own free will. I ask much of Heaven, addressing myself to my saints. Do you remember that you were a mystic? Have you really written that the liberty of the press ought not to attack republicanism? They say so in Geneva, where the people are aristocrats *à la* Calvin, or in a still more unliberal manner.

"Adieu! write to me.

"Swiss affairs will run a peaceful course and the nineteen cantons will remain."

MME. DE STAËL TO M. BENJ. CONSTANT

"30th April (1815).*

"The Constitution has satisfied me—I have, however, some objections to make to it.

"What will the Councillors of State be? Are they responsible or inviolable? What does their presence in the Constitution signify? What will the peers be? Everything has not been said in pronouncing this word. A military chamber would not be a guarantee of liberty. Will not the administration of the provinces be confided to men elected by the people? However it may be, one must praise what is praiseworthy, and I can well understand that you are pleased to have participated in it,—but what you tell me of your feeling of gratification does not seem to me to be derived entirely from the conscience. To give voice to good principles is always a great thing. Principles sometimes govern men more than men are masters of them. You know better than any one else what can be said of

* Letter already published by A. Strodtmann, "Dichterprofile."

that which touches you. I myself am inclined to understand everything, except what relates to a lack of sentiment, and in that you were not bound. I take the liberty of telling you that your conduct in my affair is much less pardonable.

"You promised, on the occasion of my daughter's marriage, to pay 40,000 of the 80,000 francs. I promised these 40,000 francs to M d' Argenson,* who reminds me of it in his last letter to Victor, who must have this sum to get settled. What can I say, except that you are now renouncing your obligations? Our arrangement, as you know, is only a present that means nothing. Think, then, of your position. How has it changed since your promise in Paris, if not for the better? In your last letter but one, you tell me that you made this promise to me and Albertine, believing that you would be a Deputy. Now, you are a Councillor of State, which brings more. Tell Fourcault, then, to yield a part of the unpaid debts to Mme. du . . . . . [illegible] . . . . You come to me now with the tale that your position cannot last. What does it matter to me what you do, or do not do, at another time, when it is now only a matter of fifteen days during which my daughter's future must be decided? We once had a correspondence which lasted for six months, during which you threatened every day to pay me by a mortgage on Vallombreuse.† You have lost nothing since, and I proved to you then that I wished to make you a present of everything, if I were the only one in question, — but now that my daughter's fate is concerned, I, as a mother, must conduct this affair with all the necessary insistence. These are disagreeable things that I will not mention again

*Marc Rene d'Argenson, second husband of the Duchess de Broglie, mother of Victor, had become an orphan at the age of ten. Possessor of a large fortune and titled estates, hereditary Governor of Vincennes, lieutenant-general, bailiff of Touraine, this blue-blooded aristocrat had all his life been a republican, and an implacable liberal. Aide-de-camp to Lafayette, a member of the Breton club, and in danger under the Terror, he retired to his estates and occupied himself solely with their amelioration, and with that of the whole province. He was a most devoted father to his adopted children. Deputy in 1815, a fine orator, and of exceedingly independent mind, he retired from office for the second and last time in 1835.

† A property that Constant possessed in common with a relation. This property apparently had been bought by Mme. De Staël. If so, she must have made a present of it to Benj. Constant.

if you get my money, and it seems to me that you could easily persuade the Emperor that, if there is now a liquidation — proportionate to last year's — they act according to the principle on which I urge my pretentions. Besides, they *would have* executed the article of the Constitution which declares that *all possessions acquired on the foundation of a law are inviolable.* My liquidation is an acquired possession, and it only depends on you to persuade the Emperor that I am a person over whom gratitude has always had more power, than any remembrance whatever, and that I desire you with all my heart to remain faithful to the Constitution. On that depends the esteem in which you will be held. Think, I conjure you, of Albertine's position, of my uneasiness on the subject, and consider it natural that, at such a time, all the means at my disposal should be employed for her. Love her then, her at least. Adieu!"

LETTER FROM MME. DE STAËL TO M. BENJ. CONSTANT

"15 May (1815).

"I do not know how to reply to your letter; it passes all that I believed of the human heart. The laws of this country concern you, as well as me, and I will fight here, but if I must lose, I shall have the bitter satisfaction of gathering together facts that will excite deep pity for a person so unhappy as to have been attached to you for fifteen years! You dare to make use of the generosity I showed you when I loved you, as of a right? And what do you say of the promise you made me in Paris, which you remember from your last letter but one? You say that my children will have the greater part of your fortune, after you. Yours! Mine; since I lend you the 80,000 francs without interest during your life, if that maintains an agreement none of whose conditions you have fulfilled, and which is not legal, since it is not authorized.

"If I had not promised this money to M. d'Argenson according to *your promise,* twice repeated in Paris, I would leave you, all that you do, and all that you are, but if I can, I will make you keep your promise; if I cannot, the conduct of each of us will at least become known; that will complete your memoirs.

"You know that a part of this money was advanced by me to your father—yet you treated him as you treat me.

"As to your fortune, I cannot conceive why you tell me what is false, when I know it as I know my own. You are to-day richer than I, you have no one to take care of, are under obligations to no one whatsoever. So you have no excuse for an action, your motives for which revolt me more than the action itself. I beg you, as you say so well, not to *oblige me*. You owe me 80,000 francs. Pay me half of it, and leave me without any further dealings with you.

"You dated the 15th May; I advise you to be fortunate, for, at present, adversity would not become you."*

LETTER FROM MME. DE STAËL TO M. BENJ. CONSTANT

"Coppet, 25th May (1815).†

"If it only concerned me, I should continue to make you a present of what I have lent you, as I was foolish enough to at other times—but you are to be blamed for the fact that my daughter's marriage cannot take place. The blame is yours because you promised 40,000 francs, and because this sum figures in the contract. I neglected to make you sign it, but as you talk to me of letters, I have one that contains this promise, in which you beg me on bended knee to allow you to participate in Albertine's happiness! What a man, who being to-day in fortunate circumstances,—O, unfortunate that we are!—does not try to be useful to my daughter! What a man, who does as much harm to a child as he has done to her mother! What a man! Imagination shudders with horror at such a proof! Every one will judge your conduct as I do, but at the moment of death the remembrance of your past life will make you shudder. However, all is over between you and me; between you and Albertine, be-

tween you and whoever is still capable of feeling. In future I shall speak to you only through lawyers, and as my daughter's guardian. Adieu!"
Address:

"To M. Benjamin de Constant,
  "Councillor of State,
"No. 2 Rue Neuve de Berry,
    "Paris.
"Faubourg du Roule."

LETTER FROM MME. DE STAËL TO
M. BENJ. CONSTANT

"Coppet, 28th May (1815).

"I did not wish to write to you again on this horrible subject, but the letters my son brought me demand a last reply. You threaten me with *my letters*. This last trait is worthy of you, worthy of you! To threaten a woman with intimate letters which may compromise her and her family, so as not to pay her the money one owes her, that is a trait lacking to M. de S . . . [illegible]. Doubtless, if that is your intention, as Albertine would suffer and my son be annoyed by it, when he has proved to the eyes of Europe that you owe me 80,000 francs,—of which, 34 *to my father* by inheritance, 18 on your note for Vallombreuse, with interest for ten years,—I will declare that a woman cannot expose herself to a man's threats of publishing her letters, and this new manner [illegible] of enriching oneself will be known, for, before you, no one has dared to conceive it. This lack of means that you proclaim after having gambled as you did all the winter, is a mockery. It pleases you to say that I will not embarrass myself for Albertine, forgetting that exile has reduced my fortune by half, and that I am charged with 20,000 francs of pensions, including Schlegel and Mlle. Rendal.* But that does not matter. You owe me 80,000 francs; your absurd agreement is proof of it. You offered me the half, my daughter is witness of this and the subject of the contract proves it.

"Besides, when I have the signature

* Benj. Constant writes in his "Jorunal Intime"; "Letter received from Mme. de Staël. She would like me to do nothing for my fortune, and to give her the little I have (charming combination)."
† Letter already published by A. Strodtmann, "Dichterprofile."

* Miss Rendal, a devoted friend of Mme. de Staël. She became acquainted with her probably in Lyons in 1809, because much attached to her, and from that time they did not leave each other again until Mme. de Staël's death. She left her, in her will, a fine diamond and an income.

of all the lawyers in this country, if you threaten me with my letters, I am ready to have it said in the Tribunal that this threat has suspended proceedings.

"So, if you are capable of a cowardice which is worse than a theft, I wish this cowardice to be known. But it will stop me, at least for æ time, for I find this conduct so atrocious, and know perfectly that neither the honor, nor the friendship, nor the despair that you have thrown over my life, nor the harm that you do to my daughter,—that none of this is anything to you, and that money alone rules your political and private life. I shall try to make you return what you owe me, because I know that should my daughter and I die of grief to-morrow, it would hurt you much less than having paid your debts. Your malignity robs you of intelligence. You write me that you wanted to break with me, *and that I held you by* . . . . * of money. I believe it,

but it is iniquitous to say it, as your intelligence tells you sometimes what you are. But take care, you have overworked the power of your talents; they will no longer save you from your character; it is too well known now. Albertine, not less wounded than I am, will testify to the offer you made her in Paris, and your place as Councillor of State cannot have changed it. You told Auguste that Mme. Dureuse did not press you. Well, then, I take Mme. Dureuse's credit, all or in part.

"Besides, it is not a question of being right; you know the truth as well as I. But what you know less well is that the unhappiness I owed to you, *the horror of the recollections of my youth*, entirely devastated by your frightful temper, have given me a firmness of will that during twenty years, if I . . * . . I should follow the suit which is going to begin. Adieu!"

* A piece of the letter is missing here.   * Here, also, a piece of the letter is missing.

(To be concluded)

The Young Goethe

By ELISABETH LUTHER CARY

THERE are two ways in which to regard a youthful intelligence. The more hackneyed, possibly the more instructive, is to seek in it the "father of the man," and attempt to find in the various and dissociated activities of a boy's life threads of connection with the serious and considered activities of his later career. The other way is to regard the different stages of our development as the "outworn cells" of the chambered nautilus without any organic connection or essential resemblance. In certain people this seems absolutely the only theory on which to account for the separateness of their age from their youth and their entire change of temperament and even of character in the course of the formative years. In the case of Goethe, however, we find certain elements of his nature as clearly revealed before he is

twenty as after he is fifty, and in spite of the great number of his intellectual interests and the lightness and swiftness with which he turned from one absorbing study to another, the growth of his mind seems to have proceeded in a singularly orderly and logical fashion almost without deviation from the line first indicated by his boyish inclinations. In the first volume of the splendid "Life of Goethe" by Dr. Bielschowsky (Putnam) which recently has been translated, the multitudinous detail gathered by this indefatigable Goethe-student displays to an industrious reader a portrait of the great German which anticipates line for line and tone for tone the aspect of his maturity and old age. Nothing, for example, could be more illustrative of his permanent temper than the description of his first semester of student life.

He came, rustic and ill-dressed, at the age of sixteen, to the gallant city of Leipsic, whither the famous university, great fairs, and an extensive book trade had combined to bring representatives of all European nations from time to time, broadening its culture and making it a centre of aristocracy and learning. Naturally enough, the first change made by Goethe was in his clothes, but he characteristically rushed to such extremes in re-furnishing his wardrobe as to become at once conspicuously foppish. He threw himself with much enthusiasm into the gay life about him, enjoying the excellent theatre and the excellent dinners, and the other agreeable experiences made possible by a well-filled purse. As soon, however, as the superficial attraction had worn off and he found that in order to win admiration he must conform in deeper matters than manners and dress to the opinion of those among whom he moved not as a superior but at most as an equal, Leipsic lost much of its charm. He found the professors, who insisted upon teaching him what he did not care to know and who could not or would not teach him concerning poetry and the classics, worthy only of his sarcasm. To shine in society he was obliged to play cards and to dance, both of which he detested, therefore he abjured society. In a word, to conform, to do what he disliked because others wished it, was as difficult for him as it is for most spirited youngsters, but with him the instinct toward essential independence went deeper than mere perverse resentment of authority. It was a part of his deliberate plan of life, and, making allowance for impulses affecting only his outer behavior, he consistently repelled any course of action that he believed would tie his hands, or, to use the favorite expression of biographers, fetter his genius. This is peculiarly obvious in his attitude of mind during his early love affairs. These were sufficiently violent, the first one occurring when he was fourteen and ending abruptly with the humiliating realization that the lovely Gretchen to whom he had given his heart considered him a child. The

later episodes were brought to their close for reasons not less closely connected with self-esteem and ambition. For Kätchen Schönkopf, the daughter of an innkeeper and a straightforward, kindly girl, he developed a sudden and fiery affection which did not in the least blind him to the fact that he had no desire to spend his life by her side. His conscience led him at length to explain this unflattering state of mind, and he writes to one of his friends: "It was hard work, but now I sit here, like Hercules who has finished all his tasks, and survey the glorious booty. It was a terrible time before the explanation; but the explanation came, and now—now I know for the first time what life is, She is the best, most amiable girl!"

A year or so later when he was twenty-one he met Frederike Brion, a bright, thoroughly educated young woman with whom he fell promptly in love. In a few months he discovered that as soon as he was bound he desired to be free, and consequently went through something the same explanation with Frederike as with Kätchen. His feeling finds expression, Dr. Bielschowsky declares, in a fairy tale or parable which relates the history of a man in love with a maiden who belongs to the dwarf kingdom. He can marry her only by consenting himself to become a dwarf, which is accomplished by his wearing a fairy ring. His new life is a merry one, but the sense of his having deliberately renounced a standard of greatness which was suited to his natural powers drives him to desperation and he files his ring in two pieces and escapes to his former world, regaining his former size. This little drama is enacted again and again by the youthful Goethe. As soon as he imagines himself doomed to the more or less restrictive life of a married man, his impatient temperament begins to file at the ring that holds him until he is free again. In 1775 he met Lili Schönemann, who charmed him, but no sooner were they betrothed than he began to storm about again in search of liberty which of course he soon found.

These episodes and others have

stirred his different critics and biographers to warm controversy. The interesting feature that distinguishes them from ordinary boy and girl attachments lightly formed and lightly broken, is the underlying sense in Goethe's mind of the importance of his freedom as well as its desirability. If he had not so richly proven his right to consider his genius he would have made rather an absurd figure as a lover in the eyes of later generations. But his cool mind kept its sway over his passionate emotions and we may imagine that he was never very near wrecking himself on any reefs of domesticity. In a recent number of the *Revue des Deux Mondes*, M. de Wyzewa discusses his influence on Eckermann, his devoted secretary, as it is disclosed by Eckermann's recently published letters. Relating the uncomfortable plight of Eckermann's betrothed, whom he has left behind him at Hanover, while he makes himself indispensable to Goethe at Weimar, M. de Wyzewa quotes from one of his letters. Eckermann has asked Goethe's advice on the subject of Jeanne's wish that they should marry and live very quietly at Weimar where Eckermann could still be of service to Goethe.

I spoke to Goethe of your situation [he writes], and told him that I thought strongly of bringing you here with me. He begged me not to decide too quickly as to that, in order that no risk be run of plunging us both in need ; for it is indispensable for me to lead here a life appropriate to the rank that I occupy. I answered him to the effect that we counted on living very retired and restricting our expenses. "No," he said, "that would be impossible for you, given the universal consideration that you have won for yourself ! Try as you might you could not strip from yourself the society of Weimar !" Then he spoke of the beautiful gowns that you would be obliged to have, and of the children that would presently be born to us. "You are an excellent man," he added, "and your *fiancée* should be a perfect being. How much I wish I could do something for you !" After which he explained to me the whole state of things at Weimar, and how his hands were tied by reason of the debts of the country and the little means at his disposal. When I told him that I thought of returning to Hanover, he strongly counselled me not to do so. He warned me that I should be too much deprived there of the companionship of intelligent and edu-

cated men, and that I might also find difficulty in obtaining employment. The result of our interview is that for the present I must guard against taking a too hasty step, but instead must work and furnish new proofs of my ability. Finally, he has given me to understand that right here and very soon something will be found for me.

In this, certainly, we hear the voice of the Goethe who renounced Kätchen and Frederike, Anna Münch and Lili Schönemann for one and the same reason, the fear of placing a yoke upon his intellectual powers which seemed to him, and indeed with truth, created for wings. It is perfectly possible that he believed such counsel the sole sort properly to be given a young man of talent, although his French critic sees in it only an "Olympian indifference" to any happiness of others that might interfere with his own comfort. It must be admitted, too, that this theory is borne out by the fact that Goethe after discouraging Eckermann's marriage for thirteen years, consents to it at last only on condition that he shall not be asked to meet the bride.

In spite, however, of the vast egoism that saved Goethe's great talents from being swallowed up in the experiences that gave him a part at least of the material for "Faust," it is impossible not to realize from Dr. Bielschowsky's painstaking delineation of him how irresistibly brilliant and vivid and delightful he was in his magnificent youth. Nor was he without unselfish impulses upon which at times he acted. When he fell in love as impetuously as usual with Charlotte Buff, the heroine of "The Sorrows of Werther," and the betrothed of Goethe's friend Kestner, he bore himself in such a way as to keep not only Charlotte's friendship but that of Kestner as well, and seems on that occasion at least to have renounced for the sake of others. In matters that did not concern his future and the development of his genius he was generous with time, thought, and strength. In his work whether it was for himself or others he was what one would expect from the author of "Faust," not merely untiring but filled with incessant enthusiasm. One of the most interesting chapters of this first volume of the "Life" is that describing his labors as Minister at Weimar. His first duty, that of training the young Duke to the responsibilites of his office and bringing his influence to bear upon him without arousing his anger, led him into compromising situations and spread the impression that he was the spur by which the Duke was pricked to extravagant conduct in a thousand directions. Dr. Bielschowsky makes very clear, however, his real moderation and the wisdom of his counsel to his good-natured sovereign. He appears to have rung all possible changes upon the fundamental precept which he addressed to the Duke in a birthday poem: "Restrain thyself; learn to forego." And apart from his mentorship over the Duke, he was wholly devoted to his political calling, wresting from it knowledge of men and government, which was enough to content him since knowledge was always the coin in which he felt himself best paid. The part he played in amateur theatricals, masquerades, etc.—a part so often descanted upon by his critics—was a small one compared to his part in the exciting game of statesmanship. He showed the true poetry of his nature in the delight he felt in his practical calling. It is not the powerfully creative mind that scorns business interests and ideals. Goethe's intelligence like Shakespeare's, transmuted the petty necessary details of his practical occupation into the significant fragments of a tremendous structure of human enterprise. Or, to speak more truly, no transmutation was needed. He saw with his imaginative vision the true relation of the small parts to the vast whole and, taking all knowledge for his province, built for himself a philosophic ideal of humanity out of such enduring materials that it bids fair to outlast the cloud-capped towers and gorgeous palaces of the most inspired dreamers as a contribution to the world's thought. His political activities have been less dwelt upon than his studies in osteology, geology, mineralogy, anatomy, and other sciences, but Dr. Bielschowsky lays special emphasis on his intelligent

systematization of the affairs of the War Commission, his reformations in the Chamber of Finance against the inclination of his free-handed prince, his revival of the mining industry at Ilmenau, and numerous other proofs of his executive talent and serious temper in official life. "That a man is made serious by serious matters is natural," he writes to his mother, "especially if one is by nature meditative and desires to promote the good and the right in the world." When at last, at the age of thirty-seven, he breaks his bonds, and starts incognito on his memorable journey to Italy, leaving behind him a quiet duchy in the serenity of which he had been the most important agent, we feel that he has made his political career as useful to his own purposes as to the welfare of the country, and is ready for the reposeful and inspiring influence of antique art.

The effect upon Goethe not merely of antique art but of every form of art with which he came into contact was extraordinary. It was not merely the æsthetically agreeable effect produced upon minds whose surface is receptive but whose composition beneath this easily enriched surface is essentially arid. The monuments of the artistic life of the far past became at once vital to him, or rather did not lose for him the vitality which so often is veiled to the commonplace vision. His sense of the continuity of man's effort sprang to his aid, and he arrived in Rome fresh from his successful struggle with contemporary problems, only to feel at home and contemporaneous with the Pantheon and the Colosseum. Characteristically he sought immediately to recreate his impressions on a basis of historical knowledge, tracing the relations between this art of the ancients and the art of Egypt by the side of which it was itself "modern art." It may well be imagined that such studies had for him none of the "dryness" commonly attributed to them, but he was not content to confine himself to study of historic art. His creative mind impelled his hand to take hold of the tool and learn what it would do for him. It is hardly to the purpose that with all his intelligence he could not make it do his will. The trouble was with his hand and eye, not with his mind. They were not his proper interpreters, but his careful and enthusiastic drill in observation reinforced by his attempts to reproduce what he saw were not wasted. No one who has ever practised an art only to make it subsidiary to another· art can question the value of his drawing, painting, and modelling to his poetry. They defined for him abstract ideas of harmony and proportion as perhaps no practice with the use of words alone could have done. They taught him new appreciation of the large forms within which detail must be kept, and they taught him too that the austere simplicity of an outline is merely the union or fusion of a thousand observations of detail. His re-reading of the manuscript of the first part of ''Faust'' on his Italian journey was well-timed, and it may fairly be argued that without the stimulation of his mind to the observation of typical forms gained from his study of antique art and his own practice in art under the influence of the antique he would hardly have past his great drama with its confusing multitudinous accumulations of observation into a form so pure and so free from the trivial and accidental. He went through the natural evolution of all artists of importance, whether poets or painters, from careful attention to and imitation of nature to choice between the essential and the non-essential and the recognition of structural harmony. In reviewing his early life as it is presented by this punctilious biographer we realize the structural harmony of his own mind and also the labor by which this harmony was acquired, the elimination from his design of all that might interfere with it and the inclusion and fostering of all that might further it. Not merely did he sacrifice the loves of his boyhood with the consistent purpose of leaving himself freedom to expand, but he strove and with success to overcome the distastes that threatened to do him an ill turn. He subjugated his horror of disease by the study and practice of medicine, working in the dissecting-room ˉwith as much thoroughness as though he had expected to become a physician. He overcame his tendency to dizziness by repeating the experiment of climbing to the highest point of the cathedral and standing there upon a ledge scarcely a square yard in size, until he was completely cured. Loud noises were distressing to him, therefore he walked by the side of drummers during the beating of the tattoo. He was secretly afraid to visit graveyards and lonely places at night, and for this reason he haunted such gruesome spots until he was unable even by intention to awaken in himself the sense of horror. Self-understanding and self-control seemed to him the necessary forerunners to greatness and there was never a moment when he did not consciously intend to be great. Writing from Weimar to his mother, who has been disquieted by reports of overwork and ill-health, he sums up his own characteristics and the effect upon him of his surroundings in a cool statement of the result of minute introspection:

Merck and several others judge my position quite falsely [he says]. They see only what I sacrifice and not what I gain ; they cannot understand that I am daily growing richer by daily giving so much. You remember the last days that I spent with you before coming here. If I had continued under such conditions, I should surely have come to a bad end. The disproportion of the narrow burgher circle to the breadth and vivacity of my nature would have driven me mad. In spite of my lively imagination and my spiritual intuition of things human, I should have remained forever unacquainted with the world and in a perpetual childhood, which usually becomes intolerable to itself and others because of its vanity and all related faults. How much more fortunate it was for me to be placed in a position of which I was in no sense master ; where through mistakes of ignorance and over-hastiness I had opportunities enough to learn to know myself and others ; where, left to myself and my fate, I passed through so many trials, which may not be necessary for many hundreds of men, but which I greatly needed for my development ! Even now how could I with my nature desire a happier condition than one which has infinite possibilities for me ? For even if new capabilities should daily develop within me, my conceptions become clearer and clearer, my strength increase, my knowledge broaden, my judgment correct itself, and my pluck grow, still I should daily find occasion to apply all these faculties both in great things and in small. You see how far I am from the hypochondriac discomfort which makes so many discontented with their lot, and that only most important considerations or very strange, unexpected developments could move me to forsake my post.

In this we have the secret if not of Goethe's genius at least of his triumph over conditions that might have served to stunt or shrivel or debase or overwhelm a duller man. He did indeed daily find occasion to apply all his faculties both in great things and small. If he made his own development the first consideration of his extremely capable mind he also lavishly spent the remarkable powers which he was at such pains to enlarge upon the slightest of the tasks that came in his way. He early showed the first attribute of real greatness,—he willingly put forth his utmost efforts for any purpose that seemed to him worthy of any effort at all. Whatever his work was he never felt himself above it or too important for it. Hence he united a kind of humility with his egoism. He was moreover entirely ready to grant importance to instruments of culture commonly underestimated or regarded as unfit for the learned. It is peculiarly appropriate, in connection with the laborious and intelligent effort that has been spent on the translation of Dr. Biel-schowsky's book, to quote from Goethe's letters to Carlyle his opinion of translation. Characteristically looking at it from two sides, that of the translator and that of the translated, he not only designates it as "one of the weightiest and worthiest affairs in the general concerns of the world," but in another letter continues with fervor:

The translator works not alone for his own nation, but likewise for the one from whose language he has taken the work. For it happens oftener than one is apt to suppose, that a nation sucks out the sap and strength of a work and absorbs it into its own inner life, so as to have no further pleasure in it, and to draw no new nourishment from it. This is especially the case with the German people, who consume far too quickly whatever is offered them, and while transforming it by various reworkings, they in a sense annihilate it. Therefore it is very salutary if what was their own should, after a time, by means of a successful translation, reappear to them endowed with fresh life.

However Goethe may seem to have changed from his tumultuous youth to his calm old age, it is easy to discern in all accounts of him at the different periods of his life ample testimony to his most valuable characteristic—an open mind. Without this he could neither have attained the inner harmony upon which he laid such stress nor could he so wisely have estimated the usefulness of largely spending largely to possess.

Laurence Hope

(After seeing her portrait in the February CRITIC)

ALTHOUGH the compass of her voice was small,
And few the strings that she could wake to life,
She sang of Love, as one who knew it held
A Heaven of sweetness and a Hell of strife.

Now she hath forced the gloomy Gates of Death,
Sooner than tarry when her mate was dead.
Cast jasmin-blossoms all about her grave,
And plant a crimson rose-tree at her head.

O. R. HOWARD THOMPSON.

Literary Tact

By MICHAEL WHITE

IN his interesting memoirs, Kropotkin tells us that at the court of the Emperor Alexander II. it was customary for the minister of state, before entering the imperial cabinet with the object of inveigling that monarch into some course, to discover from Alexander's valet in what humor his master was that morning. The minister took particular care to be on good terms with the Emperor's valet, so that he might conduct himself according to whether Alexander had slept well or otherwise overnight.

Here is where an aspiring contributor to a magazine, seeking a personal acquaintance with the editor, may find a parallel example for his own case. What the valet was to Alexander II. the office boy is to the editor. The discreet contributor will at the outset make friends with the office boy, for by so doing he can learn just what humor the editor is in and govern his actions accordingly. If, for instance, your first visit should happen to be at a time when "the boss is rip tearing mad," manifestly your best course would be to seek an interview at a more auspicious moment.

But the office boy is in a position to advance your suit further than this. He is generally keenly observant of the editorial autocrat's hobbies and failings. He can tell you, for example, whether his boss plays golf, is a Republican, or a Democrat, and how he spends his vacation.

Should the editor happen to be a lady, the office boy, knows whether she holds strong opinions upon the subject of woman's suffrage, or if her leisure interest is occupied more with higher music.

Thus having made yourself familiar with the personality of the editor, you can enter his sanctum thrice armed; because it is always well to bear in mind under such circumstances the greeting which the Emperor Shah Jehan invariably received from his emirs:

"If it is day and the Emperor says it is night we behold the moon and the stars."

But much depends upon your first interview. Nothing is more injudicious than to immediately thrust a manuscript into the editor's hand, and proceed to point out how superior your work is to anything he has already published in his magazine. By so doing you might seem to imply that his judgment has not always been infallible, which is to say the least of it indiscreet. On the contrary, as you have taken the measure of your editor by a first glance, the attitude you should adopt is one of either respectful or hearty congratulation over the unprecedented success the magazine is meeting with under his management. He cannot possibly be offended if you remark that you hear the circulation is going up by leaps and bounds in—the Middle West. This prelude should be brief; but in nine cases out of ten you will notice that it has made a favorable impression by your being invited to take a seat.

Your procedure then should be governed by circumstances, but you can diplomatically approach the object of your visit by drawing the editor's attention to the coincidence, that while he has been fortunate in securing so many of Mr. Zacheus Dewberry's stories for his magazine, your name and Mr. Dewberry's have appeared so often together in other places. As it is evident Mr. Dewberry is a favorite contributor, by thus associating your name with his it is probable the editor will thereupon express the desire to see some of your work.

This is the right moment to place your manuscript in his hand, express your gratification at having been admitted to the editorial presence, and bow yourself out. Should the office boy wink as you pass by him, and there is a quarter in your pocket, he will think none the worse of you if it is transferred into his possession.

Now as the chances are that the first contribution will be returned with more or less profound regret, it must not be supposed that your diplomacy has been all in vain. Your next move should be to discover from your friend the office boy where the editor usually goes out to lunch, and thither you should repair daily, taking a seat where he is bound to notice your presence.

Upon the first occasion you will be greeted probably with a nod and a "How's yourself," but sooner or later, possibly with the connivance of the waiter, you can manage to be seated at the same table.

But that is not the opportunity to discuss your work. That is the time, when recollecting that your editor is, say, a golf enthusiast, you should turn the conversation upon his hobby. The circulation of his magazine will be dwindling at an alarming rate if he does not promptly respond by dilating perhaps upon a new theory of his relative to putting greens, which time and again he has brought to the attention of his club committee without result. By this means you have obtained what is often a difficult matter—your editor's views upon a particular subject. So

while expressing your astonishment at the collective intellectual density of the club committee, you should carefully but surreptitiously jot down his opinions on the back of a menu or on your cuff; so that you may embody them in the next story you purpose sending him.

It will then surely be your own inferiority as a craftsman if he does not accept that story as combining in an unusual degree both human and timely interest.

There is, however, one terrible editorial rock upon which the contributor's literary bark may meet with shipwreck unless most tactfully handled. An editor will sometimes write himself under a *nom-de-plume*, and unfairly request your opinion of his unidentified work. Unlucky mortal are you, if a warning voice does not whisper in your ear, and you commit yourself to the indiscretion of saying that you are lost in amazement for the reason of its acceptance. The look, or the exclamation in response, can best be likened to the shock experienced previous to the sinking of a ship.

Keys to China by Front and Back Door

By W. E. GRIFFIS

As China emerges from mystery and obscurity, and as the miracle play of thrones and their occupants becomes a common theatre, we find less to admire in what was once professed, while our human sympathies become deeper and stronger.* The Empress Dowager of China, so often painted in the lurid colors of defamation by ignorant and even malignant foreigners, turns out to be a simple woman, who is quite attractive in many traits of her character. Marked by limitations of place, time, culture, and inheritance, she seems also possesed of the same abilities which we admire in Elizabeth of England and Catherine of Russia, while showing equal devotion to her country and people. Miss Carl

* "With the Empress Dowager." By Katharine A. Carl. Century . $2.00

may or may not have violated confidence in thus unveiling the privacies of the palace in which she was a guest. Her answer is the ready and unsurprising one that this publication is her defence against distortion and misrepresentation. Of course we do not expect her to criticise or judge harshly her hostess. That were ungracious. No doubt she is excessive in praise, while blind to the wart or to wrinkles,—and this in more senses than one. She has given us a pleasing story of observation and adventure which, beside being fascinating in itself, reveals very much of historical and antiquarian interest to those who have read widely and critically in the court life of the vassal kingdoms around the Middle Country—as the Chinese so long proudly called their realm. Both in her personality, *entourage*, costume, and tastes the Empress is interesting, but her long finger nails are not likely soon to come into fashion on this side the Pacific.

What a pair of keen eyes the jolly chaplain of His Britannic Majesty's forces garrisoning Hong Kong must have had when in the country which oppresses women, and yet is ruled by one, he took notes. The author of "How to be Happy though Married" shows us one may be blessed even though he be a Chinaman. Chaplain Hardy * has a good deal of fun to poke at "John," but he shows us our weak points even more by comparison. In many things, the man of the pigtail does not come off second best. His chapter on "Betrothal and Marriage" is delightful. He explains by hints the philosophy of the practice which veils a woman when·she is going to enter the matrimonial poke. Though a Chinese bride's veil is made of beads instead of lace, she must sightlessly enter the future, very 'much as the American maiden perforce must do. Whether talking on missionaries or Chinese mandarins, manners, clothes, or education, the contrasting characteristics of the wearer of side whiskers or of hair tails, of spirits or of mortal rogues, travelling or sitting on the verandah, the chaplain is always delightful. This is one of the most readable books about the country whose population and peculiarities are permanently exaggerated in most of our textbooks.

The tremendous quarrel in India between Lord Curzon † and General Kitchener has excited much comment on the four sides of the two oceans. What caused the strife between pen and sword ? The spurs evidently got tangled up in the civil robes, the latter being well torn; but why? As one man was married and the other was a bachelor, the trouble was laid to some phase of the eternal feminine. Nevertheless those who studied the wires

* " John Chinaman at Home." By E. J. Hardy. Scribner. $2.00

† " Tibet and Turkestan." By Oscar Terry Crosby. Putman, $2.00

and the storage batteries of politics felt sure, even long ago, that while Japan should occupy Russia in the far East, John Bull would leave no opportunity unused to grab something in central Asia. It was a sad day for both Lord Curzon and for Colonel Younghusband also, after civil ambition and military daring had done their best in scrambling, like a cat, on the roof of the world in Tibet, to be called down by orders from Whitehall, and to have their treaty of coercion virtually torn into strips. In a word, the British market-makers were surreptitiously entering the Chinese Empire, by climbing in " some other way," even at the back door of the Chinese Empire. Determined to forestall and keep out the Russians, or any other traders, they hesitated not even at scuttles and roof guards. This the American army officer, who has written a book exposing the reality, preaches loudly. He tells of his journey through old lands, high and dry, while giving wonderfully fresh and stimulating study of new conditions. His text is a medley of matters historical, descriptive, and homiletic, relating to Tibet and Turkestan. With its text, index, and brand-new map, it is a revelation of the new Asia of railways and telegraphs. Mr. Crosby has also furnished eloquent commentary upon and damning proof of the justice of Mr. Bryce's condemnation of Balfour's policy—so feeble in the far East of pre-Boxer days and so alternately unwise and vacillating in central Asia. The work is a first-class contribution toward the study of world politics, as well as of that larger sociology which shows how climate, and the excess or absence of water, as well as the altitudes and depressions in the earth's surface, influence permanently individuals and races.

Lest sentimentalist and philanthropist should forget the solid realities under the human foot and sole, a member of the British Parliament, with an eye to railways, mines, metals, markets, and highways, has refurbished his traveller's notes and impressions of three years ago and has given us a bright and brisk book on Japan, Korea, and

China.* It is full of pictures; has a map which shows at one glance of the eye what British, Russian, German, French, American, and Japanese engineers are doing, both with brain and hand, to create new highways of travel and paths from mine to market, and from the hinterlands to the seaports. He draws skilfully the contrast of life in twentieth century Japan, notes the absurdities of Korean ways, laughs at the absurdities of Chinese existence, shows us, like an orthodox Britisher, the awful dangers which come from Russian aggression, preaches the benefits of English success and ownership,

* " Far Eas'ern Impressions." By E. F. G. Hatch. A. C. McClurg & Co.

demonstrates how very desirable an arrangement with America would be, and in a final chapter discusses the effect of Japan's successes on the Asiatic mind.

However different in their points of view, spirit, motive, and method, these four books reveal to us a China that is new in potency if not yet in visible reality, even while they suggest that, instead of the disasters and woe attending the possible re-creation of Russia, the regeneration of China is to be consummated like the operation of leaven. There is indeed good ground to hope that there will be a transformation of the oldest of empires without the shattering of the vessel.

"A Reunited Anglo-Saxondom"

By THOMAS WENTWORTH HIGGINSON

IN crossing the Atlantic at different times I have been more and more impressed by the increasing cordiality between Canadians and citizens of the United States; and as far off as the Queen's Jubilee I can recall the manly bearing of one or two of those who officially represented still more distant British colonies and refused to accept knighthood because their constituents were all opposed to it. I also vividly remember the fine face and manner of Sir Wilfred Laurier when he received his degree at Oxford and had to listen from the platform to the rather boorish jokes of the undergraduates: his quiet high-bred look seeming not so much to reprove them as to ignore their very existence. To a citizen of the United States these things brought Canada and its citizens very near; and made one ask the question "Why not still nearer?"

Again, when we get such fresh and attractive literary work as that of Bliss Carman and Charles G. D. Roberts, both now residing in the United States, yet both graduates of the University of New Brunswick; when we find American authors like Longfellow and Parkman drawing the materials of their most widely known works from Canada; when the British provinces are becoming more and more a summer resort for Americans; when the post-office recognizes no separation as to mailable matter and cost,—it is impossible not to feel that, on this continent at least, the barriers of division are being steadily let down. Then come the complex ties of personal intercourse and genealogy. Being for some weeks in the Massachusetts General Hospital, last year, I found with surprise that two thirds of the nurses were from the British provinces, and then remembered that my first and best of all possible nurses—my mother —was born at St. Andrews, New Brunswick, where her father, a British army officer, was stationed at the time of her birth, and my kinsman, Sir John Wentworth, was at one time governor of New Hampshire and then of Nova Scotia. Thus close and complex are the ties which, after all, bind together the English-speaking dwellers on this continent.

There is no prospect, I suppose, that the United States and the Dominion of Canada will ever become nearer to each other in political organization, unless it be under some very wide and comprehensive tie which shall bring the whole English-speaking world under some general name, yet leave the various parts to entire individuality. In various forms and under various titles, this possibility is becoming forced upon us. Sir George Grey gave the name of "The People of One Tongue" to such a possible organization, and elsewhere spoke of it, less poetically, but in a more matter-of-fact way, as an "Anglo-American Council." Sir Walter Besant called it "The Great Reconciliation." Mr. Dicey invented a word expressly for it, namely "isopolity," or the mutual membership of citizens of England and America, each class of voters having a right of voting in both countries, so long as peace shall last among them.

On the American side, Senator Lamar long since suggested an "Anglo-Saxon League" as likely to be proposed by some future statesman; Secretary Hay suggested the possibility of a "Reunited Anglo-Saxondom," while the late Mr. A. W. Tourgée proposed in the *Contemporary Review* "an alliance between the great branches of the Anglo-Saxon family." Mr. Arthur White, in the *North American Review* for April, 1894, sought the same thing under the name of "an Anglo-American Alliance." Mr. Andrew Carnegie, meeting the special difficulty more in detail than any one would, called the proposed organization "the Reunited States of the British-American Union" and would make full provision in it for the admission even of monarchical states, on terms equal to others but not superior. This last project would evade the difficulty long since foreseen by Richard Cobden, who in 1835 in his pamphlet "England, Ireland, and America" set aside republican government as a thing destined to be forever impossible for England; and expressed the opinion that England did not "contain within herself even the germs of genuine republicanism." Against this is to be placed, on the other hand, the remark of our fellow-countryman Dr. Andrew D. White, a man who is not given to extreme radicalism, but who yet speaks of "our sister republic Great Britain" and adds, "for Great Britain is simply a republic with a monarchical figurehead, lingering along on good behavior." (Memoirs, II. 364.)

At any rate, if we once suppose it possible that the whole English-speaking world could come together — the communities, that is, for which English is the main medium of intercourse— then the name of "A Reunited Anglo-Saxondom" would not only be a good memorial of Secretary Hay, with whom it originated, but a good descriptive title until some terser final one shall take its place. We may be sure that an achievement so great will not fail for some suitable phrase to express it.

The Editor's Clearing-House

The Beauty of Laziness

How doth the little busy bee—

sings Dr. Watts when in sweetly persuasive words he seeks to turn the Sluggard from the error of his ways (we hope the great divine was never shocked by catching his pattern of industry in a lighter and more unguarded moment, staggering drunkenly over a full-blown thistle-top). But neither Dr. Watts nor the writer of Proverbs seems to realize that, however reprehensible in insect morality, indolence in a man or woman is often the jewel-case of the soul.

For when a biographer finds a trace of genuine laziness in the "god of his idolatry" it is something which must be glozed over, excused, palliated; it is regarded as a blemish rather than an important factor in his career. Even that prince of biographers, the genial Bozzy, falls into this error; after repeating Dr. Johnson's admission and assertion that he was "but a lazy fellow," Mr. Boswell hastens to assure the reader to the contrary, though much of Dr. Johnson's fame rests upon the records of those hours of tea-drinking and of coffee-house chat—the delight of his soul. How grievously would posterity have suffered had not Mr. Boswell been content to pass his life sitting by the quiet pool (rather than fountain), of the great Doctor's wisdom, and with the patience of a skilled fisherman to cast on that placid surface his tentative flies of conversation, which rarely failed of a strike.

This spice of idleness, the "sluggishness" which the Doctor deplored, occurs very frequently in men of genius. Wordsworth confessed to indolence in his youth, so did Walter Scott; statesmen such as Webster, inventors such as Watt, poets, musicians, artists—one cannot begin to name the mighty host of famous men who, at one time or another, have been in the ranks of the idlers; even Shakespeare, with his "little Latin, less Greek," gives slight evidence of youthful industry. Who can estimate the great works which have been lost to the world simply through the artist's lack in his early youth of this saving grace of laziness!

It is especially sad if a poet miss it. He, if he be an idler, a "sluggard" in Solomon's phrase, will but write when the Muse not only inspires, but fairly takes him by the shoulders and compels him; whereas, if once the microbe of industry be fastened upon him, write he must! What matters the Muse so he may find a typewriter? Much has been written of Browning's "breathlessness," his "insane swiftness," his change of style, but his poetry of the 70's seems to have suffered much also from a tireless industry; the return in his old age to something of his earlier manner may have been solely due to a slackening of his industry through sheer fatigue.

Idleness, as we have said, is one of the greatest preservatives of intellectual gifts; as camphor and moth-balls to the summering of winter garments, as alcohol to the bottled specimen, so is laziness to a budding genius.

Truth is within ourselves,

wrote Browning in "Paracelsus"; but in our faulty system of education we build about a child's mind—brick on brick— with other people's ideas until

A baffling and perverting carnal mesh
Blinds it and makes all error.

Only the idler is able to resist this evil; only the Sluggard can preserve his inner entity, for he, wrapt in his indolence as in a circumambient cloud, is unvexed by instructors and instruction; his soul is developed from within, his talent "bildet sich in der Stille."

"Go to the Ant!" cried Solomon. "Nay," answers the Sluggard, "go rather to the wise and patient caterpillar, who finds his leaf and feeds on it in placid content; who spins his cocoon and there, in seeming inertia, perfects his wings until the time comes for him to take his place in regions undreamed of in the Ant's philosophy."

So the Sluggard; he shrouds his native brilliancy in his mantle of indolence until, when the fulness of time is come, he opens

out a way
Whence the imprisoned splendor may escape—

and ye have the statesman, the philosopher, the poet.

FRANCES DUNCAN.

With More than a Single Hair

POPE said that "beauty draws us with a single hair,"—but perusal of modern fiction shows that Beauty to-day draws with a vast quantity of hair. Of course, the old-time heroines were not hairless,— they had "sunny curls," "raven locks," "golden tresses," etc. —but the novelists then did not think it necessary to go into exhaustive details. Frank Norris was one of the first of the latter-day novelists to "feature" the hair of his heroines; and whether others have simply followed his lead, or the idea is "in the air,"— no cockney pun intended,—it is certain that much descriptive talent is expended upon the hirsute adornment of the ladies of fiction.

The more conspicuous their hair is, the better; an admirer can see it at least two blocks off. In fact, the vulgar and slangy would say that they have "noisy" hair. Gold and red are the favorite colors, apparently because they can be seen the farthest off. A heroine who somehow creeps into modern fiction with only "a low knot of brown hair" must feel herself to be almost bald. Sometimes "a great mass of jetty hair towering on her head like a crown," is permitted; but this is rare. A quiet domestic little body may have "quantities of waving chestnut hair," —quantity, you see, is always insisted upon,—"coiled back so tightly from a broad, low forehead that you barely realize at first that when it is let down it forms a beautiful shimmering cloak around her that nearly touches the floor." A mild sort of siren must be satisfied with "masses of light brown hair pushed over her ears with silver combs, and falling into loops on her neck." But when it comes to the regular stunning, resplendent, triumphant heroine who is so popular just now, the type that is pet-named Princess or Duchess or My Lady by the fond author,—the irresistible being who is almost smothered in floral and confectionery offerings from her adorers, and is obliged to employ a private secretary to keep record of her conquests,—she must positively have "locks like the sun" (either the rising or the setting sun, it does not matter which). One ingenuous young person of modern fiction decides upon the profession of adventuress, because she has green eyes and "wonderful red hair" which is full of "sparks and shocks" for the electrified beholder of the opposite sex. The flaming tresses of a magazine-story beauty so impress the hero that he can think of nothing else: "He had never seen anything so tawny, so glistening, so magnificent, as the undulant masses of hair gathered up to the crown of the girl's head." One of the supernumerary characters remarks about this young lady that "you can always see her coming a mile away,"—and when introduced to the reader she is clad in a quiet little bathing costume of scarlet, with her legs, "dimpled and brown, as a child's," bared to the knee.

Red as a color either attracts or irritates, according to the species of animal that views it; but it seems to have become a fixed tradition, or superstition, of novelists that the flamboyant tint, either in the name or on the cover of a novel, is a beckoner of success; and doubly so when it flames in the locks of the heroine. Some reviewers seem to share the belief; for one of them enthusiastically queried, "Who would not want to read a novel called 'The Red-Haired Woman?'" In fact, the color has been so associated with temper, spirit, guileful fascination, etc., that it would be almost useless for a red-haired woman of real life, no matter how meek and mild she might be, to exemplify her character in her conduct; for nobody would believe in her. People would say that she was dissembling. Golden hair, however, if bright enough to glitter like a gilded signboard in the sunshine,—and if in sufficient quantities,— is almost equally popular in fiction. A novelist devotes half a column to the "amber hair" of one of his leading ladies, which was so marvellously abundant as to give scope for a bewilderingly complicated coiffure culminating on top in "golden bubbles." Another fortunate one had "the glintiest of hair, hair that curled damp on the low forehead and around the pink ears, hair that lay in a rich mass at the nape of the gleaming neck." In addition, she possessed the charm of eyes that were "of all colors, and no color,"—which suggests the paradoxical idea of a decolorized rainbow. Once we find it suggested that the amount of hair is not the only secret of female fascination: "Some men maintained that it was not the quantity nor the color of Peggy Ryle's hair that did the mischief, but simply and solely the way it grew." But the most glorious example of what "only a woman's hair" can do is found in a piece of current fiction. The heroine has hair of "meek baby-gold," that curls and waves and riots by nature, just as less blessed women have to try to make their locks do with curling tongs; and of course it is of almost superhuman length and thickness. It might seem enough for such hair to be merely ornamental; but it also proves useful. As she and a man are sailing, the boat capsizes and they are thrown into the water. They are near a small island, which they manage to reach; and as they do not wish to remain castaways any longer than necessary, they decide to signal to some passing bark. But they have nothing to signal with. Suddenly a bright idea dawns upon the lady's mind; seizing her radiant and wonderful hair in both hands, she waves it wildly as a flag of distress, "a golden banner,"—and they are promptly rescued. After this, one might almost expect to hear that some romantic heroine has made her bright-tressed head play the part of the revolving light in a lighthouse, to warn her sailor lover away from the perils of rocks and shoals. And why not? Have we not read in recent fiction of a hero who, seeking his lady in a dim conservatory, descries amid the flowery aisles "the light of her hair"?

The meditative reader wonders whether there is any connection between this Samson-like growth in fiction and the fact that hairdressers say the price of false hair has mounted amazingly of late.

J. K. WETHERILL.

The Book=Buyer's Guide

ART

Elward—On Collecting Miniatures, Enamels, and Jewelry. By Robert Elward. Longmans. 75 cents net.

Though such a book as this can hardly appeal to any very wide public, yet it should make itself distinctly useful to the man prepared to develop a hobby along the lines it lays down. The five chapters give a distinct if short summary of what is most sought after, what most rare, and what most valuable, among the miniatures, enamels, and jewelry of all ages.

Greenshields—Landscape Painting and Modern Dutch Artists. By E. B. Greenshields. Baker and Taylor. $2.00 net.

Landscape painting rarely receives the attention of one whole volume, but here is an excellent book devoted entirely to a treatment of the subject on its historical and technical sides from the awakening of the art to the present period of French impressionism and Dutch revival. The central theme from which the author attacks his subject is that every artist has painted nature not as it actually was but as it affected him. The text is concise and to the point; the half-tone illustrations admirably reproduced.

Levy—The American Art Annual, 1905–1906. Vol. V. Edited by Florence N. Levy. American Art Annual Co. $5.00.

For the editor or the man interested in the technical record of the past year of American Art such a volume stands invaluable and without competitors. The text is well illustrated with frequent half-tone illustrations of the best contemporary work of artists on this side of the Atlantic.

Miles—The Later Work of Titian. By Henry Miles. The Newnes Art Library. Warne. $1.25.

This one volume in a series of twenty on painters past and present, contains sixteen pages of sanely written comment, description, and biography concerning Titian, preceded by a photogravure frontispiece and followed by sixty-four full-page half-tone illustrations. In the series the quality of the reproductions, as well as the merit of the introductions, varies to a great extent. Here the author has written modestly and directly, but the half-tones fall below the average level. The book as a whole, however, is well worth the price and quite a find to the man looking for quantity rather than quality in reproductions of Titian's work.

Phythian—The Pre-Raphaelite Brotherhood. By J. Ernest Phythian. The Newnes Art Library. Warne. $1.25.

The text of this volume deals in a large way with the group of men among whom Dante Gabriel Rossetti made so distinct a name. The author covers his ground by chronicling the history of the movement with little or no personal comment. The half-tone reproductions have been well chosen. The book is uniform with the one on Titian.

Radford—Dante Gabriel Rossetti. By Ernest Radford. The Newnes Art Library. Warne. $1.25.

This book is a companion to the one on "The Pre-Raphaelite Brotherhood." The author has sorted with clearness such vital material concerning the life of Rossetti as may be placed in his restricted space. The illustrations have been well made, considering the price at which the volume is published.

Birney—Childhood. By Mrs. Theodore W.
Birney Stokes. $1.00 net.

Childhood in its mental, moral, and physical
aspects has evidently been the subject of much
thoughtful and loving study on the part of
the author, who is the founder and promoter
of the National Congress of Mothers. She is
singularly free from fads; does not write as if
she were the whole Law and the Prophets on
the subject of children, but by wise and
judicious suggestion she shows parents how
to know and understand the little beings they
are responsible for, and a careful perusal of
the book should bring help to many households.

George—The Menace of Privilege. By Henry
George, Jr. Doubleday, Page & Co. $1.50.

This is an able, sincere, and elaborate indict-
ment of [modern society, resting funda-
mentally on the highly questionable assertion
that the rich are getting richer, and that the
poor are getting poorer. All the well-known
evils in our industrial, political, and social
world,—and some conditions that cannot be
conceded as evils,—are described in great
detail. The temperamentally pessimistic will
find herein a mass of congenial food. In its
particulars the description is in general true,
but the resulting composite picture is as a
whole distorted and exaggerated. The net
result of such a work is a harmful one, for it
forces those who believe that progress consists
in evolution and not in revolution, and who at
the same time recognize clearly the extent of
the evils complained of, to divert their energies
from curing these evils to defending society
as a whole. For in its essence this is an attack
on social life. Its philosophy is that of France
in the eighteenth century, with its assumption
of an ideal state of nature perverted by the
very existence of society. As a remedy for
existing evils the son naturally adopts the
device of the father, namely, the single tax,
one on land equivalent to the rental value
thereof. From this follows naturally the
abolition of a protective tariff. In addition
he advocates the confiscation by the state of
all franchises granted to the public utility
corporations. The proposals are revolutionary,
and would result in making public property
the greater part of what is now private
property. Carried to their logical conclusion
George's theories would result in the abolition
of all private property, since, in whatever form
it is, private property is privilege as defined by
the author. As the work is one of considerable ability it is bound to have great influence
at a time when the people as a whole are
legitimately aroused by the corruption disclosed in financial and political circles. It is
hardly probable that the destruction of the
entire organism will commend itself as the
proper remedy for a well-diagnosed disease existing therein.

Grinnell—Social Theories and Social Facts.
By William Morton Grinnell. Putnams. $1

This is the protest of a strong individualist

against recent socialistic tendencies in the
United States, against state ownership of
railroads and other public utilities, and against
some tendencies of the trades-unions. It is not
a closely reasoned exposition, nor one characterized by breadth of view. The facts are
not critically examined to determine their real
meaning, and they are not always accurate.
Occasionally sweeping statements are made
as if the facts were well established. Yet the
book is timely, especially as it emphasizes
important facts that are usually overlooked
in the ordinary controversial discussions.
Thus, Mr. Grinnell shows that when we speak
of " the trusts" as monopolies we are incorrect,
as virtually no one of our large industrial corporations is a monopoly. Similarly he emphasizes the fact that the ownership of our railroads and industrial corporations is very
widely diffused, though popularly the managers, who usually own only a share, are
supposed to be the real owners.

**Irving—Crowell's Miniature Edition of Irving's
Select Works.** Crowell. $2.50.

Five tiny books, so small that they can be
slipped into a coat pocket, case and all, and
yet so well printed on fine India paper that
the type is agreeably legible. The five books
are; "The Sketch Book," "Christmas Sketches," "The Alhambra," "Bracebridge Hall,"
and "Tales of a Traveller." They are
bound in beautiful soft leather, with case to
match, and bear witness to the truth of the
old saying that "good things are done up in
small parcels."

Learned—Ideals of Girls. By Mrs. Frank
Learned. Stokes. $1.00.

A series of brief conventional talks on every-
day subjects, such as Manners, Personal Appearance, Friendship and Marriage, Letters
and Letter-writing. The author calls her
little essays "Talks on Character, Life, and
Culture." They have already appeared in
the Delineator.

Lodge—Life and Matter. By Sir Oliver
Lodge. Putnams. $1.00.

This little book by a well-known English
scientist is composed of stray articles, all
bearing on the subject indicated by the title.
In part it is a criticism of Haeckel's widely
read "Riddle of the Universe," and is designed
to counteract the influence of that work among
the skilled laboring classes in England. As
Haeckel has a tendency to confuse science
and philosophy, and to state as scientific
truths what were merely conjectural inferences
of varying degrees of probability, Lodge's
criticism is well founded. The two main
theses that Lodge attacks are that material
energy or terrestrial activity is insusceptible
to extra-mundane control, and that life is
merely one of the forms of material energy.
The book is not wholly critical, but in addition
Lodge develops his own views of the mystery
of life and death, of the unknown and perhaps
the forever unknowable. As a scientist he

naturally recognizes freely the purely hypothetical nature of such speculations, and consequently the acceptance of his views depends more on the temperment of the reader than on the quality of the argument.

Mabie—The Great Word. By Hamilton Wright Mabie. Dodd, Mead. $1.00.

According to Mr. Mabie, who sets forth his conviction in a series of connected essays, the "great word" is Love. He treats his subject in the largest sense, and with a delicacy of sentiment and a richness of allusion that his readers have learned to expect from him, Mr Mabie is never concerned with the promulgation of radical or startling notions; and this book, like his others, will be valued for its sane and charming conservatism.

Sainte-Beuve—Portraits of the Eighteenth Century. By C. A. Sainte-Beuve. Putnam's. $2.50.

These two volumes, of which the first is translated by Katherine Prescott Wormeley, and the second by George Burnham Ives, need no other comment than that they contain some of the most delightful of Sainte-Beuve's charming "portraits." The selections are taken from the "Causeries du Lundi," the "Portraits de Femmes," and "Portraits Littéraires," and where two or more essays on the same person have appeared in the different series they are here put together, omitting repetitions. The books are illustrated with portraits, and there is a critical introduction by Edmond Scherer.

Shaw—The Author's Apology. By Bernard Shaw. Brentano's. 80 cts.

This little pamphlet is a reprint, first of Mr. John Corbin's critical estimate of "Mrs. Warren's Profession," published in the New York *Sun;* and second, of Mr. Shaw's own preface to that play, published in the volume of "Unpleasant" plays.

BIOGRAPHY

Carus—Friedrich Schiller. By Paul Carus. Open Court Co. 75c. net.

A concise but scholarly sketch of Schiller's life and an appreciation of his poetry. Many of the copious illustrations, from old portraits, engravings, etc., are of more than usual novelty and interest.

Finck—Edvard Grieg. By Henry T. Finck. John Lane. $1.25.

A volume in the series of "Living Masters of Music," edited by Rosa Newmarch. Mr. Finck writes of the Norwegian master with almost unqualified enthusiasm. There is much new material relating to the personal side of the composer, including an account of a visit paid him at his home by Mr. Finck. The illustrations are mainly from photographs of Grieg.

MacDonnell—King Leopold II., His Rule in Belgium and the Congo. By John de Courcy MacDonnell. Cassell. $2.00.

Leopold II. in recent years has been prominently in the public eye, in part on account of the scandal in his family, in part on account of the controversy about his administration of the Independent State of the Congo. The controversy has been exceptionally acute, and printers' ink has been liberally used in it. Passengers on the Oriental express from Ostend two years ago found, probably to their surprise, that they were provided gratis with reading matter consisting of a pamphlet printed in many languages defending the Belgian king's rule in the Congo. This book is evidently a result of this controversy, and is devoted mainly to the African realm of Leopold II. The author finds all the charges against this rule false, and sustains the government on all points. Though the work has the character of special pleading, still it is not of the usually low order of such partisan publications. The author writes interestingly and graphically of conditions in the Congo, and emphasizes in detail the magnitude of the work done, and the great difficulties in doing it. He has unquestionably made out a strong case, which can be shattered only by evidence of the greatest weight.

May—Life of Johannes Brahms. By Florence May. Longmans. 2 vols. Octavo $7.00.

Unlike the recently published Tchaikovsky letters, "Johannes Brahms" will interest chiefly—perhaps exclusively—musicians and students of Brahms's work. Less stout-hearted readers will be apt to faint and grow weary at the second volume. Yet there are delightful glimpses of the Schumanns' those "divine people," as Brahms calls them, of Joachim, the composer's lifelong friend. The careful detailed tracing of Brahms's life in its relation to his work is done with the untiring faithfulness of a devoted student to a beloved master. The explanations and descriptions of many of his compositions are admirable, especially that of the noble "German Requiem." Here, especially, Miss May, shows the advantage of having been Brahms's pupil. All this will be followed with deep interest by music students, for Brahms with his intellectuality which to Tchaikovsky's slavonic temperament seemed dry and cold, with his almost austere idealism subtly inwrought with poetry and charm—Brahms in whom one sees the "romantic" movement not as a seedling, but grafted on the noble classicism of Bach and Beethoven—Brahms perhaps more than any other composer needs a sympathetic comprehension, an intimate understanding, in order to a just appreciation of his work. Valuable as undoubtedly is the painstaking collection of data, the book is somewhat overweighted by detailed accounts of programs and the like, which might have been left to an appendix, that it is rather difficult for the reader to see Brahms the man in his proper perspective. Also the author's attitude toward the great composer is so tirelessly adoring that even a devout reader wearies of constantly kneeling beside her at the shrine. The first volume is prefaced by personal reminiscences which, although readable, seem rather alien to the serious character of the book.

Mitton—Jane Austen and Her Times. By G. E. Mitton. Putnam. $2.75.

"Of Jane Austen's life there is little to tell" is the opening sentence of this book, but the author thinks there is a great deal to tell about Jane Austen's personality, and particularly as a product of her times. Naturally the book is chiefly "times," which serve as a background to a very little of Jane Austen. The position of the clergy, letters and post, society, visits, contemporary writers, and a host of other things of those times are described with the aid of extracts from journals, newspapers, letters, etc., into which are woven characters from Jane Austen's books, and little bits of her life. But notwithstanding the "made-up" nature of the book it is very readable, and the illustrations are interesting.

O'Brien—Recollections. By William O'Brien. Macmillan. $3.50.

An Irishman for a book of reminiscences, and particularly for those of one who has been so active in the national struggle for a free Ireland! Whatever may be the sympathies of the reader with reference to the political questions involved, he cannot but enjoy the genial, humorous, earnest, and patriotic pages of this volume, which not only gives us fresh views of many points in the history of the times in Ireland, but contains so many facts and anecdotes concerning his Hibernian and other contemporaries who have helped to make that history. The book brings the recollections down only to 1883, and we shall look forward with impatience to their continuation in another volume.

Robins—William T. Sherman. By Edward Robins. Jacobs. $1.25 net.

The twentieth volume in the series of "American Crisis Biographies," connected with the history of the Civil War, and quite up to the creditable standard of its predecessors. The author had a most picturesque subject, and he has improved his opportunities commendably. The Bibliography appended to the book is well compiled, filling nearly four pages.

Shand—Days of the Past: a Medley of Memories. By Alexander Innes Shand. Dutton. $3.00.

The subtitle well describes the book, which is a medley of memories of experiences in the last forty or more years in England and Scotland as a sportsman, soldier, journalist, author, and traveller, with sketches of London hotels and lodging-houses, ventures on the stock exchange, rambles among Scotch shepherds and poachers, literary reminiscence, etc., written in vivacious and free-and-easy

style not unmixed with slang—more interesting often to English than to American readers, but entertaining anywhere.

Wilkins—Mrs. Fitzherbert and George IV. By W. H. Wilkins, M. A. Longmans. $5.00 net.

For seventy years Mrs. Fitzherbert has been waiting for justice to be done her. At the request of some members of her family Mr. Wilkins undertook the writing of her biography, a task, however, that would have been incomplete had not King Edward given his permission to examine the papers that Mrs. Fitzherbert placed in Coutts's Bank in 1833. These papers were intended for publication after her death, and entirely clear up the mystery that has surrounded Mrs. Fitzherbert and her relations with George IV. Mr. Wilkins has devoted ten years to the study of the Hanoverian period, and has written sympathetically of several ladies of that race. His treatment of the present subject is no less sympathetic; he is just to George IV., and gives besides an excellent picture of the period. The book is illustrated.

FICTION

Brown—Paradise. By Alice Brown. Houghton, Mifflin. $1.50.

Miss Brown understands New England quite as well as its more famous interpreters, but it is her distinction that she has always given her imagination freer play, been content, as it were, with a less literal translation. "Paradise" is a case in point. In her detail and idiom the author has gotten very "close to the soil" indeed, while in her heroine, Barbara, she has presented a thoroughly romantic character, which she forces her New England village to assimilate. In spite of the fact that "Paradise" is sure to be called a "pretty story," it is to be lamented that Miss Brown's always interesting imagination is not a little more controlled. It would be highly unfortunate if she became literal and learned to "putter"; but Barbara, with her gauze gown and tinsel crown, her unexplained share in her "guardian's" defrauding of the public, is surely extravagant and overdone. The larger relations of life, with which the book professes to deal, it handles, after all, rather half-heartedly; its real delight lies in the pages of humorous observation, its delineations of eccentric character. Miss Brown has done bigger and more enduring work.

Crawford — Salve-Venetia. By F. Marion Crawford. 2 vols. Macmillan. $5.00.

Italy and Marion Crawford are always a good combination, and Venice gives him a fine field for his facile pen. Descriptions of scenery or places are eschewed The historical side of the picture is presented; the history is not profound,—"Gleanings" is the happy way he describes it,—but it is very readable, and, needless to say, abounds in picturesqueness.

Perhaps Mr. Pennell's illustrations are also picturesque. A great many of them are quite comprehensible to one who has not been in Venice, but occasionally he leaves more than is agreeable to the imagination. This book has already been mentioned several times in the "Lounger," which makes a longer notice unnecessary.

Huneker—Visionaries. By James Huneker. Scribner. $1.50.

Music, love, the artistic temperament, paradox, rhetorical exuberance,—readers are beginning to recognize at sight the familiar hallmarks of Mr. Huneker's method, or habit, of writing fiction. And the combination of these elements has a flavor, it must be admitted, with which it is possible to become satiated. Mr. Huneker is perhaps the most stimulating critic, in extra-academic fields, that we have, both because of his sensitive preceptions and his lively lawlessness of style. But æsthetic impressions and speculations are not, in themselves, the best material for stories, and it is this, and not at all the study of character, in which this writer is interested. His characters look like posters and talk like Mr. Huneker. Nobody will deny that the result is interesting, but it is not fiction of the first order. "The Spiral Road" is, however, an unusually impressive story, and there is scarcely one of the tales that is not based on a challenging idea. We should probably after all succeed only in depriving ourselves of entertainment if we fettered Mr. Huneker and equipped him with a duplicate of the tools that other writers use. Let him continue to soar and chant.

Kildare—The Wisdom of the Simple. A Tale of Lower New York. By Owen Kildare. Revell. $1.50.

The compelling truth of this story of tenement-house life and the interests of Wittle Street is evident in the first chapter. Mr. Kildare knows his ground, for he was reared among the scenes that he describes. He has witnessed the "glorious sport on pay-day evening" when the wife sits on the prostrate form of her husband and helps herself to handfuls of the loved one's locks, or dodges the fearful lunges of her husband's knife, when he is determined to "teach her not to get so gay and fresh." The combined humor and pathos of Martin Toner's acquaintance with old Caramel, the second-hand bookseller, is one of the best parts of the book. Probably no writer in New York is capable of presenting slum life, its needs and its temptations, as does Owen Kildare.

McVickar—Reptiles. By Henry W. McVickar. Illustrated by his own hand. Appleton. $1.50.

A clever, cynical society novel which opens by a Prologue in Teire's Tavern in Paris. Three college chums discuss marriage, and the most sceptical of them proposes a wager payable five years after marriage "that it is all the same in five years whomever you marry." The love affairs of each are ' thereafter described in turn, and sometimes in entanglement. The cold-blooded, reptile-like characteristics of certain of the *dramatis personæ* are dwelt upon at length, and emphasized by the illustrations, which might give a sensitive soul delirium tremens. The construction is jerky and unexpected at times, but altogether the story is very readable for an idle hour.

Repplier—In our Convent Days. By Agnes Repplier. Houghton, Mifflin $1.10.

It has always been Miss Repplier's distinction to succeed with whatever she has touched, beyond any one else in the same field and this holds true of her first volume of short stories, which are the best boarding-school studies that have been published in a period during which this type of material has been very generously contributed. It is of no small interest to know that those two strongly individual little girls, "Agnes" and "Elizabeth," are Miss Repplier and Mrs. Elizabeth Robbins Pennell, who once had the good fortune of being school-mates; but it is n't necessary to know this to enjoy these intensely human little histories, told with a grace and sprightliness which will make them live long. One of the first things that grown-up people forget is the fascinating complexities of little girls' minds. Miss Repplier has remembered them. Her admirable little stories are written to entertain, not to "improve" and are perhaps distinguished from all other "girls' books" ever written in that they are free from the slightest suggestion of the sentimental or the banal.

HISTORY AND TRAVEL

Avery—A History of the United States and its People. By Elroy M. Avery. Vol. II. Barrows. $6.25

This second volume of Mr. Avery's History continues the plan, announced in his first, of a genuinely "popular" and at the same time complete and thoroughly accurate work, so written as "to be actually read and easily understood, and still to avoid falling into the quicksands of partisanship and curious delusions." It covers the period from 1600 to 1661, and is copiously and elaborately illustrated with maps, facsimiles of documents, autographs, portraits, antiquities, and a multitude of other objects, many of the engravings being in colors. The typography is of the best grade throughout. The original plan was for twelve volumes, but the author now finds that it will demand fifteen, which will, however, be furnished to the original subscribers with no increase in price; and it is promised that the high standard of mechanical execution in the initial volumes shall be fully maintained to the last. The plan is a good one, and the first volume has met with such encouragement that the success of the enterprise seems to be assured.

Buley—Australian Life in Town and Country.
By E. C. Buley. Putnam. $1.20 net.

The fourth and fifth issues in the series of
"Our Asiatic Neighbours," which is rivalling
in popularity the earlier series of "Our
European Neighbours," twelve volumes of
which have already appeared and been received
with steadily increasing favor. They cover
every form and phase of life in the several
countries, and are copiously illustrated from
photographs.

**Cox—The Journeys of La Salle and his Com-
panions.** Edited by Prof. I. J. Cox. 2 vols.
Barnes. $2.00 net.

The latest issue in the series of "The Trail
Makers," which is an admirable supplement
to the formal story of American history and
exploration, giving us cheap reprints of the
personal narratives of the early discoverers
and travellers, most of which are long out of
print and comparatively inaccessible in the
libraries. La Salle's career was one of the
most eventful and dramatic in the French exploration of North America, and it was a
happy thought to include the story of it in
this neat and inexpensive series.

Duclaux—The Fields of France. By Madame
Mary Duclaux. (A. Mary F. Robinson.)
Lippincott. $6.00 net.

The fields of France are not all of that lovely
land that Mme. Duclaux writes of here. The
owner of and the worker in the fields claim a
large share of her attention. Beginning with
"A Farm in the Cantat," she describes country
life in Auvergne, that picturesque region of
sugar-loaf mountains, old castles, and dirty
but picturesque people. Her own home is the
subject of an illustration, and her relations
between peasant and master she gives very
interesting details. Of course the fields of
France cannot be written of without reference
to La Bruyère, who gave such a heart-rending
picture of the French peasant in the seventeenth century, and Arthur Young, whose
travels in France just before the outbreak of
the Revolution resulted in a book that has
become a classic on the subject of the French
peasant of that period. Mme. Duclaux does
not leave him there, but brings him quite up
to date. Two interesting chapters tell how the
poor lived in the fourteenth century, and of
life and conditions in the mediæval country
house. "A Manor in Touraine" tells more of
another class of French society than the
peasant, and "A Little Tour in Provence"
takes us through that romantic country with
a sympathetic cicerone. There are twenty
illustrations in color that lend great charm to
the book, in spite of the fact that the exigencies of color printing have sometimes
necessitated rather brighter tints than those
with which Nature favors us. Those who have
wandered much in France will enjoy this
book, and those who have not may by it conceive a desire to do so.

**James—In and Out of the old Missions of
California.** By George Wharton James.
Little, Brown. $3.00 net.

The pictures that illustrate this book create
a strong feeling of regret that these old missions should have been allowed to go to ruin.
Apart from their usefulness to the Indians,
which Mr. James estimates highly, they are
so picturesque as to supply what is a great
want in a new country. Each mission is
described in a separate chapter, its foundation,
architecture, furniture, painting, and carving.
A general account of the founding of the
missions is given, as well as of their seculari-
zation, and the author gives vent to his righteous indignation at the treatment of the
California Indians by the United States Government. The book is marred by over-much
sentimental rhetoric.

Lea—A History of the Spanish Inquisition.
By Henry Charles Lea. In four Vols.
Vol. I. Macmillan. $2.50 net.

Dr. Lea is a veteran authority on the history
of the Romish Church, having brought out in
the past forty years a succession of important
works on the subject, from his "Superstition
and Force," which has passed through four
editions since 1866, his "Sacerdotal Celibacy"
(1867), "Studies in Church History" (1869)
"History of the Inquisition in the Middle
Ages" (1888), and other important books
on related topics, down to the present work,
which he begins in his eighty-first year, and
the first instalment of which is a volume of
more than 600 pages. The opening chapters
illustrate the gradual conversion of the
Spaniards "from the most tolerant to the
most intolerant nation in Europe," through
the success of the Church in arousing the greed
and fanaticism of the people and repressing
the kindly relations with the Jews and the
Moors which had long existed. From this
the Jews were the earliest and worst sufferers,
but in the beginning of the 15th century both
Moor and Jew were victims of the cruel law
that humiliated and oppressed them almost
beyond endurance. The Inquisition was the
natural product of these conditions, and the
chapters that follow trace its growth, its increasing control of the crown, its assumption
of superiority in ecclesiastical as well as in
civil affairs, its abuses, its arrogance, its con-
flicts with the military and spiritual courts,
the popular hatred it excited and aggravated
until the general detestation of its tyranny
became a recognized fact. All this is but the
beginning of the terrible story that is to be
continued in the volumes that are to follow.

Sedgwick—A Short History of Italy. By Henry
Dwight Sedgwick. Houghton, Mifflin.
$2.00 net.

It is hard to determine for what class of readers
this book was written. It is not childish
enough for children, it does not show sufficient
research to give it value to the student, and is
far too casual in its description of many
events,—the massacre of the Albigenses, who

are not named in the account of the persecution, for instance—to be useful to persons of little knowledge but much desire to learn history.

Smith—Irish History and the Irish Question
By Goldwin Smith. McClure. $1.50.

Ever since the days of Aristotle it has been an accepted maxim of sound political thought that man is by nature a social animal, acting only in and through society. It is also being gradually recognized that history is virtually only the action and reaction of groups of associated individuals upon one another, and that political evolution consists in the conflict of such groups, and in the survival of the more fit. Sometimes the survival of the stronger group involves the physical disappearance of the weaker; more often the survival is denoted by the predominance of the language, culture, morals, and especially the political civilization of the victor. The three great factors separating group from group are differences in race, in religion and in economic interests. When all of these differences coexist, as in the case of the relations of Ireland and England, the outcome is bound to be a savage conflict. The theme offers exceptional opportunities to Goldwin Smith, and in his brilliantly-written essay he does it full justice. In an essay such as this, as in his similar survey of the history of the United States, Goldwin Smith appears to best advantage. Few writers can put as much matter in a short sentence as he can, and few are so able to suggest, by a short clause or by an allusion, facts that had to be omitted, but a knowledge of which is essential to a complete understanding of the subject. His pregnant though rather sarcastic characterization of Gladstone in connection with that statesman's sudden alliance with Parnell is worth quoting: "This retrospective imagination was strong, and having changed so much he had always present to his mind the possibility of farther change. It made his language sometimes capable of unforseen interpretation." The questions dividing the United Kingdom are still alive, and the only hope of a permanent settlement lies in the gradual abrasion of racial differences through intermarriage, in the subsidence of dogmatic religious fervor, and in the definitive settlement of the agrarian difficulties in Ireland. The hope of the future is a bright one, though the end of the difficulty is not yet in sight.

Thwaites—Early Western Travels.
Edited by Reuben Gold Thwaites. Vol. XXI. H. Clark. $4.00.

This volume of the important series of "Early Western Travels, 1748-1846" (also issued separately) contains two interesting works: (I.) John B. Wyeth's "Oregon: or a short history of a long journey from the Atlantic Ocean to the region of the Pacific, by land"; and (II.) John K. Townsend's "Narrative of Journey across the Rocky Mountains to the Columbia River." Wyeth was one of a party of twenty-four organized in 1832 by Nathaniel J. Wyeth for settling in the far West but the majority turned back on reaching St. Louis, and the author of this "short 'history" was one of the small party who left the leader four days' march beyond the Rocky Mountains, pressed on to Oregon, and later made his way back to New England. He gives us a graphic and attractive picture of early life on the plains and among the mountains. Townsend, who was a physician and naturalist, was connected with a later expedition (in 1834), and remained in the Oregon region for two years, making a voyage to the Sandwich Islands in the meantime. His narrative is written in an easy, fluent style, and is evidently based on his daily journals. The introduction and notes of the editor add much to the interest of the reprint, as throughout the series.

MISCELLANEOUS

Leonard—Who 's Who in America.
A Biographical Dictionary of Notable Living Men and Women of the United States. 1906-1907. Edited by John W. Leonard. Marquis. $3.50.

No more valuable volume of reference comes to the editor's table than "Who 's Who in America." The new "Who 's Who" is just received. It contains 346 more pages than the previous volume, but it is printed on thinner paper, so that it is no more bulky. One hesitates to criticise so admirable a work as this; at the same time those of us whose eyesight is not what it was would rather have the volume a little more bulky than to have the paper a little thinner. "Who 's Who in America" is a boon to every busy man and woman in this country and England, and it would not be without its uses on the Continent.

Sanborn—Old Time Wall Papers.
An Account of the Pictorial Papers on our Forefathers' Walls, etc. By Kate Sanborn. Literary Collector Press. $5.00.

Miss Sanborn has had a most interesting subject in old time wall papers, and she has treated it in a delightful manner. This writer devotes herself largely to old things—old houses, old furniture, old wall paper—and gives herself no end of trouble in working up her hobbies. Why no one has ever done wall papers in this way before is a mystery. Perhaps it was realized that Miss Sanborn would do it in time, and would do it well. According to the author, who has studied the matter carefully, no other book has been written on just this subject. Her collection of photographs, she tells us in her introductory note, is unique, and we can well believe it. The book is unique also. Only a limited edition of this book has been printed, which will add much to its intrinsic value.

Schillings—Flashlights in the Jungle.
By C. G. Schillings. Translated by Frederic Whyte. Doubleday, Page. $3.80 net.

Alexander had no camera; else, instead of weeping, he would have gone to Africa and taken the photograph of the zebras on page 109 of "Flashlights in the Jungle," and the photographs of the rhinoceroses, lions, baboons, elephants and leopards that come down in the night at the pools to drink, on every other page of this weird book. It is now Herr Schillings's turn and ours (who have cameras) to weep, for, unless we perfect an apparatus for doing the deep sea, there is now no other animal-world to photograph. We have read Livingstone and Stanley, Cameron and Junker, and "From the Cape to Cairo," but all of them together give no such idea of real equatorial Africa the wild, savage, untamable, beast-haunted jungle, as does this book by Herr Schillings.

I can no better describe the new and vivid impression from this work than by asking the reader to contrast the flashlight photograph of the zebras on page 109 with the photographs of the same animals on page 191 of "From the Cape to Cairo." If asked to name the most wonderful photograph, animal or other, ever taken I should say this one of the zebras by Herr Schillings. Then to that add the leopard on page 405, the gnus on 480, the lions on 356, together with the other 298, and you have the most thrilling and extraordinary animal book ever made.

In my review of the first, unauthorized edition, I said that the pictures were enough to make one afraid of his own tame dark. This fuller, authentic volume is even more realistic, and it puts the work of the author in its true light, too. He is a trained naturalist, a discoverer, whose passion and purpose are not to kill, but to study and protect the wild animals of Africa. His pluck, endurance, sincerity, and enthusiasm are as real as his pictures. The simple, almost naïve account of his bare escapes and hair-raising adventures sounds like the tales of the mighty hunters of old. But here are the pictures to back them up—every photograph an adventure, a proof of the fascinating written record.

Stevens and Darling—Practical Rowing with Scull and Sweep. by Arthur W. Stevens, and **The Effects of Training,** by Eugene A. Darling. Little, Brown. $1.00.

This primer of rowing as applied to the scull or the eight-oared shell attacks its subject in the common sense-manner of taking up each technical term of the rowing jargon, defining its requirements, and suggesting the best means of filling them. The volume is technical in treatment, and so directly to the point that it cannot fail to be of interest and of use to the oarsman. The text has been adequately illustrated by half-tone photographs. Dr. Darling's chapters on the Effects of Training are the results of a series of tests to learn more concerning the physical reaction of violent exercise, made upon the Harvard University crew. The contribution should be of undoubted value to a subject of which there is still far too little understanding.

POETRY AND VERSE

Birchall—The Book of the Singing Winds. By Sara Hamilton Birchall. Bartlett. $2.00

Those readers who some little time ago were charmed by comrade-voices singing the "Songs of Vagabondia," will recognise in this "Book of the Singing Winds" the young, fresh voice of one who should be called sister-spirit to those earlier chanters of "the Open." The poems in this dainty miniature volume number scarcely so many as their author's summers; but her twenty years of looking and listening in the world of nature, with a native gift of melody superadded, compel us to include a new and hopeful singer in the band of our nature poets. Mrs. Birchall's modest "foreword" characterizes her earliest offerings of verse as "a child's harvest of a day;" and yet we, too, may quote therefrom, bidding the "gentle reader,"

"As you pass,
Wait a moment. There's something
For you"—

And that "something" for the reader of Miss Birchall's work will increase in interest, if this young writer fulfils in future years the promise she has already given.

Graham—More Misrepresentative Men. By Harry Graham. Fox, Duffield, $1.00.

Captain Graham's hand has not lost its cunning since it produced "Ruthless Rhymes" and "Misrepresentative Men." If nothing in the present volume is quite so salient as the "Theodore Roosevelt" of last year, it is only because Henry VIII., Mr. Astor, Euclid, Sherlock Homes, and the other more or less "misrepresentative men" in the present waxwork show, are less inspiring themes than the strenuous American President. The author has a facility which, if he were a writer of serious verse, would be fatal, but in a writer of humorous skits is, so to speak, vital. His quips and cranks are numberless, and his high spirits unfailing and contagious. In an "Aftword," designed to disarm the hostile critic, the poet sings:

"To those whose intellect is small,
This work should prove a priceless treasure;
To persons who have none at all
A never-ending fount of pleasure;
A mental stimulus or tonic
To all whose idiocy is chronic."

The first series of "Misrepresentative Men," was dedicated to a portrait which was seen to be that of Miss Ethel Barrymore; the second is dedicated to E. B. Even the chronically idiotic will suspect the identity of the dedicatee! A word should be said in acknowledgment of the skill of the illustrator, Mr. Malcolm Strauss, in making his distorted portraits unmistakable likenesses of the victims of his author's amiable satires. Space may be made here to mention that Captain Graham has recently brought out through Edward Arnold of London a volume entitled "Verse and Worse."

(For list of Books Received see third page following)

Photo by Russell

HON. AUGUSTINE BIRRELL
See page 420

THE CRITIC

Vol. XLVIII   MAY, 1906   No. 5

The Lounger

LOVERS of literature were shocked to read in the daily papers on March 26th that the home of Mr. Julian Hawthorne at Yonkers on the Hudson had been partly destroyed by fire the day before, and that a number of the manuscripts of his father, Nathaniel Hawthorne, had been reduced to "pulpy masses" by the water used in extinguishing the flames. Among the MSS. that escaped the more devouring of the two elements, only to be injured by the other, one read, were "The Scarlet Letter," "The Blithedale Romance," "Septimius Felton," "The Marble Faun," and "Twice-Told Tales." The narrow escape of such priceless literary treasures was enough to make the public gasp. Needless to say, the owner received some very urgent letters bearing the same date as that of the newspaper reports; and one of his correspondents received a reply that showed how gullible he had been in assuming the correctness of a statement merely because he had seen it in print—the joke of the matter being that he himself was a veteran journalist. Mr. Hawthorne's answer—which I publish by the writer's permission—ran as follows:

"It was kind of you to sympathize with my adventure; and in return I hasten to say that nothing of national importance was involved in the event. Only my own belongings underwent the chastening of fire. None of my father's manuscripts were in the house; and most of the other family heirlooms were either saved quite, or with trifling damage. There were few of them left, anyhow. As for 'The Scarlet Letter' MS., it was destroyed about fifty-six years ago, by the negligence of our late friend, James T. Fields, who forgot to rescue it from the printers. The other books are owned by various friends of the family, and are beyond any ordinary danger of destruction. My own personal books, clothes, pictures, rugs, chairs, and tables, and other plunder, suffered, as such things will, under the attack of the elemental forces; and perhaps it is better to own nothing than to be anxious about the things one owns. Of course, for the first time in ten years, the insurance had been allowed to lapse, but my faith in insurance had been shaken by the revelations of the past few months; so that is all right, too."

❦

Shortly after the death of Mr. Paul Laurence Dunbar, the colored poet, the

COPYRIGHT 1905, BY THE CRITIC COMPANY.
ENTERED AT NEW ROCHELLE, N. Y., POST OFFICE AS SECOND-CLASS MATTER.

following announcement appeared in the *Evening Post* of this city :

Among the bright galaxy of intellectual Stars in bronzed American literature none have touched the hearts of all people and reached a more conspicuous position in belles-lettres than Mr. Dunbar. In order to perpetuate his memory and retain his genius in the minds of the young men of his race, we submit the following appeal to all men in general and young colored men in particular.

An appeal to young colored men throughout the United States:

—OBJECT—

The Erection of a Monument to
PAUL LAURENCE DUNBAR
By Francis H. Moore, Temporary Manager.

Our hero is fallen,—
The great Dunbar is gone,—
His Lyrics are our heritage,
    Then why should we mourn ?
    The noble thought
    That inspires my pen,
Is,—to raise a Monument,—
    To him,— among men.

Temporary President, Mr. J. H. Battles, No. 419 34th St., Chicago, Ill.
Temporary Treas., Mr. Geo. Sylvester, No. 836 Courtland Ave., New York (Bronx).
Temporary Secretaries, Mr. R. M. Winfrey, Mr. Harry Tibbs, No 853 Morris Ave., New York City.
Persons benevolently interested and desiring plan of action will communicate with any of the above named temporary officers. A date for meetings in New York and Chicago will be announced later.

The object is an admirable one, and THE LOUNGER wishes it every success.

꙳

A new novel by Rudyard Kipling is an event in the world of letters. It has been a long time since Mr. Kipling has given us a story that could be called a novel, for "Kim" was published five years ago. The new story is called "Robin Goodfellow and his Friends" and will be published first serially. Just how much the story has to do with our old friend, Robin Goodfellow, I do not know. I imagine, however, that the name is the only thing about the story that smacks of long ago.

꙳

I wonder how many times Mr. S. S. McClure has said that he was going to start a new magazine. It seems to me

I have heard something of this sort every year. About four years ago I met him in front of the Fifth Avenue Hotel and he told me about a new magazine he was going to start. A few weeks ago I met him in front of the Bartholdi Hotel and he told me about a new magazine he was going to start. I reminded him that he had told me a similar story several years before, but he said that he meant it this time, and that he could not back out if he wanted to, as he had ordered type, bought paper, and made the various contracts. The new magazine was to be five cents a copy, and I really believe that when Mr. McClure told me that he was going to publish it he meant every word that he said. But now I understand that he has again changed his mind, notwithstanding that he had gone so far as to make contracts for its publication.

꙳

Not for many years has Mrs. Burnett written a book that has made the sensation among its readers of "The Dawn of a To-morrow." When she took up her pen to write this story she was deeply engrossed in the writing of a novel which she considers her *magnum opus;* but the idea of "The Dawn of a To-morrow" seized her and would not be set aside. Work on the more ambitious story was postponed and the shorter story written almost under inspiration. Mrs. Burnett herself was a little sceptical as to its reception by the public, but her publishers were not. When she read the manuscript to them, which was, I believe, the way it had its first hearing, they were not only impressed by the story on its merits, but they were equally impressed with its popular value; and both of their impressions have proved prophetic. Mrs. Burnett has always written more or less "under inspiration." I do not mean that an angel from Heaven has come down and guided her hand; I merely mean that she does not write by any rule. She does not go to an office, as does Mr. Anthony Hope or Mr. Marion Crawford, for so many hours a day and write so many words within a

SARAH BERNHARDT

"THE DIVINE SARAH"

Sketched from life by Martha Duncan Beal

Mme. Bernhardt as she appeared in " La Tosca " to

an imaginative young artist

MRS. FISKE
as Leah Kleschna, recently seen at the Academy of Music, New York,
and now playing in Repertoire at the Manhattan Theatre

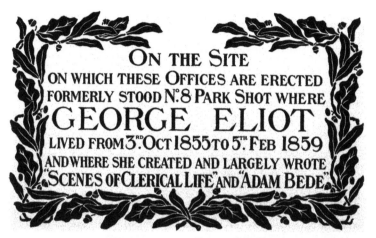

ON THE SITE
ON WHICH THESE OFFICES ARE ERECTED
FORMERLY STOOD N° 8 PARK SHOT WHERE
GEORGE ELIOT
LIVED FROM 3ʳᴰ OCT 1855 TO 5ᵀᴴ FEB 1859
AND WHERE SHE CREATED AND LARGELY WROTE
"SCENES OF CLERICAL LIFE" AND "ADAM BEDE"

given time. She writes when the mood takes her, no matter what the time or place. Usually she sits on a footstool, or perhaps on a cushion, in front of the fire, with an old atlas on her knee, her pen flying over the pages at lightning speed, tossing the sheets on the floor as they are written, until sheer exhaustion compels her to stop.

&

A list of stories and poems that were written by their writers while in jail has just been published. I could suggest many other books that might have been written in jail if their authors had had their deserts in this world. In the dark ages when men were imprisoned for debt there were a great many authors behind the bars. It was as a debtor that Leigh Hunt wrote "Rimini." It was in jail that Mr. W. T. Stead did some of his best journalistic work, though it was not for debt that Mr. Stead was incarcerated.

&

A volume of memoirs devoted to the early life of Tolstoy, compiled by one of his most intimate friends, with whom he has co-operated, will soon be published. M. Birukoff, the compiler, has also been assisted by the Countess Tolstoy, who has given him the use of her unique collection of manuscripts, letters, diaries, etc. The book will be profusely illustrated, and will be followed by two further volumes, one dealing with Tolstoy's married life and career as a novelist, the other with the period following his spiritual awakening down to the present.

&

There has been a lively time among the Richmond (England) Board of Guardians all because of a tablet erected to the memory of George Eliot by an admiring fellow-countryman, Mr. W. H. Harland. One J. Cockram, a member of the Board, spoke out in meeting and declared himself distinctly against the erection of the tablet. I quote from the *Richmond and Twickenham Times:*

Mr. Cockram objected to the place where it was going to be put, because it could be seen there. If it was put in the coal cellar he would raise no objection. He objected because the name was not a proper one. Her real name was Marian Evans. The woman's early writings were against the laws and ordinances of this country and of Christian countries. She wrote against the marriage laws, and she put her writings into practice by living with a man whilst his wife was alive. As Guardians, they should not encourage women to unite with men without the marriage bond. After the life she lived, he did not think a tablet in memory of her should be put in front of people who came for relief.

The more liberal-minded members of the Board prevailed and the tablet was erected.

❧

The edition of George Eliot's "Romola" that Messrs. A. C. McClurg & Company announce, is not to be published in Italian as I at first supposed. It is simply a new English edition of the text, edited with introduction and notes by Dr. Guido Biagi, and illustrated with 160 engravings belonging to his rare collection. Two other Italian books are announced for publication in the fall by this firm: a "History of Venice" by Pompeo Molmenti (a Roman Senator), in six volumes, with 250 illustrations—the first part in two volumes, "Venice in the Middle Ages," will be published in the fall; the second part in two volumes, "Venice in the Golden Age," will be published in the spring of 1907, and the third part "The Decadence of Venice," two volumes, will be issued in the fall of 1907—and "Byron in Italy," edited by Anna Benneson McMahan, editor of "With Shelley in Italy" and "Florence in the Poetry of the Brownings," will also be ready in the fall of 1906.

❧

Lady Henry Somerset, one of the leading lights of the W. C. T. U., who has done so much for the cause of temperance in England, has written a novel of modern London entitled "Under the Arch," which has just been published in this country. The story, while it has the attributes of the old-fashioned novel, is not lacking in modernity. Lady Henry is equally familiar with the "smart set" and the "submerged tenth." The time is during the Anglo-Boer War, and the principal figures include two soldiers, both in love with the same girl. One is killed at the front. A Socialist, naturally, plays an important part in the working out of the plot. Why, by the way, do the American publishers of the book call its author Lady Somerset? There is no such person.

T. W. H. writes from Cambridge, Mass. :

In Mr. Krehbiel's very interesting paper, "Letters of a Poet to a Musician," in the last [April] number of THE CRITIC, Mr. Krehbiel errs, I think, in assuming that the story of Rabiah originated with Mr. Hearn or that he found it "in the French." It is much more likely that he found it in Lyall's "Translations of Ancient Arabian Poetry," London, 1885, where it may be read on page 55; or, possibly, in the "Journal of the Oriental Society of Bengal," where Lyall's chapters were previously published. I am not aware that the story appeared later in *Harper's Bazaar* or that it was turned into a poem by Mr. Stoddard, as Mr. Krehbiel suggests. A metrical rendering of it by myself appeared, however, in the *Atlantic Monthly* for September, 1891; and afterwards in a volume of verses by myself and wife, entitled "Such as They Are," Boston, Roberts Bros., 1894.

❧

SUSAN BROWNELL ANTHONY
1820–1906

She sleeps: Come, cover her with
    mountain-flowers,
Who first drew breath where mighty
    Greylock climbs;
Wild-service boughs, sweet-healing
    elder-cymes,
Blossoms of ash that when a darkness
    lowers
Suffice for whiteness, clematis whose
    bowers
Hide singing birds, arbutus, creamy
    limes
Compact of honey gathered in the
    times
When thick rains fell,—as fall these
    tears of ours.
Last bring the laurels: far and high
    they throve
Where Liberty her holy vigil keeps,
Dwelt with the snows and dared the
    bolts of Jove,
To clothe with loveliness those
    barren steeps.
A thousand years will Love, through
    glen and grove,
Repeat: "Alas! how long—how late
    she sleeps!"
            AMANDA T. JONES.

❧

Just as THE CRITIC was going to press the above lines were received from Kansas. Miss Jones wrote them out of the fulness of her heart.

Courtesy of *The World's Work*

MISS SUSAN B. ANTHONY

The first "assignment" that I ever received from a New York journal was given me by the late Susan B. Anthony. I walked into the office of *The Revolution*, then published from one of a row of houses on East 23d Street, now part of the Metropolitan Life Insurance Building. Miss Anthony was sitting in front of the fire when I entered her sanctum and asked to be allowed to do some reporting. "Have you ever done any reporting?" she asked. "No, never, but I can't begin younger," I replied rather pertly. She was kind and paid no attention to the pertness of my reply but said she would give me a chance, and thereupon sent me to report a woman suffragist meeting across the street. It would interest me to see that report to-day. I tried to make it dignified and at the same time " lively reading," but I am afraid that the combination was not successful. I never saw Miss Anthony from that day, but I shall never forget her kindness to one who was to her a stranger.

Some twelve or fifteen portraits in chalk, by Mrs. Kate Rogers Nowell, were shown in April at the new Keppel galleries in 39th Street. The exhibit included the likenesses of several children, as well as a number of drawings made for reproduction in THE CRITIC and *The Outlook*. Mrs. Nowell's work is known best perhaps to the readers of the magazines, who have seen in her portraits of Mark Twain, Mrs. Edith Wharton, the Rev. Dr. Rainsford, and the late Sir Henry Irving—to name but these few—how happy have been her attempts, not merely to present a vivid likeness, but to seize and portray the characteristics of the persons of note whom she has set herself to portray. It is hard to say in which she has succeeded best— her pictures of men, or those for which women have been her sitters; while many may prefer to her portraits of older people, whether in colors or in black and white, the charming pastels that reveal her skill in capturing the fugitive moods of childhood. Practice has made her touch at once precise and facile, but patient study in Paris, in the studios of Georges Callot and L'Hermitte, laid the foundations of a style which has become as individual as it is pleasing. Mrs. Nowell has of late years given attention also to the art of the miniaturist, for which she has a special aptitude.

K. G. W. writes from East Berkshire, Vermont:

I am so pleased to be able to get any sense out of a paragraph of Henry James that I cannot withhold my opinion concerning the one you quote in the " Lounger." To me it means simply that Mr. James thinks the American crowd does better at boots and teeth than at hats. This of course fails to express the delicate *nuances* of the thought ; and although with the lack of subtle form there seems to be a lack of subtle significance, still it contains, I think, the nucleus of the paragraph. I am somewhat bewildered, however, by "the strikingly artless terms" in which " the people present their evidence of extreme consideration of the dental question." Is the reference to the broad and vulgar grins which might present such evidence, or is the artlessness shown by an excessive display of gold fillings—possibly even to gold-filled false teeth,—or does Mr. James mean only the public use of the tooth-pick ? My imagination fails me here, and I really think there should have been another paragraph redolent of observation and culture elaborating this point. But on the whole the meaning seems fairly plain.

Although Anthony Hope s "Rupert of Hentzau" is an uncopyrighted book, the authorized edition has been printed twenty-two times. The authorized publishers think that Mr. Gibson's illustrations have had much to do with the popularity of their edition, which may be more of a compliment to Mr. Gibson than it is to Mr. Hope.

Mr. H. G. Wells—one of the few authors, by the way, whose Christian names are less familiar than their initials—is among us taking notes. Already, before visiting America, he has written a series of articles on what he knows of our future: he now crosses the sea to learn something of our present. First of all, he has been surprised to find us so English—but I must avoid indiscreet anticipations, and confine myself to saying that if he has found New York like London, what will he do when he gets to Cambridge and Boston? whither he will have gone by the time these lines go to press. His friends here, new and old, have kept him busy ever since he landed: I doubt that he has lunched or dined alone since April 1st. His mail has found him at the Century Club, but he has wandered far beyond the confines of Clubland in studying social conditions in New York. Ellis Island has drawn him like a magnet; and under the wing of Mr. Steffens and Mr. Cahan he has observed the alien in his East Side café of a Sunday night. He is a keen observer, indisposed to draw on his imagination for his facts; and a delicate humorist, incapable of overlooking the human nature in the characters that embody his advanced ideas on social questions. As a literary artist and a sympathizer with the outcast and oppressed, he must shake hands very cordially with our own Mr. Howells.

The mother of Robert Louis Stevenson, Mrs. Margaret Isabella Stevenson (in England a widow drops her husband's Christian name) has published a volume of "Letters from Samoa," a companion volume to "From Saranac and Marquesas and Beyond," that cover the period of her life in Samoa until the death of her son. These letters are not only valuable as records of Stevenson's life in the islands, but are remarkable for their literary quality, which shows that Stevenson came honestly by his gift for writing.

The appointment of Mr. Bliss Perry

to the Professorship of English Literature at Harvard is singularly appropriate. Mr. Perry is an admirable successor to Ticknor, Longfellow, and Lowell, who held the chair before him. It has been vacant for twenty years, ever since Lowell gave it up. Mr. Perry was from 1886 to 1893 Professor of English at Williams College, and from 1893 to 1899 Professor of English at Princeton. He has been an editor and writer ever since his graduation from Williams in 1881. He proved so worthy a successor of the many great men who have edited the *Atlantic* that there is no doubt of his proving a worthy successor to the

Courtesy of Messrs. Scribner's Sons

MRS. M. I. STEVENSON IN 1848

great men who have occupied the chair of English Literature at Harvard. That Mr. Perry will continue the editorship of the *Atlantic Monthly* is a matter of congratulation all round.

"MARK TWAIN" AS AN "AUTOMOBILIST"

Mark Twain does not think that phonetic spelling will ever be adopted, and he says, " I am as sorry as a dog for I do love revolutions and violence." If we had not Mr. Clemens's word for it that he loved revolutions and violence we would not believe it for there never was a milder-mannered man living. By the way, Mr. Clemens has just joined the ranks of abandoned farmers. He has bought a farm in the township of Redding, Conn., several miles from a railroad, on an elevation overlooking a beautiful farming country. Mr. Clemens has not yet seen the farm. He bought it on the description of a friend, Mr. Albert Bigelow Paine, and because he heard that the old house had four fireplaces in it. Perhaps he never will see it, for Mr. Clemens has a passion for buying real estate. At one time he had four large country places on his hands, though he was living in a rented house in New York.

Mr. William Hope Hodgson, whose name I regret to say is unfamiliar to me, has written to *The Author* suggesting that as "poetry does not pay" poets might turn their talent to pecuniary account by writing epitaphs; in short, he proposes that "the poet should have equal chance with the sculptor in making beautiful the Last Abode." He goes even further and suggests that "in many cases the poet might well take the place of the sculptor, especially where the relatives of the dead are not of the wealthiest." Mr. Hodgson evidently is not aware that obituary or epitaph poetry is more of a drug in the market than any other sort. He need but refer to the mortuary columns of the Philadelphia *Ledger* to be assured of this. For a much less price than the poets of whom he writes could afford to take, the obituary notices and tombstones are liberally supplied. The late George W. Childs was humorously accused of writing these epitaphs himself. That this joke was without foundation is proved by the fact that the poetry mill of the *Ledger* still grinds.

Mrs. Felkin, better known by her maiden name, Ellen Thorneycroft Fowler, has written a new novel which is called "In Subjection," and deals, among other things, with the attitude of wives towards husbands. The publishers do not hint as to which belongs to the submerged half. In England it is said that the wives are in subjection, in America the husbands. Mrs. Felkin, being an Englishwoman, probably gives the English situation. Isabel Carnaby reappears in this book as a married woman, though the story is not a sequel to the author's first novel. In addition to Isabel Carnaby, Paul Seaton, Lord Wrexham, and one or two other characters from Mrs. Felkin's first novel appear in the pages of the new one. The scene is England, London and certain country houses being the background.

What is all this talk about an all-essay magazine? We have such a one; in fact, we have two; for what is the *North American Review* but an all essay magazine? Then there is the able *International Quarterly* which is an all-essay magazine. The *Atlantic* is nearly all essay, but certainly the other two are entirely essay. Whether an all-essay magazine pays or not is a question I am not capable of determining. Only Messrs. Harper and Messrs. Fox, Duffield & Co. can give the facts as to the pecuniary success of these reviews. Apropos of essays it may be said in all truth that this particular form of literature has not been so popular in the last decade as it is to-day. A short time ago no one cared much about publishing essays. They liked them fifty years ago, but ten, fifteen, and twenty years ago they were supplanted by descriptive articles and fiction. But now nearly every magazine publishes one or more essays, and there are no more readable pages printed than those contributed to by the essayist. THE CRITIC has always made a feature of the essay and will continue to do so.

❦

It seems to be quite a common thing nowadays for two or more members of the same family to be given over to the writing habit. There are the two Thurstons, for example, the two Wards, Elizabeth Stuart Phelps and her husband, and the two Lees, Gerald Stanley and his wife Jennette, to mention but a few. In the latter case the wife writes fiction, the husband essays. Mrs. Lee has won several prizes with her short stories. She has written two or three novels, one, "Kate Wetherill," which, though it had not a very wide sale, made a profound impression. I know some people who take it almost as their Bible. Three other books of fiction go to her credit. "Uncle William," the latest, is a New England story, and it is New England that Mrs. Lee knows the best. She lives at Northampton, Mass., and is in some way connected with Smith College. Her new story is dedicated to her husband in these lines:

Let him sing to me
Who sees the watching of the stars above the
day,

Who hears the singing of the sunrise
On its way
Through all the night,
Who outfaces skies, outsings the storms.

Let him sing to me
Who is the sky-voice, the thunder-lover,
Who hears above the winds' fast-flying shrouds,
The drifted darkness, the heavenly strife,
The singing on the sunny sides of all the clouds
Of his own life.

❦

The family of Mr. Richard Harding Davis is also a writing one. His father, the late L. Clarke Davis, was not only an editorial writer, but he was a writer of books. His mother, Rebecca Harding Davis, was a successful novelist before her son Richard was born, and she is still writing. One constantly finds her stories and essays

Courtesy of the Century Co.
JENNETTE LEE
(Mrs. G. S. Lee)

in the *Atlantic*, the *Independent*, and other periodicals. There is a Miss Nora Davis who writes novels, but she is not Mr. Richard Harding Davis's sister, who bears the same name.

Edward Carpenter, the English democratic author and poet, will soon publish through The Macmillan Company an account of his visits to the United States and Walt Whitman, 1877, and again in 1884. Carpenter has always been a great admirer of Whitman, and bears a curious resemblance to the good gray poet. In their views of life the two men were a good deal alike. Carpenter has lived on a small farm near Sheffield doing literary work, market gardening, sandal-making, and cultivating socialism as a side issue. He is not as much of a poet as

Courtesy of the Century Co.

MR. EDWARD CARPENTER

our own Walt, but he is a picturesque figure in English literature.

❧

"Il Santo," by Antonio Fogazzaro, will be published in this country by Messrs. Putnam with the title "The Saint." The book is the literary sensation of the day in Italy, where thousands of copies have been sold and scores of lectures about it been delivered. The book is characterized as "neither a romance nor an essay,

but a mixture of the epic, the lyric, the didactic, and the mystic." The character of "the saint" is a modern John the Baptist, who stands for the people of Italy, and whose interview with Pope Pius X is the most discussed episode in the book. Fogazzaro is not an unbeliever at all, but a devout Catholic.

❧

It is a curious fact that the author of the most typically American play of the past ten years is an Englishman. Mr. Charles Klein, whose play, "The Lion and the Mouse," has made the notable success of the season in New York, at the Lyceum Theatre, where it is now in its sixth month. Mr. Klein was born in London in 1867, and was educated at the North London College. Following the wish of his parents he began the study of law, but after a brief period abandoned it for the profession of writing. He came to America in 1882, and, attracted by the stage as a field for his writing ability, he became an actor so that he might study at close range the technique of the drama. His first play, "By Proxy," was produced in 1891 and ran for twelve weeks in Boston. Stimulated by this success, Klein decided to devote himself solely to playwriting. "Heartease" produced by Mr. Henry Miller, and "El Capitan," by Mr. DeWolfe Hopper, may be said to have established the author's status as a playwright and librettist. In recent years he has written "A Royal Rogue," for Mr. Jefferson de Angelis, "The Hon. John Grigsby," for Mr. Frank Keenan, and "The District Attorney," the latter one of his first plays to deal with politics, was produced by Mr. William A. Brady in New York some eight years ago. With Mr. Lee Arthur he collaborated on "The Auctioneer," in which Mr. David Warfield made his début as a "star." Mr. Klein provided for this actor "The Music Master," one of the phenomenal successes of theatrical history, for it is now in its second year in New York with no abatement of its popularity. In his latest play, "The Lion and the Mouse," Mr. Klein has again treated the subject of politics, one for which he has a pronounced predilection. The latest play by the zines, her first poem having appeared in the *Century* when she was only seventeen. Mrs. Sill is a daughter of the

Photo by Schloss

MR. CHARLES L. KLEIN
Author of the "The Lion and the Mouse," "The Music Master," etc.

way has just been "novelized" by the author.

Louise Morgan Sill, whose first volume of poems, "In Sun and Shade," was published by the Harpers on April 4th, is already widely known through the verses she has published in maga-

late Major-General Morgan L. Smith, and was born in Honolulu, H. I., during her father's consul - generalship there. She is on the editorial staff of *Harper's Magazine*.

We are to have a pocket edition of the works of George Meredith, in

Photo by Hollinger

MRS. LOUISE MORGAN SILL

sixteen volumes, bound in limp leather. The text will be the same as the Box-hill Edition. It contains enough new material and new editorial work to enable the publishers, Messrs. Scribner, to copyright it. Four volumes of the edition are now ready—"The Ordeal of Richard Feverel," "Diana of the Cross - Ways," "Sandra Belloni," and "Vittoria." Those who find Meredith rather difficult, almost as difficult as Mr. Henry James in his later manner, have nothing to complain of in such a book as "Diana of the Cross-Ways," which, by the way, is as full of real people as any novel by Mrs. Humphry Ward. We are to have a pocket edition of Tennyson also.

Messrs. Macmillan promise one in five volumes. Its contents will be: "Juvenilia" and "English Idylls" in the first volume. Volume II will give "In Memoriam," "Maud," and other poems. Volume III will consist of "Ballads and Other Poems." Volume IV will contain "The Idylls of the King," and the concluding volume the Dramas.

One of the recent surprises in magazine circles is the resignation by Mr. Charles Dwyer of the editorship of *The Delineator*, with which magazine he has been so closely identified for twenty years that one never dissociated one name from the other. The parting of the ways I believe is because of a difference of opinion between Mr. Dwyer and the business management on a matter of editorial policy. The difference must be serious to cause such a step, for Mr. Dwyer had a strong feeling of pride in the magazine which in his hands has developed from a small fashion catalogue of limited circulation into a periodical with the second largest following in the country. Hosts of his friends are interested to know what he will do next.

Mr. Rider Haggard's new novel, "The Way of the Spirit," is written in an entirely new vein for him. "In the course of a literary experience extending now, I regret to say, over more than a quarter of a century," writes Mr. Haggard, "often have I seen that he who attempts to step off the line chalked out for him by custom or opinion is apt to be driven back with stones and shoutings. Indeed, there are some who seem to think it very improper that an author should seek, however rarely, to address himself to a new line of thought or group of readers. As he began, so he must go on, they say." Mr. Haggard is wrong. A writer may make as many departures from his style as he likes. No one cares or criticises if his work does not deteriorate. We regret that Mr. Hardy is writing plays of endless length with legions of characters running through them, but

we would not regret that Mr. Hardy had turned his attention from prose to verse if he were giving us verse that was as great as his prose.

Professor Brander Matthews gives his views on the publishing of plays in a recent number of the *North American Review*. Professor Matthews is optimistic in regard to the drama, and thinks that it is especially significant that the acted drama is once more printed and published. Not only is this true of foreign playwrights, such as the French Rostand, the German Sudermann, the Italian d'Annunzio, and the Spanish Echegaray, but the English Gilbert, Jones, Pinero, Phillips, and the American Thomas and Fitch, are now in the list of those whose plays are given to the reading as well as the theatre-going public. In this connection it is interesting to know that Mr. Maurice Hewlett's play, "Pan and the Young Shepherd," which has been performed at the Court Theatre in London, will soon see the light in book form.

The portrait of Mr. Upton Sinclair which the publishers are sending around does not look as blood-thirsty as his story, "The Jungle," would make us think him to be. The face is that of an amiable, well-pleased-with-himself young man, not altogether without a sense of humor. And yet there is very little humor in anything Mr. Sinclair writes. We are told that he is now twenty-seven years old, that he was born in Baltimore, and studied at the College of the City of New York and Columbia University; that he paid his way through college by writing jokes and stories. In the picture before us, with pen in hand and pad ready to set down the inspiration, there is a look in his face of one who could write jokes; but never having seen anything but his most serious work, it is hard for me to believe that he could have written enough jokes to pay his college expenses. Mr. Sinclair has roughed it more or less in th. open. For four years he is said to have lived in shanties and tents, often subsisting on fish and game; but he probably never roughed it more absolutely than when he worked in the Chicago stockyards. It was there that he obtained the information for his latest book. Mr. Sinclair's introduction to the reading public was an unfortunate one. To attract attention he palmed off a book of fiction as fact. Few people were deceived, but every one resented the trick as they did the deception of "An Englishwoman's Love-Letters."

The spelling reformers are not such fools as the newspapers would have us think. If they intended to torture the English spelling as has been reported the credit for the so-called reform should be given to the late Josh Billings who made many thousands of dollars by phonetic spelling. Mr. Carnegie's committee have no intention, as I understand it, of changing the spelling of more than a dozen words at most.

It is an interesting announcement that the young firm of Messrs. H. S. Stone & Company have sold their entire stock, good-will, etc., to the still younger firm of Messrs. Fox, Duffield & Company, of this city. Mr. H. S. Stone continues to publish *The House Beautiful*, in Chicago, while Mr. E. M. Stone has come to New York to manage a syndicate periodical. Messrs. Dodd, Mead & Company have taken over all the Stone firm's McCutcheon books, but there were plenty of others left for Fox, Duffield & Company, among them some of those of George Bernard Shaw, Henry James, George Moore, Maeterlinck, Ibsen, H. G. Wells, Octave Thanet, David Swing, William Sharp, "Fiona MacLeod," Robert Hichens, Harold Frederic, Norman Hapgood, Clyde Fitch, Egerton Castle, and Robert Herrick.

Miss Kate Sanborn, who was one of the pioneers in the reclaiming of abandoned farms, has not forgotten that she was originally a writer. Though still an abandoned farmer Miss Sanborn has found time to bring out a most interesting and unique book about old-fashioned wall paper. One would imagine at first flush that there was nothing to say on such a subject, but Miss Sanborn has not only found a good deal to say, and to say it interestingly, but she has found an unusual lot of old papers from which she has taken illustrations. Wall paper, in the days of our grandparents, did not so much follow geometrical lines as it is apt to do to-day. Scenic patterns were popular seventy-five and a hundred years ago; and Miss Sanborn has reproduced a number of these of American, English, and French manufacture. Only a limited number of copies of the book are printed, and these are likely to be disposed of very quickly among collectors. Not only does Miss Sanborn find time for farming and book making, but she writes a column or two of lively book reviews, particularly on out-of-door subjects, for a daily paper. Her home, "Breezy Meadows," is at Metcalf, Mass.

Mr. Thomas Wright, who is well known as the author of a "Life of Edward FitzGerald" and the editor of the best collection of Cowper's letters, has written a biography of Sir Richard Burton, the famous traveller and Orientalist. Mr. Wright makes the startling announcement in his biography that " Burton's Arabian Nights " is mainly a paraphrase of Mr. John Payne's famous, or, as some people consider, infamous, translation.

Miss Marguerite Merington has laid aside the pen of the playwright for the time being and written a novel entitled "Scarlett of the Mounted." It is heralded as a distinct novelty in fiction, and as absorbing as it is witty. This we can readily believe, for Miss Merington has a pretty wit. The scene of the story is laid in the Klondike, where a girl of the sunny East and a man of the golden West meet with the usual results. Miss Merington has written the story with all the terseness of a play. There is no waste of words; it is principally dialogue, and clever dialogue at that.

❧

It is curious to note how writers often hit upon the same names for their books. There is "The Awakening" by Mrs. Deland running through the pages of *Harper's*, and there is a novel printed within a few weeks called "The Awakening," by C. Wickliffe Yulee; and there was a translation of Tolstoy's "Resurrection" called "The Awakening." I notice that the Rev. Mr. Gardenhire's new novel is called "The Long Arm," which is the name of the prize story written in collaboration, some years ago, by Mrs. Mary Wilkins Freeman and Mr. Brander Matthews.

❧

Mrs. de la Pasture, the author of "Peter's Mother" and "The Man from America," is the fortunate dramatizer of her own novels. She has made a play of "Peter's Mother," also of "The Man from America," both of which will see the footlights before very long. When an author can dramatize his or her own novels it is a good thing; but as a rule a person who is not the author, if that person is a dramatist, can do the work better. I could quote a number of instances where books that might have made a success as plays have been spoiled for the stage because the author would take a hand in the dramatization. Mr. Hall Caine, the Baroness Orczy, and Mrs. de la Pasture are exceptions to the rule. The late Paul L. Ford "collaborated" on "Janice Meredith," but I fancy he was wise enough to let the experienced dramatist have his own way.

❧

Bishop Potter has written his reminiscences of a dozen Bishops and Archbishops he has known, and the book will be published about the first of May. American and English Bishops figure in his pages. The Bishop that we would like him to write about is the Right Rev. H. C. Potter, Bishop of New York. An autobiography of this sort will probably be forthcoming some day, and it is possible that this book is merely its forerunner.

In the short preface to "Bishops and Archbishops" Bishop Potter tells an experience that he says "is largely the occasion of this volume":

On Decoration Day, 1903, as some of my readers will remember, there was unveiled, at the southeastern entrance to Central Park, in New York, the imposing equestrian statue of General W. T. Sherman, wrought by Mr. Augustus St.-Gaudens. In the evening of that day a distinguished journalist and man of letters (Hon. Whitelaw Reid) invited a few friends to meet the sculptor, quite informally, at his table. Most of the guests, and with them the host, had known General Sherman in the field, or had served with him in our great Civil War. Naturally enough,—especially after the ladies had left us,—the conversation took a reminiscent turn, and recalled scenes and incidents connected with the life of the great soldier whom New York had sought to commemorate. It is not enough to say of the recollections which were then exchanged that they were interesting—they were a great deal more—they were illuminative; and while driving home that night, past that stately equestrian statue, I found myself exclaiming to my companion, "What a regrettable fact it is that all the incidents we have heard to-night, or almost all of them, will disappear with those who have related them! They are all educated men who told us what they remembered of Grant, and Sherman, and Sheridan, and the rest; but they will never put it down on paper, I fear."

But, alas, I had not gone a great way in this pharisaic judgment of my fellows, when I was seized with the memory of official relations of my own with a distinguished and interesting body of men, the House of Bishops of the Episcopal Church, with which, in one way or another, I had been connected for nearly forty years; and with the members of which for nearly half of that time my relations, both personal and official, had been especially intimate and unreserved. The histories of many of these men have already been written; and I gladly own my indebtedness to them. But that personal note, to which I have already referred, has not always been conspicuous in them; and in some cases has never been recognized.

And in this fact must be found the explanation of the Reminiscences which follow.

❧

A collected edition of the works of Oscar Wilde will soon be brought out in London. There was an attempt made some time ago by a young New York publisher to bring out a collected edition of Wilde's books in this country, but it never got further than "The Picture of Dorian Gray." Now that an English publisher has had the courage to bring out such an edition, perhaps a New York publisher will import it. There are many of Oscar Wilde's writings that are worth while; there are others that had better be left unpublished; but if the edition is to be complete it must contain everything. A number of Wilde's books have been privately printed in England, but these, it is probable, will be found in the new edition, which will have to contain them if it is complete. In this new edition there will be an enlarged issue of his "De Profundis." The additions consist of passages which have only appeared in the German, Russian, and Italian versions of the book, and letters which Wilde wrote to a friend from Reading Gaol.

꿩

A first edition of Thoreau's first book, "A Week on the Concord and Merrimack Rivers," containing the original printer's notes, sold recently in this city at auction for $105. The manuscript edition of Thoreau's complete works, in twenty volumes, now being published by Messrs. Houghton, Mifflin & Company, contains fourteen volumes of Thoreau's Journal, which are virtually a first edition. It is said that this manuscript edition has proved almost an unexpected success. The publishers knew that it would be a success in the end, but they hardly looked for such immediate appreciation.

A Great Human Document

Written by HELEN KELLER

AT the meeting held by the Association for the Blind at the Waldorf-Astoria last month, Mr. S. L. Clemens (Mark Twain) presided, and ex-Ambassador Choate and others addressed the meeting. There is no more philanthropic work done in this country than by this association. Like most good causes, it needs money, and Mr. Herbert S. Barnes of 35 Wall Street, who is the treasurer of the association, will gladly receive donations, small or large, according to the ability of the giver. Miss Winifred Holt, 44 East 78th Street, who is secretary of the association, will answer inquiries and furnish printed material to those who are interested. In this connection I give the letter written by Miss Helen Keller to Mr. Clemens, and read by him at the Waldorf-Astoria meeting, and of which he has said: "Nothing finer has been done by a young woman since Joan of Arc confuted the lawyers when she was on trial for her life."

MY DEAR MR. CLEMENS: It is a great disappointment to me not to be with you and the other friends who have joined their strength to uplift the blind. The meeting in New York will be the greatest occasion in the movement which has so long engaged my heart; and I regret keenly not to be present and feel the inspiration of living contact with such an assembly of wit, wisdom, and philanthropy. I should be happy if I could have spelled into my hand the words as they fall from your lips, and receive, even as it is uttered, the eloquence of our newest ambassador to the blind. We have not had such advocates before. My disappointment is softened by the thought that never at any meeting was the right word so sure to be spoken. But, superfluous as all other appeal must seem after you and Mr. Choate have spoken, nevertheless, as I am a woman, I cannot be silent, and I ask you to read this letter, knowing it will be lifted to eloquence by your kindly voice.

To know what the blind man needs, you who can see must imagine what it is not to see, and you can imagine it more vividly if you remember that before your journey's end you may have to go the dark way yourself. Try to realize, what blindness means to those whose joyous activity is stricken to inactivity.

It is to live long, long days, and life is made up of days. It is to live immured, baffled, impotent, all God's world shut out. It is to sit helpless, defrauded, while your spirit strains and tugs at its fetters, and your shoulders ache for the burden they are denied, the rightful burden of labor.

The seeing man goes about his business confident and self-dependent. He does his share of the work of the world in mine, in quarry, in factory, in counting-room, asking of others no boon, save the opportunity to do a man's part, and to receive the laborer's guerdon. In an instant accident blinds him. The day is blotted out. Night envelops all the visible world. The feet which once bore him to his task with firm and confident stride, stumble and halt, and fear the forward step. He is forced to a new habit of idleness, which like a canker consumes the mind and destroys its beautiful faculties. Memory confronts him with his lighted past. Amid the tangible ruins of his life as it promised to be, he gropes his pitiful way. You have met him on your busy thoroughfares with faltering feet and outstretched hands, patiently "dredging" the universal dark, holding out for sale his petty wares, or his cap for your pennies; and this was a man with ambitions and capabilities.

It is because we know that these ambitions and capabilities can be fulfilled, that we are working to improve the condition of the adult blind. You cannot bring back the light to the vacant eyes; but you can give a helping hand to the sightless along their dark pilgrimage. You can teach them new skill. For work they once did with the aid of their eyes, you can substitute work that they can do with their hands. They ask only opportunity, and opportunity is a torch in darkness. They crave no charity, no pension, but the satisfaction that comes from lucrative toil, and this satisfaction is the right of every human being.

At your meeting New York will speak its word for the blind, and when New York speaks the world listens. The true message of New York is not the commercial ticking of busy telegraphs, but the mightier utterances of such gatherings as yours. Of late our periodicals have been filled with depressing revelations of great social evils. Querulous critics have pointed to every flaw in our civic structure. We have listened long enough to the pessimists. You once told me you were a pessimist, Mr. Clemens; but great men are usually mistaken about themselves. You are an optimist. If you were not, you would not preside at the meeting. For it is an answer to pessimism. It proclaims that the heart and the wisdom of a great city are devoted to the good of mankind, that in this, the busiest city in the world, no cry of distress goes up but receives a compassionate and generous answer. Rejoice that the cause of the blind has been heard in New York; for the day after it shall be heard round the world.

Yours sincerely,
HELEN KELLER.

Art Appreciation

By OKAKURA-KAKUZO

HAVE you heard the Taoist tale of the Taming of the Harp?

Once in the hoary ages in the Ravine of Lungmen* stood a Kiri tree, a veritable king of the forest. It reared its head to talk to the stars; its roots struck deep into the earth mingling their bronzed coils with those of the silver dragon that slept beneath. And it came to pass that a mighty wizard made of this tree a wondrous harp, whose stubborn spirit should be tamed but by the greatest of musicians. For long the instrument was treasured by the Emperor of China, but all in vain were the efforts of those who in turn tried to draw melody from its strings. In response to their utmost strivings there came from the harp but harsh notes of disdain ill-according with the songs they fain would sing. The harp refused to recognize a master.

At last came Peiwoh, the prince of harpists. With tender hand he caressed the harp as one might seek to soothe an unruly horse, and softly touched the chords. He sang of nature and the seasons, of high mountains and flowing waters, and all the memories of the tree awoke! Once more the sweet breath of spring played amidst its branches. The young cataracts as they danced down the ravine laughed to the budding flowers. Anon were heard the dreamy voices of summer with its myriad insects, the gentle pattering of rain, the wail of the cuckoo. Hark! a tiger roars,—the valley answers again. It is autumn; in the desert night sharp like a sword gleams the moon upon the frosted grass. Now winter reigns, and through the snow-filled air swirl flocks of swans, and rattling hailstones beat upon the boughs with fierce delight.

Then Peiwoh changed the key and sang of love. The forest swayed like an ardent swain deep lost in thought. On high, like a haughty maiden, swept a cloud bright and fair; but passing

*The Dragon Gorge of Honan.

trailed long shadows on the ground black like despair. Again the mood was altered: Peiwoh sang of war, of clashing steel and trampling steeds. And in the harp arose the tempest of Lungmen, the dragon rode the lightning, the thundering avalanche crashed through the hills. In ecstasy the Celestial monarch asked Peiwoh wherein lay the secret of his victory. "Sire," he replied, "others have failed because they sang but of themselves. I left the harp to choose its theme, and knew not truly whether the harp had been Peiwoh or Peiwoh were the harp."

This story well illustrates the mystery of art appreciation. The masterpiece is a symphony played upon our finest feelings. True art is Peiwoh, and we the harp of Lungmen. At the magic touch of the beautiful, the secret chords of our being are awakened, we vibrate and thrill in response to its call. Mind speaks to mind. We listen to the unspoken, we gaze upon the unseen. The master calls forth notes we know not of. Memories, long forgotten, all come back to us with a new significance. Hopes stifled by fear, yearnings that we dare not recognize, stand forth in new glory. Our mind is the canvas on which the artists lay their color; their pigments are our emotions; their chiaroscuro the light of joy, the shadow of sadness. The masterpiece is of ourselves, as we are of the masterpiece.

The sympathetic communion of minds necessary for art appreciation must be based on mutual concession. The spectator must cultivate the proper attitude for receiving the message, as the artist must know how to impart it. The tea-master, Kobori-Enshin, himself a daimyo, has left to us these memorable words: "Approach a great painting as thou wouldst approach a great prince." In order to understand a masterpiece, you must lay yourself low before it and await with bated breath its least utterance. An eminent Sung critic once made a charming confession. Said he: "In my young days I praised the master whose pictures I liked, but as my judgment matured I praised myself for liking what the masters had chosen to have me like." It is deplored that so few of us really take pains to study the moods of the masters. In our stubborn ignorance we refuse to render them this simple courtesy, and thus often miss the rich repast of beauty spread before our very eyes. A master has always something to offer, while we go hungry solely because of our own lack of appreciation.

To the sympathetic a masterpiece becomes a living reality towards which we feel drawn in bonds of comradeship. The masters are immortal, for their loves and fears live in us over and over again. It is rather the soul than the hand, the man than the technique, which appeals to us,—the more human the call the deeper is our response. It is because of this secret understanding between the master and ourselves that in poetry or romance we suffer and rejoice with the hero and heroine. Chikamatsu, our Japanese Shakespeare, has laid down as one of the first principles of dramatic composition the importance of taking the audience into the confidence of the author. Several of his pupils submitted plays for his approval, but only one of the pieces appealed to him. It was a play somewhat resembling the "Comedy of Errors," in which twin brethren suffer through mistaken identity. "This," said Chikamatsu, "has the proper spirit of the drama, for it takes the audience into consideration. The public is permitted to know more than the actors. It knows where the mistake lies, and pities the poor figures on the board who innocently rush to their fate."

The great masters both of the east and the west never forgot the value of suggestion as a means for taking the spectator into their confidence. Who can contemplate a masterpiece without being awed by the immense vista of thought presented to our consideration? How familiar and sympathetic

are they all; how cold in contrast the modern commonplace! In the former we feel the warm outpouring of a man's heart; in the latter only a formal salute. Engrossed in his technique, the modern rarely rises above himself. Like the musicians who vainly invoked the Lungmen harp, he sings only of himself. His works may be nearer science but are farther from humanity. We have an old saying in Japan that a woman cannot love a man who is truly vain, for there is no crevice in his heart for love to enter and fill up. In art vanity is equally fatal to sympathetic feeling whether on the part of the artist or the public.

Nothing is more hallowing than the union of kindred spirits in art. At the moment of meeting, the art lover transcends himself. At once he is and is not. He catches a glimpse of Infinity, but words cannot voice his delight, for the eye has no tongue. Freed from the fetters of matter his spirit moves in the rhythm of things. It is thus that art becomes akin to religion and ennobles mankind. It is this which makes a masterpiece something sacred. In the old days the veneration in which the Japanese held the work of a great artist was intense. The teamasters guarded their treasures with religious secrecy, and it was often necessary to open a whole series of boxes, one within another, before reaching the shrine itself,—the silken wrapping within whose soft folds lay the holy of holies. Rarely was the object exposed to view, and then only to the initiated.

At the time when Teaism was in the ascendency, the Taiko's generals would be better satisfied with the present of a rare work of art than a large grant of territory as a reward of victory. Many of our favorite dramas are based on the loss and recovery of a noted masterpiece. For instance, in one play the palace of Lord Hosokawa, in which was preserved the celebrated painting of Dharuma by Sessiu, suddenly takes fire through the negligence of the samurai in charge. Resolved at all hazards to rescue the precious painting, he rushes into the burning building and seizes the kake-mono only to find all means of exit cut off by the flames. Thinking only of the picture he slashes open his body with his sword, wraps his torn sleeve about the Sessiu and plunges it into the gaping wound. The fire is at last extinguished. Among the smoking embers is found a half consumed corpse within which reposes the treasure uninjured by fire. Horrible as such tales are, they illustrate the great value that we set upon a masterpiece, as well as the devotion of a trusted samurai.

We must remember, however, that art is of value only to the extent that it speaks to us. It might be a universal language if we ourselves were universal in our sympathies. Our finite nature, the power of tradition and conventionality, as well as our hereditary instincts, restrict the scope of our capacity for artistic enjoyment. Our very individuality establishes in one sense a limit to our understanding; and our æsthetic personality seeks its own affinities in the creations of the past. It is true that with cultivation our sense of art appreciation broadens, and we become able to enjoy many hitherto unrecognized expressions of beauty. But after all, we see only our own image in the universe,—our particular idiosyncrasies dictate the mode of our perceptions. The tea-masters collected only objects which fell strictly within the measure of their individual appreciation.

One is reminded in this connection of a story concerning Kobori-Enshin. Enshin was complimented by his disciples on the admirable taste he had displayed in the choice of his collection. Said they: "Each piece is such that no one could help admiring it. It shows that you had better taste than had Rikiu, for his collection could only be appreciated by one beholder in a thousand." Sorrowfully Enshin replied: "This only proves how commonplace I am. The great Rikiu dared to love only those objects which personally appealed to him, whereas I unconsciously cater to the taste of the majority. Verily, Rikiu was one in a thousand among tea-masters."

It is much to be regretted that so much of the apparent enthusiasm for art at the present day has no foundation in real feeling. In this democratic age of ours men clamor for what is popularly considered the best, regardless of their personal likings. They want the costly, not the refined; the fashionable, not the beautiful. To the masses, contemplation of illustrated periodicals, the worthy product of their own industrialism, would give more digestible food for artistic enjoyment than the Early Italians or the Ashikaga masters whom they pretend to admire. The name of the artist is more important to them than the quality of the work. As a Chinese critic complained many centuries ago, "People criticise a picture by their ear." It is this lack of genuine appreciation that is responsible for the pseudo-classic horrors that to-day greet us wherever we turn.

Another common mistake is that of confusing art with archæology. The veneration born of antiquity is one of the best traits in the human character, and fain would we have it cultivated to a greater extent. The old masters are rightly to be honored for opening the path to future enlightenment. The mere fact that they have passed unscathed through centuries of criticism and come down to us still covered with glory commands our respect. But we should be foolish indeed if we valued their achievement simply on the score of age. Yet we allow our historical sympathy to override our æsthetic discrimination. We offer flowers of approbation when the artist is safely laid in his grave. The nineteenth century, pregnant with the theory of evolution, has moreover created in us the habit of losing sight of the individual in his species. A collector is anxious to acquire specimens to illustrate a period or a school, and forgets that a single masterpiece can teach us more than any number of the mediocre products of a given period or school. We classify too much and enjoy too little. The sacrifice of the æsthetic to the so-called scientific method of exhibition has been the ban of many museums.

The claims of contemporary art cannot be ignored in any vital scheme of life. The art of to-day is that which really belongs to us: it is our own reflection. In condemning it we but condemn ourselves. We say that the present age possesses no àrt,—who is responsible for this? It is indeed a shame that despite all our rhapsodies about the ancients we pay so little attention to our own possibilities. Struggling artists, weary souls lingering in the shadow of cold disdain! In our self-centred century, what inspiration do we offer them? The past may well look with pity at the poverty of our civilization; the future will laugh at the barrenness of our art. We are destroying art in destroying the beautiful in life. Would that some great wizard might from the stem of society shape a mighty harp whose strings would resound to the touch of genius.

A Concord Note=Book

The Women of Concord—IV. Mrs. Mary Merrick Brooks and the Anti-Slavery Movement

NINTH PAPER

By F. B. SANBORN

I PERCEIVE that too little has been said in these papers of the anti-slavery activity of the women of Concord from the period of the Gisarron mob in Boston (October, 1835), which was directed against women as well as against agitators like Garrison and George Thompson, to the final emancipation under Lincoln's decree, nearly thirty years later. In all this period a Women's Anti-Slavery Society existed in Concord, the most active members of which had been from the beginning, Mrs. Mary Merrick Brooks, Mrs. Waldo Emerson, Mrs. Col. Joseph Ward, widow of a Revolutionary officer, her daughter, Miss Prudence Ward, and the ladies of the Thoreau and Dunbar and Whiting families. At the death of Mrs. Ward in 1844, her associates in the Concord Society published this memorial of her gentle and charitable character:

"Died in Concord on the 9th inst., Mrs. Prudence Ward, widow of the late Col. Joseph Ward of Boston, aged seventy-nine. Mrs. Ward has for many years been a resident of Concord, and has greatly endeared herself to many friends by the urbanity of her manners, the kindness of her heart, and that candor and charity which, while it passed over the defects of her associates as things not to be observed, at the same time sought with eagerness the bright sides to their characters, and on those alone suffered herself to dwell. This made us always feel safe and happy in her society. In addition to this she had a heart full of compassion for the suffering and the tried; which was probably the cause of her warm interest in the deeply-injured, weary, heart-broken slave. For many years she has been a faithful member of our Society, always aiding us by her purse, her sympathies, and her labors. Our hearts are tender, and our eyes fill with tears, not chiefly at our own loss, but at the loss the slave has sustained in the removal of this friend. She uniformly and consistently stood by the principles of the old pioneer Society; and we feel that indeed a great void is made in our before much-thinned ranks. But she has gone before the throne of her God and Saviour, where, we love to believe, she will still remember and be employed in the cause she loved while on earth. And we trust that her exit from us will but redouble our efforts for the relief of our suffering brethren and sisters in bonds; so that at last our end, like hers, may be peace."

This quaintly touching tribute may have been written by Maria Thoreau, the aunt of Henry, Helen, and Sophia, who were all intimate with the Ward family. Indeed, almost from their first coming to Concord in 1832-33, the mother and daughter had made their home with one or the other branch of the Thoreau family, then resident in the town. They had heard the early debates at the Concord Lyceum, when the subject of slavery was excluded; they had taken up together the cause of the Cherokee Indians in 1837, when Mrs. Brooks and the Wards and Thoreaus had caused a public meeting to be held in favor of the Indians of Georgia, and Mrs. Brooks had persuaded Emerson to write his letter to Van Buren in their behalf. Early in 1838 Miss Ward was writing to her sister, Mrs. Edmund Sewall, at Scituate, whose husband was pastor in that seashore town, and a cousin of Mrs. Alcott; and in her letters she lamented the dispersion of her young friends, the Thoreau brothers and sisters, who, she said, "are the most important part of the establishment." Helen Thoreau, the older sister, had gone to Roxbury, near Boston, to open a school for young ladies, and Sophia was then expected soon to join her there. That she did so and was busy in Roxbury botanizing and arranging her attire, will be seen by the following letter, written to Miss Prudence Ward, a botanist and flower-painter, a year later:

"Roxbury, May 5, 1839.

" My dear Miss Ward:

" I must give vent to my ecstasies by writing you about the flowers I have found. I never intended you should get a letter from me until I had forgotten that you said you would not promise to answer me if I did. Since my return to Roxbury I have been very busy, having made myself a gown,

worked half a collar like yours, made two visits, been to Boston six times, besides attending school every day.

"To proceed to business. On the 19th of April I found the *saxifraga;* April 22d I walked with the young ladies and gathered the *Viola ovata* and cinquefoil. April 26th, accompanied by nearly all my scholars, I walked over to Dorchester, and much to my surprise found the *caltha* (*palustris*) in blossom,—which we did not find in Concord (in 1838) until the third week in May. The last week in April I found the blueberry, buttercup, dandelion, and columbine in blossom. As to poor little Houstonias, I have not glimpsed one this spring.

"Miss Newton means to interest herself in botany, and thinks she can borrow ' Bigelow' of some friend. I hope she will be able to, as I have nothing but Mrs. Lincoln to refer to. The young ladies petitioned for a holiday the first of May, and invited Helen and myself to walk with them. We consented to go, but on account of the weather we were obliged to defer our walk until Friday afternoon, when, perhaps you recollect, it was very windy,—so much so that Helen declined accompanying us. We took but a short walk; however, we gathered a great many flowers. Among them was one I had never seen before, and, from its resemblance to a painting of a dog-tooth violet which you showed me, I concluded it must be that one. And upon reading the description of said violet in Mrs. .L's 'Botany,' found it agreed perfectly with the description of the *Erythronium* (yellow).

"I have concluded to walk into Boston this afternoon with Miss Newton, and must therefore cut short this epistle, as I want to take a bundle to town for E. Buttrick to carry to Concord. I wish I could write more. Please remember me to all.

"Yours in great haste,

"Sophia E. Thoreau.

" I forgot to say that the Pynes are in blossom, also the *Viola blanda.*"

At this time Sophia was not quite twenty, and Helen, the oldest of the children, was twenty-six. The "Bigelow" mentioned was the botanical work of Dr. Jacob Bigelow, and the Mrs. Lincoln was a smaller work intended for schools and private families. In 1839 Henry Thoreau had perhaps made no further progress in botanical studies than Sophia, who in after years was his companion in walks, sails, and drives, and became an accomplished letter-writer, as her published correspondence with the Ricketsons and other friends shows. Both were Latinists in some degree, for Henry wrote Helen a Latin letter in the winter of 1839-40, to which, in his mother's name, he added a Latin postcript for Sophia. In this she was informed that Sam Black, the cat, "*crebris ægrotationibus obnoxius est, quæ agilitatem et æquum animum abstulere*,"—with other bits of domestic intelligence. In the early spring of 1839, a young nephew of Miss Ward's was at the school of Henry and John Thoreau in Concord, and the first mention of the boat in which the two brothers sailed up the Merrimac occurs in a note from this lad, who, writing Sunday, April 5, said: "I have been out to sail once in Mr. Thoreau's boat; he has a very good one which he and his brother made themselves. The river was high and we sailed very fast." Five months later, in early September, 1839, Miss Ward briefly wrote to her sister an account of the going and returning of the two brothers from their excursion, now so widely known.

Henry was soon after chosen secretary of the Concord Lyceum, and continued to hold that place or some office in connection with engaging lecturers, for the next five or six years. While thus in office, he favored strongly the discussion of American slavery at the Lyceum, and procured Wendell Phillips as one of the lecturers, to introduce that topic. When, in 1842, it was announced that Phillips would lecture the following week, an elderly member, John Keyes, moved as a resolve: "That as this Lyceum is established for social and mutual improvement, the introduction of the vexed and disorganizing question of Abolitionism or Slavery should be kept

out of it." The motion failed, and Phillips lectured as announced. The same winter Bronson Alcott returned from England with his English friends, Lane and Wright, who spent the winter and spring with the Alcotts, before going to open their rural Elysium at Fruitlands, in late May, 1843. Writing to her brother George in New York, Miss Prudence Ward said (Dec. 8, 1842):

"We find the Englishmen very agreeable. We took tea with them at Mrs. Brooks's and they have passed one evening here at Mrs. Thoreau's. They and Mr. Alcott held a talk at the Marlboro Chapel in Boston, Sunday evening. Doubtless you, George, would consider them 'clean daft,' as they are as like Mr. Alcott in their views as strangers from a foreign land can well be. I should like to have them locate themselves in this vicinity. It makes a pleasant variety (to say no more) to have these different thinkers near us; and Mr. Lane we are all agreed in liking to hear talk. Our Lyceum has opened, and last evening we had 'The Philosophy of Slavery.'"

This may have been the title of Phillips's lecture; at any rate, he spoke that winter in his customary quiet manner, but uttering extreme opinions,—among other things, favoring disunion as the best remedy for slavery, and denouncing the Constitution of 1787 for its alleged protection of the national curse. When invited to lecture the next winter (Jan. 17, 1844) the same old citizen moved that he be asked to choose some other topic; alleging that his sentiments of the last winter were "vile, pernicious, and abominable." The Lyceum voted to hear him on his own chosen subject. He came and spoke for an hour and a half in "a magnificent burst of eloquence from beginning to end" as one of his hearers (possibly Helen Thoreau) wrote in the *Liberator*. This writer, signing "H. M.," went on thus:

"He charged the sin of slavery upon the religion of the country, with its 20,000 pulpits. The Church, he said, had charged Mr. Garrison with being an infidel to its teachings,—and there was some truth in it. 'I love my Master too well to be anything but infidel to the religion of my country.' Of the State he said: 'The curse of every honest man should be upon its Constitution. Could I say to Jefferson, Hancock, and Adams, after the experience of the past fifty years, "Look at the fruits of your work," they would bid me crush the parchment beneath my feet.' "

This was too much for the civil-suited conservatism of Concord, and an evening was appointed to discuss and censure the orator. " The mover of the vote of censure (the same John Keyes") says H. M., "talked an hour, quoting St. Paul about leading captive silly women, etc." Another gentleman, Samuel Hoar (father of the late Senator Hoar) occupied an hour more, with like severity, saying "It requires not a little arrogance in a stripling to assert such monstrous doctrines." He complimented Phillips on his oratory, but solemnly warned the young persons present against such exciting utterances. As he went on with his refutation, he kept asking, "What would our young Cicero say to this? How would he explain this?" etc. Phillips, who had been notified by the Thoreaus, Colonel Whiting, or some other abolitionist of the attack to be made on him, was quietly present in the back part of old vestry of the First Parish Church of Whiting, Emerson, and Dr. Ripley, and now stepped forward. "Would the gentleman like an answer here and now?" That was not the gentleman's wish at all; but there was no help for it. Phillips said, according to H. M.:

"I agree with the last speaker that this is a serious subject; otherwise I should not have devoted my life to it. Stripling as I am, I but echo the voice of the ages, of our venerable fathers, of statesmen, poets, philosophers. I do not feel accountable for my manner. In a struggle for life it is hardly fair for men looking on at ease to remark that the limbs of the combatants are not disposed with classical grace. The gentleman had painted the danger to life, liberty, and happiness that might be the consequence of doing right. The dangers he dreads are now legalized at the South. My liberty may be bought at too dear a price; if I cannot gain it except by sin, I reject it. But I would not so blaspheme God as to doubt that I shall be safe in obeying Him. Treading the dust of English law beneath my feet, I enter the Holy of Holies, and there I find written 'Thou shalt not deliver unto his master the servant which is escaped from his master unto thee; he shall dwell with you, even among you.' I throw myself upon the bosom of Infinite Wisdom. Why, the heathen has told you, 'Let justice be done, though the heavens fall,' and our old reformer answered, when warned against the danger of going to Rome, 'It is not necessary that I should live, but it is necessary that I should go to Rome.'

"Our pulpits are silent. Who ever heard our subject presented, before this movement began, of the silly women and the striplings? The first speaker accused me of ambitious motives. Had I been ambitious I should have chosen an easier path to fame. Yet I would say to you, my young friends, who have been cautioned against excitement, and advised to fold your hands in selfish ease, Throw yourself upon the altar of some noble cause! Enthusiasm is the life of the soul. To rise in the morning only to eat and drink and gather gold is a life not worth living."

His young friends, among them Henry, Helen, and Sophia Thoreau—for John had died in 1842—applauded the orator, and voted to hear him again on the same theme. He came (March, 1845), and this time Henry Thoreau reported him for the newspapers. But Miss Ward, who, since the death of her mother, had gone to visit her brother in Spencer, Mass., must be informed of the great event; and so Helen Thoreau wrote to her the next month as follows:

"CONCORD, April 27, 1845.

"DEAR MISS WARD:

"I wish to thank you for the nice long letter you sent me by Henry, in return for my little note; and also to remind you of the meeting of the American Anti-Slavery Society at the Tabernacle in New York on the 6th of May. You must not fail to attend; and I hope to meet you at the New England Convention. It is possible that George Thompson may be present from England. Can you not visit here about that time?

"Aunt Maria [Thoreau] has, I suppose, kept you informed of our controversy with the Lyceum. A hard battle, but victory at last; next winter we shall have undoubtedly a free Lyceum. Mr. Emerson says that words cannot express his admiration for the lecture of Mr. Phillips. Did you receive the paper containing Henry's article about it?

"I am glad that you liked the Hutchinsons. One of our evening meetings last May was closed with their Emancipation Song,—the whole audience rising and joining in the last stanza. George Thatcher happened to be present, and was highly delighted. Ten of the Hutchinson family sung. We are making great efforts to get them here [in Concord]. I long to see you in Concord again. We always have something stirring here. Aunt Maria will of course tell you all the news. Remember me to your brother and sister, and believe me ever yours,

"HELEN."

"Mother and Sophia send love."

This is one of the very few letters of Helen Thoreau extant. She died in June 1849, not quite thirty-seven years old.

Maria Thoreau, here mentioned, was the last survivor of the Thoreau name in America, and the genealogist and annalist of the American branch of the family. She died in 1881, at the home of her kinsman, George Thatcher, just mentioned, in Bangor. She and her two chief correspondents, Miss Ward and Miss Laura Harris, kept up a lively interchange of letters for some forty years, and these epistles, some of which I have seen, would give an interesting picture of one New England and New York circle who practised "plain living and high thinking" in a feminine way for the period preceding and immediately following the emancipation of the American slaves. The Hutchinsons, above mentioned, were that celebrated "band of young apostles" (as Mary Howitt called them) from Milford in New Hampshire, who carried their native melodies to all parts of America and Europe, during the sixty years that some of them continued to sing and play their instruments. John Hutchinson alone survives of this band now, and still occasionally lets his fine voice be heard on public occasions, though upwards of eighty years old.

For the Ward and Thoreau letters here and elsewhere edited by me, I am indebted to Miss Anna Ward of Spencer, granddaughter of Mrs. Colonel Ward. Mrs. Ward was also the grandmother of Ellen Sewall, the young lady with whom both John and Henry Thoreau were in love, as Mr. Salt has related in his English life of Thoreau.

Dr. Weininger's "Sex and Character"

Reviewed by CHARLOTTE PERKINS GILMAN

A BOOK by a German philosopher, of sufficient merit to command six editions in Germany and an English translation,* deserves serious attention from the reviewer; a book which treats at length, with profound labor of thought and wealth of study, of the woman question, deserves serious attention from the sociologist. Moreover the intense moral earnestness of this author, his evident depth of conviction, and the lofty scope of his aspirations command respect; nevertheless, to any one versed in the general facts of life, and in especial to a student of social evolution who notes the immense part played in it by the changing status of woman, there is something so paralyzingly absurd in the absolute dicta of this solemn young philosopher, that the attitude of serious attention is difficult to maintain. The author was but twenty-one when he wrote the book, and two years later he took his own life; facts of importance to the experienced observer.

Dr. Weininger himself says of his book that its special object is to answer, theoretically and practically, the woman question; that it is "an attempt to place the relation of the sexes in a new and decisive light."

Decisive he assuredly is, nothing could be more so; but the novelty of his light, or if it be light at all, is open to question.

He takes the ancient Oriental position that women have no souls, and reinforces it by the views of Greek and German philosophers and early Christian fathers, with a few sparing and cautious selections of scientific fact. To quote again from his impressive preface: "The investigation is not of details, but of principles; it does not despise the laboratory, although the help of the laboratory, with regard to the deeper problems, is limited as com-

pared with the results of introspective analysis."

This introspective analysis is the mainspring of the work; the profound lucubration of a philosophic mind; by means of which he reaches such conclusions as these:

"No men who think deeply about women retain a high opinion of them; men either despise women or they have never thought seriously about them."

"Woman, in short, has an unconscious life, man a conscious life, and the genius the most conscious life."

"Women are as much afraid of death as are men, but they have not the longing for immortality."

"A woman cannot grasp that one must act from principle."

"Woman resents any attempt to require from her that her thoughts should be logical. She may be regarded as logically insane."

"The absolute female has no ego."

"The male has everything within him. . . . It is possible for him to attain to the loftiest heights, or to sink to the lowest depths; he can become like animals, like plants, or even like women; and so there exist woman-like female men. The woman, on the other hand, can never become a man."

"I am not arguing that woman is evil and anti-moral; I state that she cannot be really evil. *She is merely non-moral.*"

These and many other vivid definitive sentences, culminating in the statement that "woman is only a function of man, a function he can raise or degrade at will, and women do not wish to be more or anything else than what man makes them," show something of the remarkable results to be attained by introspective analysis.

The first or preparatory part of the work advances a theory much of which seems reasonable and borne out by facts, namely, that sex is not manifested in two absolutely opposite types, either in humanity or lower

* "Sex and Character." By Otto Weininger. Putnam. $3.00 net.

forms; but that there is an "ideoplasm" in all our constituent cells; "Arrhenoplasm" (male plasm), Thelyplasm (female plasm), and that this distinctive plasm differs in amount not only in different persons, but in different cells of the same body. The absolute male or female he holds to be but abstract terms, like the "ideal gas" of the chemists; what we call males and females are those of preponderating amounts of one or the other plasm; and he deduces a neatly mathematical formula as to the law of sex attraction, as resting on these proportionate differences.

We are familiar with the rough working out of this principle in the often noted marriages of especially masculine men with especially feminine women, and of the more feminine men with more masculine women; but it seems somewhat precipitate to reduce these cases to this rigid measurement.

This theory, with a chapter on morbid extremes and perversions, and some sagacious suggestions as to the unwisdom of educating all boys—or all girls —exactly alike, forms his preliminary section; closing, in a chapter on "emancipated women," with the easy assertion, "A woman's demand for emancipation and her qualification for it are in direct proportion to the amount of maleness in her."

"Emancipation" he says, as he means to discuss it "is not the wish for an outward equality with man, but what is of real importance in the woman question, the deep-seated craving to acquire man's character, to attain his mental and moral freedom, to reach his real interests and his creative power. I maintain that the real female element has neither the desire nor the capacity for emancipation in this sense."

Having thus waved aside the "woman question" as a passing morbidity he then approaches the main body of the book, on "The Sexual Types."

There follow fourteen chapters of a most deep and metaphysical nature, in which we are told first that so far there is no female psychology, and that when we have one it must be written by men, she being unconscious of her own

character, and unable to express it even if she were conscious of it—and were willing to do so: that a woman thinks in "henids"—vague processes not to be called thought, and has to have a man to think for her. In short, the woman makes it a criterion of manliness that the man should be superior to her mentally, that she should be influenced and dominated by the man; and this in itself is enough to ridicule all ideas of sexual equality. "The male lives consciously, the female unconsciously," is the summary of that chapter.

There is then a discourse on talent and genius, in which it is held that the utmost any woman ever had, has, or will have, is talent; that genius is ultra-masculinity—the greatest genius is simply the most male man. It further appears that women have no real memory—only an animal-like power of "recollection."

"This peculiar continuity by which a man first realizes that he exists, that he is, and that he is in the world, is all comprehensive in the genius, limited to a few important moments in the mediocre, *and altogether lacking in women.*" (The Italics are his.)

Further we learn: "Inasmuch as woman is without continuity she can have no true reverence; as a fact, reverence is a purely male virtue. . . ." "Later I shall show how women are exactly the opposite of that which reverence means. I would rather be silent about the reverence of widows." Having no memory, he quite properly argues that woman has also no logic, which we have often heard; but he goes bravely on to assert that she has no ethics; and, being without memory, logic or ethics, we cannot blink the next horrible conclusion—that she has no ego!

From this it is but an easy step to say, "In such a being as the absolute female there are no logical and ethical phenomena, and therefore the ground for the assumption of the soul is absent." The absolute female, fortunately, is but an abstract term; nevertheless the concrete females about him are decided to be soulless and without morals.

Even modesty and compassion he denies her—the reason women make better nurses than men is because they are *unsympathetic*, they have no imagination, they do not feel with the sufferer and can therefore remain calm and helpful.

To deny souls to women is hard enough; but Mr. Weininger feels called upon to explain the curious interest in the soul which the poor creature undeniably manifests; and this he does in the following clear and delicate words: "From the side of empirical observation, no stronger proof of the soullessness of woman could be drawn than that she demands a soul in man, that she who is not good in herself demands goodness from him. The soul is a masculine character, pleasing to women in the same way and for the same purpose as a masculine body, or a well-trimmed moustache."

Little now remains to the woman but a Lamia-like body; and of this he recognizes but two types—the mother and the courtesan; the difference between which he holds is not so extreme as we have previously thought.

Even the body of the creature is next attacked, and shown to be unbeautiful—even repulsive, in itself.

All man's worship of woman's beauty comes from his love of her—he imagines beauty in her, and worships what he himself has made. Madonna-worship, for instance, is a purely masculine idea, without basis in womanhood. "Only man has an instinct for beauty, and the ideals of both manly beauty and womanly beauty have been created by man, not by woman."

Then—with a little more of this cogent reasoning—we read: "The foregoing involves the proposition that woman cannot love. Women have made no ideal of man to correspond with the male conception of the Madonna. What woman requires from man is not purity, chastity, morality, but something else. Woman is incapable of desiring virtue in a man."

And then, with a despair quite natural under the circumstances, "It is almost an insoluble riddle that woman, herself incapable of love, should attract the love of man." This riddle Mr. Weininger solves by stating that man loves not woman, but his own ideals imagined in her. "He projects his ideal of an absolutely worthy existence, the ideal that he is unable to isolate within himself, upon another human being, and this act, and this alone, is none other than love, and the significance of love."

This love he affirms is "purely spiritual, and so cannot be blemished by physical union with the beloved person," here giving us what may be taken as the keynote of the book—a mystical exaltation of the ideal, with an unspeakable grossness in apprehension of the real.

In Chapter XII, on "The Nature of Woman and Her Significance in the Universe," he is at some pains to assure us that the last thing he would advocate is the Oriental treatment of woman; and even comes forward in her defence in these magnanimous terms: "However degraded a man may be, he is immeasurably above the most superior woman, so much so that comparison and classification of the two are impossible; but even so, no one has any right to denounce or deprave woman; however inferior she must be considered." "I cannot share the view," he continues, "that women of conspicuous ability are to be regarded as morbid specimens."

These women of ability are only that much men; for the woman herself "is neither high-minded nor low-minded, strong-minded nor weak-minded. She is the opposite of all these. Mind cannot be predicated of her at all; she is mindless."

Then, seeking earnestly for some distinguishing characteristic in this vacuum, he lights upon a great luminous truth; finds one glaring distinction, applying to all women without exception, never found in men; a trait so marked, so vital, so all-inclusive and fully explanatory, that he seeks no further. What is this one womanly instinct which gives us the key to her existence? It is—her passion for *match-making!* Do not think I maliciously exaggerate; these are his words:

"But we must remember that in this, and nothing else, lies the actual essence of woman. After mature consideration of the most varied types of women, and with due regard to the special classes besides those which I have discussed, I am of opinion that the only positively general female characteristic is that of match-making, that is, her uniform willingness to further the idea of sexual union."

"All women are liars" is another sweeping conclusion; he calls it "her organic untruthfulness"; and he gives much attention to hysteria as a manifestation of this.

Under the head of hysteria he classifies all woman's poor attempts "to imitate male virtue"; and even reduces women to an inchoate condition as not being "limited formed individual entities."

"The abstract male is the image of God, the absolute something; the female, and the female element in the male, is the symbol of nothing; that is the significance of the woman in the universe," he explains, repeating, to make it more definite, "The meaning of woman is to be meaningless." "Woman is nothing but man's expression and projection of his own sexuality. Every man creates himself a woman in which he embodies himself and his own guilt. . . . Woman alone, then, is guilt; and is so through man's fault. . . . She is only a part of man, his other, ineradicable, his lower part."

Following this is an amazing chapter on Judaism, which he treats not as a race nor as a religion, but a state of mind, as has been said of Boston! To the unfortunate Jew he denies personality, dignity, aristocracy, morality, genius, humor, and even religion; then inquires, as he well may,"What then is the Jew,if he is nothing that a man can be?"

This chapter is not as extraneous as would at first appear; for, having shown Judaism to be the lowest depth, he then acclaims Jesus as the greatest moral conqueror in that, being a Jew, he rose above it; and this leads naturally to his sublime conclusion in the last chapter, that the one great answer to the whole Woman Question lies in man's gradual conquering of his lower nature, *i.e.*, woman, by an exalted and persistent celibacy. This course, steadily pursued, will gradually eliminate the accursed thing from the universe.

Of course, man will be eliminated as well, but that does not trouble this strong thinker. Moral progress is what he desires. It is only the Jew, he says, who invented the idea of "multiplying and replenishing the earth."

What we are here for is to obey the divine will, to conquer evil and attain to goodness, to a spiritual goodness and a spiritual life.

Woman is the embodied obstacle to this great end—and as such must be abjured.

The real importance of this book lies in its so fully concentrating and carrying to its logical conclusion the andro-centric view of humanity, as well as the extreme dogmas of egoistic religion. It is always well, when great questions are under discussion, to have the two sides fully and even excessively placed before us. Never before in all our literature has the ultra-masculine view of woman been so logically carried out, so unsparingly forced to its conclusion.

Those who have unconsciously held any part of these views may now see to what extreme they lead if fairly faced.

Many a wavering half-interested person might find here enough matter to force him to a definite position. If the book is read at all in America, it will probably find less acceptance than in any other country, owing to the fact that with us the humanness of women is more compellingly visible than in older lands.

It is the humanness which Mr. Weininger so wholly fails to grasp. What is human he calls male—with the unavoidable result that the woman— not being male—is not human.

We need new understanding of the immeasurable difference between sex-distinctions, which we share with other animals, and our pre-eminent race-distinction, which is beyond sex.

THE FORTUNE TELLER
By Thomas W. Dewing

Courtesy of Mr. W. K. Bixby

Thomas W. Dewing

THOMAS W. DEWING centres his thoughts on the external fascination of delicate forms as he realizes that painting, being wholly on the surface, is alone the art of presentation. Since his poetic faculties contain no desire for idiosyncrasies or superficial incidents of design, and since he appreciates that weirdness in choice of topic may show weakness as well as fertility of resource, he charms without overestimating the need of originality of subject, and paints with an imagination that never suggests incoherency or shapelessness. Therefore the inspirations of restrained sweetness that not only qualify, but thoroughly imbue his mind, turn his abilities towards disclosing the beauties of every-day surroundings, towards enriching simple motives, and slight but suggestive themes in present spheres, and towards expressing these conceptions in the most delicate and mellow terms while establishing no peculiar symbols of his fancy. With such an end to be forwarded and with a horror of anything that approaches the commonplace in result he clings to delicate technique, eliminates detail while holding that thorough knowledge of the part left out that makes its absence unnoticeable, and applies to the decorative effects of contour and control of mass a patience, a veiled strength, and a finish without pettiness that causes his work to "carry" across an exhibition hall even when crowded among paintings of contrasted values and colors. And this power of producing an impression at a distance becomes the more unusual since, nearly always, upon closer inspection, his paintings seem viewed through a soft haze or mist that strangely is never humid. As a rule his colors remain in a minor key, exquisite in their depths of silver grays, of greens, and browns, where a refinement of delicate lines and values causes them to fade and reappear in his evanescent light. Yet, as in the case of his choice of subject, he treats his drawing throughout with his usual restraint, and with the painstaking conservative qualities that give a minute and gentle care of treatment to those portions of the canvas of especial importance, the faces, the hands, and the occasional objects of still life. Also, that he may the better reinforce his control of the connotation of his atmosphere he assembles his parts with a spontaneous felicity toward a balance of unenforced symmetry of lines that with his tones focus upon some decorative spot against his tapestry-like background of soft half light and shade. Especially is all this true in the very unusual beauty of his series of ideally treated figures of women such as "The Spinet," "The Fortune Teller," and the others of like nature to which he has confined his efforts for many years. In their repose, in their pliant subtlety of poise and charm, he exhibits his power over sensitive winnowing processes, his enchantment and witchery of fine-spun workmanship. Unlike most men he displays few ups and downs in his productions, but evenly maintains his standards of elevated thoughts that seem to drift quietly through his mind directly to the conscious delicacy of his brush. All in all, the feeling of delicate intelligence and the characteristic grace and ease of his method distinguish themselves both by the excellence of its elements and by the harmony of their total effect.

—

Thomas W. Dewing, born in Boston in 1851, made his most serious study of painting during the three years between 1876 and 1879, in Paris under Jules J. Lefebre. Since that time, with the exception of one trip to Europe, he has remained in New York, gaining his thorough reputation as a painter of portraits and figure compositions. His picture "The Days" won the Clark Prize, in 1887, at the National Academy of Design, where the following year he became an academician. At one time he was also a member of the Society of American Artists, but on the foundation of the Society of Ten American Painters he resigned from the former and joined the latter body.

H. ST. G.

Great Britain's Literary Government

By WALTER LITTLEFIELD

AT a reception given three years ago by the Authors Club to Ambassador Jusserand the editor of *The Century* read a paper showing the remarkable extent to which this country had been represented abroad by men of letters. Even excluding incidental authors from the list, there was revealed a most distinguished array—from Bancroft and Irving down to Lowell and Hay—and a record of their achievements in diplomacy and statesmanship formed a gratifying contrast to the work of those men whose tenure of office began and ended in politics.

While, for obvious reasons, American Cabinets have not been conspicuous as literary bodies, the Presidential Cabinets of France have in this respect borne some resemblance to the American Corps Diplomatique, although in our sister Republic the literary element has often been a part of the harmonious whole—in individual as well as in Ministry. We are apt to overlook the fact that Jules Simon, Leon Say, Gaston Paris, de Hérédia, and the rest had achieved local fame in politics long before their writings appealed to foreign audiences. British Governments have frequently included one or two authors of exalted fame, of whom Macaulay, Lytton, and Disraeli immediately suggest themselves as examples. But it has remained for Sir Henry Campbell-Bannerman to gather together a Liberal Government in which the literary element might seem little short of indomitable were it not for the fact that the author-statesmen in question hold portfolios of a nature usually foreign to their literary achievements.

Four distinguished men of letters at once arrest the attention—John Morley, James Bryce, Augustine Birrell, and Richard Burdon Haldane; while further on, as a member of the Government without a portfolio, is Winston Churchill, who has frequently been confounded with the American author of identical name.

The fortunate chance which kept John Morley out of active politics since the fall of the Rosebery Cabinet in 1894 has been responsible for much literary activity. Toward the end of that year came "The Study of Literature"; six years later "Oliver Cromwell," and of more recent date still the monumental "Life of Gladstone" in three volumes for which the world must have waited long indeed had the three years of energy and devotion required for its composition been spent at St. Stephen's instead of in the solitude of Wimbleton Park. Parenthetically it may be remarked that Lord Rosebery's continued political obscuration has also been rich in literary expression—"Sir Robert Peel," "Napoleon, the Last Phase."

Mr. Morley, who is now Secretary of State for India, was, like his sometime political opponent, the late Lord Salisbury, a man of letters before he even thought of entering upon a political career. The most fecund period of his production extended from 1867 to 1881 and gave to the world, besides numerous articles in the *Fortnightly Review*, "Edmund Burke: An Historical Study," "Critical Miscellanies," "Voltaire," "On Compromise," "Rousseau," "More Critical Miscellanies," "Diderot and the Encyclopædists," and the "Life of Richard Cobden."

Perhaps it was this last work even more than a lifelong friendship which caused his great Liberal chief, Gladstone, to call him to the Government from his literary seclusion. At that time, 1881, he was at work on "Walpole." This did not see light until eight years later, and, together with a volume of "Studies in Literature," was the sole literary product in book form of his Ministerial career of 1881-1894. And now this foremost biographer of his time finds himself directing the Government of the Indian Empire which, aside from the economic questions which may arise, is curiously alien to his former literary themes. It

Photo by Elliott & Fry   HON. SYDNEY CHARLES BUXTON

Photo by Downey HON. JOHN MORLEY

Photo by The London Stereoscopic Co.

HON. JAMES BRYCE

would be strange indeed, however, if the archives of the Indian Office did not furnish him with inspiration and material for biographies of one or two British Viceroys whose administrations yearn for an apologist.

Very likely James Bryce, Chief Secretary for Ireland, is better known among Americans than his colleague in the Indian Office. Like him, he was a Gladstone favorite, but, unlike him, certain pledges are to be found in his writings as to how he may manipulate the functions of his present office. His recent utterances, also, reveal his policy: "In the first place, the administration of Ireland should be conciliatory. In the second, there will be an energetic and generous administration of the Land Purchase Act, and use of the powers vested in the Congested Districts Board to solve land difficulties and questions of evicted tenants in the interests of peace and order. Thirdly, it is necessary to simplify and reorganize the administrative system, and in so doing economies can be effected which will set free more funds to be used for the benefit and development of the country."

There is no hint, surely, in this proclaimed policy that the statesman who utters it is the author of "The American Commonwealth," which is regarded here as a standard work upon the growth and Constitution of the Republic, and, by the native readers of the many foreign languages in which it has appeared, as the best exposition of American institutions. This book has stood the test of forty-two years and is still unequalled in its scope.

Mr. Bryce is a very active member of the Alpine Club. He has climbed the Schreckhorn and has reached high summits in Spain, Transylvania, Poland, Iceland, and Western Asia. Not the least notable of his ascents was that of Mt. Ararat. It is an article of faith in the Armenian Church that the snow-capped summit of Noah's mountain is inaccessible. Mr. Bryce, with an escort of six Cossacks and beneath a burning sun and in a suffocating atmosphere never before experienced by him, began the ascent. One by one his companions turned back. At an altitude of 13,600 feet he found himself alone. At length he reached the summit. Two days after this exploit, an Armenian gentleman presented him to the Archimandrite of Etchmiadzin saying: "This Englishman says he has been to the top of Massis" (the Armenian name for Ararat). The venerable priest smiled sweetly. "No," he replied, "that cannot be. No one has ever been up there. It is forbidden." The story of this famous ascent was published in 1877 in a volume entitled "Transcaucasia and Ararat."

Among Mr. Bryce's more recent works may be mentioned "Impressions of South Africa," which the Salisbury Government with characteristic party obstinacy declined to heed. Later still came "Studies in History and Jurisprudence," and "Studies in Contemporary Biography." Mr. Bryce's literary activity has found expression in innumerable subjects—from the flora of the island of Arran to the Trade Marks Registration Acts. At the present moment, his new and revised edition of "Two Centuries of Irish History" may be searched for the key to his Irish policy.

Possibly the most complete man of letters in C. B.'s Government is Augustine Birrell, the new President of the Board of Education. Twenty-one years ago he published " Obiter Dicta." He was instantly recognized as an uncommon stylist, an essayist of delightful fancy and humor, while his peculiar light and varied touch caused the word "Birrelling" to pass into the language as a term of endearment among those who enjoy scholarly wit and pungent criticism. In the meantime, he has shown his capacity as a biographer of literary personages, and the urgent demands of a busy practice at Chancery Bar have neither blunted his gentle irony nor diluted his humor, notwithstanding the fact that he has laid on the altar of the Green Bags frequent libations, the most notable being " Duties and

Liabilities" of Trustees and "Copyright in Books." He is the biographer par excellence of Charlotte Brontë, William Hazlitt, and Sir William Lockwood, and has edited, not, however, without being visited by adverse criticism, an edition of Boswell's "Life of Johnson." He has also found time in the intervals of leisure from law and politics to write a Life of Andrew Marvell.

The department of philosophical criticism has distinguished represention in the Cabinet by Richard B. Haldane, the Secretary of State for War. He was educated at the Edinburgh Academy and the Edinburgh and Göttingen Universities, where he gained very high philosophical honors, and in 1876 won the Gray and Ferguson scholarships of four Scottish universities. He held the Gifford chair of philosophy in St. Andrew's University from 1902 to 1904. His publications, although well known to advanced educators in this country, are not as accessible to the public as they should be, notwithstanding the fact that, while he handles his themes in an authoritative manner, his simplicity and grace of style invite general reading. Some years ago, he published a series of volumes on philosophical criticism and wrote a standard life of Adam Smith, the founder of modern political economy. He is also the author of "Education and Empire," and, three years ago, "The Pathway to Reality." With the aid of a distinguished collaborator, he has also presented as translator "Schopenhauer's World as Will and Idea."

As these lines are being penned, word comes from England that Mr. Haldane is to contribute an introduction to a work which is now in press at George Allen's. It is entitled "Science in Public Affairs" and consists of seven essays by various writers—Mrs. Barnett, wife of Canon Barnett, writes on "City Suburbs," John A. Hobson on "Industry," and C. M. Douglas, M.D., on "Administration." Other essays treat of citizenship, physical development, and colonial expansion.

From a literary point of view, and

ignoring all saving political clauses, I may be permitted for a moment to venture beyond the Ministers who hold portfolios and touch upon one member of the Government who, although without a position in the Cabinet, has achieved distinction as an author.

When "Richard Carvel" was published in 1899, the distinguished American correspondent of the *London Times*, George W. Smalley, roundly rebuked the author for having presumed to take as a pseudonym "the name of a distinguished young Englishman of historic family already well known to letters." Many Americans had never heard of the Englishman in question, but they did know that Winston Churchill was no pseudonym, although it was many months before English readers and reviewers could digest this fact. Mr. Smalley's inexcusable rebuke made conspicuous his acquired condescending British intolerance and aroused some interest here in the English Winston Churchill, who had already written "The Story of the Malakand Field Force" and "The River War," and was just preparing to go to South Africa as the correspondent of a London paper, where he gained material to write his later books, "London to Ladysmith via Pretoria" and "Ian Hamilton's March." He is also the author of a novel, "Savrola." These later books, published through Messrs. Longmans, had made their author more or less well known to American readers, when, on the eve of his appointment as Under Secretary of State for the Colonies, he published the monumental of his father, the late Lord Randolph Churchill.

While Mr. Kipling remains as the most highly paid English author of the day, it is interesting to note that Winston Churchill received for the Life of his father £8000 down with a contingent interest reaching half the gains which may accrue after the profits of publication have yielded £12,000 to the publishers. This amount compares well with the £200 each which Macaulay received for his essays and the

Photo by Thomson

HON. WINSTON SPENCER CHURCHILL

427

£20,000 paid by a single check for his famous "History." Mr. Gladstone, whose yearly income from his pen was £3000, knew well the market temper of literary wares and always charged £200 for a review article provided the subject was "sympathetic." He is known, however, to have refused 4s., or a dollar, a word for a contribution with the topic of which he was not sympathetic.

No English politician has made such rapid strides toward a predominant position in politics as Winston Churchill during the last few months. And, recognizing the tireless energy and varied abilities and youth (he was born in 1874) of the man, it is quite likely that even his busy work in the Colonial Office and his fame as a brilliant although somewhat ill-tempered debater in the House of Commons may prove merely incidental to his literary career. He is feared quite as much by his own party as he is by the Tories. His political eminence has been partly due to skilful stage management and the gift of utilizing naturally dramatic situations. Even the publication of the brilliantly written Life of his gifted father was at the propitious moment; but when it is considered that this work compares favorably with Morley's "Gladstone," and that the author had already produced books of permanent value before his thirtieth year, the future literary career of the English Winston Churchill, although it may be punctuated by no "big sellers," like that of his older American namesake, is certainly one of promise.

Returning now to the Cabinet proper, we find a number of men who have "dabbled in literature" to some purpose. The new Postmaster-General, Sydney C. Buxton, has shown versatility as an author. Although most of his writings, like most of his life, concern politics, he has had a more or less luxurious leisure in which to record his prowess with rod and gun. His "Handbook to Political Questions" has passed through eleven editions, while his "Political Manual" is scarcely less in demand. His most ambitious work is "Finance and Politics, an Historical Study Covering the Period from 1783 to 1885." He is considered an authority on the subject of political finance.

Farther down the list is the Earl of Crewe, Lord President of the Council. Doubtless most of the members of the Cabinet have written verses at one time or another, if only in academic Latin. Lord Crewe, however, has published a volume of poems, which shows that the writer is versatile and also gifted with a fine sense of rhythm. It is called "Stray Verses." But, after all, this poet is rather a dilettante and patron of letters than a writer. He has personally tided over the age of discouragement several promising literary youths, is President of the Literary Fund, and has at Crewe Hall one of the finest libraries in the Kingdom.

Paradoxical as it may seem, the most voluminous writer in the Cabinet makes no pretension of being a man of letters. This is John Burns, President of the Local Government Board. His literary activity has been principally confined to political and sociological questions whose nature demanded strictly contemporaneous treatment so his numerous contributions; to reviews and pamphlets have not require appearance in book form.

Another member of the Cabinet may be considered as the complement of Mr. Burns, for he is a man of letters who has written nothing save a volume on fly-fishing and prefers to confine his literary ambition to collecting the works of others. We may imagine Sir Edward Grey as Secretary of State for Foreign Affairs signing a treaty with one hand, while he turns over the pages of a rare imprint with the other.

Thus it will be seen that C. B.'s Ministry is a very distinguished one from the literary point of view, and its progress or decadence will, therefore, be watched with unusual interest by literary men. As a closing word and with a final stretch to this article by way of courtesy, it may be recorded that Sir Henry Fowler, who holds a portfolio in the Cabinet as Chancellor

Photo by The London Stereoscopic Co.

THE EARL OF CREWE

Photo by The London Stereoscopic Co.

SIR. H. H. FOWLER

of the Duchy of Lancaster, is the father of Ellen Thorneycroft Fowler, whose novels, "Concerning Isabel Carnaby," "The Double Thread,"

"Place and Power," and "Kate of Kate Hall," have attained a degree of popularity in this country quite as high as in her own.

Some Recent Novels

A Study of a Woman

IN "All That Was Possible"* Mr. Howard Overing Sturgis has given us a study of a woman in an equivocal position, and has handled his subject with great skill and delicacy and with a remorseless logic that compels the reader to recognize the outcome as inevitable. For the book is the story of a woman who tries to eat her cake and have it too; to run with the hare and hunt with the hounds; to follow the primrose path although resenting its ending.

Sibyl Crofts has left the stage to become the mistress of Lord Medmenham. A woman of refinement and cultivation, her influence over the young man has been good; she has taught him to sing and cured him of gambling. But after five years the inevitable end has come: Lord Medmenham is to be married; a handsome settlement is made upon Sibyl, and, surprised to find how little she cares, she retires to a cottage in North Wales to spend the summer and decide upon her future plans.

The only gentlefolk in the neighborhood are the Henshaws, who own the big slate quarry, and Sibyl forms a chance acquaintance with young Norris Henshaw, a handsome boy of nineteen. The acquaintance is prospering when Sibyl is one day visited by Robert Henshaw, a man of thirty-five, the head of the family and cousin to Norris. With feminine intuition Norris's mother has guessed more or less accurately Sibyl Crofts's history; she dreads the influence of such a woman upon her son, and Robert has come to beg Sibyl to discourage the boy's visits. This is the beginning of an acquaintance be-

tween Robert and Sibyl, which speedily ripens into love on both sides, and then comes the struggle in the woman's mind. Shall she marry Henshaw or shall she not? There would be no deception involved, for he knows her history; and, mingled with her great love for Robert, is the desire to decide upon what will be best for him, for her love is unselfish. It would be unfair to tell the result of the struggle; it is enough to say that while it comes as a surprise, it is nevertheless perfectly logical, it is "All That Was Possible."

As may be seen, the plot is of the slightest. The author has taken an episode in a woman's life, with its results, and offered it to us for inspection and comment. Sibyl Crofts is not the vulgar, self-seeking woman so often found in such a situation, but she is unreasonable. No woman of her intelligence should be surprised if, after living openly with a man as his mistress, she should find society's doors closed to her. To do her justice, she does not utter the plaintive cry "Good women are so hard," which is so often evoked by a failure to secure social recognition, but she is guilty of the appeal to the example of George Eliot, which I suppose we shall have as long as women resent the position where their own folly has placed them.

The story is told in the form of letters, a style which seems more coming into vogue and which can be used by a clever writer with excellent results, as in the case of "The Etchingham Letters," and "The Woodhouse Correspondence." But, curiously enough, Mr. Sturgis has not availed himself of this opportunity for character-drawing. The letters, all written

* "All That Was Possible." By Howard Overing Sturgis. Putnam. $1.50.

by Sibyl, are not in the least like those of an actress. A woman who has once been successful on the stage never loses the flavor of it, but these letters might have been written by a woman of conventional society. They are only used as a vehicle for conveying facts, not as a medium for revealing character.

The book is extremely interesting, although much shorter and slighter in construction than that brilliant study of London life, "Belchamber." It is so devoid of any preaching, yet so logical in its conclusions, that no thoughtful person can read it without acquiescing in the lesson it so quietly inculcates. Particularly should it be recommended to those world-weary young persons who discourse condescendingly upon "conventional morality," meaning any of the ten commandments which they find it nconvenient to keep.

M. K. FORD.

Mr. Phillpotts Excels Himself

WE have come to expect tragedy from Mr. Phillpotts, and also to expect the tragedy to be enacted in the Dartmoor region of Devonshire. But never before has he given us tragedy of so deep and hopeless a nature, nor shown more minutely the workings of the heart, and the evolution of the mind in man and woman. Instead of the elemental passion of "The Secret Woman," we have in "The Portreeve" * a woman actuated by revenge, mercilessly ruining the life of the man who has incurred her hatred, and stopping at nothing, not even her own misfortune, in pursuance of her terrible determination. The character of the Portreeve as it unfolds itself convinces us of the inevitableness of his fate. His blind unreasoning belief in a higher Power as the source of all his fortunes and misfortunes keeps him from fighting the real author of his misery, and his gradual decay and tragic end come in these circumstances as naturally as the return of winter. These two characters are drawn with a depth of insight and power of handling that

* The Portreeve. By Eden Phillpotts. Macmillan. $1.50.

place this work at the head of the author's long list of admirable creations.

In contrast to the tragedy that is such a striking note in Mr. Phillpotts's work, we have his inimitable humor as displayed by his peasants. Abner Barkell and his friends are quite up to the standard set by the author, and their philosophy and opinions are a welcome relief to the darkness of the plot of the story. Mr. Phillpotts's descriptions of Nature have often been eulogized. They are evidently drawn from Nature herself, for he never repeats himself, and paints her with a sure and loving hand, whether in her angry, majestic, or gentle moods. The minor characters of the story are all well drawn, but the two most important ones stand out so strongly as to make one regard all else but as a delightful background. One lays down "The Portreeve" in astonishment at the inventiveness and ability that can use the same scenes and the same class of people so often, yet with increasing interest.

CHARLOTTE HARWOOD.

Mr. Moore's Symphony in Gray and Red

IF the critic of George Moore as "sensualist" and "gross materialist" would be converted, let him read "The Lake."* Except for the name on the title-page, he would not believe that the creator of "Esther Waters" wrote the book. It reveals the poet and the mystic; but, best of all, it shows that the disease of degeneracy in style and matter which appears to seize upon most modern novelists as the number of their works increases has passed him by unscathed. His "later manner" outranks his earlier.

"The Lake" is a symphony in gray, with brilliant flashes of vivid red; a fire opal whose surface is clouded and opaque except when the love element appears. Then the milky softness is submerged by the glowing ruby of intense dramatic interest.

The lake is in Ireland,—a physical

* "The Lake." By George Moore. Appleton. $1.50.

entity around which are woven poetic descriptions of nature which may be read with pleasure even by those to whom the human soul is a more interesting book than trees and birds and running streams; and it is a symbol of the metaphorical lake in every man's heart, for the crossing of which every man must ungird his loins. The actors are really only two, a young priest aged thirty-four, and a pretty schoolmistress who taught singing in his parish. The objective and the subjective are interwoven with infinite skill; the descriptions of scenery and rustic life, animate and inanimate, the petty interests of an obscure Irish parish, even the girl's state of mind, are all artfully opposed to the subtle psychology of the priest's condition, mental and moral.

The story is simple: Rose Leicester, while one of Father Grogarty's parishioners, "falls," in the ordinarily accepted meaning of the term, and is driven from Garranard by a passionate sermon which he preached upon the sin of unchastity. His conscience smites him when he realizes what he has done, and his one desire becomes to discover her whereaqouts and make tardy reparation for his hasty judgment. He learns through a letter from a Catholic priest that she has been living in London since the birth of her child, and is organist in Father O'Grady's church. At this point the narrative gives way to letters exchanged between the two, in which the ritualism of the one is contrasted with the unconventionality of the other. She travels in Holland and Germany as secretary to a Biblical exegetist and companion to his daughter. Half for pleasure of expression and half to draw out the priest, she describes the pictures she sees in Munich, The Hague, Amsterdam, Haarlem, and Cologne, and the Wagner operas in Bayreuth, quoting Ralph Ellis, her employer, as her authority in criticism. Here Moore's art is doubly apparent. Ralph Ellis is his mouthpiece, as Adrian is George Meredith's in "Richard Feverel," but with this difference: Moore's ideas of art and music are communicated to the reader indirectly and when off his guard, and at the same time Father Grogarty is made irritable by Rose's slavish adherence to the opinions of her teacher, and her parrot-like reproduction of them for his benefit. This is one of the most subtle bits in the construction of the book.

The correspondence continues until the point is reached where the priest discovers that his anxiety for her soul and his desire that she should return to his fold for safety against agnostic influence are caused only by jealousy; that he loves her and desires not only her soul but her body, and he a priest! The resemblance to "The Duel," in which Mr. Otis Skinner is playing is obvious. When this confession reaches her, Rose reveals to him that she had realized in their early acquaintance that the friendship was not entirely platonic, and she wished him to suffer and escape from the conventions and prejudices binding him as a priest, even to leave his parish, without scandal, if possible. To his question as to her feelings for Mr. Ellis she makes no reply except to say that she is bound for Central Asia with him to discover the source of the Christian River.

Father Grogarty himself is presented to us as self-deceptive, morbidly introspective, painfully exact and conscientious, and sensitive as an æolian harp. These characteristics make of him a tiresome man, and one can well understand Rose's desire to free him from his bondage of tradition.

She is his opposite: capricious, "of incurable levity of mind," he believes; impulsive, the most primitive woman he had ever known. Her spirit haunts him; he sees her in all his lonely walks as different manifestations of nature: she is a daffodil belonging to antiquity, "a thing divorced from the Christian ideal"; a fountain enchanting his senses by its joy and beauty and grace; the spirit of spring; a goddess "come down to earth to take her joy among men, an irresponsible being obedient to no human laws."

His change of attitude towards her is most subtly indicated. From believing her to be a sinner and a hopeless pagan, he hails her as his saviour.

The book is a strong plea for individualism *versus* iron-bound tradition, whether of the Catholic Church or of the Protestant; for "the mysterious lights of instinct"; for feeling rather than for ideas which pass; for nature rather than for books; for sympathy with every kind of life, good and evil; for the realization of self in all its completeness.

CAROLYN SHIPMAN WHIPPLE.

Readable but Crude

Is Miss Glasgow's study of contemporary New York life* as profoundly symbolic, after all, as her title would imply? It is a readable story, containing frequent paragraphs of observation for which "clever" is precisely the appropriate adjective; and, technically considered, the narrative is well-ordered and symmetrical. But it cannot be discovered that either Miss Glasgow's method or her point of view is strikingly new, a point that would doubtless escape comment if the book did not flaunt an implication of self-conscious novelty. But, apart from its lack of vital significance, what one most seriously misses in the story is a richness of texture and a perception, on the author's part, of the luminous contrasts of life, such qualities, in short, as made Miss Sinclair's "The Divine Fire" a memorable novel. Miss Glasgow has not seen deeply nor interpreted richly; her book is, frankly speaking, crude.

It is surely a simple and easily noted fact that it is possible for a man to attract a woman even when no more heavily equipped for capture than the following description conveys:

* "The Wheel of Life." By Ellen Glasgow. Doubleday, Page & Co. $1.50.

His handsome wooden features possessed hardly more character than was expressed by his immaculately starched shirt-front, but he was not without a certain wholly superficial attraction, half as of a sleek, well-groomed animal and half as of a masculine conceit, naked and unashamed.

Two characters of this altogether usual pattern are introduced, and the book chronicles the equally usual phenomenon that two women fell in love with them. Laura Wilde, the heroine, who escapes marrying the object of her ephemeral passion, is a poet; but will perhaps appear to have a less complex nature than has usually been attributed to her living counterparts. Her physical appearance is dwelt on to redundancy, and it is perhaps in contrast with her smile, holding "all the mystery of flame and of shadow," "her skin, which was like porcelain touched by a flame," her "illusion of mystery," that her actions appear strangely normal, if not actually commonplace. As often happens in the work of writers who fall short of genius, the minor characters have most of truth and suggestiveness. Gerty Bridewell, for instance, who pretends to no intrinsic interest of character, is a successfully sardonic little study. "Why, for instance," this luxuriously miserable young woman asks herself, "when she had been wretched with but one man on the box, should the addition of a second livery fail to produce in her the contentment of which she had often dreamed while she disconsolately regarded a single pair of shoulders?" It is a pity that Miss Glasgow's humor does not shine forth more abundantly; her work needs it. The book is a sincere and intelligent effort to approach the realities; yet after reading it one is obliged to admit that more than one obstinate veil still lies between.

OLIVIA HOWARD DUNBAR.

The Three Roses

(From the French of François Coppée)

ONE morn the sudden triumph of the spring
Beguiled me to my garden, there to see
Three lovely roses, newly opening.

Poor dainty things, that by a stern decree
Have but one short sweet summer's day to live,
For each of you what service shall there be?

" I," said the first, "love's errand shall achieve,
Breathe out my soul a snowy breast upon,
And, dying 'mid the sweetness, scarcely grieve."

"But I," the second spoke, "shall die alone
Within a churchyard, laid upon the moss
That hides a name deep carven in the stone."

Then said the third, " Of gain or seeming loss
I have the happiest lot—no service vain,
But to expire in worship 'neath the Cross."

I fell to musing in a tender strain—
On love, the passing madness of a day,
On death, and swift oblivion of its pain.

The flowers in homage sent where love holds sway,
Flowers laid upon a grave with reverent care,
Alike they die, their perfumes pass away.

It must be so. Ye new-born roses fair,
No skill your beauty shall immortalize,
Save only thine, O mystic rose of prayer!

The soul by thee exhaled shall mount the skies,
And, mingling with the censer's fragrant cloud,
Unto the very throne of God shall rise!

A. I. DU P. COLEMAN.

Afternoon Calls*

By MRS. JOHN LANE

THERE is nothing so delightful as to mingle with one's fellow-creatures. One of the charming results of this amiable human trait is afternoon calls. Of course it does happen that there is sometimes a hitch in the mingling, such as the other day when I was staying with the Jephsons. The Jephsons live in a "semi-detached," and they call it Lohengrin Lodge.

They are awfully social.

Their drawing-room has three French windows, and when you go up the drive you can look right in. The family consists of Mrs. Jephson, two daughters, a son, and an undeclared young man.

Just as we sat in the drawing-room finishing our after-lunch coffee, a four-wheeler crunched up the gravel walk. As the cab turned the curve we had a glimpse of a withered profile, surmounted by a brown front and a black lace bonnet with purple ribbons, and two black silk gloves that clutched a black card case.

"Gracious!" cried the social Mrs. Jephson, "if that is n't Miss Tomblin! For goodness' sake, let's hide!"

On his way to the front door the footman looked in for instructions. The undeclared young man and the right Miss Jephson had, in a panic, taken refuge under the piano. The brother was behind the sofa, and the other Miss Jephson was hiding behind the steel engraving of "The Christian Martyr," on a draped easel, and Mrs. Jephson was under the table. Only her feet were visible.

"Not at home," she said to the footman, with a good deal of dignity, from behind the table-cloth. The footman looked respectfully at Mrs. Jephson's feet, and never moved an eyelash, he was so well trained.

On her way back to her four-wheeler Miss Tomblin stopped for a moment and looked into the window, apparently to arrange the fuzz of her front by aid of the window-glass. All the Jephsons behind the furniture held their breath. What Miss Tomblin saw beside her front will never be known, but I have since heard that she has not called on the social Jephsons again.

It was, however, this interesting experience which directed my thoughts to the charms of friendship and the joys of mingling with one's fellow-creatures as illustrated by that delightful opportunity for modern soul-out-pourings, the afternoon call.

After serious and profound study I have come to the conclusion that the object and aim of calling is to find everybody out. If anybody is at home you are most dreadfully disappointed. I have been deeply engaged studying the philosophy of calls in company with my friend Maria, who hired a brougham for two hours and took me along, for the reason that it costs no more, and then you have a valid excuse for curtailing your call if you are so unlucky as to find any one in. For Maria is nothing if not truthful. I know just what she said and how she said it:

"I'm so sorry to go, but I have Margery Smith waiting for me in the carriage. I'm giving her an airing, poor dear; she does n't often get a chance. Sweet thing, is n't she? Especially if she has her own way,—but that's so like the Smiths!"

What she said to me when she banged the brougham door on herself was: "My dear, I thought that woman would never let me go! I would n't have called, only I thought she'd be sure to be out. I could just as well have gone there by 'bus. At any rate, she's done!" And Maria scratched her off her list with natural indignation.

"It's a great thing," and Maria thoughtfully studied her visiting list, "to call on people when you're quite

437

*Copyright, 1906, by ANNA E. LANE.

sure they 'll be out. Why, I could n't have half as many friends if I ever found them in! Now, I 've made up my mind to be gone just two hours, and I 've simply got to make eight calls. I 'll go first to the Fauntleroy-Jones, because Mrs. Fauntleroy-Jones always takes a nap till tea-time, so I 'm safe not to find her in."

The Fauntleroy-Jones are disgracefully rich, and they live in what the estate-agents describe as a " mansion," and they have columns in their drawing-room. People love to go to their dinner-parties, but hate to talk to them. When Mrs. Fauntleroy-Jones is not giving a dinner-party, she probably wanders, lonely and forsaken, among the stately columns of her drawing-room, in company with Fido, her faithful pug. As we proceeded towards that expensive part of the town where the Fauntleroy-Jones live in a sumptuous structure uplifted by plaster caryatides, Maria clutched my arm as a victoria, drawn by a thoughtful-looking horse, with a long white chin, came towards us. A red-faced, white-whiskered old gentleman, with eyes like boiled gooseberries, and a stern old lady under plumes and a Roman nose, leaned solemnly back and stared with unwinking meditation at nothing in particular.

"I declare," Maria cried, "if it is n't the Tippetts. What a mercy to have met them! I 'll call at once. Dear things!"

And as the oblivious Tippetts rolled away, Maria gave hasty instructions, and we fled in the opposite direction.

"Please hurry!" Maria cried imploringly to the coachman. "I 'm so afraid they 'll get back," she explained to me. "You can never tell!"

We landed quite out of breath at a dull green house on the side of a dingy square that looked like a favorite trysting-place for cats. A decayed summer-house invited to repose.

The Tippetts' man-servant was foreign, and Maria had to wait ages before he opened the door, and then he was still struggling with his coat.

"Nod at home," he said, out of breath. "Lady Tippett and ze General Tippett is taking of ze air," he

added by way of unnecessary explanation. He tucked Maria up with great respect, for which he got no credit, as Maria, when we drove off, remarked in a sudden burst of patriotism that foreigners might possibly take our trade, and she had heard that they did better in the way of music, and, possibly, painting, though she was no judge of such trifles, but give her an English man-servant every time; that was something no mere foreigner could ever hope to rival.

"At any rate, the Tippetts have been called on. Now for the Fauntleroy-Jones."

Our steed, which was rather given to stumbling, seemed conscious that he was expected to put his best foot foremost. We drove up with quite an air. Maria shook herself out and sailed up the front steps. Maria looks just as well from behind as she does in front, which gives her that moral support so superior to a good conscience. When you know you are all right behind, you can face the world.

An immaculate powdered being in plush said "Not at home," while a colleague in plush and flour joined him in staring over Maria's head at the brougham. Like statues in silk stockings there they stood and declined to have anything further to do with her, and they left her to open the carriage door and slam herself in.

"The insolent things!" And Maria sat up like a ramrod and breathed hard. We could not but acknowledge the perfection of the British Menial, but we felt that the suffering he caused was out of all proportion to the joy.

For reasons unexplained we still remained glued to the spot. I looked furtively up the steps. The silk stockings were permitting themselves the relaxation of a grin.

"Why don't you go?" and Maria forced her head out of the window to the detriment of her best hat.

" 'Cos you 'av'n't said where, lidy," the coachman retorted, with a sense of injury.

"I make it a point," said Maria, unfolding her philosophy of friendship, as the Fauntleroy-Jones's caryatides faded from view, "never to call on any one's 'at-home' day. At Home days are only vanity. At Home women never care about you personally. They only want you to swell the crowd, and they hate to see you any other day. That's the reason I'm calling on Mrs. Bangs-Kipper. It isn't her day."

Mrs. Bangs-Kipper is intensely "smart," and she lives in a narrow, dreary street, with a greengrocer on one side of her and a "pub" on the other side; but just around the corner is a square so aristocratic that it sheds a lustre over the whole neighborhood.

As I saw Maria's skirts swish in, I realized that my philosophic friend had made a mistake: Mrs. Bangs-Kipper was at home. For fifteen minutes I studied the street, while the driver made way for other callers; I also studied the driver's back, and saw that the fit of his coat proclaimed more than anything else that he wasn't private. It had been constructed for a big man, and it bulged at the back, and the collar scratched his ears. There was, also, a mysterious crest on his buttons, which would have puzzled the College of Arms. The only one I understood was the button that was missing.

From the study of the driver's buttons, I turned my attention to Mrs. Bangs-Kipper's callers. It struck me that they seemed satisfied with a very little of Mrs. Bangs-Kipper.

Maria stayed longer than any one, which I could not understand, seeing that time was money, but even she was being tucked in by a smart parlor-maid fifteen minutes after our arrival. Finally, when our steed had been coaxed into that slow trot sacred to "by the hour," she narrated her experiences.

"She *was* in," and Maria paused to brood over her injuries: "I haven't called on her for years, and the last time I said I'd never go again. It might have been the same call. There were four women in the room—the chilly-chintzy kind—and I didn't know one. She always sits in one place like a graven image. You take a chair be-side her and say things, and then she says things. And then somebody else comes, and you get up and stare. Nobody talks to you because you haven't been introduced, and of course you couldn't be made to talk. I sat ten minutes staring, and then I got up to go. She held out a hand like a cold fish, and smiled a long, narrow smile, like a box lid, and hoped I'd come again. I said I'd love to."

"Well, why don't you sometimes call on your friends?" I suggested, knowing Maria's rules of conduct.

Maria looked at me with her cold, prominent blue eyes. "I only went because I was sure she'd be out," she said softly, as if that explained everything.

When we reached the Simpson-Blotters and found they also were in, Maria felt that the disappointment was nearly too much to bear. It seems that by accident we had arrived at a serious function. Two small Simpson-Blotters in white and blue ribbons were flattening their noses against the dining-room windows, with a background of governess. All three were chewing.

The front door was opened with such appalling suddenness that Maria had barely time to put on her company expression. A waiter welcomed her with a look of abject relief, as if she were the first, and he was nearly discouraged. He waved her into the dining-room with a stately gesture. There were preparations on a magnificent scale, and the dining-table was pushed against the wall, but nobody was there but the Simpson-Blotter children and the governess, and all three were eating for dear life.

The danger of too great preparations is one of the most trying of social problems. When the dining-table is pushed against the wall, and there are silver urns and things, then you betray the dizzy height of your aspirations. I meditated on the different kinds of social agonies while Maria was lost to view. The trouble with too great preparations is that they are so frightfully visible. The dining-table is evidently so out of its element, and there are things on it one sees at no other time. Possibly you are the only person in the room, and so you make a good square meal—a real satisfying one —and then climb up-stairs and shake hands with your hostess. She smiles tremulously with her mouth, but there is a far-away look in her eyes as if she were listening to the front door bell. She also replies at random. All the drawing-room furniture has been pushed back, so there is a terrible vacant space in the middle, like the desert of Sahara. You timidly greet two out-of-date old ladies in the desert of Sahara—the kind who usually don't count—say maiden aunts—and you join them in looking longingly at the door for other guests. A shy man straggles in and looks forlornly about, and the maiden aunts, evidently more hopeful, ask if you have had tea.

After all, it isn't your "at home," so you have no compassion, and declare you really must be going, and though the maiden aunts implore you to stay— realizing too late your value as a human being—you murmur your way past the forlorn man to the hostess, whose ears are still at the front door, but who temporarily detaches them and clings to you. However, nothing will induce you to stay!

Yes, it takes social genius to provide just enough and not to displace the furniture too obviously

The waiter shut Maria into the brougham with evident regret. He was a loyal soul, even if only temporary, and we left him looking wistfully up and down the blank street in a vain search for other guests. As for Maria, she was so resigned, considering how she had been taken in, that I felt sure something had recompensed her for so disastrously finding the Simpson-Blotters at home. Before long I found out; it was the tea.

"Of course," she said, "the preparations were simply too ridiculous for words. It's such bad taste to have too much; still, it did me good, for I was feeling quite faint."

I was silently reflecting on my own exhausted condition when we drove up to a huge, severely simple brick structure of three sides about a court, a cross between a penitentiary and a sardine box, with some of the most pleasing characteristics of both. We paused at the principal door, and our steed settled himself solidly on his four legs. Maria was gone about two minutes, and then she flew back panting, and the hall porter banged the carriage quite respectfully. Hall porters are more broad-minded than footmen; I have even seen them respectful to a four-wheeler.

"Fancy!" Maria cried, in reminiscent horror, "Mrs. Peeples was in! I just barely escaped seeing her." I expressed the expected sympathy with her miraculous escape.

"Of course she will some day be Lady Peebles, when her brother-in-law dies," Maria explained.

"Is he ill?" I asked, with much solicitude, never having heard of the Peebles before.

"Oh, no. In fact, he's just about getting married. Mean of him, isn't it? Still, you can never tell. But to think of her being in!" and she reverted to her miraculous escape. "When I asked, the porter hesitated, and said, yes, she was in, and was I Madame Podsky!—me, Madame Podsky!" In her indignation her grammar forsook her. Her British soul revolted at the foreign name.

"I just had presence of mind enough to say, 'Oh, I see, she's only in to Madame,' and then I ran, I was so afraid he'd say he'd go up and see. What an escape! At any rate, I've called on Sophia Peebles!"

It is such a relief when one is calling in a livery carriage to circulate in those regions that most aspire to four-wheelers and hansoms. I wonder what is that subtle something about a livery carriage which prevents any one but the suburbs being taken in by it? Why had our coachman so deteriorated? What tragedy had reduced him to the universal coat of a livery stable? Why, too, did our horse have such a funny look, as if, somehow, he had forgotten to shave himself—so characteristic of the lower classes?

It was at the Crockers'—Crocker, M. P.—that Maria tore a fearful split along the whole length of her thumb trying to open the brougham door, while Crocker M.P.'s footman looked idly on from his pedestal in the front door, where he had just languidly delivered himself of "Not at home." It would have shocked him if he could have heard the tiny word that escaped Maria. It was not until we got far away from his freezing presence that she recovered her spirits. Maria never had anything social so rankle in her as Crocker M.P.'s footman. Weeks after, when I saw her again and she cried triumphantly "Crocker's out!" I couldn't understand what she meant. She explained that in the general election Crocker had been beaten out of his boots, and that, being now only an ordinary man and not a godlike M.P., he had ceased to be a coveted ornament to any dinner party. It was in this circuitous way that she revenged herself on the Crockers' footman. It was, however, when Maria directed the coachman to drive to Lambeth that I realized that she was human and in need of sympathy. Even the modest sometimes get tired of being snubbed by the menials of the rich and great!

Now, no one lives in Lambeth except the Archbishop of Canterbury. It is perhaps unnecessary to say that there is only one. So it must make it very lonely for him. The rest of the population doesn't count, and most of it circulates on the streets. What is left over is apologetic, and tries to explain how it happens to be living there. It was in Lambeth that our equipage was properly respected, and our coachman looked quite private.

Two small ragged boys darted to open the carriage door, but, discovering that we were not a vulgar four-wheeler, they hesitated. It seems there is a stern etiquette about opening cab doors! Just as they paused perplexed, an infant in a pinafore tore down to the gate for the joy of opening it. Interested neighbors paused in their occupations to watch us. Maria descended with much dignity. The maid already stood at the open door, summoned by the child in the pina-

fore. She smiled the friendly smile of the suburbs. The dear friend was of course out, but Maria's call did some good, for she cast a great glory over the establishment. The neighborhood could see that she was on visiting terms with "carriage people."

A group of the younger inhabitants of Lambeth stared at us with the engaging frankness of childhood, and a couple of unemployed gentlemen halted stolidly in the background and gazed at our worthy steed as if gauging his racing capacity. One detached himself long enough from his occupation to open the carriage door, and stretched out a very dirty palm for pennies. But though he knew a good deal, he did not know Maria. We proceeded.

There are miles of streets and houses in London that look so alike that one can't tell one from the other. Even ghosts, who have a monotonous way of going over and over the same beaten track, would be puzzled to discover here their own familiar haunting grounds. One finds, too, on careful study, that the people in these houses are all made by the gross; the principal difference is that they answer to different names.

Said Maria, "I'm going to call on the Pennaughtons."

"Oh, but your glove," I remonstrated, "how can you!" But Maria declared she had fifteen minutes to spare, and she had no intention of presenting them to the livery stable. Besides, the friendship was new and desirable. It seems this was a return call for one made on Maria when she was out. So far the flame of friendship had only been fanned by the two masculine heads of the families over a sympathetic B. & S.

We drove through an interminable avenue of plaster. Miles of bumptious plaster pillars supported miles of plaster porticoes. It was a thoroughfare that invited to a prolonged yawn. Miles of surprised-looking plaster lions kept guard on both sides of each front door.

A beneficent twilight was gently blotting out in us what was hired. I observed two different streams of carriages driving up to two separate front doors, side by side, and that two sets of adjacent lions were devouring independent callers.

It was a chilly spring evening, with the sky barred with gray and a faint acid yellow. An icy wind, whirling dust through the long street as through a tunnel, made even the lions look chilly. With the characteristic uncertainty of the British climate, it had not made up its mind whether to thaw or to freeze.

It was past five o'clock, and I had n't had my tea. "Maria," I urged, as I tried to restore the circulation in the end of my nose, "this time I 'm going in with you. If I don't have a hot cup of tea I shall have pneumonia."

"I sha n't be gone ten minutes," Maria remonstrated.

"I daresay. But those are just the ten minutes that would finish me," I said resolutely, and followed in her wake, behind a whole string of friends. For a moment we were blocked by some irresponsible affection that would persist in standing in the middle of the doorway to exchange soul-to-soul outpourings, perfectly oblivious to the impatient friends who were trying to get in and couldn 't. It 's a little way of women.

The house was of the pale blue, tufted satin kind, with oil-paintings to match, and floods of electric light. And it was all brand new, as if the Pennaughtons were only just married.

Maria, with the refined cruelty of one who has had tea, sailed past the dining-room, where picture hats were refreshing themselves with sandwiches and other convivialities. Maria is a little apt to be haughty at the wrong time, and then she throws her name at a servant as if it were a bone; sometimes he picks it up and sometimes he does n't. This time he did n't. He was a haughty butler, who seemed to have formed an unfavorable impression of the company, and in his misanthropy did n't much care what he called them. Three picture hats, one bald gentleman, and a wig were ahead of us, and the butler announced a series of names, leaving it for the hostess to disentangle

them, while he washed his hands of further responsibility.

Mrs. Pennaughton was a large and expansive person, with a wide and ingratiating smile, and she overflowed with an inexhaustible and ingratiating cordiality.

"How do? So glad to see you! Had tea?" she cried in turn to the three picture hats, the bald gentleman, and the wig, and she shook their hands in a perfect frenzy of friendship. Whereupon she propelled them forward by mere dynamic force of her welcome, and they were lost in space. They did try to resist, they smiled feebly, they made an effort to stay, but they were powerless, and we found them again in the drawing-room stranded on blue satin chairs with gilt legs, out of breath and exhausted.

"How do?" Mrs. Pennaughton cried to Maria. "How sweet of you to come! Had tea?" And she shook her hand with a fervor that finished Maria's glove. Here she caught sight of me. "How do? So glad to see you! How well you are looking! Had tea?" She held my hand and smiled like the rising sun, but while she still held my hand her expansive smile settled on the next friend, and I had been as completely forgotten as if I had never been born. The temporary quality of Mrs. Pennaughton's cordiality was immense. Maria tried to linger, but even she had to give in to the motive power of Mrs. Pennaughton's great, bland smile, and she found herself in the drawing-room before she knew it, and we joined the other guests, dotted speechlessly on blue satin chairs, and they appeared all the more gloomy by contrast with Mrs. Pennaughton's smile. We took refuge from the electric light under an imitation palm, and a gramophone began to bellow softly Caruso's latest, through which we could distinctly hear "How do? So glad to see you! Had tea?" It penetrated even through the passionate utterances of the gramophone.

"I think we 'd better be going," said Maria, who hates music. We emerged from under the imitation palm, and wedged our way through an opposing stream still advancing up-stairs, basking in Mrs. Pennaughton's smile.

"Good-bye," Maria said, taking hasty advantage of a lull.

"So glad to have seen you! Had tea?" and Mrs. Pennaughton smiled the same indefatigable smile as if she had never seen us before. "So sorry to have been out when you called," Maria hurriedly interposed, catching at Mrs. Pennaughton's fleeting attention as a drowning man catches at a straw.

"So was I," Mrs. Pennaughton began, but her gaze wandered, and she turned her voluble smile on an approaching clerical gentleman in knee-breeches.

"How do? So glad to see you! Had tea?" she cried, in an ecstasy of cordiality.

When we again emerged from between the lions, I had had tea, in spite of Maria's remonstrances.

The next door's "at home" was still being actively pursued by visitors.

"I should n't like to live next door to any one who had my at home day," Maria said meditatively, as we waited for the brougham, while we watched the next door's bosom friends file in and out.

"But is n't Mrs. Pennaughton just the sweetest thing?" she cried in admiring retrospection. "So cordial. The kind of person one could go to in any trouble."

I saw at once that Maria had been impressed — probably by the furniture.

Here a young thing with a snippy nose and a flying boa tripped past towards the next house's at home, but paused at the steps, looked over her shoulder, came back, and clutched me by the arm. It was a child with literary aspirations, but on her way to Parnassus a worldly mother obliged her to go to afternoon teas. No mother ever believes in literature as a matrimonial asset.

"I've promised to go to tea at the Pennaughtons. Do come with me," she coaxed. "I'm frightened of Mrs. Pennaughton. She never remembers me, and I've been introduced to her

five times. Some girls are known because people never remember them. I'm one," she concluded gloomily.

Here the brougham ambled up.

"My dear child," I cried, shocked, as Maria settled herself in a corner. "Don't make epigrams until you're married. A husband can't help epigrams, but it frightens off young men. Do think of your poor mother."

"Never mind mother. Come in with me, that 's a duck!"

"But, dear child, how can you be so foolish? Why, we've only just left there. I would n't go back for worlds!"

"I thought I saw you just come out of here," and if the child did n't look at the very house out of which Caruso was still vigorously roaring through the gramophone.

"Yes, of course," I assented, preparing to step into the brougham.

"But that " — the literary child gasped as one on the scent of a dramatic situation and "copy"—"but that is n't the Pennaughtons'!"

"Is n't the Pennaughtons'!" I repeated. "Not the—Maria," I cried into the brougham, "listen! We have n't been calling on the Pennaughtons at all! On whom have we been calling?"

"The Pennaughtons live next door," the literary child chimed in, and hopped with joy. "You've been calling at the wrong house."

"Maria," I repeated urgently, "do you hear? You've been calling on the wrong people. The Pennaughtons live behind the other lions."

"For mercy sake" Maria gasped in the gloom of the brougham, "on whom have I been calling!"

"I don't know," said the literary child with unholy joy, "but Mrs. Pennaughton told mother that they are new people, and they have five motor cars and the same at home day, and that is the reason she hates 'em."

"And I have lost twenty minutes," Maria wailed. "And she was so cordial. And all the time she probably wondered who I was."

"Not a bit of it," I said, cheerfully regaining my composure. "After all, what difference does it make? Friends all look alike. Come on now and call on the real Mrs. Pennaughton.''

But Maria could n't and would n't.

"I can't," she cried, in profound discouragement, "for it 'll cut into the hour. As it is I can't drive you home. I 've wasted twenty minutes on people I don't know," she wailed. "Oh, dear me! do hurry and get in and tell him 'Home.'''

So I told him "Home," and the literary child went off with that ecstatic step known only to authors who have found "copy."

Maria tried to say something, but gave it up; her feelings were too much for her. Finally she studied her bracelet watch, and I saw her face relax.

"If he has anything of a conscience he can do it within the hour," she said with a sigh of relief.

By the time she was thumping her own door knocker (within the hour) she spoke with a good deal of feeling.

"After all," she said, "what would life be without friends?"

"The friends who are out, or the friends you don't know?" I asked.

But satire is wasted on Maria.

Letters of Mme. de Staël to Benjamin Constant, Hitherto Unpublished

Edited by the BARONESS de NOLDE
Great-Granddaughter of Mme. de Constant

Translated by Charlotte Harwood

THIRD PAPER

LETTER FROM MME. DE STAËL TO M. BENJ. CONSTANT

"Coppet, 12th June (1815).

"You tell me that I am an inferior person, and to give me an example of moderation, you quote the latin passage*... '*pretaique injuria formei*,' that you think the most insulting of all for a woman, but you deceive yourself. A person who has given all her youth to a man who has destroyed her future, as the inventor of torture by slow fire might do, this person is no longer capable of self-respect. If you had treated the ugliest and stupidest servant whom you loved, as I loved you, as you have treated me, you would still be what you are: the most profoundly bitter and indelicate man on earth to-day. You tell me that for six thousand years women have complained of men who have not loved them. But for six thousand years also, men have loved money, and I do not think you have shown your-

* Incomprehensible.

self indifferent to it in the past two months. If you think that I should pay you for the pleasure of your conversation! . . . . . does my father owe you 34,000 francs for that! You tell me that my sadness made more impression on you formerly. Will you tell me if it prevented you marrying, in spite of a promise of marriage made to me, and taking to another, unknown to me, the fortune that you held from my father and me?'

"You declare that *you will speak ill of me.* I am sorry to tell you, but I have ten letters that conjure me to note that I no longer have any relations with you. If you do not know how to attack others any better than to defend yourself, you are not to be feared. Besides, if you were, do you think that you could wound me anew? There is not one spot in my heart that has not been ravaged by your persistent hatred.

"I took refuge in the past; you found it necessary to tell my daughter and myself that you had never loved a woman . . [illegible] . . the miserable insinuations of a roué that you might have spared Albertine's innocence. Finally, after your having taken from me these young days, in which, whatever you may say, I was worthy of a heart in return for mine, I wished still to retain a tie with you by the service that you could have rendered my daughter. Misfortune has struck her at eighteen years of age. One would think that all who have known you must suffer, and that you embody some perverse, supernatural power. You, who buy houses and pay for them with your winnings, as you have told me,— you, who go every evening to the foreign salons,— you do not know how to make a sacrifice for the daughter of a person who gave up to you 80,000 francs, which she would give her to-day, if she had them. I will give my poor child all that I am able to, and Heaven is my witness that, threatened with extraordinary danger the other day, I consoled myself with the thought that my death would augment her dowry. But I had promised what you had promised me, and I could not fulfil it. I have been told that the act that you made me sign, which you drew up and wrote yourself, is not legal; we shall see. But what I know is, that your pretended legacy, without mortgage or other guarantee, cannot marry Albertine. If you had made a deed with Fourcault to give her the bare ownership of 80,-000 francs, invested in real estate — I do not know if that was valuable,—you would then have been able to give the interest on it to Albertine only as long as you held your place ! . . . . In fact, if you lost it, you would be very unfortunate, but you would get something yourself. As for me, since I have seen in our liaison only a fate brought on me by the vengeance of hell, I am pursued by the idea that apparently I deserve it, that my father himself has not been able to obtain forgiveness for me.

" In short, I suffer in not being able to think of you but as a being charged with my punishment. I suffer as much as when I loved you. If I can reconcile myself with God, after having *reproached* you, I will *perhaps become*

softer. But, at this moment, *I would fly crying from any place whatsoever where I might meet you*, and it would be a pleasure to me to say so in the face of all the world. These are my feelings, but, as it is a matter now of my daughter only, if you can offer me an advantageous arrangement for her, I will accept it."

Between the letter of 12th July and the one following, written on the 21st, the battle of Waterloo took place (after which Mme. de Staël wrote paraphrasing Francis First: " Nothing is lost but honor "), and the abdication of Napoleon and the second Restoration occurred. Constant, who, after the return from Elba, had turned his coat, as we know, found himself a second time in a very bad way, and feared to be exiled. His pen saved him from it. As soon as the King arrived in Paris, he wrote him a letter of self-justification. It made the desired impression. The King, with his own hand, struck Constant's name from the list of exiles, on which it had already been written. With the keen spirit of mockery that did not spare even himself, Constant, when he heard this, said: " My memorial has persuaded the King, though it failed to convince me myself !" We read in a letter of 29th July, 1815, to his cousin Rosalie de Constant [*]: " Mme. de Staël has written me a more friendly letter than I expected, renouncing her claims to my fortune, which these latter events have not repaired." We do not believe we possess this letter of renunciation to which Constant alludes. That of the 21st July, which we publish, seems as if it must be one of those that followed it.

LETTER FROM MME. DE STAËL TO M. BENJ. CONSTANT

" Coppet, 21st July (1815).

" I wish that you believed that I am better disposed to you than I was. There are points, surely, on which we are in sympathy, but it seems to me that the conduct of the ministry must appear good to you, and one cannot

* "Letters of Benj. Constant to his Family." J. H. Menos.

apparently prevent oneself from hoping at present for the maintenance of the King and of France; there is hope for the one only by the other. I do not know what I shall do. Write me of the state of Paris: that will decide me. I have a desire for Italy, so as to let pass all this crowd of foreigners, which makes me feel bad, no matter what good it may have been able to do me. I advise two things for you, to get elected if you can, and, if you cannot, to finish your work on ' Religions,' and to publish it. They say Mme. de Constant has written to Rosalie for news of you. Mme. de Loys * and others will give you a good reception.

"The Landammann Pidou † says, that since Montesquieu ‡ there has been no work as strong as yours.

"Your talent will always sustain you. I advise you to go to Paris if you can, for it is more difficult to return here, but one must not exaggerate the hatred of parties; time appeases them.

"My son will soon see you. I hope that he will be paid, and then I shall be anxious to prove to you, by consultation with the secretary, that I was right, legally, against you; but that is no longer the question at present.

"May you be happy still, in your way. Write to me."

LETTER FROM MME. DE STAËL TO M. BENJ. CONSTANT

"11th August (1815).

"Your justification is perfect, and I felt crushed on reading it. There is no possibility of attacking you legally. None but your friends can be afflicted at the extreme mobility of your character; you have excellent answers for your enemies. As to me, if I went to Paris,

do you doubt that I would see **you as** before? If I have been able to forgive your conduct to me, would the considerations of society influence me? But if I can avoid seeing France in the condition she now is in, I earnestly desire to. If I could flatter myself that, having praised the Germans so much in adversity, they would listen to me in their hour of triumph, I would go, not to keep quiet, but to speak, for I know of nothing that can smother what is in my soul.

"But so many people in France must make them hear the truth, that it would be presumptuous to believe myself more fortunate than another. I am, then, awaiting the result of my affair, and devoting myself wholly to Albertine's future. It is my intention to go to Rome, where we shall get the dispensation ourselves. Perhaps she will be married at St. Peter's. Coppet is still more holy.

"I have shown your memorial, but in accordance with your orders, it has not left my hands. Every one says that except for the article of the 19th there would be nothing to say against you. It is the brilliance of your own talent that has done you harm. God willed that you should have everything in your hands, and that a wicked fairy should make you throw it all away. Have courage, however, above all in the cause of France; do not abandon yourself, and make for yourself steadfast principles. Assuredly Mirabeau and several others have recalled them from a greater distance than you. Party spirit will cool by degrees and the great [illegible] . . . of your life, love of liberty and talent, will reappear.

"Avoid duels; at present they would signify nothing. Society is a small thing at present; the business of the world is greater. Endure what you have not, as you have made such a great effort to relieve yourself of what you had. Your letters are of great interest to me; just now we agree; let us profit by it to write to each other. Give my son good advice about my affair. Do not think any more of the one that was in question between us." *

---

* Mme. de Loys, younger sister of the Countess de Nassau, née de Chaudieu, both aunts of Benj. Constant.

† Landammann, officer of the Swiss Government. Since 1513 Switzerland has been a confederation of thirteen cantons. Some were little city-republics, others were country-cantons and their chiefs were Landammanns. Also in the constitution of Malmaison (1801) an analogous thing was accepted. The Helvetian Republic was declared one and indivisible, and was represented by a Diet charged with the election of the Senate, from which was taken the first magistrate of the country. The latter, qualified as "Landammann of the Helvetian Republic," was invested with executive power, with the assistance of several ministers. The Pidous were a Vaudois family.

‡ The author of "Persian Letters."

* That of the 80,000 francs that Constant owed her.

" 18th August (Coppet, 1815).

"When you saw that I would return to your neighborhood, the tone of your letters changed, and those that you wrote me from Paris to London wounded me deeply. When I returned I found you like your letters : not a look, not an inflection, betrayed any recollection, and I admired you sometimes for being so witty, and at the same time so little inspired. That hurt me ; but it was better, for fifteen years of such deep feeling are a cruel wound that could be made to bleed only too easily. But let us drop that. The rejection of the liberty of the Press, and what they have said of England, have revived my old error ; but let us drop that also. I only wish to be paid, and I shall be very grateful. I wish it for Albertine ; she is so agreeable, she improves so much that there is nothing she does not deserve. I have told you that what I hope for is Victor de Broglie. Try to speak of her before him. One can praise her, certainly, without exaggerating. Her face is still more beautiful, and all the English here are enthusiastic about it. The Humboldt * family is here, three daughters, a son, a tutor, and the mother ; she is very agreeable, but her daughter is horrible. The Princess of Wales should arrive here next month, but I have no desire to wait for her. Let me know when you think I can return.

" When will the peace † deliberations be ended? I do not know why they should take long. I am still uneasy about my affairs, and I would like to be there to watch them. Will Mme. de Constant soon be in Paris? ‡ I have seen your family. Nothing has changed here but the faces. The minds are also a little faded, but otherwise all is well.

" General Filangieri has been here. He made it known to me that he wished to marry Albertine, but it was when she was so young, that it was not worth while answering. I believe he has the same wish, but he has put on a Bonapartist air.* Apropos, do you know that the Genevans are very illiberal? They . . . [illegible] . . . the acceptance of their bad constitution like little tyrants, and fear intelligence as if they were in great danger. It is comical and sad, like the world in miniature.

" I have written to tell Auguste that I believe it would be better if our name were not mentioned before the legislative body. What do you think? "

LETTER FROM MME. DE STAËL TO M. BENJ. CONSTANT

" 1st September (1815).

" The state of your health causes me much uneasiness, my dear friend. I can bear anything from you just now except your illness.

" I have found at the bottom of my heart, on pronouncing that word, emotions that I had believed to be extinct. You have been very foolish and very cruel, but you have a unique mind and faculties, and you owe it to the God who has made you thus to take scrupulous care of yourself. You can always count on my daughter and myself as friends, not such as we wished to be, but such as you have permitted us to be, and you will end by finding it is still the best of what you have.

" M. de Langallerie, † who is here, bids

---

*Charles Guillaume, Baron de Humboldt, 1767-1835, a distinguished scientist and statesman, Ambassador to Rome, then to London and Vienna. His house was an artistic and scientific centre wherever he was. A brother of the celebrated Alexander de Humboldt, he was also a member of almost all the scientific societies and academies.

† After the hundred days, Louis XVIII. returned to Paris under the protection of the Duke of Wellington, 19th July, 1815.

‡ Mme. de Constant could not rejoin her husband, because it would have been necessary to cross the allied armies before Paris, which would have made the journey very distressing.

* Charles Filangieri, Duc de Taormina, Prince of Latriano, son of the author of "La Scienza della Legislazione." He was presented when young to Napoleon, who, in consideration of his father's merits, caused him to be brought up (being an orphan) at the country's expense. On leaving college he joined the forty officers who accompanied Napoleon to Milan for his coronation. He performed prodigies of valor at the battle of Austerlitz, and was aide-de-camp to Murat. Governor of Sicily at Napoleon's downfall, he ended his career, covered with honor, in the service of Ferdinand de Bourbon.

† The Chevalier General de Langallerie, a distant relation of Benj. Constant, was one of the chiefs of the group of mystics, presided over by Mme. de Krudner, to which Benj. Constant had belonged for a short time. The Duc de Broglie gives a perfect picture of this person in his souvenir : " A little man — very round, very short, rather vain, slightly greedy, almost the same as the ribald stories of the last century showed the confessor of a convent, or director of the pious. It was difficult to restrain a smile when one heard him groaning about his poor stomach while doing justice to a good dinner, and over insomnia when one heard him happily snoring in a comfortable arm-chair. His gentle, insinuating, nasal voice was most provoking, but as soon as he was launched on pure spirituality, it was impossible not to admire the profundity and delicacy of his ideas."

me tell you that he has repeated all the conversations he had with you. Alas! What is the use? Your paper, that I lend, is much admired here by the English, and those of the Genevans who know how to read. I get word from Paris that it is very successful. Yours is a fine career, if you can teach liberty to France. You tell me that every one writes that I shall be paid. I hope so also. Fear has become so much a habit with me, that I would not spend a louis for these two millions. If they come, I hope that M. de Broglie will think of me. You see that I am modest. If you can help in this, do so. I rely entirely on your pride and your zeal in what concerns Albertine. You have written Ch. Constant * that you would perhaps stop here on your way to Germany. I hope that is only talk, for I dare to hope that you will not go. You would have the air either of being an exile, or of having failed in an attempt, if you went at present.

"I expect to start on the 15th September; you can write to me here before that. Do not forget, but address by Geneva, and not by Switzerland, which retards things. Let me have exact news of your health."

LETTER FROM MME. DE STAËL TO
M. BENJ. CONSTANT

" Coppet, 13th September (1815).

"I lead such a cruel life, always uneasy about the health of the person . . . [illegible] all my happiness lives, that I have sometimes moments of real despair. Believe me, politics are nothing beside the things that affect the heart. But let us leave that; it is like the term of existence, God alone knows what it is. An Englishman, an intelligent man whom I saw the day before yesterday, told me that he had read nothing that seemed to him so fine as your last work on political principles, and that the English

Constitution was nowhere else so well represented. If, then, circumstances should take you to England, and you should wish to write from there some facts with reflections, I think that you would have great influence; talent quickly effaces what is inconsiderate but not culpable. In this country also, you would do very well. I believe I have written you that the present Landammann Pidou,* who is really a man of very cultured intellect, spoke to me of your writings with much enthusiasm. I cannot tell you about Mme. Constant with certainty, but I have been assured that she was in Germany. Would you be right in bringing her to Paris if her relations do not remain there?

"It seems to me that the Chambers are not composed in a way to propagate liberal ideas, but one must see. What I wish is that my affairs, and the marriage to follow, were terminated. Victor and my son will join me in Italy as soon as they shall have . . . [illegible]. Write to me here always, until I give you another address.

"I have received two letters from the Emperor Alexander † in reply to mine, one of which is really superb. Such firm ideas of liberty in the head of such a man are a miracle. What I cannot conceive is why they do not get more good for France from it. What a state the Midi is in! and how calmly they take it. Party spirit has the same effect on all men.

"Sismondi ‡ is here, ill and sad to a pitiful degree. He had too much fear of unkindness to expose himself thus. I received him in my house, and Maujet, in his paper at Berne, the most impertinent of all, did not fail to say so. But what would friendship be, if one did not find it in misfortune? Besides, in political affairs I always find that there are but the . . . [illegible] . . . with whom one can count.

"Let me know what you think of the future.

"Adieu, till spring."

* Charles de Constant, his cousin and brother of Rosalie, to whom he wrote: " I hope to see you soon, for it is possible that I may go to Germany by way of Switzerland, if my wife does not join me by the end of next month. They say the roads on the shores of the Rhine are not very safe. Peace is not quite assured ; every one desires it, but that is no reason for its consummation." (" Letters of Benj. Constant to his family."—J. H Menos.)

* Note p. 446.

† The Emperor Alexander I. of Russia.

"Pisa, 14th January (1816).

"My address is Florence, Tuscany, care of MM. Donat and Orsi.

"I have had news of you continually; it would be impossible for me to ignore your fate. You do well in going to England; you will forget party spirit in France, but think well, nevertheless, before closing its doors to you by a book; imagination stops before the irreparable. I have at last obtained the dispensation from Rome, and have sent it to be legalized in Paris. Victor de Broglie and my son will bring it back, and the marriage must take place in Florence, where we shall have a protestant minister. There my plans end, for rumors of plague in the south of Italy still give me occasion· to fear exposing M. de Rocca to quarantine more than to the disease. In any case we all wish to be reunited at Coppet in June. There the *skies of our saint are spread above us*. I have ordered the statue of my father from Tieck * at Carrara, and I will place it on the great staircase at Coppet, until they come to take it from me to put up in the Hôtel de Ville.

"That will be when there is liberty in France, and as there will be liberty, it will be. Bonaparte was the real enemy of liberty in the world; it is most unfortunate that he did not die at Fontainebleau; we should then be advancing instead of retreating. What a spectacle Italy is! I no longer recognize her, for havoc has swallowed up the ruins. If you are in England I shall see you. If I live, I must marry my son to a beautiful, rich, and amiable English girl. They would make, after me, a fine dwelling-place of Coppet, where the name of my father would preside. The nearer I approach my

own end, the more I feel his hand stretching over me. If, as I hope, M. de Rocca recovers, I should be able to say I am happier now than I have ever been.

[*A piece of letter is missing here.*].

"I am much moved at Albertine's marriage, but I am very pleased. Victor is conscious of a quality in his soul, from which his mind will never make him depart. Let me have news of you. Come near us when you can, and have faith in honest people; you will always find them when you look for them."

"23rd February, Pisa, 1816.

"I leave my daughter to announce her marriage. Her feelings for you are sincere and I have never tried to lessen them. It is for her, then, to speak to you. By God's grace she is happy, and I congratulate myself more every day on having united her to a man of fine character. I wish you all the happiness you can keep. As for me, mine depends on Albertine's future, and on the restoration to health of my friend. If the other wishes are granted it will be luxury. Let us know your plans, and if England suits you."

(*The continuation is by Albertine*).

"My mother is right in saying that my feelings for you are not diminished. All the great emotions of my life make me wish to think of you and speak to you. I bless God for the choice I have made. My admiration for Victor's character increases daily. This feeling of perfect confidence in the nobility of soul of the man one marries is a great happiness. I hope, for my part, never to be unworthy of him, and we shall be able to complete each other mutually. His heart is so pure that even though he is not so religious as I would wish, it seems impossible to me that the protection of God should not descend on him, for there is only a misunderstanding of words between him and perfect belief. You see that I

---

* Friedrich Tieck, a brother of the writer, a friend of the Schlegel brothers, and through them a protégé of Mme. de Staël, born in 1776 at Berlin, and a well-known sculptor, an imitator of Greek art, many of his works are in the Berlin Museum. He made many busts, among them one of Goethe. In 1809 Bonstetten wrote to Frederike Brun: " Tieck is to arrive; nothing is droller than to hear them speak of this great artist" (at Coppet); "if one believes them, Canova and Thorwaldsen are nothing beside him."

speak of myself to you, confident of
not boring you. Send us news of
yourself in care of Messrs. Donati and
Orsi, at Florence. We are going there
to-morrow; we shall spend three months
there and then return to Switzerland.
Good-bye, dear friend. What a sad
combination of circumstances was necessary to prevent you from being present at my wedding. I would not have
believed it six years ago! But it does
not matter; love me still, and perhaps
we shall understand each other once in
this world. Victor wishes to be remembered to you; he is really most
tenderly attached to you."

Recent Histories

Reviewed by GEORGE L. BEER

IF one were to judge solely by the
number of histories published, it would
appear that history is the favorite intellectual diet of a vast multitude. The
demand is seemingly insatiable, and the
publishers see to it that this demand is,
at least partially, supplied. Yet the statistics of our public libraries do not bear
out the view that history is widely read.
Must one then perforce conclude that
the bulky volumes yearly produced by
the presses of the world in ever-increasing profusion are bought mainly for
decorative purposes, because a "gentleman's library" would be incomplete
without them? To a certain extent
this is true. It leaves out, however, two
other great factors in the demand: on
the one hand, the desire of the college
teacher to have the latest results of research in compact shape at the disposal
of his scholars, and on the other, the
rapidly growing number of public libraries, no one of which can afford to leave
off its shelves any work to any degree
authoritative. The most marked characteristic of recent historical publications,
designed primarily for the vast general
reading public, in contradistinction to
the small world of professional scholars,
is the use of the principle of co-operation. Under the supervision of an editor, whose duty is to secure uniformity
of treatment and due proportion, the
services of a number of scholars are called
into requisition, each one being assigned
the treatment of the era or subject for
which he is especially fitted. During
the last decade histories of the world,
histories of Europe, and histories of particular nations have in great numbers
been written on this general scheme.
The main aim of these works is not to
advance knowledge, but merely to put
the results of detailed research in compact and easily available shape. It
would appear that this work is greatly
overdone, as there is much useless du-
plication and consequent waste of energy. Several such works on American
history are now appearing, and two
co-operative histories of England were
started last year.* One is edited by two
competent English scholars, William
Hunt, the president of the Royal Historical Society, and Reginald Lane Poole,
the editor of the *English Historical Review*, and will narrate the political history of England in twelve large volumes
from the beginning to the opening
of the present century. The other
series is edited by C. W. C. Oman, an
indefatigable English publicist, who
was recently elected Chichele Professor of Modern History at Oxford in
succession to that virile and attractive
writer, Montagu Burrows. This series
is to be in only six volumes of approximately the same size as the Hunt
series, but it stops with the reconstruction of Europe in 1815, thus leaving out
the nineteenth century, to which the

* The Political History of England. Edited by William
Hunt and Reginald Lane Poole. Vol. II., 1066-1216, by G. B.
Adams; Vol. III., 1216-1377, by T. F. Tout; Vol. X.,
1760-1801, by William Hunt. Longmans.
A History of England. Edited by C. W. C. Oman. Vol.
II., 1066-1272, by H. W. C. Davis; Vol. IV., 1485-1603, by
Arthur D. Innes. Putnam.

Hunt series devotes two volumes. In the distribution of space to each period, the fundamental distinction between the two series is the comparatively greater attention paid to the mediæval period by that of Oman. The first three volumes of the Oman series cover the same years as the first four in the other, bringing the narrative down to the reign of the first Tudor monarch. At this period modern England really begins, and from this date on one volume in the Oman series treats the same period as is treated in two of the Hunt series. In method of treatment the two series differ in that more stress is laid on description and less on chronological narrative in the Oman series. If there is any rivalry between the two projects, it can be only of a friendly nature, for Oman, the editor of one, contributes a volume to the other.

Of the volumes thus far published that of Adams in the Hunt series covers somewhat less ground than that of Davis, but as in the main they treat of the same period, they are convenient for purposes of comparison. The two books are essentially similar in character. Both are strictly political histories, predominantly narrative and chronological in character, of the typically orthodox school of history, showing no traces of the heated and widespread controversy as to the nature and scope of history. Except for two chapters in Davis's book on general conditions in England, both bear out Freeman's dictum that "history is past politics." Seemingly this was the result of the editor's plan of the series, at least in so far as Adams—the only American contributor to either series—was concerned ; for his own unfettered ideas as to the proper treatment of history, as embodied in his "Civilization during the Middle Ages," are distinctly different. Both books are based closely on the original sources, and are distinctly solid pieces of work. From the literary standpoint that of Davis' is superior; his touch is lighter and he has boldly given in the text his own interpretation of disputed points, while calling attention in the footnotes to divergent interpretations by other au-

thorities. Adams is more cautious, and if there is any doubt, he is careful to embody it in the text. An erudite scholar, Professor Tout, takes the narrative where Adams breaks off, and carries it down to the accession of Richard II., in 1377. It is essentially similar in character to the preceding volume in the series, though it contains a short chapter on general social conditions. The descriptive and critical account of the authorities, printed as an appendix, is of noteworthy excellence.

The Tudor period, treated by Arthur D. Innes in the Oman series, is of supreme importance, but it is not by any means solely on account of this fact that this volume is by far the most interesting and readable in either series. Trevelyan's volume on the Stuart era, which appeared some time ago, is excepted from this general statement. Innes wisely discarded the stiff chronological method and the purely narrative style, and adopted a judicious combination of narration and description. He grouped large categories of connected facts for separate treatment, and in addition transgressed the narrow bounds of purely political history, describing the religious and social movements which are inseparably connected with purely political events, and make them comprehensible.

William Hunt has contributed a volume to the series he is editing, on the momentous years from 1760–1801, which include within their limits the American Revolution and also that in France, the Irish rebellion, and the subsequent union with Great Britain. The first half of this period, whose predominant feature was the separation of the continental American colonies from the mother country, has never been adequately treated in detail, nor has it as a whole, except in the case of Lecky been approached in a non-partisan spirit. The bane of English historiography is that the strong party feeling in present politics appears prominently in the discussion of past events, with the inevitably resulting distortion and exaggeration. Trevelyan is a Whig, and everything advocated by a Tory must be *ipso facto* wrong. American writers have as a rule been affected by what has been neatly called "filio-pietism," which blinded them to any faults in their ancestors and to any good qualities in their opponents. This was notoriously Bancroft's attitude. Besides, the existing mass of absolutely indispensable material in the English Record Office has never been adequately studied. Hunt has made some slight excursions into this unexplored realm, but the chief merit of his work consists, not in the new material brought to light, but in his courage in speaking the truth, both about the victors and the vanquished in the contest leading up to the independence of the United States. Though on some points he errs, especially in the treatment of the old colonial system, and though his explanation of the underlying causes of the revolt will probably have to be modified, still American readers should be grateful for an account which is human and intelligible, and brings the Revolution down from the realm of poetry into that of the humdrum world of fallible mortals in which it was fought.

Love's Blossoming.

WHEN soft on the hillside the spring winds were blowing,
　　And summer stirred sleepily under the sod,—
When through the cold earth the warm consciousness stealing
　　Brought violets voicing the whispers of God;
When out of the silence came bird notes appealing,
　　And nest-builders darted abroad on swift wing,—
Like song, in my heart, came the love of you stealing,
　　As sweet as the meadow-lark's greeting to spring.

Like blossoming May was your love's first beginning,
　　With fragrance half-wild, and a dream of a flush;
When I told you I loved you, your shy assent winning,
　　June's glorious roses were throned in your blush.
Now .   .   . deeper and dearer your love than in Junetide,
　　And goal of the midsummer bee is my goal—
For as sweets in the heart of the lily at noontide,
　　The goal of your love in the white of your soul!

　　　　　　　　　　　EDNA KINGSLEY WALLACE.

Tennyson's Annotations to "In Memoriam"

By W. J. ROLFE

MANY books on Tennyson's "In Memoriam" have been published, both in England and in this country, but no annotated edition of the poem (that is, giving the text with the commentary), so far as I am aware, appeared before mine of 1895; and this new one, edited by the present Lord Tennyson, is the only one of more recent date. According to the title page it is "annotated by the author," who left certain notes in his own handwriting, dictated others to his son, "went through the proofs and corrected them, and sanctioned their publication" under their present editorship.

The introduction by the editor is mainly taken from his "Memoir" of the poet, and includes the sketch of Arthur Hallam's life, the extract from Gladstone's review of "In Memoriam" (which Tennyson regarded as "one of the ablest"), the long and extremely interesting letter by Professor Henry Sidgwick concerning the poem, and some minor matter of the same general character; together with three omitted "sections" of the poem which the author "thought redundant," etc.

The poet's own notes, though comparatively few and brief, are of peculiar interest because of their authorship. Some of them had already appeared in Rev. Alfred Gatty's "Key" to the poem, in the third edition of which (1885) they were printed in italics; in Mr. Knowles's reminiscences of conversations with Tennyson, who read the poem to him; and elsewhere. The majority of the rest confirm the explanations given by the commentators and critics, and by myself, but occasionally they furnish fresh information on allusions and obscurities about which the critics have disagreed.

The editor's additions to his father's notes are often of interest. The question as to the poet referred to in the first stanza of the poem proper as

> him who sings
> To one clear harp in divers tones,

was settled long ago in one of Gatty's italicized notes; but, though "divers tones" is in no sense obscure, we are glad to have our editor's note upon it: " My father would often say, 'Goethe is consummate in so many different styles.'" Section xix. of the poem we might suspect was written in the neighborhood of Clevedon, but we have now the exact locality: "Written at Tintern Abbey." The poet himself remarks that the reference to the tide that "hushes half the babbling Wye" was "taken from my own observation—the rapids of the Wye are stilled by the incoming sea."

Some of the poet's notes might strike the reader as superfluous; as, for instance, when he explains "the blowing season" in xxxviii. as "the blossoming season"; but I see by reference to Gatty's book that he seems to have found it necessary to interpret it for the benefit of that reverend commentator.

The first stanza of xliv. has puzzled many people:

> How fares it with the happy dead?
> For here the man is more and more;
> But he forgets the days before
> God shut the doorways of his head.

Tennyson's note confirms the interpretation of the last line which I give in my edition—the only one possible from the context, though I may not have been the first to print it:

"Closing of the skull after babyhood. The dead after this life may have no remembrance of life, like the living babe who forgets the time before the sutures of the skull are closed; yet the babe grows in knowledge, and though the remembrance of his earliest days has vanished, yet with his increasing knowledge there comes a dreamy vision of what has been; it may be so with the dead; if so, resolve my doubts," etc.

The author of an American edition of selections from "In Memoriam" (as also of sundry schoolbooks on rhetoric, etc.) takes the allusion to be to extreme old age, the "doorways of the head" being "the senses," which are impaired or lost with the lapse of years.

In one or two instances I find a note from the poet on a passage which had seemed to me so clear that I made no reference to it in my edition; as on this stanza of xli.:

> For though my nature rarely yields
> To that vague fear implied in death,
> Nor shudders at the gulfs beneath,
> The howlings from forgotten fields.

Elsewhere in the poem Tennyson indicates his disbelief in everlasting punishment; and his son tells us that he was keenly disappointed that in the Revised Version, in the passage "Depart from me, ye cursed, into everlasting fire," the word "everlasting" had not been "altered into 'æonian' or some such word; for he never could believe that Christ would preach everlasting punishment."

His note on the present passage is, "The eternal miseries of the Inferno." His son adds: "I have thought that 'forgotten fields' implies not dwelt on, and so disregarded—a creed that is outworn; but Sir Richard Jebb writes: 'I have not been able to find any verbal parallel for the phrase "forgotten fields," or reference to the nether world. I think that "God-forgotten"—outcast— is the most probable explanation. Cf. ἄθεος in Sophocles, *O. T.* 661.'" The explanation that had occurred to the editor is certainly the correct one, and Sir Richard's is far-fetched and inadmissible.

A few of the notes are credited to Lady Tennyson, and they are among the best in the book; like this on section xcvii.: "Love finds his image everywhere. The relation of one on earth to one in the other world is as a

wife's love for her husband after a love which has been at first demonstrative. Now he is compelled to be wrapt in matters dark and deep. Although he seems distant, she knows that he loves her as well as before, for she loves him in all true faith." This is a lesson for wives withal.

Here is another of her notes—on ciii.: "I have a dream which comforts me on leaving the old home and brings me content. The departure suggests the departure of death, and my reunion with him. I have grown in spiritual grace as he has. The gorgeous sky at the end of the section typifies the glory of the hope in that which is to be."

According to a note by the poet, lxxxvi. was "written at Barmouth" (in Wales). Knowles said that Tennyson told him that "this was one of the poems he liked," and that it "was written at Bournemouth" (on the south coast of England). Both agree that the "ambrosial air" was the west wind, which at Barmouth, one would suppose, would come from the sea rather than

> over brake and bloom
> And meadow;

but the writer might have been far enough inland for this to be true, and the latter part of the description suggests that the wind was also blowing over the water. Besides, Knowles's comment is somewhat confused, for he speaks of the wind as "rolling to the *eastern* seas till it meets the *evening* star." It would have to roll round the globe to do that. The "orient star" is explained by the poet as "any rising star," which could not be "the evening star."

I note a few misprints in the commentary, the worst of which is in the editor's quotation from "Comus," where "scout" is perverted into "scent" in

> Ere the blabbing eastern scout,
> The nice morn on the Indian steep,
> From her cabin'd loophole peep.

In a note on lxxi. the visit of Tennyson and Arthur Hallam to the Pyrenees is said to have been "in 1832"; but there is a reference to the "*Memoir*, i. 51," where the date is correctly given as 1830. This journey is alluded to in the lines "In the Valley of Cauteretz," written in 1861 (though not printed until 1864) when the poet revisited the region:

All along the valley, where thy waters flow,
I walked with one I loved two and thirty years
    ago.

One might infer from the "two and thirty" that the journey was in 1829, but the dates of both visits are fixed by other evidence. Arthur Hugh Clough, who was in the Pyrenees in 1861 and met Tennyson there, refers to the poet's former visit as "thirty-one years ago." It is probable that the latter changed it in the verses for the sake of euphony. The line "I walked with one I loved two and thirty years ago" would be seriously marred if "one" were substituted for "two." Mr. Waugh, in his book on Tennyson, gives the dates of the journeys as 1830 and 1861, but refers to the former as "thirty-two years" before the latter.

I have referred above to Gladstone's tribute to Arthur Hallam quoted by Lord Tennyson in the "Memoir" and in the present volume. I also quoted it in my edition of "In Memoriam," a copy of which I sent to Gladstone. In the note acknowledging it he expressed a doubt concerning the authenticity of the passage ascribed to him, and asked me where I had found it. I referred him to the English book from which I had taken it and begged that he would inform me if it had been wrongly attributed to him, in order that I might make the necessary correction in my next edition. He did not write again, and two years later, when the "Memoir"

appeared, I found the passage quoted there and credited to Gladstone's "Gleanings of Past Years"; there it is credited to the *Quarterly Review* for October 1859. A foot-note in the book states that the sentence beginning "The writer of this paper" and ending with the quotation "I marked him," etc., "has now (1878) been added." It is curious that Gladstone, after reprinting it and adding to it in 1878, should apparently have forgotten that he wrote it.

The early reviewers of "In Memoriam" said that Tennyson had taken the form of the stanza from Lord Herbert of Cherbury, and others noted that Ben Jonson and Sir Philip Sidney had used it. No one, so far as I am aware, has observed that Shakespeare had already employed it (so far as the rhyme arrangement is concerned) in "The Phœnix and the Turtle." Tennyson said that he believed himself "the originator of the metre."

Some of Lord Herbert's stanzas are singularly Tennysonian in diction as well as rhythm—these for instance:

These eyes again thine eyes shall see,
    These hands again thine hands enfold,
    And all chaste blessings can be told
Shall with us everlasting be.

For if no use of sense remain
    When bodies once this life forsake,
    Or they could no delight partake,
    Why should they ever rise again?

And yet we may infer that Tennyson had never seen Herbert's volume, which is very rare and scarcely known even to critical students of early English poetry.

Homilies and Critical Studies

By H. W. BOYNTON

AFTER the passage of a full quarter-century, Professor Richardson's treatise on the choice and use of books * remains the most complete, the most reasonable, and one of the most readable of books hitherto written on that head. A good many such books now exist, but the comprehensive ones incline to dryness, and the brilliant ones to inconsequence. There is nothing either brilliant or haphazard about Professor Richardson's method of procedure. He defines his terms before he undertakes to use them; and evidently has a perfectly clear notion of what his whole structure is to be before he lays the first stone. Yet he is not pedantic. Each of the brief essays which make up his chapters (they were originally printed as "weekly contributions to a literary newspaper") is complete in itself; taken together they compose a thorough-going treatise. Nor is the writer's attitude toward literature hide-bound or academic. He insists that the relation between a man and a book amounts to nothing unless it is based upon enjoyment. "The real value of any book to a particular reader is to be measured by its serviceableness to that reader." And the cultivation of a taste which shall make only the best books serviceable is the object which Professor Richardson sets most clearly before the reader. In any method of determining absolutely what are the best books, he has no faith. The best books are those which have commended themselves for a long time to the best and wisest people. "In the long run nothing but truth, simplicity, purity, and a lofty purpose approves a book to the favor of the sages; and nothing else ought to approve it to the individual reader. Thus the end is reached and the choice is made, not by taking a book because a 'course of reading' commands you to do so, but because you come to see for yourself the wisdom of the selection." The writer has a word of quiet irony for the dry-as-dusts and the hundred-best-books people. For himself, he would have the pursuit of good books engaged in not as a prescribed task, but as a journey through fair regions in which the experience of most intelligent travellers promises him a profitable delight. "If we devote to books the hours or the minutes we can catch, and choose our reading with a full sense of the wideness of the field of selection and the narrowness of the time in which we can work in that field, we shall hardly go astray in our decision." It remains to be said that the original substance of the treatise is admirably supplemented by seasonable quotations of all the best things that have been said about reading by the best men, from Bacon to Schopenhauer, and from Addison to Emerson. An important part of the book is the hundred and seventy pages of "Suggestions for Household Libraries," comprising lists so varied and full as to give ample scope for selection of any one of a score of excellent private libraries; the special flavor and limitations of any given collection to depend, if Professor Richardson's counsel is followed, upon the individual bent and capacity of the given household.

The papers on books and reading in Dr. van Dyke's new volume of essays † are naturally of a more casual sort. We look to their author not for complete treatises, but for extempore homilies of an intimate and suggestive value. The speaking quality is unmistakable, we are but listening to good talk from an easy-chair or from a pulpit. Such good talk does not always stand the test of repeated readings.

For example, in his little essay on "The Flood of Books" the talker says: "Reading is a habit. Writing is a gift. Both may be cultivated. But I suppose there is this difference between them: the habit may be acquired by

" * The Choice of Books." By Charles F. Richardson. New York and London. G. P. Putnam's Sons. 1905.

† "Essays in Application." By Henry van Dyke. New York. Charles Scribner's Sons. 1905.

any who will; the gift can be developed only by those who have it in them to begin with." Definitions are dull things, but they are necessary as a basis for any intelligible generalization. By writing, Dr. van Dyke evidently means creative writing; and for that there must be a born gift. But for the highest kind of reading also there must be a born gift; it is patently untrue that anybody can acquire the art of reading, though anybody can get used to covering a certain number of pages in the course of the month or year. Anybody, on the other hand, can acquire the habit of writing. The real contrast is not between reading and writing, but between the cultivation of a habit and of an art. The problem which is under consideration is what is to be done to turn our "flood of books" to the best account. Dr. van Dyke's solution has the merit of comprehensiveness. "The only way to work it out is for the writers to try to write as well as they can, and for the publishers to publish the best that they can get, and for the great company of readers to bring a healthy appetite, a clean taste, and a good digestion to the feast that is prepared for them." We may assent to this cheerfully if we have a stomach for platform commonplaces; otherwise we shall deplore that vagueness and rhetoric should so often be the portion of the ready writer who is also an easy and applauded speaker.

How are a healthy appetite, a clean taste, and a good digestion to be cultivated? that is the really important problem; and it might be solved triumphantly if not another book were ever published. The importance of established standards of criticism is fitly emphasized: The development of public taste has been checked, says Dr. van Dyke, " by the fact that in America criticism has been so much confused with advertisement." We have ample reason to know that when the writer sets himself to it he produces valuable criticism; but it is hardly a critical faculty which we applaud vociferously when our "most effective speaker of the occasion" thus makes a platform

of the page: "We shall not need to ask any foreign critic to identify the typical American. He has arrived. He is no bully with his breeches tucked into his boots; he is no braggart with a wild, barbaric yawp. This typical American is a clear-eyed, level-headed, straightforward, educated, self-respecting gentleman with frank manners and firm convictions, who acts on the principle that

" ' The rank is but the guinea's stamp,
A man's a man for all that.' "

This is said in connection with an enumeration of the great gentlemen of American history; but it is subtly construed into a flattery. These men represent an American type; but in no sense the "typical American." The paper among the present series which is, on the whole, best worth reading, is that upon "The Creative Ideal of Education."

"There is a kind of reading," says Dr. van Dyke, "which is as passive as massage." To that kind of reading Mr. Crothers offers no opportunity. There are few appearances more innocently misleading than the nonchalance of such an essayist. He keeps us strolling in the right direction. What we take for his playthings may really be his most serviceable tools; each of his bubbles may reflect a world. In "The Pardoner's Wallet" * Mr. Crothers is less whimsical, but hardly less effective, than in "The Gentle Reader." Here he is concerned with life rather than books, and assumes the apologist for certain despised classes of humanity: the unco-guid, the ne'er-do-well, the man born an age too early or too late. The rôle of special pleader is one which especially offers itself to the discursive essayist. Often, however, as, by Mr. Chesterton, it appears to have been undertaken merely or mainly for the fun of the thing. The fun of the thing is obviously not a consideration altogether despised by Mr. Crothers; but it is never the main consideration.

* "The Pardoner's Wallet." By Samuel McChord Crothers. Boston and New York. Houghton, Mifflin, & Co. 1905

One is not in doubt as to whether these delightful homilies will bear rereading. "I suppose," says the Pardoner, "that the nature of each individual has its point of moral saturation. When this point is reached, it is of no use to continue exhortation or rebuke or any kind of didactic effort. Even the finest quality of righteous indignation will no longer soak in. With me the point of moral saturation comes when I attend successively more meetings of a reformatory and denunciatory character than nature intended me to profit by. If they are well distributed in point of time, I can take in a considerable number of good causes and earnestly reprobate an equal number of crying evils. But there is a certain monotony of rebuke which I am sure is not beneficial to persons of my disposition. That some things are wrong I admit, but when I am peremptorily ordered to believe that everything is wrong, it arouses in me a certain obstinacy of contradiction." This is his modest way of putting it; his actual mode of procedure is not founded on hyperbole and paradox. He always has something distinct and reasonable to say, and, being a true humorist, it is his way to be often quaint, and hardly ever fantastic. His most serious word, perhaps, is spoken in defence, or rather recognition, of "the land of the large and charitable air." Hardly has there been a finer celebration of the West as "a state of mind"; a purer and freer America. "The psychological West begins at the point of interest where the centre of interest suddenly shifts from the day before yesterday to the day after to-morrow. Great expectations are treated with the respect that elsewhere had been reserved for accomplished facts. There is a stir in the air as if Humanity were a new family just setting up housekeeping. What a fine house it is, and how much room there is on the ground floor. What a great show it will make when all the furniture is in! There is no time now for finishing touches, but all will come in due order. There is need for unskilled labor and plenty of

it. Let every able-bodied man lend a hand."

Readers who are unacquainted with Mr. Crothers's graver manner will do well to get hold of his recent Ingersoll Lecture on Immortality, now published in a little volume.[*] Its substance is condensed, or rather suggested, by the final sentence: "Conscious of the divine quality of the present life, one can afford to wait for the thing which does not yet appear." .

Elisabeth Luther Cary would appear to have done, in her study of Henry James,[†] pretty much all for him that it is possible for an ardent disciple to do at this time. That the biographer or critic of contemporary or late lamented writers should be first of all an ardent admirer is now a popular theory. Perhaps, for such a purpose, that extreme of *parti pris* is better than the other. But the world as a whole is disposed toward neither extreme; and is quite as likely to refuse a nibble of something it does not especially like the look of, when requested to swallow it whole as when advised to nibble at it with caution. It would be a pity for us to turn away from Henry James; he is good nibbling, at least.

And this fact it may be salutary for us to keep in mind when, after reading the present monograph, we find ourselves still averse to a Jacobite gorge. When we have been told of James that "the interrogation of the invisible united to an unremitting effort toward completeness of evocation constitutes his extraordinary distinction" — we must realize that we are bidden to no casual banquet. The critic is, however, by no means a mouther of large phrases; the one in question is, one must own, intelligible enough in its context. If now and then the apparently irresistible tendency in followers of James to imitate his invertebrate

* "The Endless Life." By Samuel McChord Crothers. Boston and New York. Houghton, Mifflin, & Co. 1905.

† "The Novels of Henry James: A Study." By Elisabeth Luther Cary. New York and London. G. P. Putnam's Sons. 1905.

periods is manifest, the style is of the best according to its school. Richness and subtlety of texture are the qualities admired in the master's work; and simplicity of line would not be looked for from a disciple. Miss Cary is not a hesitant chronicler of James's career. She asks no quarter for those portions of his work which seem to many well-disposed persons to o'erleap themselves not a little, in the direction of a mere elaborate tenuity. She observes a steady growth in power from "Roderick Hudson" to "The Golden Bowl." His technical curiosity, his ability to represent life pictorially by a multiplicity of fine observations, runs hand in hand with a curiosity far more unusual and far more difficult to satisfy, a curiosity as to moral states and responsible affections." There is no denying that both these kinds of curiosity are manifested at their extreme in "The Wings of a Dove" and "The Golden Bowl." Nowhere is Mr. James's power of presenting character by a process of slow increment, nowhere is what Mrs. Cary admirably calls his "decorative fancy," more in evidence. Whether these later stories give evidence also of "an imagination of the most vital sort" is a question less readily to be answered by most of us. We have here, at all events, a strong and reasonable argument in the affirmative. Mrs. Cary believes Mr. James to be a consummate artist; and, as such, possessed of an imagination as strong as his intellect and his moral sense. The thorough bibliography appended gives the book added value as a manual.

Mr. Woodberry's monograph on Swinburne is * also in no slight sense

* "Swinburne." By George Edward Woodberry. Contemporary Men of Letters Series. New York. McClure, Phillips & Co. 1905.

the work of a disciple; as those who are familiar with the critic's poetry (and it is far too little known) must feel. "Liberty, melody, passion, fate, nature, love, and fame, are the seven chords which the poet's hand, from its first almost boyhood touch upon the lyre, has swept now for two-score years with music that has been blown through the world." Somewhat curiously, it seems, the passion of liberty is placed first in order of importance; "the simplest aspect of his genius lies in his revolutionary songs." This love of human freedom, however, was no more than Swinburne's other passions, the outgrowth of direct personal experience of life. Mr. Woodberry lays much stress upon his scholarship, his "provenience from literature;" and admits that "the revolutionary cause, even, was for him a literary heirloom from the poets." This we can very well credit. There is, indeed, only one aspect of Swinburne which obviously does not derive from literature. He is the supreme poet of the love of the body as detached from, though always yearning toward, the love of the spirit. He is not Pagan; he is not Christian; he is neither a faun nor a *roué*. He is the voice of a desire which knows itself to be sterile:

" For desire is a respite from love, and the flesh not the heart is her fuel."

This is not the languid note of decadence: it is a cry of torture such as may be heard in any sophisticated age from this or that uneasy spirit which finds in the summons of the body a constraint equally imperious and debasing. It is the greatest of all such cries which the world has yet heard; it was not "provenient" from literature, but from a human soul.

"Fiona Macleod"

By LILIAN REA

THE death of the well-known English critic and poet, William Sharp, has made public the fact of his identity with Fiona Macleod, the Highland poet and romancist. Now that the revelation has been made, it seems allowable to discuss the question of this wonderful dual personality—a question which lies deeper than the mere fact of a man hiding his identity under the pseudonym of a woman. Knowing Mr. Sharp intimately for many years, I can not only vouch for the reality of his being Fiona Macleod (which has been doubted by Dr. Robertson Nicoll, the editor of the English *Bookman*, and others), but it was my privilege to watch the development of the woman's side of his nature in her personality, as well as to hear his own explanation of these two souls that "dwelt in one breast." In him seemed to live again the child of Hermes and Aphrodite, the twain that became one flesh—man and woman in one. At times Hermes was predominant, working along the lines of art and literary criticism, research, and occasional strange, but essentially virile, fancies. Again, the woman would blot out all trace of the critic and compiler, in wild flights of fancy, intuition, and mysticism—wherein her genius usually manifested itself.

Much wonder has been expressed in the English papers that Mr. Sharp never revealed his identity as Fiona Macleod even after her success became assured. After the publication of the "Sin-Eater" especially, one of her strongest books, much curiosity was felt as to who the author really was: William Sharp was strongly suspected first of all; then his wife; then a syndicate of young Celtic writers; Mr. W. B. Yeats and Miss Norah Hopper in conjunction, Miss Maud Gonne, the well-known Irish politician, and even a broken-down journalist in Fleet Street were taxed with it, but the excitement gradually died down, and Miss Macleod was accepted as a literary fact.

Personally I should explain Mr. Sharp's unbroken reticence on this point by a certain delicacy which he felt in acknowledging his belief to the world at large that a woman's soul really lived within himself in dual unity with his distinct man's nature. Such a phenomenon is not a mere mythological fancy, but has existed in many ages of the world, and Mr. Sharp was, in my opinion, an example of that strange phase of nature. Be that as it may, while his two styles approach each other closely on the mystical side—as in William Sharp's "Vistas," for instance, and any of Miss Macleod's books—they are usually very distinct, and Dr. Robertson Nicoll, in refuting the possibility of their identity, voices the idea that at once occurs to the reader familiar with Mr. Sharp's own writing in first reading a book of Fiona Macleod's. He is reported to base his doubt on the opinion that "Fiona Macleod's best work discloses knowledge and power which Mr. Sharp did not possess." One feels instinctively that Fiona Macleod was a more inspired writer than William Sharp—that she may have been *his* model, but one that *he* could never equal: that in her work there is a touch of genius never perceptible in his. Both he and his friends who were in the secret looked upon her as quite a distinct personality; he himself always spoke of her either as "Miss Macleod" or "Fiona," and it was in her that he had most pride. Himself Highland born, he loved to claim for this other half of his a life in the Hebrides remote from the sordid world where he had been obliged to live for many years: she was his dream self—she could do all and dream all that he would never be able to—she could not only give herself up to a passionate love of Nature and lead a life of intimate comradeship with it, but it was not essential for her to mix with the Sassenach: she was free to be a real Celt with the "Celtic joy in the life of Nature," the Celtic vision, the visionary rapture and passion of the poet. The description of Lora, the heroine of Miss Macleod's first book, "Pharais," is autobiographical of this dream self, as are also certain portions of "Green Fire": Innisron, for instance, in the first-named, representing the far-away island where she was supposed to be born, the historic island of Iona.

In 1893, shortly after writing, as William Sharp, the woman's letters in the book called "A Fellowe and His Wife"—the man's letters being written by Blanche Willis Howard — Fiona Macleod published her first long story, "Pharais" (Paradise), her first literary experiment having been a short story entitled "The Last Fantasy of James Achanna"—a name which frequently reappears in the volume of the "Sin-Eater." This story was declined by the *Scots Observer*, but the refusal was accompanied by words of such genuine encouragement that Miss Macleod showed her appreciation of the editor's criticism by never again offering it for publication. "Pharais" is too mystical and romantic ever to become a widely read or popular work—its characters are not creatures of flesh and blood, but dream figures, whose motions are graceful and beautiful even though they themselves may never come into direct relation with the passions and problems, circumstances and environment, of real people. It, like all of her books, is full of that *Anima Celtica* for the keeping alive of which she and so many others have striven ardently, and which she herself thus describes:

Blue are the hills that are far from us. Dear saying of the Gael whose soul as well as whose heart speaks therein. Far hills, recede, recede ! Dim veils of blue, woven from within and without, haunt us, allure us, always, always !

Another quality that the practical half of this dual personality relegated to his dream self was a deep Panthe-

ism—a Scottish Pantheism, to be sure, and one that differs from the Greek even as the wild scenery of the remote Hebrides differs from the soft airs and warm tints of the Grecian Isles. Deeply spiritual, and impregnated with a strong sense of mystery and dread, it is the outcome of the close observation of the person who has lived by night and by day, in storm and in fair weather, upon the sea and among the hills—it is full of an intimate fellowship and close alliance with Nature which can be expressed only by the half-human, mythological creatures of the woods and water. This instinct is intense throughout "Pharais": the young Alastair, the hero, upon whom madness — the "mind-dark"— has come, quite naturally wandering to the sea, and living there among the rocks like a wild thing.

Yet, even as all "Pharais" is full of the sea mist and charm, so the next book, "The Mountain Lovers," interprets the beauty of pine woods and of sparkling waters tumbling down from the high hills. The story here is treated in a more dramatic and less lyric manner, and though the human relations remain the least satisfactory part of the book, still the mountain breezes often clear away the mist.

But, in spite of the alluring charm of these two romances, critics agree that Fiona Macleod's best work is found in the short barbaric tales and tragic stories of the Scottish Islands contained in a volume entitled, after the tragic tale which opens the collection, "The Sin-Eater." There are those even among the Scottish people themselves who deny the assertion that the inheritance of the Gael is "the beauty of the world, the pathos of life, the gloom, the fatalism, the spiritual glamour," understanding least of all the gloom; and to such these stories of Fiona Macleod's will not so much appeal as to those others who, like Oscar Wilde, cry out for mystery in art, to them who love weird imaginings for their very remoteness from everyday life. They were dedicated to George Meredith "in gratitude and homage: and as the Prince of Celtdom," and ever since reading this book, he has been one of Miss Macleod's great admirers, writing her soon after that he was in the habit of reading almost every day the story of Alison Achanna, the "Anointed Man" —a story which describes how Alison Achanna, when lying in the heather one day, was touched with the Fairy Ointment, and how ever afterwards he saw the most hideous and sordid sides of life with the white light of beauty upon them.

Two distinct strains are apparent in the volume of short tales entitled "The Washer of the Ford, and other Legendary Moralities," i. e., the spiritual and the barbaric: "The Song of the Sword," "The Laughter of the Queen," and the "Flight of the Culdees" are full of the angry clashing of steel, the swift approach of the war-galleys, and the flamelike leaping up of the passions of those early, solitary, and bloodthirsty Celts; while "The Last Supper," "The Fisher of Men," "Ula and Urla," "The Three Marvels of Hy," and "Muime Chriosd, the Foster Mother of Christ," illustrate the author's romantic and imaginative spirituality, her power of weaving with the mediæval magic of such well-known scenes as the Last Supper and the Repentance of the Magdalen the most modern psychology, and of enriching their everlasting significance with the continuous development of thought and experience through the ages. They are, in fact—to use the words of her own superscription to one of the Spiritual Tales—"beautiful things made new."

The prose romance of "Green Fire" goes back again to the purely Celtic spirit of the blue hills that recede. The scene of the first and last chapters is laid in Brittany, the others have the Hebrides as background: in it, as the title promises, there is everywhere the magic of Spring in Nature as in life.

O green fire of life, pulse of the world! O Love! O Youth! O Dream of Dreams! . . . . . .

In the beauty of the world lies the ultimate redemption of our mortality. When we shall become at one with nature in a sense profounder even than the poetic imaginings of most of us, we shall understand what we now fail to discern. The arrogance of those who would have the stars as candles for our night, and the universe as a pleasaunce for our thought, will be as impossible as their blind fatuity who say we are of dust briefly vitalized, that we shall be dust again, with no fragrance saved from the rude bankruptcy of life, no beauty raised up against the sun to bloom anew.

"From the Hills of Dream" is the significant title of a collection of all the love poems and lyric runes which are scattered throughout the several books Fiona Macleod has published, containing as well a great many poems which have not appeared elsewhere. The last section, entitled "The Silence of Amor," consists of twenty five prose fancies steeped in the atmosphere of love yet never naming the word. Love is here a vague longing, "a wandering voice, a flame-winged lute player whom none sees but for a moment, in a rainbow shimmer of joy, or a sudden lightning flare of passion"—love engendered on the Hills of Dream. The poet sings:

O come, come to me, Weaver of Dream !

and it is in the island solitude that, in these days of restless striving and impatient haste, the Weaver of Dream is most surely to be found. The inspiration of this book is shown in the first poem:

Across the silent stream
Where the slumber shadows go,
From the blue Hills of Dream
I have heard the west wind blow.

Who hath seen that fragrant land
Who hath seen that unscanned west ?
Only the listless hand
And the unpulsing breast.

But when the west wind blows
I see moon-lances gleam
Where the Host of Faerie flows
Athwart the Hills of Dream.

And a strange song I have heard
By a shadowy stream,
And the singing of a snow-white bird
On the Hills of Dream.

In addition to the books mentioned, Fiona Macleod wrote a number of others, among them: "The Dominion of Dreams," "The Devine Adventure," and two or three plays, all with the same general characteristics; but none of her work has, in my opinion, ever surpassed the volume of "The Sin-Eater" in power and imaginative beauty.

With the passing of William Sharp "across the silent stream where the slumber shadows go," Fiona Macleod has retired forever to the Hills of Dream, her home, from whence her voice comes out into this prosaic, hurrying world of ours with its message to the Few—to those who listen in the throbbing noontide, alone on the hills or on the sea, to the message of Nature. Through her, this voice tells of the strength and beauty of the body, of the close kinship of Man with Beast and Bird, with Flower and Tree, speaking its message, moreover, in words beautiful and rhythmic.

Idle Notes

By AN IDLE READER.

I HAVE been a novel-reader since the tender age of half-past five, when I *The Lean Years* wrestled with "John Godfrey's Fortunes," that plump, substantial volume in which Bayard Taylor mingled certain of his own youthful experiences with those of his hero. Is anybody else now alive, I wonder, who read "John Godfrey's Fortunes"? The wood-sawyer in the back yard (whose name was also Taylor) was the object of my awed observation, for I had an inner assurance that he wrote the book, though the secret of its authorship seemed to be known only to myself, and I shrank from confiding it to any grown-up.

It is a far cry from those days to these, but having read all the good novels and most of the bad ones published in the meantime, I am quite positive that in the last two years the sacred fires have been waning. Just as fiction has become an accepted fact and all the text-books are telling that the development of the novel is one of the significant symptoms of our generation, suddenly the development of the novel is checked. The great names begin to turn out fiction that is a little dry, a little wooden as compared to the masterpieces of their prime. Is this true, or is it that the palate of the taster is failing? At all events, one no longer sits up o' nights to finish Mr. Henry James, or snaps at whoever interrupts the perusal of Mrs. Ward. And the five really arresting novels of the last twelve-month have been "Broke of Covenden," "The Divine Fire," "The Morals of Marcus Ordeyne," "The Shadow of Life," and "The House of Mirth." I mean, these are the books that, pre-eminently, bring fresh sensations to the novel-taster's palate, and give him anew the thrill that comes of finding in them something of life, sincerity, power, piquancy, or charm.

By the way, did no one but myself object to the "logical conclusion" of *Mrs. Wharton's Logical Conclusions* Mrs. Wharton's great novel on the ground that it was not logical? Lily Bart at her worst was too good to fight her world with its own weapons—hence her defeat. Had she been of a fibre to meet calumny with blackmail, all would have gone merrily. If, then, she does not belong to her apparent world, she does belong not so much to the Heaven to which she is condignly sent, as to some earthly circle where the folk are finer and their morals more civilized than in Bertha Dorset's set. Lily's real standards of behavior entitle her to a safe conduct from Vanity Fair to some less brutalizing environment, and any fair-minded creator would have provided her with one.

An overdose of chloral may be, in reality, a satisfactory substitute for a happy life, but while we are still on this side the grave, the demonstration is a little incomplete. Of course if Selden had not been a weak-kneed, finical, super-refined, yet unnecessarily low-minded cad (I would speak candidly with him, as man to man, if we could meet) Lily's fate would have been different. But making him such as he is, is one of Mrs. Wharton's most realistic strokes. In spite of humanity's long belief to the contrary, the real truth is that men never do make efficient substitutes for a kindly Providence in the working out of women's lives.

Probably writers never reflect upon the eagerness with which readers of a critical bias follow their development, or upon the pleasure the latter feel when that development is adequate and up to the promise of its start.

The Evolution of Miss Sedgwick

It is some seven years since I began to consider Miss Sedgwick's talent affectionately and—like a good child—in all that time it has never given me an hour's uneasiness. It has not followed the line one would have prophesied, nor the line of least resistance, but this makes it only the more interesting.

Her first novel, "The Dull Miss Archinard," showed clearly the genuine story-teller's gift, together with the power of making detail significant and absorbing. In "The Confounding of Camelia" there was added to these qualities a pretty psychology and a clear but not obtrusive ethical bias. As her talent stood, at that time, she seemed likely to become an up-to-date Miss Austen with a deeper sense of the seriousness of life. "The Rescue" was a most unusual achievement along a different line. Restrained, concise, dramatic, striking, it was a *tour de force* in that it made exquisite a theme—the love of a young man for a woman seventeen years his senior—which is by nature ridiculous or pathetic. The book still remains her unsurpassed

artistic achievement, not because her development has faltered, but because it has again changed direction. "Paths of Judgment" sunk the story more or less, and went deeply into the psychology of three futile, selfish souls of assorted types. These characters are set forth as completely as Mr. Henry James might do it, but make less exhausting demands upon the reader's intelligence and imagination than Mr. James's creations have done of late. Her new novel,"The Shadow of Life," is almost without incident, and the interest depends upon the sharply contrasted philosophical beliefs held by hero and heroine. This sounds difficult, but is not.

In "The Shadow of Life" Miss Sedgwick has written "an impossible love-story" with immense skill, delicacy, and grace. The book records the inner life of a man whose thoughts have more validity for him than his feelings —a type despised of Nature but treated here with grave consideration.

"The Shadow of Life"

Gavan Palairet and Elspeth Gifford were child-friends. At fourteen Gavan is most unchildlike, selfless, and attaching. He is capable of intense affection and he has also that keen sense of the Divine which is seemingly innate in certain rare natures. At that age he knows that he would be unspeakably unwilling to live without God in the world, and yet is temperamentally Buddhistic. "I am often so frightened. I get so lost sometimes that I can hardly believe that Some One is near me. And then the fear becomes a sort of numbness so that I hardly seem there myself. It's only loneliness while I melt and melt away into nothing. Even now when I look at that sky, the feeling creeps and creeps, that dreadful loneliness where there isn't any 'I' left to know that it's only—only a feeling."

This is Gavan the child. Gavan the man loses his hold on his religious faith, and seeking through the philosophies of the schools for truth finds only the finite self dissolving, a contradiction, and "its sense of moral freedom upon which are built all the valuations of life and all its sanctions, a self-deception."

By temperament it is easy for him to detach himself from Life the Dream, that is always seeking to draw him back and break him upon the Wheel of Things. It has no firm grasp of him even when he loves the grown-up Elspeth, who is the very lovely incarnation of an opposite philosophy, Elspeth who loves life and and trusts it even while it slays her, believing always in "selves and love."

Only tragedy can result from the conflict of such natures. In actual life, love would probably be stronger than philosophy, but Gavan as Miss Sedgwick has conceived him is a thoroughly convincing if also a thoroughly exasperating character. Only one thing about him seems unlikely. So far as I have observed the evolutions of child-nature into maturity, the children who are born with that especial apprehension of the Divine never lose it. Philosophies fall from them harmlessly, and they measure religions by their own inner certitudes. Granting that Gavan might mislay his faith, the rest is inevitable.

If Miss Sedgwick were not herself, the critic might be tempted to deplore the fact that psychology or philosophy should preoccupy one who has also the rarer and more beneficent gift of making incident and detail alive for us. But, being Miss Sedgwick and writing, as she so evidently does, to please herself, to see what she can do, the one thing certain concerning her next piece of work is that it will bear no resemblance to "The Shadow of Life."

There could be no more acute contrast in heroes than between Gavan Palairet and the "Uncle William" of Mrs. Lee's new book. They are at opposite ends of the social scale, for Uncle William is a Nova Scotia fisherman, but he is, none the less, a finished expert in the art of living. All the philosophers from Spinoza to Schopenhauer taught poor Gavan, "drugged

The Sunshine of Life

with thought," nothing so valuable as the smallest bit of Uncle William's philosophy. He and Elspeth would have understood each other, and, just possibly, he might have done more than she for Gavan's mystic sickness of the mind. Where Gavan is Thought's fool, Uncle William is Life's sage.

Uncle William is big, benignant, gentle, and shrewd; he is slow and has even felt the imputation of "shif'less," but he has learned that "*Livin's* the thing to live for . . . the's a great deal of fun in it if you go at it right," and in every last atom of his body and soul he is "comf'tabul." Time belongs to him and the world, and even to pass him in the street is tonic. "Men who never saw him again recalled his face sometimes at night as they wakened for a minute from sleep. The big smile reached to them across time and gave them a sense of the goodness of life before they turned again and slept."

He not only knows—as, after a fashion, we all do—that a man's life consists not in the abundance of his possessions, but he is even aware—knowledge vouchsafed to few men—that excitement, interest, does not depend upon action. " 'It ain't exactly the things that happen.'— He broke off looking at something far away. 'I 've had things happen to me —shipwreck, you know—winds a blowin' and sousin' the deck—and a-gettin' out the boats and yellin' and shoutin'—seems 's if it ought to' a' been excitin'. But, Lord! 't wan't nuthin' to what I 've felt other times—times when it was all still—like on the island here—and big—so 's 't you kind o' hear suthin' comin' to ye over the water. Why, some days it 's been so 's I 'd feel 's if I 'd *bust* if I did n't do suthin'—suthin' to let off steam.' "

There is a story about an artist and his love, charming young people they are, but one values them most because they give Uncle William a chance to demonstrate himself. To my mind, as an antidote for nervous prostration and a general bracer, Uncle William throws the popular Mrs. Wiggs completely in the shade.

Fiction and Reform

By ELLIOTT FLOWER

THESE are great days for financial, political, and all other kinds of practical reform, but is the credit for this apportioned fairly?

A Governor here and a Mayor there and a District Attorney somewhere else deal vigorous and effective blows to corruption, and the public applauds. They are great men—incorruptible and strong men. Well, they are. I have no desire to detract in the least from the credit due them. In every case it has required courage and strength to fight the intrenched forces of evil. They have, in many cases, risked promising futures in what seemed to be a hopeless battle against existing conditions, and that they have, occasionally, profited in popularity as a result of their victories does not in the least affect the estimate of their sincerity and courage. Others, of whom we no longer hear, have wrecked their political prospects, and sometimes their material fortunes, in efforts to do what these men have done and are doing.

Why, then, should the reform leaders be so uniformly successful now? Are they stronger and more capable men?

Possibly. There can be no doubt that it is easier to elect fearlessly independent men to office now than it was a few years ago, so it may be that these are more capable and more courageous than certain others, of equally good intentions, who preceded them in office. The awakened public is looking at the man rather than at the party label, and the awakened public is also helping the man.

That explains a great deal. Some of these "strong men," who are accomplishing so much now, could not have done it ten years ago. Most of them admit it themselves. "We have had the support of the public," they say, in explanation of their success. This means the active, and not merely the passive, support of the public. So far as public affairs are concerned, the American public sleeps a good part of the time, and, when it does wake up, it usually does little more than turn over and go to sleep again. This time it has remained awake—not only has it remained awake, but it has been getting wider awake every minute.

Why? Have these practical reform leaders awakened it and rallied it to their support?

In a measure, yes; but it was prepared for this awakening by "graft" fiction. Among those who have helped Governor Folk and Governor LaFollette and District Attorney Jerome and Mayor Weaver and all the other agents and agencies for reform in both politics and business are David Graham Phillips, Brand Whitlock, Will Payne, William Allen White, Frank Norris, Guy Wetmore Carryl, Alfred Henry Lewis, Francis Lynde, Edwin LeFevre, Forrest Crissey, and many others who have dealt with "graft" in their novels and short stories. Not even Lawson may take all the credit for the exposure of the insurance scandals. Before him came the "graft" fiction, to educate the public up to an understanding of finance and financial methods. Without that preliminary, I doubt very much that the Lawson articles would have attracted more than brief, and possibly frivolous, comment, for we are disposed to take a light view of everything.

I have no wish to reflect on the value of the serious and earnest articles on political and business evils. They have done an immense amount of good, but you must interest your public before you can teach it. We all knew long ago that there was "grafting" in both politics and business, and that the "grafting" in the one was so related to the "grafting" in the other that it was almost impossible to consider them separately. There have been learned and thoughtful articles on the subject in the magazines, and the newspapers have discussed it in forceful editorials. But we forgot about it soon after reading, and many of us did not read such things at all; they were not entertaining, and we were not sure that we understood them. In the form of fiction, however, they were entertaining.

The American admires cleverness. Whether he approves or disapproves of the morals of a clever man, he admires his cleverness. The men in these stories of "graft" were invariably clever, whether they shone in politics or business, so the stories proved interesting. And they showed how things were done. Whether good or evil triumphed, the result was the same: a more intimate knowledge of devious ways, that prepared the reader for the awakening to come. He began to understand the game. You might have hammered at him editorially for ten years without giving him any very clear conception of what it was all about, but fiction told him. Fiction did not bring it home to him that this was an evil that threatened him personally, but it prepared him for that knowledge. After the fiction, he read the other things more understandingly: he had been lured into learning enough to appreciate the more thoughtful discussions of the subject, and he soon found that he had a personal interest in it. The conditions described in that novel or short story, that he had found so interesting, were not imaginary conditions of an imaginary place; they were actual conditions existing in his own city or State. The thing became very real to him, and he wanted to know more about it. The articles that had hardly arrested his attention before were now of absorbing interest: he was ready for anything that dealt with the subject that had assumed such importance, and he read all that related to it, including more novels and stories.

No one of these stories can be said to have accomplished a particular, concrete thing. Great reforms have been credited to certain novels in the past, but, in most instances, it has seemed to me more likely that the novel came along at the psychological

moment to direct attention to a reform for which the public was already pretty well prepared, just as certain public officials have appeared on the stage at the opportune moment for success. We always remember the man who was first over the enemy's ramparts, but we sometimes forget the leaders who fell before the ramparts were reached. However, whether or not single stories have been responsible for reforms at other times, that certainly is not the case in this instance. All the innumerable "graft" stories have helped. Without them, very likely the public would have awakened in time, but certainly not so soon, and some of the men now so successful would have been buried by the "graft" forces before this. We would simply remember them, if we remembered them at all, as misguided or impractical men who meant well.

Of course the public was ready for this fiction. Finance and politics were attractive subjects, to which its attention had been called by many surprising successes, and it had heard enough of "graft" to be ready to take it up in entertaining form. I give no great credit to the authors for high moral purpose, further than the desire of every honest man that the influence of his work shall be good and not harmful. The stories were no part of a deliberate reform plan, but were written primarily to entertain. The authors, like the men who were instrumental in carrying out the reforms, aimed at success. It is seldom indeed that a man accepts public office solely as a public duty. He may intend to do his whole duty to the public, and there may seem to be a material sacrifice, but ambition and the honor of the office are strong impelling motives. It is seldom also that an article or a story is written solely as a public duty, but that is no reason for taking from it the credit for what it accomplishes. I have written some of this "graft" fiction myself, and I confess that I was always looking for the story and not trying to drive home a moral lesson. Still, my investigations in the search for material uncovered conditions that were startling to me, and these conditions I tried to picture faithfully for the reader. I presume it has been the same with other writers. Indeed, I am disposed to think that the stories, if a great "purpose" lay back of them, would not be so interesting and would not penetrate so far. It is easy to reach the student, but it is not so easy to reach the man who does not go outside of his business, except for occasional entertainment. Fiction did it —the fiction of political and business "spoils," of the many ways of juggling with votes and money. The fiction of Wall Street and high finance was quite as illuminating as the fiction of State capitols, congressional districts, and city wards, for it all came to the same end: the bamboozling of the public and the evasion, if not the violation, of the law. You can't successfully separate the fields of "graft," for "shady" politics and "shady" business go hand in hand. A particular story or a particular incident may seem to pertain wholly to one or the other, but you will always find, if you go deep enough, that they are interdependent.

So the public—the ordinarily heedless and unthinking public—began to wake up. It was able to hear and understand what was said to it on this subject in a more serious way; it became interested in the facts as well as the fiction. The short stories, especially in the periodicals of low price, reached even those who see little of the more pretentious novels, and an audience was prepared for the man who had any suggestion to make. If the suggestion looked good, and the man seemed to have strength and sincerity, the audience was ready to help him make a practical trial of it. But the main point is, that, whether he addressed it with tongue or pen, he had his audience—an attentive and an earnest audience,—and this was largely given to him by "graft" fiction.

Some of the writers I have mentioned have also discussed the evils of politics and business in other ways, but I am considering only their fiction. That is what first caught the attention of a part of the public that could be reached in no other way—a part of the public that is very earnest when aroused, but that ordinarily gives no attention to ethical essays, and discounts all political statements.

So, when you throw up your hat for Jerome or Folk, or even President Roosevelt, please remember that the writers of fiction have helped to make possible some of the splendid things they have done; that they at least did much in the primary education of the public; that they prepared it for the more advanced lessons; that they strengthened the determination that has held it steadfast; and that, without this help, some of the reform idols of to-day probably would lie shattered in the wake of some political "machine" or some juggernaut of what Lawson calls "The System." Without this, there would not yet be a public sentiment that makes the honest official fearless in his investigations, and the unscrupulous one fearful. Without this, some of our municipal "good government" organizations would hardly have achieved the full measure of success that has attended their efforts. Without this, some of the good men never would have reached office at all. It is worth remembering, if only as an illustration of the fact that the man who lays the last brick is not necessarily the only one who has been engaged in the construction of the house.

The Editor's Clearing-House

Need Journalism Destroy Literature?

IT is beyond all things sobering and pathetic to see a man in grave need of a weapon, nervously fingering a perfect and efficient revolver, and finally casting it from him ignorant of its power.

This, it seems to me, is what Mr. Julian Hawthorne has done in his recent article in THE CRITIC which he called "Is Journalism the Destroyer of Literature?" He very properly laments the decadence of the modern press, he gracefully defines literature, he compares it with the journalistic work of to-day, he sagely notices that the two are unalike, and then, though his country is sore-pressed by this insistent force of evil, he chucks away his revolver and says "there is no hope."

If ever a man had a weapon in his hand to meet the attack of another weapon, that man is Mr. Hawthorne. His name is great, he has many natural talents, he is on the staff of one of the most widely read papers in the world, and I believe he is within point-blank range of the very mark he would wish to strike.

Mr. Hawthorne would be the first to admit that the press is a gigantic power, and that it is under the most delicate control of the editorial conning tower, and yet when he sees its broadsides turned against the cause of common decency, he wrings his hands and writes a charming essay defining literature.

He laments that it is a fact that news is necessary, and can and should be told only in the simplest way. But, after all, what better definition of literature can be given than that it is that sort of writing which most perfectly conveys the meaning of the author? It is not necessary that facts should be dealt with in a matter-of-fact way. Does Macaulay's work become less like literature because he chronicles human affairs? Does William James forfeit all claim to literary style because he writes of dull science and illumines it with the fire of his imagination?

Is it not within the bounds of possibility that even our every-day news should be so well and so clearly set forth that the value of that matter could be easily judged, and the author's manner be a source of delight instead of disgust? That would indeed be a press to be proud of, and in the time of that millennium, ours would be—

A land of lovely speech where every tone is fashioned
By generations of emotions, high and sweet,
Of thought and deed and bearing lofty and impassioned;
A land of golden calm, grave forms, and fretless feet.

We do not expect that yet, but unless we hitch our wagon to a star we shall be hopelessly mired in muck of our own creation. It is only the most obvious and every-day sort of practicality to set before oneself a hopelessly high ideal.

What we need, then, is to re-wed literature with journalism, for surely God hath joined them together, and it was man who put them asunder.

Let the young men fresh from the universities do this thing. We want eager, scornful men, with high-carried standards and deliberately chosen aims. We are fast sickening of these feeble fellows who dabble in the slime and weep the senile tears of sentimentality, looking up now and then to watch the effect on the public. Honor and sentiment and humor are as much in place in our daily press, God knows, as in our daily life, and are less often found there.

With a few honorable exceptions, those editorial writers in New York who are not callow sneerers are stupid folk who write without style, wit, or wisdom, pandering to the wants of a public which learns its wants from them.

Mr. Hawthorne has said that "the Newspaper is the characteristic voice of the age," and leaves us sunk in despair because it would seem we live in such evil days. Let him carry out his

469

own simile to its logical conclusion. Was there ever a voice that could not be benefited by training? School the voice to be delicate and flexible, to show accurately the emotion that moves the singer, and then, but not till then—judge your age by it.

LANGDON WARNER.

The Book=Buyer's Guide

ART

Meynell—Giovanni Bellini. By Everard Meynell. Newnes Art Library. Warne. $1.25.
This latest addition to a series of twenty volumes on painters past and present has all of the good qualities in its sixty-five illustrations and clear text that have placed its companions on so firm a basis.

Staley—Fra Angelico. By Edgecumbe Staley. Newnes Art Library. Warne. $1.25.
As in the case of the nineteen companion volumes of the series, this book contains an excellent photogravure frontispiece, sixty-four half-tone reproductions of Fra Angelico's work, and an excellent life of the painter by Mr. Staley. Both the text and the illustrations are of such an excellent quality that the volume should have a firmly established place on the shelves of the student desiring a general view of the period.

BELLES LETTRES

Carter—The Religion of Numa. By Jesse Benedict Carter. Macmillan. $1.00.
This is a very valuable short study of an interesting and in some respects a difficult subject. The author is a pupil of Wissowas, and he acknowledges his indebtedness to his teacher and to Mr. Warde Fowler. But he has treated his materials in his own way and has written a volume which is in many respects original. After pointing out the weakness of the "Indo-Germanic theory," of which the philologists have been so fond, Mr. Carter goes on to discuss, largely in the light of anthropological discoveries, the origin and character of the gods of early Rome who flourished in the days of the half-legendary Numa. To those unfamiliar with Roman religion except in its later developments, the idea that these gods arose out of ancestor worship and that they had no connection whatever with the Grecian deities, will be novel, but of the fact there is no doubt. Mr. Carter traces the changes due to the changing character of the Roman people, until, despite the multiplicity of gods and goddesses, or perhaps because of it, the old Roman religion was dead.

Gladden—The New Idolatry. By Washington Gladden. McClure, Phillips & Co. $1.20.
In this volume of essays, Dr. Gladden claims the authorship of the phrase "tainted money" and elaborates the idea contained in it. His protests, in various forms, against the "enthronement of Mammon" are entirely safe, even conservative; they have been made many times before. The essays are really adapted only for oral delivery. They verge upon platitude and will scarcely stimulate thought.

Helm—Aspects of Balzac. By W. H. Helm. Pott. $1.00.
The manifold aspects of Balzac have been carefully studied, and are presented in short studies of his methods, the "Women of the Human Comedy," the "Men of the Human Comedy," Balzac's "Comédie Anglaise," a chapter on "Balzac and Dickens," deprecating the easy criticism that calls Balzac the French Dickens," and points out the resemblances and differences beween them. Mr. Helm is evidently a great admirer and lover of Balzac, and shows a thorough appreciation of his great qualities without blindness to his defects. His book is a useful addition to Balzac literature.

James—English Hours. By Henry James. Houghton, Mifflin. $3.00.
Reviewers are sometimes accused of not reading the books they review, but cannot the blame be laid sometimes on the books? No such blame can be laid on this one, for even the most hardened reviewer will get genuine pleasure from its pages. The keen and just appreciation of the English character, customs, and surroundings will appeal to any one who has been in England, and there is plenty left for those who have not. Through all the mists and fogs of England—not only the very real London article, but also the metaphorical one—Mr. James's eyes have pierced to what lies beyond. He has weighed England in the balances and not found her wanting, and, though not blind to her failings, her charm pervades all his pages, and in its turn finds a complement in the charm of his style.

Lane—The Champagne Standard. By Mrs. John Lane. Lane. $1.50.
Spontaneous wit united with keen judgment makes this volume a delightful one. Mrs. Lane writes amusingly of the difference of living customs in this country and England, where she has made her home since her second marriage. She cannot resign American conveniences without a pang, and finds home without speaking-tubes a dreary abode. Instead of agreeing with the idea that London is a cheaper place to live in than New York, she finds it dearer. The steam-laundry is an institution especially abhorred by her. It costs, she says, "one pound a week to keep up to the pearl-grey standard." English ser-

vants are, in Mrs. Lane's opinion, more difficult to deal with than American, because of their hard and fast ideas as to the exact nature of their duties. Moreover, "the English servant despises a kind and considerate mistress as not knowing her place." Mrs. Lane's clever essays are never ill-natured; she touches up the foibles of life above and below stairs on both sides of the Atlantic in brisk but kindly fashion. The volume is one which every one with a sense of humor should not fail to enjoy.

Mencken—George Bernard Shaw: His Plays. By Henry L. Mencken. Luce. $1.00.

If the writer of this book had Mr. Shaw's sense of humor he would be less eager to claim for that amusing and erratic dramatist a kinship with Darwin and "the fight against orthodoxy." Orthodoxy has survived many hard knocks, and it is not very likely that any thrust from Mr. Shaw will give it its death blow. One suspects that the esoteric doctrines which both the author and his admirers profess to find in "Man and Superman" and the rest of the plays are, after all, only part of the joke. There is such a thing as taking a clever *farceur* too seriously.

Merriam—The Negro and the Nation. By George S. Merriam. Holt. $1.75.

A history of the growth of the negro problem distinguished throughout by fairness. The author defends the theories of the abolitionists none the less warmly because he recognizes the folly of some of their acts. He is just to the Southern whites as well as generous to the Southern blacks, and recognizes the fact that the atrocities practised by a few slave-owners were by no means universal. An admirable account of the John Brown episode and of the impeachment of President Johnson is given. The final chapter is devoted to a consideration of the best way of helping the negro in the future.

Pritchett—What Is Religion? By Henry S. Pritchett. Houghton, Mifflin. $1.00.

President Pritchett gives some thoroughly sound advice in his talks to young men. There is no cant or priggishness about these earnest addresses; they are of the kind which ought to serve as the "word in season." They deal with such subjects as "What is truth?" and "What is religion?" in a practical manner far more likely to influence young men in the right direction than more eloquent addresses which depart more from the vital questions to be discussed. Many persons other than students will find food for thought in the little volume.

Thackeray—The New Sketch Book. By W. M. Thackeray. Edited by Robert S. Garnett. Rivers, London.

A collection of eleven papers, discovered by Mr. Garnett in the *Foreign Quarterly Review* (1842-1844), and now first recognized as Thackeray's. They are mostly reviews of French books (Victor Hugo, Dumas, Lemaitre, Eugène Scribe, Eugène Sue, and others), and, though not up to the standard of Thackeray's later work, bear unmistakable marks of his hand, with scattered paragraphs in his most characteristic vein. The editor, moreover, in his introduction and appendix, gives much collateral evidence of various kinds, to confirm his identification of the authorship. Altogether the volume is a notable addition to Thackeray literature, and unexpected withal after the careful search of so many biographers and critics for unacknowledged matter from his pen.

Warner—Famous Introductions to Shakespeare's Plays. Edited with an Introduction, etc., by Beverley Warner. Dodd, Mead. $2.50 net.

This collection of eighteenth-century Shakespearian matter includes the prefaces to the editions of Rowe, Pope, Theobald, Hammer, Warburton, Johnson, Steevens, Capell, Reed, and Malone, with that of the player-editors of the Folio of 1623; to whom, by the way, Dr. Warner gives the credit of being "really editors," assuming that the "changes and alterations in the Folio [from the Quartos] presuppose an editor's hand," and that it is probable that the other plays (not previously issued in quarto form) "received the same attention"—a view which we are inclined to think few scholars and critics will accept. Besides the introduction, which calls for no especial comment, very brief biographical notices of the authors of the prefaces are given, and occasional explanatory notes. These prefaces with two or three exceptions, have little other than historical interest, but as they are mostly inaccessible except in the original editions and in the "Variorum" of 1821, many students and critical readers of Shakespeare will be glad to have them in this convenient reprint. We note a few misprints ("Auxene" for "Auxerre," "Siliklo" for "Sinklo," etc.), and now and then a strange slip on the part of the editor, as (p. 11) the statement that "Thos. Fletcher" (instead of John Fletcher) is admitted to have had a hand in the play of "Henry VIII."

BIOGRAPHY

Barine—Louis XIV. and La Grande Mademoiselle. By Arvède Barine. Putnam.

The proof of the merit of Mme. Barine's work lies in the fact that one is eager to read it in spite of the very bad translation. It is a thoughtful study of the life of the Grande Mademoiselle, and the results of the abortive revolution for which she was so largely responsible. Mme. Barine sees in the effect produced on Louis XIV. by the Fronde the germ of the causes of the great Revolution. This period of the King's life has not been so fully noticed as the later years with which St. Simon has made us so familiar, though it embraces perhaps the most important part of his career. The description of the poverty of the country in these early years, and of the King's making himself absolute monarch, of his forcing the effacement of the aristocracy and abandonment of Paris, show how the seeds of the Revolution were sown. A striking picture of the times is given in the story of Louis's marriage, also in the description of the Court journeys. The extraordinary love-affair of Lauzun and the Grande Mademoiselle alone would make this book worth reading, but there are a host of other details of these earlier years of Louis XIV., and to a subject replete with picturesque interest Mme. Barine has done full justice. The book is fully illustrated from original paintings and engravings.

Brown—Life of Oliver Ellsworth By William Garrott Brown. Macmillan. $2.00 net.
A biography of a prominent character in our Colonial and Revolutionary periods and the years of constitutional organization that immediately followed, and perhaps of more interest for its historical and political matter than for that which is of a personal nature. The life of the man was not particularly eventful, but his official work and relations were important, and the record of them includes much information which is not readily, if at all, to be found elsewhere.

Gapon—The Story of My Life. By Father George Gapon. Dutton. $3.00 net.
The author of this book might have lived and died unknown to the world at large but for the St. Petersburg massacre of January 22, 1905. Then the figure of the priest who led the workingmen to demand audience of the Tsar suddenly flashed into vivid distinctness. The story that fills half his pages need not be repeated here. It is told with vigor and deep feeling. Father Gapon's whole career had qualified him for the post he filled on that fatal day, when peaceable citizens, seeking redress for grievances, were shot down in cold blood by the troops. His sincerity has been questioned since his flight from Russia, and it has even been intimated that he deliberately led his deluded followers into a trap. But an unprejudiced reading of his story leaves the impression that this accusation is quite groundless. Certainly from the time he became a priest he has devoted himself with apparent whole-heartedness to the toiling and suffering masses. He writes simply and naturally about himself, describing his peasant youth, his early religious aspirations and doubts, his philanthropic and missionary work. His view of the condition of the Russian Church is not flattering, and he predicts for autocracy a *débacle* like that of the French Revolution. Possibly his statements require a few grains of salt, but they are none the less interesting.

Henderson—Mary Queen of Scots. By T. F. Henderson. 2 volumes. Imported by Scribners. $6.00 net.
"Age cannot wither nor custom stale her infinite variety" was written of Cleopatra, and surely the same must be true of Mary Queen of Scots, for biographies of her fall

almost as thick as leaves in Vallombrosa. In spite of Dr. Hay Fleming's biographic work, Major Hume's treatment of her love-affairs, Mr. Lang's "Mystery," with its ingenious Casket Letter theory, and Mr. Hewlett's sensuous "Queen's Quair," Mr. Henderson has found means to compose a book of much interest, which will probably, however, satisfy neither the friends nor enemies of Mary Stuart entirely. Fate of an inexorable kind is the chief factor in her life, as seen by the author. He leans to the human side of history, rather than to the externals of customs, habits, social conditions, etc., seeking to read the heart of the nation in the hearts of the actors in the contest that raged around the Scottish Queen. And he succeeds in giving an excellent idea of the changing conditions of thought, political and religious, and a good picture of the men who wrought the ruin of the Queen. Not less well drawn is her own portrait, unbiassed by sentiment, and with evident desire to do her justice, and no less evident belief in her guilt; there is shown also keen appreciation of Elizabeth's cunning power, and the contrast between the rival Queens is well brought out. The book begins with Mary's birth, and follows her fortunes closely throughout her stormy career, no time or space being wasted on the gossip that forms so large a part of some "Lives." Mr. Henderson deals with the Casket Letters in an appendix, and makes out a good case for their authenticity. He utterly refutes Mr. Lang's forgery theory, calling it "heroic self-sacrifice on behalf of a historical myth." It is a pity that several mistakes have been allowed to creep into the text, and that, in giving the date of the month, in nearly every instance the date of the year has been omitted; also that the author has permitted himself the use of so many unusual words. The illustrations are exceedingly numerous, and it seems as if a diligent search must have been made for portraits, not of Mary alone, but of those who came into the sphere of her history.

Hubback—Jane Austen's Sailor Brothers. By J. H. and Edith C. Hubback. Lane. $3.50 net.
To the true "Janean" every book about Miss Austen has some interest, however superfluous it may appear to others. That two of her brothers were naval officers, most of us know; and it was a happy thought to deal with their careers, to give extracts from their logs and letters, and to recall from their sister's novels Captain Wentworth, William Price, and the rest, in whose lineaments some of their features may perhaps be traced. If it be true, as has been suggested with some plausibility, that Miss Austen drew in Anne Elliot—to many of us the most charming of her heroines—a woman whose experience she had shared, it may be equally true that in Captain Wentworth some one not a brother sat for the portrait. In the present volume there are passages interesting in themselves, apart from their connection with the Austen family; but when all is said and done it was

written for the Janeans, and they will best appreciate it.

Hume—The Wives of Henry the Eighth. By Martin Hume. McClure. $3.50 net.

The six consorts of Henry the VIIIth are important by reason of the part his marriages took in the Reformation. This is the way the author regards and treats them. Putting aside the picturesque side of the Queens, he sees in them the tools used by politicians to sway the King as they desired. Naturally, the greater part of the book is devoted to Katherine of Aragon and Anne Boleyn, Henry's declaration of himself as the head of the Church having been the outcome of these two marriages. But the author does not regard Henry as the far-seeing statesman he is sometimes represented as being, but rather as the sensualist used by both parties in the struggle that ended in the Reformation. His character is dealt with justly, but the white-wash of Mr. Froude is not used by Mr. Hume, who, on the contrary, calls him a "whited sepulchre." Katherine of Aragon, too, has to step down from the pedestal on which Shakespeare placed and others maintained her, and appears with all her failings, and bereft of none of her virtues. There is an absence of sentimental feeling for the Queens, and the book is more a political study of the causes of the Reformation than of the lives of the Queens as women, but it does not lose interest in consequence.

Ober—Columbus. By Frederick A. Ober. Heroes of American History. Harper. $1.00 net.

A life of the great discoverer well calculated to interest young people in his personality. Mr. Ober shows Columbus as a much injured man—as indeed he was,—and describes vividly the many difficulties which he encountered in carrying out the projects of his genius. A middle ground is generally followed in moot points. It is assumed that Columbus may readily have had access to the Norse manuscripts but that the supposition is incapable of proof.

Winchester—The Life of John Wesley. By C. T. Winchester. Macmillan. $1.50 net.

Professor Winchester's view of the founder of Methodism is in some respects different from the usual one. He points out that Wesley was the child of his age in his distrust of enthusiasm. He laid great stress upon an intelligent faith, and endeavored himself to be clear, candid, and logical. That he could have carried on his especial work within the Anglican Church, had the bishops of his day held more statesmanlike ideas as to their duty, is plain enough; in fact, he never abandoned that Church, nor did he desire his followers to do so. Yet the logic of events made the organization of a distinctive Methodist body inevitable. Professor Winchester tells the story of Wesley's career sympathetically, though not in a partisan spirit, and he

brings out the character and personality of the man better, on the whole, than any of Wesley's previous biographers have done.

BOOKS FOR THE YOUNG

Maunder—The Plain Princess and Other Stories. By I. Maunder. With a preface by Andrew Lang. Illustrated by M. W. Taylor and M. D. Baxter. Longmans. $1.50.

If a child doesn't like this book, he ought. It is a charming affair; the drawings are admirable and the book also benefits by Mr. Lang's delightful preface, though without it, the Plain Princess is well worth knowing, and the Land of Reasonwhy worth a visit.

Rankin—The Girls of Gardenville. By Carroll Watson Rankin. Holt. $1.25.

Wholesome stories of the doings of the "Sweet Sixteen Club" of Gardenville. The sixteen heroines are natural, lively girls whose pleasures and trials would be of interest to other young people between the ages of twelve to sixteen years. The tone of the book is commendable; it teaches sound principles without being priggish.

FICTION

Alexander—Judith. By Grace Alexander. Bobbs-Merrill. $1.50.

It is a pity that Miss Alexander did not choose a more distinctive title for her pleasantly written little tale of ante-bellum times in Camden; Judith is a name that suggests a far different heroine than hers, who after marrying for duty the man she does not love is rewarded by his death and a second marriage, with the man she does love. The novelty of the story, such as it is, lies rather in the atmosphere than in the plot. Some of the scenes are well done, and the characters stand out with a good degree of boldness.

Anonymous—The Princess Priscilla's Fortnight. By the author of "Elizabeth and her German Garden." Scribner. $1.50.

We like "Elizabeth's" charming egotism, and we greatly prefer her when she concerns herself with her own intimate affairs. The authorship of "Priscilla" is recognizable, but the book is a far flimsier fabric than the earlier stories. Priscilla's adventures are a shade too preposterous for genuine enjoyment. The imaginative quality of the book is not high, and though a whimsical charm of style counts for much, it is hardly enough, in this case, to carry the reader through to the end unwearied. If "Elizabeth" belongs to the very considerable group of authors who are forever haunted and tormented by a first success, her public is not, after all, to blame.

Benson—The Angel of Pain. By E. F. Benson. Lippincott. $1.50.

A great change has taken place in Mr. Benson's style within the last several years. The difference between that of "Mammon and Company" and his latest novel is almost startling. He has a fine idea in "The Angel of Pain," but he is not wholly successful in developing it. He endeavors to show through the medium of four principal characters the necessity of pain in the world. Three of the people are real; the fourth is a shadow. Mr. Benson makes a mistake in his dalliance with the supernatural. In this book it destroys the verisimilitude. The reader loses his belief in the reality of the personages after Tom Merivale's mysterious death. Mr. Benson has gained much in solidity; he can no longer be called merely clever. But he has lost in vitality. The reader feels no great desire to know what happens to any one of the people in the book, with the single exception of Evelyn Dundas, the artist. "The Angel of Pain" is an interesting novel; it is hardly an absorbing one. Apparently Mr. Benson has not even yet found himself.

Boyce—The Eternal Spring. By Neith Boyce. Macmillan. $1.50.

Sentimentality runs riot in this story of young love in Italy. All the characters, including the hero, are fluffy and most of them are hysterical. Mrs. Hapgood has written better fiction than this and will probably write more in the future. The apparent moral of this sugary tale is that only the young have the right to love and that a woman over thirty ought to be dead and buried.

Brown—The Sacred Cup. By Vincent Brown. Putnam. $1.50.

A story of English life admirably told. The plot hinges on a problem of the familiar kind, but none of the ordinarily attendant vulgarity is revealed in its development. The characters are all well drawn; that of the little rector, Mr. Jerred, is conspicuous for a rarely fine combination of humor and pathos. This is not a novel to appeal to the class of readers who delight in the morbid revelations of the pseudo-realist. Its reserve is its most striking quality and it is one worthy of high praise. This is altogether the best piece of fiction written by Mr. Brown.

Burnett—The Dawn of To-morrow. By Frances Hodgson Burnett. Scribner. $1.

A vividly told sketch of the experiences of a rich man who, miserable beyond endurance from one cause and another, determines to put an end to his life. He goes to a cheap lodging-house and expects to kill himself before another morning. He has planned things so that he thinks his identity will remain unknown. He goes out in the fog to buy a revolver and comes in contact with a number of poor people. The possibilities revealed to him of helping humanity change the entire current of his life and he thinks of "to-morrow" as the beginning of a new life on earth instead of the entrance to a state of annihilation. Nothing that Mrs. Burnett has written in years has made the impression or enjoyed the popularity of this story.

Castle—The Heart of Lady Anne. By Agnes and Egerton Castle. With Illustrations in color by Ethel Franklin Betts and numerous decorations by Frederick Garrison Hall. Stokes. $1.50.

If Henrietta Crossman has not exhausted the characteristics of "Sweet Kitty Bellairs" and her *Enorage* here is another dainty book of dresden china people ripe for her art. Lady Anne is an English shrew in miniature, with French training and an English husband to act as her Petruchio. The story of her taming is charmingly told, and the entire make-up of the book is an accord with its spirit—lavendar and gold covers, four illustrations in color, and blue and black initials and half-titles for the chapters. The combined effect of language and illustrations is engaging.

Cooke—Chronicles of the Little Tot. By Edmund Vance Cooke. Dodge. $1.50.

"The Chronicles of the Little Tot" should make both universal and tender appeal,—not alone to those who are the Little Tot's immediate vassals and slaves, but to the wider circle of child-lovers, as well. There is a naïve, exquisite sympathy with the (alleged) workings of the baby mind,—a laughing and benevolent understanding of parental idolatries, whether of the maternal or the paternal order; and withal, there is excellent metrical craft in this collection, whereby the author's sympathy and understanding are carried direct to the hearts of his readers—even if we might at times, spare something from his characteristic method of clever punning. But his "Creepers," "Cruisers," and "Climbers," mark various stages in the career of Little Young Mortality and lead us to that riper period of infancy chronicled so deftly and inimitably in "Willie's Letter to His Teacher," said letter being the worried product of "Young Hopeful," who is torn between his father's old-fashioned insistence upon the indispensableness of instruction in the Three R's and his teacher's devotion to the "modern system of enriched education" in vogue in some of our public schools. Mr. Cooke's "Chronicles" have not excluded the note of pathos, which is heard (much in the spirit and pitch of Emerson's "Threnody") in "The Little Boy Who Left Us," and, again, in the delicate lyric, "At Night."

Crockett—Fishers of Men. By S. R. Crockett. Appleton. $1.50.

Persons who love Scotland can hardly fail to appreciate Mr. Crockett, for even at his worst his local color is deftly applied. It would be too harsh a judgment, perhaps, to say that in this book he is at his worst; but he is certainly not at his best. He seems to be trying to imitate certain distinguished contemporaries, and that is always a dangerous experiment. In this case the result is a painful lack of reality.

Dillon—In Old Bellaire By Mary Dillon. Century. $1.50.

A romance of the Civil War in which the

leading characters are a pretty but very puritanical New England school-teacher and a typical young Southerner. Bellaire is really Carlisle, Pennsylvania. The most attractive feature of the story is the manner in which the author has imprisoned the atmosphere of the old-fashioned college town, investing it with real charm.

Eyre—The Girl in Waiting. By Archibald Eyre. Luce. $1.50.

This is an unpretentious tale of a rich girl masquerading as a poor one and coming under suspicion as a dangerous character. There is a young man in the case, of course, and circumstances shape themselves, equally of course, to bring the two together. Mr. Eyre writes pleasantly and cleverly and enables the reader to avoid ennui for an idle hour.

Gardenhire—The Long Arm. By S. M. Gardenhire. Harpers. $1.50.

The clever detective will never lose his charm for a certain order of mind. Personally, we do not find LeDroit Conners as entertaining as Old Sleuth, although perhaps his methods are more subtle. In any case Mr. Gardenhire's book need not be seriously considered as literature.

Graham—The Wizard's Daughter. By Margaret Collier Graham. Houghton, Mifflin and Co. $1.25.

Very capably handled stories of simple Western life, women's tragedies, for the most part, told without relieving contrasts. Their grim and harsh atmosphere would scarcely be tolerable if it were not for the essential truth, and therefore, in a sense, the beauty, of each tale.

Horton—The Edge of Hazard. By George Horton. Bobbs-Merrill. $1.50.

It is fortunate for the novelist that the supply of princesses who are willing to marry Americans holds out. Mr. Horton has discovered another in the person of Elizabeth Romanovna, whom Frederick Courtland Hardy, erst of Boston's "smart set," going to Russia to take a business position, was able by his straight shooting to save from deadly peril. The enmity of the Princess's cousin and the love of a Japanese girl keep him and his revolver busy to the last. An excellent story—for people who merely wish to be amused.

Maartens—The Healers. By Maarten Maartens. Appleton. $1.50.

The eminent Dutch novelist who writes in English has written in this very long and somewhat inchoate novel a study of the physiological view of therapeutics versus the psychical. There are many brilliant passages in the book, but as a whole it leaves a confused impression upon the mind of the reader. There are too many characters and the threads of the story are hopelessly involved. "Dorothea" showed a tendency on the part of Mr. Maartens to let his ideas overrun him, and in his latest work of fiction this artistic license is still more apparent. The result of this

serious mistake is materially to injure alike the beauty and the force of his literary style. Cleverness and power are both evident in "The Healers," but it is a most unsatisfying work of fiction.

Macdonald—The Sea Maid. By Ronald Macdonald. Holt. $1.50.

A story based on the common "desert island" plot, told uncommonly well. Mr. Macdonald has plenty of humor and skill in characterization. By this means he makes the familiar "casting away" device into an eminently readable and amusing bit of fiction. Of its kind "The Sea Maid" is good.

Macnaughtan—A Lame Dog's Diary. By S. Macnaughtan. Dodd, Mead. $1.50.

A pleasing bit of fiction which does not draw too heavily upon the reader's nervous endurance. Life in a sort of Cranfordian village is depicted in the diary of a man, still young, who has lost a leg in the Boer War. Later there are Scotch scenes which recall the author's former amusing volume, "The Fortune of Christina McNab." A graceful but not novel love-story is interwoven with the humorous sketches.

Martin—Sabina. A Story of the Amish. By Helen Reimensnyder Martin. Century. $1.25.

This story is the product of close observation. Nobody would dream of questioning its accuracy. But the reader's frame of mind is one of curiosity rather than of sympathetic interest. The "manners and customs" of a strange tribe may have a quaint and half-humorous flavor; but an exposition of them does not fascinate or absorb. To her really pitiful heroine, Sabina, the author has attributed a psychic power which she vouches for, in her preface, as based on fact. But this is, of course, a doubtful recommendation for fiction.

Merejkowski—Peter and Alexis. By Dmitri Merejkowski. Putnam. $1.50.

The concluding novel in its author's trilogy entitled "Christ and Anti-Christ." It is a powerfully impressive study of unlovely characters among revolting conditions. Merejkowski finds little that is inspiring in Russia at the beginning of the eighteenth century and his study of the royal father and son, Peer the Great and Alexis, is one of the most terrible pictures conceivable. Alexis, between whom and the present Tsar a resemblance has been traced, is a weak, morbid, craven, pitiful figure, a kind of exemplification of Death-in-Life, who haunts the reader for days. The unutterable scene of the Tsar's murder of his son is a supreme test of the reader's hardihood, for Russian literature can contain nothing more appalling. The present publication of the book, with the light that it throws on the Romanoff character, is peculiarly timely.

Moore—Love Alone is Lord. By F. Frankfort
Moore. Putnam. $1.50.

Another version of Lord Byron's fascinating
life. Mr. Moore represents Mary Chaworth
as the woman whom Byron loved deepest
and longest. Familiar, even popularly familiar, as Byron's story has become, it is retold
here with a great deal of zest and vigor and
easily holds the reader's attention to the very
end. Apparently few novelists are able to
invent characters that can rival in interest
this real-life hero.

Olmsted—The Nonchalante. By Stanley Olmsted. Holt. $1.25.

A rather cleverly written story of three Americans, two men and a girl, in Germany. The
heroine, Dixie Bilton, is cheerfully indifferent
to the feelings of any one but her own.
The author has succeeded, however, in giving
her some genuine fascination. The style is
too obviously imitative of that of Mr. James.

Orczy—The Scarlet Pimpernel. By Baroness
Orczy. Putnam. $1.50.

A brilliantly vivid story, abounding in dramatic incident, of Paris and London in the
year 1792. Unusually effective use has been
made of the abundant material this period
affords, and the variety of scene and situation, as well as the mystery, of "The Scarlet
Pimpernel" are likely to keep the most
critical reader interested to the end. Photographs of the leading situations in the story,
as represented by Julia Neilson and Fred
Terry and their company, are used as illustrations.

Osbourne—Wild Justice. By Lloyd Osbourne.
Appleton. $1.25.

Stories of life in Hawaii and Samoa which
reveal Mr. Osbourne as a much better writer
than might be thought from "Baby Bullet."
The tales all have a swing in the telling and
show that the author is in his own field.
There is plenty of humor in them and an
occasional bit of real pathos. "The Security
of the High Seas" and "Old Dibs" are especially good.

**Quick—Double Trouble or, Every Hero His
Own Villain.** By Herbert Quick. With
illustrations by Orson Lowell. Bobbs-
Merrill. $1.50.

This title has a good, old-fashioned ring, such
as novels used to provide in days of yore.
The key-note is found in the quatrain from
the "Secret ritual of the A. O. C. M." (whatever that may be!): "Pervasive woman! in
our hours of ease, our cloud-dispeller, tem-
pering storm to breeze! But when our dual
selves the pot sets bubbling, our cares providing, and our doubles troubling!" The particular troubler is the woman represented not
only in an illustration (page 28), but also in
colors on the outside wrapper. She sits poised
on a kind of dais, one foot on a tiger skin, the
other lifted in the air, addressing herself to
young Amidon, a scared-looking youth with
his left hand spread awkwardly over his
chest and his right curled up behind him.
This same man is the person who caught in
his arms "the blast-furnace of hair, the strik-

ing hat and the pleasantly rounded figure"
of an unknown guest as she "descended,
partly flying, partly falling, partly sliding
down the baluster—a whirl of superheated
hair, swirling skirts, and wide, appealing eyes
of delf blue." No wonder he continued to look
awkward, with such adventures.

Quiller-Couch—The Mayor of Troy. By A.
T. Quiller-Couch. Scribner. $1.50.

"Years ago," explains Mr. Quiller-Couch, in
the prologue of this delightful story, "I
promised myself to write a treatise on the lost
Mayors of Cornwall." This volume carries
out in part that singular but commendable
intention. A writer with a delicate and significant touch and entirely congenial material
is the best of companions, and the "Mayor
of Troy" has a fragrance and a flavor which
must be felt at first hand. Summaries and
analyses would be far from conveying it.

Shaw—The Irrational Knot. By Bernard
Shaw. Brentano's. $1.50.

In his characteristically exuberant and entertaining preface, Mr. Shaw remarks that he
cannot see, for the life of him, why people
should wish to read a crude novel that he
wrote in his early twenties;—but if they do—.
It is true that the most significant points in
the story are taken up and developed in the
author's later work, and so far as its opinions
and contentions go it may safely be ignored.
The Shaw-reading public knows pretty well
by this time what the dramatist thinks of
marriage, the irrational knot. But Mr. Shaw,
whatever he lacked at twenty-five, did not
lack wit; and readers who delight in his energetic paradoxes will find plenty to repay them
for reading this voluminous story.

Sinclair—The Jungle. By Upton Sinclair.
Doubleday, Page. $1.50.

"An elemental odor, raw and crude; it was
rich, almost rancid, sensual, strong." Mr.
Sinclair's words apply as well to his own novel
as to the Chicago stockyards, where the scene
of it is laid. In describing the horrors through
which his characters live and move and have
their being, he adopts the pseudo-realistic
method of Zola, but he has no spark of Zola's
genius in compensation. How far his book
represents actual conditions we need not
attempt to decide; that it contains some
exaggeration is plain. To consider it as a
work of art would be futile; to discuss it as a
tract would lead us too far afield.

Smith—The Wood Fire in No. 3. By F.
Hopkinson Smith. Scribner. $1.50.

No lurking, ungracious disappointment is concealed beneath the fair and open pages of
this companionable volume. Mr. Hopkinson
Smith is as good a story-teller as ever, and as
loyal an adherent of the old school that told
a story for the story's sake. There are nine
stories in this volume, more or less loosely
connected, and all in a vein of genial, charitable reminiscence. They may best be read

not through cool, critical spectacles, but under the circumstances which purport to have produced them—a wood fire, a pipe, and sympathetic companionship.

Spofford—Old Washington. By Harriet Prescott Spofford. Little, Brown. $1.50.

Five stories, good as such, but better as pictures of life and society at the capital as it was after the Civil War, forty or more years ago—a period which, with the changes that have taken place in this comparatively short period, seems "old" indeed. History and fiction are most agreeably combined in this delineation of it by one who was personally familiar with its varied and vanishing phases.

Tooker—Under Rocking Skies. By L. Frank Tooker. Century. $1.50.

A straightforward sea-romance, told simply and without subtleties or complications. The book will not offer a strong lure to over-sophisticated readers, nor is it written with marked distinction, but it has a genuine sea-flavor, a wholesome tone, and a certain degree of humor. Distinctly á readable story.

Wheat—The Third Daughter. By Mrs. Lu. Wheat. Los Angeles. Oriental Publishing. $1.50.

This is an unusually good story of Chinese home life, and withal thoroughly trustworthy in its pictures of Chinese thought, environment, and habit at home and in California. Even if it does teach powerfully some of the fruits of the wisdom of the Far East, such as the longevity of China, and the splendid physical condition of her people after ages of struggle, the moral is not tacked on as a bit of adornment, but is what the story itself carries.

HISTORY AND TRAVEL

Armstrong—The Heroes of Defeat. By William Jackson Armstrong. Clarke.

It is well that a generation too much given to the worship of success should now and then pause to contemplate those who failed to reach the goal. The six "heroes of defeat" chosen by Mr. Armstrong are, with one exception, little known. This exception, of course, is Kosciusko, long a favorite in fiction, as in history. Americans remember, if vaguely, Tecumseh, and Vercingetorix has been preserved to immortality by his great antagonist; Schamyl, Abdel Kader, and Scanderbeg are not even names to the average reader. Mr. Armstrong tells the stories of all these with some skill, though his style is considerably marred by flights that suggest stump oratory.

Bradley—In the March and Borderland of Wales. By A. G. Bradley. Houghton. $3.00

The illustrations alone are worth the price of this book; not that this statement is meant to disparage the text, for that is full of romantic and historic tales of the places depicted

by the artist, and one is the worthy complement of the other. One of the most picturesque parts of the United Kingdom has been chosen as the subject, which receives full justice from author and artist.

Goil—A Yankee in Pigmy Land. By William Edward Geil. Dodd, Mead.

As long as Little Jack Horner lives in nursery lore, so long will the pigmies of Africa be the subject of increasing interest. Stanley gave these human mites of darkest Africa their name, but Geil has told us more about them, perhaps, than any other explorer. We remember his lively book on the people of interior China, and with this work as a standard of comparison vote this latest story of personal experience and of rich human sympathy fully as interesting, while much more moving. Both text and pictures are tremendously realistic, and, to be frank, excite both disgust and pity. Mr. Geil tells not only about the little Jack Horners of the forest world, but depicts eloquently the energies of Christian missionaries in their determined effort to let in the light of Christianity and civilization. These men and women are working hard at the levers of education and industrial training that will bring to the Africans, both in body and mind, to hand and to eye, something more closely approaching the semblance of humanity than anything now visible in their assets of existence. Geil made a journey across Africa from Mombasa through the great pigmy forest to Banana on the west coast. In his narrative we have so much fun and frolic, from the author's overflowing animal spirits and fluent pen, that we sometimes are in doubt whether to take him seriously or in a Pickwickian sense. On Congoland much light is cast. The formula for correct living is almost Beorhavian in its brevity—"If you perspire, you can live well in Congo."

Greene—The Development of Religious Liberty in Connecticut. By M. Louise Greene, Houghton. $2.00 net.

A monograph much enlarged and elaborated from three earlier and briefer essays on the same subject which have been very favorably received, one of them having won the Strauss prize at Brown University. Connecticut was more modern in her progress toward religious liberty than most other parts of New England, and yet liberal or radical thinkers there "found early and late an uncomfortable atmosphere and restricted liberties." How the movement for the divorce of Church and State began, progressed, and finally triumphed is ably and fully told in this volume of five hundred pages; and the appendix gives lists of authorities on the successive periods and a complete bibliography of the literature of the subject.

Joubert—The Fall of Tsardom. By Carl Joubert. Lippincott. $2.00 net.

Those familiar with Mr. Joubert's previous books about Russia will readily understand that the present volume strikes and spares not the whole system of government of which Nicholas II. is the unfortunate representative. Although Mr. Joube.t was not a Russian, he identified himself thoroughly with the aims of the Russian Revolutionary party; and his writings secured so large an audience that his recent death must be a distinct loss to that party. It cannot be said that in these pages he gives an accurate picture of social and political conditions; his pen is distinctly that of an advocate. For example he criticises the secret societies for the purposeless crimes they commit, but at the same time he defends the "revolutionary committee" for sanctioning assassination "in extreme cases." Purely constitutional reform is in his opinion hopeless; the Tsardom is a deadly growth that must be plucked up by the roots. The theories which the author promulgates, however, are less interesting than the experiences he describes. These at least convince the reader, whatever his theories as to the remedy, that the disease is desperate grown; and so, perhaps, only by desperate appliances is it to be relieved. Those interested in current movements in Russia should not overlook this account of them.

Laut—The Vikings of the Pacific. By A. C. Laut. Macmillan. $2.00 net.
The title is figurative rather than literal, as none of the "Vikings" was from Scandinavia, though one of them is a Dane. The others are the outlaw hunters of Russia, the Polish pirate Benyowsky, the English Cook and Vancouver, Robert Gray of Boston, who discovered the Columbia River, with Drake, Ledyard, and other soldiers of fortune who made explorations on the Pacific coast of America. Their adventures and achievements are well told, and copiously illustrated with maps, portraits, views of scenery, etc.

Lee—The Spirit of Rome. By Vernon Lee. Lane. $1.50 net.
These notes of travel glow with color, and the wonder and enchantment of Rome. They cover a period of ten years, but might just as well cover two or two hundred. It is the eternal spirit of Rome that Vernon Lee has caught, and some of it descends on us in reading her book.

Little—Round About my Pekin Garden. By Mrs. Archibald Little. Lippincott. $5.00 net.
In her former books on China Mrs. Little gave us very graphic accounts of life in the country before the Boxer troubles; and this record of her return thither in these recent years is equally interesting for its description of the present condition of things. She has had exceptional opportunities for seeing China in all its phases of society and life from the highest to the lowest, and her keen observation and careful study of what she sees make the book one of the most trustworthy of its class. It photographs the Chinese man and the Chinese woman to the intellectual vision

as vividly as the abundant photographic illustrations, which are of extraordinary excellence and finish, bring them before the outer eye. The text is as truly pictorial as the pictures. The discussion of the social and political problems of the country and the times, though incidental and fragmentary, is sensible and shrewd. Altogether the book is to be commended quite without qualification.

Meeker—Pioneer Reminiscences of Puget Sound. By Ezra Meeker. Hanford. $3.
A big book which would have been better if the author had had the literary experience and skill needed for discreetly condensing large portions of it. Other portions are all the more interesting for their detail and diffusiveness, bringing the pioneer life and adventure more distinctly before us. The early wars with the Indians, for instance, are minutely and graphically chronicled, and we are glad to have many particulars which the historian of the period would omit. The illustrations of scenery and life and the portraits are good in their way.

Remington—The Way of an Indian. By Frederick Remington. Fox, Duffield.
A remarkably realistic life-history of a typical Indian. Mr. Remington has long been noted as almost the only illustrator who has succeeded in portraying Indians successfully. In this book he displays the same power of getting inside the red man's skin, alike in text and illustrations. He shows us an Indian who has every appearance of being true to life, and neither a white man painted copper-colored nor a fiend incarnate, although in certain characteristics he is not far from the latter according to our ideas.

MISCELLANEOUS

Anderson—The Country Town. By Wilbert L. Anderson. Baker, Taylor. $1.00.
Mr. Anderson takes a somewhat different view of the country town from that generally held. He argues that the growth of the cities has been made possible by the natural multiplication of population, that the rural districts are "in partnership" with the cities, and that there is no rural exodus which leaves a mere remnant of the people in the country. On the contrary, the growth of cities implies a growth in farming communities that supply city wants. Furthermore, the country towns are in closer and more vital connection with the outside world than they were once. This study of existing conditions will be found valuable even by those who do not agree with all the conclusions reached.

Decharme—Euripides and the Spirit of his Dramas. By Paul Decharme. Translated by James Loeb. Macmillan. $3.00 net.
The scholarly French professor has done excellent work in this discussion of the Greek

tragedian, and the book has been accurately and attractively "Englished" by the translator. The headings of the chapters will suggest the author's method of dealing with his subject: "Life and Character of Euripides"; "Relations of Euripides with Philosophers and Sophists"; his "Criticism of Religious Traditions"; his "Philosophical Views"; his treatment of "Society"; "Political Views"; "Choice of Subjects"; "Dramatic Situations"; "Action," and other matters of dramatic art. As the author says in his preface, "Euripides is the most modern of the Greek tragic poets"; but at the same time he is "an elusive poet, not easy to comprehend," and the modern reader, even if not unfamiliar with Greek, needs just such help in understanding his character, his philosophy, and his art as this critical study affords. It will therefore be welcome to the classical student no less than to the general public of cultivated and thoughtful readers. The analytical index of a dozen pages is a commendable feature.

Dresser—Health and the Inner Life. An Analytical and Historical Study of Spiritual Healing Theories, with an Account of the Life and Teachings of P. P. Quimby. By Horatio Dresser. Putnam. $1.35 net.

Mr. Dresser's last book has the great virtue of presenting abstract truths concretely, in good literary style, which is quite unusual in works of this class. The manner is such that students of psychology are not discouraged in their efforts to find ideas. The great drawback with most writers on "mental" subjects is that they hide their ignorance by many high-sounding terms and eloquent verbosities. Mr. Dresser's book is an exposition of the beliefs of Mr. Quimby, who was the "healer" of Mrs. Eddy, and the source of her inspiration.

Gilman—The Launching of a University, and other Papers. By Daniel Coit Gilman. Dodd, Mead. $2.50 net.

Ideals of education have greatly changed within the past quarter of a century, and in this change such an institution as Johns Hopkins University at Baltimore has played no small part. Something more than half of Dr. Gilman's interesting volume is given up to recalling the circumstances of its origin, its aims, and achievements. The incomplete part of this record concerns Dr. Gilman himself, to whom, as President of the institution from its foundation until 1902, no slender portion of the credit is due. Johns Hopkins, like Harvard and Cornell, had to undergo some misrepresentation in its early days from those who held sectarian views of the function of teaching; but it lived down obloquy on this score and contributed immeasurably to the intellectual life of the nation by the complete freedom of research its conductors established. The idea of post-graduate study has spread widely of late, and it is easy to forget the obligation to the institution which did so much to promote such study. Dr. Gilman has many charming reminiscences to relate of men more or less connected with the history

of Johns Hopkins—of Huxley, Freeman Rowland, Sylvester, Lanier, Child, and others. The papers in the volume not directly connected with Johns Hopkins are mainly on educational subjects. They are written with unfailing kindliness of spirit and they throw pleasant sidelights upon the character and career of the distinguished writer.

Moore—Aurelian. By Spencer Moore. Longmans.

A drama of the later Roman Empire in four acts and an interlude, in which some liberties are taken with historical facts, but not greater than the usual license allows. It seems to us hardly up to the average of modern efforts in the same line, mediocre as these mostly are.

Sabin—When You Were a Boy. By Edwin L. Sabin. With fifty pictures by Frederic Dorr Steele. Baker, Taylor. $1.50.

There are some books that even hardened reviewers do not give away. They are kept to add to their circulating library of "recent books recommended." Of such a nature is Mr. Sabin's delightful volume of sketches of boy life. Like Mrs. Gardiner's "Heart of a Girl" it is not meant for children (except grown ones). The difference between the two books is the difference between boys and girls, objective rather than subjective. The transitions of feeling and experience are not always nicely shaded, as they might be by the mechanical device of spaces or asterisks, but the literary jolts are pardonable when the true boyishness of the narrative is considered, e. g. the tale of a bent pin, and "speaking" in school. The illustrations are capital and add fully one half to the charm.

Saint Maur—A Self-Supporting Home. By Kate V. Saint Maur. Macmillan. $1.75 net.

Divided into months, the whole work of a small farm is given, and it all seems very possible and delightful. Poultry and vegetables are the chief supports of this home, but the cow and the calf also receive attention, rabbits, cats, the family horse, the bee, and our friend the dog add variety, and the pictures make one feel that the country is really the right place to live in. The author's figures show that everything can be made profitable if properly managed.

Schermerhorn—House Hints. By C. E. Schermerhorn. House Hints Co. 50c.

If you wish to build, buy, improve, or rent a house you can make no better beginning than by laying hands on this little pamphlet on practical home building and equipping. The author has here discussed every essential detail pertaining to site, construction, plumbing, and furnishing, in a simple, direct, and unusually condensed manner. The text is planned in a fashion that makes individual details most accessible.

Seaman—The Real Triumph of Japan. By
Louis Livingston Seaman, M.D., LL.D.
Appleton. $1.50.

Major Seaman expatiates further in this volume upon the same theme exploited by him
in his former account of his experiences with
the Japanese army—the success of the Japanese officials in preventing and curing disease.
The reasons for this remarkable record are the
simple, non-irritating food of the Japanese soldier, the obedience to orders of the surgeons
invariably displayed, and the thorough preparation and constant vigilance of those in
charge of the health of the army. Major Seaman considers this a greater victory than that
won on the field of battle, and makes an
earnest plea for similar measures in the American army. The points are all well made, and
the book is deserving of more careful consideration than "From Tokio through Manchuria
with the Japanese," as it enlarges upon the
reasons for the statements made in that
readable volume.

Spargo—The Bitter Cry of the Children. By
John Spargo. Macmillan. $1.50.

The author of this rather painfully interesting
study brings many facts to show that a large
proportion of the children of the poor suffer
from actual physical hunger. The evil results
of insufficient nutrition are, he points out,
manifold. Rickets or rachitis is induced by
under-feeding in a very large number of cases.
The rickety child is an easy prey for other
diseases of all kinds and has small chance of
recovery from illness. Epilepsy and tuber-
culosis are especially likely to attack a sufferer
from rickets, either in childhood or maturity.
Not hospitals alone but prisons as well, declares Mr. Spargo, are filled with the victims
of hunger. He considers food more important
than sanitary conditions. Ignorance is, of
course, in some cases responsible for improper
feeding, but not, he thinks, so much so as
poverty. Other evils, such as unhealthful
employment, in the lives of poor children are
also discussed. It may be that there is some
exaggeration in the accounts of suffering, but
the facts seem, for the most part, to be only
too well attested.

Woods—Heredity in Royalty. By Frederick
Adams Woods, M.D. Holt. $3.00.

Dr. Woods adds an important link in the chain
of evidence in support of the theories of Dr.
Francis Galton. Dr. Galton, it will be remembered, has framed the law of heredity,
which would make each child inherit one-half
of his make-up from his parents, one-half the
remaining half from his grandparents, one-
half the remaining fourth from his great-
grandparents, and so on indefinitely. To
prove this by examples he has selected various
persons of note in the world's history. Dr.
Woods takes the royal families of Europe
and traces the influences in each scion. By
this method there can be no possibility of
arbitrary selection of favorable examples of
the heredity theory, and it is, also, easier to
learn the pedigree of royal personages than of

others. The author considers both mental
and moral power. He has ten grades of each
and each subject is put in one of these,
receiving the corresponding number; a man
or woman may be in only the fourth grade
morally, although mentally he belongs in the
fifth. These numbers enable the author to
arrive at mathematical deductions as to the
force of the heredity law. After considering
the characteristics of each family in turn, Dr.
Woods takes up the correlative study of the
results of his investigations. He finds that
"there is a very distinct correlation in royalty
between mental and moral qualities." Further, he believes that "heredity is almost the
entire cause" for both, and that environment
plays a very small part, probably none worth
considering, in producing characteristics. Dr.
Woods has made a valuable contribution to
the heredity theories; but it would be easy
to show the flaws in his system by which such
extreme conclusions as his would be weakened.

POETRY AND VERSE

Coleridge—The Poetical Works of Lord Byron.
Edited, with a Memoir, by Ernest Hartley
Coleridge. Imported by Scribner. $1.50
net.

In this compact, well-printed volume of 1120
pages we have all the poems included in
Murray's seven-volume edition of 1898-1904,
with a memoir of fifty pages, all of Byron's
own notes with a few trifling exceptions, and
copious historical and explanatory notes by
the editor. The entire work has been subjected to a fresh and thorough revision since
the appearance of the larger edition, with
special reference to orthography and punctu-
ation.

The text of this edition was collated with
the original manuscripts, so far as they were
available, and may therefore be considered
as final and authoritative. Here and there
however, we meet with readings that are
doubtful and perplexing. One of the most
notable of these is in the 97th stanza of the
second canto of "Childe Harold."

This is, we believe, the pointing of the early
editions except that they have a semicolon
at the end of the seventh line. Murray's
"revised" text of 1884, if we may trust Tozer's Oxford edition of 1885, changes this
semicolon to a mark of interrogation. Tozer
explains 6 and 7 thus; "despite weariness
(still), in the countenance, which they (Revel
and Laughter) force to wear a cheerful aspect."
On the following lines he remarks: "The construction is involved, but the meaning apparently is—'Revel and Laughter distort the
cheek so as to feign.'" Dr. W. J. Rolfe, in his
edition of 1886, joins 6 and 7 to what follows,
making "they" refer to "Smiles". He believes that this was the poet's intention, the
semicolon after "pique" being used instead
of a comma, as in repeated instances where
there are several commas indicating minor
subdivisions in the sentence. He has
"changed scores of these semicolons to commas in order to make the pointing conform
to the best usage of the present day."

(For list of books received see third page following.)

M. JEAN JAURÈS

Vol. XLVIII   **JUNE, 1906**   **No. 6**

The Lounger

M. JEAN JAURÈS, the author of "Studies in Socialism," is one of the most prominent socialists in Europe as well as one of the strongest personalities in French political life to-day. His personal organ, published in Paris, *L'Humanité*, contains an article a day signed by him, and expresses his policy in every department of life. M. Jaurès is an *intellectuel*. He graduated at the head of his class at the École Normale Supérieure, and has been twice Professor of Philosophy at Toulouse. During an interval of four years in his parliamentary career he wrote a history of the French Revolution that is said by some authorities to be based on a more careful study of original documents than any other history of the period. But it is as a political leader and orator that he is best known and most successful. He is a member of the Chamber of Deputies, and his speeches are probably the most fiery and eloquent delivered before that body. This collection of his writings was made by Miss Mildred Minturn, of this city, who is the translator of the book.

The authorized biography of that delightful artist, Mr. Walter Crane, will soon appear with the title "Fifty Years of an Artist's Life." Among its attractions will be reproductions of a number of drawings by Mr. Crane which have not heretofore been published. In the days of our youth Walter Crane, Kate Greenaway, and Ralph Caldecott added much sweetness to our lives. A new Caldecott book, a new Greenaway book, or a new Crane book did much to increase the joy of Christmas time. Now Caldecott is dead, Miss Greenaway is dead, but Crane still lives. Long may he wave!

Mr. Horace Thompson Carpenter has given me permission to publish this interesting letter concerning his recent trip to Italy:

While over in Italy with Mr. F. Marion Crawford recently working out some illustrations for one or two of this author's novels, it was my good fortune to be on more than one unusually interesting trip with this genial author. The last but not least delightful was a cruise on his schooner yacht "Alda," the transformed New York pilot boat which you will remember he navigated across the ocean himself.

At Gaeta, one of our harbor seeking points, we were ashore long enough to be whirled up a long wall-bound road behind one of those sturdy little Sardinian ponies, to that wonderful and impressive pile, the home of Cicero. Here, in a great field half-way up the mountain side, overlooking the beautiful bay and sea, surrounded by orange groves, towered the great massive, half-ruined structure. And here I snapped my little modern kodak which resulted in the accompanying photograph. It seemed very fitting that I should be able to get Mr.

Crawford and his youngest daughter, Miss Claire, just here. And particularly for this reason. Earlier in the season while in Rome, I had happily been taken by Mr. Crawford to the Colonna palace. Here I was turned loose, with free sketch book, in those beautifully frescoed halls. Vastly deep-set casement windows opened out upon the most charming of courtyards where tropical plants and trees and rare flowers surrounded a soul-inspiring fountain. And to the music of this plashing talisman (the music of falling water is the one accompaniment to which is written almost everything that comes from the pen of this author) what is likely to be one of the most interesting literary, undertakings in the world of Italian literature, was discussed and agreement entered into between the noted archæologist, Professor Tommasato—who has had charge of the wonderful Colonna archives for many years—and Mr. Crawford. An agreement which can only be hinted at here, but which practically turns into Mr. Crawford's hands unused and undreamed of material of the greatest importance in the mediæval history of Italy which is to gradually develop into a tangible historical record that will be of inestimable value. You will doubtless say I am wandering from my first subject. But the connection is here. The final consummation of the agreement of this important work was postponed until a further conference, and that to be on board the yacht "Alda." And it was at Porto D'Anzio a day or two prior to our call at Gaeta that Profesor Tommasato had boarded the "Alda," and the privileges and rights of the entire material of the Colonna archives much of which had been classified under Professor Tommasato's learned direction had been transferred to Mr. Crawford. Our dinner under the awning of the "Alda's" deck that evening served to perfection by an immaculately uniformed, well trained crew—for the splendid looking fellows of that particular crew are wonders whether as sailors or attendants—will not soon be forgotten. The jolly unending good humor of the archæologist, the charming and accomplished daughter of the author-navigator, and the author himself a host such as one may find in his own inimitable Mr. Isaacs, the soft lapping of the ripples against the side of the boat, the sweet cadence of far away notes of the returning fishermen, the time, the setting, the occasion, all made it ideal. And so I think you will understand when I say that just after this resurrecting of long buried Colonna material—buried so far as the public was concerned—and the final signing of the bond, as it were, it seemed quite fitting to find the author of "Ava Roma Immortalis," "Salve Venetia," and a wealth of literature besides, before the Tomba di Cicerone in the quietness of the Gaeta hills and recording, so far as the camera may, a moment which seemed to the writer full of significance and of more than ordinary interest. And I send you this thinking it will prove of interest to you and your CRITIC friends who, I know, are for the most part friends of Mr. Crawford.

⁂

By the way, if Boston believes that Mr. and Mrs. Ernest Fenollosa are "Sidney McCall," Boston has overshot the mark—for once. The true identity of "Sidney McCall" will, if the present plan is carried out, be revealed about next Christmas time. I have this on authority of one whose name you would recognize if I felt at liberty to mention it. The same person tells me that "The Breath of the Gods" has won much praise in the Orient, especially from members of the Japanese Parliament, who say that Hagonè is a wonderful and faithful portrayal of the old feudal daimyo. "I found this book a well-spring of joy, in contrast with the pseudo-Japanese stuff put forth of late years," writes an enthusia t from the West.

⁂

Professor Nevil Monroe Hopkins, who writes the complete novelette, "The Strange Case of Doctor North" for the May *Lippincott*, has done the world a greater service than that of amusing it with a detective story. He has invented a system for the preventing of the bursting of water-pipes by freezing. Prof. Hopkins's friends will not be recruited from the plumbing fraternity.

⁂

A novel by Mr. Richard Whiteing, "Ring in the New," is out in England. Mr. Whiteing has been engaged on the story for two years. The scene is laid mainly in London. Mr. Whiteing's best-known book is "No. 5 John Street," which attracted general attention here and in England.

⁂

The London *Academy* accuses Mr. W. S. Harwood of having coined a new word—Burbankitis—and enters a protest against his gushing tone in writing about his hero's "New Creations in Plant Life." The saying, "Save us

F. M. CRAWFORD AND DAUGHTER.

from our friends," is as true as it is old. I wonder how Mr. Burbank enjoyed reading this paragraph:

He counts no day completed in which he has not said a cheery good morning to his aged mother, now faring near the century line, looked after her with the utmost devotion during all its hours, and tenderly kissed her good night at the going down of the sun.

Has it anything to do with "New Creations in Plant Life" that the new creator gives his aged mother a "cheery good-morning" and "kisses her tenderly at the going down of the sun"? Mr. Burbank is doing great things in horticulture, but many of them have yet to be proved. Mr. Harwood has just published a book partly on Mr. Burbank called "The New Earth," the title of which explains itself. Mr. Harwood, who, by the way, has contributed a number of entertaining articles to the pages of this magazine, is the Boswell of Mr. Burbank. Everything that the latter does is to be told to the world by this writer, the horticulturist himself being the man with the hoe rather than the man with the pen.

.2%

Mme. Nasimoff, the Russian actress, who has been so much admired by the discriminating since her sojourn in this country, is studying English with a view to appearing on the American stage. Mme. Nasimoff has already made good progress, and by the beginning of the new year, if not sooner, I will venture to say that her English will be almost free of foreign accent. The manager who secures this actress as one of his stars will have reason to be congratulated. Mme. Nasimoff has not only great charm and magnetism but she is a rare artist. She is a very young woman, being still in her early twenties. I do not know a word of Russian, but I did know the plot of "The Abyss," in which she has one of her strongest parts, and I could follow the story and the action sufficiently well not to lose the meaning of an expression or a gesture. It was a wonderful performance, and not only is the manager who secures Mme. Nasimoff to be

congratulated, but the entire theatre-going public may congratulate itself upon the acquisition of this gifted young woman for our stage.

.2%

From time to time I have printed in this column some of the criticisms of school-boys and girls on the authors whom they have been reading. I find in *The Sun* a number of criticisms made by school-boys in old Greenwich village, a section of this city, which are most interesting not only for the point of view but the manner of expression:

"Once there was a Jew who lived in Venice. He was a mean, hard hearted man what never lend money without taking great interest off. Antonio went to Shylock one day and asked him for the lend of 3,000 ducats."

Another Shakespeare student lapses into biography:—

"William Shakespeare was born at Stratford-on-Avon in 1564. He received his knowledge and learnment at the free grammar school of Stratford. He has written many plays and published them in different languages. After his marriage he became a great actor in London and received 200 lbs. a week."

.2%

Mr. Frank Richardson, whose portrait is here reproduced, has written a number of books, but nothing more amusing than "The Secret Kingdom," which is really a humorous satire on contemporary novelists rather than a mere novel. England calls him one of her cleverest young novelists, and I think there can be no doubt on this subject. "He seems to find time," says *The Tattler*, "in the intervals of his strenuous life as a social butterfly and a genial clubman to write about two novels a year." The Rev. Cyrus Townsend Brady is not much more prolific than this.

.2%

Miss Ruth St. Denis, over the stage name of "Rhada," has danced herself into success. She began in vaudeville and worked up to drawing-rooms. "Society" is pleased to indorse her, and she has now gone to England where it is said that the aristocracy is waiting to throw its drawing-rooms

MR. LUTHER BURBANK
(The Plant Wizard)

MISS ST. DENIS— 'RHADA"
The Indian Dancer

open to her. Miss St. Denis has undoubtedly hit upon a novelty in the way of dancing. Not only are her poses marvellous, but her illusions are equally marvellous. In her famous "Cobra" dance, with her jewelled fingers she makes one think that the snakes are there writhing and twisting before one's eyes; but they are no more real snakes than are those that are said to have haunted the dreams of Edgar Allan Poe.

⁂

The publishers of "The Lady of the Decoration" are disturbed because the rumor has gone forth that the name of the author of the story is a household word. They tell me that while they hope that the name of "Frances Little" may become famous, and have certain reasons for believing that it will, it is not so now, for this is her first work. The letters are bona-fide and were written to a lady in the West, whose name is a household word, and who advised the writer of them to weave in a bit of plot and let her offer the book to the Century Company. This was done, and the book was quickly accepted, but it was not written by the author who offered it for publication. The book is attracting attention in London already.

⁂

Miss Jane E. Duncan, a strenuous Scotchwoman, has penetrated the wilds of Thibet, and written a description of her journeyings. Miss Duncan is a traveller and not a sportswoman. Sportswomen she says are not liked by sportsmen, and are the cause of much strong language among sportsmen in Thibet, and in the plains indignant remarks are made about globe-trotting women shooting animals that men, living all their lives in India, have never so much as seen. If they do not kill anything, they are accused of shooting wild and disturbing the game to no purpose; if they get some heads the men are furiously jealous and say the shikari has shot them, or imposed upon them in some way.

The hero of "Frank Danby's" new novel, "The Sphinx's Lawyer," has ideas of his own as to man's evening dress:

The pearls in his shirt-front were black, the buttons of his waistcoat were of the most delicate workmanship, serpenting in diamonds around blue enamel, his sleeve-links were pink pearls set à jour.

A little later on she says:

The expanse of white shirt with its be-gemmed studs, the double-breasted white waistcoat, with its jewelled buttons, accentuating his remarkable personality.

"Frank Danby" knows that this is not "correct style," or I suppose that she does, for while women are no better at describing men's dress than men are in describing the clothes that women wear, this would be a little too unconventional.

⁂

"All for the Love of a Lady," Elinor Macartney Lane's new book, is a romance of Scotland in feudal days. Its heroes are two little boys, of bellicose dispositions, but their chivalrous devotion to the heroine shows them to be true knights at heart. The tale, though considerably shorter, is said to be quite as charmingly told as the author's other great success, "Nancy Stair." Mrs. Lane has made a dramatization of the story, which will make a pretty play. She is now in North Carolina, where she has been working all the winter on a new novel.

⁂

Mrs. Kenneth-Brown, who was Miss Demetra Vaka, a Greek, has just completed a novel of Greek and Turkish life that is said to be as unusual in plot as it is in its characters. There are few persons with Mrs. Kenneth - Brown's knowledge of the inside life of Greece and Turkey, who have her command of English. Before her marriage she was a teacher of French in a fashionable New York boarding-school. Now she is living on her husband's estate in Virginia.

⁂

"Sandy from the Sierras" is the title of a new story by Mr. Richard Barry, author of "Port Arthur," which was, if I mistake not, the first volume published by the young firm of Moffat, Yard & Company. "Port Arthur" was an account of the recent great siege. The new book is a novel with the scene laid in San Francisco, where the author is now writing up the earthquake and the conditions that it has caused.

❧

I spoke some time ago of husbands and wives who are writers. Among those that I did not mention, but should have, are Mr. and Mrs. Cale Young Rice. Mrs. Rice, as is well-known, is the author of "Mrs. Wiggs," "Lovey Mary," etc. She was Miss Hegan when she wrote "Mrs. Wiggs," Mrs. Rice when she wrote "Lovey Mary." Mr. Rice is a poet. He writes dramatic verse, which has been complimented not only by poets but by actors. Mrs. Fiske finds some of it superior, poetically and dramatically, to Stephen Phillips's work; while Mr. Richard Mansfield has been greatly impressed with Mr. Rice's play, "David," and "derived a sense of personal encouragement from the evidence of so fine and lofty a product for the stage." Speaking of Mr. Mansfield, that actor has a most interesting article in the May number of the *Atlantic Monthly* on "Man and the Actor." It is the study of the meaning of an actor's life and the existing conditions of the American stage. Mr. Mansfield is as clever a writer as he is an actor. His writing is not always confined to essays. I recall with pleasure a most charming book for grown-up children called "Blown Away: a Nonsense Book."

❧

Mr. Richard Harding Davis has for a time turned his back upon the fishing port of Marion, Mass., to become a farmer in this State. The writing of plays makes it necessary for him to be nearer New York, so that he bought a farm not many miles from the rush and roar of the town; but it is far enough away to be peaceful and quiet, and yet near enough for Mr. Davis's many

friends to drop in upon him for weekends. In the group before us we have Mr. Davis, his brother, Mr. Charles Belmont Davis, Mr. Melville E. Stone, late of the firm of H. S. Stone & Company, now with the *Associated Sunday Magazines*, a newspaper syndicate supplement issued from this city, and Mr. Peter Finley Dunne, known to the world as "Mr. Dooley."

❧

Mr. Richard Harding Davis's "The Galloper" will be published in book form during the summer with some other of his plays.

❧

It is interesting news that Mr. Ripley Hitchcock has resigned his connection with Messrs. A. S. Barnes & Company to become associated with Messrs. Harper & Brothers. If Mr. Hitchcock does as well by Messrs. Harper as he has by the two other houses of which he has been an important factor, the Franklin Square firm is to be congratulated. Mr. Hitchcock not only knows how to suggest books, but he knows a good manuscript when he sees it, as was proved by his quick acceptance of "David Harum." This manuscript covered some eight hundred or a thousand forbidding pages. Though mostly typewritten, it was interlined and rewritten, and anything but attractive to a publisher's reader. Mr. Hitchcock, however, pegged away at it and induced the author to cut it down and polish it up; and the result was a fortune to every one concerned. It will be remembered that Mr. Hitchcock made the dramatization of the novel, which was played with such great success by Mr. W. H. Crane.

❧

This admirable sculptured likeness of Mr. Booker T. Washington was made for the Tuskegee School by Miss Leila Usher. Miss Usher has done an excellent piece of work. To be sure she had a good subject, but that is not everything. In another picture we see the artist at work upon another bust, in which, although the face is turned away from us, we recog-

MR. MELVILLE E. STONE   MR. C. B. DAVIS   MR. R. H. DAVIS   MR. P. F. DUNNE

THE DOOR STEP AT MR. R. H. DAVIS'S FARM, MT. KISCO, N. Y.

BUST OF MR. BOOKER T. WASHINGTON
By Miss Lelia Usher

MISS LELIA USHER

493

nize the beard of Mr. Robert Underwood Johnson, associate editor of the *Century Magazine*.

⁂

A biographical edition of Stevenson's writings, the one to which the author's widow has contributed most interesting introductions, somewhat in the manner of the biographical edition of Thackeray, will soon be published in England. One would suppose that this edition would have been published in England simultaneously with the edition published in this country by Messrs. Scribner; but this has not been the case, for it is only now that England is talking about its publication in that country. It is not, however, as though England had no edition of Stevenson. There are many of them, none more delightful to the eye than the Edinburgh Edition, of which only a limited number was published. Still another is announced with introductions by Mr. Gosse.

⁂

I read in a London paper that "the American Mr. Winston Churchill has written a play which has been successfully produced in New York. It is called 'The Title Mart,' and it is about to be issued here as a volume." This is all true except the "successfully produced." I fancy that if Mr. Churchill was interviewed on this subject he would not speak of the production as a successful one.

⁂

Those who always imagined the late Walter Pater to be a stern and severe person, much above frivolity of any kind, will be surprised when they read Mr. A. C. Benson's monograph on him in the English Men of Letters Series. Mr. Benson tells us that far from being a man of "strained and affected solemnity," Pater loved easy talk and simple laughter. Nothing amused Mr. Pater more than the Gilbert and Sullivan operas, and he is said to have laughed till his sides ached over "Ruddigore," and, later, Mr. Pinero's "Magistrate."

The London publishers' advertisements are big with the announcements of American books. Among those that are attracting most attention on the other side of the water are "Lady Baltimore" and Mrs. Burton Harrison's "Latter-Day Sweethearts." It is not only American fiction that England is enjoying, for I notice an announcement of sets of Emerson's Essays by two publishers, and a volume of Mr. Bliss Carman's Poems, together with one of Mr. Charles G. D. Roberts's out-of-door books. But Mr. Roberts and Mr. Carman are only half American. They are, if I am rightly informed, Canadians by birth and education.

⁂

The interesting announcement is made that Swinburne's "Atalanta in Calydon" is to be performed upon the stage in London during the present month. There is a good deal that is dramatic in Swinburne's writings, and I have often wondered that some of them have not been adapted for stage purposes. We have had Browning and Tennyson and Longfellow on the stage, but never Swinburne, as far as I know.

⁂

Miss Agnes C. Laut, the author of "Lords of the North" and several other exciting stories of the northwest, has just returned from England, where she has made some very remarkable discoveries along her line of research. It would not be fair for me to say just what these discoveries are, but I betray no confidence in saying that she has found chests full of manuscripts that are priceless for her purposes. Miss Laut expects to go back to this new historical gold mine in the course of a few weeks. The results of the more important of her researches will be made known through the pages of *Harper's Magazine*.

⁂

It is announced that "A Magdalen's Husband," by Mr. Vincent Brown, will soon be seen on the stage with

MISS ELLEN TERRY
Whose fifty years on the stage has just been celebrated
with great enthusiasm in England
From her latest photograph

MR. VINCENT BROWN

Mrs. Leslie Carter as the Magdalen. The author and Mr. Belasco are making the play, I understand. A new novel by Mr. Brown is just issued. It is called "The Sacred Cup," and there is undoubtedly a play in this story also. It is, however, a man's part. Now that Mr. Brown has a taste of the excitement and profit of play-writing, he will probably adapt all his stories for the stage. He is fortunate if he can do it himself. There are not many authors who can write stories and plays as well. Mr. Richard Harding Davis is one of the exceptions to the rule.

Miss May Sinclair, author of the "Divine Fire," says that she thinks in the country and works in the city. Before she began to write novels, nine years ago, Miss Sinclair wrote verse and philosophic criticisms. She is a student of the Greek classics, and of Elizabethan literature, with fiction for a pastime. Her favorite novelists are Balzac, Meredith Turguéneff, Thackeray, Henry James and George Gissing.

⁂

An édition de luxe of that rarely fascinating book, the Autobiography of

Benvenuto Cellini, is published by L. C. Page & Co. Cellini was one of the foremost artists of his day, winning equal success as a goldsmith, an engraver, and a sculptor. Because of a duelling affair early in his life, he was obliged to fly from Florence to Rome, where he did much work for Pope Clement VI. Later he went to Paris and executed several commissions for Francis I. Catherine de Medicis was also one of his patrons. His autobiography is one of the frankest of books, as his life was one of the busiest and the gayest.

When Mr. Andrew Carnegie was on his recent tour in Ohio and Canada, gathering up several additional doctorates and making some excellent speeches, he spent a day at Kenyon College, of which he promptly became "the youngest alumnus." A feature of the occasion at Kenyon was the singing of the undergraduates at the banquet. Among other impromptu songs in honor of their guest there was sung, with great effect,

A BALLAD OF ANDREW

When Andrew was a little lad
He had no books to read,
And so he built a library
His intellect to feed.
Whene'er he saw a useful book
Says he, " I will put that in ";
And German, French, and Scots he took
But nary Greek nor Latin.

So diligent a lad, I fear,
Will not be seen again ;
He labored fourteen hours a day,
And read the other ten.
But when his money all was spent,
Says he, " So poor I feel,

There 's nothing left for me to do
But make a little steel."

Then everybody bought his steel
And paid him such a price
That Andrew was a millionaire
In just about a trice.
But now he felt a fearful fear
That rose to such a pitch
It haunted him by day and night—
The fear of dying rich.

He did not want the charge to stand
On the eternal docket
That A. Carnegie had expired
With money in his pocket.
Says he, " To keep from such a fate
I 'll alter my char–ac–ter :
I 'll leave off making steel, and be
Henceforth a benefactor."

In theologic zeal he gave
An organ to a church,
And then endowed an " Institute
Of Biblical Research."
He saw that college profs die poor
In spite of their endeavor ;
He filled their pockets up with cash
And now they 'll live forever.

He saw that we Americans
In courage are but zeros ;
He spent ten million dollars to
Transform us into heroes.
He saw we could n't spell. Says he
While tears his eyes did fill,
" Spell just as badly as you please,
And I will pay the bill."

What things are lovely, true, and pure,
Of good report and right,
On these our Andrew thinks, and these
He helps with all his might.
So here 's to Andrew Carnegie,
And when he 's called above,
He may go poor in pocket, but
He will go rich in love.

The Illustrations that Do Not Illustrate

More than once THE LOUNGER has called attention to illustrations in novels that do not illustrate. Within a few days of each other I have received three communications on the subject. Here is the first:

It is a fact patent to all that artists in general and particular have a supreme disregard for the text in the matter which they illustrate. I believe this fact has been touched upon at various times, but it seems to me that writers and publishers should rise *en masse*, and demand adherence to the text. A departure from it is careless, inartistic, and often ludicrous. Also, it is inexcusable—at least to one of the laity. I know that artists are privileged beings, that they are supposed to possess attributes which would blast a common mortal, and move in an atmosphere of rarefied ether and dreamy eyes : that they are often worshipped by women and looked at askance by men. And yet, beneath all their glamour and highmightiness, they are nothing but poor, puny mortals like the rest of us. They eat, and sleep, and wear clothes, and get sick, and have the doctor. Then why should they be given the right of way above their fellow artisans who labor with letters and words? Let a poor author use an adjective incorrectly, or dare to change the color of his heroine's eyes (and we all know there are eyes which *do* change color) and such a torrent of ridicule, opprobrium, and irony will flow upon his defenceless head that he will almost vow never to put pen to paper again. But in this very book where such a slip as we have mentioned may inadvertently creep in, we behold some illustrations, exquisitely done, and reproduced with commendable faithfulness, but entirely inconsistent with the story which they aim to picture. We look upon the drawing as a work of art purely, and admire its conception, its execution, its graceful and harmonious lines. But when we glance at the words beneath the picture and read "She lowered her parasol and turned towards him haughtily," then raise our eyes a few inches and gaze upon a vision of feminine loveliness with a knight of society kneeling humbly at her feet tying her boot—then we are apt to swear softly (if we be men) and call the artist an ugly name.

There is sufficient provocation. If it is carelessness, there is no excuse, for there can be no compromise between art of any kind and slip-shod methods. If it is callous indifference to the universal fitness of things—a presumptuous reliance upon the faulty prerogative assumed by the profession, there is still no excuse. The practice should be discouraged and discountenanced. For instead of making a beautiful whole from the conjunction of pen and brush, a result which we have a perfect right to expect, behold! we have two separate and distinct things well done in themselves, but ruthlessly joined together without regard to the niceties of detail which is the sign manual and hall-mark of all greatness.

Whatever the cause, for mercy's sake let it be removed! It would be entirely superfluous for me to cite examples to illustrate my point. Simply turn to the book or magazine you were reading last night, and you will in all probability find that your hero is wearing a straw hat instead of a derby ; that your heroine is in a carriage when she should be on horseback, and that the wrecked automobile has bumped into a tree instead of a stone wall. And in the corner at the foot of the picture you 'll find a name you can't make out, but it may represent some big artist.

We want pictures to our stories and books ; you, and I, and almost everybody. I regret to add that no doubt there are some who don't care a snap whether the girl of the plot is dancing when the author humbly suggested that she was boating, or not. In the furious rush of this good day of grace there are some who don't have time to look closely. They fling a quick glance at the picture and plunge again into the story. But there are others of us who are lazy, and who like for things to be rational and right. Especially when it is just as easy for the facile brush to produce a golfing costume as it is an evening one. So we of the cult of the leather chair wonder where on earth the man who made that picture got his authority for an attitude or an item of dress of which the innocent writer of the tale never dreamed. We don't know ; I warrant the author don't ; I suppose the artist would stare at you for an upstart if you were to ask him.

Let 's have a reformation. Let the writers who write and the publishers who publish insist that the artist be consistent with the material entrusted to him to picture—and he will! That 's where his living comes from.

EDWIN CARLILE LITSEY.

Here is the second. It comes from San Francisco:

The ineptitudes of so called illustrations have become so common that every one expects them—even in the " best sellers." But it seems to a more or less constant reader of these magazines that the portrait picture by Mr. Albert Sterner in the January *Century* of Mme. de Pastourelles in Mrs. Ward 's story is the most flagrant and irritating of any.

One of the most intelligent and capable of living novelists spends almost a page of delightful description of the portrait—superbly dressed in marvellous white velvet and sables—of a complex and exquisite woman. The painter and his model are alone in his studio with the exception of a mild duenna knitting in a corner. And the illustrator gives us simply the Kitty of Mrs. Ward's last story a trifle larger and longer, with the same pose and a gown more suitable for one's room than the creation in which Mrs. Ward tells us the lady was dressed. He places somebody else in the picture though the text plainly tells us that the two men came in after the sitting was over.

If illustrations in the best magazines are to be no better than the Sunday supplements—and by heaven they are often much worse—such carelessness as this might pass along with so much other of the kind. But here was an opportunity to do a really splendid bit of work. The story deals with painting and painters and here was a chance to create a real portrait such as it was supposed the artist of the story had done—something that made all his critics sit up and wonder who this country man was that could paint like that. If your gentle readers will compare the text and the picture they will become at once as ungentle as the undersigned and we may bye and bye be able to demand better things—even of Mr. Sterner.

DOROTHEA MOORE.

The third comes in the form of verse:

Without doubt, she was slender and queenly—
    That's here, in plain print—and the white
Flower-face that looked down, so serenely,
    When the prince told his passion, that night.
The artist's conception should fit, like—
    (Where's the cut? Frontispiece—and unsigned)
Oh, dear! This is not the least bit like
    I'd pictured her out in my mind.

And the hero (a man with a gnawing
    Remorse for—oh, ages!—of sin)
Here he looms, in a misty wash-drawing—
    Smooth-shaved and (of course) with cleft chin.
He'd a *beard* (from the first I divined this)
    And some years, any body could see,
But the fatuous dolt who designed this
    Libel "opp. page 53."

Her mother—a pleasant old lady—
    Shows up here like a girl of eighteen;
And the woman whose past was so shady
    Looks as some youthful saint might, I ween;
The uncle is limned, tall, and courtly,
    When he should have been made short and fat.

(The text? Well, it says he was "portly")
    —Anyway, he did *not* look like *that.*

Here's the hero again—with eye-glasses;
    No, I'm wrong—that's his father; and this
Is a mountainous matron, who passes
    (In half-tone) for the pert little Miss.
I would n't, for one, be caught trusting
    This rector (vignette) with a pin,
While the villain (it's simply disgusting)
    Is another young boy with a chin.

I declare, such obtuseness seems wilful—
    And yet, I suppose, it can't be.
What a pity, a pencil so skilful
    Should utterly lack sympathy!
Who's the writer? Let's see ..." Trite Temptations
    By Dane Harding." (Old English—red ink)
And—what's this? " *With Sixteen Illustrations
    By the Author.*"...Well, what—do—you—think!

FRANK PRESTON SMART.

On the top of all this comes the publishers' side of the story in the form of a printed note from Messrs. Harper:

The recent exhibition in New York of Albert Sterner's drawings, including the originals for "The Marriage of William Ashe" serves to call to mind some of the obstacles that may confront an artist. When Mr. Sterner undertook the commission to illustrate Mrs. Ward's novel, he was living in Münich, where he found great difficulty in securing good English models. A long and tiresome search revealed one man who consented to pose for a short time. Mr. Sterner thus obtained one drawing of "William Ashe," and then had a life-size plaster bust of the man made, which he used as model for the remainder of the series. Then rows upon rows of stout and rosy German maidens were passed in review before the artist in the vain hope of discovering a suitable original for the sprightly "Lady Kitty"; but at last Mr. Sterner was forced to betake himself to London to find the slender girl with the oval face and dark eyes now familiar to us as "Lady Kitty." For a time Mr. Sterner occupied Mrs. Ward's beautiful country house, in daily consultation with the author, discussing, altering, and amending; but his endeavor is more than justified by the result, for his illustrations for the novel really illustrate a quality in pictorial work that is, unfortunately, very rare.

Mr. Sterner's pictures are so good, so much more than mere illustrations why should one care whether they illustrate or not!

The Minor Crimes*

By MRS. JOHN LANE

IT has always seemed to me that it is not the great scoundrels who make the world so very annoying and unsafe, but, rather, the well-meaning but dangerous criminals of the minor crimes, some of the worst of whom are probably lurking in the very bosom of one's otherwise blameless family. Sometimes I actually think that a good many gentlemen languishing in penitentiaries and expiating a single crime are not half so objectionable as those worthy and respected citizens who can look a policeman in the eye without trembling, and yet who commit those awful crimes for which an innocent and unsuspecting criminal code has, in its guilelessness, decreed no punishment.

An umbrella or a cane have within them potentialities for evil which are perfectly appalling. Many a worthy gentleman who goes to church on Sundays accompanied by his umbrella, and offers up a silent prayer into the lining of his hat as he stands at the head of his pew, is really a menace to the public, for as he files out, after having just requested to have his sins forgiven him, he is more likely than not to carry that umbrella across his shoulder, or high under his arm, where the point endangers the eyesight of his fellow-man; or he drags it in such a way that unwary sinners trip over it and make remarks that are distinctly out of place in the sanctuary.

Yes, umbrellas and canes are among the most dangerous of modern weapons. More harm is done by umbrellas poking and maiming mankind than by the deadliest ammunition known in warfare. In view of this, one would like to suggest modestly to the War Office that a regiment equipped with umbrellas to be hoisted in the midst of an unsuspecting enemy, would do untold damage. Also regiments armed with sticks carried over the shoulder and playfully twiddled, would cause an amount of destruction compared to which a Maxim. gun, no matter how lively, but laboring under the disadvantage of being miles off, wouldn't be in it. Even in private life there is nothing so destructive as an umbrella, especially in the irresponsible grasp of a woman. The umbrella seems to be endowed with a sentient existence all its own, and its gambols, when not fatal, are of a most painful playfulness. Really, the owners of some umbrellas deserve a long sentence with hard labor much more than many an erring man whose crime has been possibly more ostentatious but less subtle.

Another very dangerous instrument for the annihilation of the human race is the fruit peel irresponsible citizens of all ages and classes scatter over the pavement. I don't see my way to utilize this danger in warfare—though that may be trustfully left to our warlords,—but one can study samples of the fatal effects when a bit of peel—the kind of fruit is really immaterial—invites the unwary to sit upon the pavement with appalling suddenness, upon which the earth is strewn with miscellaneous property characteristic of the unwary, such as muffs, sticks, umbrellas, bowler hats, the daily paper, that last sweet ballad "Let me kiss him for his mother," a pair of spectacles, a batch of laundry done up to look like a brief, and two kippers that emerge bashfully out of a brown-paper parcel. What martyr to a bit of peel has not felt the immortal stars detached from heaven to find a temporary resting-place in his head! I consider an infant with an orange, with all that means of danger, as more menacing to the public peace than a turmoil of mistaken but well-meaning anarchists in Trafalgar Square, who merely talk about bombs. Talk about bombs! Why, what bomb is so dangerous as the irresponsible peel of an orange!

Another terrible instrument of the

* Copyright in the United States, 1906, by ANNIE E. LANE.

minor crimes is music. Music is an awful weapon in the hands of minor criminals next-door, or in flats. I once lived near a villain who tried to play the French horn; a French horn is a brass instrument with an independent will of its own. You blow in one thing, and the chances are that it will come out something quite different. For six months he practised playing "She never told her love" from 9.30 P. M. until midnight. If she had only lived up to it! Finally the cruel instrument moved; but now the very sight of a French horn in an orchestra makes me quail! A piano is another frightful instrument of torture. I always feel rather sorry for the Inquisition that it missed this magnificent opportunity for directing a fearful weapon against the defenceless and the oppressed. The most hardened heretic, after having the C major scale with variations, and other five-finger exercises decorated with false notes, drummed into his ears by an innocent child next-door for days and nights, will be glad and happy to confess to anything, if only to escape with a remnant of reason. If the Inquisition could only have known!

Pianos in hotel parlors are another scourge. The medium of torture is usually a travelling infant plumped before the keys to keep it quiet while "Mother" refreshes her intellect with fashion papers six months old. Or an elderly maiden lady wanders in, who claws mid-Victorian melodies out of the key-board with stiff and feeble fingers. Then there are always one or two girls in the latest thing in hair-fluffs, who bolt in and make a bee-line for the piano and bang away at the latest Gaiety tunes till the windows rattle, and an elderly man in a corner, who is taking a nap behind the illustrated paper, rises in wrath and ostentatiously scowls his way out. Yes, music is the cruelest of the fine arts, and ought to be chained and padlocked and not turned loose on a long-suffering public under pain of instant death.

Connected with music there is another dangerous criminal, and that is the amateur musical critic. He is always armed with the score, and he labors under the delusion that the audience is stone-deaf. He *is* a trial to the sufferers about him! Glare at him with double-distilled venom and he remains quite unmoved. He is always accompanied by a kindred soul with long hair that has an inward curl, and he wears the necktie of genius, which is soft. There is nothing I so loathe as a score! The pages are always turned so that the rattle comes in with the *pianissimo,* just when the conductor stands on the tips of his toes and broods over the orchestra as if ready for flight.

The amateur critic despises people who cannot follow a score, and sometimes he commits murder with his eye if some innocent victim ventures to whisper. But he does not hesitate to talk pretty loud himself. But he has the divine right because he has the score. At ardent climaxes he kindly hums the melody, and when the orchestra has perpetrated the last crash, he bursts into perfect ecstasies of abuse, because there 's no sense in praising anything; for that only shows you don't know.

All critics are very awful people, because one never knows when one's own turn may come; but on studying the theatrical critic one observes that he, too, labors under the fond delusion that the audience is deaf, or if it is n't deaf, that it has come to hear a running commentary on the play and the players, who are referred to by their private names. So it is a little discouraging when one has paid for one's seat, and one's soul is bathed in illusion, to hear Polydorus the brave, who is on the point of rescuing the Christian martyr in white cashmere from the lions in the arena, referred to as Podkins; Podkins being his name in private life. Nor is it convincing to have a *sotto-voce* synopsis of the Christian martyr's rather giddy private life as an accompaniment to her sufferings on the stage. I cannot help thinking that if the critics had to pay for their seats as we humble sufferers do, they would approach the Drama with more respect.

Did you ever sit behind the kind man who has taken a deaf friend to the theatre and obligingly repeats titbits of the speeches to him as well as a running description of the plot? It is particularly discouraging for the surrounding sufferers when the deaf gentleman, who has but a vague idea of the story, mistakes the tragedy for a comedy!

Among others there are what may be called the silent crimes. Reading-rooms at Clubs are the scenes of some of the most awful of these. What is it in newspapers that exercises such an unholy effect on otherwise blameless and honest gentlemen who, away from their baleful influence, could not be induced to possess themselves dishonestly of a penny? But study them in the Club reading-room and see them make a dive for all the newspapers within reach! Trembling with eagerness and cupidity, they collect them in a mountainous pile—leaving out only one, always the most popular of the illustrated—and upon these they sit; whereupon, with the illustrated one as a screen, they sleep the sleep of the unjust, which in this erring world is always very peaceful and sound. Brother clubmen venture within the radius of their snores, and glare, but it is the unwritten etiquette of Clubs that what you sit on becomes yours by a kind of divine right. No, newspapers are not constructed only for a diffusion of knowledge.

Perhaps of the entire human anatomy nothing is more admirably adapted for crime than elbows. It is amazing the execution that can be done by a judicious use of these usually sharp instruments of destruction. They are conceded to be an essentially feminine weapon: and yet I have seen them used with great success by men. I, myself, have had the honor to come in violent contact with the elbows of a great dignitary of the Church, when we were both making for the same railway carriage of a special train—the object being a garden party. I always acknowledge the divine supremacy of man, and I did so again as he plunged victoriously into the only vacant seat and gave me, in parting—as I stood lost on the platform—the heavenly benediction of his smile.

The prevailing characteristic of the age is undoubtedly bashfulness. Who has not seen a weak but determined woman triumphantly hold a bashful humanity at bay while she kept three vacant seats in a crowded hall for belated friends? Nobody ventures to take those empty chairs she has appropriated by a right sacred to herself. The world passes furiously but shyly by, and leaves the gentle pirate triumphant.

Then, who has not met that travelling criminal, also the foe of the bashful, who, armed with kit-bags, hold-alls, dressing-case, shawl straps, and those brown-paper parcels so characteristic of the British traveller, plumps them in three of the corners of the only empty railway carriage of a popular train, and himself into the fourth, and so buried behind the genial shelter of a newspaper, permits other harassed travellers to look wildly in, but, on being confronted by seats so obviously reserved, tear madly on, vanquished though unconvinced. The experienced traveller behind his paper has then the joy of seeing them race up and down the platform in a flight of frenzy, or cling to the harassed guard, who has a shilling in his pocket for which he could not conscientiously account to the railway company.

Then, too, some of the most dangerous weapons for the perpetration of the minor crimes are children. I remember with terror a small boy of eight whose laudable ambition in life was, of course, to be a pirate.

But to become a pirate a pistol is indispensable, and so his fond parents procured for him a revolver. I was visiting at their country place when it arrived, in company with a stock of cartridges. The next morning the dear child came down to breakfast with the weapon of destruction loaded to the muzzle and hanging from his neck by a string. I nearly fainted over my bacon and eggs.

"He'll kill somebody, sure," I prophesied, "and I won't stay here a moment if he is going to wear that dreadful thing as a necklace."

So, after much coaxing from his

proud father, the young pirate was persuaded to temporarily divest himself of his weapon and to lay it on the table beside his porridge. He bolted his breakfast and flew off with the war-whoop of an Indian chief, and made the landscape so unsafe with his am-munition that I took the earliest afternoon train back to my quiet home.

"You are such an old maid," my friend said scornfully as we parted, "no wonder children don't appeal to you." "It isn't that, dear girl," I said, conscious of a want of heroism, "but I should be mortified to death to be killed by a little boy."

In this connection I cannot overlook the terrible danger, also, of unloaded weapons. It is always the unloaded weapon which, pointed playfully at you, immediately blows your head off. Not the other person's, but yours. I never can reconcile myself to the result. But retribution is a funny thing, and I find it is usually meted out to the in-nocent. One would like to advocate the use of unloaded weapons in warfare. The effect would be so deadly.

To return to the irresponsible young as destroyers. Have you ever had a small child of inquiring mind come to spend the day, in company of a dot-ing mother who is so old a friend that she asks the price of everything, and feels quite at home? After some study I have come to the conclusion that the direct way to a child's brain is *via* his tongue. At any rate, before that dear child left for home he had licked every-thing in my possession. What he couldn't get into his mouth he sampled. I have a sacred collection of Old Eng-lish glass which stands about on things, and I always dust it myself for fear, but before the child had left he had licked the whole collection, and when I feebly remonstrated my friend said I was selfish. And when he smashed my pet Jacobite glass—the gem of the whole and worth pounds—she was quite indifferent, and said she knew I had picked it up outside a rag-shop for sixpence, and she'd much rather give me a shilling for it than have me frighten the little innocent by looking so cross.

Another sinister weapon most dan-gerous to society is a door. A heavy door slammed with an accelerated impetus can do any amount of damage to the innocent coming behind. Every door has its own private and pet dan-ger, but to get the best results open it as far as it will go, don't look back, and just let it slam for all it is worth. The result is always successful, for you are sure to hit somebody. Why, the other day a light-hearted slammer broke an innocent nose that was fol-lowing on behind. One is conscious of a want of discrimination in the decrees of fate, or it wouldn't have been that blameless nose that was so sacrificed. Swearing is a great safety-valve for the passions, and it is less reprehensible than murder, though there are occasions when a little judicious murder might really be overlooked.

Some of the most terrible of the silent crimes are committed by the Casual. The criminal proclivities of the Casual are amazing, and what makes it all the worse is that the Cas-ual are usually so very amiable; but that is probably due to their leaving all the unpleasant emotions to others. Still, one of their engaging peculiarities is that they do hate having anybody else casual to them. On the same principle, probably, that one can con-template the sufferings of one's friends with great fortitude, though one has a distinct aversion to suffering oneself. It is also interesting to note that the Casual are called by different names according to the society in which they move. In the lowest class, where peo-ple still show their feelings, they are called rude, but as they ascend in the social scale they are not called rude, but just casual, which is really the same thing only it sounds more refined.

Of course, it isn't the great who are casual, but the imitation great. The Casual are always unpunctual. When a man begins to feel his greatness sprout, he realizes that it is due to his dignity always to come late; it's the first step, and it shows that he is get-ting on. The next step—by this time he feels that he has arrived and that he is Great,—he forgets to come at all. Some of the Casual have made the crime of coming late a fine art. To time their belated and longed-for presence so to arrive, as it were, at the boiling point, is indeed a great and fine art. To arrive at the dramatic moment at a dinner-party when, in her relief, the hostess greets you with an exaggerated effusiveness, and so gives your arrival an importance which it would never have had had you come in time, is a Social Triumph.

Punctuality is an unamiable virtue and very plebeian in every one but a king. It is always the punctual who lose their tempers waiting for the unpunctual, and to lose your temper is the thin end of the wedge for the perpetration of the worst crimes. I suppose the angels are always unpunctual, or they would n't be so sweet-tempered. I don't believe the punctual are ever destined to be angels, for already on earth they get so soured. So one cannot help thinking that Heaven must be a rather unpunctual place.

It is the Casual who borrow your books and forget to return them. A friend of mine bought a stray volume at Sotheby's to replace one that had disappeared years before out of a priceless set, and when he opened it his own book-plate stared him cheerfully in the face, and the criminal had gone to that bourne where he was safe even from the wrath of a collector. Possibly he was only casual, but the result was the same.

Books seem to exercise a wicked influence on human beings. Besides the books that are borrowed and never returned, there are those poor victims that leave your shelves so upright and neat, and they return with broken backs and rings on their covers and dog-ears on the corners of their melancholy pages, and here and there a hardened drop of candle-grease to suggest midnight vigils. Much better never to see them again than to see them in such a pitiable plight.

Among other silent victims to the minor crimes is the poor and humble author. Not only do his immortal works not circulate with that vivacity

which he could wish, but well-meaning friends try to borrow his last book from him, so as to save swelling the lordly revenues of the circulating library by tuppence. If the dear, kind world could only be made to comprehend that even an author cannot live on laurels only!

Then there are those benevolent people who, to encourage the author, ask the humble man to give them his dear little book autographed. Even the meekest of authors sometimes wonders in perplexity "Why?" Do we, when we are so lucky as to know a brewer, ask him as a compliment to himself to send us a barrel of beer to remind us of him? When we circulate in society and meet a distinguished tailor, do we beg him to present us with a new suit of clothes made invaluable by his autograph? Do we ask a railway director, at whose house we may happen to dine, to send us a free pass over his roads? Not usually. What would these prosperous gentlemen say to the mere suggestion? But the poor author is always the uncomplaining victim of an inexpensive patronage, and really he can afford it less than most!

Another weapon of destruction essentially feminine but none the less deadly because of that, is the hat-pin. It is probably the invention of some misanthrope aching to exterminate the human race. It is the modern dagger, and has infinite possibilities in the way of low-down tragedy eminently suitable for police courts when not for the higher social circles. Considering its death-dealing qualities, it is a source of real dramatic interest to see the feminine hat bristle with half a dozen of these terrible weapons, preferably with their cruel points protruding inches beyond the hat, and yet to realize that, up to the present, there has been no legislation against these innocent criminals. What would we say if our fathers and husbands carried about in their respectable pockets six-shooters loaded to the hilt? Now, is not a hat-pin as dangerous to society as a loaded revolver? A girl, no matter how pretty, who bristles with the points of obtrusive hat-pins is a menace to the public welfare and should be legislated against, like mobs and invasions.

Society simply bristles with criminals. Even dinners, usually threatening only to the digestion, have been turned into ruthless weapons for the destruction of the Shy. The agony of a bashful man who is called upon unexpectedly by an easy and fluent chairman to answer to a toast, is something which mere words cannot describe. The terror which ties his knees into double bow-knots, and makes of his voice something which either hits the roof of his head or rises out of the soles of his boots, is an anguish to which no one can do justice. The sufferer is probably not a drivelling idiot in private life, but nobody would suppose so to judge by the few remarks he pumps out of his parched throat and emits in instalments by the aid of a tongue like red-hot and very heavy lead. His jaws creak with an awful stiffness, as if they were carved out of pasteboard; he glares frantically about and sees nothing, and does awful things with his table-napkin, and finally, having given up all earthly hope, he plumps wildly down and no amount of champagne can make him forgive the genial man who has encouraged him to make such an ass of himself. Yes, society is full of agonies as well as crimes.

There is one criminal in society one would dearly like to see exterminated, and that is the beast who, having, by some contemptible and underhand method, become acquainted with your best after-dinner stories, accompanies your recital—and you are in capital form—with an ingratiating grin like a hyena, and a benevolent and confirmatory nodding of his head, and just as you have nearly reached your climax, and the guests are hanging spell-bound on your words and are rewarding you with anticipatory chuckles, this beast bursts out with your point just five seconds before you can reach the winning post. This is another instance when a little manslaughter should be excused.

On the other hand, there is that innocent sufferer, the man who forgets his point. Society is full of people who would be perfectly delightful if they could only remember what they meant to say. If any enterprising publisher would collect the speeches that are never made, and the anecdotes that have everything but a point, as well as the jokes that are forgotten, he would produce volumes of thrilling interest. The other night at a dinner-party we were favored by a most delightful anecdote about the fair Melusine, who, as everybody knows, was half a woman and half a serpent. The excellent gentleman who was entertaining us with the story got, however, slightly mixed as to the particular beast into which the fair Melusine was partly turned. His point was intended to be that the husband of the fair Melusine was singularly fortunate because his wife was a serpent only half the time. At which climax he could confidently reckon on frantic hilarity both from the married men as well as the more innocent bachelors. Unfortunately, in the excitement of recital, he couldn't think of the animal required for the point. Nothing would come to his agitated consciousness but a whale. So, when he said with a smile, which grew more uncertain as he approached his climax, that the husband of the fair Melusine was singularly lucky as his wife was a whale only half the time, even the most charitable of diners-out looked perplexed and vainly tried to see the joke, and rewarded him with perfunctory smiles that were pathetic. The man sent me the point on a post-card the very next morning.

There is no end to dinner crimes. The other evening I was at a great banquet, for which a very impressive personage, all hung with stars and things, had been captured as ornamental chairman. Behind his noble back were draped the flags of those two great nations that have two independent pieces of poetry and one tune. The toast-master hovered anxiously over the eminent chairman, and as I looked into the chairman's red face, decorated with mid-Victorian whiskers,

I had a dreadful suspicion that he knew but vaguely why he was there. Like the immortal brook, the speeches proceeded to flow on forever. Finally, a busy little committee-man darted up to the noble chairman and whispered frantically into his ear, and I felt at once, from the jerks of his head, that he referred to a lonely man, one remove from the chairman, who bore on his features the stamp of America as well as an only partly concealed dissatisfaction. The committee-man retired, and the toast-master in stentorian accents cried, "Silence for your noble chairman!" Whereupon the noble chairman rose to those feet his ancestors had so cruelly endowed with gout, and vouchsafed us his best British eloquence.

As I listened I happened, accidentally, to look at the lonely gentleman with the dissatisfied expression, and I observed samples of different emotions chasing across his expressive features.   .

"Ladies and gentlemen," said the noble chairman after a great deal of eloquence that got lost behind his shirt collar, "I have the gratification of introducing to you one of the most distinguished citizens of the great Republic, a man famous in her councils, and even more famous in the still greater republic of letters; a man whose name is a household word, ladies and gentlemen, Major-General Jabez B. Tompkins of America."

Here, as the noble chairman looked benevolently across at the dissatisfied stranger, the stranger met his glance with unconcealed malevolence.

"Hopkins!" he hissed across at the noble chairman. "My name is Hopkins!"   .

For a moment the chairman was staggered, but then he came gallantly to his own rescue.

"The fact is, ladies and gentlemen, the name that is a—a—in fact, a household word is—is—in fact, is Hopkins." Whereupon he sat down rapidly amid thunders of applause.

Yes, it is the minor crimes that make the world so dangerous and unsafe and life so trying. It would be so comforting if Parliament would legislate against them! Only the result would be that most of the inhabitants of this erring world would be in penitentiaries, which might be somewhat of a drawback. Still, it would be nice if one could at least chop off the heads of a few of these genial criminals, if only as an example.

The world is alarmingly full of well-intentioned criminals who are all the more dangerous because there are no laws to protect one against them. Parliament really ought to do something for us, only the trouble is that probably Parliament itself consists entirely of minor criminals.

Still, it does make laws such as they are, and if it would only make it a penal offence to be casual, to slam doors, to forget to come, to tell the other man's best story, and heaps of other crimes, the result would be quite as beneficial and important as its penal laws for the major crimes. A gentleman who commits a murder knows what will happen to him if he is ever caught, and so he discreetly avoids society and usually doesn't do it again. But the gentleman who keeps your dinner waiting for half an hour is not punished—no one arrests him, no one chops off his head—so he repeats his offence over and over again, and society has no earthly redress. In fact, he is a bold, bad character whom we constantly invite in spite of his crimes, and his motto of conduct is "Don't care a d—n."

If Parliament would only come to the rescue and consider the awful importance of the minor crimes, what a beneficent effect it would have on the temper of the world!

And, indeed, after a serious study of life, one comes to the conclusion that there are really no minor crimes, but that all, even the little bits of ones, are major, dreadfully major—though possibly in disguise.

Telephones and Letter=Writing

By ANDREW LANG

"I HAD her over the phone this morning." These words, applied by one fair lady to another, in an American novel, conveyed no meaning to my mind. How do you have a person over a phone? "Over the coals" is an old expression, of unknown origin, but of a certain significance. Reading on in the American novel, I gathered, from the context, that to have a person over a phone meant to converse with him or her through a telephone.

This is a mechanical advantage of our age which I have never employed. I tried it once. I tried, being at the station of Clovenford, on the Tweed, to talk to somebody at Galashiels, a distance of four or five miles. But I could not hear a word that he said, and am therefore unable to be certain as to whether he heard a word that I said. Perhaps the *phone* may not have been *tele* enough, and did not carry the distance. I do not know what the range of a telephone is, nor whether you can have a person over a phone by Marconi's wireless system. Telephones are only known to me in the kind of novels which a man reads in bed, hoping that they will send him to sleep. In one romance of this sort, "The Crimson Blind," a good deal of the action and still more of the conversation are transacted by aid of the telephone. The characters are always at it, busy in unmasking a terrible villain, and they find that the instrument works satisfactorily and is quite safe. This is not always so; in another novel, the hero, who is foreman of a jury in a murder case, thinks that he is discussing the mystery with the girl of his heart, far away (this was a long-range telephone), but he is really conversing with another lady, who, as far as I have read the story, seems likely to be detected as the First or Second Murderess. (On research, she was not; the murderer was the Counsel for the Defence.) Such are the inconveniences and perils of telephones, which ought to be noted by the foremen of juries. Is

it not possible to "tap" the wires of a telephone (if they have wires), or otherwise to overhear what is being said? Lothian Dodd, in "The Wrecker," did hear what the wicked attorney was saying, at his end, which had a great effect on the plot.

The telephone, if audible to others than the beloved object, is quite as unsafe as love letters, which you can compose with caution, keeping office copies, like a Scotsman known in story. But when conversing through a telephone, and holding amorous discourse, with intentions perhaps honorable, but certainly vague, how are you to know that the lady's solicitor is not listening and making a note of it, at the farther end? Conspirators ought to be chary of using the telephone, cyphered letters are much safer, at least if Government has not the key to the cypher, which it has, in fact, usually purchased from one of the daring sons of freedom concerned in the plot.

Perhaps my notions of the perils connected with the telephone are inaccurate. If they were so great as they appear, the phone would not be the substitute for pen and ink, and would not be destroying the art of letter-writing, which it is doing, as I am credibly informed. Let us rejoice that the thing was not discovered sooner! If Horace Walpole could have chatted with Horace Mann, in Florence, by telephone; or Madame de Sévigné with her daughter; or Thackeray with Mrs. Brookfield; or Mr. Stevenson, from Samoa, with Mr. Gosse and others, our literature would be the poorer. It is true that we should also be spared the painfully dull correspondence which pads out volumes of "Life and Letters," but, after all, we need not read these, unless we are conscientious reviewers, which is far from probable.

The art of letter-writing does seem to be in decay, and no wonder, for few people have time to read a long letter, at all events a long letter much alarms

507

them. They put it away, meaning to read it after dinner, but they read the evening newspaper, and forget about the letter. Lovers do write, no doubt, to each other, because of the lingering tradition that it is the proper thing to do in their situation. When the effusions occasionally reach the public eye, they do not remind us of Horace Walpole, or even of the Portuguese Nun, who wrote the famous five or six letters to the young officer, but he had ridden away, and never answered.

Ladies also write to old friends of their own sex : men never write to each other if they can help it. The virtue, or vice, of ladies' letters is to be too historical, they are usually records of events other than momentous, and bulletins of the health and dresses of acquaintances. Of course, they may contain witty comments, and then they are, and always have been, the best kind of letters, though one is not sure that women have written more of them than men, or more, at least, that have been given to the world. However, to-day, women sometimes take pains to be entertaining in their epistles, and men, as a rule, do not. A modern Atticus would not read the letters of Cicero, if a modern Cicero wrote them. If they contained news, he could get the news much earlier from the newspapers, which now know everything, and sometimes know it right. Literary men do not write letters, if they have a good idea they keep it, and make copy of it, and a friend can read it much more easily in print than in the handwriting of many literary men. Mr. Stevenson was the last letter-writer, because he lived so far away from almost everybody who shared his interests. He could only talk to them with the pen, whereas people in town see each other in those clubs where people do talk to each other ; in many clubs they scrupulously shun conversation. Indeed talk is mainly done through telephones, or a brief telegram is sent, and letters are only written to men of business, or to others who are, for the moment, involved in business, such as trustees, parents and guardians, Members of Parliament; and, by bores, to men of letters whom they do not know, and who do not want to hear from them. "The old order changes," as the poet justly remarks, and the art of spelling, even, may come to be lost, as by the lady letter-writer, of conservative opinions, who described a certain newspaper as a " wrotton wradical wrag."

The Spring Call

By THOMAS HARDY

(From the *Cornhill*)

Down Wessex way, when spring's a-shine,
    The blackbird's " purr-ty de-urr ! "
In Wessex accents marked as mine,
    Is heard afar and near.

He flutes it strong, as if in song
    No R's of feebler tone
Than his appear in " purr-ty de-urr ! "
    Have blackbirds ever known.

Yet they pipe "prittie deerh !" I glean,
    Beneath a Scottish sky,
And "pehty deaw !" amid the treen
    Of Middlesex or nigh.

While some folk say—perhaps in play—
    Who know the Irish isle,
'T is " purrity dare ! " in treeland there
    When songsters would beguile.

Well : I'll say what the listening birds
    Say, hearing " purr-ty de-urr ! "—
"However strangers sound such words,
    That's how we sound 'em *he-urr*.

"Yes, in this clime at pairing-time
    As soon as eyes can see her,
At eve or day, the proper way
    To call is ' purr-ty de-urr ! '"

Idle Notes

By AN IDLE READER

Is there just as much niceness as there ever was, or is the quantity of the precious stuff diminishing? Mr. Owen Wister thinks that it is, and he has written "Lady Baltimore" to help preserve the record of a very special type of social distinction and charm. The story—which might have been called "The South Carolinians"—deals with an outsider's sojourn in the city he calls "the most appealing, the most lovely, the most wistful town in America." By telling the story only as the outsider learned it, in shreds and fragments, Mr. Wister increased the difficulty of his task immensely, and made the amiable Augustus, his spokesman, seem at times unduly inquiring, but one must always grant a novelist the point on which to place his lever, or he cannot lift up a world before our eyes, and then, if Augustus is somewhat curious, at least his curiosity is most affectionate and admiring. The characters of whom Mr. Henry James has written in late years are even more feverishly interested in "making out" things about one another, but they do it as an intellectual game, while Augustus does it in a thoroughly warm-hearted, human way. Augustus, in fact, is no end nice himself, and that is why he loves the Southern city full of history and memories, with its exquisite old ladies, its charming young ones, and why he doesn't wish John Mayrant, the fine contemporary flower of the old traditions, to marry Hortense Rieppe, a very beautiful, up-to-date girl who "looks like a steel wasp," and requires for her amusement yachts, automobiles, millions—all the paraphenalia of what Augustus calls "the yellow rich."

Just in passing—there *is* something very special about the Southern gentlewoman of the last generation. I do not know "Kings Port," but I pay my thanks to the kindly stars that I have known contemporaries of the ladies St. Michael, women of their type.

What it is about them, tongue cannot tell. It is not that they were more delicately bred or held to finer traditions than certain other worshipful ladies in the North. It is atmosphere, perhaps. But just as Paderewski's playing throws music into the air and makes it visible until you see the texture of it as if it were a glitter of old lace and gems, so do some of these elder women make you conscious of the fineness and beauty of the texture of life. Clouds lift, horizons widen; the imagination stirs as well as the heart, and the eye sees visions of all the exquisite things of mortality. This is not a rhapsody. I am just trying to tell you how it is. Some natures have the "singing quality" in their touch on life, as the Polish pianist has it on the ivory keys.

That is a charming chapter of "Lady Baltimore" where Augustus and young John Mayrant sit on the tombs in the old graveyard and deplore the passing of America's classic age, of the manners and characters of the old school. "We're no longer a small people living and dying for a great idea; we're a big people living and dying for money," declares Augustus delightfully. "And these ladies of yours, well, they have made me homesick for a national and social past which I never saw, but which my old people knew. They're like legends still living. In their quiet, clean-cut faces I seem to see a reflection of the old, serene candle-light we all once talked and danced in. . . . Such quiet faces are gone now in the breathless, competing North; ground into oblivion between the clashing trades of the competing men and the clashing jewels and chandeliers of their competing wives—while yours have lingered on, spared by your very adversity. And that's why I shall miss your old people when they follow mine—because they're the last of their kind, the end of the chain, the bold, original stock, the great race that made our glory grow and saw that it did grow through thick and thin, the good old native blood of independence."

Some half dozen years ago, an old gentleman wrote to the New York *Sun* an arraignment of the social life of that city, comparing it with the days preceding the Civil War. At that time, he averred, people of position avoided the display of wealth as vulgar. The quality of personal distinction was the thing prized, and "the discrimination to recognize it was deemed evidence of the validity of a title to social superiority." With the loss of this discrimination (he thought it wholly lost nowadays) had departed "the graciousness which used to be considered the attribute and test of good breeding"— that graciousness whose loss Mr. Wister mourns for the North and still finds in the South.

The obvious outer truth of these strictures cannot be denied, but I sometimes feel rebelliously in behalf of my own generation that all has not been told. It is true that great wealth is the severest test of character Providence has yet devised; it is true that "the yellow .rich" are paramount in most large cities, and that the higher tradition of personal distinction seems in eclipse—but in the smaller cities and the towns it is still markedly in evidence. The towns! What if our social salvation is yet to come out of them? How many of them does Mr. Wister intimately know? They contain a far greater proportion of the old blood of our independence than the cities, and it tells in their daily life. I remember perceiving hazily in my youth that the nice people of the smaller places seemed to have more time to be nice in than did the city-dwellers. There is leisure still left in them, and with leisure come dignity and graciousness. Perhaps when the gentle secrets of the towns are all revealed, it will be seen that there is just as much niceness as there ever was; it is only the distribution that is different.

But if this is wrong and all modern society is really tainted with vulgarity and rushing down the primrose path in devil-wagons, then let us remember for our consolation that Mr. Howells thinks distinction is not a Christian trait. Of course we don't agree with him; neither does Margaret Baillie-Saunders, whose clever novel, "Saints in Society," attempts a demonstration of precisely the converse. It tells the history of a young Christian-Socialist printer and his wife who are tested with the great test of rapidly acquired wealth and prominence. Before these things begin to arrive, Mark Hading is a man of distinction, for he believes in humanity and works for it, and his face shows forth the glory of his dream. His wife is just a good-looking, rather sulky London girl who loves cheap finery as if it were the ultimate joy. But when her husband begins to rise she casts about for some directions for "becoming a lady" in order to keep step with him. Her own idea is that ladies avoid work and cultivate a scornful expression. The first assistance she receives is the impression, derived from a chance conversation, that "a lady helps her husband and does kindnesses to little children." These are simple directions, but hers is a simple soul. She adopts the idea and it makes her over, as ideas will if they are taken seriously. She achieves character, presence, usefulness, even beauty by its aid, while her husband steadily deteriorates, losing his ideals, his religion, everything worth having, in the crucible of prosperity. All the distinction in the family changes hands and comes into Chloris's possession, so entirely does the writer regard it as one of the things of the spirit. The reader is not quite sure that everything would have happened just so. The author may be a little arbitrary —but the book interests and half convinces.

I do not know whether the intended moral of Lady Henry Somerset's novel is that which I found in it, but it seems to indicate with great clearness the futility, for a woman, of loving the wrong man. Lady Cliffe and Elizabeth

"Saints in Society"

"Under the Arch"

both make this mistake; they are both, also, young, fervent, imaginative, charming. The man in question falls in love first with one and then with the other, and the novelist offers no explanation of him or apology for him. He just does, that's all. Happily his sense of honor is as uncertain as his affections, and this failing in him ultimately results in the deliverance of both women from the bondage of their sentiment for him. Lady Cliffe goes into a decline, but Elizabeth lives to be happy with a better, if a less interesting, man. But in each case the woman loses much. Lady Cliffe neglects her husband for her unreal affection, and he slips out of life before she finds herself. Elizabeth suffers more, being less sentimental, but her loss is not so irretrievable for she employs herself in useful settlement work as a method of forgetting her own unhappiness.

The book is full of vivid little touches and sharply contrasting sketches of London life in the West End and the East. It is in these pictures that the greatest strength of the book lies. Better even than the impressive mother who devoutly believes that grief *must* be assuaged by mourning fresh from Paris, are the children of the slums, and "the rag and bone lady" who falls down on the pavement and lies happily upon her back for half an hour talking to the strip of blue night sky, telling the stars all her history and how "the blind man 'e 'stole my farden, but Lawd in 'eaven will pity me." She has begun to pray when a passing policeman offers to help her home and to bed, an offer which she declines to accept until he has prompted her, petition by petition, through "Our Father," explaining as she thanks him, "T ain't often I gets time to siy my prayers, but when I do, I likes to siy 'em right." Such things are not invented; they are seen.

The Muck=Rake as a Circulation Boomer

By F. HOPKINSON SMITH

(In an Interview)

PUBLICITY through the medium of the daily press and the magazines of the United States has assumed such a vicious form in some instances that it has done the American people much harm. Under the guise of exposing graft, corruption, or whatever title we may be pleased to give it, some of the mediums of publicity have magnified petty faults and grossly exaggerated conditions merely for the sake of commercialism —to increase their circulation. Agitation for reform has served as a pretext for attacks upon men and women which were entirely unwarranted, but one of the most baneful tendencies of this stuff, which is unfit to be called literature, is its wholesale slander of our country and our people. For example, to read the well-termed "yellow journals" of the Metropolis, one well might think that the purity of its women was a misnomer, that those who do not drink, smoke, or gamble are the exception and not the rule. In certain alleged magazines we read articles defaming the United States Senate, which every American should regard as the most honorable legislative body in the world —which it is. Men in public life are made the targets of slanderous criticism. Even our customs, the people as a whole are defamed by the so-called writers in their greed for the money offered them by those who are willing to debase their pages in the interest of commercialism.

So it is that this great evil of abuse has gotten to be a colossal scheme to make money by doing the greatest harm to men who do not deserve it. The people are laboring under the mis.

apprehension of believing that these men in high places are all wrong-doers and that the newspapers and magazines are defenders of the public good in exposing them, but they are not. They are on the scent for scandal and blackmail because that sort of stuff is salable, and in most cases for that reason alone. They are merely pandering to a public taste which craves these things, but at what cost? At the cost of increasing the spirit of Anarchism in this country! This means of turning abuse into cash is like throwing sharp stones and mud into a flower garden; spraying a bunch of orchids with the filth of a sewer; after the harm is done, it is useless to try to make amends.

Nothing has seemed safe from the attacks of the critics. Even the food we eat is tainted with graft and poison according to their accounts. Yet only a few days ago a New York chemist prepared a meal out of chemicals, and one which was in no way injurious to the partaker. Of course some exposures are necessary, but in most cases this agitation has gone too far. Among the food products, take for example oleomargarine. We who have refined tastes in our eating prefer cow's butter to beef butter; but to the poor man who has been accustomed to the other, there is really no difference, except in price. Down South I remember an old darky who for years had been fond of green cheese. He found out that he had n't been eating green cheese at all, but wagon grease instead. Did he write a magazine article? No; the fact that he had eaten and enjoyed it before his discovery led him to believe that he could continue to eat it with a relish—and he still included "green cheese" in his daily menu.

As I have intimated, this sort of publicity has one very dangerous tendency in sowing the seed of anarchy. We must remember that the sensational periodical and newspaper circulates widely among the classes of our people who do not appreciate that much of the stuff they read is exaggerated or utterly untrue. They do not realize that many of the men who occupy high places are the victims of false attacks. They get distorted ideas of those who deserve to stand high in their estimation. Their standard of citizenship is lowered by reading such articles and having the substance preached to them by labor agitators. So they are left dissatisfied. Their peace of mind is taken away and replaced by unrest and discontent.

To show how baseless are some of the tirades about our country and our people, let us contrast the United States with other nations. Ask the world traveller, American or European, and he will say that nowhere abroad is there a country which has the cleanliness that we have—moral, physical, civic, national—in no one of these ways can any of them compare with our cleanliness, and yet we are held up in the light of public censure as though no good thing could come out of America. Everything and everybody seems tainted with dishonesty or daubed with mud slung by some hysterical publisher, who thus sees a chance to increase his circulation.

But we cannot afford to let this literary mud-throwing continue—nor will we for long. Our people are very busy, and they have much to do. Much escapes us in our working hours because we are all absorbed in our labor. But when a thing is brought before our notice in all its force, we take hold of it with all our might and then the reaction comes. The cheap magazines and yellow press are not reformers—and that the masses will learn very soon. When they do learn this, there will be a revolution in popular beliefs which will counteract in a measure the harm that is being done by these alarmists. But let us hope that the revulsion of feeling comes soon.

The American creed, by nature, is optimism and hard work, for there is no real happiness without work. God Almighty gives us the sun every morning, and that sun is bound to shine so long as the world lasts. A cloud may come between you and the sun now and then, but why waste time worrying about that cloud, when you know God's sunshine is just behind it?

Greatness

I.

WHAT makes a man great?   Is it houses and land?
　　Is it argosies dropping their wealth at his feet?
　　Is it multitudes shouting his name in the street?
Is it power of brain?   Is it skill of hand?
Is it writing a book?   Is it guiding the State?
Nay, nay, none of these can make a man great.

II.

The crystal burns cold with its beautiful fire,
　　And is what it is; it can never be more;
　　The acorn, with something wrapped warm at the core,
In quietness says, "To the oak I aspire."
That something in seed and in tree is the same—
What makes a man great is his greatness of aim.

III.

What is greatness of aim?   Your purpose to trim
　　For bringing the world to obey your behest?
　　Oh no, it is seeking God's perfect and best,
Making something the same both in you and in Him.
Love what He loves, and child of the sod,
Already you share in the greatness of God.

SAMUEL V. COLE.

MR. WALTER PACH

By William M. Chase

William M. Chase

WILLIAM M. CHASE, one of the most talented leaders of American painters of portraits, creates results that possess the rare quality of representing things as they should appear to normal eyes, untinged by any preconceived sentiment of his imagination. Naturally, then, his tendency is not primarily to lay stress on a feeling for form, or a desire for composition, or charm of line, for its own sake. Therefore he never shows any inclination to deal with the half tangible, or with theoretic ideals, or with personified connotations of the vague, or the half-imagined. He leaves the dramatic field to the stage, the story-telling realm to literature. He aims his ambition rather towards selecting tangible facts, apparently common in shape and color, but truly of alluring charm, as they pass him day by day. These he places before us with the understanding that it is not the novel production but the well-done, clearly-wrought effort that merits praise. To such an end he strikes unerringly the significant details of the external aspect of the world. He finds the enjoyment of his work in simulating the effect of a gule of light falling upon some pleasing spot. He takes pleasure in' the keen and sincere rendering of the texture-fabric of a screen. His chief possession, a possession that few hold in duplicate, is an eye that sees what it should see with a thoroughly vital and accurate vision, that does not see at all what should be best avoided, and that directs his hand towards securing a permanent reminder of the best of what it has absorbed. During late years he has confined himself more and more closely to treating still life and figure studies. There, luckily, with greater aptness than in other directions his free and vigorous handling of his clever brush gives him a facility of color modelling and a versatility that breeds realism. Yet, though based upon this aloof condition of mind by which the eye seems to communicate directly with the hand, his portraits never display his technique at the expense of some poor mortal's character, never result in the conventionally expected cruel or analytical categories that represent each sitter as a man or woman of many faults and few virtues. On the contrary he combines his understanding of a uniquely spontaneous method of bringing out the pleasant emotions stored in the most common of everyday surroundings with a distinct sympathy for the object he is to reproduce. He loves his tools, loves his medium of expression, loves his world, and paints it as it spreads before his eyes that are direct and strong. He never attempts to soothe his audience with dreamy studies of mystic abstractions, but he gives them paintings that are awake, paintings that are true and full of beauty, and paintings that snap with potentiality.

William Merrit Chase was born in 1849 in Franklin, Indiana. He carried on his early work at the age of twenty-five under B. F. Hayes in Indianapolis, and later under J. O. Eaton in New York. Then before finally establishing himself in the United States he took the customary tour abroad, where he became one of the disciples of the Munich School of Art, studying there under Wagner, and Piloty. His work on this side of the Atlantic first attracted attention in 1876. Since that time he has made his way to the front rank of portrait and still life painters, winning, among other prizes, a gold medal in the Paris Exposition of 1900.

H. St.-G.

The MacDowell Club

A New Force in the Art Life of New York

By LAWRENCE GILMAN

MR. GEORGE MOORE, in his "Evelyn Innes," refers with excusable vivacity to the "absurd idea" propounded by Richard Wagner in the heat of controversy "that all the arts were to wax to one art in the music drama,—that even sculpture was to be represented by attitudes of the actors and actresses"; and Mr. Moore makes ungentle sport of such emphatic exponents of the Bayreuth idea as that most ponderable of *Isoldes*, Rosa Sucher, who was wont to "walk about with her hands raised and posed above her head in the conventional, statuesque attitude designed for the decoration of beer gardens." Wagner's amiable theory concerning the fusion of all the arts into one—that of the lyric drama—has been regarded, one may not deny, with somewhat less than universal seriousness; yet a not unrelated, though far older, ideal —that of the fertilization of one art by another—has, one conceives, a very considerable prospect of increasing realization.

It is known to his friends that the correlation of the different arts was a subject very dear to the heart of that distinguished American music-maker whose lamentable affliction is filling the minds of those who best know how to appreciate his singular and persuasive genius. For Edward MacDowell, the inter-relation of the arts—the rich and unexpected results made possible by the reaction one upon the other of music, painting, literature, and sculpture—was more than an æsthetic abstraction, a concept to be vaguely held or idly dreamed upon; it was, for him, a vital principle of artistic procedure. It was made constantly manifest in his work, almost from the first; and especially is it evident in those extraordinarily sensitive and imaginative tone-poems of his later period, in which an exquisite poetic vision has ordered the outflow of the musical thought. From first to last he has been not so much the master of a superb and distinguished order of musical eloquence, — although he was very completely that,—as the poet alive to all manner of quickening experiences, who chose to re-utter those experiences in a vivified form of musical speech.

That ideals and convictions such as his should have found some sort of objective perpetuation, now that he may no longer effectually uphold them, is perhaps as natural as it is fortunate. No less idealistic a motive than this underlies the purposes of the recently organized MacDowell Club of New York, which, in an embryonic form, came into existence just a year ago—on May 31, 1905, and which has moved with astonishing strides toward its present influential and significant position in the artistic activities of this town. The Club has now very nearly three hundred members, and its Advisory Board is so widely representative as to include these writers, musicians, painters, actors, architects, sculptors, and men and women of affairs: Mr. William F. Apthorp, Miss Cecilia Beaux, Madame Sarah Bernhardt, Mr. George De Forest Brush, Mr. John Burroughs, Mr. John La Farge, Mr. Henry T. Finck, Mr. Daniel C. French, Mr. Henry Fuller, Mrs. John L. Gardner, Mr. Augustus Saint Gaudens, Mr. Richard Watson Gilder, Mr. Philip Hale, Mr. Henry Lee Higginson, Mr. William Dean Howells, Mr. James Huneker, Mr. Robert Underwood Johnson, Mr. John Lane, Mr. Seth Low, Mr. Charles McKim, Mr. Frederick MacMonnies, Mr. William Mason, Mr. Howard Mansfield, Mr. Richard Mansfield, Mr. Horatio W. Parker, Mr. Emil Paur, Mr. Wassily Safonoff, Mr. Templeton Strong, Mr. Frederick A. Stock, and Mr. Owen Wister.

The purposes of the Club are thus officially declared: "To emphasize the nobility of Art as a whole; and the fundamental unity of the arts; and to broaden their appreciation and influence. To study and demonstrate the

tion." In that last clause is contained a sufficiently concise announcement of a purpose which, to many, suggests the most admirable of the Club's func-

Copyright by Estelle Huntington Huggins.

MR. EDWARD MACDOWELL
From his latest photograph made by Estelle Huntington Huggins.

correlation of the drama, literature, and music; architecture, painting, and sculpture; and the other fine arts. To aid in the extension of the knowledge of æsthetic principles; and to bring into prominence special works of art that are deserving of broader recogni-

tions: that of promoting and exhibiting whatever, in any of the arts, is at once new, significant, and unrecognized. It is primarily for this purpose that the Club's By-Laws provide for a number of yearly private meetings at which works "especially fitted to exemplify

THE GARDEN AT MR. MACDOWELL'S COUNTRY HOME AT PETERBORO, N. H.

MR. MACDOWELL'S LOG CABIN IN THE WOODS AT PETERBORO, N. H.

MR. MACDOWELL'S PLACE AT PETERBORO, N. H., IN WINTER.

the finer purposes of the several arts" shall be presented, and for "at least one annual public presentation . . . of the works of some artist or artists, whether of music, literature, the drama, painting, sculpture, or architecture; the selection to be made by the directors."

The evolution of the Club toward its present estate may be interesting to trace. It had its genesis, appropriately enough, in the "artist-class" which Mr. MacDowell organized among his pupils during the last years of his activity, as composer and teacher, and which was composed of those students of the piano who disclosed particular ability. From time to time a semi-public lesson was arranged for this class, and to it were bidden a limited number of auditors who knew how to appreciate the stimulating and suggestive promptings of the poet-composer whom a grotesque fate cast, for the best years of his life, in the somewhat confining rôle of a preceptor of youth. At the final meeting of this class, about a year ago, it became known that Mr. MacDowell was far from well, and that there was small possibility of his being able to continue the class during the following winter. It was regretted that the meetings had come to an end, and several plans were suggested for carrying them on in permanent form. The result was the formation of the nucleus of the Mac-Dowell Club, which began at once to take definite shape. I cannot better trace the subsequent development of the Club than by quoting from a singularly lucid account of its history prepared by Mrs. MacDowell:

"The impetus which hastened the growth of the Club to its present proportions came from an unexpected source. Mr. MacDowell's home in Peterboro, where, for the past ten years, he has spent most of his summers, and where practically all his creative work has been done during those years, was very dear to him. Undoubtedly the imagination which colored his thoughts in his work and plans helped also to idealize this home. When he bought it, it was a deserted farm of about eighty acres with a little cottage on it dating from Colonial days. The hand-made nails, the birch-bark lining the walls between the boards and the shingles, the old spinning-wheels still in the attic, the flint-lock found behind one of the stone fences, the tansy and lilacs—all these seemed a message to him from a bygone civilization, and in a way it was. As the years went on, Mr. MacDowell brought back the worn-out fields to their original value, and built himself in the midst of a sixty-acre forest a log cabin study where he worked and meditated. The old cottage was transformed into a low, rambling house, with a large, detached music-room. Barns were built, and gardens sprang up in all directions. As the years went by, Mr. MacDowell longed to feel assured that after his death and that of his wife the place might remain intact, and that it might, in some small way, help the development of art in this country. His supreme faith in the artistic future

of America strengthened this desire. Lack of funds to endow any plan in connection with the Peterboro house, and the assurance of his lawyer that such a bequest would have to be in connection with some corporation in order to insure its stability, seemed, however, to preclude any possibility of carrying out his ideas. The formation of the American Academy at Rome, where music was put on an equal footing with the other arts, renewed his Peterboro ideals, but the corporation was still lacking. As his mind grew more cloudy, his anxiety about Peterboro became acute, and was a constant source of unhappiness to him. The formation of the MacDowell Club of New York suddenly brought relief to the situation, and he hailed with delight the suggestion that the place should be given to it.

"In a letter which he wrote last year to the trustees of the Academy of Rome he tried to formulate some plan in regard to the four-year musical scholarship planned for that institution. He expressed strongly his opinion as to the influence he felt the different arts must have on each other when brought into close contact, though he doubted whether the musical student should live for more than three or four months of each year in Rome. That he should study in other European countries went without saying, but he trusted that the time would come when it would be felt just as necessary for the student to be sent back to America for a portion of his four years. In describing Peterboro in this connection, I wish to show that it is admirably planned for a miniature imitation of an American Academy, and what Mr. MacDowell hoped was that it might be used for a few months of each year as a resting spot for several students in all the arts, professional or otherwise, where quiet work and close companionship could be had, a modest sum being paid for board in order to clear it of a possible accusation of its being a charitable institution; and although no teaching need be done for the present, future years might evolve there a summer school.

"Last October, when Mr. MacDowell's hopeless condition became generally known, the feeling grew that the Club should stand on a broader basis than had at first been contemplated, although the difficulty of getting people together in New York, and the rapidity with which the membership grew, made the problem a formidable one.   There arose also the need of incorporating the Club, to enable it to receive the gift of the Peterboro home, which its donors were anxious to have immediately accomplished,—naturally reserving to themselves entire control of the property while they lived. Thus the organization came finally to its present estate."

During the season now ending, the Club has held a number of exhibition meetings that have yielded some notable occasions. Music of significance and value—some of it virtually unknown—has been performed by Miss Ruth Deyo, a young and hitherto unrecognized American pianist of striking gifts; by the Olive Mead Quartet; by Miss Maud Powell; by Mr. Sigismund Stojowski; by Mr. Gwilym Miles; by Mrs. Emma Juch Wellman, and others. There have been exhibitions of paintings by Mr. Orlando Rouland, Mr. Arthur Davies, and Mr. Ben-Ali Haggin; talks by Mr. E. H. Blashfield and Mr. Herbert Adams, upon aspects of painting and sculpture; the reading of an unforgettable poem, addressed to MacDowell, by Mr. Richard Watson Gilder; and a remarkably complete, persuasive, and beautiful exemplification of the possibilities of the arts in combination, in the shape of some exquisite tableaux arranged by Mr. John W. Alexander, accompanied by illustrative readings by Mrs. Le Moyne, and by some of MacDowell's music played by Miss Deyo.

It is, even now, a record which gives promise of an ultimately achieved fulfilment of the purposes of an artist who served his art with unvarying steadfastness, dignity, and ardor; and it is capable of almost unlimited development.

Ballade Song

When twilight's purples pass to gray
    And stars emerge in majesty,
When Night's dim fingers close the day
    And all is hush and ecstasy,—
From the fond homes of Memory,
In immemorial murmuring,
    Supreme, illusive, comes to me
The song that I shall never sing.

The words allure, delude, delay,
    Kiss, captivate, combine, agree,
Flash, quiver, tantalize, and play,
    Then soar in matchless harmony:—
I thrill with unconjectured glee
To catch the final faultless ring,—
    When sudden fades, and utterly,
The song that I shall never sing.

The voice of bird from budding spray,
    When winter dies by spring's decree,—
The flush and perfume of the May,
    Which quicken meadow, field, and
        tree,—
Vague throbs of far-heard melody,
The perfect poise of perfect wing,
    Are hints of what might chance to be
The song that I shall never sing.

Envoy

Friend, I would give all else for fee,
    If by the forfeit I could bring
To my poor brain the power to free
    The song that I shall never sing.
                              A. T. Schumann.

THE ARCH AT COPPA'S
Decorations by Aitken

San Francisco's Famous Bohemian Restaurant*

By MABEL CROFT DEERING

Eeny, meeny, mince, moe,
A fig for Care and a fig for Woe.

IMAGINE two attenuated figures sitting at a table, one of them holding up two fingers, not for Zwei Bier, alas! but for two figs which a waiter bears aloft on a spinning tray—all that poor Care and Woe can afford!

In such delightful foolery have the wall frescoes at Coppa's, San Francisco's famous Bohemian restaurant, been done. There is no central idea; there is no general scheme of decoration. Everything was done just by chance and on the spur of the moment, and no panel has anything at all to do with

*Written some months ago this article on Coppa's famous restaurant is particularly interesting from the fact that it is the only downtown restaurant in San Francisco unhurt by the earthquake or fire, and is the only building standing in what is known as the Latin Quarter.

any other panel. On the one next to dull Care, for instance, is a very rotund man eating macaroni underneath the legend, "Paste makes waist."

The mural decoration of Coppa's is a delightful illustration of the amateur spirit, for the entire work was a labor of love. The story of it is interesting. Coppa is a fat and locally famous chef who learned the divine art of feeding in Turin, with a post graduate course in Paris. He came to San Francisco years ago by way of Guatemala, where there are many good appetites. For a while he cooked at Martinelli's, the Italian café in San Francisco's Latin Quarter where many gourmets gathered in an older day, and where Paderewski always dines when he visits the far West. From there Coppa went to the old Poodle Dog, and at last set up in business for himself. Though a past master of the cuisine his business was not as successful as his ragouts. Something seemed to be the matter.

In all his wanderings through other men's kitchens, however, there was one faithful little coterie which followed Coppa, and when he finally settled in a tiny place of his own these faithful ones became the nucleus of his trade. They were artists and writers for the most part, many of them members of the Bohemian Club, and though they were not rich they were appreciative.

One day about a year ago the Bohemian Club gave an exhibition of fine photographs which were displayed on a screen of gray cartridge paper twenty-five feet long by ten feet high. The day after the pictures were removed from the screen a number of Bohemians worked far into the night ornamenting this virgin surface with grotesque caricatures of club members. Some of these were pleasant and some of them were not, but they made a sensation. The material used was kindergarten chalk in various colors.

That night at Coppa's one of the artists remarked to Felix, Coppa's young and good-looking partner, "It 's fearfully dark here, old man. Why don't you have some light?"

"We 're going to," said Felix. "We are going to have new paper and more lights and be fixed up fine."

"Great" said one of the fellows. "Get gray paper, Coppa, and we 'll fix it up for you. Like the screen," he remarked to his table companions.

One Monday when the faithful came to dine they found the little Montgomery Street café lined with hideous bright red paper with an impossible moulding of red and gold, and Coppa rubbing his plump hands with delight.

"Awful," said the artists, while Coppa's face fell. Only the arrival of the ravioli restored the *status quo*.

So Coppa was told to provide kindergarten chalk, which he did in abundance, though not without anxious inquiries as to what they purposed to do to his beautiful red paper.

"Never you mind," they said. "It will be all right. You 'll like it when it 's done."

Queerly enough, Coppa's is closed on Sunday. It is an oddly un-Bohemain custom and results in much loss of patronage, but Coppa likes one day a week in the country.

The first Sunday three men worked. They were Porter Garnett of the *Argonaut* staff, who writes and draws with equal facility; Perry Newberry, a newspaper artist and "Bobby" Aitken, the best-known sculptor of the West, a number of whose statues ornament San Francisco streets and squares, to say nothing of the Spreckels marble music-stand in Golden Gate Park, though his best-known work is probably "Art Lured by Bohemia," which ornaments the Jinks Room of the Bohemian Club.

Coppa had spread a cold luncheon for the willing workers, and, with a touching trust not confined to wall paper, had left the sideboard open. For the three men it was a lark, like the famous publication of that name which was intended merely as a hoax on the public, to last for one issue, and whose year of life made such a stir in the literary world. The three decided to have fun with the Philistines and to let their fancies run away with them. The most inconsequential fooleries began to cover the wall. Nothing had anything to do with anything else, and if you attempt any sort of orderly progression you end in despair.

The first cartoon placed on the wall showed a large continent surrounded by water, and on it a huge red lobster offers a claw to a long-haired man in a corduroy jacket, while a winged head which looks like Shakespeare hovers above. The picture was Porter Garnett's, and the idea is that the lobster and the poet meet on common ground in Bohemia. Mr. Aitken decorated the arch which faces the entrance in fine bold strokes and the spandrels show two nude figures, one of which bears aloft a smoking fowl and the other a fish. A green frog very much flattened forms the keystone of the arch. Literal-minded people gravely survey these figures and say that they are out of drawing, which is part of the joke. Underneath the figures is

FATHER TIME UNDER THE CLOCK
By Porter Garnett

the refrain of a Bohemian song known only to the elect.

That same first day Mr. Newberry contributed two figures, arms about waists, wandering up Telegraph Hill in the moonlight. As Coppa's is in the very shadow of the Hill this bit of realism may be considered as reminiscent of transient after-dinner affections.

After thers fit tremendous burst of energy, the frescoes languished, the artistic enthusiasm leaked away, and Coppa thought he was destined to go through life with only part of his beautiful red wall paper spoiled by pastels which wouldn't wash off. The Spring and Summer, when all grasshoppers wish to dance, came on, the beautiful California country beckoned to the artists and poets, and it was some time before they worked again. One day the enthusiastic fit came back. Zavier Martinez, a picturesque-looking, impressionist-painting Mexican artist returned from his native country where he had been sketching, and, being an old patron of Coppa's, he fell in enthusiastically with the idea. One of the best panels at the left of the

"BEFORE THE GRINGO CAME"

entrance had been reserved for Martinez, and his first work showed two figures, typical of the Latin Quarter of
Paris, where Martinez spent five years,
during which time he was the favorite
of Whistler and Carriere and, among
other things, did illustrations for *Gil
Blas*. These typical figures, a man
and a woman, are at either side of a big
mirror of the conventional sort, but
there is nothing conventional about
the next panel, which is also the work
of Martinez. It is called "Before the
Gringo Came," after Gertrude Ather-
ton's novel, and shows a table at
Coppa's in the good old days before
conventionality came to sample Coppa's dishes and to ogle the Bohemians.

A number of men appear in the picture, all portraits. There are three
women, but these are said to be "just
anybody," though one might wager
something and not lose. The men are
Martinez, Newberry, Garnett, Sterling, who wears a laurel crown for his
"Testimony of the Suns," Gelett Bur-

gess, Lafler, editor of the *Argonaut*,
and Maynard Dixon, painter of Arizona scenes and frontier life. One
man clasps a girl about the waist, not
noticing that her free hand presses that
of another man. A girl with a crown
of Titian hair smokes a cigarette with
Maynard Dixon. It all suggests Mimi
and Musetta.

All this freedom and easiness has
disappeared. The place is proper
enough now if it ever were anything
else. "We used to sing and talk, you
know," the Bohemians say regretfully.
It is their own fault; their pictures
made Coppa's one of the sights of the
town and put the place in the class
with Madame Begué's in New Orleans,
and that Parisian café decorated by
students of the Latin Quarter under
the direction of Florence Lundborg.
You are likely to be turned away from
Coppa's unless you have bespoken a
table, and Coppa beams as he counts
the sheckels his pictures and his shabby
friends have brought him.

The gulf between those who go to
Coppa's because it is "the thing" and
those who have always gone there
forms the theme of another cartoon by
Garnett, in which a lady with a lorgnon
says to her evening-coated escort,
"Freaks?" He replies, "Yes, artists,"
to which the long-haired ones at a
neighboring table are saying, "Rasta-
quoueres? Oui, cretins." Rastaquou-
eres, in the Latin Quarter, it may be
explained, meant originally a Philistine
who hailed from southern countries.

In July, Gelett Burgess arrived from
the eastern states and the decorations
at Coppa's received a new impetus.
Burgess added several Goop panels in
his characteristic style. He also contributed the "Josephine est morte,"
after a Latin Quarter song. Josephine is, of course, a Goop. Burgess
also suggested a number of quotations.

These quotations, which dot the
walls but have nothing to do with the
pictures, range from heaven to hell and
back again. They are intentionally
cryptic and "designed to keep the
Philistine guessing." As a matter of
fact they range from Rabelais to Alice
in Wonderland, taking in Kant by the

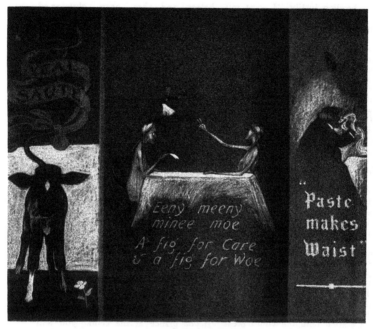

CARTOON BY SPENCER WRIGHT

way, and the best-read man in the world would be puzzled by some of them. There is, for instance, the "Something terrible is going to happen" from Oscar Wilde's "Salome," and Whistler's famous retort when classed with Velasquez, "Why drag in Velasquez?" "It is a crime" is from Martinez's unpublished conversations, and the literary miner may dig up for himself, "O love, dead, and your adjectives still in you" and "You cannot argue with the choice of the soul."

> The blue-eyed vampire, sated at her feet,
> Smiles bloodily against the leprous moon,

is from an unpublished poem by George Sterling, and is not likely to be in demand as a motto for the ordinary *salle à manger;*.

Besides these, there are numberless bits from Villon, naturally popular with these unconventional diners, from Verlaine and other vagabond poets, many of them in the picturesque French of other times. One of the ideas was to have as many languages represented as possible—also to the bewilderment of the stranger—and beside Hebrew there appears in the Greek character above the clock, "Business to-morrow." The clock, by the way, is supported on the soles of the feet of Father Time who, lying on his back, spins an hour-glass on one hand, a Chianti bottle on the other.

The Goop who represents the muse of nonsense, placed there by the author of the Purple Cow, beams across the room at a baby in a high chair. The baby has the tangled black mane of Martinez and his flaunting red tie. His milk bottle contains Martinez's favorite tipple, absinthe, and the infant is bawling lustily, "I want my Tagliarini."

Above all this miscellany of quotation and illustration is a frieze of prowling black cats, all headed in one direction. 'T is queer how these figures seem to be moving, as though they walked on a roof, looking in through attic windows at Pierrot and Columbine. As a matter of fact, the cats were designed by Martinez, a stencil was made, and the cats were appliqued on the wall. In spite of the strong similarity each cat seems to have an individuality, and several have eyeballs painted in. These cats are all to have gold paper eyes—some day. Below the cats are a string of names— the Coppa Temple of Fame. The delightful thing about these names is the juxtaposition of the past great with the shifting present. The names follow in their order: Aristotle, Newberry, Velasquez, Isabel I., Dante, Martinez, Villon, Buttsky, Rabelais, Garnett, Goethe, Maisie, Nietzsche, Burgess, Whistler, Lafler, Sappho, Sterling, Verlaine, Aitken.

Could anything be more grotesque than the juxtaposition of Maisie and Goethe? Of course it is to be expected that the eternal feminine would press close to the famous lover, but "Maisie" is such an inconsequential name —such a legacy from a sentimental mother. "Maisie" is the "Christian" name of a young woman who does magazine work in San Francisco, and who is a great favorite with the little group which has made Coppa's famous. "Buttsky" is the nickname of the wife of one of the decorators, and Isabel I. was a well-known San Francisco newspaper woman now in New York, who was known during her western sojourn as the queen of Bohemia. She still lives as Isabel the First. In the Temple of Fame Nietzsche was mispelled, but in the claws of the cat above, taken out by force, no doubt, may be seen the missing "Z." The cat above Dante's name casts most languishing eyes at the Italian poet

below and has been christened "Beatrice."

I said that one must secure a table in advance if one would not be turned away from Coppa's, but there is one table at which there is always room. It is a rectangular table, almost in the middle of the room, and at it the original patrons of the place dine. There may be ten persons standing up and but two Bohemians at this table, but the other seats remain sacredly empty. At this table are often to be seen the men who decorated the wall, including Spencer Wright, who does bookbinding and who contributed the "Eeny, meeny, minee, moe," Anna Strunsky, who collaborated with Jack London in the Kempton–Wace Letters—an enthusiastic little Russian nihilist—London, himself, Lafler of the *Argonaut*, and a few newspaper men who have been admitted to the inner circle. They and they alone may add to the company at the "Round Table."

Straying in by chance you might think that you had discovered the original of Du Maurier's Little Billee or the prototypes for Rudolpho and his friends from La Boheme, so strange are the clothes, so unfamiliar the talk. If you glance at the ceiling you will see black footprints there—footprints which approach the Bohemian table at an orderly pace. Apparently the owner of the feet sees something interesting, for his steps suddenly lengthen and, in a trice, his feet are cuddled beside a much smaller pair of soles and you see the marks of chair-legs drawn close together. The prints of the chair-legs ornament the ceiling at a point which is just above the Bohemian table.

If you be too polite to stare, you may listen to the conversation at this interesting table.

Sometimes the talk does not scintillate because the worry of daily bread sits on the Bohemian brow; but suddenly the cloud lifts, glasses clink, and some one proposes a toast and all goes merrily again.

Holman Hunt's Pre=Raphaelitism

By ELISABETH LUTHER CARY

MR. HOLMAN HUNT'S two large and interesting volumes* are avowedly iconoclastic in purpose. He prepares his readers at the start for rather desperate measures and for an account of the Pre-Raphaelites that shall differ from all others and place the Brotherhood on a new footing before the world, which continues to regard it with mild but certain interest. It is almost a disappointment, therefore, to find that, while Mr. Hunt has conscientiously been painting in his background, most of the facts he has to set forth have leaked out in one form and another, and it must be owned that his strenuous denial of Rossetti's authority among the Brothers reads a little ungenerously and wears the disagreeable look of surplusage. It already quite generally has been conceded, I think, that Rossetti was not typically a Pre-Raphaelite, a point upon which Mr. Hunt lays stress, and it is also known that Hunt and Millais were the first to make a compact to go to nature for teaching. This going to nature, too, is what most people now understand by Pre-Raphaelitism—certainly there are few readers of intelligence who confound the movement with the mediævalism which Rossetti displayed in his early designs. What is not, perhaps, so well known is the fact stated by Mr. Hunt that both he and Rossetti agreed at the start in thinking that "a man's work must be the reflex of a living image in his own mind, and not the icy double of the facts themselves. It will be seen that we were never realists," he adds. "I think art would have ceased to have the slightest interest for any of us had the object been only to make a representation, elaborate or unelaborate, of a fact in nature. . . . In agreeing to use the utmost elaboration in painting our first pictures, we never meant more than to insist that the practice was essential

for training the eye and hand of the young artist; we should not have admitted that the relinquishment of this habit of work by a matured painter would make him less a Pre-Raphaelite." Truly enough the little band, with the exception perhaps of Millais, were never realists, but when Rossetti himself threw off to a degree the habit of representing minute detail, he threw off all that united him to the Brethren, and became the one painter of his generation who used his art to express a strongly poetic intelligence. If he never produced a great work, tried by the standard of the masters, he at least never produced any work which did not contain both a pictorial and a poetic idea, and he never failed to impress those ideas with adequate subordination of any detail that might interfere with them. If Millais was the painter of the group, Rossetti indubitably was the poet, and there is no one now likely to quarrel with the designation of Mr. Hunt as the Pre-Raphaelite, *par excellence*. Perhaps he was always the only exclusively Pre-Raphaelite painter in England in the sense he gives to the term. To release his fellows from the long misplaced badge is probably as much a matter of justice to them as to the ideal for which, at heart, they did not stand. And at the present date there is certainly no necessity of standing out against Mr. Hunt's earnest affirmation that Rossetti was not the leader of the movement. That Millais and Hunt were the leaders, that they, by continuing to exhibit in the face of detraction, bore the heat of the day, that Rossetti showed little "corporate spirit" in retiring from public exhibitions and in separating himself at the beginning from the Brotherhood, exhibiting his picture in advance of their pictures and in another gallery, must of course be conceded by all openminded persons, and requires no special discussion. That Rossetti was indebted almost solely to Hunt and hardly at

*" Pre-Raphaelitism and the Pre-Raphaelite Brotherhood." By Holman Hunt. Macmillan. 2 vols., $10.00.

529

all to Madox Brown for guidance "through the portals of original picture-painting in oil" is very interesting as must be any statement regarding the early training of a man of genius. "He might possibly, in course of time, and after many mischances, have got through this dreaded gate, but had he not been very closely, thoughtfully, and affectionately guided by me, hour by hour, in my studio for seven or eight months, I unhesitatingly maintain that he could not ever have appeared as a painter in 1849, and not even in 1850, if ever. The nature of the service he received from his successive masters can best be judged by considering the two oil studies done under Brown, one a copy of 'Angels Watching the Crown of Thorns,' the other from the group of bottles which had driven Gabriel to desperation before he came to me, and which, some years afterwards, he partly transformed in idle mood by the addition of a female on a couch in the background. Any intelligent person can compare them with 'The Girlhood of the Virgin ' painted under my auspices, and they may then estimate whether Brown's course of instruction or mine most led to Rossetti's becoming a master in his art. That the drilling I prescribed was so successful arose greatly, beyond doubt, from his own unswerving energy and determination." This puts the case clearly and positively enough, and there is little chance hereafter that Mr. Hunt will be denied the honor—by no means an empty one—of having been, for one important year, Rossetti's master. It is not entirely pertinent, but it is tempting to consider what might have been if Fantin-Latour, instead of the leader of the Pre-Raphaelites, had stood by Rossetti's side at this time of the young Italian's impressionable period; if, instead of toiling over wet-white technique, Rossetti had been inspired to emulate the beautiful limpid painting of Fantin. No doubt the result would have been much the same. If Rossetti had not sufficiently the pure painter's sense to get himself out from a bad method into a good one he had, nevertheless, too much individuality to

make it fair to lay at the door of others the contraction of his genius.

As for the rest of the book—the parts that have nothing to do with setting right the popular conception of that boyish revolution of more than half a century ago—it would be difficult to imagine anything more wonderful than its detail, more astounding than its naïve elaboration. As a record of indefatigable labor, of persistent painstaking, of the "dogged as does it" that universally commands respect from the Anglo-Saxon race, the pages inspire something almost like pity. If, as many of us now believe, Pre-Raphaelitism even in its unperverted significance was not the right track for the student of art to follow, it is fairly terrible to count in retrospect the cost of following it for so devoted a pilgrim. Mr. Hunt reveals the progress step by step, from the time that he, at the age of four, made a paint brush from a lock of his hair, through all the subsequent years of disappointment, effort, and self-reliance. That he multiplied his difficulties by his travels to the East for the purpose of studying local types and local conditions for his religious paintings is a characteristic feature of his struggle towards truth of representation. His stories of poverty and real physical hardship have in them no suggestion of self-pity. It was in the day's work for him to go without meat from a mixture of economy and Shelley-worship, just as it was a matter of course for him to risk theft and assault and the deadly plague to put the right kind of sky behind his Scapegoat, and make sure of the anatomy of his dead camel.

The tone of the long narrative is by no means that of gloom, and as the celebrities of the author's later acquaintance are brought in—almost as informally as Rossetti was in the habit of bringing in school companions to share Hunt's meagre dinners—a certain dry humor enlivens the plentiful anecdote. We see Tennyson very clearly cut against the contemporary background and apparently greatly enjoying his own "unflinching truthfulness of nature." This sublimely dis-

agreeable quality was in full force upon the occasion of a festivity which
was sprung upon the would-be recluse by Mrs. Prinsep. "Mrs. Prinsep
took occasion to present a gentleman
as 'the Editor of the *Midnight
Beacon.*' Tennyson silently blinked
at him with his head craned. The
lady felt need of overcoming the
awkwardness of the position and
ejaculated, 'Mr. Tennyson is delighted to make your acquaintance!' Tennyson, with the stranger
still standing waiting, turned to Mrs.
Prinsep and said inquiringly, but without petulance, 'What made you say
that? I did not say that I was
delighted to make his acquaintance';
and this query dispersed the little
group with the best grace each could
assume, leaving Tennyson unintended
master of the situation." Later at
dinner the poet addressed his sonorous
voice to Hunt, who was sitting opposite, saying, "In this company there
ought to be Lady Somers, whose
beauty I have heard so much extolled.
I can't see her anywhere; is she here?"
Hunt found himself in some embarrassment at the necessity of answering
such a question aloud, but he did his
best. Tennyson soon showed perplexity, put up his right hand, and waved
it from side to side, saying, "Your
voice sounds like the piping of a little
bird in the storm." A quite different
story is told of Thackeray. Some of
Thackeray's old school-fellows were to
dine together on a Wednesday evening
and he was besought to join them. He
declined on the plea of being behind
hand with his writing, and having set
aside that Wednesday to go down to
some quiet lodgings he had taken for
the purpose and "make big innings."
On the way home from the dinner the
party drove up to these lodgings and
shouted Thackeray's name under the
one lighted window. "Very calm and
terribly sober" he came to the door and
let them in, and upstairs on the table
they beheld a writing-pad with some
sheets of note paper on the table, the
upper sheet bearing about twelve lines
of Thackeray's neat, small writing,
with a blank space at the bottom. He
was promply charged with having given

up his pleasure to no purpose, and
sadly admitted that it was true. The
teller of the tale concluded by asking
Hunt, with indignation, if he called
that being a genius!

Taking the book as a whole, it
seems, despite its prolixity, curiously
incomplete. As the history of a movement in art it is a failure, since through
the multiplicity of its detail we lose
the general effect—the forest, minute
as in itself it is, cannot be seen for the
trees. The reason perhaps lies in the
fact that, according to Mr. Hunt, there
really was no movement to record.
At the end of his thousand pages, he
frankly remarks: "It is stultifying in
writing a history of Pre-Raphaelitism to
be compelled to avow that our impul-
sively formed Brotherhood was a tragic
failure almost from the beginning, and
that we became the victims of the in-
discretions of our allies." So far as
we can detach a general impression of
the ideal for which the young Millais
and the young Hunt stood, it combined
the breaking with conventionalism, the
return to nature as a model, and the
negation of mediævalism. The last
point is that which Mr. Hunt most
fervently presses, and it is of course
the one which separates him most
completely from Rossetti. But what
really placed Rossetti apart from his
fellows was not his mediævalism or his
faithlessness to the principles of the P.
R. B. It was his great imagination.
We may doubt in all sincerity whether,
if he had waited properly to exhibit
together with his Brethren in the
Academy, and loyally had abstained
from disclosing the meaning of the
cabalistic letters to the jeering public,
if no one had published his influence
upon his companions as, rightly or
wrongly, his brother conceived it, he
would not still have remained in men's
minds as the "leader of the Pre-Raphaelites." So great is the power of
imagination that it constitutes in itself
a priority with which facts of time and
theory have little to do. However
much, for example, Thomas Lodge
might make us believe that Shakespeare was not the original and only
creator of "As You Like It"; it would
be difficult for him to make us feel it.

The Lion and the Mouse:

A Story of American Life To-Day *

By CHARLES KLEIN

Novelized from the Play, by ARTHUR HORNBLOW

" *The Lion and the Mouse*," *by Mr. Charles Klein, is the most successful play pro-*
duced in New York in many years. Only its own author has touched its record, for in
" *The Music Master* " *he has written a play that has run through two seasons without any*
falling off in popularity. " *The Lion and the Mouse* " *was accepted by Mr. Henry B.*
Harris as soon as he had finished reading the manuscript. He saw its possibilities, got his
company together, and produced it at the Lyceum Theatre, where it has been running "*to*
capacity " *since its production in the early fall ; and it is likely to run on into next season,*
with only a short intermission in the summer to give the actors a much needed rest. Soon
after the success of the play in New York a company was sent to Chicago, where it was
played to packed houses for four weeks. On the last day of the engagement occurred some-
thing unprecedented in theatrical annals, three performances being giving in one day—at
eleven in the morning, two in the afternoon, and again at night. This success was repeated
in San Francisco the company getting away only a few days before the earthquake.
One reason for the great success of " *The Lion and the Mouse* " *is that it bears so di-*
rectly on an exciting topic of the day—trusts and their makers. No one could see the play
without realizing its adaptability to the purposes of a novel. Mr. Arthur Hornblow, the
editor of the Theatre Magazine, was one of the first to realize its book possibilities, and in
collaboration with the author he has made this " *novelization* "—*to use an awkward but use-*
ful word.
THE CRITIC *has been fortunate enough to secure the serial rights in this story, of which*
unusually large instalments will be printed beginning with the present issue. The reader
will not have to wait longer than three months to get the whole story.

I

THERE was unwonted bustle in the usually sleepy and dignified New York offices of the Southern and Transcontinental Railroad Company in lower Broadway. The supercilious, well-groomed clerks who, on ordinary days, are far too preoccupied with their own personal affairs to betray the slightest interest in anything not immediately concerning them, now condescended to bestir themselves and, gathered in little groups, conversed in subdued, eager tones. The slim, nervous fingers of half a dozen haughty stenographers, representing as many different types of business femininity, were busily rattling the keys of clicking typewriters, each of their owners intent on reducing with all possible despatch the mass of letters which lay piled up in front of her. Through the heavy plate-glass swinging doors, leading to the elevators and thence to the street, came and went an army of messengers and telegraph boys, noisy and insolent.

Through the open windows the hoarse shouting of news-venders, the rushing of elevated trains, the clanging of street cars, with an occasional feverish dash of an ambulance — all these familiar noises of a great city had the far-away sound peculiar to top floors of the modern sky-scraper. The day was warm and sticky, as is not uncommon in early

Copyright, 1906, by the G. W. Dillingham Company

May, and the overcast sky and a distant rumbling of thunder promised rain before night.

The big express elevators, running smoothly and swiftly, unloaded every few moments a number of prosperous-looking men who, chatting volubly and affably, made their way immediately through the outer offices towards another and larger inner office on the glass door of which was the legend "Directors' Room. Private." Each comer gave a patronizing nod in recognition of the deferential salutation of the clerks. Earlier arrivals had preceded them, and as they opened the door there issued from the Directors' Room a confused murmur of voices, each different in pitch and tone, some deep and deliberate, others shrill and nervous, but all talking earnestly and with animation as men do when the subject under discussion is of common interest. Now and again a voice was heard high above the others, denoting anger in the speaker, followed by the pleading accents of the peacemaker, who was arguing his irate colleague into calmness. At intervals the door opened to admit other arrivals, and through the crack was caught a glimpse of a dozen directors, some seated, some standing near a long table covered with green baize.

It was the regular quarterly meeting of the directors of the Southern and Transcontinental Railroad Company, but it was something more than mere routine that had called out a quorum of such strength and which made to-day's gathering one of extraordinary importance in the history of the road. That the business on hand was of the greatest significance was easily to be inferred from the concerned and anxious expression on the directors' faces and the eagerness of the employés as they plied each other with questions.

"Suppose the injunction is sustained?" asked a clerk in a whisper. "Is not the road rich enough to bear the loss?"

The man he addressed turned impatiently to the questioner:

"That's all you know about railroading. Don't you understand that this suit we have lost will be the entering wedge for hundreds of others? The very existence of the road may be at stake. And between you and me," he added in a lower key, "with Judge Rossmore on the bench we never stood much show. It's Judge Rossmore that scares 'em, not the injunction. They've found it easy to corrupt all the other Supreme Court judges, but Judge Rossmore is one too many for them. You could no more bribe him than you could have bribed Abraham Lincoln."

"But the newspapers say that he, too, has been caught accepting $50,000 worth of stock for that decision rendered in the Great Northwestern case?"

"Lies! All those stories are lies," replied the other emphatically. Then looking cautiously around to make sure no one overheard, he added contemptuously: "The big interests fear him and they're inventing these lies to try to injure him. They might as well try to blow up Gibraltar. The fact is the public is seriously aroused this time and the railroads are in a panic."

It was true. The railroad, which heretofore had considered itself superior to law, had found itself checked in its career of outlawry and oppression. The railroad, this modern octopus of steam and steel that stretches its greedy tentacles out over the land had at last been brought to book.

At first, when the country was in the earlier stages of its development, the railroad appeared in the guise of a public benefactor. It brought to the markets of the East the produce of the South and West. It opened up new and inaccessible territory and made oases of waste places. It brought to the city coal, lumber, food, and other prime necessaries of life, taking back to the farmer and the woodsman in exchange, clothes and other manufactured goods. Thus, little by little, the railroad wormed itself into the affections of the people and gradually became an indispensable part of the life it had itself created. Tear up the railroad and life itself is extinguished.

So, when the railroad found it could not be dispensed with, it grew dissatisfied with the size of its earnings. Legitimate profits were not enough. Its directors cried out for bigger dividends and from then on the railroad became a conscienceless tyrant, fawning on those it feared and crushing without mercy those who were defenceless. It raised its rates for hauling freight, discriminating against certain localities without reason or justice, and favoring other points where its own interests lay. By corrupting government officials and other unlawful methods it appropriated lands, and there was no escape from its exactions and brigandage. Other roads were built, and for a brief period there was held out the hope of relief that invariably comes from honest competition. But the railroad either absorbed its rivals or pooled interests with them, and thereafter there were several masters instead of one.

Soon the railroads began to war among themselves, and in a mad scramble to secure business at any price they cut each other's rates and unlawfully entered into secret compacts with certain big shippers, permitting the latter to enjoy lower freight rates than their competitors. The smaller shippers were soon crushed out of existence in this way. Competition was throttled and prices went up, making the railroad barons richer and the people poorer. That was the beginning of the giant Trusts, the greatest evil American civilization has yet produced, and one which, unless checked, will inevitably lead this country into the throes of civil strife.

From out this quagmire of corruption and rascality emerged the Colossus, a man so stupendously rich and with such unlimited powers for evil that the world has never looked upon his like. The fabled Crœsus, whose fortune was estimated at only eight millions in our money, was a pauper compared with John Burkett Ryder, whose holdings no man could count, but which were approximately estimated at a thousand millions of dollars. The railroads had created the Trust, the ogre of corporate greed, of which Ryder was the incarnation, and in time the Trust became master of the railroads, which, after all, seemed but retributive justice.

John Burkett Ryder, the richest man in the world—the man whose name had spread to the farthest corners of the

earth because of his wealth, and whose money, instead of being a blessing, promised to become not only a curse to himself but a source of dire peril to all mankind—was a genius born of the railroad age. No other age could have brought him forth; his peculiar talents fitted exactly the conditions of his time. Attracted early in life to the newly discovered oil fields of Pennsylvania, he became a dealer in the raw product and later a refiner, acquiring with capital, laboriously saved, first one refinery, then another. The railroads were cutting each other's throats to secure the freight business of the oil men, and John Burkett Ryder saw his opportunity. He made secret overtures to the road guaranteeing a vast amount of business if he could get exceptionally low rates, and the illegal compact was made. His competitors, undersold in the market, stood no chance, and one by one they were crushed out of existence. Ryder called these manœuvres "business"; the world called them brigandage. But the Colossus prospered and slowly built up the foundations of the extraordinary fortune which is the talk and the wonder of the world to-day. Master now of the oil situation, Ryder succeeded in his ambition of organizing the Empire Trading Company, the most powerful, the most secretive, and the most wealthy business institution the commercial world has known.

Yet with all this success John Burkett Ryder was still not content. He was now a rich man, richer by many millions than he ever dreamed he could ever be, but still he was unsatisfied. He became money mad. He wanted to be richer still, to be the richest man in the world, the richest man the world had ever known. And the richer he got the stronger the idea grew upon him with all the force of a morbid obsession. He thought of money by day, he dreamt of it at night. No matter by what questionable device it was to be procured, more gold and more must flow into his already overflowing coffers. So each day, instead of spending the rest of his years in peace, in the enjoyment of the wealth he had accumulated, he went down-town like any twenty-dollar-a-week clerk to the tall building in lower Broadway and, closeted with his associates, toiled and plotted to make more money.

He acquired vast copper mines and secured control of this and that railroad. He had invested heavily in the Southern and Transcontinental road and was chairman of its board of directors. Then he and his fellow conspirators planned a great financial coup. The millions were not coming in fast enough. They must make a hundred millions at one stroke. They floated a great mining company to which the public was invited to subscribe. The scheme having the endorsement of the Empire Trading Company no one suspected a snare, and such was the magic of John Ryder's name that gold flowed in from every point of the compass. The stock sold away above par the day it was issued. Men deemed themselves fortunate if they were even granted an allotment. What matter if, a few days later, the house of cards came tumbling down, and a dozen suicides were strewn along Wall Street, that sinister thoroughfare which, as a wit has said, has a graveyard at one end and the river at the other! Had Ryder any twinges of conscience? Hardly. Had he not made a cool twenty millions by the deal?

Yet this commercial pirate, this Napoleon of finance, was not a wholly bad man. He had his redeeming qualities, like most bad men. His most pronounced weakness, and the one that had made him the most conspicuous man of his time, was an entire lack of moral principle. No honest or honorable man could have amassed such stupendous wealth. In other words, John Ryder had not been equipped by Nature with a conscience. He had no sense of right, or wrong, or justice where his own interests were concerned. He was the prince of egoists. On the other hand, he possessed qualities which, with some people, count as virtues. He was pious and regular in his attendance at church and, while he had done but little for charity, he was known to have encouraged the giving of alms by the members of his family, which con-

sisted of a wife, whose timid voice was rarely heard, and a son Jefferson, who was the destined successor to his gigantic estate.

Such was the man who was the real power behind the Southern and Transcontinental Railroad. More than any one else Ryder had been aroused by the present legal action, not so much for the money interest at stake as that any one should dare to thwart his will. It had been a pet scheme of his, this purchase for a song, when the land was cheap, of some thousand acres along the line, and it is true that at the time of the purchase there had been some idea of laying the land out as a park. But real-estate values had increased in astonishing fashion, the road could no longer afford to carry out the original scheme, and had attempted to dispose of the property for building purposes, including a right of way for a branch road. The news, made public in the newspapers, had raised a storm of protest. The people in the vicinity claimed that the railroad secured the land on the express condition of a park being laid out, and in order to make a legal test they had secured an injunction, which had been sustained by Judge Rossmore of the United States Circuit Court.

These details were hastily told and re-told by one clerk to another as the babel of voices in the inner room grew louder, and more directors kept arriving from the ever-busy elevators. The meeting was called for three o'clock. Another five minutes and the chairman would rap for order. A tall, strongly built man with white moustache and kindly smile emerged from the Directors' Room and, addressing one of the clerks, asked:

" Has Mr. Ryder arrived yet? "

The alacrity with which the employé hastened forward to reply would indicate that his interlocutor was a person of more than ordinary importance.

" No, Senator, not yet. We expect him any minute." Then with a deferential smile he added : " Mr. Ryder usually arrives on the stroke, sir."

The senator gave a nod of acquiescence and, turning on his heel, greeted with a grasp of the hand and affable smile his fellow-directors as they passed in by twos and threes.

Senator Roberts was in the world of politics what his friend John Burkett Ryder was in the world of finance—a leader of men. He began life in Wisconsin as an errand boy, was educated in the public schools, and later became clerk in a dry-goods store, finally going into business for his own account on a large scale. He was elected to the Legislature, where his ability as an organizer soon won the confidence of the men in power, and later was sent to Congress, where he was quickly initiated in the game of corrupt politics. In 1885 he entered the United States Senate. He soon became the acknowledged leader of a considerable majority of the Republican senators, and from then on he was a power to be reckoned with. A very ambitious man with a great love of power and few scruples, it is little wonder that only the practical or dishonest side of politics appealed to him. He was in politics for all there was in it and he saw in his lofty position only a splendid opportunity for easy graft.

He was not slow to enter into such alliances with corporate interests seeking influence at Washington as would enable him to accomplish this purpose, and in this way he had met and formed a strong friendship with John Burkett Ryder. Each being a master in his own field was useful to the other. Neither was troubled with qualms of conscience, so they never quarrelled. If the Ryder interests needed anything in the Senate, Roberts and his followers were there to attend to it. Just now the cohort was marshalled in defence of the railroads against the attacks of the new Rebate bill. In fact, Ryder managed to keep the Senate busy all the time. When, on the other hand, the senators wanted anything—and they often did—Ryder saw that they got it, lower rates for this one, a fat job for that one, not forgetting themselves. Senator Roberts was already a very rich man, and although the world often wondered where he got it, no one had the courage to ask him.

But the Republican leader was stirred with an ambition greater than that of controlling a majority in the Senate. He had a daughter, a marriageable young woman who, at least in her father's opinion, would make a desirable wife for any man. His friend Ryder had a son, and this son was the only heir to the greatest fortune ever amassed by one man, a fortune which, at its present rate of increase, by the time the father died and the young couple were ready to inherit, would probably amount to over *six billions of dollars.* Could the human mind grasp the possibilities of such a colossal fortune? It staggered the imagination. Its owner, or the man who controlled it, would be master of the world. Was not this a prize any man might well set himself out to win? The senator was thinking of it now as he stood exchanging banal remarks with the men who accosted him. If he could only bring off that marriage he would be content. The ambition of his life would be attained. There was no difficulty as far as John Ryder was concerned. He favored the match and had often spoken of it. Indeed, Ryder desired it, for such an alliance would naturally further his business interests in every way. Roberts knew that his daughter Kate had more than a liking for Ryder's handsome son. Moreover, Kate was practical, like her father, and had sense enough to realize what it would mean to be the mistress of the Ryder fortune. No, Kate was all right, but there was Master Jefferson to reckon with. It would take two in this case to make a bargain.

Jefferson Ryder was, in truth, an entirely different man from his father. It was difficult to realize that both had sprung from the same stock. A college-bred boy with all the advantages his father's wealth could give him, he had inherited from the parent only those characteristics which would have made him successful even if born poor—activity, pluck, application, dogged obstinacy, alert mentality. To these qualities he added what his father sorely lacked— a high notion of honor, a keen sense of right and wrong. He had the honest man's contempt for meanness of any description, and he had little patience with the lax so-called business morals of the day. For him a dishonorable or dishonest action could have no apologist, and he could see no difference between the crime of the hungry wretch who stole a loaf of bread and the coal baron who systematically robbed both his employés and the public. In fact, had he been on the bench he would probably have acquitted the human derelict who, in despair, had appropriated the prime necessary of life, and sent the over-fed conscienceless coal baron to jail.

"Do unto others as you would have others do unto you." This simple and fundamental axiom Jefferson Ryder had adopted early in life, and it had become his religion, the only one, in fact, that he had. He was never pious like his father, a fact much regretted by his mother, who could see nothing but eternal damnation in store for her son because he never went to church and professed no orthodox creed. She knew him to be a good lad, but to her simple mind a conduct of life based merely on a system of moral philosophy was the worst kind of paganism. There could be, she argued, be no religion, and assuredly no salvation, outside the dogmatic teachings of the Church. But otherwise Jefferson was a model son and, with the exception of this bad habit of thinking for himself on religious matters, really gave her no anxiety. When Jefferson left college, his father took him into the Empire Trading Company with the idea of his eventually succeeding him as head of the concern, but the different views held by father and son on almost every subject soon led to stormy scenes that augured anything but well for the continuation of the arrangement. Senator Roberts was well aware of these unfortunate independent tendencies in John Ryder's son, and while he devoutly desired the consummation of Jefferson's union with his daughter, he quite realized that the young man was a nut that was going to be exceedingly hard to crack.

"Hello, Senator, you're always on time."

Disturbed in his reflections, Senator Roberts looked up and saw the extended hand of a red-faced, corpulent man,

one of the directors. He was no favorite with the senator, but the latter was too keen a man of the world to make enemies uselessly, so he condescended to place two fingers in the outstretched fat palm.

"How are you, Grimsby? Well, what are we going to do about this injunction? The case has gone against us. I knew Judge Rossmore's decision would be for the other side. Public opinion is aroused. The press——"

Mr. Grimsby's red face grew more apoplectic as he blurted out:

"Public opinion and the press be d——d. Who cares for public opinion? What is public opinion, anyhow? This road can manage its own affairs or it can't. If it can't I for one quit railroading. The press! Pshaw! It's all graft, I tell you. It's nothing but a strike! I never knew one of these virtuous outbursts that wasn't. First the newspapers bark ferociously to advertise themselves; then they crawl round and whine like a cur. And it usually costs something to fix matters."

The senator smiled grimly.

"No, no, Grimsby—not this time. It's more serious than that. Hitherto the road has been unusually lucky in its bench decisions——"

The senator gave a covert glance round to see if any long ears were listening. Then he added:

"We can't expect always to get a favorable decision like that in the Cartwright case, when franchise rights valued at nearly five millions were at stake. Judge Stollman proved himself a true friend in that affair."

Grimsby made a wry grimace as he retorted:

"Yes, and it was worth it to him. A Supreme Court judge don't get a cheque for $20,000 every day. That represents two years' pay."

"It might represent two years in jail if it were found out," said the senator, with a forced laugh.

Grimsby saw an opportunity, and he could not resist the temptation. Bluntly he said:

"As far as jail's concerned, others might be getting their deserts there too."

The senator looked keenly at Grimsby from under his white eyebrows. Then in a calm, decisive tone he replied :

"It's no question of a cheque this time. The road could not buy Judge Rossmore with $200,000. He is absolutely unapproachable in that way."

The apoplectic face of Mr. Grimsby looked incredulous.

It was hard for these men who plotted in the dark, and cheated the widow and the orphan for love of the dollar, to understand that there were in the world, breathing the same air as they, men who put honor, truth, and justice above mere money - getting. With a slight tinge of sarcasm he asked :

"Is there any man in our public life who is unapproachable from some direction or other?"

"Yes, Judge Rossmore is such a man. He is one of the few men in American public life who takes his duties seriously. In the strictest sense of the term, he serves his country instead of serving himself. I am no friend of his, but I must do him that justice."

He spoke sharply, in an irritated tone, as if resenting the insinuation of this vulgarian that every man in public life had his price. Roberts knew that the charge was true as far as he and the men he consorted with were concerned, but sometimes the truth hurts. That was why he had for a moment seemed to champion Judge Rossmore which, seeing that the judge himself was at that very moment under a cloud, was an absurd thing for him to do.

He had known Rossmore years before when the latter was a city magistrate in New York. That was before he, Roberts, had become a political grafter and when the decent things in life still appealed to him. The two men, although having few interests in common, had seen a good deal of one another until Roberts went to Washington when their relations were completely severed. But he had always watched Rossmore's career, and when he was made a judge of the Supreme Court at a comparatively early age he was sincerely glad. If anything could have convinced Roberts that success can come in public life to a man who pursues it by honest

methods it was the success of James Rossmore. He could never help feeling that Rossmore had been endowed by Nature with certain qualities which had been denied to him, above all that ability to walk straight through life with skirts clean which he had found impossible himself. To-day Judge Rossmore was one of the most celebrated judges in the country. He was a brilliant orator and a splendid after-dinner speaker. He was considered the most learned and able of all the members of the judiciary, and his decisions were noted as much for their fearlessness as for their wisdom. But what was far more, he enjoyed a reputation for absolute integrity. Until now, no breath of slander, no suspicion of corruption, had ever touched him. Even his enemies acknowledged that. And that is why there was a panic to-day among the directors of the Southern and Transcontinental Railroad. This honest, upright man had been called upon in the course of his duty to decide matters of vital importance to the road, and the directors were ready to stampede because, in their hearts, they knew the weakness of their case and the strength of the judge.

Grimsby, unconvinced, returned to the charge.

"What about these newspaper charges? Did Judge Rossmore take a bribe from the Great Northwestern or didn't he? You ought to know."

"I do know," answered the senator cautiously and somewhat curtly, "but until Mr. Ryder arrives I can say nothing. I believe he has been inquiring into the matter. He will tell us when he comes."

The hands of the large clock in the outer room pointed to three. An active, dapper little man with glasses and with books under his arm passed hurriedly from another office into the Directors' Room.

"There goes Mr. Lane with the minutes. The meeting is called, Where's Mr. Ryder?"

There was a general move of the scattered groups of directors towards the committee room. The clock overhead began to strike. The last stroke had not quite died away when the big swinging doors from the street were thrown open and there entered a tall, thin man, gray-headed, and with a slight stoop, but keen-eyed and alert. He was carefully dressed in a well-fitting frock coat, white waistcoat, black tie, and silk hat.

It was John Burkett Ryder, the Colossus.

II

At fifty-five, John Burkett Ryder was surprisingly well preserved. With the exception of the slight stoop, already noted, and the rapidly thinning snow-white hair, his step was as light and elastic, and his brain as vigorous and alert, as in a man of forty. Of old English stock, his physical make-up presented all those strongly marked characteristics of our race which, sprung from Anglo-Saxon ancestry, but modified by nearly three hundred years of different climate and customs, has produced the distinct and true American type, as easily recognizable among the family of nations as any other of the earth's children. Tall and distinguished-looking, Ryder would have attracted attention anywhere. Men who have accomplished much in life usually bear plainly upon their persons the indefinable stamp of achievement, whether of good or evil, which renders them conspicuous among their fellows. We turn after a man in the street and ask, Who is he? And nine times out of ten the object of our curiosity is a man who has made his mark—a successful soldier, a famous sailor, a celebrated author, a distinguished lawyer, or even a notorious crook.

There was certainly nothing in John Ryder's outward appearance to justify Lombroso's sensational description of him: " A social and physiological freak, a degenerate and a prodigy of turpitude who, in the pursuit of money, crushes with the insensibility of a steel machine every one who stands in his way." On the contrary, Ryder, outwardly at least, was a prepossessing-looking man. His head was well-shaped, and he had an intellectual brow,

while power was expressed in every gesture of his hands and body. Every inch of him suggested strength and resourcefulness. His face, when in good humor, frequently expanded in a pleasant smile, and he had even been known to laugh boisterously, usually at his own stories, which he rightly considered very droll, and of which he possessed a goodly stock. But in repose his face grew stern and forbidding, and when his prognathous jaw, indicative of will-power and bull-dog tenacity, snapped to with a click-like sound, those who heard it knew that squalls were coming.

But it was John Ryder's eyes that were regarded as the most reliable barometer of his mental condition. Wonderful eyes they were, strangely eloquent and expressive, but their most singular feature was that they possessed the uncanny power of changing color like a cat's. When their owner was at peace with the world, and had temporarily shaken off the cares of business, his eyes were of the most restful, beautiful blue, like the sky after sunrise on a Spring morning, and looking into their serene depths it seemed absurd to think that this man could ever harm a fly. His face, while under the spell of this kindly mood, was so benevolent and gentle, so frank and honest, that you felt there was nothing in the world—purse, honor, wife, child—that, if needs be, you would not entrust to his keeping.

When this period of truce was ended, when the plutocrat was once more absorbed in dominating the political as well as the industrial machinery of the nation, then his eyes took on a snakish, greenish hue, and one could plainly read in them the cunning, the avariciousness, the meanness, the insatiable thirst for gain that had made this man the most unscrupulous money-getter of his time. But his eyes had still another color, and when this last transformation took place those dependent on him, and even his friends, quaked with fear. For they were his eyes of anger. On these dreaded occasions his eyes grew black as darkest night and flashed fire as lightning rends the thunder-cloud. Almost ungovernable fury was, indeed, the weakest spot in John Ryder's armor, for in these moments of appalling wrath he was reckless of what he said or did—friendship, self-interest, prudence—all were sacrificed.

Such was the Colossus on whom all eyes were turned as he entered. Instantly the conversations stopped as by magic. The directors nudged each other and whispered. Instinctively, Ryder singled out his crony, Senator Roberts, who advanced with effusive gesture:

" Hello, Senator! "

"You're punctual as usual, Mr. Ryder. I never knew you to be late!"

The great man chuckled, and the little men standing around, listening breathlessly, chuckled in respectful sympathy, and they elbowed and pushed one another in their efforts to attract Ryder's notice, like so many cowardly hyenas not daring to approach the lordly wolf. Senator Roberts made a remark in a low tone to Ryder, whereupon the latter laughed. The bystanders congratulated each other silently. The great man was pleased to be in a good humor. And as Ryder turned with the senator to enter the Directors' Room the light from the big windows fell full on his face, and they noticed that his eyes were of the softest blue.

" No squalls to-day," whispered one.

"Wait and see," retorted a more experienced colleague. " Those eyes are more fickle than the weather."

Outside the sky was darkening, and drops of rain were already falling. A flash of lightning presaged the coming storm.

Ryder passed on and into the Directors' Room, followed by Senator Roberts and the other directors, procession being brought up by the dapper little secretary bearing the the minutes.

The long room, with its narrow centre table covered with green baize, was filled with directors scattered in little groups and all talking at once with excited gesture. At the sight of Ryder the chattering stopped as if by common consent, and the only sound audible was of the shuffling of feet and the moving of chairs as the directors took their places around the long table.

With a nod here and there Ryder took his place in the chairman's seat and rapped for order. Then at a sign from the chair the dapper little secretary began in a monotonous voice to read the minutes of the previous meeting. No one listened, a few directors yawned. Others had their eyes riveted on Ryder's face, trying to read there if he had devised some plan to offset the crushing blow of this adverse decision, which meant a serious loss to them all. He, the master mind, had served them in many a like crisis in the past. Could he do so again? But John Ryder gave no sign. His eyes, still of the same restful blue, were fixed on the ceiling watching a spider marching with diabolical intent on a wretched fly that had become entangled in its web. And as the secretary ambled monotonously on, Ryder watched and watched until he saw the spider seize the helpless prey and devour it. Fascinated by the spectacle, which doubtless suggested to him some analogy to his own methods, Ryder sat motionless, his eyes fastened on the ceiling, until the sudden stopping of the secretary's reading aroused him and told him that the minutes were finished. Quickly they were approved, and the chairman proceeded as rapidly as possible with the regular business routine. That disposed of, the meeting was ready for the chief business of the day. Ryder then calmly proceeded to present the facts in the case.

Some years back the road had acquired as an investment some thousands of acres of land located in the outskirts of Auburndale, on the line of their road. The land was bought cheap, and there had been some talk of laying part of it out as a public park. This promise had been made at the time in good faith, but it was no condition of the sale. If, afterwards, owing to the rise in the value of real estate, the road found it impossible to carry out the original idea, surely they were masters of their own property! The people of Auburndale thought differently and, goaded on by the local newspapers, had begun action in the courts to restrain the road from diverting the land from its alleged original purpose. They had succeeded in getting the injunction, but the road had fought it tooth and nail and finally carried it to the Supreme Court, where Judge Rossmore, after reserving his opinion, had finally upheld the injunction and decided against the railroad. That was the situation, and he would now like to hear from the members of the board.

Mr. Grimsby rose. Self-confident and noisily loquacious, as most men of his class are in simple conversation, he was plainly intimidated at speaking before such a crowd. He did not know where to look nor what to do with his hands, and he shuffled uneasily on his feet, while streams of nervous perspiration ran down his fat face, which he mopped repeatedly with a big colored handkerchief. At last, taking courage, he began:

"Mr. Chairman, for the past ten years this road has made bigger earnings in proportion to its carrying capacity than any other railroad in the United States. We have had fewer accidents, less injury to rolling stock, less litigation and bigger dividends. The road has been well managed and,"— here he looked significantly in Ryder's direction,—"there has been a big brain behind the manager. We owe you that credit, Mr. Ryder!"

Cries of "Hear! Hear!" came from all round the table.

Ryder bowed coldly, and Mr. Grimsby continued:

"But during the last year or two things have gone wrong. There has been a lot of litigation, most of which has gone against us, and it has cost a heap of money. It reduced the last quarterly dividend very considerably, and the new complication — this Auburndale suit, which also has gone against us — is going to make a still bigger hole in our exchequer. Gentlemen, I don't want to be a prophet of misfortune, but I'll tell you this — unless something is done to stop this hostility in the courts you and I stand to lose every cent we have invested in the road. This suit which we have just lost means a hundred others. What I would ask our chairman is what has become of his former good relations with the Supreme Court, what has become of his influence, which never failed us? What are these rumors regarding Judge Rossmore? He is charged in the newspapers with having accepted a present from a road in whose favor he handed down a very valuable decision. How is it that this road cannot reach Judge Rossmore and make him presents?"

The speaker sat down, flushed and breathless. The expression on every face showed that the anxiety was general. The directors glanced at Ryder, but his face was expressionless as marble. Apparently he took not the slightest interest in this matter which so agitated his colleagues.

Another director rose. He was a better speaker than Mr. Grimsby, but his voice had a hard, rasping quality that smote the ears unpleasantly. He said:

"Mr. Chairman, none of us can deny what Mr. Grimsby has just put before us so vividly. We are threatened not with one, but with a hundred such suits, unless something is done either to placate the public or to render its attacks harmless. Rightly or wrongly, the railroad is hated by the people, yet we are only what railroad conditions compel us to be. With the present fierce competition, no fine question of ethics can enter into our dealings as a business organization. With an irritated public and press on one side, and a hostile judiciary on the other, the outlook certainly is far from bright. But is the judiciary hostile? Is it not true that we have been singularly free from litigation until recently, and that most of the decisions were favorable to the road? Judge Rossmore is the real danger. While he is on the bench the road is not safe. Yet all efforts to reach him have failed and will fail. I do not take any stock in the newspaper stories regarding Judge Rossmore. They are preposterous. Judge Rossmore is too strong a man to be got rid of so easily."

The speaker sat down and another rose, his arguments being merely a reiteration of those already heard. Ryder did not listen to what was being said.

Why should he? Was he not familiar with every possible phase of the game? Better than these men who merely talked, he was planning how the railroad and all his other interests could get rid of this troublesome judge.

It was true. He who controlled legislatures and dictated to Supreme Court judges had found himself powerless when each turn of the legal machinery had brought him face to face with Judge Rossmore. Suit after suit had been decided against him and the interests he represented, and each time it was Judge Rossmore who had handed down the decision. So for years these two men had fought a silent but bitter duel in which principle on the one side and attempted corruption on the other were the gauge of battle. Judge Rossmore fought with the weapons which his oath and the law directed him to use, Ryder with the only weapons he understood—bribery and corruption. And each time it had been Rossmore who had emerged triumphant. Despite every manœuvre his experience could suggest, notwithstanding every trick that could be played to undermine his credit and reputation, Judge Rossmore stood higher in the country's confidence than when he was first appointed.

So when Ryder found he could not corrupt this honest judge with his gold, he decided to destroy him with calumny. He realized that the sordid methods that had succeeded with other judges would never prevail with Rossmore, so he plotted to take away from this man the one thing he cherished most, even more dearly than wife or daughter—his honor. He would ruin him by defaming his character, and so skilfully would he accomplish his work that the judge himself would realize the hopelessness of resistance. No scruples embarrassed Ryder in arriving at this determination. From his point of view he was fully justified. "Business is business. He hurts my interests; therefore I remove him." So he argued, and he considered it no more wrong to wreck the happiness of this honorable man than he would to have shot a burglar in self-defence. So having thus tranquillized

his conscience he had gone to work in his usual manner, and his success had surpassed his most sanguine expectations.

This is what he had done.

Like many of our public servants whose labors are compensated only in niggardly fashion by an inconsiderate country, Judge Rossmore was a man of but moderate means. His income as Justice of the Supreme Court was $10,000 a year, but for a man in his position, having a certain appearance to keep up, it little more than kept the wolf from the door. He lived quietly but comfortably in New York City with his wife and his daughter Shirley, an attractive young woman who had graduated from Vassar and had shown a marked taste for literature. The daughter's education had cost a good deal of money, and this, together with life insurance and other incidentals of keeping house in New York, had about taken all he had. But he had managed to save a little, and those years when he could put by a fifth of his salary the judge considered himself lucky. Secretly, he was proud of his comparative poverty. At least the world could never ask him "where he got it."

Ryder was well acquainted with Judge Rossmore's private means. The two men had met at a dinner, and although Ryder had tried to cultivate the acquaintance, he never received much encouragement. Ryder's son Jefferson, too, had met Miss Shirley Rossmore and been much attracted to her, but the father having more ambitious plans for his heir quickly discouraged all attentions in that direction. He himself, however, continued to meet the judge casually, and one evening he contrived to broach the subject of profitable investments. The judge admitted that by careful hoarding and much stinting he had managed to save up a few thousand dollars which he was anxious to invest in something good.

Quick as the keen-eyed vulture swoops down on its prey the wily financier seized the opportunity thus presented. And he took so much trouble in answering the judge's inexperienced questions, and generally made himself so agreeable that the judge found himself regretting that he and Ryder had, by force of circumstances, been opposed to each other in public life so long. Ryder strongly recommended the purchase of Alaskan Mining stock, a new and booming enterprise which had lately become very active in the market. Ryder said he had reasons to believe that the stock would soon advance, and now there was an opportunity to get it cheap. The judge was sincerely grateful for this apparently disinterested advice, and wrote two letters to Ryder, one in which he thanked him for the trouble he had taken, and another in which he asked him again if he was sure the company was financially sound, as the investment he contemplated making represented all his savings. He added in the second letter that he had received stock for double the amount of his investment and that being a perfect child in business transactions he had been unable to account for the extra $50,000 worth until the secretary of the company had written him assuring him that everything was in order. These letters Ryder kept.

A few days after he had made the investment the judge was surprised to receive certificates of stock for double the amount he had paid for. At the same time he received a letter from the secretary of the company explaining that the additional stock was pool stock, and not to be marketed at the present time. It was in the nature of a bonus to which he was entitled as one of the early shareholders. The letter was full of verbiage and technical details of which the judge understood nothing, but he thought it very liberal of the company, and putting the stock away in his safe soon forgot all about it. Had he been a business man he would have scented peril. He would have realized that he had now in his possession $50,000 worth of stock for which he had not paid a cent, and furthermore had deposited it when a reorganization came. ·

From that time on the Alaskan Mining Company underwent mysterious changes. New capitalists gained control and the name was altered to the Great Northwestern Mining Company. Then it became involved in litigation, and one suit, the outcome of which meant millions to the company, was carried to the Supreme Court, where Judge Rossmore was sitting. The judge had by this time forgotten all about the company in which he owned stock. He did not even recall its name. He only knew vaguely that it was a mine and that it was situated in Alaska. Could he dream that the Great Northwestern Mining Company and the company to which he had entrusted his few thousands were one and the same? In deciding on the merits of the case presented to him right seemed to him to be plainly with the Mining Company, and he rendered a decision to that effect. It was an important decision, involving a large sum, and for a day or two it was talked about. But as it was the opinion of the most learned and honest judge on the bench no one dreamed of questioning it.

But very soon ugly paragraphs began to appear in the newspapers. One paper asked if it were true that Judge Rossmore owned stock in the Great Northwestern Mining Company which had recently benefited so signally by his decision. Interviewed by a reporter, Judge Rossmore indignantly denied being interested in any way in the company. Thereupon, the same paper returned to the attack stating that the judge must surely be mistaken as the records showed a sale of stock to him at the time the company was known as the Alaskan Mining Company. When he read this the Judge was overwhelmed. It was true then? They had not slandered him. It was he who had lied, but how innocently! how innocently!

His daughter Shirley, who was his greatest friend and comfort, was then in Europe. She had gone to the Continent to rest, after working for months on a novel which she had just published. But to his old and tried friend, ex-Judge Stott, Judge Rossmore explained the facts as they were. Stott shook his head. " It 's a conspiracy!"

he cried. "And that man Ryder is behind it." Rossmore refused to believe that any man could so deliberately try to encompass another's destruction, but when more newspaper stories came out he began to realize that Stott was right and that his enemies had indeed dealt him a deadly blow. One newspaper boldly stated that Judge Rossmore was down on the mining company's book for $50,000 more stock than he had paid for, and it went on to ask if this were payment for the favorable decision just rendered. Rossmore, helpless, child-like as he was in business matters, now fully realized the seriousness of his position. "My God! My God!" he cried, as he bowed his head down on his desk. And for a whole day he remained closeted in his library, no one venturing near him.

As John Ryder sat there sphinx-like at the head of the directors' table he reviewed all this in his mind. His own part in the work was now done and he had come to this meeting to-day to tell them of his triumph.

The speaker, to whom he had paid such scant attention, resumed his seat, and there followed a pause and an intense silence which was broken only by the pattering of the rain against the big windows. The directors turned expectantly to Ryder, waiting for him to speak. What could the Colossus do now to save the situation? Cries of "the Chair! the Chair!" arose on every side. Senator Roberts leaned over to Ryder and whispered something in his ear.

With an acquiescent gesture, John Ryder tapped the table with his gavel and rose to address his fellow-directors. Instantly the room was silent again as the tomb. One might have heard a pin drop, so intense was the attention. All eyes were riveted on the chairman. The air itself seemed charged with electricity, that needed but a spark to set it ablaze.

Speaking deliberately and dispassionately, the Master Dissembler began.

They had all listened carefully, he said, to what had been stated by previous speakers. The situation no doubt was very critical, but they had weathered worse storms and he had every reason to hope they would outlive this storm. It was true that public opinion was greatly incensed against the railroads and, indeed, against all organized capital, and was seeking to injure them through the courts. For a time this agitation would hurt business and lessen the dividends, for it meant not only smaller annual earnings, but a lot of money which would have to be spent in Washington.

The eyes of the listeners who were hanging on every word involuntarily turned in the direction of Senator Roberts, but the latter, who at that moment was busily engaged in rummaging among a lot of papers, seemed to have missed this significant allusion to the road's expenses in the District of Columbia. Ryder continued:

In his experience such waves of reform were periodical and soon wear themselves out, when things go on just as they did before. Much of the agitation, doubtless, was a strike for graft. They would have to go down in their pockets, he supposed, and then these yellow newspapers and these yellow magazines that were barking at their heels would let them go. But in regard to the particular case now at issue —this Auburndale decision — there had been no way of preventing it. Influence had been used, but to no effect. The thing to do now was to prevent any such disasters in the future by removing the author of them.

The directors bent eagerly forward. Had Ryder really got some plan up his sleeve after all? The faces around the table looked brighter, and the directors cleared their throats and settled themselves down in their chairs as audiences do in the theatre when the drama is reaching its climax.

The board, continued Ryder with icy calmness, had perhaps heard, and also seen in the newspapers, the stories regarding Judge Rossmore and his alleged connection with the Great Northwestern Mining Company. Perhaps, they had not believed these stories. It was only natural. He had not believed them himself. But he had taken the trouble to inquire into the matter very carefully, and he regretted to say that the stories were true. In fact, they were no longer denied by Judge Rossmore himself.

The directors looked at each other in amazement. Gasps of astonishment, incredulity, satisfaction were heard all over the room. The rumors were true, then. Was it possible? Incredible!

Investigation, Ryder went on, had shown that Judge Rossmore was not only interested in the company in whose favor, as Judge of the Supreme Court, he had rendered an important decision, but what was worse, he had accepted from that company a valuable gift — that is $50,000 worth of stock — for which he had given absolutely nothing in return unless, as some claimed, the weight of his influence on the bench. These facts were very ugly and so unanswerable that Judge Rossmore did not attempt to answer them, and the important news which he, Ryder had to announce to his fellow-directors that afternoon, was that Judge Rossmore's conduct would shortly be made the subject of an inquiry by Congress.

This was the spark that was needed to ignite the electrically charged air. A wild cry of triumph went up from this band of jackals only too willing to fatten their bellies at the cost of another man's ruin, and one director, in his enthusiasm, rose excitely in his chair and demanded a vote of thanks for John Ryder.

Ryder coldly opposed the motion. No thanks were due to him, he said deprecatingly, nor did he think the occasion called for congratulations of any kind. It was surely a sad spectacle to see this honored judge, this devoted father, this blameless citizen threatened with ruin and disgrace on account of one false step. Let them rather sympathize with him and his family in their misfortune. He had little more to tell. The Congressional inquiry would take place immediately, and in all probability a demand would be made upon the Senate for Judge Rossmore's impeachment. It was, he added, almost unnecessary for him to remind the Board that, in the event of impeachment, the adverse decision in the Auburndale case would be annulled and the road would be entitled to a new trial.

Ryder sat down, and pandemonium broke loose, the delighted directors tumbling over each other in their eagerness to shake hands with the man who had saved them. Ryder had given no hint that he had been a factor in the working up of this case against their common enemy, in fact he had appeared to sympathize with him, but the directors knew well that he and he alone had been the master mind which had brought about the happy result.

On a motion to adjourn, the meeting broke up, and every one began to troop towards the elevators. Outside, the rain was now coming down in torrents, and the lights that everywhere dotted the great city only paled when every few moments a vivid flash of lightning rent the enveloping gloom.

Ryder and Senator Roberts went down ir the elevator together. When they reached the street the Senator inquired in a low tone:

"Do you think they really believed Rossmore was influenced in his decision?"

Ryder glanced from the lowering clouds overhead to his electric brougham which awaited him at the curb and replied indifferently:

"Not they. They don't care. All they want to believe is that he is to be impeached. The man was dangerous and had to be removed—no matter by what means. He is our enemy—my enemy—and I never give quarter to my enemies."

As he spoke, his prognathous jaw snapped to with a click-like sound, and in his eyes now coal-black were glints of fire. At the same instant there was a blinding flash, accompanied by a terrific crash, and the splinters of the flag-pole on the building opposite, which had been struck by a bolt, fell at their feet.

"A good or a bad omen?" asked the Senator, with a nervous laugh. He was secretly afraid of lightning, but was ashamed to admit it.

"A bad omen for Judge Rossmore!" rejoined Ryder coolly, as he slammed to the door of the cab, and the two men drove rapidly off in the direction of Fifth Avenue.

III

Of all the spots on this fair, broad earth where the jaded globe-wanderer, surfeited with hackneyed sight-seeing, may sit in perfect peace and watch the world go by, there is none more fascinating nor one presenting a more brilliant panorama of cosmopolitan life than that famous corner on the Paris boulevards, formed by the angle of the Boulevard des Capucines and the Place de l'Opéra. Here, on the " terrace " of the Café de la Paix, with its white and gold façade and long French windows, and its innumerable little marble-topped tables and rattan chairs, one may sit for hours at the trifling expense of a few *sous*, undisturbed even by the tip-seeking *garçon*, and, if one happens to be a student of human nature, find keen enjoyment in observing the world-types, representing every race and nationality under the sun, that pass and re-pass in a steady, never ceasing, exhaustless stream. The crowd surges to and fro past the little tables, occasionally toppling over a chair or two in the crush, moving up or down the great boulevards, one procession going to the right, in the direction of the Church of the Madeleine, the other to the left, heading toward the historic Bastille, both really going nowhere in particular, but ambling gently and good humoredly along enjoying the sights—and life!

Paris, queen of cities! Light-hearted, joyous, radiant Paris! The playground of the nations, the Mecca of the pleasure-seekers, the city beautiful! Paris—the siren, frankly immoral, always seductive, ever caressing! City of a thousand political convulsions, city of a million crimes—her streets have run with human blood, horrors unspeakable have stained her history, civil strife has scarred her monuments, the German conqueror insolently has bivouacked within her walls. Yet, like a virgin undefiled, she shows no sign of storm and stress, she offers her dimpled cheek to the rising sun, and when fall the shadows of night and a billion electric bulbs flash in the siren's crown, her resplendent, matchless beauty dazzles the world!

As the supreme reward of virtue, the good American is promised a visit to Paris when he dies. Those, however, of our sagacious fellow-countrymen who can afford to make the trip, usually manage to see Lutetia before crossing the river Styx. Most Americans like Paris—some like it so well that they have made it their permanent home—although it must be added that in their admiration they rarely include the Frenchman. For that matter, we are not as a nation particularly fond of any foreigner, largely because we do not understand him, while the foreigner for his part is quite willing to return the compliment. He gives the Yankee credit for commercial smartness, which has built up America's great material prosperity ; but he has the utmost contempt for our acquaintance with art, and no profound respect for us as scientists.

Is it not indeed fortunate that every nation finds itself superior to its neighbor ? If this were not so each would be jealous of the other, and would cry with envy like a spoiled child who cannot have the moon to play with. Happily, therefore, for the harmony of the world, each nation cordially detests the other, and the much exploited " brotherhood of man " is only a figure of speech. The Englishman, confident that he is the last word of creation, despises the Frenchman, who, in turn, laughs at the German, who shows open contempt for the Italian, while the American, conscious of his superiority to the whole family of nations, secretly pities them all.

The most serious fault which the American—whose one god is Mammon and chief characteristic hustle—has to find with his French brother is that he enjoys life too much, is never in a hurry, and, what to the Yankee mind is hardly respectable, has a habit of playing dominoes during business hours. The Frenchman retorts that his American brother, clever person though he be, has one or two things still to learn. He has, he declares, no philosophy of life. It is true that he has learned the trick of making money, but in the things which go to satisfy the soul he is still strangely lacking. He thinks he is enjoying life, when really he is ignorant of what life is. He admits it is not the American's fault, for he has never been taught how to enjoy life. One must be educated to that as everything else. All the American is taught is to be in a perpetual hurry and to make money no matter how. In this mad daily race for wealth he bolts his food, not stopping to masticate it properly, and consequently suffers all his life from dyspepsia. So he rushes from the cradle to the grave, and what's the good, since he must one day die like all the rest?

And what, asks the foreigner, has the American hustler accomplished that his slower-going Continental brother has not done as well? Are finer cities to be found in America than in Europe, do Americans paint more beautiful pictures, or write more learned or more entertaining books, has America made greater progress in science? Is it not a fact that the greatest inventors and scientists of our time—Marconi who gave to the world wireless telegraphy, Professor Curie who discovered radium, Pasteur who found a cure for rabies, Santos Dumont who has almost succeeded in navigating the air, Professor Röntgen who discovered the X-ray—are not all these immortals Europeans? And those two greatest mechanical inventions of our day, the automobile and the submarine boat, were they not first introduced and perfected in France before we in America woke up to appreciate their use? Is it, therefore, not possible to take life easily and still achieve?

The logic of these arguments, set forth in *Le Soir* in an article on the New World, appealed strongly to Jefferson Ryder as he sat in front of the Café de la Paix, sipping a sugared vermouth. It was five o'clock, the magic hour of the *aperitif*, when the glutton taxes his wits to deceive his stomach and work up an appetite for renewed gorging. The little tables were all occupied with the usual before-dinner crowd. There were a good many foreigners, mostly English and Americans and a few Frenchmen, obviously from the provinces, with only a sprinkling of real Parisians.

Jefferson's acquaintance with the French language was none too profound, and he had to guess at half the words in the article, but he understood enough to follow the writer's arguments. Yes, it was quite true, he thought, the American idea of life was all wrong. What was the sense of slaving all one's life, piling up a mass of money one cannot possibly spend, when there is only one life to live? How much saner the man who is content with enough and enjoys life while he is able to. These Frenchmen, and indeed all the Continental nations, had solved the problem. The gaiety of their cities, and this exuberant joy of life they communicated to all about them, were sufficient proofs of it.

Fascinated by the gay scene around him Jefferson laid the newspaper aside. To the young American, fresh from prosaic money-mad New York, the City of Pleasure presented indeed a novel and beautiful spectacle. How different, he mused, from his own city with its one fashionable throughfare—Fifth Avenue—monotonously lined for miles with hideous, brownstone residences, and showing little real animation except during the Saturday afternoon parade when the interests of the smart set, male and female, centred chiefly in such exciting diversions as going to Huyler's for soda, taking tea at the Waldorf, and trying to outdo each other in dress and show. New York certainly was a dull place with all its boasted cosmopolitanism. There was no denying that. Destitute of any natural beauty, handicapped by its cramped geographical position between two rivers, made unsightly by gigantic sky-scrapers and that noisy monstrosity, the Elevated Railroad, having no interests in anything not immediately connected with dollars, it was a city to dwell in and make money in, but hardly a city to *live* in. The millionaires were building white-marble palaces, taxing the ingenuity and the originality of the native architects, and thus to some extent relieving the general ugliness and drab commonplaceness, while the merchant princes had begun to invade the lower end of the avenue with handsome shops. But in spite of all this, in spite of its pretty girls—and Jefferson insisted that in this one important particular New York had no peer—in spite of its comfortable theatres and its wicked Tenderloin, and its Rialto made so brilliant at night by thousands of elaborate electric signs, New York still had the subdued air of a provincial town, compared with the exuberant gaiety, the multiple attractions, the beauties, natural and artificial, of cosmopolitan Paris.

The boulevards were crowded, as usual at that hour, and the crush of both vehicles and pedestrians was so great as to permit of only a snail-like progress. The clumsy three-horse omnibuses — Madeleine - Bastille — crowded inside and out with passengers and with their neatly uniformed drivers and conductors, so different in appearance and manner from our own slovenly street-car rowdies, were endeavoring to breast a perfect sea of *fiacres* which, like a swarm of mosquitoes, appeared to be trying to go in every direction at once, their drivers vociferating torrents of vituperous abuse on every man, woman, or beast unfortunate enough to get in their way. As a dispenser of unspeakable profanity, the Paris *cocher* has no equal. He is unique, no one can approach him. He also enjoys the reputation of being the worst driver in the world. If there is any possible way in which he can run down a pedestrian or crash into another vehicle he will do it, probably for the reason that it gives him another opportunity to display his choice stock of picturesque expletives.

But it was a lively, good-natured crowd and the fashionably gowned women and the well-dressed men, the fakirs hoarsely crying their catch-penny devices, the noble boulevards lined as far as the eye could reach with trees in full foliage, the magnificent Opera House with its glided dome glistening in the warm sunshine of a June afternoon, the broad avenue directly opposite, leading in a splendid straight line to the famous Palais Royal, the almost dazzling whiteness of the houses and monuments, the remarkable cleanliness and excellent condition of the sidewalks and streets, the gaiety and richness of the shops and restaurants, the picturesque kiosks where they sold newspapers and flowers—all this made up a picture so utterly unlike anything he was familiar with at home that Jefferson sat spellbound, delighted.

Yes, it was true, he thought, the foreigner had indeed learned the secret of enjoying life. There was assuredly something else in the world beyond mere money-getting. His father was a slave to it, but he would never be. He was resolved on that. Yet, with all his ideas of emancipation and progress, Jefferson was a thoroughly practical young man. He fully understood the value of money and the possession of it was as sweet to him as to other men. Only he would never soil his soul in acquiring it dishonorably. He was convinced that society as at present organized was all wrong and that the feudalism of the middle ages had simply given place to a worse form of slavery—capitalistic driven labor, which had resulted in the actual iniquitous conditions, the enriching of the rich and the impoverishment of the poor. He was familiar with the socialistic doctrines of the day and had taken a keen interest in this momentous question, this dream of a regenerated mankind. He had read Karl Marx and other socialistic writers, and while his essentially practical mind could hardly approve all their programme for reorganizing the State, some of which seemed to him utopian, extravagant, and even undesirable, he realized that the socialistic movement was growing rapidly all over the world, and the day was not far distant when in America, as to-day in Germany and France, it would be a formidable factor to reckon with.

But until the socialistic millennium arrived and society was reorganized, money, he admitted, would remain the lever of the world, the great stimulus to effort. Money supplied not only the necessities of life but also its luxuries, everything the material desire craved for, and so long as money had this magic purchasing power, so long would men lie and cheat and rob and kill for its possession. Was life worth living without money? Could one travel and enjoy the glorious spectacles Nature affords—the rolling ocean, the majestic mountains, the beautiful lakes, the noble rivers — without money? Could the book-lover buy books, the art-lover purchase pictures? Could one have fine houses to live in, or all sorts of modern conveniences to add to one's comfort, without money? The philosophers declared contentment to be happiness, arguing that the hod-carrier was likely to be happier in his hut than the millionaire in his palace, but was not that mere animal contentment, the happiness that knows no higher state, the ignorance of one whose eyes have never been raised to the heights?

No, Jefferson was no fool. He loved money for what pleasure, intellectual or physical, it could give him, but he would never allow money to dominate his life as his father had done. His father, he knew well, was not a happy man, neither happy himself nor respected by the world. He had toiled all his life to make his vast fortune and now he toiled to take care of it. The galley slave led a life of luxurious ease compared with John Burkett Ryder. Baited by the yellow newspapers and magazines, investigated by State committees, dogged by process-servers haunted by beggars, harassed by blackmailers, threatened by kidnappers, frustrated in his attempts to bestow charity by the cry "tainted money" — certainly the lot of the world's richest man was far from being an enviable one.

That is why Jefferson had resolved to strike out for himself. He had warded off the golden yoke which his father proposed to put on his shoulders, declining the lucrative position made for him in the Empire Trading Company, and he had gone so far as to refuse also the private income his father offered to settle on him. He would earn his own living. A man who has his bread buttered for him seldom accomplishes anything, he had said, and while his father had appeared to be angry at this open opposition to his will, he was secretly pleased at his son's grit. Jefferson was thoroughly in earnest. If needs be, he would forego the great fortune that awaited him rather than be forced into questionable business methods against which his whole manhood revolted.

Jefferson Ryder felt strongly about these matters, and gave them more thought than would be expected of most young men with his opportunities. In fact, he was unusually serious for his age. He was not yet thirty, but he had done a great deal of reading, and he took a keen interest in all the political and sociological questions of the hour. In personal appearance, he was the type of man that both men and women like—tall and athletic looking, with smooth face and clean-cut features. He had the steel-blue eyes and the fighting jaw of his father, and when he smiled he displayed two even rows of very white teeth. He was popular with men, being manly, frank, and cordial in his relations with them, and women admired him greatly, although they were somewhat intimidated by his grave and serious manner. The truth was that he was rather diffident with women, largely owing to lack of experience with them.

He had never felt the slightest inclination for business. He had the artistic temperament strongly developed, and his personal tastes had little in common with Wall Street and its feverish stock manipulating. When he was younger, he had dreamed of a literary or art career. At one time he had even had thoughts of going on the stage. But it was to art that he turned finally. From an early age he had shown considerable skill as a draughtsman, and later a two-years course at the Academy of Design convinced him that this was his true vocation. He had begun by illustrating for the book publishers and for the magazines, meeting at first with the usual rebuffs and disappointments, but, refusing to be discouraged, he had kept on and soon the tide turned. His drawings began to be accepted. They appeared first in one magazine, then in another, until one day, to his great joy, he received an order from an important firm of publishers for six wash-drawings to be used in illustrating a famous novel. This was the beginning of his real success. His illustrations were talked about almost as much as the book, and from that time on everything was easy. He was in great demand by the publishers, and very soon the young artist, who had begun his career of independence on nothing a year so to speak, found himself in a handsomely appointed studio in Bryant Park, with more orders coming in than he could possibly fill, and enjoying an income of little less than $8000 a year. The money was all the sweeter to Jefferson in that he felt he had himself earned every cent of it. This summer he was giving himself a well-deserved vacation, and he had come to Europe partly to see Paris and the other art centres about which his fellow-students at the Academy raved, but principally—although this he did not acknowledge even to himself—to meet in Paris a young woman in whom he was more than ordinarily interested — Shirley Rossmore, daughter of Judge Rossmore, of the United States Supreme Court, who had come abroad to recuperate after the labors on her new novel, "The American Octopus," a book which was then the talk of two hemispheres.

Jefferson had read half a dozen reviews of it in as many American papers that afternoon at the *New York Herald's* reading-room in the Avenue de l' Opéra, and he chuckled with glee as he thought how accurately this young woman had described his father. The book had been published under the pseudonym "Shirley Green," and he alone had been admitted into the secret of authorship. The critics all conceded that it was the book of the year, and that it portrayed with a pitiless pen the personality of the biggest figure in the commercial life of America. "Although," wrote one reviewer, "the leading character in the book is given another name, there can be no doubt that the author intended to give to the world a vivid pen portrait of John Burkett Ryder. She has succeeded in presenting a remarkable character study of the most remarkable man of his time."

He was particularly pleased with the reviews, not only for Miss Rossmore's

sake, but also because his own vanity was gratified. Had he not collaborated on the book to the extent of acquainting the author with details of his father's life, and his characteristics, which no outsider could possibly have learned? There had been no disloyalty to his father in doing this. Jefferson admired his father's smartness, if he could not approve his methods. He did not consider the book an attack on his father, but rather a powerfully written pen picture of an extraordinary man.

Jefferson had met Shirley Rossmore two years before at a meeting of the Schiller Society, a pseudo-literary organization gotten up by a lot of old fogies for no useful purpose, and at whose monthly meetings the poet who gave the society its name was probably the last person to be discussed. He had gone out of curiosity, anxious to take in all the freak shows New York had to offer, and he had been introduced to a tall girl with a pale, thoughtful face and firm mouth. She was a writer, Miss Rossmore told him, and this was also her first visit to the evening receptions of the Schiller Society. Half apologetically she added that it was likely to be her last, for, frankly, she was bored to death. But she explained that she had to go to these affairs, as she found them useful in gathering material for literary use. She studied types and eccentric characters, and this seemed to her a capital hunting-ground. Jefferson, who, as a rule, was timid with girls and avoided them, found this girl quite unlike the others he had known. Her quiet, forceful demeanor appealed to him strongly, and he lingered with her, chatting about his work, which had so many interests in common with her own, until refreshments were served, when the affair broke up. This first meeting had been followed by a call at the Rossmore residence, and the acquaintance had kept up until Jefferson, for the first time since he came to manhood, was surprised and somewhat alarmed at finding himself strangely and unduly interested in a person of the opposite sex.

The young artist's courteous manner,

his serious outlook on life, his high moral principles, so rarely met with nowadays in young men of his age and class, could hardly fail to appeal to Shirley, whose ideals of men had been somewhat rudely shattered by those she had hitherto met. Above all, she demanded in a man the refinement of the true gentleman, together with strength of character and personal courage. That Jefferson Ryder came up to this standard she was soon convinced. He was certainly a gentleman; his views on a hundred topics of the hour expressed in numerous conversations assured her as to his principles, while a glance at his powerful physique left no doubt possible as to his courage. She rightly guessed that this was no *poseur* trying to make an impression and gain her confidence. There was an unmistakable ring of sincerity in all his words, and his struggle at home with his father and his subsequent brave and successful fight for his own independence and self-respect more than substantiated all her theories. And the more Shirley let her mind dwell on Jefferson Ryder and his blue eyes and serious manner, the more conscious she became that the artist was encroaching more upon her thoughts and time than was good either for her work or for herself.

So their casual acquaintance grew into a real friendship and comradeship. Further than that Shirley promised herself it should never go. Not that Jefferson had given her the slightest hint that he entertained the idea of making her his wife one day, only she was sophisticated enough to know the direction in which run the minds of men who are abnormally interested in one girl, and long before this Shirley had made up her mind that she would never marry. Firstly, she was devoted to her father and could not bear the thought of ever leaving him; secondly, she was fascinated by her literary work and she was practical enough to know that matrimony, with its visions of slippers and cradles, would be fatal to any ambition of that kind. She liked Jefferson immensely, more, perhaps, than any man she had yet met, and she

did not think any the less of him because of her resolve not to get entangled in the meshes of Cupid. In any case he had not asked her to marry him—perhaps the idea was far from his thoughts. Meantime, she could enjoy his friendship freely without fear of embarrassing entanglements.

When, therefore, she first conceived the idea of portraying in the guise of fiction the personality of John Burkett Ryder, the Colossus of finance whose vast and ever-increasing fortune was fast becoming a public nuisance, she naturally turned to Jefferson for assistance. She wanted to write a book that would be talked about, and which at the same time would open the eyes of the public to this growing peril in their midst—this monster of insensate and unscrupulous greed who, by sheer weight of his ill-gotten gold, was corrupting legislators and judges and trying to enslave the nation. The book, she argued, would perform a public service in awakening all to the common danger. Jefferson fully entered into her views and had furnished her with the information regarding his father that she deemed of value. The book had proven a success beyond their most sanguine expectations, and Shirley had come to Europe for a rest after the many weary months of work that it took to write it.

The acquaintance of his son with the daughter of Judge Rossmore had not escaped the eagle eye of Ryder, Sr., and much to the financier's annoyance, and even consternation, he had ascertained that Jefferson was a frequent caller at the Rossmore home. He immediately jumped at the conclusion that this could mean only one thing, and fearing what he termed "the consequences of the insanity of immature minds," he had summoned Jefferson peremptorily to his presence. He told his son that all idea of marriage in that quarter was out of the question for two reasons: One was that Judge Rossmore was his most bitter enemy, the other was that he had hoped to see Jefferson, his destined successor, marry a woman of whom he, Ryder, Sr., could approve. He knew of such a woman, one who would make a far more desirable mate than Miss Rossmore. He alluded, of course, to Kate Roberts, the pretty daughter of his old friend, the Senator. The family interests would benefit by this alliance, which was desirable from every point of view. Jefferson had listened respectfully until his father had finished and then grimly said that only one point of view had been overlooked—his own. He did not care for Miss Roberts; he did not think she really cared for him. The marriage was out of the question. Whereupon Ryder, Sr., had fumed and raged, declaring that Jefferson was opposing his will as he always did, and ending with the threat that if his son married Shirley Rossmore without his consent he would disinherit him.

Jefferson was cogitating on these incidents of the last few months when suddenly a feminine voice which he quickly recognized called out in English:

"Hallo! Mr. Ryder."

He looked up and saw two ladies, one young, the other middle aged, smiling at him from an open *fiacre* which had drawn up to the curb. Jefferson started from his seat, upsetting his chair and startling two nervous Frenchmen in his hurry, and hastened out, hat in hand.

"Why, Miss Rossmore, what are you doing out driving?" he asked. "You know you and Mrs. Blake promised to dine with me to-night. I was coming round to the hotel in a few moments."

Mrs. Blake was a younger sister of Shirley's mother. Her husband had died a few years previously, leaving her a small income, and when she had heard of her niece's contemplated trip to Europe she had decided to come to Paris to meet her and incidentally to chaperone her. The two women were stopping at the Grand Hotel close by, while Jefferson had found accommodations at the Athenée.

Shirley explained. Her aunt wanted to go to the dressmaker's, and she herself was most anxious to go to the Luxembourg Gardens to hear the music. Would he take her? Then they could meet Mrs. Blake at the hotel at seven o'clock and all go to dinner. Was he willing?

Was he? Jefferson's face fairly glowed. He ran back to his table on the *terrasse* to settle for his Vermouth, astonished the waiter by not stopping to notice the short change he gave him, and rushed back to the carriage.

A dirty little Italian girl, shrewd enough to note the young man's attention to the younger of the American women, wheedled up to the carriage and thrust a bunch of flowers in Jefferson's face.

"*Achetez des fleurs, monsieur, pour la jolie dame?*"

Down went Jefferson's hand in his pocket and, filling the child's hand with small silver, he flung the flowers in the carriage. Then he turned inquiringly to Shirley for instructions so he could direct the *cocher*. Mrs. Blake said she would get out here. Her dressmaker was close by, in the Rue Auber, and she would walk back to the hotel to meet them at seven o'clock. Jefferson assisted her to alight and escorted her as far as the *porte-cochère* of the modiste's, a couple of doors away. When he returned to the carriage, Shirley had already told the coachman where to go. He got in and the *fiacre* started.

"Now," said Shirley, "tell me what you have been doing with yourself all day."

Jefferson was busily arranging the faded carriage rug about Shirley, spending more time in the task perhaps than was absolutely necessary, and she had to repeat the question.

"Doing?" he echoed with a smile, "I've been doing two things — waiting impatiently for seven o'clock and incidentally reading the notices of your book."

"Tell me, what do the papers say?"

Settling herself comfortably back in the carriage, Shirley questioned Jefferson with eagerness, even anxiety. She had been impatiently awaiting the arrival of the newspapers from "home," for so much depended on this first effort. She knew her book had been praised in some quarters, and her publishers had written her that the sales were bigger every day, but she was curious to learn how it had been received by the reviewers.

In truth, it had been no slight achievement for a young writer of her inexperience, a mere tyro in literature, to attract so much attention with her first book. The success almost threatened to turn her head, she had told her aunt laughingly, although she was sure it could never do that. She fully realized that it was the subject rather than the skill of the narrator that counted in the book's success, also the fact that it had come out at a timely moment, when the whole world was talking of the Money Peril. Had not President Roosevelt, in a recent sensational speech, declared that it might be necessary for the State to curb the colossal fortunes of America, and was not her hero, John Burkett Ryder, the richest of them all? Any way they looked at it, the success of the book was most gratifying.

While she was an attractive, aristocratic-looking girl, Shirley Rossmore had no serious claims to academic beauty. Her features were irregular, and the firm and rather thin mouth lines disturbed the harmony indispensable to plastic beauty. Yet there was in her face something far more appealing — soul and character. The face of the merely beautiful woman expresses nothing, promises nothing. It presents absolutely no key to the soul within, and often there is no soul within to have a key to. Perfect in its outlines and coloring, it is a delight to gaze upon, just as is a flawless piece of sculpture, yet the delight is only fleeting. One soon grows satiated, no matter how beautiful the face may be, because it is always the same, expressionless and soulless. "Beauty is only skin deep," said the philosopher, and no truer dictum was ever uttered. The merely beautiful woman, who posseses only beauty and nothing else, is kept so busy thinking of her looks, and is so anxious to observe the impression her beauty makes on others, that she has neither the time nor the inclination for matters of greater importance. Sensible men,

as a rule, do not lose their hearts to women whose only assets are their good looks. They enjoy a flirtation with them, but seldom care to make them their wives. The marrying man is shrewd enough to realize that domestic virtues will be more useful in his household economy than all the academic beauty ever chiselled out of block marble.

Shirley was not beautiful, but hers was a face that never failed to attract attention. It was a thoughtful and interesting face, with an intellectual brow and large, expressive eyes, the face of a woman who had both brain power and ideals, and yet who, at the same time, was in perfect sympathy with the world. She was fair in complexion, and her fine brown eyes, alternately reflective and alert, were shaded by long dark lashes. Her eyebrows were delicately arched, and she had a good nose. She wore her hair well off the forehead, which was broader than in the average woman, suggesting good mentality. Her mouth, however, was her strongest feature. It was well shaped, but there were firm lines about it that suggested unusual will power. Yet it smiled readily, and when it did there was an agreeable vision of strong, healthy-looking teeth of dazzling whiteness. She was a little over medium height and slender in figure, and carried herself with that unmistakable air of well-bred independence that bespeaks birth and culture. She dressed stylishly, and while her gowns were of rich material, and of a cut suggesting expensive modistes, she was always so quietly attired and in such perfect taste that after leaving her one could never recall what she had on.

At the special request of Shirley, who wanted to get a glimpse of the Latin Quarter, the driver took a course down the Avenue de l'Opéra, that magnificent thoroughfare which starts at the Opéra and ends at the Théâtre Français, and which, like many others that go to the beautifying of the capital, the Parisians owe to the much-despised Napoleon III. The cab, Jefferson told her, would skirt the Palais Royal and follow the Rue de Rivoli until it came to the Châtelet, when it would cross the Seine and drive up the Boulevard St. Michel—the students' boulevard—until it reached the Luxembourg Gardens. Like most of his kind, the *cocher* knew less than nothing of the art of driving, and he ran a reckless, zig-zag flight, in and out, forcing his way through a confusing maze of vehicles of every description, pulling first to the right, then to the left, for no good purpose that was apparent, and averting only by the narrowest of margins half a dozen bad collisions. At times the *fiacre* lurched in such alarming fashion that Shirley was visibly perturbed, but when Jefferson assured her that all Paris cabs travelled in this crazy fashion and nothing ever happened, she was comforted.

"Tell me," she repeated, "what do the papers say about the book?"

"Say?" he echoed. "Why, simply that you've written the biggest book of the year, that's all!"

"Really! Oh, do tell me all they said!" She was fairly excited now, and in her enthusiasm she grasped Jefferson's broad, sunburnt hand which was lying outside the carriage rug. He tried to appear unconscious of the contact, which made his every nerve tingle, as he proceeded to tell her the gist of the reviews he had read that afternoon.

"Isn't that splendid!" she exclaimed, when he had finished. Then she added quickly:

"I wonder if your father has seen it?"

Jefferson grinned. He had something on his conscience, and this was a good opportunity to get rid of it. He replied laconically.

"He probably has read it by this time. I sent him a copy myself."

The instant the words were out of his mouth he was sorry, for Shirley's face had changed color.

"You sent him a copy of 'The American Octopus'?" she cried. "Then he'll guess who wrote the book."

"Oh, no, he won't," rejoined Jefferson calmly. "He has no idea who sent it to him. I mailed it anonymously."

Shirley breathed a sigh of relief. It was so important that her identity should remain a secret. As daughter of a Supreme Court judge she had to be most careful. She would not embarrass

her father for anything in the world. But it was smart of Jefferson to have sent Ryder, Sr., the book, so she smiled graciously on his son as she asked:

"How do you know he got it? So many letters and packages are sent to him that he never sees himself."

"Oh, he saw your book all right," laughed Jefferson. "I went to the house to say good-bye to him and mother before sailing, and I found him in the library reading it."

They both laughed, feeling like mischievous children who had played a successful trick on the hokey-pokey man. Jefferson noted his companion's pretty dimples and fine teeth, and he thought how attractive she was, and stronger and stronger grew the idea within him that this was the woman who was intended by Nature to share his life. Her slender hand still covered his broad, sunburnt one, and he fancied he felt a slight pressure. But he was mistaken. Not the slightest sentiment entered into Shirley's thoughts of Jefferson. She regarded him only as a good comrade with whom she had secrets she confided in no one else. To that extent, and to that extent alone, he was privileged above other men. Suddenly he asked her:

"Have you heard from home recently?"

A soft light stole into the girl's face. Home! Ah, that was all she needed to make her cup of happiness full. Intoxicated with this new sensation of a first literary success, full of the keen pleasure this visit to the beautiful city was giving her, bubbling over with the joy of life, happy in the almost daily companionship of the man she liked most in the world after her father, there was only one thing lacking—home! She had left New York only a month before, and she was homesick already. Her father she missed most. She was fond of her mother, too, but the latter, being somewhat of a nervous invalid, had never been to her quite what her father had been. The playmate of her childhood, companion of her girlhood, her friend and adviser in womanhood, Judge Rossmore was to his daughter the ideal man and father. Answering Jefferson's question she said:

"I had a letter from father last week. Everything was going on at home as when I left. Father says he misses me sadly, and that mother is ailing as usual."

She smiled, and Jefferson smiled too. They both knew by experience that nothing really serious ailed Mrs. Rossmore, who was a good deal of a hypochondriac, and always so filled with aches and pains that, on the few occasions when she really felt well, she was genuinely alarmed.

The *fiacre* by this time had emerged from the Rue de Rivoli and was rolling smoothly along the fine wooden pavement in front of the historic Conciergerie prison where Marie Antoinette was confined before her execution. Presently they recrossed the Seine, and the cab, dodging the tram-car rails, proceeded at a smart pace up the "Boule Mich," which is the familiar diminutive bestowed by the students upon that broad avenue which traverses the very heart of their beloved *Quartier Latin*. On the left frowned the scholastic walls of the learned Sorbonne, in the distance towered the majestic dome of the Pantheon where Rousseau, Voltaire, and Hugo lay buried.

Like most of the principal arteries of the French capital, the boulevard was generously lined with trees, now in full bloom, and the sidewalks fairly seethed with a picturesque throng in which mingled promiscuously frivolous students, dapper shop clerks, sober citizens, and frisky, flirtatious little *ouvrières*, these last being all hatless, as is characteristic of the work-girl class, but singularly attractive in their neat black dresses and dainty low-cut shoes. There was also much in evidence another type of female whose extravagance of costume and boldness of manner loudly proclaimed her profession.

On either side of the boulevard were shops and cafés, mostly cafés, with every now and then a *brasserie*, or beer hall. Seated in front of these establishments, taking their ease as if beer sampling constituted the only real interest in their lives, were hundreds of students, reckless and dare-devil, and suggesting almost anything except serious study. They all wore frock coats and tall silk hats, and some of the latter were wonderful specimens of the hatter's art. Some of the more eccentric students had long hair down to their shoulders, and wore baggy peg-top trousers of extravagant cut, which hung in loose folds over their sharp-pointed boots. On their heads were queer plug hats with flat brims.

Shirley laughed outright and regretted that she did not have her kodak to take back to America some idea of their grotesque appearance, and she listened with amused interest as Jefferson explained that these men were notorious *poseurs*, aping the dress and manners of the old-time student as he flourished in the days of Randolph and Mimi and the other immortal characters of Murger's Bohemia. Nobody took them seriously except themselves, and for the most part they were bad rhymsters of decadent verse. Shirley was astonished to see so many of them busily engaged smoking cigarettes and imbibing glasses of a pale-green beverage, which Jefferson told her was absinthe.

"When do they read?" she asked. "When do they attend lectures?"

"Oh," laughed Jefferson, "only the old-fashioned students take their studies seriously. Most of the men you see there are from the provinces, seeing Paris for the first time, and having their fling. Incidentally they are studying life. When they have sown their wild oats and learned all about life—provided they are still alive and have any money left—they will begin to study books. You would be surprised to know how many of these young men, who have been sent to the University at a cost of goodness knows what sacrifices, return to their native towns in a few months wrecked in body and mind, without having once set foot in a lecture room, and, in fact, having done nothing except inscribe their names on the rolls."

Shirley was glad she knew no such men, and if she ever married and had a son she would pray God to spare her that grief and humiliation. She herself knew something about the sacrifices parents make to secure a college education for their children. Her father had sent her to Vassar. She was a product of the much-sneered-at higher education for women, and all her life she would be grateful for the advantages given her. Her liberal education had broadened her outlook on life and enabled her to accomplish the little she had. When she graduated her father had left her free to follow her own inclinations. She had little taste for social distractions, and still she could not remain idle. For a time she thought of teaching to occupy her mind, but she knew she lacked the necessary patience, and she could not endure the drudgery of it, so, having won honors at college in English composition, she determined to try her hand at literature. She wrote a number of essays and articles on a hundred different subjects which she sent to the magazines, but they all came back with politely worded excuses for their rejection. But Shirley kept right on. She knew she wrote well; it must be that her subjects were not suitable. So she adopted new tactics, and persevered until one day came a letter of acceptance from the editor of one of the minor magazines. They would take the article offered—a sketch of college life—and as many more in similar vein as Miss Rossmore could write. This success had been followed by other acceptances and other commissions, until at the present time she ·was a well-known writer for the leading publications. Her great ambition had been to write a book, and "The American Octopus," published under an assumed name, was the result.

The cab stopped suddenly in front of beautiful glided gates. It was the Luxembourg, and through the tall railings they caught a glimpse of well-kept lawns, splashing fountains, and richly dressed children playing. From the distance came the stirring strains of a brass band.

The coachman drove up to the curb and Jefferson jumped down, assisting Shirley to alight. In spite of Shirley's protest Jefferson insisted ·on paying.

"*Combien?*" he asked the *cocher.*

The jehu, a surly, thick-set man with a red face and small, cunning eyes like a ferret, had already sized up his fares for two *sacré* foreigners whom it would be flying in the face of Providence not to cheat, so with unblushing effrontery he answered:

"*Dix francs, Monsieur!*" And he held up ten fingers by way of illustration.

Jefferson was about to hand up a ten-franc piece when Shirley indignantly interfered. She would not submit to such an imposition. There was a regular tariff and she would pay that and nothing more. So, in better French than was at Jefferson's command, she exclaimed:

"Ten francs? *Pourquoi dix francs?* I took your cab by the hour. It is exactly two hours. That makes four francs." Then to Jefferson she added: "Give him a france for a *pourboire*— that makes five francs altogether."

Jefferson, obedient to her superior wisdom, held out a five-franc piece, but the driver shrugged his shoulders disdainfully. He saw that the moment had come to bluster so he descended from his box fully prepared to carry out his bluff. He started in to abuse the two Americans whom in his ignorance he took for English.

"Ah, you *sale Anglais!* You come to France to cheat the poor Frenchman. You make me work all afternoon and then pay me nothing. ´Not with this coco! I know my rights and I 'll get them too."

All this was hurled at them in a patois French, almost unintelligible to Shirley, and wholly so to Jefferson. All he knew was that the fellow's attitude was becoming unbearably insolent and he stepped forward with a gleam in his eye that might have startled the man had he not been so busy shaking his fist at Shirley. But she saw Jefferson's movement and laid her hand on his arm.

"No, no, Mr. Ryder—no scandal, please. Look, people are beginning to come up! Leave him to me. I know how to manage him."

With this the daughter of a United States Supreme Court judge proceeded to lay down the law to the representative of the most lazy and irresponsible class of men ever let loose in the streets of a civilized community. Speaking with an air of authority, she said :

"Now look here, my man, we have no time to bandy words with you. I took your cab at 3.30. It is now 5.30. That makes two hours. The rate is two francs an hour, or four francs in all. We offer you five francs, and this includes a franc *pourboire*. If this settlement does not suit you we will get into your cab and you will drive us to the nearest police-station where the argument can be continued."

The man's jaw dropped. He was obviously outclassed. These foreigners knew the law as well as he did. He had no desire to accept Shirley's suggestion of a trip to the police-station, where he knew he would get little sympathy, so, grumbling and giving vent under his breath to a volley of strange oaths, he grabbed viciously at the five-franc piece Jefferson held out and, mounting his box, drove off.

Proud of their victory, they entered the gardens, following the sweet-scented paths until they came to where the music was. The band of an infantry regiment was playing, and a large crowd had gathered. Many people were sitting on the chairs provided for visitors for the modest fee of two sous; others were promenading round and round a great circle having the musicians in its centre. The dense foliage of the trees overhead afforded a perfect shelter from the hot rays of the sun, and the place was so inviting and interesting, so cool, and so full of sweet perfumes and sounds, appealing to and satisfying the senses, that Shirley wished they had more time to spend there. She was very fond of a good brass band, especially when heard in the open air. They were playing Strauss's *Blue Danube*, and the familiar strains of the delightful waltz were so infectious that both were seized by a desire to get up and dance.

There was constant amusement, too, watching the crowd, with its many original and curious types. There were serious college professors, with gold-rimmed spectacles, buxom *nounous* in their uniform cloaks and long ribbon streamers, nicely dressed children romping merrily but not noisily, more

queer-looking students in shabby frock coats, tight at the waist, trousers too short, and comical hats, stylishly dressed women displaying the latest fashions, brilliantly uniformed army officers strutting proudly, dangling their swords —an attractive and interesting crowd, so different, thought the two Americans, from the cheap, evil-smelling, ill-mannered mob of aliens that invades their own Central Park the days when there is music, making it a nuisance instead of a pleasure. Here every one belonged apparently to the better class; the women and children were richly and fashionably dressed, the officers looked smart in their multi-colored uniforms, and, no matter how one might laugh at the students, there was an atmosphere of good-breeding and refinement everywhere which Shirley was not accustomed to see in public places at home. A sprinkling of workmen and people of the poorer class was to be seen here and there, but they were in the decided minority. Shirley, herself a daughter of the Revolution, was a staunch supporter of the immortal principles of democracy and of the equality of man before the law. But all other talk of equality was the greatest sophistry and charlatanism. There could be no real equality so long as some people were cultured and refined and others were uneducated and vulgar. Shirley believed in an aristocracy of brains and soap. She insisted that no clean person, no matter how good a democrat, should be expected to sit close in public places to persons who were not on speaking terms with the bath-tub. In America this foolish theory of a democracy, which insists on throwing all classes, the clean and the unclean, promiscuously together, was positively revolting, making travelling in the public vehicles almost impossible, and it was not much better in the public parks. In France—also a republic—where they likewise paraded conspicuously the clap-trap "Égalité, Fraternité," they managed these things far better. The French lower classes knew their place. They did not ape the dress, nor frequent the resorts of those above them in the social scale.

The distinction between the classes was plainly and properly marked, yet this was not antagonistic to the ideal of true democracy ; it had not prevented the son of a peasant from becoming President of the French Republic. Each district in Paris had its own amusements, its own theatres, its own parks. It was not a question of capital refusing to fraternize with labor, but the very natural desire of persons of refinement to mingle with clean people rather than to rub elbows with the Great Unwashed.

"Isn't it delightful here?" said Shirley. "I could stay here forever, couldn't you?"

"With you—yes," answered Jefferson, with a significant smile.

Shirley tried to look angry. She strictly discouraged these conventional, sentimental speeches which constantly flung her sex in her face.

"Now, you know I don't like you to talk that way, Mr. Ryder. It's most undignified. Please be sensible."

Quite subdued, Jefferson relapsed into a sulky silence. Presently he said :

"I wish you wouldn't call me Mr. Ryder. I meant to ask you this before. You know very well that you've no great love for the name, and if you persist you'll end by including me in your hatred of the hero of your book."

Shirley looked at him with amused curiosity.

"What do you mean?" she asked. "What do you want me to call you?"

"Oh, I don't know," he stammered, rather intimidated by this self-possessed young woman who looked him calmly through and through. "Why not call me Jefferson? Mr. Ryder is so formal."

Shirley laughed outright, a merry, unrestrained peal of honest laughter, which made the passers-by turn their heads and smile, too, commenting the while on the stylish appearance of the two Americans whom they took for sweethearts. After all, reasoned Shirley, he was right. They had been together now nearly every hour in the day for over a month. It was absurd to call him Mr. Ryder. So, addressing him with mock gravity, she said :

"You're right, Mr. Ryder—I mean Jefferson. You're quite right. You

are Jefferson from this time on, only remember"—here she shook her gloved finger at him warningly—"mind you behave yourself ! No more such sentimental speeches as you made just now."

Jefferson beamed. He felt at least two inches taller, and at that moment he would not have changed places with any one in the world. To hide the embarrassment his gratification caused him he pulled out his watch and exclaimed :

"Why, it's a quarter past six. We shall have all we can do to get back to the hotel and dress for dinner."

Shirley rose at once, although loath to leave.

"I had no idea it was so late," she said. "How the time flies!" Then mockingly she added : "Come, Jefferson—be a good boy and find a cab."

They passed out of the Gardens by the gate facing the Théâtre de l'Odéon, where there was a long string of *fiacres* for hire. They got into one and in fifteen minutes they were back at the Grand Hotel.

At the office they told Shirley that her aunt had already come in and gone to her room, so she hurried up-stairs to dress for dinner while Jefferson proceeded to the Hotel de l'Athenée on the same mission. He had still twenty-five minutes before dinner time, and he needed only ten minutes for a wash and to jump into his dress-suit, so, instead of going directly to his hotel, he sat down at the Café de la Paix. He was thirsty, and calling for a Vermouth *frappé* he told the *garçon* to bring him also the American papers.

The crowd on the boulevard was denser than ever. The business offices and some of the shops were closing, and a vast army of employés, homeward bound, helped to swell the sea of humanity that pushed this way and that.

But Jefferson had no eyes for the crowd. He was thinking of Shirley. What singular, mysterious power had this girl acquired over him? He, who had scoffed at the very idea of marriage only a few months before, now desired it ardently, anxiously! Yes, that was what his life lacked—such a woman to be his companion and helpmate! He loved her—there was no doubt of that. His every thought, waking and sleeping, was of her, all his plans for the future included her. He would win her if any man could. But did she care for him? Ah, that was the cruel, torturing uncertainty! She appeared cold and indifferent, but perhaps she was only trying him. Certainly she did not seem to dislike him.

The waiter returned with the Vermouth and the newspapers. All he could find were the *London Times*, which he pronounced T-e-e-m-s, and some issues of the *New York Herald*. Jefferson idly turned over the pages of the *Herald*. The papers were nearly a month old, but he did not care for that. His thoughts were still running on Shirley, and he was paying little attention to what he was reading. Suddenly, however, his eyes rested on a headline which made him sit up with a start. It read as follows:

JUDGE ROSSMORE IMPEACHED

JUSTICE OF THE SUPREME COURT TO BE TRIED ON BRIBERY CHARGES

The despatch, which was dated Washington two weeks back, went on to say that serious charges affecting the integrity of Judge Rossmore had been made the subject of Congressional inquiry, and that the result of the inquiry was so grave that a demand for impeachment would be at once sent to the Senate. It added that the charges grew out of the recent decision in the Great Nothwestern Mining Company case, it being alleged that Judge Rossmore had accepted a large sum of money on condition of his handing down a decision favorable to the company.

Jefferson was thunderstruck. He read the despatch over again to make sure there was no mistake. No, it was very plain—Judge Rossmore of Madison Avenue. But how preposterous, what a calumny! The one judge on the bench at whom one could point and say with absolute conviction: "There goes an honest man!" And this judge was to be tried on a charge of bribery! What could be the meaning of it? Something terrible must have happened since Shirley's departure from home, that was certain. It meant her immediate return to the States and, of course, his own. He would see what could be done. He would make his father use his great influence. But how could he tell Shirley? Impossible, he could not! She would not believe him if he did. She would probably hear from home in some other way. They might cable. In any case he would say nothing yet. He paid for his Vermouth and hurried away to his hotel to dress.

It was just striking seven when he re-entered the courtyard of the Grand Hotel. Shirley and Mrs. Blake were waiting for him. Jefferson suggested having dinner at the Café de Paris, but Shirley objected that as the weather was warm it would be more pleasant to dine in the open air, so they finally decided on the Pavillon d'Armonville where there was music and where they could have a little table to themselves in the garden.

They drove up the stately Champs Élysées, past the monumental Arc de Triomphe, and from there down to the Bois. All were singularly quiet. Mrs. Blake was worrying about her new gown, Shirley was tired, and Jefferson could not banish from his mind the terrible news he had just read. He avoided looking at Shirley until the latter noticed it and thought she must have offended him in some way. She was more sorry than she would have him know, for, with all her apparent coldness, Jefferson was rapidly becoming very indispensable to her happiness.

They dined sumptuously and delightfully with all the luxury of surroundings and all the delights of cooking that the French culinary art can perfect. A single glass of champagne had put Shirley in high spirits and she had tried hard to communicate some of her good humor to Jefferson, who, despite all her efforts, remained quiet and preoccupied. Finally losing patience she asked him bluntly:

"Jefferson, what's the matter with

you to-night? You've been sulky as a bear all evening."

Pleased to see she had not forgotten their compact of the afternoon in regard to his name, Jefferson relaxed somewhat and said apologetically:

"Excuse me, I've been feeling a bit seedy, lately. I think I need another sea voyage. That's the only time when I feel really first-class—when I'm on the water."

The mention of the sea started Shirley to talk about her future plans. She wasn't going back to America until September. She had arranged to make a stay of three weeks in London and then she would be free. Some friends of hers from home, a man and his wife who owned a steam yacht, were arranging a trip to the Mediterranean, including a run over to Cairo. They had asked her and Mrs. Blake to go and she was sure they would ask Jefferson, too. Would he go?

There was no way out of it. Jefferson tried to work up some enthusiasm for this yachting trip, which he knew very well could never come off, and it cut him to the heart to see this poor girl joyously making all these preparations and plans, little dreaming of the domestic calamity which at that very moment was hanging over her head.

It was nearly ten o'clock when they had finished. They sat a little longer listening to the gypsy music, weird and barbaric. Very pointedly, Shirley remarked:

"I for one preferred the music this afternoon."

"Why?" inquired Jefferson, ignoring the petulant note in her voice.

"Because you were more amiable!" she retorted rather crossly.

This was their first misunderstanding, but Jefferson said nothing. He could not tell her the thoughts and fears that had been haunting him all night. Soon afterward they re-entered their cab and returned to the boulevards which were ablaze with light and gayety. Jefferson suggested going somewhere else, but Mrs. Blake was tired and Shirley, now quite irritated at what she considered Jefferson's unaccountable unsociability, declined somewhat abruptly. But she could never remain angry long, and when they said good-night she whispered demurely:

"Are you cross with me, Jeff?"

He turned his head away and she saw that his face was singularly drawn and grave.

"Cross—no. Good-night. God bless you!" he said hoarsely, gulping down a lump that rose in his throat. Then grasping her hand he hurried away.

Completely mystified, Shirley and her companion turned to the office to get the key of their room. As the man handed it to Shirley he passed her also a cablegram which had just come. She changed color. She did not like telegrams. She always had a dread of them, for with her sudden news was usually bad news. Could this, she thought, explain Jefferson's strange behavior? Trembling, she tore open the envelope and read:

COME HOME AT ONCE.

MOTHER.

(*To be continued.*)

Smoky Torches in Franklin's Honor

By RICHARD MEADE BACHE

A WRITER remarked, just before the Bicentenary Celebration of Franklin's birth, that, considering that we were then so near to the date of the event, few articles regarding him were appearing in the press. I could not agree with him then, still less could I agree with him now, if he be of the same mind, for articles on Franklin have verged on superfluity. But I had observed, and still regard as surprising, that both then and at the time of the celebration, we should find speeches about him and articles printed about him full of egregious errors. Not long since a man wrote that Franklin had printed the first paper in this country. I am moved to say something in the matter, because I recognize how hard it is to drive from their lairs long-established popular errors, and how insuperably hard it would be ever to dispose of some of them, should they be confirmed at this time, when final appraisement is being attempted of Franklin's true value, scientifically, literarily, and patriotically.

I doubt not what the verdict of any candid man would be in answer to the question, If he regards as tolerable the statement made by Mr. George A. Post, in his after-dinner speech in New York before the Pennsylvania Society, in which he summarized Franklin's official service at home and abroad by remarking, that it is wonderful that his example has not led to the formation of a society in this country whose motto would be never to resign office. Was it a joke? Then it was, as being on a serious subject, inadmissible; was, in a word, *une mauvaise plaisanterie.* Was it serious? Then it was out of place in an entertainment in Franklin's honor, and betrayed the profoundest ignorance of his career. No one acquainted with the details of Franklin's official life could truthfully say such a thing. Even as early, relatively, to his long life, as Franklin's second official visit to England, he dejectedly wrote to his son of his homesickness and of his desire to return permanently to America; and, in the latter part of his stay in France, he thrice, at long intervals, vainly sought relief from his office as plenipotentiary. Mr. Post's statement must have been read by at least a million people. Such apparently authentic judgments are likely to do irreparable injury to Franklin's fair fame, so vast is the expanse of human credulity, so deep its tendency to believe of fellow-men the worst.

There is much published on this subject which is beyond reproach, much of which this cannot be said, and much, also, which contains many gross as well as petty errors. I am pleased to be able to note that the article, "Franklin's Place in Literature" by Professor Albert H. Smyth, the author of the ten-volume edition of Franklin's Life, now appearing from the press, is satisfactory within the narrow limits to which it is confined. So, also, is that of Mr. Edward Robins, "Franklin the Man," as one should have had reason to expect from reading his duodecimo volume, "Benjamin Franklin," published a few years ago. The posthumous article of the Hon. John Hay is admirable. So is that of the Hon. Joseph H. Choate, reproduced from his inaugural address, on July 23, 1903, as President of the Birmingham and Midland Institute, England. I regret to see, however, that he seems not fully acquainted with the incident of Franklin's wearing his celebrated ceremonial dress on the occasion of his signing the treaties with France, not the treaty of peace with Great Britain; for he merely says, with reference to the point:

"At the signing of one of the treaties in Paris, Franklin is said to have worn the same old suit of spotted Manchester velvet which he had worn on the fatal day at the Cockpit, years before, when Wedderburn attacked him, showing how deeply on that occasion the iron had entered into his soul."

Much turns upon the point. Nothing could have induced Franklin to wear, at the signing of the treaty of peace with Great Britain, the ceremonial dress in which he was clad when Wedderburn made his disgraceful attack upon him before the applauding Lords in Council. *The Gentleman's Magazine*, of London, settled this point more than a century ago. I tried to help to the same renewed necessity a few years ago, by an article that I published in *The Pennsylvania Magazine of History and Biography*. But the hydra-headed tendency of error requires another check, and perhaps many more blows to give quietus; no one, it almost seems, can ever adequately even sear its many germinative necks.

Franklin felt so delicately towards England at the close of the Revolutionary War that, as a letter from him to his friend, Mrs. Hewson, in London, proves, he relinquished his intention to make her a visit at that time, lest it might be accounted triumphant. Later, touching at Southampton, on his return to America from France, he scarcely left his ship. The treaty of peace between America and Great Britain was largely (although John Adams was the chief American commissioner in the framing of it) the product, in its favorable aspects, of Franklin's continued warm friendships with some of the principal men of England. Franklin, who would not wound the susceptibilities of Englishmen by a visit to London, was not the man who could have worn the significant ceremonial dress in signing the treaty of peace with Great Britain. The fact is, that it was on the occasion of his signing the two treaties with the French that he wore the dress with its inseparable significance; a significance, too, which he did not deny when questioned about it. He had been the chief influence in inducing France to join her fortunes with America's when he signed the treaties with her relating to war and commerce.

I have already spoken appreciatingly of four articles and, doubtless, there are others which I should similarly regard, had I had the opportunity of seeing them. Of two more I shall make later favorable mention here. The remarks just made with regard to Mr. Choate's article are of no moment as affecting my view of the admirable character of his contribution as a whole. I have merely availed myself of an omission in it to introduce, in the interest of the reader, an important subject which was thoroughly discussed in bygone days and finally settled in the manner indicated.

What shall we think, however, of an article of a different kind from these that have been mentioned, "Franklin in Europe," by Dr. Ellis Paxson Oberholtzer? He starts out very well, but, after a page or so, we come upon these extraordinary statements:

"Franklin had much more common-sense than learning, and, like all men with whom mother-wit is the chief article of equipment, a good many deficiencies appeared when he was brought face to face with those who were made wise by books. . . . To Franklin, history, political science, and such branches of learning were practically unknown. He shone by an epigram, a witty speech, a clever parry or thrust, winding his way up to and among the learned with his interest in lightning-rods, stoves, and many utilitarian projects, with what we call shrewdness in private life; while, in public walks, it becomes diplomacy. It was in France that Franklin's political philosophy was acquired, and his mind was there attainted [sic] with the doctrines of Rousseau, Turgot, and a large group of writers and workers, the natural fruit of whose agitations was the French Revolution. . . . In this great matter [the bubbling of the political cauldron before the outburst of the French Revolution] Franklin erred. His mind was open, and he was ready to embrace intellectual swindles, because true learning was strange to him, in spite of his degrees and decorations, his Philosophical Society, his scientific papers, and his restless curiosity to discover, to know, and to improve. His service in politics was performed with the aid of his mother-wit, which is sometimes said to be better than the wisdom of ages, though a study of

Franklin's life impressively shows us the limitations set upon the self-made man in at least one direction, the philosophy and science of government. . . . What Franklin would have been in this age, under a different set of circumstances, we do not know, and it is needless to speculate about it. That no man could be regarded as a scientist to-day, on the strength of observations such as Franklin's, will be granted universally. That no one would be sent abroad, as he was, to represent us for a quarter of a century, to wear wool hats, mingle his locks with Voltaire's, while crowds acclaimed the dawn of a new social and political era, and receive the laurel wreaths and kisses bestowed upon him by French women, is tolerably clear. . . .''

I do not think that any one has heretofore heard that Franklin was sent abroad incidentally to wear woollen hats and to mingle his locks with Voltaire's, to say nothing of the crowning and kissing. Personally, I don't believe it. As a matter of detail, it would be well to mention that Franklin himself describes his *cap*, not hat, as fur, and says nothing anywhere about mingling his locks, which is not a French fashion, and would have been, at best, figurative with the hairless Voltaire. The kissing took place entirely by foreign, not domestic request.

The question here is biographical. Is the portraiture just given in quotation anywhere near the truth? I think that it is as much unlike Franklin as if it had been designedly so made. Can any one imagine a more perfect travesty of the truth about him? Does not even the average reader of his life know that he was a student of philosophy, history, the science of government, and much else, from his earliest years; that he was an omnivorous reader throughout all his long life, in every variety of literature and in science; that he had, as vehicles for obtaining information, a working knowledge of several languages; that he, for years, associated intimately with some of the first statesmen of Europe and his own country; that, in a word,

he possessed all the learning that any one could absorb in the span of the longest life?

The writer of the account quoted forgets that Franklin was recognized by the foremost scientists of Europe as their equal. He finds that Franklin could have no standing in science at the present day. He thus ignores the fundamental canon of criticism, that a man must be judged in every sphere of thought with reference to the times in which he lived. Lord Bacon expressly dissented from the Copernican Theory of our planetary system, and speaks, in his ''Novum Organon,'' of the pungency of spice, as possibly analogous to fire, and therefore worth investigation to ascertain if they belong to the same category of existences. Much more, too, he speculates about in matters that are known at the present day to be childish notions. Yet Lord Bacon it was who first efficiently directed men's minds to the value of the practice of careful induction, much neglected then in favor of wild deduction.

The product of the daily labors of every scientist is provisional, subject, and subjected by him, to revision as long as he lives, and by others after he is dead; and forasmuch as it is always so, are successive generations of scientists enabled to build higher and higher upon foundations laid by their predecessors. Not only was Franklin conversant with the science of his times, but scientists of the present day are in accord in stating that there is not much to revise of what he thought of as true. Just when he, as he himself says, was looking forward to an existence in which he could devote himself exclusively to scientific pursuits, he was whirled away by the political exigencies of the period to the career of statesmanship. The ultimate nature of the agency which was the chief object of his study, neither he nor any one else will ever know. It would have been bootless for him, even if he had had the time, to dwell upon some of its phenomena. We may rest assured that, in speaking of electricity, he merely used terms generally adopted, two of which he himself invented, and no more believed in electricity as fluid than we do. So dense is general ignorance, even as to his electrical discoveries, that not one man in a hundred knows the full significance of the theory and action of the lightning-rod.

The article by Mr. Le Roy Ruggles, "A Few Things Recalled by the Franklin Centenary," is very different from the preceding, is quite good, in fact, from its thorough sanity. He has made a mistake, however, in the course of telling an anecdote about Franklin, where he speaks of Dr. Cooper's having replied to Franklin's remark to him, before Franklin went to France, that the public had eaten his flesh, and now seemed resolved to pick his bones, "Ah, I approve their taste, for the nearer the bone the sweeter the meat!"

The letter is extant which Franklin wrote from Philadelphia, not before his going to, but after his return from, France. He there says:

"But I had not firmness enough to resist the unanimous desire of my country folks ; and I find myself harnessed again in their service for another year [as President of Pennsylvania]. They engrossed the prime of my life. They have eaten my flesh, and seem resolved now to pick my bones."

So, with the correction of the time, about ten years, the reply, too, as if made in conversation, also requires the correction as to words that I have made. Thus myths are born. I once contributed to Max Müller's list a modern one, full grown in forty years, where a hill, which had been called after Napoleon's mother, *Madame Mère*, had become known as *Mad Mare's Hill*, with reference to an imaginary wild horse which had held it against all comers.

An article written by Miss Emma Repplier, entitled "Franklin's Trials as a Benefactor," is well worth perusal. In the safe ark of the American Philosophical Society's Hall, she skimmed through the great collection of original manuscripts that had once belonged to Franklin, and thus was able to produce the interesting story of how he was bedevilled in Paris by all sorts of strangers, from near and far, with requests that were sometimes almost demands

for appointments, recommendation, money; in fact, for everything that is ordinarily supposed to flow only from the source of the most intimate personal acquaintance. Their writers grotesquely pose before him in the guise of reflections in the mirror of their own conceit, through descriptions of their military capacity, their claim to recognition for all sorts of reasons without reason; while Franklin's endorsements on their missives illustrate, in turn, his awakened sympathy, beneficence, or contempt, as his spirit is moved by the individual character of the demand upon him.

Of course, if misrepresentations about Franklin have occurred on account of imperfect knowledge of him among speakers and writers, at dinners and in magazines, newspapers have not been exempt. I wrote three newspaper corrections under the quasi-anonimity of my initials; but tired of that procedure, I am led to this as somewhat less ephemeral. I cannot but attribute many of the published misstatements about Franklin to the hastiness of men who undertake to speak or write at a moment's notice upon the subject. It is dangerous to pick up the first book at hand and to rely upon everything there said. All books are not trustworthy, and no one book is perfect. There is no acquisition of accurate knowledge possible without examination of various presentations of a subject. I find lapses about Franklin even in Professor Bach McMaster's "Benjamin Franklin as a Man of Letters." He states that Franklin's celebrated "Polly Baker Tale" is to be found in *The Pennsylvania Gazette*. Two well-known bibliophiles of whom I know searched for it there in vain. Franklin himself once indicated, in the course of a conversation, that the tale was to be found there. But his memory may have failed him after the lapse of so many years as had occurred, for he was speaking then as an old man of what he believed had occurred when he was a young one. It may be left an open question as to where the "Polly Baker Tale" was first published, but we cannot leave as an open question

Professor McMaster's statement that Franklin was buried in "the yard of Christ Church." Of course he knows that Franklin is buried at the corner of Fifth and Arch streets, Philadelphia, the burying-ground belonging to Christ Church, but what he says has a very different meaning. There are burial-vaults in the yard of Christ Church itself, several squares away from where Franklin is buried. Therefore the quoted statement is misleading. It is also stated by Professor McMaster that the papers which Franklin left in America when he went to France, and which were molested where they were stored, were partly "picked up by Benjamin Bache." It was Richard Bache, Franklin's son-in-law, who recovered the remains of the papers. Benjamin Franklin Bache, a lad, Franklin's eldest grandson by his daughter, Mrs. Richard Bache, was with his grandfather in France. Professor McMaster speaks of Lord Le Despencer's requesting Franklin to assist Sir Francis Dashwood in abridging the Book of Common Prayer of the Church of England. But Sir Francis Dashwood and Lord Le Despencer were one and the same person. Sir Francis Dashwood became Lord Le Despencer.

Now, if mistakes like these can occur in a book written by an historian, it ought to be evident how important it is to look at any subject, as far as possible, through original documents, and from the point of view of different annalists. A few months ago, while waiting in the office of a publisher, I casually picked up a show-book of short biographies of eminent men, and there alighted on a biography of Franklin of only a page or two in length. Short as it was, however, it contained a glaring mistake, in the statement that Franklin had brought about the opening with prayer of the daily sessions of the Constitutional Convention. But, although it is true that Franklin offered a resolution that the sessions should be opened with prayer, and reinforced his proposition by an admirable address, the resolution did not pass.

Poor Richard, the name by which the supposititious *Richard Saunders* was known as the author of Franklin's Almanac, reminds us, in the course of his own manufacturing of sayings and of his culling them from every source, that we are all apt to forget our debts. From whom to Franklin is any debt due, from whom especially is any due. To what place on earth did the creditor, Franklin, belong; to Boston, to Philadelphia, or to the whole civilized world? Notwithstanding, that when, as a young man, I sat near the Hon. Robert C. Winthrop, when he delivered his oration on the occasion of the inauguration of the statue of Franklin in Printing House Square, Boston, and heard Franklin called by him the great Bostonian, when I had always thought of him as belonging to Philadelphia, I was, nevertheless, inclined to think of him ever afterwards as the property of neither, as having lived in the closest spiritual communion, not only in those places, but in England and France, and therefore as having been, beyond any man of whom we have known, truly cosmopolitan. If we must judge for him between Boston and Philadelphia, be it so. By the ties of affection, we find him tenderly attached to the home of his parents and of his boyhood associations, and to Philadelphia by those of his descendants, to the second generation, and by those of his immediate friends and neighbors, to the end of his life. He loved both Boston and Philadelphia dearly, with his magnificent tenderness of heart, which seemed to embrace all humanity. He could truly have said with Vergil, so far as his relations to Boston and Philadelphia are concerned, "*Mantua me genuit, Calabri rapuit.*"

I must concede, however, that Boston was first in recognizing her indebtedness to Franklin. *Poor Richard* was right in reminding us that we are prone to forget our debts, and we can add, without fear of contradiction from him, were he alive, that having at last been brought to think of paying, we are prone also to forget how long we have been guilty of neglect. My memory goes not back to the contrary thought that Franklin was ever deemed in his native place the great Bostonian. I do not believe that there ever was such a time. My knowledge, on the other hand, as to the stirring of the popular heart in Philadelphia regarding him need not go back more than twenty years to find its first manifestations since his death. Philadelphia has always been deemed what she calls conservative, what the outside world calls slow to move and be moved. But, if she be slow in movement, she has also a characteristic trait that tends in time to countervail her neglect. Once started on a course, she is thorough in the way in which she carries out a change of base. She showed on this occasion of *The Franklin Centenary Celebration* a tendency to be volcanic. The American Philosophical Society was the principal vent around which portents of rumblings were early heard as the time approached for the celebration, from which its fires were communicated to the whole outlying region, ending with the most magnificent *feu-de-joie* in Franklin's honor as the greatest of the founders of his day.

It were best, for the reasons given, because they are the truest, to regard Franklin, not as the great Bostonian, nor as the great Philadelphian, but as a great American, one to whom America is unspeakably indebted, one who, as Lord Chatham said, is an honor to human nature. On the 17th of January, 1706, genius was born, through Boston, to the English race and men; a star, then of the smallest magnitude, but one which was finally, in its zenith path, destined to shed lustre over England, France, and the little Colonies of America, grown finally to empire under its auspices and other kindly aspects of the skies, until, at last, in 1790, it sank to rest forever on the horizon where its benign light first appeared. Strictly speaking, Franklin does not belong exclusively even to America. Before the Revolution, he was strongly drawn to England, for he was for years a thoroughly loyal Englishman; afterwards, he was still more strongly drawn to France, through temperamental affinity with her people, which influences men largely, independent of their native clime. If, however, from the aggregate, in birth and love and deeds, he belongs more intimately than elsewhere to America, we should not forget that he truly belongs more largely than to any place to humanity, through the fact of his breadth of being and inclusive love and thought and labor for all mankind.

Why Not a Thackeray Club?

By LEWIS MELVILLE

A FEW weeks ago I was dining as a guest at the Samuel Pepys Club, an assembly of gentlemen who, to judge from their interesting conversation, had apparently made the study of the "Diary" the main feature of their lives; and though I am aware that, with perhaps two or three exceptions, this was not the case, yet the majority of those present were undoubtedly experts in all concerning Pepys and his times. After dinner, when the company had drunk in silence the toast of the evening, the immortal memory of Samuel Pepys, there came the singing of some of Pepys's verses and other popular ballads of his day, as well as a recitation of the famous soliloquy " To be or not to be,' taken from Pepys's music-books; and in addition was read by a well-known authority a most interesting paper on " The Collection of Ballads in the Pepysian Library at Magdalene College, Cambridge."

So delighted was I with the evening's entertainment that I wondered why admirers of most authors did not band themselves together in such associations. There are, of course, the Omar Club, the Johnson Club, Browning Societies *galore*, and the Boz Club and the Dickens Fellowship, the last with innumerable branches all over the world. But, I thought, why are there not more of these associations? What are the lovers of other great writers doing—the lovers of Fielding, Goldsmith, Sheridan, Thackeray, for instance, all "clubbable" fellows — the very men to be made the excuse for such pleasant literary gatherings?

Thackeray, for one, was *par excellence* the clubman, Bohemian, social, literary. Was it not at some Shakespearian birthday dinner that he spoke of his favorite club?—"We, the happy initiated, never speak of it as the Garrick: to us it is 'the G.', 'the little G.', 'the dearest little place in the world.'" But he was also a member of many other clubs, although the Travellers would not have him, fearing to see themselves in some future novel by the great man — the Reform, the Athenæum, the Fielding (the title of which was chosen by him), the Cyder Cellars (the club which must not be confounded with the tavern), that came into existence because the Garrick Club would not serve suppers at a late hour — a *very* late hour I suspect; in the Whittington, and "Our Club." What a pleasant picture of Thackeray in that last-mentioned place has Mr. Jefferson conjured up: "I cannot conceive him to have ever been seen to greater advantage than when he was sitting with a party of his congenial comrades at 'Our Club,' gossiping tenderly about dead authors, artists, and actors, and in the kindliest spirit about living notabilities. It was very pleasant to watch the white-haired veteran, and also to hear him (though at best he sang indifferently) whilst he trolled forth his favorite ballads touching 'Little Billee' and 'Father Martin Luther.' Better still it was to regard the radiant gratification of his face whilst Horace Mayhew sang 'The Mahogany Tree,' perhaps the finest and most soul-stirring of Thackeray's social songs, or was throwing his soul into the passionate 'Marseillaise.'"

Thackeray seems never to have been happier than when at one of his clubs surrounded by his friends, although even at the Garrick Club there was a rift in his lute: a member whose presence irritated him and who, discover-

ing his power, was not averse to the exercise of it. Sir Francis Burnand has told us how Thackeray was one night telling a story in the smoking-room when his persecutor entered, and, to the surprise of all present, the great man hesitated, stammered, and then stopped, whereupon the new arrival exasperated him with the encouraging words, delivered with the most irritating air of patronage: "Proceed, sweet warbler, your story interests me much." There are many good stories told of Thackeray as clubman. It was to the Garrick he took Mr. Herman Merivale as a boy to dinner, and years after Mr. Merivale asked him if he remembered the occasion. "Why, yes, of course, and what is more, I remember I gave you beefsteak and apricot omelette." Mr. Merivale, then still a young man, was delighted that his company should have made so great an impression; but his complacency was rudely disturbed when the novelist, with twinkling eye, added, "Yes, I always gave boys beefsteak and apricot omelettes." Another amusing anecdote is told of Thackeray at the Reform Club. On an evening when he was to dine with some great personage, he happened to see on the *menu* of the day "Beans and Bacon." That was too much for him, and straightway he wrote to his host, telling him he could not have the pleasure of dining with him after all, as he had just met a very old friend whom he had not seen for years, and from whom he could not tear himself.

Why should there not foregather admirers, critical or otherwise, of—as Mr. Walter Jerrold has so aptly phrased it—the larger Thackeray? What interesting and amusing arguments could there be around the mahogany concerning the various aspects of this many-sided man of letters, who, besides the novels that are more or less familiar to all, wrote poems, satires, parodies, short stories, art criticism, reviews of books, and innumerable skits for *Punch ;* and in a day when most are concerned to point out the technical faults of Thackeray the artist, some one might be found courageous enough to insist upon the wonderful merits of his drawings as illustrations. For my part, I rank Thackeray as the best illustrator of his own books, and I regret that he let Doyle illustrate "The Newcomes"; for, although the latter's plates are technically far superior, there is lacking a certain *je ne sais quoi* which the other usually supplied. And now, before Mr. M. H. Spielmann sees this heresy in print, may the heavens fall!

Why, then, should there not be a Titmarsh Club or a Thackeray Fellowship—with its dinners, discussions, and pilgrimages, and perhaps also with a companion journal to the admirably conducted "Dickensian"?

The providing of the dinners and discussions would present no difficulty, but in the matter of outings, always an attractive feature of these associations, Titmarshians would be at a marked disadvantage to the Omarites and the Dickensians, since for them there is of course no Gad's Hill or Woodbridge. It is accepted that there must be some *raison d'être* for the pilgrimage, which may be the birthplace or a residence of the author whose works have inspired the club, or it may be made to a scene prominent in one of his books.

Thackeray's birthplace is out of the question, the Pumpernickel of "Vanity Fair" is too far, and for the rest there is little of the Thackeray country outside London. His schools at Chiswick and Charterhouse are always within walking distance, and all his homes are in the heart of the metropolis: Albion Street, "Jorum" Street, Onslow Square, Palace Green, still stand; the St. James's Street lodgings have gone, and I am not aware that the Jermyn Street house has been more closely identified than "within a few doors of the Museum of Geology." Still, the outlook is not entirely hopeless. There are the homes of the Crawleys in Hampshire, but I do not know whether they have been traced within the boundaries of that county. There are Ottery St. Mary and Exeter and Sidmouth, the Clavering St. Mary and Chatteris and Baymouth of "Pendennis." There is Winchester, where Harry Esmond came back and was seen by Lady Castlewood

in the Cathedral during the singing of the anthem, "When the Lord turned the captivity of Zion we were like them that dream"—that return of the wanderer, the description of which is, perhaps, the finest thing in Thackeray. There is Clevedon Court, the original of Castlewood, and also the Winchelsea of "Denis Duval." There are many who would have an unassailable right to membership. Firstly, those, but a handful now, who knew him in the flesh, prominent among whom would be Sir Theodore Martin and Mr. Justin McCarthy, who was to have dined with the novelist the very day he went to the silent land. Then, the small number of writers who, consciously or unconsciously, owe so much to the master, and so might join—Mr. W. E. Norris, Mr. Percy White, and Mr. G. S. Street; and those who have contributed admirable illustrations to his text—Mr. Furniss, whose wonderful sketches to "Major Gahagan" linger in the memory, Mr. Linley Sambourne, Mr. Hugh Thomson, Mr. C. E. Brock, who has taken all the prose works for his province, and the rest of the talented band. Lastly, but not by any means the least worthy, the numerous critics and editors, and all those, in fact, who know and love their Thackeray—Mr. Frederick Greenwood, Sir Francis Burnand, Mr. W. L. Courtney, Mr. Andrew Lang, Sir Frank Marzials, Mr. Charles Whibley, Mr. M. H. Spielmann, Mr. Walter Jerrold (the editor of Mr. Dent's excellent edition), Mr. G. K. Chesterton, Mr. Stephen Gwynne, Mr. William Archer, Mr. R. S. Garnett, of *The New Sketch Book* fame, Mr. A. A. Jack, and others too numerous to mention.

The American contingent would be strong, although there can be few surviving who knew the great man; but important trans-Atlantic members of a Titmarsh Club would be Mr. Frederick S. Dickson, the great authority upon Thackeray's bibliography; Major William H. Lambert, whose collection of the novelist's works is world-famous; and General James Grant Wilson, the author of the recently published "Thackeray in the United States."

The Book=Buyer's Guide

Egan—The Ghost in Hamlet, and Other Essays.
By Maurice Francis Egan. McClurg.
$1.00 net.

The author of this scholarly collection of
essays is professor of English literature in
the Catholic University of America. His
subjects are mostly from Shakespeare. Besides a second one on Hamlet, he deals with
"Some Phases of Shakespearean Interpretation"; "Some Pedagogical Uses of Shakespeare"; "Lyrism in Shakespeare's Comedies";
"The Greatest of Shakespeare's Contemporaries"(Calderon); "Imitators of Shakespeare"
(mainly devoted to a comparison of Tennyson's "Becket" and Aubrey de Vere's "St.
Thomas of Canterbury," the latter being
placed far above the former as a delineation
of the great Chancellor and Primate); "The
Comparative Method in Literature"; "A
Definition of Literature"; and "The Ebb and
Flow of Romance." All show great breadth
of reading and study, keen and sympathetic
criticism, and sound educational judgment.
The two Hamlet papers seem to us the least
able, but perhaps only because we cannot
agree with the author's solution of the insoluble problem, though his discussion of it is
none the less interesting. Students and
teachers of Shakespeare and of literature in
general will find the book eminently worth
their attention.

Heisch—Art and Craft of the Author. By
C. E. Heisch. Grafton Press. $1.00 net.

In a sense it is true of prose writers as of poets
that they are born, not made. It might even
be said that in these days it is of more consequence to discourage people from writing than
to encourage them. Yet there are beginners
in the art of authorship—it may perhaps be
called an art, though Mr. Heisch suggests in
his title that it is a craft as well—who will
appreciate and profit by the admirable suggestions contained in these pages. They will
find here a discussion of principles rather than
of details; but the principles are firmly grasped
and lucidly expounded. Mr. Heisch is not
concerned to point out any easy road to success. He wisely lays stress upon the fact that
a man must have something to say before he
can say it. Nor has he any patience with
scamped and hasty work. To take one's
calling seriously is a prime requisite. Authors
with some experience as well as beginners
will find profit in these pages.

**Hunt—Literature: Its Principles and Prob-
lems.** By Theodore W. Hunt. Funk &
Wagnalls. $1.20 net.

It is somewhat difficult to understand just
what class of readers Dr. Hunt wished to
reach when he wrote this book. His discussion of principles is occasionally elementary,
and yet his statements have hardly sufficient
lucidity to meet the needs of students. When
he designs to emphasize a phrase he puts it

in capitals. Thus we hear of the Appreciation
of Letters, of Mental and Moral Enfranchise-
ment, of the Liberal Professions, of the Philosophic Method. But there is really very little
explanation of the meaning of these terms.
Dr. Hunt's ideas are sane enough, in the main,
but he fails to set them forth in a very orderly
manner. He is too apt, indeed, to fall into
the quotation habit as practised by novices
in composition. Arnold says this, and Lowell
says that, and how true it is that—then come
the inverted commas. We would not be understood as depreciating a book that is in
many respects stimulating and suggestive.
But it would be the grossest flattery to say
that it is well written, or that one's appreciation of the best in literature is forwarded by
the perusal of it.

Wilson—Making the Most of Ourselves. By
Calvin Dill Wilson. A. C. McClurg. $1.00.

Elementary talks on self-cultivation, free
from pretentiousness and sentimentality, and
containing a good deal of sense. For young
men and women who are at a groping and
impressionable age and who have not had
"advantages," this book ought to be of far
greater value than most of its kind. It is
not addressed to mature readers.

BIOGRAPHY.

Brady—The True Andrew Jackson. By Cyrus
T. Brady. Lippincott. $2.00 net.

Mr. Brady is a sturdy admirer of Jackson,
but this account of his character and career
is not likely to affect greatly the general
judgment. The adjective which is the distinguishing mark of the series to which this
volume belongs could hardly have been worse
applied. Mr. Brady's picture is neither true
nor plausible. The necessity of dealing with
his subject topically rather than chronologi-
cally may have hampered him somewhat; but
even so he manifests no clear conception of
the issues in which Jackson played so large a
part. Nor has he contributed anything original to the discussion. He has thrown together
odds and ends of quotations from every possible source. He cites former biographers *ad
libitum*, and when these fail repeats *in extenso*
the impressions of those who met his hero
casually. It must be said that the antagonism
which Jackson aroused was not due wholly to
unreasoning prejudice, as Mr. Brady suggests.
In the affair of Mrs. Eaton, for example, he
assumed an attitude for which there was no
excuse. Indeed, throughout his career he was
inclined, like Macbeth, to use "barefaced
power" and "bid his will avouch it." The
defence of his dealings with the United States
Bank is a conspicuous instance of special
pleading that fails to accomplish its object.
The opportunity to write a satisfactory life
of Jackson has by no means passed, but it is
plain that Mr. Brady is not the man to take
advantage of it.

Conover—Memories of a Great Schoolmaster.
By James P. Conover. Houghton, Mifflin. $1.50 net.

The schoolmaster was Rev. Dr. Henry A. Coit, who for almost forty years was at the head of St. Paul's School, Concord, N. H.; and this tribute to his memory is from the pen of one who after being his pupil became associated with him as a teacher. It is an interesting account of the remarkable growth of a boy's boarding-school under the management of a scholarly, energetic, and devoted man, with marked personal magnetism combined with keen and sympathetic understanding of boy nature. Like Dr. Arnold, to whom he has been compared, he had the rare gift of inspiring the school with a religious tone while keeping in touch with the natural tastes and tendencies of the students who heartily loved and honored him. The book will be particularly welcome to the large company of St. Paul's alumni, as well as to all who are interested in secondary education.

Macfall—Whistler: Butterfly, Wasp, Wit, Master of the Arts, Enigma. By Haldane Macfall. Luce & Co. 75c. net.

A brief, vivacious, and highly eulogistic sketch of the man and the artist; the first booklet in the "Spirit of the Age Series," the aim of which is announced to be "to present to the readers a living, marching [sic], personality, breathing with the individuality characteristic of the person." It is illustrated with photographic copies of four of Whistler's paintings.

Reid—Memoirs of Sir Wemyss Reid, 1842-1885. Ed. by Stuart J. Reid. Cassell.

The author of this autobiography was a well-known English journalist of considerable influence; to his pen we are also indebted for two authoritative biographies, those of W. E. Forster and of Lord Houghton. His own life, so far as it is here recorded, is not of great interest, for while his character was of sterling quality, it was essentially of that commonplace type which, though it has made the Anglo-Saxon predominant throughout the world, is of greater interest in the aggregate than in the individual instance. It is the foundation on which the success of England and of America rests. Nor did Reid do anything of exceptional interest during these years, and finally he has little of importance to record about others more prominent in the life of the day. It therefore seems egotistic to offer to the world, even if it is done posthumously, a series of such unimportant reminiscences. The interesting matter in the volume could be presented in less than a score of pages. In all probability this general view would be modified were the second volume, which is to complete the autobiography, at hand. This volume, covering the last two decades, has been withheld for political reasons. During these years Reid was in the inner councils of the Liberal party, of which he was an uncritically ardent adherent, and unquestionably he should be in a position to throw much valuable light on recent English political life.

Rothschild—Lincoln, Master of Men. By Alonzo Rothschild. Houghton, Mifflin. $3.

Mr. Rothschild has taken great pains in the preparation of this volume; he has delved into all sorts of unlikely places to find the material for his study of Lincoln. The point of the book is to show that the essential quality in Lincoln's mental make-up was his masterfulness. From early youth this tendency made itself evident. Both physically and mentally Lincoln was very loath to be beaten. This feeling sometimes showed itself in ways unworthy of his nobler self, but more often in support of his fine traits. Mr. Rothschild gives chapter and verse for every statement made by him, but wisely does not confuse the clearness of the text by interpolations of authorities. The story is well and forcibly told and the style is admirably terse.

Simpson—Robert Louis Stevenson. By E. Blantyre Simpson. Luce & Co. 75c. net.

The second issue in the "Spirit of the Age Series." The illustrations are four portraits of Stevenson, including that painted by Count Nerli in Samoa.

Taylor—The Life of Queen Henrietta Maria. By I. A. Taylor. Dutton. $7.50 net.

Considering the important part that Henrietta Maria played in a momentous period of English history it is strange that so few biographies of her exist. The present volume covers her stormy life from infancy to death, and necessarily includes much of the history of events leading to the Civil Wars, and of the French Court under Louis XIII and Anne of Austria as Regent. Henrietta's character is drawn with justice not untempered by mercy; quotations from her correspondence aid in telling a very clear and interesting story of her influence over Charles I and the causes that led to his martyrdom. The illustrations are from contemporary portraits.

Thompson—Party Leaders of the Time. By Charles Willis Thompson. Dillingham. $1.75 net.

In this volume Mr. Thompson deals for the most part with living public men. He has come into contact with them during his service as a newspaper correspondent at Washington, and his design in these pages is to make them real figures to his readers. As he has an eye for revealing personal details and a sense of the picturesque he succeeds admirably in his design. It should be said he does not descend to backstairs gossip. Even where he is not altogether laudatory he is not unkindly. The leaders of the Senate and House, certain Cabinet officers, and a few politicians elsewhere form the subjects of his sketches.

Wilson—Joseph Jefferson: Reminiscences of a Fellow Player. By Francis Wilson. Scribner.

Every lover of Joseph Jefferson—and their name is legion upon legion—will be grateful for this pleasant record of genial and sympa-

The Book-Buyer's Guide

thetic personal reminiscences; and all the more because Mr. Jefferson did *not* have—as some hypercritical critic has wished that he might have had—the opportunity of "blue-pencilling" the whole of it, as he did that portion of it which describes the "all star" tour of "The Rivals." But his sole objection there was that it put his friend "in the light of a hero-worshipper" and himself "on a theatrical throne chair with an assumed air of modesty, but slily acquiescing in the praise." As it is, the author will not resent the imputation of being in a sense a hero-worshipper, for he was honestly one, and his hero, who was in reality one of the most modest of men, is now in no danger of being suspected of slily winking at his worshipper's eulogies. The reader at the same time may congratulate himself on getting many apt and shrewd remarks of dear old "Rip," which he never suspected that the listener would make a note of, and many capital anecdotes of the man and his friends to the printing of which he might too scrupulously have objected. Personally we should be sorry to miss a single sentence of all this matter.

The author of the book, while necessarily having to place himself rather prominently before the reader, is equally modest and felicitous in his brief preface—so brief that we may quote it entire in this brief notice:

"Those who seek the facts of his life, and the standard and accepted estimates of Jefferson's work and art, will find them in the adequate pages of Mr. William Winter. Those who would acquaint themselves with the ineffable charm of his personality must linger over the pages of the comedian's Autobiography, a book to be mentioned only with Colley Cibber's 'Apology,' equal in interest, beyond it in charm. The present writer has aimed merely to set down the remembrances, mostly anecdotal, which were his over a number of years in connection with the subject of this sketch."

This exactly expresses the character and purpose of the book, which is an appropriate and welcome supplement to Mr. Winter's Life of Jefferson and the Autobiography.

The illustrations, many of which are unique, include no less than fifteen photographs of Mr. Jefferson, others taken from his paintings, views of his home at "Crow's Nest," and his grave, and portraits of the actors in the "all star" performance of "The Rivals."

FICTION

Adams—Cattle Brands. By Andy Adams. Houghton, Mifflin. $1.50.

These stories of the real cowboy are by one who may justly lay claim to be the "greatest living authority" upon the life which he so well depicts. To many people they will seem more enjoyable than the longer stories by Mr. Adams. Their merit lies wholly in the obvious truth to life of the scenes.

Barr—The Triumphs of Eugene Valmont. By Robert Barr. Appleton. $1.50.

The ex-chief of the detective force of Paris is supposed to be the narrator of these tales.

Not all of them, however, are records of complicated adventures. One of them, for example, relates the manner in which a man was reclaimed from the clutches of absinthe and anarchy by the resolute action of the ubiquitous Valmont. One of the best of the tales is the first which takes the famous "Queen's Necklace" as the basis of its plot. The stories are readable but not absorbing.

Bacheller—Silas Strong. By Irving Bacheller. Harper. $1.50.

It is a relief to find that Mr. Bacheller has left the ancient Romans and returned to his proper field. The scene of his new book is the Adirondacks. Its principal character is of the same type as other men of the woods and fields drawn by this writer. The love story approaches the absurd rather closely. Were it not for the old backwoodsman the book would have little reason for being. "Uncle Silas" leavens—to a certain extent—the whole lump by his amusing peculiarities and shrewd sayings.

Beach—The Spoilers. By Rex E. Beach. Harper. $1.50.

Probably it is the "actuality" of this coarse-fibred tale which will make it popular. Mr. Beach has collected his documents, human and other, on the spot and the picture of life in the gold regions of Alaska is doubtless accurate enough; the judicial conspiracy which occupies so large a portion of his pages has been already exposed by him in the magazines. But the trouble is that as a novelist he has no artistic restraint. He mistakes vulgarity for strength and brute force for manliness; and he discusses without reserve matters which emphatically demand discreet treatment.

Bernstein—Contrite Hearts. By Herman Bernstein. Wessels. $1.25.

An emotional study of certain tragedies of Russian life. In its pictures of facts and conditions the book is entirely convincing, but as a story it is not signally impressive and the later portions, whose scenes are in New York, among the exiled Jews, are of lesser value. There is probably not so much art in the book as deep sincerity of intention.

Bindloss—Alton of Somasco. By Harold Bindloss. Stokes. $1.50.

British Columbia is the *mise en scène* of this novel of love and adventure. The interest of the plot is fairly well sustained, but the book is carelessly written and the characters occasionally behave in a manner entirely out of keeping with their supposed position in life. There is plenty of excitement in the incidents.

Castle—"If Youth but Knew." By Agnes and Egerton Castle. Macmillan. $1.50.

The Castles tell a fantastic tale of Westphalia during the reign of Jerome Bonaparte in their latest novel. The joy of life and love, the poetry of youth, are the theme of the story and constitute its charm. The most fascinating character in the story is a mysterious fiddler who acts as the good genius of the lovers.

Cheney—The Challenge. By Warren Cheney. Bobbs-Merrill. $1.50.

An unfamiliar setting may or may not be an advantage in a novel. Mr. Cheney makes good use of such a setting, however, in this tale of Alaska in the Russian days. His characters are very much alive, too, and the reader who begins the tale will wish to finish it.

Frothingham—The Evasion. By Eugenia Brooks Frothingham. Houghton, Mifflin. $1.50.

Miss Frothingham has not quite fulfilled in this novel the promise which many persons discerned in "The Turn of the Road." The faith of the reader in the possibility of the incidents is strained more than once to the breaking point. The whole story hinges on a misunderstanding as to which of two men was caught cheating at cards. It seems inconceivable that the woman who loved Richard Copeland should have been deceived so completely as to his real character. The novel has much that is admirable, much that is clever; but it lacks balance. It interests the reader, but it cannot fail to disappoint him in part. It is so good that one wishes it were better. Miss Frothingham should studiously avoid the morbid and overstrained effects which are her most serious menace as a novelist.

Gray—The Great Refusal. By Maxwell Gray. Appleton. $1.50.

Dullness is a quality never before associated with the productions of this writer. Unprofitable her novels may have been; but they were not dull. Unhappily this is the most unmistakable fault of "The Great Refusal." Departing entirely from her ordinary range of plots, with their invariable one dramatic scene, the author has taken the theories of the founders of Brotherland as her theme. Her faults of style are much more obvious in pragmatical fiction than in novels of the "Silence of Dean Maitland" type and become unbearable in portions of this wearisome volume. The manner is that of Mrs. Henry Wood in the once famous and still read "East Lynne" and the matter is not as good. An atmosphere of unreality prevades the novel from the first page to the last.

Hale—A Motor Car Divorce. By Louise Closser Hale. Dodd, Mead. $1.50.

Mrs. Hale's variation of the automobile theme is briskly sketchy and entertaining but lacks coherence as a piece of fiction. Amusing as the idea of the story is, the plot lacks the element of probability. However, the descriptions of the incidents of a trip through Europe are clever and with Mr. Hale's drawings make a volume slight in substance but attractive none the less.

Harker—Paul and Fiammetta. By L. Allen Harker. Scribner. $1.25.

Mrs. Kate Douglas Wiggin introduces the author of this charming story of child life in England to an American audience. Mrs. Harker understands young people thoroughly and writes of them with sympathy and humor. She has, moreover, a delightful style. The story is one in which young folk and those who have not forgotten the pleasures of youth will find much to enjoy.

Harry—The Conquest of Jerusalem. By Myriam Harry. Turner. $1.50.

This story of modern Jerusalem is really a study of what is known as the "artistic" temperament worked out in a morbid fashion. Hélie's apostasy from the Roman Catholic religion upon his marriage with a deaconess of the Protestant Church destroys eventually the religious instinct in his nature. Many of the details of the novel are revolting. It is unwholesome and unpleasant.

Lancaster—The Spur. By G. B. Lancaster. Doubleday, Page & Co. $1.50.

A caddish kind of "literary gent" finds on an Australian sheep farm a wonderful writer of tales—a Kipling in the rough—and makes a bargain with him, agreeing to educate him and exploit his genius on condition that he submits to absolute control of his services for a term of years. The fetters thus forged do not gall at first. The young fellow gets his training and experience and fully justifies the confidence of the promoter. But when the inevitable woman calls and Shylock demands his pound of flesh the result is tragic. The tale as a whole has many merits; the Samoan scenes are both picturesque and novel; but the author unfortunately falls into a certain exasperating preciosity of style which interferes seriously with the reader's enjoyment. Indeed there are whole chapters that perplex and bewilder even the most patient explorer of the writer's mental processes.

Lipsett—A Summer in the Apple-Tree Inn. By Ella Partridge Lipsett. Holt. $1.25.

A pleasing story for children is this account of the good times enjoyed by four young people in the little house fitted up for them by a gracious aunt and named by her the "Apple-Tree Inn." All kinds of delightful resources are contained within the four walls of this play-house. The little folk have other good times besides those in the "inn"; and pass a very happy summer.

Lloyd—Six Stars. By Nelson Lloyd. Scribner. $1.50.

Mr. Lloyd has a pleasing vein of quiet humor and he depicts the village life of Six Stars in this series of sketches with good-natured satire which makes the book very readable. But his people talk as no Americans ever talked and seem rather palpably created out of whole cloth. The transposition of the V and the W in certain words is a case in point. One would like to know of any Americans who committed this Wellerism. Mr. Lloyd probably would consider this an over-literal criticism; but amusing as several of the stories are, the fault is a real one.

Long—Seffy; A Little Comedy of Country Manners. By John Luther Long. Illustrations by C. D. Williams. Bobbs-Merrill. $1.50.

"Seffy" is a man's name. Sephenijah P. Baumgartner, Jr., was his full name, but even that knowledge does not always help the reader to differentiate between him and Sally, his sweetheart, especially as the name appears over the picture of a woman on the paper wrapper of the book. The story is slight but fairly interesting. The delicate lavender tracery borders on each page do not seem particularly appropriate for a tale in which tragedy is prominent.

Lynde—The Quickening. By Francis Lynde. Bobbs-Merrill. $1.50.

Novels that begin with the hero's or heroine's childhood run the risk of boring the reader. The first chapters of "The Quickening" conduct Thomas Jefferson Gordon from the day of his "conversion", at the age of twelve, to that of his return from "Tech" to save his father's business from conscienceless promoters. The real interest of the narrative begins after these preliminary stages are passed. Mr. Lynde gives us what is presumably a faithful picture of the new South, and many of his characters are well drawn; but the novel as a whole is not convincing. There was no good reason why Tom should have undergone so much suspicion for another's fault. But if novelists had to be reasonable, what would become of the "best sellers"? Mr. Lynde is no worse offender on this head than many another.

McCall—The Breath of the Gods. By Sidney McCall. Little, Brown. $1.50.

The scene of "Sidney McCall's" second novel is laid partly in Washington, partly in Japan, and the latter portion is the better. The story is of an American diplomat and his family stationed in Japan, after political life in this country. The characters are American, Japanese, and French. The customs of Japan and the peculiar ethical point of view, almost incomprehensible to the occidental mind, are portrayed by a man to whom they are perfectly familiar. The sacrifice of the young Japanese wife at the end seems fantastic to any but an oriental, yet the spirit of the east is thereby expressed. The dual personality of "the author" is artistically concealed, so that it is well-nigh impossible to say (from the construction) who wrote what part.

McCutcheon—Cowardice Court. By George Barr McCutcheon. Dodd, Mead. $1.25.

By all the ingenious devices of padding and ornamentation known to the printing craft, the publishers have managed to make what is really a longish short story into a novelette for separate publication. There is a pleasing vein of sentiment in it, and it is accompanied by some pretty colored pictures.

Michelson—A Yellow Journalist. By Miriam Michelson. Appleton. $1.50.

Never was a book more appropriately named. Yellow journalism with all its vulgarity, slang, and slipshod slapdash, simply reeks—there is no other word—in these pages. It must be admitted that Miss Michelson is possessed of a very vivacious and snappy style, that may make her work entertaining to those who can stand yellow journalism unexcused by daily news.

Mighels—Chatwit, the Man-Talk Bird. By Philip Verrill Mighels. Harper. $1.50.

Rather different from the ordinary animal story, patterned after the style of Mr. Thompson-Seton, is this tale of a magpie whose knowledge of human speech involves him in many complications with his fellow-beasts. Several of the incidents are amusing and original.

Parry—The Scarlet Empire. By David M. Parry. Bobbs-Merrill. $1.50.

A model Social Democracy many leagues under the sea is depicted in this tale of unusual adventures. An American finds his way into this commonwealth, and soon has his cherished notions as to the delights of socialism disabused by seeing it put into practice. Eventually he makes his escape with a beautiful Atlantian with whom he has fallen in love and rejoices greatly to find himself once more in the country once so despised by him.

Potter—The Genius. By Margaret Potter. Harpers. $1.50.

A much better piece of fiction than Miss Potter's latest previous book, but not free from neurotic tendencies. The public is informed that it is the first of a trilogy dealing with Russian life. The hero is obviously a perverted study of Tschaikovsky. The false impressions of the personality of the great Russian composer are hardly justifiable, and the entirely untrue picture of Anton Rubinstein is one to arouse indignation in persons who cherish deep admiration for the services performed by him to the cause of music in Russia. This is the best written and the sanest of any of Miss Potter's books. It is impossible, however, to approve such liberties as she has taken with the lives of men so lately dead. In the case of Tschaikovsky, or Ivan Gregoriev, as he is called in the novel, the personal details are entirely different from the real ones; with Rubinstein it is the characteristics which have been distorted.

Powell—The Prisoner of Ornith Farm. By Frances Powell. Scribner. $1.50.

In the days of Mrs. Radcliffe and of Horace Walpole's Gothic castles such a story as this might have seemed plausible. But Miss Powell makes too severe a demand upon our credulity in asking us to believe that the extraordinary events she narrates could happen on the banks of the Hudson River. Her story is melodrama of the baldest sort. Doubtless it would greatly impress audiences at the "ten, twenty, and thirty" theatres.

Ray—Hearts and Creeds. By Anna Chapin Ray. Little, Brown . $1.50.

Miss Ray is less successful as a whole in fiction for adults than in her admirable stories for young people. This is by no means as good as "The Dominant Strain" although the author is obviously familiar with her *milieu.* The plot is based upon the marked separation between the French and English races in Quebec, as in other Canadian cities. The chief fault to be found with the novel is that it is too "talky." The characters are not always logically developed and the heroine is too unpleasant to arouse the interest of the reader, while her French husband seems a tame and unexciting person. For once, Miss Ray's usual brisk fashion of telling a story has apparently deserted her.

Saltus—The Perfume of Eros. By Edgar Saltus Wessell. $1.25.

A highly unnecessary story, containing not so very much, after all, of the scent to which the title alludes. The book's superficial smartnesses fail to conceal its lack of serious intention.

Seawell—The Château of Montplaisir. By Molly Eliot Seawell. Appleton. $1.50.

This trivial tale is quite unworthy of the author of "Children of Destiny." It revolves about the adventures of a young Frenchman of noble family who inherits a dilapidated château and an old Frenchman who fancies himself a member of that family and proposes to adopt the other and repair the dilapidation. With the advent of a very lively old lady and her niece various complications ensue. These cannot be truthfully described as particularly amusing. However, they will occupy an idle hour.

Sienkiewicz—On the Field of Glory. An historical novel of the time of King John Sobieski by Henry Sienkiewicz. Translated from the Polish original by Jeremiah Curtin. Little, Brown. $1.50.

Somebody has wisely remarked that if Russian names could be anglicized, the pleasure of reading Russian novels would be intensified fifty per cent. What is an Anglo-Saxon reader to do, for example, with Mateush, Marek, Lukash, and Yan, the Bukoyemski brothers, who are as impossible to differentiate for the average reader as two sets of Siamese twins? Even Turgenieff and Tolstoy, the most interesting of Russian writers, get on one's nerves at times because of the superfluity of nominal prefixes and suffixes, which have little meaning to English-speaking readers. It requires a strong individuality in a novel nowadays to attach itself permanently to a given name.

In this translation from Sienkiewicz, Mr Curtin uses the Polish original, and the result is highly satisfactory. The English is idiomatic, yet the atmosphere is distinctly foreign. The story itself is in the usual manner of Sienkiewicz, a vivid narrative of events, with a trifle of psychology as a bye-product; objective and discursive as contrasted with Turgenieff (the master), subjective and succinct. The picture of Pan Gideon's party speeding over the snow, pursued by wolves, and protected by the four brothers with the unrememberable names, is not soon forgotten. It is like a Schreyer painting. Incidentally Mr. Curtin's dedication to Sir Thomas G. Shaughnessy (a name almost Russian in its combination of consonants), "President of the Canadian Pacific Railroad," with its mention of his fondness for books, appears somewhat forced in its explanation, unless it has an underlying motive.

Silberrad—Curayl. By Una L. Silberrad. Doubleday, Page. $1.50.

Although several of the characters in this novel are not wholly convincing, it is one so much above the average in literary merit and interest that one is not inclined to condemn this defect too unsparingly. The worst fault lies in the excess of brutality—as far as artistic effect is concerned—with which the unspeakable Sir William Goyt and the equally detestable Delmer are endowed. Beatrice Curayl's sorrows strike the reader as rather sordid on this account. After all both of these men should have been gentlemen; and they behave with a vulgarity which would be discreditable to a navvy.

Strang—Brown of Moukden. By Herbert Strang. Putnam. $1.50.

Already this popular writer for boys has written one story of the Russo-Japanese War, but in this he gives another brisk tale based upon the recent contest. While "Kobo" had for its hero a Japanese boy, the latest story shows the contest from the Russian side. Mr. Strang has a permanent place in juvenile affection and he deserves it because he knows how to put plenty of "ginger" into a story without infusing adventitious excitement into the plot and thus making the book unwholesome.

Thruston—Called to the Field. By Lucy Meacham Thruston. Little, Brown. $1.50.

Unlike many writers of war-time stories Miss Thruston knows the South thoroughly and can picture the scenes without effort. So this little story of a young wife in the Civil War possesses an attractiveness which could hardly be expected in a tale new neither in plot nor theme. The charm of the home life of the brave little woman, her husband, and her father, lends the book a distinctly pleasing atmosphere.

(For list of Books Received see twelfth page following.)

The Critic

VOL. XLVIII. JANUARY-JUNE, 1906

INDEX

Lightning Source UK Ltd.
Milton Keynes UK
UKHW021326100219
336936UK00006B/533/P